QUANTITATIVE INVESTMENT ANALYSIS

CFA Institute is the premier association for investment professionals around the world, with over 85,000 members in 129 countries. Since 1963 the organization has developed and administered the renowned Chartered Financial Analyst® Program. With a rich history of leading the investment profession, CFA Institute has set the highest standards in ethics, education, and professional excellence within the global investment community, and is the foremost authority on investment profession conduct and practice.

Each book in the CFA Institute Investment Series is geared toward industry practitioners along with graduate-level finance students and covers the most important topics in the industry. The authors of these cutting-edge books are themselves industry professionals and academics and bring their wealth of knowledge and expertise to this series.

QUANTITATIVE INVESTMENT ANALYSIS

Second Edition

Richard A. DeFusco, CFA

Dennis W. McLeavey, CFA

Jerald E. Pinto, CFA

David E. Runkle, CFA

BICENTENNIAL
1807
WILEY
2007
BICENTENNIAL

John Wiley & Sons, Inc.

Published by John Wiley & Sons, Inc., Hoboken, New Jersey.
Published simultaneously in Canada.

For general information on our other products and services or for technical support, please contact our Customer Care Department within the United States at (800) 762-2974, outside the United States at (317) 572-3993 or fax (317) 572-4002.

Wiley also publishes its books in a variety of electronic formats. Some content that appears in print may not be available in electronic formats. For more information about Wiley products, visit our Web site at www.wiley.com.

Library of Congress Cataloging-in-Publication Data:

Quantitative investment analysis / Richard A. DeFusco . . . [et al.].—
2nd ed.
      p. cm.—(The CFA Institute investment series)
   Includes bibliographical references.
   ISBN-13 978-0-470-05220-4 (cloth)
   ISBN-10 0-470-05220-1 (cloth)
  1. Investment analysis—Mathematical models.   I. DeFusco, Richard Armand.
   HG4529.Q35 2006
   332.601'5195—dc22

                             2006052578

Printed in the United States of America.

10 9 8 7 6 5

CONTENTS

Foreword   xiii

Acknowledgments   xvii

Introduction   xix

CHAPTER 1
The Time Value of Money   1

1   Introduction   1
2   Interest Rates: Interpretation   1
3   The Future Value of a Single Cash Flow   3
    3.1 The Frequency of Compounding   8
    3.2 Continuous Compounding   10
    3.3 Stated and Effective Rates   12
4   The Future Value of a Series of Cash Flows   13
    4.1 Equal Cash Flows—Ordinary Annuity   13
    4.2 Unequal Cash Flows   15
5   The Present Value of a Single Cash Flow   15
    5.1 Finding the Present Value of a Single Cash Flow   15
    5.2 The Frequency of Compounding   17
6   The Present Value of a Series of Cash Flows   19
    6.1 The Present Value of a Series of Equal Cash Flows   19
    6.2 The Present Value of an Infinite Series of Equal Cash Flows—Perpetuity   23
    6.3 Present Values Indexed at Times Other Than $t = 0$ 24
    6.4 The Present Value of a Series of Unequal Cash Flows   26
7   Solving for Rates, Number of Periods, or Size of Annuity Payments   27
    7.1 Solving for Interest Rates and Growth Rates   27
    7.2 Solving for the Number of Periods   30
    7.3 Solving for the Size of Annuity Payments   30
    7.4 Review of Present and Future Value Equivalence   35
    7.5 The Cash Flow Additivity Principle   36

CHAPTER 2
Discounted Cash Flow Applications   **39**

1   Introduction   39
2   Net Present Value and Internal Rate of Return   39
   2.1   Net Present Value and the Net Present Value Rule   40
   2.2   The Internal Rate of Return and the Internal Rate of
       Return Rule   42
   2.3   Problems with the IRR Rule   45
3   Portfolio Return Measurement   47
   3.1   Money-Weighted Rate of Return   47
   3.2   Time-Weighted Rate of Return   49
4   Money Market Yields   54

CHAPTER 3
Statistical Concepts and Market Returns   **61**

1   Introduction   61
2   Some Fundamental Concepts   61
   2.1   The Nature of Statistics   62
   2.2   Populations and Samples   62
   2.3   Measurement Scales   63
3   Summarizing Data Using Frequency Distributions   65
4   The Graphic Presentation of Data   72
   4.1   The Histogram   73
   4.2   The Frequency Polygon and the Cumulative Frequency
       Distribution   74
5   Measures of Central Tendency   76
   5.1   The Arithmetic Mean   77
   5.2   The Median   81
   5.3   The Mode   84
   5.4   Other Concepts of Mean   85
6   Other Measures of Location: Quantiles   94
   6.1   Quartiles, Quintiles, Deciles, and Percentiles   94
   6.2   Quantiles in Investment Practice   98
7   Measures of Dispersion   100
   7.1   The Range   100
   7.2   The Mean Absolute Deviation   101
   7.3   Population Variance and Population Standard
       Deviation   103
   7.4   Sample Variance and Sample Standard Deviation   106
   7.5   Semivariance, Semideviation, and Related Concepts   110
   7.6   Chebyshev's Inequality   111
   7.7   Coefficient of Variation   113
   7.8   The Sharpe Ratio   115
8   Symmetry and Skewness in Return Distributions   118
9   Kurtosis in Return Distributions   123
10 Using Geometric and Arithmetic Means   127

CHAPTER 4
Probability Concepts — 129

1 Introduction — 129
2 Probability, Expected Value, and Variance — 129
3 Portfolio Expected Return and Variance of Return — 152
4 Topics in Probability — 161
  4.1 Bayes' Formula — 161
  4.2 Principles of Counting — 166

CHAPTER 5
Common Probability Distributions — 171

1 Introduction — 171
2 Discrete Random Variables — 171
  2.1 The Discrete Uniform Distribution — 173
  2.2 The Binomial Distribution — 175
3 Continuous Random Variables — 185
  3.1 Continuous Uniform Distribution — 186
  3.2 The Normal Distribution — 189
  3.3 Applications of the Normal Distribution — 197
  3.4 The Lognormal Distribution — 200
4 Monte Carlo Simulation — 206

CHAPTER 6
Sampling and Estimation — 215

1 Introduction — 215
2 Sampling — 215
  2.1 Simple Random Sampling — 216
  2.2 Stratified Random Sampling — 217
  2.3 Time-Series and Cross-Sectional Data — 219
3 Distribution of the Sample Mean — 221
  3.1 The Central Limit Theorem — 222
4 Point and Interval Estimates of the Population Mean — 225
  4.1 Point Estimators — 225
  4.2 Confidence Intervals for the Population Mean — 227
  4.3 Selection of Sample Size — 233
5 More on Sampling — 235
  5.1 Data-Mining Bias — 236
  5.2 Sample Selection Bias — 238
  5.3 Look-Ahead Bias — 240
  5.4 Time-Period Bias — 240

CHAPTER 7
Hypothesis Testing — 243

1 Introduction — 243
2 Hypothesis Testing — 244

3   Hypothesis Tests Concerning the Mean   253
    3.1 Tests Concerning a Single Mean   254
    3.2 Tests Concerning Differences between Means   261
    3.3 Tests Concerning Mean Differences   265
4   Hypothesis Tests Concerning Variance   269
    4.1 Tests Concerning a Single Variance   269
    4.2 Tests Concerning the Equality (Inequality) of Two Variances   271
5   Other Issues: Nonparametric Inference   275
    5.1 Tests Concerning Correlation: The Spearman Rank
         Correlation Coefficient   276
    5.2 Nonparametric Inference: Summary   279

CHAPTER 8
Correlation and Regression   281

1   Introduction   281
2   Correlation Analysis   281
    2.1 Scatter Plots   281
    2.2 Correlation Analysis   282
    2.3 Calculating and Interpreting the Correlation Coefficient   283
    2.4 Limitations of Correlation Analysis   287
    2.5 Uses of Correlation Analysis   289
    2.6 Testing the Significance of the Correlation Coefficient   297
3   Linear Regression   300
    3.1 Linear Regression with One Independent Variable   300
    3.2 Assumptions of the Linear Regression Model   303
    3.3 The Standard Error of Estimate   306
    3.4 The Coefficient of Determination   309
    3.5 Hypothesis Testing   310
    3.6 Analysis of Variance in a Regression with One Independent Variable   318
    3.7 Prediction Intervals   321
    3.8 Limitations of Regression Analysis   324

CHAPTER 9
Multiple Regression and Issues in Regression Analysis   325

1   Introduction   325
2   Multiple Linear Regression   325
    2.1 Assumptions of the Multiple Linear Regression Model   331
    2.2 Predicting the Dependent Variable in a Multiple Regression Model   336
    2.3 Testing Whether All Population Regression Coefficients Equal Zero   338
    2.4 Adjusted R^2 340
3   Using Dummy Variables in Regressions   341
4   Violations of Regression Assumptions   345
    4.1 Heteroskedasticity   345
    4.2 Serial Correlation   351
    4.3 Multicollinearity   356

4.4 Heteroskedasticity, Serial Correlation, Multicollinearity:
   Summarizing the Issues 359
5 Model Specification and Errors in Specification 359
   5.1 Principles of Model Specification 359
   5.2 Misspecified Functional Form 360
   5.3 Time-Series Misspecification (Independent Variables Correlated
      with Errors) 368
   5.4 Other Types of Time-Series Misspecification 372
6 Models with Qualitative Dependent Variables 372

CHAPTER 10
Time-Series Analysis 375

1 Introduction 375
2 Challenges of Working with Time Series 375
3 Trend Models 377
   3.1 Linear Trend Models 377
   3.2 Log-Linear Trend Models 380
   3.3 Trend Models and Testing for Correlated Errors 385
4 Autoregressive (AR) Time-Series Models 386
   4.1 Covariance-Stationary Series 386
   4.2 Detecting Serially Correlated Errors in an Autoregressive Model 387
   4.3 Mean Reversion 391
   4.4 Multiperiod Forecasts and the Chain Rule of Forecasting 391
   4.5 Comparing Forecast Model Performance 394
   4.6 Instability of Regression Coefficients 397
5 Random Walks and Unit Roots 399
   5.1 Random Walks 400
   5.2 The Unit Root Test of Nonstationarity 403
6 Moving-Average Time-Series Models 407
   6.1 Smoothing Past Values with an n-Period Moving Average 407
   6.2 Moving-Average Time-Series Models for Forecasting 409
7 Seasonality in Time-Series Models 412
8 Autoregressive Moving-Average Models 416
9 Autoregressive Conditional Heteroskedasticity Models 417
10 Regressions with More than One Time Series 420
11 Other Issues in Time Series 424
12 Suggested Steps in Time-Series Forecasting 425

CHAPTER 11
Portfolio Concepts 429

1 Introduction 429
2 Mean–Variance Analysis 429
   2.1 The Minimum-Variance Frontier and Related Concepts 430
   2.2 Extension to the Three-Asset Case 439
   2.3 Determining the Minimum-Variance Frontier for Many Assets 442
   2.4 Diversification and Portfolio Size 445

2.5 Portfolio Choice with a Risk-Free Asset   449
2.6 The Capital Asset Pricing Model   458
2.7 Mean–Variance Portfolio Choice Rules: An Introduction   460
3 Practical Issues in Mean–Variance Analysis   464
3.1 Estimating Inputs for Mean–Variance Optimization   464
3.2 Instability in the Minimum-Variance Frontier   470
4 Multifactor Models   473
4.1 Factors and Types of Multifactor Models   474
4.2 The Structure of Macroeconomic Factor Models   475
4.3 Arbitrage Pricing Theory and the Factor Model   478
4.4 The Structure of Fundamental Factor Models   484
4.5 Multifactor Models in Current Practice   485
4.6 Applications   493
4.7 Concluding Remarks   509

Appendices   **511**

References   **521**

Glossary   **527**

About the CFA Program   **541**

About the Authors   **543**

Index   **545**

FOREWORD

HOW QUANTITATIVE INVESTMENT ANALYSIS CAN IMPROVE PORTFOLIO DECISION MAKING

I am a Quant. By my own self-admission, I use quantitative investment techniques in the management of investment portfolios. However, when I tell people that I am a Quant, they often respond: "But Mark, aren't you a lawyer?" Well, yes, but . . .

The fact is that Quants come from all walks of life. Whether we are called Quants, Quant Jocks, Gear Heads, Computer Monkeys, or any of the other monikers that are attached to investors who like to scribble equations on a piece of paper, we all share a common denominator—the use of quantitative analysis to make better investment decisions. You don't have to be a rocket scientist with a Ph.D. in an esoteric mathematical field to be a Quant (although there are, I suspect, several former rocket scientists who have found working in the financial markets to be both fun and profitable). Anyone can become a Quant—even a lawyer.

But let's take a step back. Why should any investor want to use quantitative tools in the management of investment portfolios? There are three reasons why Quants are so popular.

First, the financial markets are very complicated places. There are many interwoven variables that can affect the price of securities in an investment portfolio. For example, the stock price of a public company can be affected by macroeconomic factors such as the level of interest rates, current account deficits, government spending, and economic cycles. These factors may affect the cost of capital at which a corporation finances its new projects, or influence the spending patterns of the company's customers, or provide economic impetus through government spending programs.

In addition to macro variables, the value of a company's stock can be affected by factors that are peculiar to the company itself. Factors such as cash flow, working capital, book-to-market value, earnings growth rates, dividend policy, and debt-to-equity ratios affect the individual value of each public company. These are considered to be the fundamental factors that have an impact on the specific company as opposed to the broader stock market.

Then we come to the financial market variables that affect a company's valuation. Its "beta" or measure of systematic risk will impact the expected return for the company and, in turn, its stock price. The famous Capital Asset Pricing Model that measures a stock's beta is really just a linear regression equation of the type described in Chapter 8.

Last, there are behavioral variables that can affect security values. Such behavior as herding, overconfidence, overreaction to earnings announcements, and momentum trading can all impact the price of a company's stock. These behavioral variables can have a lasting impact on a stock price (remember the technology bubble of 1998–2001 when tech stocks were going to take over the world?) as well as generate a significant amount of "noise" around a security's true value.

Considering all of these variables together at one time to determine the true value of a security can be an overwhelming task without some framework in which to analyze their impact. It is simply not possible for the human mind alone (at least, not mine) to be able to weigh the impact of individual company specific factors such as price-to-earnings ratios, macroeconomic variables such as government spending programs, investor behavioral patterns such as momentum trading, and other potentially influential variables in a rigorous fashion within the human brain.

This is where *Quantitative Investment Analysis* can help. Factor modeling techniques such as those described in Chapter 11 can be used to supplement the intuition of the human mind to produce a quantitative framework that digests the large number of plausible variables that can impact the price of a security. Further, given the many variables that can affect a security's value, it is not possible to consider each variable in isolation. The economic factors that cause a security's price to go up or down are interwoven in a complex web such that the variables must be considered together to determine their collective impact on the price of a security.

This is where the value of Chapters 8 and 9 are most useful. These two chapters provide the basic knowledge for building regression equations to study the impact of economic factors on security prices. The regression techniques provided in Chapters 8 and 9 can be used to filter out which variables have a significant impact on the price of a security, and which variables just provide "noise."

In addition, Chapter 9 introduces the reader to "dummy variables." Despite their name, you don't have to be a dummy like me to use them. Dummy variables are a neat way to study different states of the world and their impact on security prices. They are often referred to as "binary" variables because they divide the world into two states for observation, for example, financial markets up versus financial markets down; Republicans in control of the White House versus Democrats in control of the White House; Chicago Cubs win (almost never) versus Chicago Cubs lose; and so on. This last variable—the record of the Chicago Cubs—I can attest has no impact on security valuations, although, as a long-standing and suffering Cub fan, it does have an impact on my morale.

As another example, consider a recent research paper where I studied the behavior of private equity managers in the way they price their private equity portfolios depending on whether the public stock markets were doing well versus when the public stock markets were doing poorly. To conduct this analysis, I ran a regression equation using dummy variables to divide the world into two states: up public stock markets versus down public stock markets. By using dummy variables in this manner, I was able to observe different behavioral patterns of private equity managers in how they marked up or down their private equity portfolios depending on the performance of the public stock markets.

The second reason *Quantitative Investment Analysis* will add value to the reader is that it provides the basic tools to consider a breadth of economic factors and securities. It is not only the fact that there are many interwoven economic variables that impact the value of a security, the sheer number of securities in the market place can be daunting. Therefore, most investors only look at a subset of the investable securities in the market.

Consider the U.S. stock market. Generally, this market is divided into three categories based on company size: large-cap, mid-cap, and small-cap stocks. This division is less so because there might be "size" effects in valuation, but rather, because of the pragmatic limitation that asset managers simply cannot analyze stocks beyond a certain number. So traditional fundamental investors select different parts of the U.S. stock market in which to conduct their security analysis. However, the division of the stock market into size categories effectively establishes barriers for investment managers. There is no reason, for example, why a portfolio manager with insight into how earnings surprises affect stock prices cannot invest across the whole range of stock market capitalization.

This is where Chapters 6 and 7 can be useful. The quantitative skills of sampling, estimation, and hypothesis testing can be used to analyze large baskets of data. This allows portfolio managers to invest across a broad universe of stocks, breaking down traditional barriers such as cap-size restrictions. When viewed in this light, quantitative analysis does not displace the fundamental stock picking skills of traditional asset managers. Rather, quantitative analysis extends the portfolio manager's insight with respect to company, macro, and market variables to a broader array of investment opportunities.

This also has implications for the statistical tools and probability concepts provided in Chapters 3 and 4. The larger the data set to be analyzed the greater the reliability of the parameter estimation derived from that data set. Breadth of economic analysis will improve not only the statistical reliability of the quantitative analysis, but will also increase the predictability of the relationships between economic factors and stock price movement. The statistical tools provided in this book allow the portfolio manager to realize the full potential of his or her skill across a larger universe of securities than may have previously been achieved.

Another example might help. Every year the California Public Employees' Retirement System (CalPERS), my former employer, publishes a list of the most poorly governed companies in the United States. This list has now been published for 16 years and has been very successful. Early on in the process, the selection was conducted on a subset of the U.S. stock market. However, this process has evolved to consider every U.S. stock held in CalPERS's portfolio regardless of stock market capitalization range. This requires the analysis of up to 1,800 stocks every year based on both economic factors and governance variables. The sheer number of securities in this data sample could not be analyzed without the application of quantitative screening tools to expand the governance universe for CalPERS.

Last, *Quantitative Investment Analysis* can provide a certain amount of discipline to the investment process. We are all human, and as humans, we are subject to making mistakes. If I were to recount all of the investment mistakes that I have made over my career, this Foreword would exceed the length of the chapters in this book. Just as a brief example, one of my "better calls" was Starbucks Coffee. Early on when Starbucks was just getting started, I visited one of their shops to see what the buzz was all about. At that time a Latte Grande was selling for about $1.50. I recall that I thought this was an outrageous price and I can remember distinctly saying: "Oh, this is a dumb idea, this will never catch on!" Ah yes . . .

So back to quantitative techniques—how can they help? In this instance, they could have helped me remove my human biases and to think more analytically about Starbucks' prospects. If I had taken the time to conduct an empirical review using the quantitative tools provided in this text, I would have seen the fundamental value underlying that buck-fifty Latte.

The fact is that we are all subject to behavioral biases such as overconfidence, momentum, and overreaction. Not only can these be analyzed as discussed above, they can be revealed and discounted when we make our investment decisions. Perhaps the single biggest behavioral hurdle to overcome for investors is the inability to sell a security when its value declines. All too often we become almost emotionally attached to the securities in our portfolio such that we find it hard to sell a security that begins to decline in price.

Yet, this is precisely, where *Quantitative Investment Analysis* can help because it is dispassionate. Quantitative tools and modeling techniques can take the emotion and cognitive biases out of the portfolio decision-making process. As portfolio managers, our goal is to be objective, critical, and demanding. Unfortunately, sometimes our embedded habits and opinions can get in the way. However, quantitative models are unemotional and they can root out our cognitive biases in a way that we simply cannot do ourselves by looking in the mirror (in fact, when I look in the mirror I see someone who is six feet and four inches tall and incredibly good looking but then my wife Mary reminds me that I am only six feet and one inch tall and she had better offers).

All in all, the investor will appreciate the methods, models, and techniques provided in this text. This book serves as an excellent introduction to those investors who are just beginning to use quantitative tools in their portfolio management process as well as an excellent reference guide for those already converted. Quantitative investing is not difficult to grasp—even a lawyer can do it.

MARK J. P. ANSON
CEO, Hermes Pensions Management
CEO, British Telecomm Pension Scheme
mark@hermes.co.uk

ACKNOWLEDGMENTS

We would like to thank the many individuals who played important roles in producing this book.

Robert R. Johnson, CFA, Managing Director of the CFA and CIPM Programs Division, saw the need for specialized curriculum materials and initiated this project. We appreciate his support for the timely revision of this textbook. Senior executives in the CFA Program Division have generously given their advice and time in the writing of both editions of this book. Philip J. Young, CFA, provided continuous assistance in writing the book's learning outcome statements and participated in final manuscript reviews. Jan R. Squires, CFA, contributed an orientation stressing motivation and testability. Mary K. Erickson, CFA, made contributions to the accuracy of the text. John D. Stowe, CFA, supplied suggestions for revising several chapters.

The Executive Advisory Board of the Candidate Curriculum Committee provided invaluable input: James Bronson, CFA, Chair; Peter Mackey, CFA, Immediate Past Chair; and members, Alan Meder, CFA, Victoria Rati, CFA, and Matt Scanlan, CFA, as well as the Candidate Curriculum Committee Working Body.

The manuscript reviewers for this edition were Philip Fanara, Jr., CFA; Jane Farris, CFA; David M. Jessop; Lisa M. Joublanc, CFA; Asjeet S. Lamba, CFA; Mario Lavallee, CFA; William L. Randolph, CFA; Eric N. Remole; Vijay Singal, CFA; Zoe L. Van Schyndel, CFA; Charlotte Weems, CFA; and Lavone F. Whitmer, CFA. We thank them for their excellent work.

We also appreciate the many comments received from those who used the first edition.

Jacques R. Gagne, CFA, Gregory M. Noronha, CFA, and Sanjiv Sabherwal provided highly detailed proofreading of the individual chapters. We thank each for their dedicated and painstaking work. We are also indebted to Dr. Sabherwal for his expert assistance in running regressions, revising in-chapter examples, and creating some of the end-of-chapter problems/solutions.

Fiona D. Russell provided incisive copyediting that substantially contributed to the book's accuracy and readability.

Wanda A. Lauziere of the CFA Program Division, the project manager for the revision, expertly guided the manuscript from planning through production and made many other contributions to all aspects of the revision.

Finally, we thank Ibbotson Associates of Chicago for generously providing us with EnCorr Analyzer^{TM}.

INTRODUCTION

CFA Institute is pleased to provide you with this Investment Series covering major areas in the field of investments. These texts are thoroughly grounded in the highly regarded CFA Program Candidate Body of Knowledge (CBOK®) that draws upon hundreds of practicing investment professionals and serves as the anchor for the three levels of the CFA Examinations. In the year this series is being launched, more than 120,000 aspiring investment professionals will each devote over 250 hours of study to master this material as well as other elements of the Candidate Body of Knowledge in order to obtain the coveted CFA charter. We provide these materials for the same reason we have been chartering investment professionals for over 40 years: to improve the competency and ethical character of those serving the capital markets.

PARENTAGE

One of the valuable attributes of this series derives from its parentage. In the 1940s, a handful of societies had risen to form communities that revolved around common interests and work in what we now think of as the investment industry.

Understand that the idea of purchasing common stock as an investment—as opposed to casino speculation—was only a couple of decades old at most. We were only 10 years past the creation of the U.S. Securities and Exchange Commission and laws that attempted to level the playing field after robber baron and stock market panic episodes.

In January 1945, in what is today CFA Institute *Financial Analysts Journal*, a fundamentally driven professor and practitioner from Columbia University and Graham-Newman Corporation wrote an article making the case that people who research and manage portfolios should have some sort of credential to demonstrate competence and ethical behavior. This person was none other than Benjamin Graham, the father of security analysis and future mentor to a well-known modern investor, Warren Buffett.

The idea of creating a credential took a mere 16 years to drive to execution but by 1963, 284 brave souls, all over the age of 45, took an exam and launched the CFA credential. What many do not fully understand was that this effort had at its root a desire to create a profession where its practitioners were professionals who provided investing services to individuals in need. In so doing, a fairer and more productive capital market would result.

A profession—whether it be medicine, law, or other—has certain hallmark characteristics. These characteristics are part of what attracts serious individuals to devote the energy of their life's work to the investment endeavor. First, and tightly connected to this Series, there must be a body of knowledge. Second, there needs to be some entry requirements such as those required to achieve the CFA credential. Third, there must be a commitment to continuing education. Fourth, a profession must serve a purpose beyond one's direct selfish interest. In this case, by properly conducting one's affairs and putting client interests first, the investment professional can work as a fair-minded cog in the wheel of the incredibly productive global capital markets. This encourages the citizenry to part with their hard-earned savings to be redeployed in fair and productive pursuit.

As C. Stewart Sheppard, founding executive director of the Institute of Chartered Financial Analysts said, "Society demands more from a profession and its members than it does from a professional craftsman in trade, arts, or business. In return for status, prestige, and autonomy, a profession extends a public warranty that it has established and maintains conditions of entry, standards of fair practice, disciplinary procedures, and continuing education for its particular constituency. Much is expected from members of a profession, but over time, more is given."

"The Standards for Educational and Psychological Testing," put forth by the American Psychological Association, the American Educational Research Association, and the National Council on Measurement in Education, state that the validity of professional credentialing examinations should be demonstrated primarily by verifying that the content of the examination accurately represents professional practice. In addition, a practice analysis study, which confirms the knowledge and skills required for the competent professional, should be the basis for establishing content validity.

For more than 40 years, hundreds upon hundreds of practitioners and academics have served on CFA Institute curriculum committees sifting through and winnowing all the many investment concepts and ideas to create a body of knowledge and the CFA curriculum. One of the hallmarks of curriculum development at CFA Institute is its extensive use of practitioners in all phases of the process.

CFA Institute has followed a formal practice analysis process since 1995. The effort involves special practice analysis forums held, most recently, at 20 locations around the world. Results of the forums were put forth to 70,000 CFA charterholders for verification and confirmation of the body of knowledge so derived.

What this means for the reader is that the concepts contained in these texts were driven by practicing professionals in the field who understand the responsibilities and knowledge that practitioners in the industry need to be successful. We are pleased to put this extensive effort to work for the benefit of the readers of the Investment Series.

BENEFITS

This series will prove useful both to the new student of capital markets, who is seriously contemplating entry into the extremely competitive field of investment management, and to the more seasoned professional who is looking for a user-friendly way to keep one's knowledge current. All chapters include extensive references for those who would like to dig deeper into a given concept. The workbooks provide a summary of each chapter's key points to help organize your thoughts, as well as sample questions and answers to test yourself on your progress.

For the new student, the essential concepts that any investment professional needs to master are presented in a time-tested fashion. This material, in addition to university study and reading the financial press, will help you better understand the investment field. I believe that the general public seriously underestimates the disciplined processes needed for the best investment firms and individuals to prosper. These texts lay the basic groundwork for many of the processes that successful firms use. Without this base level of understanding and an appreciation for how the capital markets work to properly price securities, you may not find competitive success. Furthermore, the concepts herein give a genuine sense of the kind of work that is to be found day to day managing portfolios, doing research, or related endeavors.

The investment profession, despite its relatively lucrative compensation, is not for everyone. It takes a special kind of individual to fundamentally understand and absorb the teachings from this body of work and then convert that into application in the practitioner world. In fact, most individuals who enter the field do not survive in the longer run. The aspiring professional should think long and hard about whether this is the field for him or herself. There is no better way to make such a critical decision than to be prepared by reading and evaluating the gospel of the profession.

The more experienced professional understands that the nature of the capital markets requires a commitment to continuous learning. Markets evolve as quickly as smart minds can find new ways to create an exposure, to attract capital, or to manage risk. A number of the concepts in these pages were not present a decade or two ago when many of us were starting out in the business. Hedge funds, derivatives, alternative investment concepts, and behavioral finance are examples of new applications and concepts that have altered the capital markets in recent years. As markets invent and reinvent themselves, a best-in-class foundation investment series is of great value.

Those of us who have been at this business for a while know that we must continuously hone our skills and knowledge if we are to compete with the young talent that constantly emerges. In fact, as we talk to major employers about their training needs, we are often told that one of the biggest challenges they face is how to help the experienced professional, laboring under heavy time pressure, keep up with the state of the art and the more recently educated associates. This series can be part of that answer.

CONVENTIONAL WISDOM

It doesn't take long for the astute investment professional to realize two common characteristics of markets. First, prices are set by conventional wisdom, or a function of the many variables in the market. Truth in markets is, at its essence, what the market believes it is and how it assesses pricing credits or debits on those beliefs. Second, as conventional wisdom is a product of the evolution of general theory and learning, by definition conventional wisdom is often wrong or at the least subject to material change.

When I first entered this industry in the mid-1970s, conventional wisdom held that the concepts examined in these texts were a bit too academic to be heavily employed in the competitive marketplace. Many of those considered to be the best investment firms at the time were led by men who had an eclectic style, an intuitive sense of markets, and a great track record. In the rough-and-tumble world of the practitioner, some of these concepts were considered to be of no use. Could conventional wisdom have been more wrong? If so, I'm not sure when.

During the years of my tenure in the profession, the practitioner investment management firms that evolved successfully were full of determined, intelligent, intellectually curious investment professionals who endeavored to apply these concepts in a serious and disciplined manner. Today, the best firms are run by those who carefully form investment hypotheses and test them rigorously in the marketplace, whether it be in a quant strategy, in comparative shopping for stocks within an industry, or in many hedge fund strategies. Their goal is to create investment processes that can be replicated with some statistical reliability. I believe those who embraced the so-called academic side of the learning equation have been much more successful as real-world investment managers.

THE TEXTS

Approximately 35 percent of the Candidate Body of Knowledge is represented in the initial four texts of the series. Additional texts on corporate finance and international financial statement analysis are in development, and more topics may be forthcoming.

One of the most prominent texts over the years in the investment management industry has been Maginn and Tuttle's *Managing Investment Portfolios: A Dynamic Process*. The third edition updates key concepts from the 1990 second edition. Some of the more experienced members of our community, like myself, own the prior two editions and will add this to our library. Not only does this tome take the concepts from the other readings and put them in a portfolio context, it also updates the concepts of alternative investments, performance presentation standards, portfolio execution and, very importantly, managing individual investor portfolios. To direct attention, long focused on institutional portfolios, toward the individual will make this edition an important improvement over the past.

Quantitative Investment Analysis focuses on some key tools that are needed for today's professional investor. In addition to classic time value of money, discounted cash flow applications, and probability material, there are two aspects that can be of value over traditional thinking.

First are the chapters dealing with correlation and regression that ultimately figure into the formation of hypotheses for purposes of testing. This gets to a critical skill that many professionals are challenged by: the ability to sift out the wheat from the chaff. For most investment researchers and managers, their analysis is not solely the result of newly created data and tests that they perform. Rather, they synthesize and analyze primary research done by others. Without a rigorous manner by which to understand quality research, not only can you not understand good research, you really have no basis by which to evaluate less rigorous research. What is often put forth in the applied world as good quantitative research lacks rigor and validity.

Second, the last chapter on portfolio concepts moves the reader beyond the traditional capital asset pricing model (CAPM) type of tools and into the more practical world of multifactor models and to arbitrage pricing theory. Many have felt that there has been a CAPM bias to the work put forth in the past, and this chapter helps move beyond that point.

Equity Asset Valuation is a particularly cogent and important read for anyone involved in estimating the value of securities and understanding security pricing. A well-informed professional would know that the common forms of equity valuation—dividend discount modeling, free cash flow modeling, price/earnings models, and residual income models (often known by trade names)—can all be reconciled to one another under certain assumptions. With a deep understanding of the underlying assumptions, the professional investor can better understand what other investors assume when calculating their valuation estimates. In my prior life as the head of an equity investment team, this knowledge would give us an edge over other investors.

Fixed Income Analysis has been at the frontier of new concepts in recent years, greatly expanding horizons over the past. This text is probably the one with the most new material for the seasoned professional who is not a fixed-income specialist. The application of option and derivative technology to the once staid province of fixed income has helped contribute to an explosion of thought in this area. And not only does that challenge the professional to stay up to speed with credit derivatives, swaptions, collateralized mortgage securities, mortgage backs, and others, but it also puts a strain on the world's central banks to provide oversight and the risk of a correlated event. Armed with a thorough grasp of the new exposures, the professional investor is much better able to anticipate and understand the challenges our central bankers and markets face.

I hope you find this new series helpful in your efforts to grow your investment knowledge, whether you are a relatively new entrant or a grizzled veteran ethically bound to keep up to date in the ever-changing market environment. CFA Institute, as a long-term committed participant of the investment profession and a not-for-profit association, is pleased to give you this opportunity.

Jeff Diermeier, CFA
President and Chief Executive Officer
CFA Institute
September 2006

QUANTITATIVE INVESTMENT ANALYSIS

CHAPTER 1

THE TIME VALUE OF MONEY

1. INTRODUCTION

As individuals, we often face decisions that involve saving money for a future use, or borrowing money for current consumption. We then need to determine the amount we need to invest, if we are saving, or the cost of borrowing, if we are shopping for a loan. As investment analysts, much of our work also involves evaluating transactions with present and future cash flows. When we place a value on any security, for example, we are attempting to determine the worth of a stream of future cash flows. To carry out all the above tasks accurately, we must understand the mathematics of time value of money problems. Money has time value in that individuals value a given amount of money more highly the earlier it is received. Therefore, a smaller amount of money now may be equivalent in value to a larger amount received at a future date. The **time value of money** as a topic in investment mathematics deals with equivalence relationships between cash flows with different dates. Mastery of time value of money concepts and techniques is essential for investment analysts.

The chapter is organized as follows: Section 2 introduces some terminology used throughout the chapter and supplies some economic intuition for the variables we will discuss. Section 3 tackles the problem of determining the worth at a future point in time of an amount invested today. Section 4 addresses the future worth of a series of cash flows. These two sections provide the tools for calculating the equivalent value at a future date of a single cash flow or series of cash flows. Sections 5 and 6 discuss the equivalent value today of a single future cash flow and a series of future cash flows, respectively. In Section 7, we explore how to determine other quantities of interest in time value of money problems.

2. INTEREST RATES: INTERPRETATION

In this chapter, we will continually refer to interest rates. In some cases, we assume a particular value for the interest rate; in other cases, the interest rate will be the unknown quantity we seek to determine. Before turning to the mechanics of time value of money problems, we must illustrate the underlying economic concepts. In this section, we briefly explain the meaning and interpretation of interest rates.

Time value of money concerns equivalence relationships between cash flows occurring on different dates. The idea of equivalence relationships is relatively simple. Consider the following exchange: You pay $10,000 today and in return receive $9,500 today. Would you accept this arrangement? Not likely. But what if you received the $9,500 today and paid the $10,000 one year from now? Can these amounts be considered equivalent? Possibly, because a payment of $10,000 a year from now would probably be worth less to you than a payment of $10,000 today. It would be fair, therefore, to **discount** the $10,000 received in one year; that is, to cut its value based on how much time passes before the money is paid. An **interest rate**, denoted r, is a rate of return that reflects the relationship between differently dated cash flows. If $9,500 today and $10,000 in one year are equivalent in value, then $10,000 − $9,500 = $500 is the required compensation for receiving $10,000 in one year rather than now. The interest rate—the required compensation stated as a rate of return—is $500/$9,500 = 0.0526 or 5.26 percent.

Interest rates can be thought of in three ways. First, they can be considered required rates of return—that is, the minimum rate of return an investor must receive in order to accept the investment. Second, interest rates can be considered discount rates. In the example above, 5.26 percent is that rate at which we discounted the $10,000 future amount to find its value today. Thus, we use the terms "interest rate" and "discount rate" almost interchangeably. Third, interest rates can be considered opportunity costs. An **opportunity cost** is the value that investors forgo by choosing a particular course of action. In the example, if the party who supplied $9,500 had instead decided to spend it today, he would have forgone earning 5.26 percent on the money. So we can view 5.26 percent as the opportunity cost of current consumption.

Economics tells us that interest rates are set in the marketplace by the forces of supply and demand, where investors are suppliers of funds and borrowers are demanders of funds. Taking the perspective of investors in analyzing market-determined interest rates, we can view an interest rate r as being composed of a real risk-free interest rate plus a set of four premiums that are required returns or compensation for bearing distinct types of risk:

$$r = \text{Real risk-free interest rate} + \text{Inflation premium} + \text{Default risk premium}$$
$$+ \text{Liquidity premium} + \text{Maturity premium}$$

- The **real risk-free interest rate** is the single-period interest rate for a completely risk-free security if no inflation were expected. In economic theory, the real risk-free rate reflects the time preferences of individuals for current versus future real consumption.
- The **inflation premium** compensates investors for expected inflation and reflects the average inflation rate expected over the maturity of the debt. Inflation reduces the purchasing power of a unit of currency—the amount of goods and services one can buy with it. The sum of the real risk-free interest rate and the inflation premium is the **nominal risk-free interest rate**.[1] Many countries have governmental short-term debt whose interest rate can be considered to represent the nominal risk-free interest rate in that country. The interest rate on a 90-day U.S. Treasury bill (T-bill), for example, represents the nominal risk-free interest rate over that time horizon.[2] U.S. T-bills can be bought and sold in large quantities with minimal transaction costs and are backed by the full faith and credit of the U.S. government.

---

[1]Technically, 1 plus the nominal rate equals the product of 1 plus the real rate and 1 plus the inflation rate. As a quick approximation, however, the nominal rate is equal to the real rate plus an inflation premium. In this discussion we focus on approximate additive relationships to highlight the underlying concepts.

[2]Other developed countries issue securities similar to U.S. Treasury bills. The French government issues BTFs or negotiable fixed-rate discount Treasury bills (*Bons du Trésor à taux fixe et à intérêts précomptés*) with maturities of 3, 6, and 12 months. The Japanese government issues a short-term Treasury bill with maturities of 6 and 12 months. The German government issues at discount both Treasury financing

- The **default risk premium** compensates investors for the possibility that the borrower will fail to make a promised payment at the contracted time and in the contracted amount.
- The **liquidity premium** compensates investors for the risk of loss relative to an investment's fair value if the investment needs to be converted to cash quickly. U.S. T-bills, for example, do not bear a liquidity premium because large amounts can be bought and sold without affecting their market price. Many bonds of small issuers, by contrast, trade infrequently after they are issued; the interest rate on such bonds includes a liquidity premium reflecting the relatively high costs (including the impact on price) of selling a position.
- The **maturity premium** compensates investors for the increased sensitivity of the market value of debt to a change in market interest rates as maturity is extended, in general (holding all else equal). The difference between the interest rate on longer-maturity, liquid Treasury debt and that on short-term Treasury debt reflects a positive maturity premium for the longer-term debt (and possibly different inflation premiums as well).

Using this insight into the economic meaning of interest rates, we now turn to a discussion of solving time value of money problems, starting with the future value of a single cash flow.

3. THE FUTURE VALUE OF A SINGLE CASH FLOW

In this section, we introduce time value associated with a single cash flow or lump-sum investment. We describe the relationship between an initial investment or **present value** (PV), which earns a rate of return (the interest rate per period) denoted as r, and its **future value** (FV), which will be received N years or periods from today.

The following example illustrates this concept. Suppose you invest $100 (PV = $100) in an interest-bearing bank account paying 5 percent annually. At the end of the first year, you will have the $100 plus the interest earned, $0.05 \times \$100 = \$5$, for a total of $105. To formalize this one-period example, we define the following terms:

$$PV = \text{present value of the investment}$$

$$FV_N = \text{future value of the investment } N \text{ periods from today}$$

$$r = \text{rate of interest per period}$$

For $N = 1$, the expression for the future value of amount PV is

$$FV_1 = PV(1 + r) \tag{1-1}$$

For this example, we calculate the future value one year from today as $FV_1 = \$100(1.05) = \$105$.

Now suppose you decide to invest the initial $100 for two years with interest earned and credited to your account annually (annual compounding). At the end of the first year (the

---

paper (*Finanzierungsschätze des Bundes* or, for short, *Schätze*) and Treasury discount paper (*Bubills*) with maturities up to 24 months. In the United Kingdom, the British government issues gilt-edged Treasury bills with maturities ranging from 1 to 364 days. The Canadian government bond market is closely related to the U.S. market; Canadian Treasury bills have maturities of 3, 6, and 12 months.

beginning of the second year), your account will have $105, which you will leave in the bank for another year. Thus, with a beginning amount of $105 (PV = $105), the amount at the end of the second year will be $105(1.05) = $110.25. Note that the $5.25 interest earned during the second year is 5 percent of the amount invested at the beginning of Year 2.

Another way to understand this example is to note that the amount invested at the beginning of Year 2 is composed of the original $100 that you invested plus the $5 interest earned during the first year. During the second year, the original principal again earns interest, as does the interest that was earned during Year 1. You can see how the original investment grows:

Original investment	$100.00
Interest for the first year ($100 × 0.05)	5.00
Interest for the second year based on original investment ($100 × 0.05)	5.00
Interest for the second year based on interest earned in the first year (0.05× $5.00 interest on interest)	0.25
Total	$110.25

The $5 interest that you earned each period on the $100 original investment is known as **simple interest** (the interest rate times the principal). **Principal** is the amount of funds originally invested. During the two-year period, you earn $10 of simple interest. The extra $0.25 that you have at the end of Year 2 is the interest you earned on the Year 1 interest of $5 that you reinvested.

The interest earned on interest provides the first glimpse of the phenomenon known as **compounding**. Although the interest earned on the initial investment is important, for a given interest rate it is fixed in size from period to period. The compounded interest earned on reinvested interest is a far more powerful force because, for a given interest rate, it grows in size each period. The importance of compounding increases with the magnitude of the interest rate. For example, $100 invested today would be worth about $13,150 after 100 years if compounded annually at 5 percent, but worth more than $20 million if compounded annually over the same time period at a rate of 13 percent.

To verify the $20 million figure, we need a general formula to handle compounding for any number of periods. The following general formula relates the present value of an initial investment to its future value after N periods:

$$\text{FV}_N = \text{PV}(1 + r)^N \qquad (1\text{-}2)$$

where r is the stated interest rate per period and N is the number of compounding periods. In the bank example, $\text{FV}_2 = \$100(1 + 0.05)^2 = \$110.25$. In the 13 percent investment example, $\text{FV}_{100} = \$100(1.13)^{100} = \$20,316,287.42$.

The most important point to remember about using the future value equation is that the stated interest rate, r, and the number of compounding periods, N, must be compatible. Both variables must be defined in the same time units. For example, if N is stated in months, then r should be the one-month interest rate, unannualized.

A time line helps us to keep track of the compatibility of time units and the interest rate per time period. In the time line, we use the time index t to represent a point in time a stated number of periods from today. Thus the present value is the amount available for investment today, indexed as $t = 0$. We can now refer to a time N periods from today as $t = N$. The time line in Figure 1-1 shows this relationship.

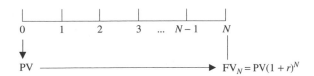

FIGURE 1-1   The Relationship Between an Initial Investment, PV, and Its Future Value, FV

In Figure 1-1, we have positioned the initial investment, PV, at $t = 0$. Using Equation 1-2, we move the present value, PV, forward to $t = N$ by the factor $(1 + r)^N$. This factor is called a future value factor. We denote the future value on the time line as FV and position it at $t = N$. Suppose the future value is to be received exactly 10 periods from today's date ($N = 10$). The present value, PV, and the future value, FV, are separated in time through the factor $(1 + r)$.[10]

The fact that the present value and the future value are separated in time has important consequences:

- We can add amounts of money only if they are indexed at the same point in time.
- For a given interest rate, the future value increases with the number of periods.
- For a given number of periods, the future value increases with the interest rate.

To better understand these concepts, consider three examples that illustrate how to apply the future value formula.

EXAMPLE 1-1   The Future Value of a Lump Sum with Interim Cash Reinvested at the Same Rate

You are the lucky winner of your state's lottery of $5 million after taxes. You invest your winnings in a five-year certificate of deposit (CD) at a local financial institution. The CD promises to pay 7 percent per year compounded annually. This institution also lets you reinvest the interest at that rate for the duration of the CD. How much will you have at the end of five years if your money remains invested at 7 percent for five years with no withdrawals?

Solution: To solve this problem, compute the future value of the $5 million investment using the following values in Equation 1-2:

$$PV = \$5,000,000$$

$$r = 7\% = 0.07$$

$$N = 5$$

$$FV_N = PV(1 + r)^N$$

$$= \$5,000,000(1.07)^5$$

$$= \$5,000,000(1.402552)$$

$$= \$7,012,758.65$$

At the end of five years, you will have \$7,012,758.65 if your money remains invested at 7 percent with no withdrawals.

In this and most examples in this chapter, note that the factors are reported at six decimal places but the calculations may actually reflect greater precision. For example, the reported 1.402552 has been rounded up from 1.40255173 (the calculation is actually carried out with more than eight decimal places of precision by the calculator or spreadsheet). Our final result reflects the higher number of decimal places carried by the calculator or spreadsheet.[3]

EXAMPLE 1-2   The Future Value of a Lump Sum with No Interim Cash

An institution offers you the following terms for a contract: For an investment of ¥2,500,000, the institution promises to pay you a lump sum six years from now at an 8 percent annual interest rate. What future amount can you expect?

Solution: Use the following data in Equation 1-2 to find the future value:

$$PV = ¥2,500,000$$

$$r = 8\% = 0.08$$

$$N = 6$$

$$FV_N = PV(1 + r)^N$$

$$= ¥2,500,000(1.08)^6$$

$$= ¥2,500,000(1.586874)$$

$$= ¥3,967,186$$

You can expect to receive ¥3,967,186 six years from now.

Our third example is a more complicated future value problem that illustrates the importance of keeping track of actual calendar time.

---

[3]We could also solve time value of money problems using tables of interest rate factors. Solutions using tabled values of interest rate factors are generally less accurate than solutions obtained using calculators or spreadsheets, so practitioners prefer calculators or spreadsheets.

EXAMPLE 1-3   The Future Value of a Future Lump Sum

A pension fund manager estimates that his corporate sponsor will make a $10 million contribution five years from now. The rate of return on plan assets has been estimated at 9 percent per year. The pension fund manager wants to calculate the future value of this contribution 15 years from now, which is the date at which the funds will be distributed to retirees. What is that future value?

Solution: By positioning the initial investment, PV, at $t = 5$, we can calculate the future value of the contribution using the following data in Equation 1-2:

$$PV = \$10,000,000$$

$$r = 9\% = 0.09$$

$$N = 10$$

$$FV_N = PV(1 + r)^N$$

$$= \$10,000,000(1.09)^{10}$$

$$= \$10,000,000(2.367364)$$

$$= \$23,673,636.75$$

This problem looks much like the previous two, but it differs in one important respect: its timing. From the standpoint of today ($t = 0$), the future amount of $23,673,636.75 is 15 years into the future. Although the future value is 10 years from its present value, the present value of $10 million will not be received for another five years.

$10,000,000 ⟶ $23,673,636.75

FIGURE 1-2   The Future Value of a Lump Sum, Initial Investment; Not at $t = 0$

As Figure 1-2 shows, we have followed the convention of indexing today as $t = 0$ and indexing subsequent times by adding 1 for each period. The additional contribution of $10 million is to be received in five years, so it is indexed as $t = 5$ and appears as such in the figure. The future value of the investment in 10 years is then indexed at $t = 15$; that is, 10 years following the receipt of the $10 million contribution at $t = 5$. Time lines like this one can be extremely useful when dealing with more-complicated problems, especially those involving more than one cash flow.

In a later section of this chapter, we will discuss how to calculate the value today of the $10 million to be received five years from now. For the moment, we can use Equation 1-2. Suppose the pension fund manager in Example 1-3 above were to receive $6,499,313.86 today from the corporate sponsor. How much will that sum be worth at the end of five years? How much will it be worth at the end of 15 years?

$$PV = \$6,499,313.86$$

$$r = 9\% = 0.09$$

$$N = 5$$

$$FV_N = PV(1 + r)^N$$

$$= \$6,499,313.86(1.09)^5$$

$$= \$6,499,313.86(1.538624)$$

$$= \$10,000,000 \text{ at the five-year mark}$$

and

$$PV = \$6,499,313.86$$

$$r = 9\% = 0.09$$

$$N = 15$$

$$FV_N = PV(1 + r)^N$$

$$= \$6,499,313.86(1.09)^{15}$$

$$= \$6,499,313.86(3.642482)$$

$$= \$23,673,636.74 \text{ at the 15-year mark}$$

These results show that today's present value of about $6.5 million becomes $10 million after five years and $23.67 million after 15 years.

3.1. The Frequency of Compounding

In this section, we examine investments paying interest more than once a year. For instance, many banks offer a monthly interest rate that compounds 12 times a year. In such an arrangement, they pay interest on interest every month. Rather than quote the periodic monthly interest rate, financial institutions often quote an annual interest rate that we refer to as the **stated annual interest rate** or **quoted interest rate**. We denote the stated annual interest rate by r_s. For instance, your bank might state that a particular CD pays 8 percent compounded monthly. The stated annual interest rate equals the monthly interest rate multiplied by 12. In this example, the monthly interest rate is $0.08/12 = 0.0067$ or 0.67 percent.[4] This rate is strictly a quoting convention because $(1 + 0.0067)^{12} = 1.083$, not 1.08; the term $(1 + r_s)$ is not meant to be a future value factor when compounding is more frequent than annual.

---

[4]To avoid rounding errors when using a financial calculator, divide 8 by 12 and then press the %i key, rather than simply entering 0.67 for %i, so we have $(1 + 0.08/12)^{12} = 1.083000$.

With more than one compounding period per year, the future value formula can be expressed as

$$\text{FV}_N = \text{PV}\left(1 + \frac{r_s}{m}\right)^{mN} \tag{1-3}$$

where r_s is the stated annual interest rate, m is the number of compounding periods per year, and N now stands for the number of years. Note the compatibility here between the interest rate used, r_s/m, and the number of compounding periods, mN. The periodic rate, r_s/m, is the stated annual interest rate divided by the number of compounding periods per year. The number of compounding periods, mN, is the number of compounding periods in one year multiplied by the number of years. The periodic rate, r_s/m, and the number of compounding periods, mN, must be compatible.

EXAMPLE 1-4   The Future Value of a Lump Sum with Quarterly Compounding

Continuing with the CD example, suppose your bank offers you a CD with a two-year maturity, a stated annual interest rate of 8 percent compounded quarterly, and a feature allowing reinvestment of the interest at the same interest rate. You decide to invest $10,000. What will the CD be worth at maturity?

Solution: Compute the future value with Equation 1-3 as follows:

$$PV = \$10,000$$

$$r_s = 8\% = 0.08$$

$$m = 4$$

$$r_s/m = 0.08/4 = 0.02$$

$$N = 2$$

$$mN = 4(2) = 8 \text{ interest periods}$$

$$\text{FV}_N = \text{PV}\left(1 + \frac{r_s}{m}\right)^{mN}$$

$$= \$10,000(1.02)^8$$

$$= \$10,000(1.171659)$$

$$= \$11,716.59$$

At maturity, the CD will be worth $11,716.59.

The future value formula in Equation 1-3 does not differ from the one in Equation 1-2. Simply keep in mind that the interest rate to use is the rate per period and the exponent is the number of interest, or compounding, periods.

EXAMPLE 1-5   The Future Value of a Lump Sum with Monthly Compounding

An Australian bank offers to pay you 6 percent compounded monthly. You decide to invest A\$1 million for one year. What is the future value of your investment if interest payments are reinvested at 6 percent?

Solution: Use Equation 1-3 to find the future value of the one-year investment as follows:

$$PV = A\$1,000,000$$

$$r_s = 6\% = 0.06$$

$$m = 12$$

$$r_s/m = 0.06/12 = 0.0050$$

$$N = 1$$

$$mN = 12(1) = 12 \text{ interest periods}$$

$$FV_N = PV\left(1 + \frac{r_s}{m}\right)^{mN}$$

$$= A\$1,000,000(1.005)^{12}$$

$$= A\$1,000,000(1.061678)$$

$$= A\$1,061,677.81$$

If you had been paid 6 percent with annual compounding, the future amount would be only A\$1,000,000(1.06) = A\$1,060,000 instead of A\$1,061,677.81 with monthly compounding.

3.2. Continuous Compounding

The preceding discussion on compounding periods illustrates discrete compounding, which credits interest after a discrete amount of time has elapsed. If the number of compounding periods per year becomes infinite, then interest is said to compound continuously. If we want to use the future value formula with continuous compounding, we need to find the limiting value of the future value factor for $m \to \infty$ (infinitely many compounding periods per year) in Equation 1-3. The expression for the future value of a sum in N years with continuous compounding is

$$FV_N = PVe^{r_s N} \tag{1-4}$$

The term $e^{r_s N}$ is the transcendental number $e \approx 2.7182818$ raised to the power $r_s N$. Most financial calculators have the function e^x.

EXAMPLE 1-6   The Future Value of a Lump Sum with Continuous Compounding

Suppose a $10,000 investment will earn 8 percent compounded continuously for two years. We can compute the future value with Equation 1-4 as follows:

$$PV = \$10{,}000$$

$$r_s = 8\% = 0.08$$

$$N = 2$$

$$FV_N = PVe^{r_sN}$$

$$= \$10{,}000e^{0.08(2)}$$

$$= \$10{,}000(1.173511)$$

$$= \$11{,}735.11$$

With the same interest rate but using continuous compounding, the $10,000 investment will grow to $11,735.11 in two years, compared with $11,716.59 using quarterly compounding as shown in Example 1-4.

Table 1-1 shows how a stated annual interest rate of 8 percent generates different ending dollar amounts with annual, semiannual, quarterly, monthly, daily, and continuous compounding for an initial investment of $1 (carried out to six decimal places).

As Table 1-1 shows, all six cases have the same stated annual interest rate of 8 percent; they have different ending dollar amounts, however, because of differences in the frequency of compounding. With annual compounding, the ending amount is $1.08. More frequent compounding results in larger ending amounts. The ending dollar amount with continuous compounding is the maximum amount that can be earned with a stated annual rate of 8 percent.

Table 1-1 also shows that a $1 investment earning 8.16 percent compounded annually grows to the same future value at the end of one year as a $1 investment earning 8 percent compounded semiannually. This result leads us to a distinction between the stated annual

TABLE 1-1   The Effect of Compounding Frequency on Future Value

Frequency	r_s/m	mN	Future Value of $1
Annual	$8\%/1 = 8\%$	$1 \times 1 = 1$	$\$1.00(1.08) = \$1.08$
Semiannual	$8\%/2 = 4\%$	$2 \times 1 = 2$	$\$1.00(1.04)^2 = \$1.081600$
Quarterly	$8\%/4 = 2\%$	$4 \times 1 = 4$	$\$1.00(1.02)^4 = \$1.082432$
Monthly	$8\%/12 = 0.6667\%$	$12 \times 1 = 12$	$\$1.00(1.006667)^{12} = \$1.083000$
Daily	$8\%/365 = 0.0219\%$	$365 \times 1 = 365$	$\$1.00(1.000219)^{365} = \$1.083278$
Continuous			$\$1.00e^{0.08(1)} = \$1.083287$

interest rate and the **effective annual rate** (EAR).[5] For an 8 percent stated annual interest rate with semiannual compounding, the EAR is 8.16 percent.

3.3. Stated and Effective Rates

The stated annual interest rate does not give a future value directly, so we need a formula for the EAR. With an annual interest rate of 8 percent compounded semiannually, we receive a periodic rate of 4 percent. During the course of a year, an investment of $1 would grow to $1(1.04)^2 = 1.0816, as illustrated in Table 1-1. The interest earned on the $1 investment is $0.0816 and represents an effective annual rate of interest of 8.16 percent. The effective annual rate is calculated as follows:

$$\text{EAR} = (1 + \text{Periodic interest rate})^m - 1 \tag{1-5}$$

The periodic interest rate is the stated annual interest rate divided by m, where m is the number of compounding periods in one year. Using the example in Table 1-1, we can solve for EAR as follows: $(1.04)^2 - 1 = 8.16$ percent.

    The concept of EAR extends to continuous compounding. Suppose we have a rate of 8 percent compounded continuously. We can find the EAR in the same way as above by finding the appropriate future value factor. In this case, a $1 investment would grow to $1e^{0.08(1.0)} = 1.0833. The interest earned for one year represents an effective annual rate of 8.33 percent and is larger than the 8.16 percent EAR with semiannual compounding because interest is compounded more frequently. With continuous compounding, we can solve for the effective annual rate as follows:

$$\text{EAR} = e^{r_s} - 1 \tag{1-6}$$

We can reverse the formulas for EAR with discrete and continuous compounding to find a periodic rate that corresponds to a particular effective annual rate. Suppose we want to find the appropriate periodic rate for a given effective annual rate of 8.16 percent with semiannual compounding. We can use Equation 1-5 to find the periodic rate:

$$0.0816 = (1 + \text{Periodic rate})^2 - 1$$

$$1.0816 = (1 + \text{Periodic rate})^2$$

$$(1.0816)^{1/2} - 1 = \text{Periodic rate}$$

$$1.04 - 1 = \text{Periodic rate}$$

$$4\% = \text{Periodic rate}$$

---

[5]Among the terms used for the effective annual return on interest-bearing bank deposits are annual percentage yield (APY) in the United States and equivalent annual rate (EAR) in the United Kingdom. By contrast, the **annual percentage rate** (APR) measures the cost of borrowing expressed as a yearly rate. In the United States, the APR is calculated as a periodic rate times the number of payment periods per year and, as a result, some writers use APR as a general synonym for the stated annual interest rate. Nevertheless, APR is a term with legal connotations; its calculation follows regulatory standards that vary internationally. Therefore, "stated annual interest rate" is the preferred general term for an annual interest rate that does not account for compounding within the year.

To calculate the continuously compounded rate (the stated annual interest rate with continuous compounding) corresponding to an effective annual rate of 8.33 percent, we find the interest rate that satisfies Equation 1-6:

$$0.0833 = e^{r_s} - 1$$

$$1.0833 = e^{r_s}$$

To solve this equation, we take the natural logarithm of both sides. (Recall that the natural log of e^{r_s} is $\ln e^{r_s} = r_s$.) Therefore, $\ln 1.0833 = r_s$, resulting in $r_s = 8$ percent. We see that a stated annual rate of 8 percent with continuous compounding is equivalent to an EAR of 8.33 percent.

4. THE FUTURE VALUE OF A SERIES OF CASH FLOWS

In this section, we consider series of cash flows, both even and uneven. We begin with a list of terms commonly used when valuing cash flows that are distributed over many time periods.

- An **annuity** is a finite set of level sequential cash flows.
- An **ordinary annuity** has a first cash flow that occurs one period from now (indexed at $t = 1$).
- An **annuity due** has a first cash flow that occurs immediately (indexed at $t = 0$).
- A **perpetuity** is a perpetual annuity, or a set of level never-ending sequential cash flows, with the first cash flow occurring one period from now.

4.1. Equal Cash Flows—Ordinary Annuity

Consider an ordinary annuity paying 5 percent annually. Suppose we have five separate deposits of $1,000 occurring at equally spaced intervals of one year, with the first payment occurring at $t = 1$. Our goal is to find the future value of this ordinary annuity after the last deposit at $t = 5$. The increment in the time counter is one year, so the last payment occurs five years from now. As the time line in Figure 1-3 shows, we find the future value of each $1,000 deposit as of $t = 5$ with Equation 1-2, $FV_N = PV(1 + r)^N$. The arrows in Figure 1-3 extend from the payment date to $t = 5$. For instance, the first $1,000 deposit made at $t = 1$ will compound over four periods. Using Equation 1-2, we find that the future value of the first deposit at $t = 5$ is $1,000(1.05)^4 = \$1,215.51$. We calculate the future value of all other payments in a similar fashion. (Note that we are finding the future value at $t = 5$, so the last payment does not earn any interest.) With all values now at $t = 5$, we can add the future values to arrive at the future value of the annuity. This amount is $5,525.63.

We can arrive at a general annuity formula if we define the annuity amount as A, the number of time periods as N, and the interest rate per period as r. We can then define the future value as

$$FV_N = A[(1 + r)^{N-1} + (1 + r)^{N-2} + (1 + r)^{N-3} + \cdots + (1 + r)^1 + (1 + r)^0]$$

which simplifies to

$$FV_N = A\left[\frac{(1 + r)^N - 1}{r}\right] \tag{1-7}$$

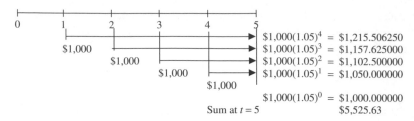

FIGURE 1-3   The Future Value of a Five-Year Ordinary Annuity

The term in brackets is the future value annuity factor. This factor gives the future value of an ordinary annuity of $1 per period. Multiplying the future value annuity factor by the annuity amount gives the future value of an ordinary annuity. For the ordinary annuity in Figure 1-3, we find the future value annuity factor from Equation 1-7 as

$$\left[\frac{(1.05)^5 - 1}{0.05}\right] = 5.525631$$

With an annuity amount $A = \$1,000$, the future value of the annuity is $1,000(5.525631) = $5,525.63$, an amount that agrees with our earlier work.

The next example illustrates how to find the future value of an ordinary annuity using the formula in Equation 1-7.

EXAMPLE 1-7   The Future Value of an Annuity

Suppose your company's defined contribution retirement plan allows you to invest up to €20,000 per year. You plan to invest €20,000 per year in a stock index fund for the next 30 years. Historically, this fund has earned 9 percent per year on average. Assuming that you actually earn 9 percent a year, how much money will you have available for retirement after making the last payment?

Solution: Use Equation 1-7 to find the future amount:

$$A = €20,000$$

$$r = 9\% = 0.09$$

$$N = 30$$

$$\text{FV annuity factor} = \frac{(1 + r)^N - 1}{r} = \frac{(1.09)^{30} - 1}{0.09} = 136.307539$$

$$\text{FV}_N = €20,000(136.307539)$$

$$= €2,726,150.77$$

Assuming the fund continues to earn an average of 9 percent per year, you will have €2,726,150.77 available at retirement.

TABLE 1-2   A Series of Unequal Cash Flows and Their
Future Values at 5 Percent

Time	Cash Flow	Future Value at Year 5
$t = 1$	\$1,000	$\$1,000(1.05)^4 =$ \$1,215.51
$t = 2$	\$2,000	$\$2,000(1.05)^3 =$ \$2,315.25
$t = 3$	\$4,000	$\$4,000(1.05)^2 =$ \$4,410.00
$t = 4$	\$5,000	$\$5,000(1.05)^1 =$ \$5,250.00
$t = 5$	\$6,000	$\$6,000(1.05)^0 =$ \$6,000.00
		Sum = \$19,190.76

4.2. Unequal Cash Flows

In many cases, cash flow streams are unequal, precluding the simple use of the future value annuity factor. For instance, an individual investor might have a savings plan that involves unequal cash payments depending on the month of the year or lower savings during a planned vacation. One can always find the future value of a series of unequal cash flows by compounding the cash flows one at a time. Suppose you have the five cash flows described in Table 1-2, indexed relative to the present ($t = 0$).

All of the payments shown in Table 1-2 are different. Therefore, the most direct approach to finding the future value at $t = 5$ is to compute the future value of each payment as of $t = 5$ and then sum the individual future values. The total future value at Year 5 equals \$19,190.76, as shown in the third column. Later in this chapter, you will learn shortcuts to take when the cash flows are close to even; these shortcuts will allow you to combine annuity and single-period calculations.

5. THE PRESENT VALUE OF A SINGLE CASH FLOW

5.1. Finding the Present Value of a Single Cash Flow

Just as the future value factor links today's present value with tomorrow's future value, the present value factor allows us to discount future value to present value. For example, with a 5 percent interest rate generating a future payoff of \$105 in one year, what current amount invested at 5 percent for one year will grow to \$105? The answer is \$100; therefore, \$100 is the present value of \$105 to be received in one year at a discount rate of 5 percent.

Given a future cash flow that is to be received in N periods and an interest rate per period of r, we can use the formula for future value to solve directly for the present value as follows:

$$\text{FV}_N = \text{PV}(1 + r)^N$$

$$\text{PV} = \text{FV}_N \left[\frac{1}{(1 + r)^N} \right] \tag{1-8}$$

$$\text{PV} = \text{FV}_N (1 + r)^{-N}$$

We see from Equation 1-8 that the present value factor, $(1 + r)^{-N}$, is the reciprocal of the future value factor, $(1 + r)^N$.

EXAMPLE 1-8   The Present Value of a Lump Sum

An insurance company has issued a Guaranteed Investment Contract (GIC) that promises to pay $100,000 in six years with an 8 percent return rate. What amount of money must the insurer invest today at 8 percent for six years to make the promised payment?

Solution: We can use Equation 1-8 to find the present value using the following data:

$$FV_N = \$100,000$$

$$r = 8\% = 0.08$$

$$N = 6$$

$$PV = FV_N(1 + r)^{-N}$$

$$= \$100,000 \left[\frac{1}{(1.08)^6} \right]$$

$$= \$100,000(0.6301696)$$

$$= \$63,016.96$$

We can say that $63,016.96 today, with an interest rate of 8 percent, is equivalent to $100,000 to be received in six years. Discounting the $100,000 makes a future $100,000 equivalent to $63,016.96 when allowance is made for the time value of money. As the time line in Figure 1-4 shows, the $100,000 has been discounted six full periods.

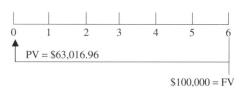

FIGURE 1-4   The Present Value of a Lump Sum to Be Received at Time $t = 6$

EXAMPLE 1-9   The Projected Present Value of a More Distant Future Lump Sum

Suppose you own a liquid financial asset that will pay you $100,000 in 10 years from today. Your daughter plans to attend college four years from today, and you want to know what the asset's present value will be at that time. Given an 8 percent discount rate, what will the asset be worth four years from today?

Solution: The value of the asset is the present value of the asset's promised payment. At $t = 4$, the cash payment will be received six years later. With this information, you can solve for the value four years from today using Equation 1-8:

$$FV_N = \$100,000$$

$$r = 8\% = 0.08$$

$$N = 6$$

$$PV = FV_N(1 + r)^{-N}$$

$$= \$100,000 \left[\frac{1}{(1.08)^6} \right]$$

$$= \$100,000(0.6301696)$$

$$= \$63,016.96$$

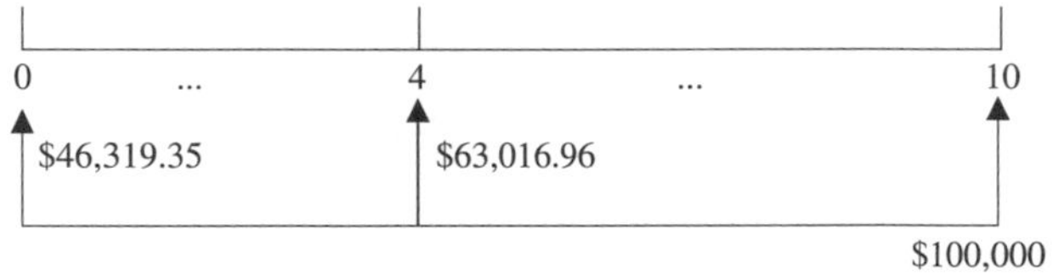

FIGURE 1-5   The Relationship between Present Value and Future Value

The time line in Figure 1-5 shows the future payment of $100,000 that is to be received at $t = 10$. The time line also shows the values at $t = 4$ and at $t = 0$. Relative to the payment at $t = 10$, the amount at $t = 4$ is a projected present value, while the amount at $t = 0$ is the present value (as of today).

Present value problems require an evaluation of the present value factor, $(1 + r)^{-N}$. Present values relate to the discount rate and the number of periods in the following ways:

- For a given discount rate, the farther in the future the amount to be received, the smaller that amount's present value.
- Holding time constant, the larger the discount rate, the smaller the present value of a future amount.

5.2. The Frequency of Compounding

Recall that interest may be paid semiannually, quarterly, monthly, or even daily. To handle interest payments made more than once a year, we can modify the present value formula (Equation 1-8) as follows: Recall that r_s is the quoted interest rate and equals the periodic interest rate multiplied by the number of compounding periods in each year. In general, with more than one compounding period in a year, we can express the formula for present value as

$$PV = FV_N \left(1 + \frac{r_s}{m}\right)^{-mN} \tag{1-9}$$

where

m = number of compounding periods per year
r_s = quoted annual interest rate
N = number of years

The formula in Equation 1-9 is quite similar to that in Equation 1-8. As we have already noted, present value and future value factors are reciprocals. Changing the frequency of compounding does not alter this result. The only difference is the use of the periodic interest rate and the corresponding number of compounding periods.

The following example illustrates Equation 1-9.

EXAMPLE 1-10   The Present Value of a Lump Sum with Monthly Compounding

The manager of a Canadian pension fund knows that the fund must make a lump-sum payment of C$5 million 10 years from now. She wants to invest an amount today in a GIC so that it will grow to the required amount. The current interest rate on GICs is 6 percent a year, compounded monthly. How much should she invest today in the GIC?

Solution: Use Equation 1-9 to find the required present value:

$$FV_N = C\$5,000,000$$

$$r_s = 6\% = 0.06$$

$$m = 12$$

$$r_s/m = 0.06/12 = 0.005$$

$$N = 10$$

$$mN = 12(10) = 120$$

$$PV = FV_N \left(1 + \frac{r_s}{m}\right)^{-mN}$$

$$= C\$5,000,000(1.005)^{-120}$$

$$= C\$5,000,000(0.549633)$$

$$= C\$2,748,163.67$$

In applying Equation 1-9, we use the periodic rate (in this case, the monthly rate) and the appropriate number of periods with monthly compounding (in this case, 10 years of monthly compounding, or 120 periods).

6. THE PRESENT VALUE OF A SERIES OF CASH FLOWS

Many applications in investment management involve assets that offer a series of cash flows over time. The cash flows may be highly uneven, relatively even, or equal. They may occur over relatively short periods of time, longer periods of time, or even stretch on indefinitely. In this section, we discuss how to find the present value of a series of cash flows.

6.1. The Present Value of a Series of Equal Cash Flows

We begin with an ordinary annuity. Recall that an ordinary annuity has equal annuity payments, with the first payment starting one period into the future. In total, the annuity makes N payments, with the first payment at $t = 1$ and the last at $t = N$. We can express the present value of an ordinary annuity as the sum of the present values of each individual annuity payment, as follows:

$$PV = \frac{A}{(1 + r)} + \frac{A}{(1 + r)^2} + \frac{A}{(1 + r)^3} + \cdots + \frac{A}{(1 + r)^{N-1}} + \frac{A}{(1 + r)^N} \qquad (1\text{-}10)$$

where

A = the annuity amount
r = the interest rate per period corresponding to the frequency of annuity payments (for example, annual, quarterly, or monthly)
N = the number of annuity payments

Because the annuity payment (A) is a constant in this equation, it can be factored out as a common term. Thus the sum of the interest factors has a shortcut expression:

$$PV = A \left[\frac{1 - \dfrac{1}{(1 + r)^N}}{r} \right] \qquad (1\text{-}11)$$

In much the same way that we computed the future value of an ordinary annuity, we find the present value by multiplying the annuity amount by a present value annuity factor (the term in brackets in Equation 1-11).

EXAMPLE 1-11   The Present Value of an Ordinary Annuity

Suppose you are considering purchasing a financial asset that promises to pay €1,000 per year for five years, with the first payment one year from now. The required rate of return is 12 percent per year. How much should you pay for this asset?

Solution: To find the value of the financial asset, use the formula for the present value of an ordinary annuity given in Equation 1-11 with the following data:

$$A = \text{€}1{,}000$$

$$r = 12\% = 0.12$$

$$N = 5$$

$$PV = A \left[\frac{1 - \dfrac{1}{(1+r)^N}}{r} \right]$$

$$= \text{€}1{,}000 \left[\frac{1 - \dfrac{1}{(1.12)^5}}{0.12} \right]$$

$$= \text{€}1{,}000(3.604776)$$

$$= \text{€}3{,}604.78$$

The series of cash flows of €1,000 per year for five years is currently worth €3,604.78 when discounted at 12 percent.

Keeping track of the actual calendar time brings us to a specific type of annuity with level payments: the annuity due. An annuity due has its first payment occurring today ($t = 0$). In total, the annuity due will make N payments. Figure 1-6 presents the time line for an annuity due that makes four payments of $100.

As Figure 1-6 shows, we can view the four-period annuity due as the sum of two parts: a $100 lump sum today and an ordinary annuity of $100 per period for three periods. At a 12 percent discount rate, the four $100 cash flows in this annuity due example will be worth $340.18.[6]

Expressing the value of the future series of cash flows in today's dollars gives us a convenient way of comparing annuities. The next example illustrates this approach.

FIGURE 1-6   An Annuity Due of $100 per Period

[6]There is an alternative way to calculate the present value of an annuity due. Compared to an ordinary annuity, the payments in an annuity due are each discounted one less period. Therefore, we can modify Equation 1-11 to handle annuities due by multiplying the right-hand side of the equation by $(1 + r)$:

$$PV(\text{Annuity due}) = A\{[1 - (1 + r)^{-N}]/r\}(1 + r).$$

EXAMPLE 1-12   The Present Value of an Immediate Cash Flow Plus an Ordinary Annuity

You are retiring today and must choose to take your retirement benefits either as a lump sum or as an annuity. Your company's benefits officer presents you with two alternatives: an immediate lump sum of $2 million or an annuity with 20 payments of $200,000 a year with the first payment starting today. The interest rate at your bank is 7 percent per year compounded annually. Which option has the greater present value? (Ignore any tax differences between the two options.)

Solution: To compare the two options, find the present value of each at time $t = 0$ and choose the one with the larger value. The first option's present value is $2 million, already expressed in today's dollars. The second option is an annuity due. Because the first payment occurs at $t = 0$, you can separate the annuity benefits into two pieces: an immediate $200,000 to be paid today ($t = 0$) and an ordinary annuity of $200,000 per year for 19 years. To value this option, you need to find the present value of the ordinary annuity using Equation 1-11 and then add $200,000 to it.

$$A = \$200,000$$

$$N = 19$$

$$r = 7\% = 0.07$$

$$PV = A \left[\frac{1 - \dfrac{1}{(1+r)^N}}{r} \right]$$

$$= \$200,000 \left[\frac{1 - \dfrac{1}{(1.07)^{19}}}{0.07} \right]$$

$$= \$200,000(10.335595)$$

$$= \$2,067,119.05$$

The 19 payments of $200,000 have a present value of $2,067,119.05. Adding the initial payment of $200,000 to $2,067,119.05, we find that the total value of the annuity option is $2,267,119.05. The present value of the annuity is greater than the lump sum alternative of $2 million.

We now look at another example reiterating the equivalence of present and future values.

EXAMPLE 1-13   The Projected Present Value of an Ordinary Annuity

A German pension fund manager anticipates that benefits of €1 million per year must be paid to retirees. Retirements will not occur until 10 years from now at time $t = 10$. Once benefits begin to be paid, they will extend until $t = 39$ for a total of 30 payments. What is the present value of the pension liability if the appropriate annual discount rate for plan liabilities is 5 percent compounded annually?

Solution: This problem involves an annuity with the first payment at $t = 10$. From the perspective of $t = 9$, we have an ordinary annuity with 30 payments. We can compute the present value of this annuity with Equation 1-11 and then look at it on a time line.

$$A = €1,000,000$$

$$r = 5\% = 0.05$$

$$N = 30$$

$$PV = A \left[\frac{1 - \dfrac{1}{(1 + r)^N}}{r} \right]$$

$$= €1,000,000 \left[\frac{1 - \dfrac{1}{(1.05)^{30}}}{0.05} \right]$$

$$= €1,000,000(15.372451)$$

$$= €15,372,451.03$$

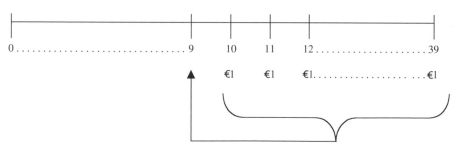

FIGURE 1-7   The Present Value of an Ordinary Annuity with First Payment at Time $t = 10$ (in millions)

On the time line, we have shown the pension payments of €1 million extending from $t = 10$ to $t = 39$. The bracket and arrow indicate the process of finding the present value of the annuity, discounted back to $t = 9$. The present value of the pension benefits as of $t = 9$ is €15,372,451.03. The problem is to find the present value today (at $t = 0$).

Now we can rely on the equivalence of present value and future value. As Figure 1-7 shows, we can view the amount at $t = 9$ as a future value from the vantage point of $t = 0$. We compute the present value of the amount at $t = 9$ as follows:

$$\text{FV}_N = €15{,}372{,}451.03(\text{the present value at } t = 9)$$

$$N = 9$$

$$r = 5\% = 0.05$$

$$\text{PV} = \text{FV}_N(1 + r)^{-N}$$

$$= €15{,}372{,}451.03(1.05)^{-9}$$

$$= €15{,}372{,}451.03(0.644609)$$

$$= €9{,}909{,}219.00$$

The present value of the pension liability is €9,909,219.00.

Example 1-13 illustrates three procedures emphasized in this chapter:

- finding the present or future value of any cash flow series;
- recognizing the equivalence of present value and appropriately discounted future value; and
- keeping track of the actual calendar time in a problem involving the time value of money.

6.2. The Present Value of an Infinite Series of Equal Cash Flows—Perpetuity

Consider the case of an ordinary annuity that extends indefinitely. Such an ordinary annuity is called a perpetuity (a perpetual annuity). To derive a formula for the present value of a perpetuity, we can modify Equation 1-10 to account for an infinite series of cash flows:

$$\text{PV} = A \sum_{t=1}^{\infty} \left[\frac{1}{(1 + r)^t} \right] \tag{1-12}$$

As long as interest rates are positive, the sum of present value factors converges and

$$\text{PV} = \frac{A}{r} \tag{1-13}$$

To see this, look back at Equation 1-11, the expression for the present value of an ordinary annuity. As N (the number of periods in the annuity) goes to infinity, the term $1/(1 + r)^N$ goes to 0 and Equation 1-11 simplifies to Equation 1-13. This equation will reappear when we value dividends from stocks because stocks have no predefined life span. (A stock paying constant dividends is similar to a perpetuity.) With the first payment a year from now, a perpetuity of $10 per year with a 20 percent required rate of return has a present value of $10/0.2 = $50.

Equation 1-13 is valid only for a perpetuity with level payments. In our development above, the first payment occurred at $t = 1$; therefore, we compute the present value as of $t = 0$.

Other assets also come close to satisfying the assumptions of a perpetuity. Certain government bonds and preferred stocks are typical examples of financial assets that make level payments for an indefinite period of time.

EXAMPLE 1-14   The Present Value of a Perpetuity

The British government once issued a type of security called a consol bond, which promised to pay a level cash flow indefinitely. If a consol bond paid £100 per year in perpetuity, what would it be worth today if the required rate of return were 5 percent?

Solution: To answer this question, we can use Equation 1-13 with the following data:

$$A = £100$$
$$r = 5\% = 0.05$$
$$PV = A/r$$
$$= £100/0.05$$
$$= £2,000$$

The bond would be worth £2,000.

6.3. Present Values Indexed at Times Other Than $t = 0$

In practice with investments, analysts frequently need to find present values indexed at times other than $t = 0$. Subscripting the present value and evaluating a perpetuity beginning with $100 payments in Year 2, we find $PV_1 = \$100/0.05 = \$2,000$ at a 5 percent discount rate. Further, we can calculate today's PV as $PV_0 = \$2,000/1.05 = \$1,904.76$.

Consider a similar situation in which cash flows of $6 per year begin at the end of the 4th year and continue at the end of each year thereafter, with the last cash flow at the end of the 10th year. From the perspective of the end of the third year, we are facing a typical seven-year ordinary annuity. We can find the present value of the annuity from the perspective of the end of the third year and then discount that present value back to the present. At an interest rate of 5 percent, the cash flows of $6 per year starting at the end of the fourth year will be worth $34.72 at the end of the third year ($t = 3$) and $29.99 today ($t = 0$).

The next example illustrates the important concept that an annuity or perpetuity beginning sometime in the future can be expressed in present value terms one period prior to the first payment. That present value can then be discounted back to today's present value.

EXAMPLE 1-15   The Present Value
of a Projected Perpetuity

Consider a level perpetuity of £100 per year with its first payment beginning at $t = 5$. What is its present value today (at $t = 0$), given a 5 percent discount rate?

Solution: First, we find the present value of the perpetuity at $t = 4$ and then discount that amount back to $t = 0$. (Recall that a perpetuity or an ordinary annuity has its first payment one period away, explaining the $t = 4$ index for our present value calculation.)

i. Find the present value of the perpetuity at $t = 4$:

$$A = £100$$
$$r = 5\% = 0.05$$
$$PV = A/r$$
$$= £100/0.05$$
$$= £2,000$$

ii. Find the present value of the future amount at $t = 4$. From the perspective of $t = 0$, the present value of £2,000 can be considered a future value. Now we need to find the present value of a lump sum:

$$FV_N = £2,000 \text{(the present value at } t = 4)$$
$$r = 5\% = 0.05$$
$$N = 4$$
$$PV = FV_N(1 + r)^{-N}$$
$$= £2,000(1.05)^{-4}$$
$$= £2,000(0.822702)$$
$$= £1,645.40$$

Today's present value of the perpetuity is £1,645.40.

As discussed earlier, an annuity is a series of payments of a fixed amount for a specified number of periods. Suppose we own a perpetuity. At the same time, we issue a perpetuity obligating us to make payments; these payments are the same size as those of the perpetuity we own. However, the first payment of the perpetuity we issue is at $t = 5$; payments then continue on forever. The payments on this second perpetuity exactly offset the payments received from the perpetuity we own at $t = 5$ and all subsequent dates. We are left with level nonzero net cash flows at $t = 1, 2, 3$, and 4. This outcome exactly fits the definition of an annuity with four payments. Thus we can construct an annuity as the difference between two perpetuities with equal, level payments but differing starting dates. The next example illustrates this result.

EXAMPLE 1-16   The Present Value of an Ordinary Annuity
as the Present Value of a Current Minus Projected Perpetuity

Given a 5 percent discount rate, find the present value of a four-year ordinary annuity
of £100 per year starting in Year 1 as the difference between the following two level
perpetuities:

Perpetuity 1   £100 per year starting in Year 1 (first payment at $t = 1$)

Perpetuity 2   £100 per year starting in Year 5 (first payment at $t = 5$)

Solution: If we subtract Perpetuity 2 from Perpetuity 1, we are left with an ordinary
annuity of £100 per period for four years (payments at $t = 1, 2, 3, 4$). Subtracting the
present value of Perpetuity 2 from that of Perpetuity 1, we arrive at the present value of
the four-year ordinary annuity:

i. $PV_0(\text{Perpetuity 1}) = £100/0.05 = £2,000$
ii. $PV_4(\text{Perpetuity 2}) = £100/0.05 = £2,000$
iii. $PV_0(\text{Perpetuity 2}) = £2,000/(1.05)^4 = £1,645.40$
iv. $PV_0(\text{Annuity}) \quad = PV_0(\text{Perpetuity 1}) - PV_0(\text{Perpetuity 2})$
         $= £2,000 - £1,645.40$
         $= £354.60$

The four-year ordinary annuity's present value is equal to $£2,000 - £1,645.40 = £354.60$.

6.4. The Present Value of a Series of Unequal Cash Flows

When we have unequal cash flows, we must first find the present value of each individual
cash flow and then sum the respective present values. For a series with many cash flows, we
usually use a spreadsheet. Table 1-3 lists a series of cash flows with the time periods in the
first column, cash flows in the second column, and each cash flow's present value in the third
column. The last row of Table 1-3 shows the sum of the five present values.

   We could calculate the future value of these cash flows by computing them one at a
time using the single-payment future value formula. We already know the present value of

TABLE 1-3   A Series of Unequal Cash Flows and Their Present
Values at 5 Percent

Time Period	Cash Flow	Present Value at Year 0
1	$1,000	$1,000(1.05)^{-1} =$ $952.38
2	$2,000	$2,000(1.05)^{-2} =$ $1,814.06
3	$4,000	$4,000(1.05)^{-3} =$ $3,455.35
4	$5,000	$5,000(1.05)^{-4} =$ $4,113.51
5	$6,000	$6,000(1.05)^{-5} =$ $4,701.16
		Sum $= $15,036.46

this series, however, so we can easily apply time-value equivalence. The future value of the series of cash flows from Table 1-2, $19,190.76, is equal to the single $15,036.46 amount compounded forward to $t = 5$:

$$PV = \$15,036.46$$

$$N = 5$$

$$r = 5\% = 0.05$$

$$FV_N = PV(1 + r)^N$$

$$= \$15,036.46(1.05)^5$$

$$= \$15,036.46(1.276282)$$

$$= \$19,190.76$$

7. SOLVING FOR RATES, NUMBER OF PERIODS, OR SIZE OF ANNUITY PAYMENTS

In the previous examples, certain pieces of information have been made available. For instance, all problems have given the rate of interest, r, the number of time periods, N, the annuity amount, A, and either the present value, PV, or future value, FV. In real-world applications, however, although the present and future values may be given, you may have to solve for either the interest rate, the number of periods, or the annuity amount. In the subsections that follow, we show these types of problems.

7.1. Solving for Interest Rates and Growth Rates

Suppose a bank deposit of €100 is known to generate a payoff of €111 in one year. With this information, we can infer the interest rate that separates the present value of €100 from the future value of €111 by using Equation 1-2, $FV_N = PV(1 + r)^N$, with $N = 1$. With PV, FV, and N known, we can solve for r directly:

$$1 + r = FV/PV$$

$$1 + r = €111/€100 = 1.11$$

$$r = 0.11, \text{ or } 11\%$$

The interest rate that equates €100 at $t = 0$ to €111 at $t = 1$ is 11 percent. Thus we can state that €100 grows to €111 with a growth rate of 11 percent.

As this example shows, an interest rate can also be considered a growth rate. The particular application will usually dictate whether we use the term "interest rate" or "growth rate." Solving Equation 1-2 for r and replacing the interest rate r with the growth rate g produces the following expression for determining growth rates:

$$g = (FV_N/PV)^{1/N} - 1 \qquad (1\text{-}14)$$

Following are two examples that use the concept of a growth rate.

EXAMPLE 1-17   Calculating a Growth Rate (1)

For 1998, Limited Brands, Inc., recorded net sales of $8,436 million. For 2002, Limited Brands recorded net sales of $8,445 million, only slightly higher than in 1998. Over the four-year period from the end of 1998 to the end of 2002, what was the rate of growth of Limited Brands' net sales?

Solution: To solve this problem, we can use Equation 1-14, $g = (FV_N/PV)^{1/N} - 1$. We denote net sales in 1998 as PV and net sales in 2002 as FV_4. We can then solve for the growth rate as follows:

$$g = \sqrt[4]{\$8,445/\$8,436} - 1$$
$$= \sqrt[4]{1.001067} - 1$$
$$= 1.000267 - 1$$
$$= 0.000267$$

The calculated growth rate of approximately 0.03 percent a year, barely more than zero, confirms the initial impression that Limited Brands' net sales were essentially flat during the 1998–2002 period.

EXAMPLE 1-18   Calculating a Growth Rate (2)

In Example 1-17, we found that Limited Brands' compound growth rate of net sales was close to zero for 1998 to 2002. As a retailer, Limited Brands' sales depend both on the number of stores (or selling square feet or meters) and sales per store (or sales per average selling square foot or meter). In fact, Limited Brands decreased its number of stores during the 1998–2002 period. In 1998, Limited Brands operated 5,382 stores, whereas in 2002 it operated 4,036 stores. In this case, we can speak of a positive compound rate of decrease or a negative compound growth rate. What was the growth rate in number of stores operated?

Solution: Using Equation 1-14, we find

$$g = \sqrt[4]{4,036/5,382} - 1$$
$$= \sqrt[4]{0.749907} - 1$$
$$= 0.930576 - 1$$
$$= -0.069424$$

The rate of growth in stores operated was approximately −6.9 percent during the 1998–2002 period. Note that we can also refer to −6.9 percent as the compound annual growth rate because it is the single number that compounds the number of stores in 1998 forward to the number of stores in 2002. Table 1-4 lists the number of stores operated by Limited Brands from 1998 to 2002.

TABLE 1-4   Number of Limited Brands Stores, 1998–2002

Year	Number of Stores	$(1 + g)_t$	t
1998	5,382		0
1999	5,023	5,023/5,382 = 0.933296	1
2000	5,129	5,129/5,023 = 1.021103	2
2001	4,614	4,614/5,129 = 0.899591	3
2002	4,036	4,036/4,614 = 0.874729	4

Source: www.limited.com.

Table 1-4 also shows 1 plus the one-year growth rate in number of stores. We can compute the 1 plus four-year cumulative growth in number of stores from 1998 to 2002 as the product of quantities (1 + one-year growth rate). We arrive at the same result as when we divide the ending number of stores, 4,036, by the beginning number of stores, 5,382:

$$\frac{4,036}{5,382} = \left(\frac{5,023}{5,382}\right)\left(\frac{5,129}{5,023}\right)\left(\frac{4,614}{5,129}\right)\left(\frac{4,036}{4,614}\right)$$

$$= (1 + g_1)(1 + g_2)(1 + g_3)(1 + g_4)$$

$$0.749907 = (0.933296)(1.021103)(0.899591)(0.874729)$$

The right-hand side of the equation is the product of 1 plus the one-year growth rate in number of stores operated for each year. Recall that, using Equation 1-14, we took the fourth root of 4,036/5,382 = 0.749907. In effect, we were solving for the single value of g which, when compounded over four periods, gives the correct product of 1 plus the one-year growth rates.[7]

In conclusion, we do not need to compute intermediate growth rates as in Table 1-4 to solve for a compound growth rate g. Sometimes, however, the intermediate growth rates are interesting or informative. For example, during one year (2000), Limited Brands increased its number of stores. We can also analyze the variability in growth rates when we conduct an analysis as in Table 1-4. How did Limited Brands maintain approximately the same revenues during the period although it operated increasingly fewer stores? Elsewhere in Limited Brands' disclosures, the company noted that its sales per average selling square foot increased during the period.

---

[7]The compound growth rate that we calculate here is an example of a geometric mean, specifically the geometric mean of the growth rates. We define the geometric mean in the chapter on statistical concepts.

The compound growth rate is an excellent summary measure of growth over multiple time periods. In our Limited Brands example, the compound growth rate of -6.9 percent is the single growth rate that, when added to 1, compounded over four years, and multiplied by the 1998 number of stores operated, yields the 2002 number of stores operated.

7.2. Solving for the Number of Periods

In this section, we demonstrate how to solve for the number of periods given present value, future value, and interest or growth rates.

EXAMPLE 1-19   The Number of Annual Compounding Periods Needed for an Investment to Reach a Specific Value

You are interested in determining how long it will take an investment of €10,000,000 to double in value. The current interest rate is 7 percent compounded annually. How many years will it take €10,000,000 to double to €20,000,000?

Solution: Use Equation 1-2, $FV_N = PV(1 + r)^N$, to solve for the number of periods, N, as follows:

$$(1 + r)^N = FV_N/PV = 2$$
$$N \ln(1 + r) = \ln(2)$$
$$N = \ln(2)/\ln(1 + r)$$
$$= \ln(2)/\ln(1.07) = 10.24$$

With an interest rate of 7 percent, it will take approximately 10 years for the initial €10,000,000 investment to grow to €20,000,000. Solving for N in the expression $(1.07)^N = 2.0$ requires taking the natural logarithm of both sides and using the rule that $\ln(x^N) = N \ln(x)$. Generally, we find that $N = [\ln(FV/PV)]/\ln(1 + r)$. Here, $N = \ln(€20,000,000/€10,000,000)/\ln(1.07) = \ln(2)/\ln(1.07) = 10.24$.[8]

7.3. Solving for the Size of Annuity Payments

In this section, we discuss how to solve for annuity payments. Mortgages, auto loans, and retirement savings plans are classic examples of applications of annuity formulas.

---

[8]To quickly approximate the number of periods, practitioners sometimes use an ad hoc rule called the **Rule of 72**: Divide 72 by the stated interest rate to get the approximate number of years it would take to double an investment at the interest rate. Here, the approximation gives $72/7 = 10.3$ years. The Rule of 72 is loosely based on the observation that it takes 12 years to double an amount at a 6 percent interest rate, giving $6 \times 12 = 72$. At a 3 percent rate, one would guess it would take twice as many years, $3 \times 24 = 72$.

EXAMPLE 1-20   The Annuity Payments Needed to Reach a
Future Value with Monthly Compounding

You are planning to purchase a $120,000 house by making a down payment of
$20,000 and borrowing the remainder with a 30-year fixed-rate mortgage with monthly
payments. The first payment is due at $t = 1$. Current mortgage interest rates are
quoted at 8 percent with monthly compounding. What will your monthly mortgage
payments be?

Solution: The bank will determine the mortgage payments such that at the stated
periodic interest rate, the present value of the payments will be equal to the amount
borrowed (in this case, $100,000). With this fact in mind, we can use Equation 1-11,

$$PV = A \left[\frac{1 - \dfrac{1}{(1+r)^N}}{r} \right]$$, to solve for the annuity amount, A, as the present value

divided by the present value annuity factor:

$$PV = \$100,000$$

$$r_s = 8\% = 0.08$$

$$m = 12$$

$$r_s/m = 0.08/12 = 0.006667$$

$$N = 30$$

$$mN = 12 \times 30 = 360$$

$$\text{Present value annuity factor} = \frac{1 - \dfrac{1}{[1 + (r_s/m)]^{mN}}}{r_s/m} = \frac{1 - \dfrac{1}{(1.006667)^{360}}}{0.006667}$$

$$= 136.283494$$

$$A = PV/\text{Present value annuity factor}$$

$$= \$100,000/136.283494$$

$$= \$733.76$$

The amount borrowed, $100,000, is equivalent to 360 monthly payments of $733.76
with a stated interest rate of 8 percent. The mortgage problem is a relatively straightforward application of finding a level annuity payment.

Next, we turn to a retirement-planning problem. This problem illustrates the complexity
of the situation in which an individual wants to retire with a specified retirement income.
Over the course of a life cycle, the individual may be able to save only a small amount during

the early years but then may have the financial resources to save more during later years. Savings plans often involve uneven cash flows, a topic we will examine in the last part of this chapter. When dealing with uneven cash flows, we take maximum advantage of the principle that dollar amounts indexed at the same point in time are additive—the **cash flow additivity principle**.

EXAMPLE 1-21   The Projected Annuity Amount Needed to Fund a Future Annuity Inflow

Jill Grant is 22 years old (at $t = 0$) and is planning for her retirement at age 63 (at $t = 41$). She plans to save \$2,000 per year for the next 15 years ($t = 1$ to $t = 15$). She wants to have retirement income of \$100,000 per year for 20 years, with the first retirement payment starting at $t = 41$. How much must Grant save each year from $t = 16$ to $t = 40$ in order to achieve her retirement goal? Assume she plans to invest in a diversified stock-and-bond mutual fund that will earn 8 percent per year on average.

Solution: To help solve this problem, we set up the information on a time line. As Figure 1-8 shows, Grant will save \$2,000 (an outflow) each year for Years 1 to 15. Starting in Year 41, Grant will start to draw retirement income of \$100,000 per year for 20 years. In the time line, the annual savings is recorded in parentheses (\$2) to show that it is an outflow. The problem is to find the savings, recorded as X, from Year 16 to Year 40.

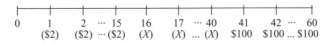

FIGURE 1-8   Solving for Missing Annuity Payments (in thousands)

Solving this problem involves satisfying the following relationship: the present value of savings (outflows) equals the present value of retirement income (inflows). We could bring all the dollar amounts to $t = 40$ or to $t = 15$ and solve for X.

Let us evaluate all dollar amounts at $t = 15$ (we encourage the reader to repeat the problem by bringing all cash flows to $t = 40$). As of $t = 15$, the first payment of X will be one period away (at $t = 16$). Thus we can value the stream of Xs using the formula for the present value of an ordinary annuity.

This problem involves three series of level cash flows. The basic idea is that the present value of the retirement income must equal the present value of Grant's savings. Our strategy requires the following steps:

1. Find the future value of the savings of \$2,000 per year and index it at $t = 15$. This value tells us how much Grant will have saved.

2. Find the present value of the retirement income at $t = 15$. This value tells us how much Grant needs to meet her retirement goals (as of $t = 15$). Two substeps are necessary. First, calculate the present value of the annuity of $100,000 per year at $t = 40$. Use the formula for the present value of an annuity. (Note that the present value is indexed at $t = 40$ because the first payment is at $t = 41$.) Next, discount the present value back to $t = 15$ (a total of 25 periods).

3. Now compute the difference between the amount Grant has saved (Step 1) and the amount she needs to meet her retirement goals (Step 2). Her savings from $t = 16$ to $t = 40$ must have a present value equal to the difference between the future value of her savings and the present value of her retirement income.

Our goal is to determine the amount Grant should save in each of the 25 years from $t = 16$ to $t = 40$. We start by bringing the $2,000 savings to $t = 15$, as follows:

$$A = \$2,000$$

$$r = 8\% = 0.08$$

$$N = 15$$

$$FV = A\left[\frac{(1 + r)^N - 1}{r}\right]$$

$$= \$2,000\left[\frac{(1.08)^{15} - 1}{0.08}\right]$$

$$= \$2,000(27.152114)$$

$$= \$54,304.23$$

At $t = 15$, Grant's initial savings will have grown to $54,304.23.

Now we need to know the value of Grant's retirement income at $t = 15$. As stated earlier, computing the retirement present value requires two substeps. First, find the present value at $t = 40$ with the formula in Equation 1-11; second, discount this present value back to $t = 15$. Now we can find the retirement income present value at $t = 40$:

$$A = \$100,000$$

$$r = 8\% = 0.08$$

$$N = 20$$

$$PV = A\left[\frac{1 - \dfrac{1}{(1 + r)^N}}{r}\right]$$

$$= \$100,000\left[\frac{1 - \dfrac{1}{(1.08)^{20}}}{0.08}\right]$$

$$= \$100,000(9.818147)$$

$$= \$981,814.74$$

The present value amount is as of $t = 40$, so we must now discount it back as a lump sum to $t = 15$:

$$FV_N = \$981,814.74$$

$$N = 25$$

$$r = 8\% = 0.08$$

$$PV = FV_N(1 + r)^{-N}$$

$$= \$981,814.74(1.08)^{-25}$$

$$= \$981,814.74(0.146018)$$

$$= \$143,362.53$$

Now recall that Grant will have saved \$54,304.23 by $t = 15$. Therefore, in present value terms, the annuity from $t = 16$ to $t = 40$ must equal the difference between the amount already saved (\$54,304.23) and the amount required for retirement (\$143,362.53). This amount is equal to $\$143,362.53 - \$54,304.23 = \$89,058.30$. Therefore, we must now find the annuity payment, A, from $t = 16$ to $t = 40$ that has a present value of \$89,058.30. We find the annuity payment as follows:

$$PV = \$89,058.30$$

$$r = 8\% = 0.08$$

$$N = 25$$

$$\text{Present value annuity factor} = \left[\frac{1 - \dfrac{1}{(1 + r)^N}}{r} \right]$$

$$= \left[\frac{1 - \dfrac{1}{(1.08)^{25}}}{0.08} \right]$$

$$= 10.674776$$

$$A = PV/\text{Present value annuity factor}$$

$$= \$89,058.30/10.674776$$

$$= \$8,342.87$$

Grant will need to increase her savings to $8,342.87 per year from $t = 16$ to $t = 40$ to meet her retirement goal of having a fund equal to $981,814.74 after making her last payment at $t = 40$.

7.4. Review of Present and Future Value Equivalence

As we have demonstrated, finding present and future values involves moving amounts of money to different points on a time line. These operations are possible because present value and future value are equivalent measures separated in time. Table 1-5 illustrates this equivalence; it lists the timing of five cash flows, their present values at $t = 0$, and their future values at $t = 5$.

To interpret Table 1-5, start with the third column, which shows the present values. Note that each $1,000 cash payment is discounted back the appropriate number of periods to find the present value at $t = 0$. The present value of $4,329.48 is exactly equivalent to the series of cash flows. This information illustrates an important point: A lump sum can actually generate an annuity. If we place a lump sum in an account that earns the stated interest rate for all periods, we can generate an annuity that is equivalent to the lump sum. Amortized loans, such as mortgages and car loans, are examples of this principle.

To see how a lump sum can fund an annuity, assume that we place $4,329.48 in the bank today at 5 percent interest. We can calculate the size of the annuity payments by using Equation 1-11. Solving for A, we find

$$A = \frac{PV}{\dfrac{1 - [1/(1 + r)^N]}{r}}$$

$$= \frac{\$4,329.48}{\dfrac{1 - [1/(1.05)^5]}{0.05}}$$

$$= \$1,000$$

Table 1-6 shows how the initial investment of $4,329.48 can actually generate five $1,000 withdrawals over the next five years.

To interpret Table 1-6, start with an initial present value of $4,329.48 at $t = 0$. From $t = 0$ to $t = 1$, the initial investment earns 5 percent interest, generating a future value

TABLE 1-5   The Equivalence of Present and Future Values

Time	Cash Flow	Present Value at $t = 0$	Future Value at $t = 5$
1	$1,000	$1,000(1.05)^{-1} = $952.38	$1,000(1.05)^4 = $1,215.51
2	$1,000	$1,000(1.05)^{-2} = $907.03	$1,000(1.05)^3 = $1,157.63
3	$1,000	$1,000(1.05)^{-3} = $863.84	$1,000(1.05)^2 = $1,102.50
4	$1,000	$1,000(1.05)^{-4} = $822.70	$1,000(1.05)^1 = $1,050.00
5	$1,000	$1,000(1.05)^{-5} = $783.53	$1,000(1.05)^0 = $1,000.00
		Sum: $4,329.48	Sum: $5,525.64

TABLE 1-6   How an Initial Present Value Funds an Annuity

Time Period	Amount Available at the Beginning of the Time Period	Ending Amount Before Withdrawal	Withdrawal	Amount Available After Withdrawal
1	$4,329.48	$4,329.48(1.05) = $4,545.95	$1,000	$3,545.95
2	$3,545.95	$3,545.95(1.05) = $3,723.25	$1,000	$2,723.25
3	$2,723.25	$2,723.25(1.05) = $2,859.41	$1,000	$1,859.41
4	$1,859.41	$1,859.41(1.05) = $1,952.38	$1,000	$952.38
5	$952.38	$952.38(1.05) = $1,000	$1,000	$0

of $4,329.48(1.05) = $4,545.95. We then withdraw $1,000 from our account, leaving $4,545.95 − $1,000 = $3,545.95 (the figure reported in the last column for time period 1). In the next period, we earn one year's worth of interest and then make a $1,000 withdrawal. After the fourth withdrawal, we have $952.38, which earns 5 percent. This amount then grows to $1,000 during the year, just enough for us to make the last withdrawal. Thus the initial present value, when invested at 5 percent for five years, generates the $1,000 five-year ordinary annuity. The present value of the initial investment is exactly equivalent to the annuity.

Now we can look at how future value relates to annuities. In Table 1-5, we reported that the future value of the annuity was $5,525.64. We arrived at this figure by compounding the first $1,000 payment forward four periods, the second $1,000 forward three periods, and so on. We then added the five future amounts at $t = 5$. The annuity is equivalent to $5,525.64 at $t = 5$ and $4,329.48 at $t = 0$. These two dollar measures are thus equivalent. We can verify the equivalence by finding the present value of $5,525.64, which is $5,525.64 \times (1.05)^{-5} = $4,329.48. We found this result above when we showed that a lump sum can generate an annuity.

To summarize what we have learned so far: A lump sum can be seen as equivalent to an annuity, and an annuity can be seen as equivalent to its future value. Thus present values, future values, and a series of cash flows can all be considered equivalent as long as they are indexed at the same point in time.

7.5. The Cash Flow Additivity Principle

The cash flow additivity principle—the idea that amounts of money indexed at the same point in time are additive—is one of the most important concepts in time value of money mathematics. We have already mentioned and used this principle; this section provides a reference example for it.

Consider the two series of cash flows shown on the time line in Figure 1-9. The series are denoted A and B. If we assume that the annual interest rate is 2 percent, we can find the future value of each series of cash flows as follows. Series A's future value is $100(1.02) + $100 = $202. Series B's future value is $200(1.02) + $200 = $404. The future value of (A + B) is $202 + $404 = $606 by the method we have used up to this point. The alternative way to find the future value is to add the cash flows of each series, A and B (call it A + B), and then find the future value of the combined cash flow, as shown in Figure 1-9.

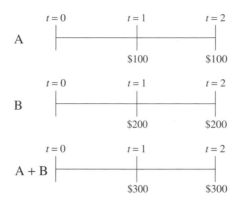

FIGURE 1-9   The Additivity of Two Series of Cash Flows

The third time line in Figure 1-9 shows the combined series of cash flows. Series A has a cash flow of $100 at $t = 1$, and Series B has a cash flow of $200 at $t = 1$. The combined series thus has a cash flow of $300 at $t = 1$. We can similarly calculate the cash flow of the combined series at $t = 2$. The future value of the combined series (A + B) is $300(1.02) + \$300 = \$606$—the same result we found when we added the future values of each series.

The additivity and equivalence principles also appear in another common situation. Suppose cash flows are $4 at the end of the first year and $24 (actually separate payments of $4 and $20) at the end of the second year. Rather than finding present values of the first year's $4 and the second year's $24, we can treat this situation as a $4 annuity for two years and a second-year $20 lump sum. If the discount rate were 6 percent, the $4 annuity would have a present value of $7.33 and the $20 lump sum a present value of $17.80, for a total of $25.13.

CHAPTER 2

DISCOUNTED CASH FLOW APPLICATIONS

1. INTRODUCTION

As investment analysts, much of our work includes evaluating transactions involving present and future cash flows. In the chapter on the time value of money (TVM), we presented the mathematics needed to solve those problems and illustrated the techniques for the major problem types. In this chapter we turn to applications. Analysts must master the numerous applications of TVM or discounted cash flow analysis in equity, fixed income, and derivatives analysis as they study each of those topics individually. In this chapter, we present a selection of important TVM applications: net present value and internal rate of return as tools for evaluating cash flow streams, portfolio return measurement, and the calculation of money market yields. Important in themselves, these applications also introduce concepts that reappear in many other investment contexts.

The chapter is organized as follows. Section 2 introduces two key TVM concepts, net present value and internal rate of return. Building on these concepts, Section 3 discusses a key topic in investment management, portfolio return measurement. Investment managers often face the task of investing funds for the short term; to understand the choices available, they need to understand the calculation of money market yields. The chapter thus concludes with a discussion of that topic in Section 4.

2. NET PRESENT VALUE AND INTERNAL RATE OF RETURN

In applying discounted cash flow analysis in all fields of finance, we repeatedly encounter two concepts, net present value and internal rate of return. In the following sections we present these keystone concepts.

We could explore the concepts of net present value and internal rate of return in many contexts, because their scope of application covers all areas of finance. Capital budgeting, however, can serve as a representative starting point. Capital budgeting is important not only in corporate finance but also in security analysis, because both equity and fixed income analysts must be able to assess how well managers are investing the assets of their companies. There are three chief areas of financial decision-making in most businesses. **Capital budgeting** is the allocation of funds to relatively long-range projects or investments. From the perspective of capital budgeting, a company is a portfolio of projects and investments. **Capital structure** is the choice of long-term financing for the investments the company wants to make. **Working capital management** is the management of the company's short-term assets (such as inventory) and short-term liabilities (such as money owed to suppliers).

2.1. Net Present Value and the Net Present Value Rule

Net present value (NPV) describes a way to characterize the value of an investment, and the net present value rule is a method for choosing among alternative investments. The **net present value** of an investment is the present value of its cash inflows minus the present value of its cash outflows. The word "net" in net present value refers to subtracting the present value of the investment's outflows (costs) from the present value of its inflows (benefits) to arrive at the net benefit.

The steps in computing NPV and applying the NPV rule are as follows:

1. Identify all cash flows associated with the investment—all inflows and outflows.[1]
2. Determine the appropriate discount rate or opportunity cost, r, for the investment project.[2]
3. Using that discount rate, find the present value of each cash flow. (Inflows have a positive sign and increase NPV; outflows have a negative sign and decrease NPV.)
4. Sum all present values. The sum of the present values of all cash flows (inflows and outflows) is the investment's net present value.
5. Apply the **NPV rule**: If the investment's NPV is positive, an investor should undertake it; if the NPV is negative, the investor should not undertake it. If an investor has two candidates for investment but can only invest in one (i.e., mutually exclusive projects), the investor should choose the candidate with the higher positive NPV.

What is the meaning of the NPV rule? In calculating the NPV of an investment proposal, we use an estimate of the opportunity cost of capital as the discount rate. The opportunity cost of capital is the alternative return that investors forgo in undertaking the investment. When NPV is positive, the investment adds value because it more than covers the opportunity cost of the capital needed to undertake it. So a company undertaking a positive NPV investment increases shareholders' wealth. An individual investor making a positive NPV investment increases personal wealth, but a negative NPV investment decreases wealth.

When working problems using the NPV rule, it will be helpful to refer to the following formula:

$$NPV = \sum_{t=0}^{N} \frac{CF_t}{(1+r)^t} \qquad (2\text{-}1)$$

---

[1] In developing cash flow estimates, we observe two principles. First, we include only the **incremental cash flows** resulting from undertaking the project; we do not include sunk costs (costs that have been committed prior to the project). Second, we account for tax effects by using after-tax cash flows. For a full discussion of these and other issues in capital budgeting, see Brealey and Myers (2003).

[2] The **weighted-average cost of capital** (WACC) is often used to discount cash flows. This value is a weighted average of the after-tax required rates of return on the company's common stock, preferred stock, and long-term debt, where the weights are the fraction of each source of financing in the company's target capital structure. For a full discussion of the issues surrounding the cost of capital, see Brealey and Myers (2003).

where

    CF_t = the expected net cash flow at time t

    N = the investment's projected life

     r = the discount rate or opportunity cost of capital

As always, we state the inputs on a compatible time basis: If cash flows are annual, N is the project's life in years and r is an annual rate. For instance, suppose you are reviewing a proposal that requires an initial outlay of \$2 million ($CF_0 = -\$2$ million). You expect that the proposed investment will generate net positive cash flows of $CF_1 = \$0.50$ million at the end of Year 1, $CF_2 = \$0.75$ million at the end of Year 2, and $CF_3 = \$1.35$ million at the end of Year 3. Using 10 percent as a discount rate, you calculate the NPV as follows:

$$NPV = -\$2 + \$0.50/(1.10) + \$0.75/(1.10)^2 + \$1.35/(1.10)^3$$

$$= -\$2 + \$0.454545 + \$0.619835 + \$1.014275$$

$$= \$0.088655 \text{ million}$$

Because the NPV of \$88,655 is positive, you accept the proposal under the NPV rule.

    Consider an example in which a research and development program is evaluated using the NPV rule.

EXAMPLE 2-1   Evaluating a Research and Development Program Using the NPV Rule

As an analyst covering the RAD Corporation, you are evaluating its research and development (R&D) program for the current year. Management has announced that it intends to invest \$1 million in R&D. Incremental net cash flows are forecasted to be \$150,000 per year in perpetuity. RAD Corporation's opportunity cost of capital is 10 percent.

    1. State whether RAD's R&D program will benefit shareholders, as judged by the NPV rule.
    2. Evaluate whether your answer to Part 1 changes if RAD Corporation's opportunity cost of capital is 15 percent rather than 10 percent.

Solution to 1: The constant net cash flows of \$150,000, which we can denote as $\overline{CF}$, form a perpetuity. The present value of the perpetuity is $\overline{CF}/r$, so we calculate the project's NPV as

    $NPV = CF_0 + \overline{CF}/r = -\$1,000,000 + \$150,000/0.10 = \$500,000$

With an opportunity cost of 10 percent, the present value of the program's cash inflows is \$1.5 million. The program's cost is an immediate outflow of \$1 million; therefore, its net present value is \$500,000. As NPV is positive, you conclude that RAD Corporation's R&D program will benefit shareholders.

Solution to 2: With an opportunity cost of capital of 15 percent, you compute the NPV as you did above, but this time you use a 15 percent discount rate:

$$NPV = -\$1,000,000 + \$150,000/0.15 = \$0$$

With a higher opportunity cost of capital, the present value of the inflows is smaller and the program's NPV is smaller: At 15 percent, the NPV exactly equals $0. At NPV = 0, the program generates just enough cash flow to compensate shareholders for the opportunity cost of making the investment. When a company undertakes a zero-NPV project, the company becomes larger but shareholders' wealth does not increase.

2.2. The Internal Rate of Return and the Internal Rate of Return Rule

Financial managers often want a single number that represents the rate of return generated by an investment. The rate of return computation most often used in investment applications (including capital budgeting) is the internal rate of return (IRR). The internal rate of return rule is a second method for choosing among investment proposals. The **internal rate of return** is the discount rate that makes net present value equal to zero. It equates the present value of the investment's costs (outflows) to the present value of the investment's benefits (inflows). The rate is "internal" because it depends only on the cash flows of the investment; no external data are needed. As a result, we can apply the IRR concept to any investment that can be represented as a series of cash flows. In the study of bonds, we encounter IRR under the name of yield to maturity. Later in this chapter, we will explore IRR as the money-weighted rate of return for portfolios.

Before we continue, however, we must add a note of caution about interpreting IRR: Even if our cash flow projections are correct, we will realize a compound rate of return that is equal to IRR over the life of the investment *only if* we can reinvest all interim cash flows at exactly the IRR. Suppose the IRR for a project is 15 percent but we consistently reinvest the cash generated by the project at a lower rate. In this case, we will realize a return that is less than 15 percent. (This principle can work in our favor if we can reinvest at rates above 15 percent.)

To return to the definition of IRR, in mathematical terms we said the following:

$$NPV = CF_0 + \frac{CF_1}{(1 + IRR)^1} + \frac{CF_2}{(1 + IRR)^2} + \cdots + \frac{CF_N}{(1 + IRR)^N} = 0 \qquad (2\text{-}2)$$

Again, the IRR in Equation 2-2 must be compatible with the timing of the cash flows. If the cash flows are quarterly, we have a quarterly IRR in Equation 2-2. We can then state the IRR on an annual basis. For some simple projects, the cash flow at $t = 0$, CF_0, captures the single capital outlay or initial investment; cash flows after $t = 0$ are the positive returns to the investment. In such cases, we can say $CF_0 = -$Investment (the negative sign indicates an outflow). Thus we can rearrange Equation 2-2 in a form that is helpful in those cases:

$$Investment = \frac{CF_1}{(1 + IRR)^1} + \frac{CF_2}{(1 + IRR)^2} + \cdots + \frac{CF_N}{(1 + IRR)^N}$$

For most real-life problems, financial analysts use software, spreadsheets, or financial calculators to solve this equation for IRR, so you should familiarize yourself with such tools.[3]

The investment decision rule using IRR, the **IRR rule**, states the following: "Accept projects or investments for which the IRR is greater than the opportunity cost of capital." The IRR rule uses the opportunity cost of capital as a **hurdle rate**, or rate that a project's IRR must exceed for the project to be accepted. Note that if the opportunity cost of capital is equal to the IRR, then the NPV is equal to 0. If the project's opportunity cost is less than the IRR, the NPV is greater than 0 (using a discount rate less than the IRR will make the NPV positive). With these comments in mind, we work through two examples that involve the internal rate of return.

EXAMPLE 2-2   Evaluating a Research and Development Program Using the IRR Rule

In the previous RAD Corporation example, the initial outlay is $1 million and the program's cash flows are $150,000 in perpetuity. Now you are interested in determining the program's internal rate of return. Address the following:

1. Write the equation for determining the internal rate of return of this R&D program.
2. Calculate the IRR.

Solution to 1: Finding the IRR is equivalent to finding the discount rate that makes the NPV equal to 0. Because the program's cash flows are a perpetuity, you can set up the NPV equation as

$$NPV = -\text{Investment} + \overline{CF}/IRR = 0$$

$$NPV = -\$1,000,000 + \$150,000/IRR = 0$$

or as

$$\text{Investment} = \overline{CF}/IRR$$

$$\$1,000,000 = \$150,000/IRR$$

Solution to 2: We can solve for IRR as IRR = $150,000/$1,000,000 = 0.15 or 15 percent. The solution of 15 percent accords with the definition of IRR. In Example 2-1, you found that a discount rate of 15 percent made the program's NPV equal to 0. By definition, therefore, the program's IRR must be 15 percent. If the opportunity cost of capital is also 15 percent, the R&D program just covers its opportunity costs and neither

---

[3]In some real-world capital budgeting problems, the initial investment (which has a minus sign) may be followed by subsequent cash inflows (which have plus signs) and outflows (which have minus signs). In these instances, the project can have more than one IRR. The possibility of multiple solutions is a theoretical limitation of IRR.

increases nor decreases shareholder wealth. If it is less than 15 percent, the IRR rule indicates that management should invest in the program because it more than covers its opportunity cost. If the opportunity cost is greater than 15 percent, the IRR rule tells management to reject the R&D program. For a given opportunity cost, the IRR rule and the NPV rule lead to the same decision in this example.

EXAMPLE 2-3   The IRR and NPV Rules Side by Side

The Japanese company Kageyama Ltd. is considering whether or not to open a new factory to manufacture capacitors used in cell phones. The factory will require an investment of ¥1,000 million. The factory is expected to generate level cash flows of ¥294.8 million per year in each of the next five years. According to information in its financial reports, Kageyama's opportunity cost of capital for this type of project is 11 percent.

1. Determine whether the project will benefit Kageyama's shareholders using the NPV rule.
2. Determine whether the project will benefit Kageyama's shareholders using the IRR rule.

Solution to 1: The cash flows can be grouped into an initial outflow of ¥1,000 million and an ordinary annuity of five inflows of ¥294.8 million. The expression for the present value of an annuity is $A[1 - (1 + r)^{-N}]/r$, where A is the level annuity payment. Therefore, with amounts shown in millions of Japanese yen,

$$\text{NPV} = -1,000 + 294.8[1 - (1.11)^{-5}]/0.11$$
$$= -1,000 + 1,089.55 = 89.55$$

Because the project's NPV is positive ¥89.55 million, it should benefit Kageyama's shareholders.

Solution to 2: The IRR of the project is the solution to

$$\text{NPV} = -1,000 + 294.8[1 - (1 + \text{IRR})^{-5}]/\text{IRR} = 0$$

This project's positive NPV tells us that the internal rate of return must be greater than 11 percent. Using a calculator, we find that IRR is 0.145012 or 14.50 percent. Table 2-1 gives the keystrokes on most financial calculators.

Because the IRR of 14.50 percent is greater than the opportunity cost of the project, the project should benefit Kageyama's shareholders. Whether it uses the IRR rule or the NPV rule, Kageyama makes the same decision: Build the factory.

TABLE 2-1   Computing IRR

Notation Used on Most Calculators	Numerical Value for This Problem
N	5
%*i* **compute**	X
PV	$-1,000$
PMT	294.8
FV	n/a ($=0$)

In the previous example, value creation is evident: For a single ¥1,000 million payment, Kageyama creates a project worth ¥1,089.55 million, a value increase of ¥89.55 million. Another perspective on value creation comes from converting the initial investment into a capital charge against the annual operating cash flows that the project generates. Recall that the project generates an annual operating cash flow of ¥294,800,000. If we subtract a capital charge of ¥270,570,310 (the amount of a five-year annuity having a present value of ¥1,000 million at 11 percent), we find ¥294,800,000 − ¥270,570,310 = ¥24,229,690. The amount of ¥24,229,690 represents the profit in each of the next five years after taking into account opportunity costs. The present value of a five-year annuity of ¥24,229,690 at an 11 percent cost of capital is exactly what we calculated as the project's NPV: ¥89.55 million. Therefore, we can also calculate NPV by converting the initial investment to an annual capital charge against cash flow.

2.3. Problems with the IRR Rule

The IRR and NPV rules give the same accept or reject decision when projects are independent—that is, when the decision to invest in one project does not affect the decision to undertake another. When a company cannot finance all the projects it would like to undertake—that is, when projects are mutually exclusive—it must rank the projects from most profitable to least. However, rankings according to IRR and NPV may not be the same. The IRR and NPV rules rank projects differently when

- the size or scale of the projects differs (measuring size by the investment needed to undertake the project), or
- the timing of the projects' cash flows differs.

When the IRR and NPV rules conflict in ranking projects, we should take directions from the NPV rule. Why that preference? The NPV of an investment represents the expected addition to shareholder wealth from an investment, and we take the maximization of shareholder wealth to be a basic financial objective of a company. To illustrate the preference for the NPV rule, consider first the case of projects that differ in size. Suppose that a company has only €30,000 available to invest.[4] The company has available two one-period investment projects described as A and B in Table 2-2.

---

[4]Or suppose the two projects require the same physical or other resources, so that only one can be undertaken.

TABLE 2-2   IRR and NPV for Mutually Exclusive Projects of Different Size

Project	Investment at $t = 0$	Cash Flow at $t = 1$	IRR	NPV at 8%
A	−€10,000	€15,000	50%	€3,888.89
B	−€30,000	€42,000	40%	€8,888.89

Project A requires an immediate investment of €10,000. This project will make a single cash payment of $15,000 at $t = 1$. Because the IRR is the discount rate that equates the present value of the future cash flow with the cost of the investment, the IRR equals 50 percent. If we assume that the opportunity cost of capital is 8 percent, then the NPV of Project A is €3,888.89. We compute the IRR and NPV of Project B as 40 percent and €8,888.89, respectively. The IRR and NPV rules indicate that we should undertake both projects, but to do so we would need €40,000—more money than is available. So we need to rank the projects. How do the projects rank according to IRR and NPV?

The IRR rule ranks Project A, with the higher IRR, first. The NPV rule, however, ranks Project B, with the higher NPV, first—a conflict with the IRR rule's ranking. Choosing Project A because it has the higher IRR would not lead to the largest increase in shareholders' wealth. Investing in Project A effectively leaves €20,000 (€30,000 minus A's cost) uninvested. Project A increases wealth by almost €4,000, but Project B increases wealth by almost €9,000. The difference between the two projects' scale creates the inconsistency in the ranking between the two rules.

IRR and NPV can also rank projects of the same scale differently when the timing of cash flows differs. We can illustrate this principle with Projects A and D, presented in Table 2-3.

TABLE 2-3   IRR and NPV for Mutually Exclusive Projects with Different Timing of Cash Flows

Project	CF_0	CF_1	CF_2	CF_3	IRR	NPV at 8%
A	− €10,000	€15,000	0	0	50.0%	€3,888.89
D	− €10,000	0	0	€21,220	28.5%	€6,845.12

The terms CF_0, CF_1, CF_2, and CF_3 represent the cash flows at time periods 0, 1, 2, and 3. The IRR for Project A is the same as it was in the previous example. The IRR for Project D is found as follows:

$$-10,000 + \frac{21,220}{(1 + IRR)^3} = 0$$

The IRR for Project D is 28.5 percent, compared with 50 percent for Project A. IRRs and IRR rankings are not affected by any external interest rate or discount rate because a project's cash flows alone determine the internal rate of return. The IRR calculation furthermore assumes reinvestment at the IRR, so we generally cannot interpret them as achievable rates of return. For Project D, for example, to achieve a 28.5 percent return we would need to earn 28.5 percent on €10,000 for the first year, earn 28.5 percent on €10,000(1.285) = €12,850 the second year, and earn 28.5 percent on €10,000(1.285)^2 = €16,512.25 the third year.[5] A reinvestment rate such as 50 percent or 28.5 percent may be quite unrealistic. By contrast, the calculation of NPV uses an external market-determined discount rate, and reinvestment is assumed to take place at that discount rate. NPV rankings can depend on the external discount rate chosen. Here, Project D has a larger but more distant cash inflow (€21,220 versus €15,000). As a result, Project D has a higher NPV than Project A at lower discount rates.[6] The NPV rule's assumption about reinvestment rates is more realistic and more economically relevant because it incorporates the market-determined opportunity cost of capital as a discount rate. As a consequence, the NPV is the expected addition to shareholder wealth from an investment.

In summary, when dealing with mutually exclusive projects, choose among them using the NPV rule when the IRR rule and NPV rule conflict.[7]

3. PORTFOLIO RETURN MEASUREMENT

Suppose you are an investor and you want to assess the success of your investments. You face two related but distinct tasks. The first is **performance measurement**, which involves calculating returns in a logical and consistent manner. Accurate performance measurement provides the basis for your second task, **performance appraisal**.[8] Performance measurement is thus of great importance for all investors and investment managers because it is the foundation for all further analysis.

In our discussion of portfolio return measurement, we will use the fundamental concept of **holding period return** (HPR), the return that an investor earns over a specified holding period. For an investment that makes one cash payment at the end of the holding period, HPR = $(P_1 - P_0 + D_1)/P_0$, where P_0 is the initial investment, P_1 is the price received at the end of the holding period, and D_1 is the cash paid by the investment at the end of the holding period.

Particularly when we measure performance over many periods, or when the portfolio is subject to additions and withdrawals, portfolio performance measurement is a challenging task. Two of the measurement tools available are the money-weighted rate of return measure and the time-weighted rate of return measure. The first measure we discuss, the money-weighted rate of return, implements a concept we have already covered in the context of capital budgeting: internal rate of return.

3.1. Money-Weighted Rate of Return

The first performance measurement concept that we will discuss is an internal rate of return calculation. In investment management applications, the internal rate of return is called the

---

[5]The ending amount €10,000(1.285)^3 = €21,218 differs from the €21,220 amount listed in Table 2-3 because we rounded IRR.

[6]There is a crossover discount rate above which Project A has a higher NPV than Project D. This crossover rate is 18.94 percent.

[7]Technically, different reinvestment rate assumptions account for this conflict between the IRR and NPV rules. The IRR rule assumes that the company can earn the IRR on all reinvested cash flows, but the NPV rule assumes that cash flows are reinvested at the company's opportunity cost of capital. The NPV assumption is far more realistic. For further details on this and other topics in capital budgeting, see Brealey and Myers (2003).

[8]The term "performance evaluation" has been used as a synonym for performance appraisal. In later chapters we will discuss one performance appraisal tool, the Sharpe ratio.

TABLE 2-4   Cash Flows

Time	Outlay
0	$200 to purchase the first share
1	$225 to purchase the second share

	Proceeds
1	$5 dividend received from first share (and not reinvested)
2	$10 dividend ($5 per share × 2 shares) received
2	$470 received from selling two shares at $235 per share

money-weighted rate of return because it accounts for the timing and amount of all dollar flows into and out of the portfolio.[9]

To illustrate the money-weighted return, consider an investment that covers a two-year horizon. At time $t = 0$, an investor buys one share at $200. At time $t = 1$, he purchases an additional share at $225. At the end of Year 2, $t = 2$, he sells both shares for $235 each. During both years, the stock pays a per-share dividend of $5. The $t = 1$ dividend is not reinvested. Table 2-4 shows the total cash inflows and outflows.

The money-weighted return on this portfolio is its internal rate of return for the two-year period. The portfolio's internal rate of return is the rate, r, for which the present value of the cash inflows minus the present value of the cash outflows equals 0, or

$$PV(\text{outflows}) = PV(\text{inflows})$$

$$\$200 + \frac{\$225}{(1 + r)} = \frac{\$5}{(1 + r)} + \frac{\$480}{(1 + r)^2}$$

The left-hand side of this equation details the outflows: $200 at time $t = 0$ and $225 at time $t = 1$. The $225 outflow is discounted back one period because it occurs at $t = 1$. The right-hand side of the equation shows the present value of the inflows: $5 at time $t = 1$ (discounted back one period) and $480 (the $10 dividend plus the $470 sale proceeds) at time $t = 2$ (discounted back two periods).

To solve for the money-weighted return, we use either a financial calculator that allows us to enter cash flows or a spreadsheet with an IRR function.[10] The first step is to group net cash flows by time. For this example, we have $-\$200$ for the $t = 0$ net cash flow, $-\$220 = -\$225 + \$5$ for the $t = 1$ net cash flow, and $480 for the $t = 2$ net cash flow. After entering these cash flows, we use the spreadsheet's or calculator's IRR function to find that the money-weighted rate of return is 9.39 percent.[11]

Now we take a closer look at what has happened to the portfolio during each of the two years. In the first year, the portfolio generated a one-period holding period return of

---

[9]In the United States, the money-weighted return is frequently called the dollar-weighted return. We follow a standard presentation of the money-weighted return as an IRR concept.

[10]In this particular case we could solve for r by solving the quadratic equation $480x^2 - 220x - 200 = 0$ with $x = 1/(1 + r)$, using standard results from algebra. In general, however, we rely on a calculator or spreadsheet software to compute a money-weighted rate of return.

[11]Note that the calculator or spreadsheet will give the IRR as a periodic rate. If the periods are not annual, we annualize the periodic rate.

($5 + $225 − $200)/$200 = 15 percent. At the beginning of the second year, the amount invested is $450, calculated as $225 (per share price of stock) × 2 shares, because the $5 dividend was spent rather than reinvested. At the end of the second year, the proceeds from the liquidation of the portfolio are $470 (as detailed in Table 2-4) plus $10 in dividends (as also detailed in Table 2-4). So in the second year the portfolio produced a holding period return of ($10 + $470 − $450)/$450 = 6.67 percent. The mean holding period return was (15% + 6.67%)/2 = 10.84 percent. The money-weighted rate of return, which we calculated as 9.39 percent, puts a greater weight on the second year's relatively poor performance (6.67 percent) than the first year's relatively good performance (15 percent), as more money was invested in the second year than in the first. That is the sense in which returns in this method of calculating performance are "money weighted."

As a tool for evaluating investment managers, the money-weighted rate of return has a serious drawback. Generally, the investment manager's clients determine when money is given to the investment manager and how much money is given. As we have seen, those decisions may significantly influence the investment manager's money-weighted rate of return. A general principle of evaluation, however, is that persons or entities should be judged only on the basis of their own actions, or actions under their control. An evaluation tool should isolate the effects of the investment manager's actions. The next section presents a tool that is effective in that respect.

3.2. Time-Weighted Rate of Return

An investment measure that is not sensitive to the additions and withdrawals of funds is the time-weighted rate of return. In the investment management industry, the time-weighted rate of return is the preferred performance measure. The **time-weighted rate of return** measures the compound rate of growth of $1 initially invested in the portfolio over a stated measurement period. In contrast to the money-weighted rate of return, the time-weighted rate of return is not affected by cash withdrawals or additions to the portfolio. The term "time-weighted" refers to the fact that returns are averaged over time. To compute an exact time-weighted rate of return on a portfolio, take the following three steps:

1. Price the portfolio immediately prior to any significant addition or withdrawal of funds. Break the overall evaluation period into subperiods based on the dates of cash inflows and outflows.
2. Calculate the holding period return on the portfolio for each subperiod.
3. Link or compound holding period returns to obtain an annual rate of return for the year (the time-weighted rate of return for the year). If the investment is for more than one year, take the geometric mean of the annual returns to obtain the time-weighted rate of return over that measurement period.

Let us return to our money-weighted example and calculate the time-weighted rate of return for that investor's portfolio. In that example, we computed the holding period returns on the portfolio, Step 2 in the procedure for finding time-weighted rate of return. Given that the portfolio earned returns of 15 percent during the first year and 6.67 percent during the second year, what is the portfolio's time-weighted rate of return over an evaluation period of two years?

We find this time-weighted return by taking the geometric mean of the two holding period returns, Step 3 in the procedure above. The calculation of the geometric mean exactly mirrors the calculation of a compound growth rate. Here, we take the product of 1 plus the holding period return for each period to find the terminal value at $t = 2$ of \$1 invested at $t = 0$. We then take the square root of this product and subtract 1 to get the geometric mean. We interpret the result as the annual compound growth rate of \$1 invested in the portfolio at $t = 0$. Thus we have

$$(1 + \text{Time-weighted return})^2 = (1.15)(1.0667)$$

$$\text{Time-weighted return} = \sqrt{(1.15)(1.0667)} - 1 = 10.76\%$$

The time-weighted return on the portfolio was 10.76 percent, compared with the money-weighted return of 9.39 percent, which gave larger weight to the second year's return. We can see why investment managers find time-weighted returns more meaningful. If a client gives an investment manager more funds to invest at an unfavorable time, the manager's money-weighted rate of return will tend to be depressed. If a client adds funds at a favorable time, the money-weighted return will tend to be elevated. The time-weighted rate of return removes these effects.

In defining the steps to calculate an exact time-weighted rate of return, we said that the portfolio should be valued immediately prior to any significant addition or withdrawal of funds. With the amount of cash flow activity in many portfolios, this task can be costly. We can often obtain a reasonable approximation of the time-weighted rate of return by valuing the portfolio at frequent, regular intervals, particularly if additions and withdrawals are unrelated to market movements. The more frequent the valuation, the more accurate the approximation. Daily valuation is commonplace. Suppose that a portfolio is valued daily over the course of a year. To compute the time-weighted return for the year, we first compute each day's holding period return:

$$r_t = \frac{\text{MVE}_t - \text{MVB}_t}{\text{MVB}_t}$$

where MVB_t equals the market value at the beginning of day t and MVE_t equals the market value at the end of day t. We compute 365 such daily returns, denoted $r_1, r_2, \ldots, r_{365}$. We obtain the annual return for the year by linking the daily holding period returns in the following way: $(1 + r_1) \times (1 + r_2) \times \cdots \times (1 + r_{365}) - 1$. If withdrawals and additions to the portfolio happen only at day's end, this annual return is a precise time-weighted rate of return for the year. Otherwise, it is an approximate time-weighted return for the year.

If we have a number of years of data, we can calculate a time-weighted return for each year individually, as above. If r_i is the time-weighted return for year i, we calculate an annualized time-weighted return as the geometric mean of N annual returns, as follows:

$$r_{TW} = [(1 + r_1) \times (1 + r_2) \times \cdots \times (1 + r_N)]^{1/N} - 1$$

Example 2-4 illustrates the calculation of the time-weighted rate of return.

EXAMPLE 2-4   Time-Weighted Rate of Return

Strubeck Corporation sponsors a pension plan for its employees. It manages part of the equity portfolio in-house and delegates management of the balance to Super Trust Company. As chief investment officer of Strubeck, you want to review the performance of the in-house and Super Trust portfolios over the last four quarters. You have arranged for outflows and inflows to the portfolios to be made at the very beginning of the quarter. Table 2-5 summarizes the inflows and outflows as well as the two portfolios' valuations. In the table, the ending value is the portfolio's value just prior to the cash inflow or outflow at the beginning of the quarter. The amount invested is the amount each portfolio manager is responsible for investing.

TABLE 2-5   Cash Flows for the In-House Strubeck Account and the Super Trust Account

	Quarter			
	1	2	3	4
In-House Account				
Beginning value	$4,000,000	$6,000,000	$5,775,000	$6,720,000
Beginning of period inflow (outflow)	$1,000,000	($500,000)	$225,000	($600,000)
Amount invested	$5,000,000	$5,500,000	$6,000,000	$6,120,000
Ending value	$6,000,000	$5,775,000	$6,720,000	$5,508,000
Super Trust Account				
Beginning value	$10,000,000	$13,200,000	$12,240,000	$5,659,200
Beginning of period inflow (outflow)	$2,000,000	($1,200,000)	($7,000,000)	($400,000)
Amount invested	$12,000,000	$12,000,000	$5,240,000	$5,259,200
Ending value	$13,200,000	$12,240,000	$5,659,200	$5,469,568

Based on the information given, address the following:

1. Calculate the time-weighted rate of return for the in-house account.
2. Calculate the time-weighted rate of return for the Super Trust account.

Solution to 1: To calculate the time-weighted rate of return for the in-house account, we compute the quarterly holding period returns for the account and link them into an annual return. The in-house account's time-weighted rate of return is 27 percent, calculated as follows:

$$1Q \ HPR: r_1 = (\$6,000,000 - \$5,000,000)/\$5,000,000 = 0.20$$

$$2Q \ HPR: r_2 = (\$5,775,000 - \$5,500,000)/\$5,500,000 = 0.05$$

$$3Q \ HPR: r_3 = (\$6,720,000 - \$6,000,000)/\$6,000,000 = 0.12$$

4Q HPR: $r_4 = (\$5,508,000 - \$6,120,000)/\$6,120,000 = -0.10$

$(1 + r_1)(1 + r_2)(1 + r_3)(1 + r_4) - 1 = (1.20)(1.05)(1.12)(0.90) - 1 = 0.27$ or 27%

Solution to 2: The account managed by Super Trust has a time-weighted rate of return of 26 percent, calculated as follows:

1Q HPR: $r_1 = (\$13,200,000 - \$12,000,000)/\$12,000,000 = 0.10$

2Q HPR: $r_2 = (\$12,240,000 - \$12,000,000)/\$12,000,000 = 0.02$

3Q HPR: $r_3 = (\$5,659,200 - \$5,240,000)/\$5,240,000 = 0.08$

4Q HPR: $r_4 = (\$5,469,568 - \$5,259,200)/\$5,259,200 = 0.04$

$(1 + r_1)(1 + r_2)(1 + r_3)(1 + r_4) - 1 = (1.10)(1.02)(1.08)(1.04) - 1 = 0.26$ or 26%

The in-house portfolio's time-weighted rate of return is higher than the Super Trust portfolio's by 100 basis points.

Having worked through this exercise, we are ready to look at a more detailed case.

EXAMPLE 2-5 Time-Weighted and Money-Weighted Rates of Return Side by Side

Your task is to compute the investment performance of the Walbright Fund during 2003. The facts are as follows:

- On 1 January 2003, the Walbright Fund had a market value of $100 million.
- During the period 1 January 2003 to 30 April 2003, the stocks in the fund showed a capital gain of $10 million.
- On 1 May 2003, the stocks in the fund paid a total dividend of $2 million. All dividends were reinvested in additional shares.
- Because the fund's performance had been exceptional, institutions invested an additional $20 million in Walbright on 1 May 2003, raising assets under management to $132 million ($100 + $10 + $2 + $20).
- On 31 December 2003, Walbright received total dividends of $2.64 million. The fund's market value on 31 December 2003, not including the $2.64 million in dividends, was $140 million.
- The fund made no other interim cash payments during 2003.

Based on the information given, address the following:

1. Compute the Walbright Fund's time-weighted rate of return.

2. Compute the Walbright Fund's money-weighted rate of return.
3. Interpret the differences between the time-weighted and money-weighted rates of return.

Solution to 1: Because interim cash flows were made on 1 May 2003, we must compute two interim total returns and then link them to obtain an annual return. Table 2-6 lists the relevant market values on 1 January, 1 May, and 31 December as well as the associated interim four-month (1 January to 1 May) and eight-month (1 May to 31 December) holding period returns.

TABLE 2-6   Cash Flows for the Walbright Fund

1 January 2003	Beginning portfolio value = $100 million
1 May 2003	Dividends received before additional investment = $2 million
	Ending portfolio value = $110 million
	Holding period return = $\dfrac{\$2 + \$10}{\$100} = 12\%$
	New investment = $20 million
	Beginning market value for last 2/3 of year = $132 million
31 December 2003	Dividends received = $2.64 million
	Ending portfolio value = $140 million
	Holding period return = $\dfrac{\$2.64 + \$140 - \$132}{\$132} = 8.06\%$

Now we must geometrically link the four- and eight-month returns to compute an annual return. We compute the time-weighted return as follows:

$$\text{Time-weighted return} = 1.12 \times 1.0806 - 1 = 0.2103$$

In this instance, we compute a time-weighted rate of return of 21.03 percent for one year. The four-month and eight-month intervals combine to equal one year. (Taking the square root of the product 1.12×1.0806 would be appropriate only if 1.12 and 1.0806 each applied to one full year.)

Solution to 2: To calculate the money-weighted return, we find the discount rate that sets the present value of the outflows (purchases) equal to the present value of the inflows (dividends and future payoff). The initial market value of the fund and all additions to it are treated as cash outflows. (Think of them as expenditures.) Withdrawals, receipts, and the ending market value of the fund are counted as inflows. (The ending market value is the amount investors receive on liquidating the fund.) Because interim cash flows have occurred at four-month intervals, we must solve for the four-month internal rate of return. Table 2-6 details the cash flows and their timing.
    The present value equation (in millions) is as follows:

$$\text{PV(outflows)} = \text{PV(inflows)}$$

$$\$100 + \frac{\$2}{(1+r)^1} + \frac{\$20}{(1+r)^1} = \frac{\$2}{(1+r)^1} + \frac{\$2.64}{(1+r)^3} + \frac{\$140}{(1+r)^3}$$

The left-hand side of the equation shows the investments in the fund or outflows: a \$100 million initial investment followed by the \$2 million dividend reinvested and an additional \$20 million of new investment (both occurring at the end of the first four-month interval, which makes the exponent in the denominator 1). The right-hand side of the equation shows the payoffs or inflows: the \$2 million dividend at the first four-month interval followed by the \$2.64 million dividend and the terminal market value of \$140 million (both occurring at the end of the third four-month interval, which makes the exponent in the denominator 3). The second four-month interval has no cash flow. We can bring all the terms to the right of the equal sign, arranging them in order of time. After simplification,

$$0 = -\$100 - \frac{\$20}{(1+r)^1} + \frac{\$142.64}{(1+r)^3}$$

Using a spreadsheet or IRR-enabled calculator, we use -100, -20, 0, and \$142.64 for the $t=0, t=1, t=2$, and $t=3$ net cash flows, respectively.[12] Using either tool, we get a four-month IRR of 6.28 percent. The quick way to annualize this is to multiply by 3. A more accurate way is $(1.0628)^3 - 1 = 0.20$ or 20 percent.

Solution to 3: In this example, the time-weighted return (21.03 percent) is greater than the money-weighted return (20 percent). The Walbright Fund's performance was relatively poorer during the eight-month period, when the fund owned more shares, than it was overall. This fact is reflected in a lower money-weighted rate of return compared with time-weighted rate of return, as the money-weighted return is sensitive to the timing and amount of withdrawals and additions to the portfolio.

The accurate measurement of portfolio returns is important to the process of evaluating portfolio managers. In addition to considering returns, however, analysts must also weigh risk. When we worked through Example 2-4, we stopped short of suggesting that in-house management was superior to Super Trust because it earned a higher time-weighted rate of return. With risk in focus, we can talk of risk-adjusted performance and make comparisons—but only cautiously. In later chapters, we will discuss the Sharpe ratio, an important risk-adjusted performance measure that we might apply to an investment manager's time-weighted rate of return. For now, we have illustrated the major tools for measuring the return on a portfolio.

4. MONEY MARKET YIELDS

In our discussion of internal rate of return and net present value, we referred to the opportunity cost of capital as a market-determined rate. In this section, we begin a discussion of discounted cash flow analysis in actual markets by considering short-term debt markets.

To understand the various ways returns are presented in debt markets, we must discuss some of the conventions for quoting yields on money-market instruments. The **money market**

[12] By convention, we denote outflows with a negative sign, and we need 0 as a placeholder for $t=2$.

is the market for short-term debt instruments (one-year maturity or less). Some instruments require the issuer to repay the lender the amount borrowed plus interest. Others are **pure discount instruments** that pay interest as the difference between the amount borrowed and the amount paid back.

In the U.S. money market, the classic example of a pure discount instrument is the U.S. Treasury bill (T-bill) issued by the federal government. The **face value** of a T-bill is the amount the U.S. government promises to pay back to a T-bill investor. In buying a T-bill, investors pay the face amount less the discount, and receive the face amount at maturity. The **discount** is the reduction from the face amount that gives the price for the T-bill. This discount becomes the interest that accumulates, because the investor receives the face amount at maturity. Thus, investors earn a dollar return equal to the discount if they hold the instrument to maturity. T-bills are by far the most important class of money-market instruments in the United States. Other types of money-market instruments include commercial paper and bankers' acceptances, which are discount instruments, and negotiable certificates of deposit, which are interest-bearing instruments. The market for each of these instruments has its own convention for quoting prices or yields. The remainder of this section examines the quoting conventions for T-bills and other money-market instruments. In most instances, the quoted yields must be adjusted for use in other present value problems.

Pure discount instruments such as T-bills are quoted differently from U.S. government bonds. T-bills are quoted on a **bank discount basis**, rather than on a price basis. The bank discount basis is a quoting convention that annualizes, based on a 360-day year, the discount as a percentage of face value. Yield on a bank discount basis is computed as follows:

$$r_{BD} = \frac{D}{F}\frac{360}{t} \qquad\qquad (2\text{-}3)$$

where

        r_{BD} = the annualized yield on a bank discount basis

         D = the dollar discount, which is equal to the difference between the face value of the bill, F, and its purchase price, P_0

         F = the face value of the T-bill

          t = the actual number of days remaining to maturity

      360 = bank convention of the number of days in a year

The bank discount yield (often called simply the discount yield) takes the dollar discount from par, D, and expresses it as a fraction of the face value (not the price) of the T-bill. This fraction is then multiplied by the number of periods of length t in one year (that is, $360/t$), where the year is assumed to have 360 days. Annualizing in this fashion assumes simple interest (no compounding). Consider the following example.

EXAMPLE 2-6   The Bank Discount Yield

Suppose a T-bill with a face value (or par value) of \$100,000 and 150 days until maturity is selling for \$98,000. What is its bank discount yield?

Solution: For this example, the dollar discount, D, is $2,000. The yield on a bank discount basis is 4.8 percent, as computed with Equation 2-3:

$$r_{BD} = \frac{\$2,000}{\$100,000} \frac{360}{150} = 4.8\%$$

The bank discount formula takes the T-bill's dollar discount from face or par as a fraction of face value, 2 percent, and then annualizes by the factor $360/150 = 2.4$. The price of discount instruments such as T-bills is quoted using discount yields, so we typically translate discount yield into price.

Suppose we know the bank discount yield of 4.8 percent but do not know the price. We solve for the dollar discount, D, as follows:

$$D = r_{BD} F \frac{t}{360}$$

With $r_{BD} = 4.8$ percent, the dollar discount is $D = 0.048 \times \$100,000 \times 150/360 = \$2,000$. Once we have computed the dollar discount, the purchase price for the T-bill is its face value minus the dollar discount, $F - D = \$100,000 - \$2,000 = \$98,000$.

Yield on a bank discount basis is not a meaningful measure of investors' return, for three reasons. First, the yield is based on the face value of the bond, not on its purchase price. Returns from investments should be evaluated relative to the amount that is invested. Second, the yield is annualized based on a 360-day year rather than a 365-day year. Third, the bank discount yield annualizes with simple interest, which ignores the opportunity to earn interest on interest (compound interest).

We can extend Example 2-6 to discuss three often-used alternative yield measures. The first is the holding period return over the remaining life of the instrument (150 days in the case of the T-bill in Example 2-6). It determines the return that an investor will earn by holding the instrument to maturity; as used here, this measure refers to an unannualized rate of return (or periodic rate of return). In fixed income markets, this holding period return is also called a **holding period yield** (HPY).[13] For an instrument that makes one cash payment during its life, HPY is

$$\text{HPY} = \frac{P_1 - P_0 + D_1}{P_0} \tag{2-4}$$

where

$P_0 = $ the initial purchase price of the instrument
$P_1 = $ the price received for the instrument at its maturity
$D_1 = $ the cash distribution paid by the instrument at its maturity (i.e., interest)

---

[13] Bond-market participants often use the term "yield" when referring to total returns (returns incorporating both price change and income), as in yield to maturity. In other cases, yield refers to returns from income alone (as in current yield, which is annual interest divided by price). As used in this book and by many writers, holding period yield is a bond market synonym for holding period return, total return, and horizon return.

When we use this expression to calculate the holding period yield for an interest-bearing instrument (for example, coupon-bearing bonds), we need to observe an important detail: The purchase and sale prices must include any **accrued interest** added to the trade price because the bond was traded between interest payment dates. Accrued interest is the coupon interest that the seller earns from the last coupon date but does not receive as a coupon, because the next coupon date occurs after the date of sale.[14]

For pure discount securities, all of the return is derived by redeeming the bill for more than its purchase price. Because the T-bill is a pure discount instrument, it makes no interest payment and thus $D_1 = 0$. Therefore, the holding period yield is the dollar discount divided by the purchase price, HPY $= D/P_0$, where $D = P_1 - P_0$. The holding period yield is the amount that is annualized in the other measures. For the T-bill in Example 2-6, the investment of \$98,000 will pay \$100,000 in 150 days. The holding period yield on this investment using Equation 2-4 is (\$100,000 − \$98,000)/\$98,000 = \$2,000/\$98,000 = 2.0408 percent. For this example, the periodic return of 2.0408 percent is associated with a 150-day period. If we were to use the T-bill rate of return as the opportunity cost of investing, we would use a discount rate of 2.0408 percent for the 150-day T-bill to find the present value of any other cash flow to be received in 150 days. As long as the other cash flow has risk characteristics similar to those of the T-bill, this approach is appropriate. If the other cash flow were riskier than the T-bill, then we could use the T-bill's yield as a base rate, to which we would add a risk premium. The formula for the holding period yield is the same regardless of the currency of denomination.

The second measure of yield is the **effective annual yield** (EAY). The EAY takes the quantity 1 plus the holding period yield and compounds it forward to one year, then subtracts 1 to recover an annualized return that accounts for the effect of interest-on-interest.[15]

$$EAY = (1 + HPY)^{365/t} - 1 \qquad (2\text{-}5)$$

In our example, we can solve for EAY as follows:

$$EAY = (1.020408)^{365/150} - 1 = 1.050388 - 1 = 5.0388\%$$

This example illustrates a general rule: The bank discount yield is less than the effective annual yield.

The third alternative measure of yield is the **money market yield** (also known as the **CD equivalent yield**). This convention makes the quoted yield on a T-bill comparable to yield quotations on interest-bearing money-market instruments that pay interest on a 360-day basis. In general, the money market yield is equal to the annualized holding period yield; assuming a 360-day year, $r_{MM} = (HPY)(360/t)$. Compared to the bank discount yield, the money market yield is computed on the purchase price, so $r_{MM} = (r_{BD})(F/P_0)$. This equation

---

[14]The price with accrued interest is called the **full price**. Trade prices are quoted "clean" (without accrued interest), but accrued interest, if any, is added to the purchase price. For more on accrued interest, see Fabozzi (2004).

[15]Effective annual yield was called the effective annual rate (Equation 1-5) in the chapter on the time value of money.

TABLE 2-7   Three Commonly Used Yield Measures

Holding Period Yield (HPY)	Effective Annual Yield (EAY)	Money Market Yield (CD Equivalent Yield)
$HPY = \dfrac{P_1 - P_0 + D_1}{P_0}$	$EAY = (1 + HPY)^{365/t} - 1$	$r_{MM} = \dfrac{360 r_{BD}}{360 - (t)(r_{BD})}$

shows that the money market yield is larger than the bank discount yield. In practice, the following expression is more useful because it does not require knowing the T-bill price:

$$r_{MM} = \frac{360 r_{BD}}{360 - (t)(r_{BD})} \tag{2-6}$$

For the T-bill example, the money market yield is $r_{MM} = (360)(0.048)/[360 - (150)(0.048)]$ = 4.898 percent.[16]

Table 2-7 summarizes the three yield measures we have discussed.

The next example will help you consolidate your knowledge of these yield measures.

EXAMPLE 2-7   Using the Appropriate Discount Rate

You need to find the present value of a cash flow of $1,000 that is to be received in 150 days. You decide to look at a T-bill maturing in 150 days to determine the relevant interest rate for calculating the present value. You have found a variety of yields for the 150-day bill. Table 2-8 presents this information.

TABLE 2-8   Short-Term Money Market Yields

Holding period yield	2.0408%
Bank discount yield	4.8%
Money market yield	4.898%
Effective annual yield	5.0388%

Which yield or yields are appropriate for finding the present value of the $1,000 to be received in 150 days?

Solution: The holding period yield is appropriate, and we can also use the money market yield and effective annual yield after converting them to a holding period yield.

---

[16]Some national markets use the money market yield formula, rather than the bank discount yield formula, to quote the yields on discount instruments such as T-bills. In Canada, the convention is to quote Treasury bill yields using the money market formula assuming a 365-day year. Yields for German Treasury discount paper with a maturity less than one year and French BTFs (T-bills) are computed with the money market formula assuming a 360-day year.

- *Holding period yield* (2.0408 percent). This yield is exactly what we want. Because it applies to a 150-day period, we can use it in a straightforward fashion to find the present value of the $1,000 to be received in 150 days. (Recall the principle that discount rates must be compatible with the time period.) The present value is

$$PV = \frac{\$1,000}{1.020408} = \$980.00$$

Now we can see why the other yield measures are inappropriate or not as easily applied.

- *Bank discount yield* (4.8 percent). We should not use this yield measure to determine the present value of the cash flow. As mentioned earlier, the bank discount yield is based on the face value of the bill and not on its price.
- *Money market yield* (4.898 percent). To use the money market yield, we need to convert it to the 150-day holding period yield by dividing it by (360/150). After obtaining the holding period yield $0.04898/(360/150) = 0.020408$, we use it to discount the $1,000 as above.
- *Effective annual yield* (5.0388 percent). This yield has also been annualized, so it must be adjusted to be compatible with the timing of the cash flow. We can obtain the holding period yield from the EAY as follows:

$$(1.050388)^{150/365} - 1 = 0.020408$$

Recall that when we found the effective annual yield, the exponent was 365/150, or the number of 150-day periods in a 365-day year. To shrink the effective annual yield to a 150-day yield, we use the reciprocal of the exponent that we used to annualize.

In Example 2-7, we converted two short-term measures of annual yield to a holding period yield for a 150-day period. That is one type of conversion. We frequently also need to convert periodic rates to annual rates. The issue can arise both in money markets and in longer-term debt markets. As an example, many bonds (long-term debt instruments) pay interest semiannually. Bond investors compute IRRs for bonds, known as yields to maturity (YTM). If the semiannual yield to maturity is 4 percent, how do we annualize it? An exact approach, taking account of compounding, would be to compute $(1.04)^2 - 1 = 0.0816$ or 8.16 percent. This is what we have been calling an effective annual yield. An approach used in U.S. bond markets, however, is to double the semiannual YTM: $4\% \times 2 = 8\%$. The yield to maturity calculated this way, ignoring compounding, has been called a **bond-equivalent yield**. Annualizing a semiannual yield by doubling is putting the yield on a **bond-equivalent basis**. In practice, the result, 8 percent, would be referred to simply as the bond's yield to maturity. In money markets, if we annualized a six-month-period yield by doubling it, in order to make the result comparable to bonds' YTMs, we would also say that the result was a bond-equivalent yield.

CHAPTER 3

STATISTICAL CONCEPTS AND MARKET RETURNS

1. INTRODUCTION

Statistical methods provide a powerful set of tools for analyzing data and drawing conclusions from them. Whether we are analyzing asset returns, earnings growth rates, commodity prices, or any other financial data, statistical tools help us quantify and communicate the data's important features. This chapter presents the basics of describing and analyzing data, the branch of statistics known as descriptive statistics. The chapter supplies a set of useful concepts and tools, illustrated in a variety of investment contexts. One theme of our presentation, reflected in the chapter's title, is the demonstration of the statistical methods that allow us to summarize return distributions.[1] We explore four properties of return distributions:

- where the returns are centered (central tendency),
- how far returns are dispersed from their center (dispersion),
- whether the distribution of returns is symmetrically shaped or lopsided (skewness), and
- whether extreme outcomes are likely (kurtosis).

These same concepts are generally applicable to the distributions of other types of data, too.

The chapter is organized as follows. After defining some basic concepts in Section 2, in Sections 3 and 4 we discuss the presentation of data: Section 3 describes the organization of data in a table format, and Section 4 describes the graphic presentation of data. We then turn to the quantitative description of how data are distributed: Section 5 focuses on measures that quantify where data are centered, or measures of central tendency. Section 6 presents other measures that describe the location of data. Section 7 presents measures that quantify the degree to which data are dispersed. Sections 8 and 9 describe additional measures that provide a more accurate picture of data. Section 10 discusses investment applications of concepts introduced in Section 5.

2. SOME FUNDAMENTAL CONCEPTS

Before starting the study of statistics with this chapter, it may be helpful to examine a picture of the overall field. In the following, we briefly describe the scope of statistics and its branches

---

[1] Ibbotson Associates (www.ibbotson.com) generously provided much of the data used in this chapter. We also draw on Dimson, Marsh, and Staunton's (2002) history and study of world markets, as well as other sources.

of study. We explain the concepts of population and sample. Data come in a variety of types, affecting the ways they can be measured and the appropriate statistical methods for analyzing them. We conclude by discussing the basic types of data measurement.

2.1. The Nature of Statistics

The term **statistics** can have two broad meanings, one referring to data and the other to method. A company's average earnings per share (EPS) for the last 20 quarters or its average returns for the past 10 years are statistics. We may also analyze historical EPS to forecast future EPS or use the company's past returns to infer its risk. The totality of methods we employ to collect and analyze data is also called statistics.

Statistical methods include descriptive statistics and statistical inference (inferential statistics). **Descriptive statistics** is the study of how data can be summarized effectively to describe the important aspects of large data sets. By consolidating a mass of numerical details, descriptive statistics turns data into information. **Statistical inference** involves making forecasts, estimates, or judgments about a larger group from the smaller group actually observed. The foundation for statistical inference is probability theory, and both statistical inference and probability theory will be discussed in later chapters. Our focus in this chapter is solely on descriptive statistics.

2.2. Populations and Samples

Throughout the study of statistics we make a critical distinction between a population and a sample. In this section, we explain these two terms as well as the related terms "parameter" and "sample statistic."[2]

- **Definition of Population.** A **population** is defined as all members of a specified group.

Any descriptive measure of a population characteristic is called a **parameter**. Although a population can have many parameters, investment analysts are usually concerned with only a few, such as the mean value, the range of investment returns, and the variance.

Even if it is possible to observe all the members of a population, it is often too expensive in terms of time or money to attempt to do so. For example, if the population is all telecommunications customers worldwide and an analyst is interested in their purchasing plans, she will find it too costly to observe the entire population. The analyst can address this situation by taking a sample of the population.

- **Definition of Sample.** A **sample** is a subset of a population.

In taking a sample, the analyst hopes it is characteristic of the population. The field of statistics known as sampling deals with taking samples in appropriate ways to achieve the objective of representing the population well. A later chapter addresses the details of sampling.

Earlier, we mentioned statistics in the sense of referring to data. Just as a parameter is a descriptive measure of a population characteristic, a sample statistic (statistic, for short) is a descriptive measure of a sample characteristic.

---

[2] This chapter introduces many statistical concepts and formulas. To make it easy to locate them, we have set off some of the more important ones with bullet points.

- **Definition of Sample Statistic**.   A **sample statistic** (or **statistic**) is a quantity computed from or used to describe a sample.

We devote much of this chapter to explaining and illustrating the use of statistics in this sense. The concept is critical also in statistical inference, which addresses such problems as estimating an unknown population parameter using a sample statistic.

2.3. Measurement Scales

To choose the appropriate statistical methods for summarizing and analyzing data, we need to distinguish among different **measurement scales** or levels of measurement. All data measurements are taken on one of four major scales: nominal, ordinal, interval, or ratio.

Nominal scales represent the weakest level of measurement: They categorize data but do not rank them. If we assigned integers to mutual funds that follow different investment strategies, the number 1 might refer to a small-cap value fund, the number 2 to a large-cap value fund, and so on for each possible style. This nominal scale categorizes the funds according to their style but does not rank them.

Ordinal scales reflect a stronger level of measurement. Ordinal scales sort data into categories that are ordered with respect to some characteristic. For example, the Morningstar and Standard & Poor's star ratings for mutual funds represent an ordinal scale in which one star represents a group of funds judged to have had relatively the worst performance, with two, three, four, and five stars representing groups with increasingly better performance, as evaluated by those services.

An ordinal scale may also involve numbers to identify categories. For example, in ranking balanced mutual funds based on their five-year cumulative return, we might assign the number 1 to the top 10 percent of funds, and so on, so that the number 10 represents the bottom 10 percent of funds. The ordinal scale is stronger than the nominal scale because it reveals that a fund ranked 1 performed better than a fund ranked 2. The scale tells us nothing, however, about the difference in performance between funds ranked 1 and 2 compared with the difference in performance between funds ranked 3 and 4, or 9 and 10.

Interval scales provide not only ranking but also assurance that the differences between scale values are equal. As a result, scale values can be added and subtracted meaningfully. The Celsius and Fahrenheit scales are interval measurement scales. The difference in temperature between $10°C$ and $11°C$ is the same amount as the difference between $40°C$ and $41°C$. We can state accurately that $12°C = 9°C + 3°C$, for example. Nevertheless, the zero point of an interval scale does not reflect complete absence of what is being measured; it is not a true zero point or natural zero. Zero degrees Celsius corresponds to the freezing point of water, not the absence of temperature. As a consequence of the absence of a true zero point, we cannot meaningfully form ratios on interval scales.

As an example, $50°C$, although five times as large a number as $10°C$, does not represent five times as much temperature. Also, questionnaire scales are often treated as interval scales. If an investor is asked to rank his risk aversion on a scale from 1 (extremely risk-averse) to 7 (extremely risk-loving), the difference between a response of 1 and a response of 2 is sometimes assumed to represent the same difference in risk aversion as the difference between a response of 6 and a response of 7. When that assumption can be justified, the data are measured on interval scales.

Ratio scales represent the strongest level of measurement. They have all the characteristics of interval measurement scales as well as a true zero point as the origin. With ratio scales, we can meaningfully compute ratios as well as meaningfully add and subtract amounts within the scale. As a result, we can apply the widest range of statistical tools to data measured on a ratio scale. Rates of return are measured on a ratio scale, as is money. If we have twice as much money, then we have twice the purchasing power. Note that the scale has a natural zero—zero means no money.

EXAMPLE 3-1   Identifying Scales of Measurement

State the scale of measurement for each of the following:

1. Credit ratings for bond issues.[3]
2. Cash dividends per share.
3. Hedge fund classification types.[4]
4. Bond maturity in years.

Solution to 1: Credit ratings are measured on an ordinal scale. A rating places a bond issue in a category, and the categories are ordered with respect to the expected probability of default. But the difference in the expected probability of default between AA— and A+, for example, is not necessarily equal to that between BB— and B+. In other words, letter credit ratings are not measured on an interval scale.

Solution to 2: Cash dividends per share are measured on a ratio scale. For this variable, 0 represents the complete absence of dividends; it is a true zero point.

Solution to 3: Hedge fund classification types are measured on a nominal scale. Each type groups together hedge funds with similar investment strategies. In contrast to credit ratings for bonds, however, hedge fund classification schemes do not involve a ranking. Thus such classification schemes are not measured on an ordinal scale.

Solution to 4: Bond maturity is measured on a ratio scale.

Now that we have addressed the important preliminaries, we can discuss summarizing and describing data.

---

[3]Credit ratings for a bond issue gauge the bond issuer's ability to meet the promised principal and interest payments on the bond. For example, one rating agency, Standard & Poor's, assigns bond issues to one of the following ratings, given in descending order of credit quality (increasing probability of default): AAA, AA+, AA, AA—, A+, A, A—, BBB+, BBB, BBB—, BB+, BB, BB—, B, CCC+, CCC—, CC, C, CI, D. For more information on credit risk and credit ratings, see Fabozzi (2004a).

[4]"Hedge fund" refers to investment vehicles with legal structures that result in less regulatory oversight than other pooled investment vehicles such as mutual funds. Hedge fund classification types group hedge funds by the kind of investment strategy they pursue.

3. SUMMARIZING DATA USING FREQUENCY DISTRIBUTIONS

In this section, we discuss one of the simplest ways to summarize data—the frequency distribution.

- **Definition of Frequency Distribution.** A **frequency distribution** is a tabular display of data summarized into a relatively small number of intervals.

Frequency distributions help in the analysis of large amounts of statistical data, and they work with all types of measurement scales.

Rates of return are the fundamental units that analysts and portfolio managers use for making investment decisions, and we can use frequency distributions to summarize rates of return. When we analyze rates of return, our starting point is the holding period return (also called the total return).

- **Holding Period Return Formula.** The holding period return for time period t, R_t, is

$$R_t = \frac{P_t - P_{t-1} + D_t}{P_{t-1}} \qquad (3\text{-}1)$$

where

P_t = price per share at the end of time period t

P_{t-1} = price per share at the end of time period $t - 1$, the time period immediately preceding time period t

D_t = cash distributions received during time period t

Thus the holding period return for time period t is the capital gain (or loss) plus distributions divided by the beginning-period price. (For common stocks, the distribution is a dividend; for bonds, the distribution is a coupon payment.) Equation 3-1 can be used to define the holding period return on any asset for a day, week, month, or year simply by changing the interpretation of the time interval between successive values of the time index, t.

The holding period return, as defined in Equation 3-1, has two important characteristics. First, it has an element of time attached to it. For example, if a monthly time interval is used between successive observations for price, then the rate of return is a monthly figure. Second, rate of return has no currency unit attached to it. For instance, suppose that prices are denominated in euros. The numerator and denominator of Equation 3-1 would be expressed in euros, and the resulting ratio would not have any units because the units in the numerator and denominator would cancel one another. This result holds regardless of the currency in which prices are denominated.[5]

With these concerns noted, we now turn to the frequency distribution of the holding period returns on the S&P 500 Index.[6] First, we examine annual rates of return; then we

---

[5]Note, however, that if price and cash distributions in the expression for holding period return were not in one's home currency, one would generally convert those variables to one's home currency before calculating the holding period return. Because of exchange rate fluctuations during the holding period, holding period returns on an asset computed in different currencies would generally differ.

[6]We use the total return series on the S&P 500 from January 1926 to December 2002 provided by Ibbotson Associates.

look at monthly rates of return. The annual rates of return on the S&P 500 calculated with Equation 3-1 span the period January 1926 to December 2002, for a total of 77 annual observations. Monthly return data cover the period January 1926 to December 2002, for a total of 924 monthly observations.

We can state a basic procedure for constructing a frequency distribution as follows:

- **Construction of a Frequency Distribution**.

    1. Sort the data in ascending order.
    2. Calculate the range of the data, defined as Range = Maximum value − Minimum value.
    3. Decide on the number of intervals in the frequency distribution, k.
    4. Determine interval width as Range/k.
    5. Determine the intervals by successively adding the interval width to the minimum value, to determine the ending points of intervals, stopping after reaching an interval that includes the maximum value.
    6. Count the number of observations falling in each interval.
    7. Construct a table of the intervals listed from smallest to largest that shows the number of observations falling in each interval.

    In Step 4, when rounding the interval width, round up rather than down, to ensure that the final interval includes the maximum value of the data.

As the above procedure makes clear, a frequency distribution groups data into a set of intervals.[7] An **interval** is a set of values within which an observation falls. Each observation falls into only one interval, and the total number of intervals covers all the values represented in the data. The actual number of observations in a given interval is called the **absolute frequency**, or simply the frequency. The frequency distribution is the list of intervals together with the corresponding measures of frequency.

To illustrate the basic procedure, suppose we have 12 observations sorted in ascending order: −4.57, −4.04, −1.64, 0.28, 1.34, 2.35, 2.38, 4.28, 4.42, 4.68, 7.16, and 11.43. The minimum observation is −4.57 and the maximum observation is +11.43, so the range is +11.43 − (−4.57) = 16. If we set $k = 4$, the interval width is 16/4 = 4. Table 3-1 shows the repeated addition of the interval width of 4 to determine the endpoints for the intervals (Step 5).

Thus the intervals are [−4.57 to −0.57), [−0.57 to 3.43), [3.43 to 7.43), and [7.43 to 11.43].[8] Table 3-2 summarizes Steps 5 through 7.

TABLE 3-1
Endpoints of Intervals

−4.57 + 4.00 =	−0.57
−0.57 + 4.00 =	3.43
3.43 + 4.00 =	7.43
7.43 + 4.00 =	11.43

---

[7]Intervals are also sometimes called classes, ranges, or bins.
[8]The notation [−4.57 to −0.57) means −4.57 ≤ observation < −0.57. In this context, a square bracket indicates that the endpoint is included in the interval.

TABLE 3-2   Frequency Distribution

Interval		Absolute Frequency
A	$-4.57 \leq$ observation < -0.57	3
B	$-0.57 \leq$ observation < 3.43	4
C	$3.43 \leq$ observation < 7.43	4
D	$7.43 \leq$ observation ≤ 11.43	1

Note that the intervals do not overlap, so each observation can be placed uniquely into one interval.

In practice, we may want to refine the above basic procedure. For example, we may want the intervals to begin and end with whole numbers for ease of interpretation. We also need to explain the choice of the number of intervals, k. We turn to these issues in discussing the construction of frequency distributions for the S&P 500.

We first consider the case of constructing a frequency distribution for the annual returns on the S&P 500 over the period 1926 to 2002. During that period, the return on the S&P 500 had a minimum value of -43.34 percent (in 1931) and a maximum value of $+53.99$ percent (in 1933). Thus the range of the data was $+54\% - (-43\%) = 97\%$, approximately. The question now is the number k of intervals into which we should group observations. Although some guidelines for setting k have been suggested in statistical literature, the setting of a useful value for k often involves inspecting the data and exercising judgment. How much detail should we include? If we use too few intervals, we will summarize too much and lose pertinent characteristics. If we use too many intervals, we may not summarize enough.

We can establish an appropriate value for k by evaluating the usefulness of the resulting interval width. A large number of empty intervals may indicate that we are trying to organize the data to present too much detail. Starting with a relatively small interval width, we can see whether or not the intervals are mostly empty and whether or not the value of k associated with that interval width is too large. If intervals are mostly empty or k is very large, we can consider increasingly larger intervals (smaller values of k) until we have a frequency distribution that effectively summarizes the distribution. For the annual S&P 500 series, return intervals of 1 percent width would result in 97 intervals and many of them would be empty because we have only 77 annual observations. We need to keep in mind that the purpose of a frequency distribution is to *summarize* the data. Suppose that for ease of interpretation we want to use an interval width stated in whole rather than fractional percents. A 2 percent interval width would have many fewer empty intervals than a 1 percent interval width and effectively summarize the data. A 2 percent interval width would be associated with $97/2 = 48.5$ intervals, which we can round up to 49 intervals. That number of intervals will cover $2\% \times 49 = 98\%$. We can confirm that if we start the smallest 2 percent interval at the whole number -44.0 percent, the final interval ends at $-44.0\% + 98\% = 54\%$ and includes the maximum return in the sample, 53.99 percent. In so constructing the frequency distribution, we will also have intervals that end and begin at a value of 0 percent, allowing us to count the negative and positive returns in the data. Without too much work, we have found an effective way to summarize the data. We will use return intervals of 2 percent, beginning with $-44\% \leq R_t < -42\%$ (given as "-44% to -42%" in the table) and ending with $52\% \leq R_t \leq 54\%$. Table 3-3 shows the frequency distribution for the annual total returns on the S&P 500.

TABLE 3-3   Frequency Distribution for the Annual Total Return on the S&P 500, 1926–2002

Return Interval	Frequency	Relative Frequency	Cumulative Frequency	Cumulative Relative Frequency
−44.0% to −42.0%	1	1.30%	1	1.30%
−42.0% to −40.0%	0	0.00%	1	1.30%
−40.0% to −38.0%	0	0.00%	1	1.30%
−38.0% to −36.0%	0	0.00%	1	1.30%
−36.0% to −34.0%	1	1.30%	2	2.60%
−34.0% to −32.0%	0	0.00%	2	2.60%
−32.0% to −30.0%	0	0.00%	2	2.60%
−30.0% to −28.0%	0	0.00%	2	2.60%
−28.0% to −26.0%	1	1.30%	3	3.90%
−26.0% to −24.0%	1	1.30%	4	5.19%
−24.0% to −22.0%	1	1.30%	5	6.49%
−22.0% to −20.0%	0	0.00%	5	6.49%
−20.0% to −18.0%	0	0.00%	5	6.49%
−18.0% to −16.0%	0	0.00%	5	6.49%
−16.0% to −14.0%	1	1.30%	6	7.79%
−14.0% to −12.0%	0	0.00%	6	7.79%
−12.0% to −10.0%	4	5.19%	10	12.99%
−10.0% to −8.0%	7	9.09%	17	22.08%
−8.0% to −6.0%	1	1.30%	18	23.38%
−6.0% to −4.0%	1	1.30%	19	24.68%
−4.0% to −2.0%	1	1.30%	20	25.97%
−2.0% to 0.0%	3	3.90%	23	29.87%
0.0% to 2.0%	2	2.60%	25	32.47%
2.0% to 4.0%	0	0.00%	25	32.47%

Return Interval	Frequency	Relative Frequency	Cumulative Frequency	Cumulative Relative Frequency
4.0% to 6.0%	4	5.19%	29	37.66%
6.0% to 8.0%	4	5.19%	33	42.86%
8.0% to 10.0%	1	1.30%	34	44.16%
10.0% to 12.0%	3	3.90%	37	48.05%
12.0% to 14.0%	1	1.30%	38	49.35%
14.0% to 16.0%	1	1.30%	39	50.65%
16.0% to 18.0%	2	2.60%	41	53.25%
18.0% to 20.0%	6	7.79%	47	61.04%
20.0% to 22.0%	3	3.90%	50	64.94%
22.0% to 24.0%	5	6.49%	55	71.43%
24.0% to 26.0%	2	2.60%	57	74.03%
26.0% to 28.0%	1	1.30%	58	75.32%
28.0% to 30.0%	1	1.30%	59	76.62%
30.0% to 32.0%	5	6.49%	64	83.12%
32.0% to 34.0%	4	5.19%	68	88.31%
34.0% to 36.0%	0	0.00%	68	88.31%
36.0% to 38.0%	4	5.19%	72	93.51%
38.0% to 40.0%	0	0.00%	72	93.51%
40.0% to 42.0%	0	0.00%	72	93.51%
42.0% to 44.0%	2	2.60%	74	96.10%
44.0% to 46.0%	0	0.00%	74	96.10%
46.0% to 48.0%	1	1.30%	75	97.40%
48.0% to 50.0%	0	0.00%	75	97.40%
50.0% to 52.0%	0	0.00%	75	97.40%
52.0% to 54.0%	2	2.60%	77	100.00%

Note: The lower class limit is the weak inequality (≤) and the upper class limit is the strong inequality (<).
Source: Frequency distribution generated with Ibbotson Associates EnCorr Analyzer.

Table 3-3 includes three other useful ways to present data, which we can compute once we have established the frequency distribution: the relative frequency, the cumulative frequency (also called the cumulative absolute frequency), and the cumulative relative frequency.

- **Definition of Relative Frequency**.   The **relative frequency** is the absolute frequency of each interval divided by the total number of observations.

The **cumulative relative frequency** cumulates (adds up) the relative frequencies as we move from the first to the last interval. It tells us the fraction of observations that are less than the upper limit of each interval. Examining the frequency distribution given in Table 3-3, we see that the first return interval, −44 percent to −42 percent, has one observation; its relative frequency is 1/77 or 1.30 percent. The cumulative frequency for this interval is 1 because only one observation is less than −42 percent. The cumulative relative frequency is thus 1/77 or 1.30 percent. The next return interval has zero observations; therefore, its cumulative frequency is 0 plus 1 and its cumulative relative frequency is 1.30 percent (the cumulative relative frequency from the previous interval). We can find the other cumulative frequencies by adding the (absolute) frequency to the previous cumulative frequency. The cumulative frequency, then, tells us the number of observations that are less than the upper limit of each return interval.

As Table 3-3 shows, return intervals have frequencies from 0 to 7 in this sample. The interval encompassing returns between −10 percent and −8 percent ($-10\% \leq R_t < -8\%$) has the most observations, seven. Next most frequent are returns between 18 percent and 20 percent ($18\% \leq R_t < 20\%$), with six observations. From the cumulative frequency column, we see that the number of negative returns is 23. The number of positive returns must then be equal to $77 - 23$, or 54. We can express the number of positive and negative outcomes as a percentage of the total to get a sense of the risk inherent in investing in the stock market. During the 77-year period, the S&P 500 had negative annual returns 29.9 percent of the time (that is, 23/77). This result appears in the fifth column of Table 3-3, which reports the cumulative relative frequency.

The frequency distribution gives us a sense of not only where most of the observations lie but also whether the distribution is evenly distributed, lopsided, or peaked. In the case of the S&P 500, we can see that more than half of the outcomes are positive and most of those annual returns are larger than 10 percent. (Only 11 of the 54 positive annual returns—about 20 percent—were between 0 and 10 percent.)

Table 3-3 permits us to make an important further point about the choice of the number of intervals related to equity returns in particular. From the frequency distribution in Table 3-3, we can see that only five outcomes fall between −44 percent and −16 percent and between 38 percent and 54 percent. Stock return data are frequently characterized by a few very large or small outcomes. We could have collapsed the return intervals in the tails of the frequency distribution by choosing a smaller value of k, but then we would have lost the information about how extremely poorly or well the stock market had performed. A risk manager may need to know the worst possible outcomes and thus may want to have detailed information on the tails (the extreme values). A frequency distribution with a relatively large value of k is useful for that. A portfolio manager or analyst may be equally interested in detailed information on the tails; however, if the manager or analyst wants a picture only of where most of the observations lie, he might prefer to use an interval width of 4 percent (25 intervals beginning at −44 percent), for example.

The frequency distribution for monthly returns on the S&P 500 looks quite different from that for annual returns. The monthly return series from January 1926 to December

TABLE 3-4   Frequency Distribution for the Monthly Total Return on the S&P 500,
January 1926 to December 2002

Return Interval	Absolute Frequency	Relative Frequency	Cumulative Absolute Frequency	Cumulative Relative Frequency
−30.0% to −28.0%	1	0.11%	1	0.11%
−28.0% to −26.0%	0	0.00%	1	0.11%
−26.0% to −24.0%	1	0.11%	2	0.22%
−24.0% to −22.0%	1	0.11%	3	0.32%
−22.0% to −20.0%	2	0.22%	5	0.54%
−20.0% to −18.0%	2	0.22%	7	0.76%
−18.0% to −16.0%	2	0.22%	9	0.97%
−16.0% to −14.0%	3	0.32%	12	1.30%
−14.0% to −12.0%	5	0.54%	17	1.84%
−12.0% to −10.0%	6	0.65%	23	2.49%
−10.0% to −8.0%	20	2.16%	43	4.65%
−8.0% to −6.0%	30	3.25%	73	7.90%
−6.0% to −4.0%	54	5.84%	127	13.74%
−4.0% to −2.0%	90	9.74%	217	23.48%
−2.0% to 0.0%	138	14.94%	355	38.42%
0.0% to 2.0%	182	19.70%	537	58.12%
2.0% to 4.0%	153	16.56%	690	74.68%
4.0% to 6.0%	126	13.64%	816	88.31%
6.0% to 8.0%	58	6.28%	874	94.59%
8.0% to 10.0%	21	2.27%	895	96.86%
10.0% to 12.0%	14	1.52%	909	98.38%
12.0% to 14.0%	6	0.65%	915	99.03%
14.0% to 16.0%	2	0.22%	917	99.24%
16.0% to 18.0%	3	0.32%	920	99.57%
18.0% to 20.0%	0	0.00%	920	99.57%
20.0% to 22.0%	0	0.00%	920	99.57%
22.0% to 24.0%	0	0.00%	920	99.57%
24.0% to 26.0%	1	0.11%	921	99.68%
26.0% to 28.0%	0	0.00%	921	99.68%
28.0% to 30.0%	0	0.00%	921	99.68%
30.0% to 32.0%	0	0.00%	921	99.68%
32.0% to 34.0%	0	0.00%	921	99.68%
34.0% to 36.0%	0	0.00%	921	99.68%
36.0% to 38.0%	0	0.00%	921	99.68%
38.0% to 40.0%	2	0.22%	923	99.89%
40.0% to 42.0%	0	0.00%	923	99.89%
42.0% to 44.0%	1	0.11%	924	100.00%

Note: The lower class limit is the weak inequality (≤) and the upper class limit is the strong inequality
(<). The relative frequency is the absolute frequency or cumulative frequency divided by the total
number of observations.
Source: Frequency distribution generated with Ibbotson Associates EnCorr Analyzer.

2002 has 924 observations. Returns range from a minimum of approximately −30 percent to a maximum of approximately +43 percent. With such a large quantity of monthly data we must summarize to get a sense of the distribution, and so we group the data into 37 equally spaced return intervals of 2 percent. The gains from summarizing in this way are substantial. Table 3-4 presents the resulting frequency distribution. The absolute frequencies appear in the second column, followed by the relative frequencies. The relative frequencies are rounded to two decimal places. The cumulative absolute and cumulative relative frequencies appear in the fourth and fifth columns, respectively.

The advantage of a frequency distribution is evident in Table 3-4, which tells us that the vast majority of observations (599/924 = 65 percent) lie in the four intervals spanning −2 percent to +6 percent. Altogether, we have 355 negative returns and 569 positive returns. Almost 62 percent of the monthly outcomes are positive. Looking at the cumulative relative frequency in the last column, we see that the interval −2 percent to 0 percent shows a cumulative frequency of 38.42 percent, for an upper return limit of 0 percent. This means that 38.42 percent of the observations lie below the level of 0 percent. We can also see that not many observations are greater than +12 percent or less than −12 percent. Note that the frequency distributions of annual and monthly returns are not directly comparable. On average, we should expect the returns measured at shorter intervals (for example, months) to be smaller than returns measured over longer periods (for example, years).

Next, we construct a frequency distribution of average inflation-adjusted returns over 1900−2000 for 16 major equity markets.

EXAMPLE 3-2   Constructing a Frequency Distribution

How have equities rewarded investors in different countries in the long run? To answer this question, we could examine the average annual returns directly.[9] The worth of a nominal level of return depends on changes in the purchasing power of money, however, and internationally there have been a variety of experiences with price inflation. It is preferable, therefore, to compare the average real or inflation-adjusted returns earned by investors in different countries. Dimson, Marsh, and Staunton (2002) presented authoritative evidence on asset returns in 16 countries for the 101 years 1900−2000. Table 3-5 excerpts their findings for average inflation-adjusted returns.

Table 3-6 summarizes the data in Table 3-5 into six intervals spanning 4 percent to 10 percent.

As Table 3-6 shows, there is substantial variation internationally of average real equity returns. Three-fourths of the observations fall in one of three intervals: 6.0 to 7.0 percent, 7.0 to 8.0 percent, or 9.0 to 10.0 percent. Most average real equity returns are between 6.0 percent and 10 percent; the cumulative relative frequency of returns less than 6.0 percent was only 12.50 percent.

---

[9]The average or arithmetic mean of a set of values equals the sum of the values divided by the number of values summed. To find the arithmetic mean of 101 annual returns, for example, we sum the 101 annual returns and then divide the total by 101. Among the most familiar of statistical concepts, the arithmetic mean is explained in more detail later in the chapter.

TABLE 3-5 Real (Inflation-Adjusted) Equity Returns: Sixteen Major Equity Markets, 1900–2000

Country	Arithmetic Mean
Australia	9.0%
Belgium	4.8%
Canada	7.7%
Denmark	6.2%
France	6.3%
Germany	8.8%
Ireland	7.0%
Italy	6.8%
Japan	9.3%
Netherlands	7.7%
South Africa	9.1%
Spain	5.8%
Sweden	9.9%
Switzerland	6.9%
United Kingdom	7.6%
United States	8.7%

Source: Dimson, Marsh, and Staunton (2002), Table 4-3. Swiss equities date from 1911.

TABLE 3-6 Frequency Distribution of Average Real Equity Returns

Return Interval	Absolute Frequency	Relative Frequency	Cumulative Absolute Frequency	Cumulative Relative Frequency
4.0% to 5.0%	1	6.25%	1	6.25%
5.0% to 6.0%	1	6.25%	2	12.50%
6.0% to 7.0%	4	25.00%	6	37.50%
7.0% to 8.0%	4	25.00%	10	62.50%
8.0% to 9.0%	2	12.50%	12	75.00%
9.0% to 10%	4	25.00%	16	100.00%

Note: Relative frequencies are rounded to sum to 100%.

4. THE GRAPHIC PRESENTATION OF DATA

A graphical display of data allows us to visualize important characteristics quickly. For example, we may see that the distribution is symmetrically shaped, and this finding may influence which probability distribution we use to describe the data. In this section, we discuss the histogram, the frequency polygon, and the cumulative frequency distribution as methods for displaying data graphically. We construct all of these graphic presentations with the information contained in the frequency distribution of the S&P 500 shown in either Table 3-3 or Table 3-4.

4.1. The Histogram

A histogram is the graphical equivalent of a frequency distribution.

- **Definition of Histogram.**   A **histogram** is a bar chart of data that have been grouped into a frequency distribution.

The advantage of the visual display is that we can see quickly where most of the observations lie. To see how a histogram is constructed, look at the return interval $18\% \leq R_t < 20\%$ in Table 3-3. This interval has an absolute frequency of 6. Therefore, we erect a bar or rectangle with a height of 6 over that return interval on the horizontal axis. Continuing with this process for all other return intervals yields a histogram. Figure 3-1 presents the histogram of the annual total return series on the S&P 500 from 1926 to 2002.

In the histogram in Figure 3-1, the height of each bar represents the absolute frequency for each return interval. The return interval $-10\% \leq R_t < -8\%$ has a frequency of 7 and is represented by the tallest bar in the histogram. Because there are no gaps between the interval limits, there are no gaps between the bars of the histogram. Many of the return intervals have zero frequency; therefore, they have no height in the histogram.

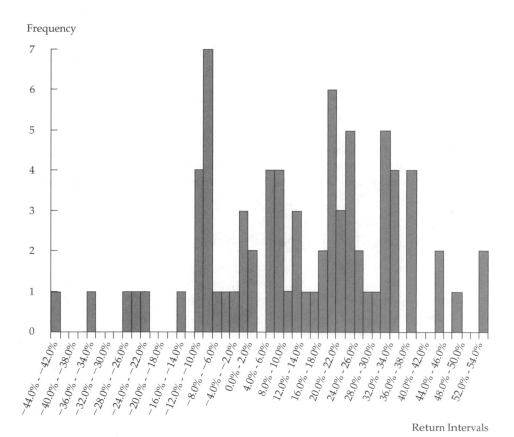

FIGURE 3-1   Histogram of S&P 500 Annual Total Returns: 1926 to 2002
Source: Ibbotson EnCorr Analyzer.

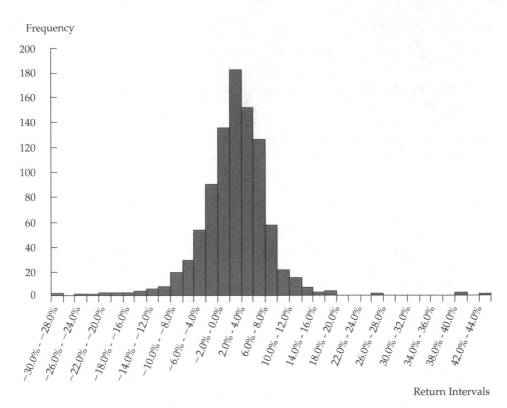

FIGURE 3-2   Histogram of S&P 500 Monthly Total Returns: January 1926 to December 2002

Figure 3-2 presents the histogram for the distribution of monthly returns on the S&P 500. Somewhat more symmetrically shaped than the histogram of annual returns shown in Figure 3-1, this histogram also appears more bell-shaped than the distribution of annual returns.

4.2. The Frequency Polygon and the Cumulative Frequency Distribution

Two other graphical tools for displaying data are the frequency polygon and the cumulative frequency distribution. To construct a **frequency polygon**, we plot the midpoint of each interval on the x-axis and the absolute frequency for that interval on the y-axis; we then connect neighboring points with a straight line. Figure 3-3 shows the frequency polygon for the 924 monthly returns for the S&P 500 from January 1926 to December 2002.

In Figure 3-3, we have replaced the bars in the histogram with points connected with straight lines. For example, the return interval 0 percent to 2 percent has an absolute frequency of 182. In the frequency polygon, we plot the return-interval midpoint of 1 percent and a frequency of 182. We plot all other points in a similar way.[10] This form of visual display adds a degree of continuity to the representation of the distribution.

---

[10]Even though the upper limit on the interval is not a return falling in the interval, we still average it with the lower limit to determine the midpoint.

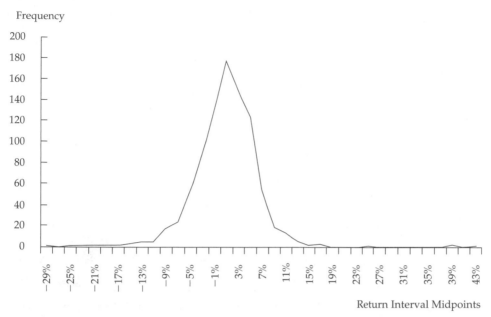

Frequency

Return Interval Midpoints

FIGURE 3-3   Frequency Polygon of S&P 500 Monthly Total Returns: January 1926 to December 2002
Source: Ibbotson Associates.

Another form of line graph is the cumulative frequency distribution. Such a graph can plot either the cumulative absolute or cumulative relative frequency against the upper interval limit. The cumulative frequency distribution allows us to see how many or what percent of the observations lie below a certain value. To construct the cumulative frequency distribution, we graph the returns in the fourth or fifth column of Table 3-4 against the upper limit of each return interval. Figure 3-4 presents a graph of the cumulative absolute distribution for the monthly returns on the S&P 500. Notice that the cumulative distribution tends to flatten out when returns are extremely negative or extremely positive. The steep slope in the middle of Figure 3-4 reflects the fact that most of the observations lie in the neighborhood of −2 percent to 6 percent.

We can further examine the relationship between the relative frequency and the cumulative relative frequency by looking at the two return intervals reproduced in Table 3-7. The first return interval (0 percent to 2 percent) has a cumulative relative frequency of 58.12 percent. The next return interval (2 percent to 4 percent) has a cumulative relative frequency of 74.68 percent. The change in the cumulative relative frequency as we move from one interval to the next is the next interval's relative frequency. For instance, as we go from the first return interval (0 percent to 2 percent) to the next return interval (2 percent to 4 percent), the change in the cumulative relative frequency is 74.68% − 58.12% = 16.56%. (Values in the table have been rounded to two decimal places.) The fact that the slope is steep indicates that these frequencies are large. As you can see in the graph of the cumulative distribution, the slope of the curve changes as we move from the first return interval to the last. A fairly small slope for the cumulative distribution for the first few return intervals tells us that these return intervals do not contain many observations. You can go back to the frequency distribution in Table 3-4 and verify that the cumulative absolute frequency is only 23 observations (the

Cumulative Frequency

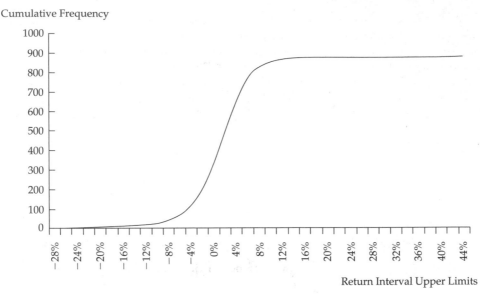

FIGURE 3-4   Cumulative Absolute Frequency Distribution of S&P 500 Monthly Total Returns: January 1926 to December 2002
Source: Ibbotson Associates.

TABLE 3-7   Selected Class Frequencies for the S&P 500 Monthly Returns

Return Interval	Absolute Frequency	Relative Frequency	Cumulative Absolute Frequency	Cumulative Relative Frequency
0.0% to 2.0%	182	19.70%	537	58.12%
2.0% to 4.0%	153	16.56%	690	74.68%

cumulative relative frequency is 2.49 percent) up to the 10th return interval (-12 percent to -10 percent). In essence, the slope of the cumulative absolute distribution at any particular interval is proportional to the number of observations in that interval.

5. MEASURES OF CENTRAL TENDENCY

So far, we have discussed methods we can use to organize and present data so that they are more understandable. The frequency distribution of an asset class's return series, for example, reveals the nature of the risks that investors may encounter in a particular asset class. As an illustration, the histogram for the annual returns on the S&P 500 clearly shows that large positive and negative annual returns are common. Although frequency distributions and histograms provide a convenient way to summarize a series of observations, these methods are just a first step toward describing the data. In this section we discuss the use of quantitative measures that explain characteristics of data. Our focus is on measures of central tendency and other measures of location or location parameters. A **measure of central tendency** specifies where the data are centered. Measures of central tendency are probably more widely used than any other statistical measure because they can be computed and applied easily. **Measures of location** include not only measures of central tendency but other measures that illustrate the location or distribution of data.

In the following subsections we explain the common measures of central tendency—the arithmetic mean, the median, the mode, the weighted mean, and the geometric mean. We also explain other useful measures of location, including quartiles, quintiles, deciles, and percentiles.

5.1. The Arithmetic Mean

Analysts and portfolio managers often want one number that describes a representative possible outcome of an investment decision. The arithmetic mean is by far the most frequently used measure of the middle or center of data.

- **Definition of Arithmetic Mean**. The **arithmetic mean** is the sum of the observations divided by the number of observations.

We can compute the arithmetic mean for both populations and samples, known as the population mean and the sample mean, respectively.

5.1.1. The Population Mean The population mean is the arithmetic mean computed for a population. If we can define a population adequately, then we can calculate the population mean as the arithmetic mean of all the observations or values in the population. For example, analysts examining the fiscal 2002 year-over-year growth in same-store sales of major U.S. wholesale clubs might define the population of interest to include only three companies: BJ's Wholesale Club (NYSE: BJ), Costco Wholesale Corporation (Nasdaq: COST), and Sam's Club, part of Wal-Mart Stores (NYSE: WMT).[11] As another example, if a portfolio manager's investment universe (the set of securities she must choose from) is the Nikkei–Dow Jones Average, the relevant population is the 225 shares on the First Section of the Tokyo Stock Exchange that compose the Nikkei.

- **Population Mean Formula**. The **population mean**, μ, is the arithmetic mean value of a population. For a finite population, the population mean is

$$\mu = \frac{\sum_{i=1}^{N} X_i}{N} \tag{3-2}$$

where N is the number of observations in the entire population and X_i is the ith observation.

The population mean is an example of a parameter. The population mean is unique; that is, a given population has only one mean. To illustrate the calculation, we can take the case of the population mean of current price-to-earnings ratio (P/E) of stocks of U.S. companies running major wholesale clubs as of the beginning of September 2003. As of that date, the current P/Es for BJ, COST, and WMT were 16.73, 22.02, and 29.30, respectively, according to First Call/Thomson Financial. Thus the population mean current P/E on that date was $\mu = (16.73 + 22.02 + 29.30)/3 = 68.05/3 = 22.68$.

---

[11]A wholesale club implements a store format dedicated mostly to bulk sales in warehouse-sized stores to customers who pay membership dues. As of the early 2000s, those three wholesale clubs dominated the segment in the United States.

5.1.2. The Sample Mean   The sample mean is the arithmetic mean computed for a sample. Many times we cannot observe every member of a set; instead, we observe a subset or sample of the population. The concept of the mean can be applied to the observations in a sample with a slight change in notation.

- **Sample Mean Formula**. The **sample mean** or average, $\overline{X}$ (read "X-bar"), is the arithmetic mean value of a sample:

$$\overline{X} = \frac{\sum_{i=1}^{n} X_i}{n} \tag{3-3}$$

where n is the number of observations in the sample.

Equation 3-3 tells us to sum the values of the observations (X_i) and divide the sum by the number of observations. For example, if the sample of P/E multiples contains the values 35, 30, 22, 18, 15, and 12, the sample mean P/E is $132/6 = 22$. The sample mean is also called the arithmetic average.[12] As we discussed earlier, the sample mean is a statistic (that is, a descriptive measure of a sample).

Means can be computed for individual units or over time. For instance, the sample might be the 2003 return on equity (ROE) for the 300 companies in the Financial Times Stock Exchange (FTSE) Eurotop 300, an index of Europe's 300 largest companies. In this case, we calculate mean ROE in 2003 as an average across 300 individual units. When we examine the characteristics of some units at a specific point in time (such as ROE for the FTSE Eurotop 300), we are examining **cross-sectional data**. The mean of these observations is called a cross-sectional mean. On the other hand, if our sample consists of the historical monthly returns on the FTSE Eurotop 300 for the past five years, then we have **time-series data**. The mean of these observations is called a time-series mean. We will examine specialized statistical methods related to the behavior of time series in the chapter on times-series analysis.

Next, we show an example of finding the sample mean return for equities in 16 European countries for 2002. In this case, the mean is cross-sectional because we are averaging individual country returns.

EXAMPLE 3-3   Calculating a Cross-Sectional Mean

The MSCI EAFE (Europe, Australasia, and Far East) Index is a free float-adjusted market capitalization index designed to measure developed-market equity performance excluding the United States and Canada.[13] As of the end of 2002, the EAFE consisted of 21 developed market country indexes, including indexes for 16 European markets, 2

---

[12] Statisticians prefer the term "mean" to "average." Some writers refer to all measures of central tendency (including the median and mode) as averages. The term "mean" avoids any possibility of confusion.
[13] The term "free float-adjusted" means that the weights of companies in the index reflect the value of the shares actually available for investment.

Australasian markets (Australia and New Zealand), and 3 Far Eastern markets (Hong Kong, Japan, and Singapore).

Suppose we are interested in the local currency performance of the 16 European markets in the EAFE in 2002, a severe bear market year. We want to find the sample mean total return for 2002 across these 16 markets. The return series reported in Table 3-8 are in local currency (that is, returns are for investors living in the country). Because this return is not stated in any single investor's home currency, it is not a return any single investor would earn. Rather, it is an average of returns in 16 local currencies.

TABLE 3-8   Total Returns for European Equity Markets, 2002

Market	Total Return in Local Currency
Austria	−2.97%
Belgium	−29.71%
Denmark	−29.67%
Finland	−41.65%
France	−33.99%
Germany	−44.05%
Greece	−39.06%
Ireland	−38.97%
Italy	−23.64%
Netherlands	−34.27%
Norway	−29.73%
Portugal	−28.29%
Spain	−29.47%
Sweden	−43.07%
Switzerland	−25.84%
United Kingdom	−25.66%

Source: www.mscidata.com.

Using the data in Table 3-8, calculate the sample mean return for the 16 equity markets in 2002.

Solution: The calculation applies Equation 3-3 to the returns in Table 3-8: $(−2.97 − 29.71 − 29.67 − 41.65 − 33.99 − 44.05 − 39.06 − 38.97 − 23.64 − 34.27 − 29.73 − 28.29 − 29.47 − 43.07 − 25.84 − 25.66)/16 = −500.04/16 = −31.25$ percent.

In Example 3-3, we can verify that seven markets had returns less than the mean and nine had returns that were greater. We should not expect any of the actual observations to equal the mean, because sample means provide only a summary of the data being analyzed. As an analyst, you will often need to find a few numbers that describe the characteristics of the distribution. The mean is generally the statistic that you will use as a measure of the typical outcome for a distribution. You can then use the mean to compare the performance of

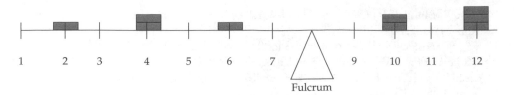

When the fulcrum is placed at 8, the bar is perfectly balanced.

FIGURE 3-5   Center of Gravity Analogy for the Arithmetic Mean

two different markets. For example, you might be interested in comparing the stock market performance of investments in Pacific Rim countries with investments in European countries. You can use the mean returns in these markets to compare investment results.

5.1.3. Properties of the Arithmetic Mean   The arithmetic mean can be likened to the center of gravity of an object. Figure 3-5 expresses this analogy graphically by plotting nine hypothetical observations on a bar. The nine observations are 2, 4, 4, 6, 10, 10, 12, 12, and 12; the arithmetic mean is $72/9 = 8$. The observations are plotted on the bar with various heights based on their frequency (that is, 2 is one unit high, 4 is two units high, and so on). When the bar is placed on a fulcrum, it balances only when the fulcrum is located at the point on the scale that corresponds to the arithmetic mean.

As analysts, we often use the mean return as a measure of the typical outcome for an asset. As in the example above, however, some outcomes are above the mean and some are below it. We can calculate the distance between the mean and each outcome and call it a deviation. Mathematically, it is always true that the sum of the deviations around the mean equals 0. We can see this by using the definition of the arithmetic mean shown in Equation 3-3, multiplying both sides of the equation by n: $n\overline{X} = \sum_{i=1}^{n} X_i$. The sum of the deviations from the mean can thus be calculated as follows:

$$\sum_{i=1}^{n}(X_i - \overline{X}) = \sum_{i=1}^{n} X_i - \sum_{i=1}^{n} \overline{X} = \sum_{i=1}^{n} X_i - n\overline{X} = 0$$

Deviations from the arithmetic mean are important information because they indicate risk. The concept of deviations around the mean forms the foundation for the more complex concepts of variance, skewness, and kurtosis, which we will discuss later in this chapter.

An advantage of the arithmetic mean over two other measures of central tendency, the median and mode, is that the mean uses all the information about the size and magnitude of the observations. The mean is also easy to work with mathematically.

A property and potential drawback of the arithmetic mean is its sensitivity to extreme values. Because all observations are used to compute the mean, the arithmetic mean can be pulled sharply upward or downward by extremely large or small observations, respectively. For example, suppose we compute the arithmetic mean of the following seven numbers: 1, 2, 3, 4, 5, 6, and 1,000. The mean is $1,021/7 = 145.86$ or approximately 146. Because the magnitude of the mean, 146, is so much larger than that of the bulk of the observations (the first six), we might question how well it represents the location of the data. In practice, although an extreme value or outlier in a financial dataset may only represent a rare value in the population, it may also reflect an error in recording the value of an observation, or an observation generated from a different population from that producing the other observations in the sample. In the latter two cases in particular, the arithmetic mean could be misleading. Perhaps the most common approach in such cases is to report the median in place of or in addition to the mean.[14] We discuss the median next.

5.2. The Median

A second important measure of central tendency is the median.

- **Definition of Median.**   The **median** is the value of the middle item of a set of items that has been sorted into ascending or descending order. In an odd-numbered sample of n items, the median occupies the $(n + 1)/2$ position. In an even-numbered sample, we define the median as the mean of the values of items occupying the $n/2$ and $(n + 2)/2$ positions (the two middle items).[15]

Earlier we gave the current P/Es of three wholesale clubs as 16.73, 22.02, and 29.30. With an odd number of observations ($n = 3$), the median occupies the $(n + 1)/2 = 4/2 = 2$nd position. The median P/E was 22.02. The P/E value of 22.02 is the "middlemost" observation: One lies above it, and one lies below it. Whether we use the calculation for an even- or odd-numbered sample, an equal number of observations lie above and below the median. A distribution has only one median.

A potential advantage of the median is that, unlike the mean, extreme values do not affect it. The median, however, does not use all the information about the size and magnitude of the observations; it focuses only on the relative position of the ranked observations. Calculating the median is also more complex; to do so, we need to order the observations from smallest to largest, determine whether the sample size is even or odd, and, on that basis, apply one of two calculations. Mathematicians express this disadvantage by saying that the median is less mathematically tractable than the mean.

To demonstrate finding the median, we use the data from Example 3-3, reproduced in Table 3-9 in ascending order, of the 2002 total return for European equities. Because this sample has 16 observations, the median is the mean of the values in the sorted array that occupy the $16/2 = 8$th and $18/2 = 9$th positions. Norway's return occupies the eighth position with a return of -29.73 percent, and Belgium's return occupies the ninth

---

[14]Other approaches to handling extreme values involve variations of the arithmetic mean. The **trimmed mean** is computed by excluding a stated small percentage of the lowest and highest values and then computing an arithmetic mean of the remaining values. For example, a 5 percent trimmed mean discards the lowest 2.5 percent and the largest 2.5 percent of values and computes the mean of the remaining 95 percent of values. A trimmed mean is used in sports competitions when judges' lowest and highest scores are discarded in computing a contestant's score. A **Winsorized mean** assigns a stated percent of the lowest values equal to one specified low value, and a stated percent of the highest values equal to one specified high value, then computes a mean from the restated data. For example, a 95 percent Winsorized mean sets the bottom 2.5 percent of values equal to the 2.5th percentile value and the upper 2.5 percent of values equal to the 97.5th percentile value. (Percentile values are defined later.)

[15]The notation M_d is occasionally used for the median. Just as for the mean, we may distinguish between a population median and a sample median. With the understanding that a population median divides a population in half while a sample median divides a sample in half, we follow general usage in using the term "median" without qualification, for the sake of brevity.

TABLE 3-9   Total Returns for European Equity
Markets, 2002 (in ascending order)

No.	Market	Total Return in Local Currency
1	Germany	−44.05%
2	Sweden	−43.07%
3	Finland	−41.65%
4	Greece	−39.06%
5	Ireland	−38.97%
6	Netherlands	−34.27%
7	France	−33.99%
8	Norway	−29.73%
9	Belgium	−29.71%
10	Denmark	−29.67%
11	Spain	−29.47%
12	Portugal	−28.29%
13	Switzerland	−25.84%
14	United Kingdom	−25.66%
15	Italy	−23.64%
16	Austria	−2.97%

Source: www.mscidata.com.

position with a return of −29.71 percent. The median, as the mean of these two returns, is $(-29.73 - 29.71)/2 = -29.72$ percent. Note that the median is not influenced by extremely large or small outcomes. Had Germany's total return been a much lower value or Austria's total return a much larger value, the median would not have changed.

Using a context that arises often in practice, Example 3-4 shows how to use the mean and median in a sample with extreme values.

EXAMPLE 3-4   Median and Arithmetic Mean: The Case of the Price–Earnings Ratio

Suppose a client asks you for a valuation analysis on the seven-stock U.S. common stock portfolio given in Table 3-10. The stocks are equally weighted in the portfolio. One valuation measure that you use is P/E, the ratio of share price to earnings per share (EPS). Many variations exist for the denominator in the P/E, but you are examining P/E defined as current price divided by the current mean of all analysts' EPS estimates for the company for the current fiscal year ("Consensus Current EPS" in the table).[16] The values in Table 3-10 are as of 11 September 2003. For comparison purposes, the consensus current P/E on the S&P 500 was 23.63 at that time.

Using the data in Table 3-10, address the following:

---

[16]For more information on price multiples, see Stowe, Robinson, Pinto, and McLeavey (2002).

1. Calculate the arithmetic mean P/E.
2. Calculate the median P/E.
3. Evaluate the mean and median P/Es as measures of central tendency for the above portfolio.

TABLE 3-10   P/Es for a Client Portfolio

Stock	Consensus Current EPS	Consensus Current P/E
Exponent Inc. (Nasdaq: EXPO)	1.23	13.68
Express Scripts (Nasdaq: ESRX)	3.19	19.07
General Dynamics (NYSE: GD)	4.95	17.56
Limited Brands (NYSE: LTD)	1.06	15.60
Merant plc (Nasdaq: MRNT)	0.03	443.33
Microsoft Corporation (Nasdaq: MSFT)	1.11	25.61
O'Reilly Automotive, Inc. (Nasdaq: ORLY)	1.84	21.01

Source: First Call/Thomson Financial.

Solution to 1: The mean P/E is $(13.68 + 19.07 + 17.56 + 15.60 + 443.33 + 25.61 + 21.01)/7 = 555.86/7 = 79.41$.

Solution to 2: The P/Es listed in ascending order are:

$$13.68 \quad 15.60 \quad 17.56 \quad 19.07 \quad 21.01 \quad 25.61 \quad 443.33$$

The sample has an odd number of observations with $n = 7$, so the median occupies the $(n + 1)/2 = 8/2 = 4$th position in the sorted list. Therefore, the median P/E is 19.07.

Solution to 3: Merant's P/E of approximately 443 tremendously influences the value of the portfolio's arithmetic mean P/E. The mean P/E of 79 is much larger than the P/E of six of the seven stocks in the portfolio. The mean P/E also misleadingly suggests an orientation to stocks with high P/Es. The mean P/E of the stocks excluding Merant, or excluding the largest- and smallest-P/E stocks (Merant and Exponent), is below the S&P 500's P/E of 23.63. The median P/E of 19.07 appears to better represent the central tendency of the P/Es.

It frequently happens that when a company's EPS is close to zero—at a low point in the business cycle, for example—its P/E is extremely high. The high P/E in those circumstances reflects an anticipated future recovery of earnings. Extreme P/E values need to be investigated and handled with care. For reasons related to this example, analysts often use the median of price multiples to characterize the valuation of industry groups.

5.3. The Mode

The third important measure of central tendency is the mode.

- **Definition of Mode**.   The **mode** is the most frequently occurring value in a distribution.[17]

A distribution can have more than one mode or even no mode. When a distribution has one most frequently occurring value, the distribution is said to be unimodal. If a distribution has two most frequently occurring values, then it has two modes, and we say it is bimodal. If the distribution has three most frequently occurring values, then it is trimodal. When all the values in a data set are different, the distribution has no mode because no value occurs more frequently than any other value.

Stock return data and other data from continuous distributions may not have a modal outcome. When such data are grouped into intervals, however, we often find an interval (possibly more than one) with the highest frequency: the **modal interval** (or intervals). For example, the frequency distribution for the monthly returns on the S&P 500 has a modal interval of 0 percent to 2 percent, as shown in Figure 3-2; this return interval has 182 observations out of a total of 924. The modal interval always has the highest bar in the histogram.

The mode is the only measure of central tendency that can be used with nominal data. When we categorize mutual funds into different styles and assign a number to each style, the mode of these categorized data is the most frequent mutual fund style.

EXAMPLE 3-5   Calculating a Mode

Table 3-11 gives the credit ratings on senior unsecured debt as of September 2002 of nine U.S. department stores rated by Moody's Investors Service. In descending order of credit quality (increasing expected probability of default), Moody's ratings are Aaa, Aa1, Aa2, Aa3, A1, A2, A3, Baa1, Baa2, Baa3, Ba1, Ba2, Ba3, B1, B2, B3, Caa, Ca, and C.[18]

Using the data in Table 3-11, address the following concerning the senior unsecured debt of U.S. department stores:

1. State the modal credit rating.
2. State the median credit rating.

Solution to 1: The group of companies represents seven distinct credit ratings, ranging from A2 to B1. To make our task easy, we first organize the ratings into a frequency distribution.

All credit ratings have a frequency of 1 except for Baa1, which has a frequency of 3. Therefore, the modal credit rating of U.S. department stores as of the date of the

---

[17]The notation M_o is occasionally used for the mode. Just as for the mean and the median, we may distinguish between a population mode and a sample mode. With the understanding that a population mode is the value with the greatest probability of occurrence, while a sample mode is the most frequently occurring value in the sample, we follow general usage in using the term "mode" without qualification, for the sake of brevity.

[18]For more information on credit risk and credit ratings, see Fabozzi (2004a).

Moody's report was Baa1. Moody's considers bonds rated Baa1 to be medium-grade obligations—they are neither highly protected nor poorly secured.

TABLE 3-11   Senior Unsecured Debt Ratings: U.S. Department Stores, September 2002

Company	Credit Rating
Dillards, Inc.	Ba3
Federated Department Stores, Inc.	Baa1
Kohl's Corporation	A3
May's Department Stores Company	A2
Neiman Marcus Group, Inc.	Baa2
Nordstom, Inc.	Baa1
Penney, JC, Company, Inc.	Ba2
Saks Incorporated	B1
Sears, Roebuck and Co.	Baa1

Source: Moody's Investors Service.

Solution to 2: For the group, $n = 9$, an odd number. The group's median occupies the $(n + 1)/2 = 10/2 = 5$th position. We see from Table 3-12 that Baa1 occupies the fifth position. Therefore, the median credit rating as of September 2002 was Baa1.

TABLE 3-12   Senior Unsecured Debt Ratings: U.S. Department Stores, Distribution of Credit Ratings

Credit Rating	Frequency
A2	1
A3	1
Baa1	3
Baa2	1
Ba2	1
Ba3	1
B1	1

5.4. Other Concepts of Mean

Earlier we explained the arithmetic mean, which is a fundamental concept for describing the central tendency of data. Other concepts of mean are very important in investments, however. In the following, we discuss such concepts.

5.4.1. The Weighted Mean

The concept of weighted mean arises repeatedly in portfolio analysis. In the arithmetic mean, all observations are equally weighted by the factor $1/n$ (or $1/N$). In working with portfolios, we need the more general concept of weighted mean to allow different weights on different observations.

To illustrate the weighted mean concept, an investment manager with $100 million to invest might allocate $70 million to equities and $30 million to bonds. The portfolio has a weight of 0.70 on stocks and 0.30 on bonds. How do we calculate the return on this portfolio?

TABLE 3-13 Total Returns for Canadian
Equities and Bonds, 1998–2002

Year	Equities	Bonds
1998	−1.6%	9.1%
1999	31.7%	−1.1%
2000	7.4%	10.3%
2001	−12.6%	8.0%
2002	−12.4%	8.7%

Source: www.fidelity.ca and www.money.msn.ca.

The portfolio's return clearly involves an averaging of the returns on the stock and bond investments. The mean that we compute, however, must reflect the fact that stocks have a 70 percent weight in the portfolio and bonds have a 30 percent weight. The way to reflect this weighting is to multiply the return on the stock investment by 0.70 and the return on the bond investment by 0.30, then sum the two results. This sum is an example of a weighted mean. It would be incorrect to take an arithmetic mean of the return on the stock and bond investments, equally weighting the returns on the two asset classes.

Consider a portfolio invested in Canadian stocks and bonds in which the stock component is indexed on the S&P/TSX Composite Index and the bond component is indexed on the RBC Capital Markets Canadian Bond Market Index. These indexes represent the broad Canadian equity and bond markets, respectively. The portfolio manager allocates 60 percent of the portfolio to Canadian stocks and 40 percent to Canadian bonds. Table 3-13 presents total returns for these indexes for 1998 to 2002.

- **Weighted Mean Formula.** The **weighted mean** $\overline{X}_w$ (read "X-bar sub-w") for a set of observations $X_1, X_2, \ldots, X_n$ with corresponding weights of $w_1, w_2, \ldots, w_n$ is computed as

$$\overline{X}_w = \sum_{i=1}^{n} w_i X_i \tag{3-4}$$

where the sum of the weights equals 1; that is, $\sum_i w_i = 1$.

In the context of portfolios, a positive weight represents an asset held long and a negative weight represents an asset held short.[19]

The return on the portfolio under consideration is the weighted average of the return on Canadian stocks and Canadian bonds (the weight on stocks is 0.60; that on bonds is 0.40). Apart from expenses, if the portfolio tracks the indexes perfectly, we find, using Equation 3-4, that

---

[19]The formula for the weighted mean can be compared to the formula for the arithmetic mean. For a set of observations $X_1, X_2, \ldots, X_n$, let the weights $w_1, w_2, \ldots, w_n$ all equal $1/n$. Under this assumption, the formula for the weighted mean is $(1/n) \sum_{i=1}^{n} X_i$. This is the formula for the arithmetic mean. Therefore, the arithmetic mean is a special case of the weighted mean in which all the weights are equal.

$$\text{Portfolio return for 1998} = w_{\text{stock}} R_{\text{stock}} + w_{\text{bonds}} R_{\text{bonds}}$$
$$= 0.60(-1.6\%) + 0.40(9.1\%)$$
$$= 2.7\%$$

It should be clear that the correct mean to compute in this example is the weighted mean and not the arithmetic mean. If we had computed the arithmetic mean for 1998, we would have calculated a return equal to $1/2(-1.6\%) + 1/2(9.1\%) = (-1.6\% + 9.1\%)/2 = 3.8\%$. Given that the portfolio manager invested 60 percent in stocks and 40 percent in bonds, the arithmetic mean would underweight the investment in stocks and overweight the investment in bonds, resulting in a number for portfolio return that is too high by 1.1 percentage points $(3.8\% - 2.7\%)$.

Now suppose that the portfolio manager maintains constant weights of 60 percent in stocks and 40 percent in bonds for all five years. This method is called a constant-proportions strategy. Because value is price multiplied by quantity, price fluctuation causes portfolio weights to change. As a result, the constant-proportions strategy requires rebalancing to restore the weights in stocks and bonds to their target levels. Assuming that the portfolio manager is able to accomplish the necessary rebalancing, we can compute the portfolio returns in 1999, 2000, 2001, and 2002 with Equation 3-4 as follows:

$$\text{Portfolio return for 1999} = 0.60(31.7) + 0.40(-1.1) = 18.6\%$$

$$\text{Portfolio return for 2000} = 0.60(7.4) + 0.40(10.3) = 8.6\%$$

$$\text{Portfolio return for 2001} = 0.60(-12.6) + 0.40(8.0) = -4.4\%$$

$$\text{Portfolio return for 2002} = 0.60(-12.4) + 0.40(8.7) = -4.0\%$$

We can now find the time-series mean of the returns for 1998 through 2002 using Equation 3-3 for the arithmetic mean. The time-series mean total return for the portfolio is $(2.7 + 18.6 + 8.6 - 4.4 - 4.0)/5 = 21.5/5 = 4.3$ percent.

Instead of calculating the portfolio time-series mean return from portfolio annual returns, we can calculate the arithmetic mean bond and stock returns for the five years and then apply the portfolio weights of 0.60 and 0.40, respectively, to those values. The mean stock return is $(-1.6 + 31.7 + 7.4 - 12.6 - 12.4)/5 = 12.5/5 = 2.5$ percent. The mean bond return is $(9.1 - 1.1 + 10.3 + 8.0 + 8.7)/5 = 35.0/5 = 7.0$ percent. Therefore, the mean total return for the portfolio is $0.60(2.5) + 0.40(7.0) = 4.3$ percent, which agrees with our previous calculation.

EXAMPLE 3-6   Portfolio Return as a Weighted Mean

Table 3-14 gives information on the estimated average asset allocation of Canadian pension funds as well as four-year asset class returns.[20]

---

[20] In Table 3-14, equities are represented by the S&P/TSX Composite Index, U.S. equities by the S&P 500, international (non–North American) equities by the MSCI EAFE Index, bonds by the Scotia Capital Markets Universe Bond Index, mortgages by the Scotia Capital Markets Mortgage Index, real estate by the Standard Life Investments pooled real estate fund, and cash and equivalents by 91-day T-bills.

TABLE 3-14   Asset Allocation for Average Canadian Pension Fund as of 31 March 2003

Asset Class	Asset Allocation (Weight)	Asset Class Return (%)
Equities	34.6	0.6
U.S. equities	10.8	−9.3
International equities	6.4	−10.5
Bonds	34.0	6.0
Mortgages	1.3	9.0
Real estate	4.5	10.2
Cash and equivalents	8.4	4.2

Source: Standard Life Investments, Inc.

Using the information in Table 3-14, calculate the mean return earned by the average Canadian pension fund over the four years ending 31 March 2003.

Solution: Converting the percent asset allocation to decimal form, we find the mean return as a weighted average of the asset class returns. We have

$$
\begin{aligned}
\text{Mean portfolio return} =\ & 0.346(0.6\%) + 0.108(-9.3\%) + 0.064(-10.5\%) \\
& + 0.340(6.0\%) + 0.013(9.0\%) + 0.045(10.2\%) \\
& + 0.084(4.2\%) \\
=\ & 0.208\% - 1.004\% - 0.672\% + 2.040\% \\
& + 0.117\% + 0.459\% + 0.353\% \\
=\ & 1.5\%
\end{aligned}
$$

The previous examples illustrate the general principle that a portfolio return is a weighted sum. Specifically, a portfolio's return is the weighted average of the returns on the assets in the portfolio; the weight applied to each asset's return is the fraction of the portfolio invested in that asset.

Market indexes are computed as weighted averages. For market-capitalization indexes such as the CAC-40 in France or the S&P 500 in the United States, each included stock receives a weight corresponding to its outstanding market value divided by the total market value of all stocks in the index.

Our illustrations of weighted mean use past data, but they might just as well use forward-looking data. When we take a weighted average of forward-looking data, the weighted mean is called **expected value**. Suppose we make one forecast for the year-end level of the S&P 500 assuming economic expansion and another forecast for the year-end level of the S&P 500 assuming economic contraction. If we multiply the first forecast by the probability of expansion and the second forecast by the probability of contraction and then add these weighted forecasts, we are calculating the expected value of the S&P 500 at year-end. If we take a weighted average of possible future returns on the S&P 500, we are computing the S&P 500's expected return. The probabilities must sum to 1, satisfying the condition on the weights in the expression for weighted mean, Equation 3-4.

5.4.2. The Geometric Mean   The geometric mean is most frequently used to average rates of change over time or to compute the growth rate of a variable. In investments, we frequently use the geometric mean to average a time series of rates of return on an asset or a portfolio or to compute the growth rate of a financial variable such as earnings or sales. In the chapter on the time value of money, for instance, we computed a sales growth rate (Example 1-17). That growth rate was a geometric mean. Because of the subject's importance, in a later section we will return to the use of the geometric mean and offer practical perspectives on its use. The geometric mean is defined by the following formula.

- **Geometric Mean Formula**.   The **geometric mean**, G, of a set of observations $X_1, X_2, \ldots,$ X_n is

$$G = \sqrt[n]{X_1 X_2 X_3 \ldots X_n} \tag{3-5}$$

  with $X_i \geq 0$ for $i = 1, 2, \ldots, n$.

Equation 3-5 has a solution, and the geometric mean exists, only if the product under the radical sign is non-negative. We impose the restriction that all the observations X_i in Equation 3-5 are greater than or equal to zero. We can solve for the geometric mean using Equation 3-5 directly with any calculator that has an exponentiation key (on most calculators, y^x). We can also solve for the geometric mean using natural logarithms. Equation 3-5 can also be stated as

$$\ln G = \frac{1}{n} \ln(X_1 X_2 X_3 \ldots X_n)$$

or as

$$\ln G = \frac{\sum_{i=1}^{n} \ln X_i}{n}$$

When we have computed $\ln G$, then $G = e^{\ln G}$ (on most calculators, the key for this step is e^x).

Risky assets can have negative returns up to -100 percent (if their price falls to zero), so we must take some care in defining the relevant variables to average in computing a geometric mean. We cannot just use the product of the returns for the sample and then take the nth root because the returns for any period could be negative. We must redefine the returns to make them positive. We do this by adding 1.0 to the returns expressed as decimals. The term $(1 + R_t)$ represents the year-ending value relative to an initial unit of investment at the beginning of the year. As long as we use $(1 + R_t)$, the observations will never be negative because the biggest negative return is -100 percent. The result is the geometric mean of $1 + R_t$; by then subtracting 1.0 from this result, we obtain the geometric mean of the individual returns R_t. For example, the returns on Canadian stocks as represented by the S&P/TSX Composite Index during the 1998–2002 period were given in Table 3-13 as $-0.016, 0.317, 0.074, -0.126,$ and -0.124, putting the returns into decimal form. Adding 1.0 to those returns produces 0.9840, 1.317, 1.074, 0.874, and 0.876. Using Equation 3-5 we have $\sqrt[5]{(0.9840)(1.317)(1.074)(0.874)(0.876)} = \sqrt[5]{1.065616} = 1.012792$. This number is 1 plus the geometric mean rate of return. Subtracting 1.0 from this result, we have $1.012792 - 1.0 = 0.012792$ or approximately 1.3 percent. The geometric mean return for Canadian stocks during the 1998–2002 period was 1.3 percent.

An equation that summarizes the calculation of the geometric mean return, R_G, is a slightly modified version of Equation 3-5 in which the X_i represent "1 + return in decimal form." Because geometric mean returns use time series, we use a subscript t indexing time as well.

$$1 + R_G = \sqrt[T]{(1 + R_1)(1 + R_2) \dots (1 + R_T)}$$

$$1 + R_G = \left[\prod_{t=1}^{T} (1 + R_t) \right]^{\frac{1}{T}}$$

which leads to the following formula:

- **Geometric Mean Return Formula.** Given a time series of holding period returns $R_t, t = 1, 2, \dots, T$, the geometric mean return over the time period spanned by the returns R_1 through R_T is

$$R_G = \left[\prod_{t=1}^{T} (1 + R_t) \right]^{\frac{1}{T}} - 1 \qquad (3\text{-}6)$$

We can use Equation 3-6 to solve for the geometric mean return for any return data series. Geometric mean returns are also referred to as compound returns. If the returns being averaged in Equation 3-6 have a monthly frequency, for example, we may call the geometric mean monthly return the compound monthly return. The next example illustrates the computation of the geometric mean while contrasting the geometric and arithmetic means.

EXAMPLE 3-7   Geometric and Arithmetic Mean Returns (1)

As a mutual fund analyst, you are examining, as of early 2003, the most recent five years of total returns for two U.S. large-cap value equity mutual funds.

Based on the data in Table 3-15, address the following:

1. Calculate the geometric mean return of SLASX.
2. Calculate the arithmetic mean return of SLASX and contrast it to the fund's geometric mean return.
3. Calculate the geometric mean return of PRFDX.
4. Calculate the arithmetic mean return of PRFDX and contrast it to the fund's geometric mean return.

Solution to 1: Converting the returns on SLASX to decimal form and adding 1.0 to each return produces 1.162, 1.203, 1.093, 0.889, and 0.830. We use Equation 3-6 to find SLASX's geometric mean return:

TABLE 3-15   Total Returns for Two Mutual Funds, 1998–2002

Year	Selected American Shares (SLASX)	T. Rowe Price Equity Income (PRFDX)
1998	16.2%	9.2%
1999	20.3%	3.8%
2000	9.3%	13.1%
2001	−11.1%	1.6%
2002	−17.0%	−13.0%

Source: American Association of Individual Investors (AAII).

$$R_G = \sqrt[5]{(1.162)(1.203)(1.093)(0.889)(0.830)} - 1$$

$$= \sqrt[5]{1.127384} - 1 = 1.024270 - 1 = 0.024270$$

$$= 2.43\%$$

Solution to 2:   For SLASX, $\overline{R} = (16.2 + 20.3 + 9.3 - 11.1 - 17.0)/5 = 17.7/5 =$ 3.54%. The arithmetic mean return for SLASX exceeds the geometric mean return by $3.54 - 2.43 = 1.11\%$ or 111 basis points.

Solution to 3: Converting the returns on PRFDX to decimal form and adding 1.0 to each return produces 1.092, 1.038, 1.131, 1.016, and 0.870. We use Equation 3-6 to find PRFDX's geometric mean return:

$$R_G = \sqrt[5]{(1.092)(1.038)(1.131)(1.016)(0.870)} - 1$$

$$= \sqrt[5]{1.133171} - 1 = 1.025319 - 1 = 0.025319$$

$$= 2.53\%$$

Solution to 4:   For PRFDX, $\overline{R} = (9.2 + 3.8 + 13.1 + 1.6 - 13.0)/5 = 14.7/5 =$ 2.94%. The arithmetic mean for PRFDX exceeds the geometric mean return by $2.94 - 2.53 = 0.41\%$ or 41 basis points. The table below summarizes the findings.

TABLE 3-16   Mutual Fund Arithmetic and Geometric Mean Returns: Summary of Findings

Fund	Arithmetic Mean	Geometric Mean
SLASX	3.54%	2.43%
PRFDX	2.94%	2.53%

In Example 3-7, for both mutual funds, the geometric mean return was less than the arithmetic mean return. In fact, the geometric mean is always less than or equal to the arithmetic mean.[21] The only time that the two means will be equal is when there is no variability in the observations—that is, when all the observations in the series are the same.[22] In Example 3-7, there was variability in the funds' returns; thus for both funds, the geometric mean was strictly less than the arithmetic mean. In general, the difference between the arithmetic and geometric means increases with the variability in the period-by-period observations.[23] This relationship is also illustrated by Example 3-7. Even casual inspection reveals that the returns of SLASX are more variable than those of PRFDX, and consequently, the spread between the arithmetic and geometric mean returns is larger for SLASX (111 basis points) than for PRFDX (41 basis points).[24] The arithmetic and geometric mean also rank the two funds differently. Although SLASX has the higher arithmetic mean return, PRFDX has the higher geometric mean return. How should the analyst interpret this result?

The geometric mean return represents the growth rate or compound rate of return on an investment. One dollar invested in SLASX at the beginning of 1998 would have grown to $(1.162)(1.203)(1.093)(0.889)(0.830) = \$1.127$, which is equal to 1 plus the geometric mean return compounded over five periods: $(1.0243)^5 = \$1.127$, confirming that the geometric mean is the compound rate of return. For PRFDX, one dollar would have grown to a larger amount, $(1.092)(1.038)(1.131)(1.016)(0.870) = \$1.133$, equal to $(1.0253)^5$. With its focus on the profitability of an investment over a multiperiod horizon, the geometric mean is of key interest to investors. The arithmetic mean return, focusing on average single-period performance, is also of interest. Both arithmetic and geometric means have a role to play in investment management, and both are often reported for return series. Example 3-8 highlights these points in a simple context.

EXAMPLE 3-8   Geometric and Arithmetic Mean Returns (2)

A hypothetical investment in a single stock initially costs €100. One year later, the stock is trading at €200. At the end of the second year, the stock price falls back to the original purchase price of €100. No dividends are paid during the two-year period. Calculate the arithmetic and geometric mean annual returns.

Solution: First, we need to find the Year 1 and Year 2 annual returns with Equation 3-1.

$$\text{Return in Year } 1 = 200/100 - 1 = 100\%$$

---

[21] This statement can be proved using Jensen's inequality that the average value of a function is less than or equal to the function evaluated at the mean if the function is concave from below—the case for $\ln(X)$.

[22] For instance, suppose the return for each of the three years is 10 percent. The arithmetic mean is 10 percent. To find the geometric mean, we first express the returns as $(1 + R_t)$ and then find the geometric mean: $[(1.10)(1.10)(1.10)]^{1/3} - 1.0 = 10$ percent. The two means are the same.

[23] We will soon introduce standard deviation as a measure of variability. Holding the arithmetic mean return constant, the geometric mean return decreases for an increase in standard deviation.

[24] We will introduce formal measures of variability later. But note, for example, the 20.4 percentage point swing in returns between 2000 and 2001 for SLASX versus the 11.5 percentage point for PRFDX.

> Return in Year 2 $= 100/200 - 1 = -50\%$
>
> The arithmetic mean of the annual returns is $(100\% - 50\%)/2 = 25\%$.
>
> Before we find the geometric mean, we must convert the percentage rates of return to $(1 + R_t)$. After this adjustment, the geometric mean from Equation 3-6 is $\sqrt{2.0 \times 0.50} - 1 = 0\%$.
>
> The geometric mean return of 0 percent accurately reflects that the ending value of the investment in Year 2 equals the starting value in Year 1. The compound rate of return on the investment is 0 percent. The arithmetic mean return reflects the average of the one-year returns.

5.4.3. The Harmonic Mean   The arithmetic mean, the weighted mean, and the geometric mean are the most frequently used concepts of mean in investments. A fourth concept, the harmonic mean, $\overline{X}_H$, is appropriate in a limited number of applications.[25]

- **Harmonic Mean Formula**.   The **harmonic mean** of a set of observations $X_1, X_2, \ldots, X_n$ is

$$\overline{X}_H = n / \sum_{i=1}^{n} (1/X_i) \tag{3-7}$$

with $X_i > 0$ for $i = 1, 2, \ldots, n$.

The harmonic mean is the value obtained by summing the reciprocals of the observations—terms of the form $1/X_i$—then averaging that sum by dividing it by the number of observations n, and, finally, taking the reciprocal of the average.

The harmonic mean may be viewed as a special type of weighted mean in which an observation's weight is inversely proportional to its magnitude. The harmonic mean is a relatively specialized concept of the mean that is appropriate when averaging ratios ("amount per unit") when the ratios are repeatedly applied to a fixed quantity to yield a variable number of units. The concept is best explained through an illustration. A well-known application arises in the investment strategy known as **cost averaging**, which involves the periodic investment of a fixed amount of money. In this application, the ratios we are averaging are prices per share at purchases dates, and we are applying those prices to a constant amount of money to yield a variable number of shares.

Suppose an investor purchases €1,000 of a security each month for $n = 2$ months. The share prices are €10 and €15 at the two purchase dates. What is the average price paid for the security?

In this example, in the first month we purchase €1,000/€10 = 100 shares, and in the second month we purchase €1,000/€15 = 66.67, or 166.67 shares in total. Dividing the total euro amount invested, €2,000, by the total number of shares purchased, 166.67, gives an average price paid of €2,000/166.67 = €12. The average price paid is in fact the harmonic mean of the asset's prices at the purchase dates. Using Equation 3-7, the harmonic mean

---

[25]The terminology "harmonic" arises from its use relative to a type of series involving reciprocals known as a harmonic series.

price is $2/[(1/10) + (1/15)] = €12$. The value €12 is less than the arithmetic mean purchase price $(€10 + €15)/2 = €12.5$. However, we could find the correct value of €12 using the weighted mean formula, where the weights on the purchase prices equal the shares purchased at a given price as a proportion of the total shares purchased. In our example, the calculation would be $(100/166.67)€10.00 + (66.67/166.67)€15.00 = €12$. If we had invested varying amounts of money at each date, we could not use the harmonic mean formula. We could, however, still use the weighted mean formula in a manner similar to that just described.

A mathematical fact concerning the harmonic, geometric, and arithmetic means is that unless all the observations in a dataset have the same value, the harmonic mean is less than the geometric mean, which in turn is less than the arithmetic mean. In the illustration given, the harmonic mean price was indeed less than the arithmetic mean price.

6. OTHER MEASURES OF LOCATION: QUANTILES

Having discussed measures of central tendency, we now examine an approach to describing the location of data that involves identifying values at or below which specified proportions of the data lie. For example, establishing that 25, 50, and 75 percent of the annual returns on a portfolio are at or below the values $-0.05, 0.16$, and 0.25, respectively, provides concise information about the distribution of portfolio returns. Statisticians use the word **quantile** (or **fractile**) as the most general term for a value at or below which a stated fraction of the data lies. In the following, we describe the most commonly used quantiles—quartiles, quintiles, deciles, and percentiles—and their application in investments.

6.1. Quartiles, Quintiles, Deciles, and Percentiles

We know that the median divides a distribution in half. We can define other dividing lines that split the distribution into smaller sizes. **Quartiles** divide the distribution into quarters, **quintiles** into fifths, **deciles** into tenths, and **percentiles** into hundredths. Given a set of observations, the yth percentile is the value at or below which y percent of observations lie. Percentiles are used frequently, and the other measures can be defined with respect to them. For example, the first quartile (Q_1) divides a distribution such that 25 percent of the observations lie at or below it; therefore, the first quartile is also the 25th percentile. The second quartile (Q_2) represents the 50th percentile, and the third quartile (Q_3) represents the 75th percentile because 75 percent of the observations lie at or below it.

When dealing with actual data, we often find that we need to approximate the value of a percentile. For example, if we are interested in the value of the 75th percentile, we may find that no observation divides the sample such that exactly 75 percent of the observations lie at or below that value. The following procedure, however, can help us determine or estimate a percentile. The procedure involves first locating the position of the percentile within the set of observations and then determining (or estimating) the value associated with that position.

Let P_y be the value at or below which y percent of the distribution lies, or the yth percentile. (For example, P_{18} is the point at or below which 18 percent of the observations lie; $100 - 18 = 82$ percent are greater than P_{18}.) The formula for the position of a percentile in an array with n entries sorted in ascending order is

$$L_y = (n+1)\frac{y}{100} \tag{3-8}$$

where y is the percentage point at which we are dividing the distribution and L_y is the location (L) of the percentile (P_y) in the array sorted in ascending order. The value of L_y may or may not be a whole number. In general, as the sample size increases, the percentile location calculation becomes more accurate; in small samples it may be quite approximate.

As an example of the case in which L_y is not a whole number, suppose that we want to determine the third quartile of returns for 2002 (Q_3 or P_{75}) for the 16 European equity markets given in Table 3-8. According to Equation 3-8, the position of the third quartile is $L_{75} = (16 + 1)75/100 = 12.75$, or between the 12th and 13th items in Table 3-9, which ordered the returns into ascending order. The 12th item in Table 3-9 is the return to equities in Portugal in 2002, -28.29 percent. The 13th item is the return to equities in Switzerland in 2002, -25.84 percent. Reflecting the "0.75" in "12.75," we would conclude that P_{75} lies 75 percent of the distance between -28.29 percent and -25.84 percent.

To summarize:

- When the location, L_y, is a whole number, the location corresponds to an actual observation. For example, if Italy had not been included in the sample, then $n + 1$ would have been 16 and, with $L_{75} = 12$, the third quartile would be $P_{75} = X_{12}$, where X_i is defined as the value of the observation in the ith ($i = L_{75}$) position of the data sorted in ascending order (i.e., $P_{75} = -28.29$).
- When L_y is not a whole number or integer, L_y lies between the two closest integer numbers (one above and one below), and we use **linear interpolation** between those two places to determine P_y. Interpolation means estimating an unknown value on the basis of two known values that surround it (lie above and below it); the term "linear" refers to a straight-line estimate. Returning to the calculation of P_{75} for the equity returns, we found that $L_y = 12.75$; the next lower whole number is 12 and the next higher whole number is 13. Using linear interpolation, $P_{75} \approx X_{12} + (12.75 - 12)(X_{13} - X_{12})$. As above, in the 12th position is the return to equities in Portugal, so $X_{12} = -28.29$ percent; $X_{13} = -25.84$ percent, the return to equities in Switzerland. Thus our estimate is $P_{75} \approx X_{12} + (12.75 - 12)(X_{13} - X_{12}) = -28.29 + 0.75[-25.84 - (-28.29)] = -28.29 + 0.75(2.45) = -28.29 + 1.84 = -26.45$ percent. In words, -28.29 and -25.84 bracket P_{75} from below and above, respectively. Because $12.75 - 12 = 0.75$, using linear interpolation we move 75 percent of the distance from -28.29 to -25.84 as our estimate of P_{75}. We follow this pattern whenever L_y is non-integer: The nearest whole numbers below and above L_y establish the positions of observations that bracket P_y and then interpolate between the values of those two observations.

Example 3-9 illustrates the calculation of various quantiles for the dividend yield on the components of a major European equity index.

EXAMPLE 3-9   Calculating Percentiles, Quartiles, and Quintiles

The DJ EuroSTOXX 50 is an index of Europe's 50 largest publicly traded companies as measured by market capitalization. Table 3-17 shows the dividend yields on the 50 component stocks in the index as of mid-2003, ranked in ascending order.

TABLE 3-17   Dividend Yields on the Components of the DJ EuroSTOXX 50

No.	Company	Dividend Yield	No.	Company	Dividend Yield
1	AstraZeneca	0.00%	26	UBS	2.65%
2	BP	0.00%	27	Tesco	2.95%
3	Deutsche Telekom	0.00%	28	Total	3.11%
4	HSBC Holdings	0.00%	29	GlaxoSmithKline	3.31%
5	Credit Suisse Group	0.26%	30	BT Group	3.34%
6	L'Oréal	1.09%	31	Unilever	3.53%
7	SwissRe	1.27%	32	BASF	3.59%
8	Roche Holding	1.33%	33	Santander Central	
9	Munich Re Group	1.36%		Hispano	3.66%
10	General Assicurazioni	1.39%	34	Banco Bilbao Vizcaya	
11	Vodafone Group	1.41%		Argentaria	3.67%
12	Carrefour	1.51%	35	Diageo	3.68%
13	Nokia	1.75%	36	HBOS	3.78%
14	Novartis	1.81%	37	E.ON	3.87%
15	Allianz	1.92%	38	Shell Transport and Co.	3.88%
16	Koninklije Philips		39	Barclays	4.06%
	Electronics	2.01%	40	Royal Dutch	
17	Siemens	2.16%		Petroleum Co.	4.27%
18	Deutsche Bank	2.27%	41	Fortis	4.28%
19	Telecom Italia	2. 27%	42	Bayer	4.45%
20	AXA	2.39%	43	DaimlerChrysler	4.68%
21	Telefonica	2.49%	44	Suez	5.13%
22	Nestlé	2.55%	45	Aviva	5.15%
23	Royal Bank of Scotland		46	Eni	5.66%
	Group	2.60%	47	ING Group	6.16%
24	ABN-AMRO		48	Prudential	6.43%
	Holding	2.65%	49	Lloyds TSB	7.68%
25	BNP Paribas	2.65%	50	AEGON	8.14%

Source: http://france.finance.yahoo.com accessed 8 July 2003.

Using the data in Table 3-17, address the following:

1. Calculate the 10th and 90th percentiles.
2. Calculate the first, second, and third quartiles.
3. State the value of the median.
4. How many quintiles are there, and to what percentiles do the quintiles correspond?
5. Calculate the value of the first quintile.

Solution to 1: In this example, $n = 50$. Using Equation 3-8, $L_y = (n + 1)y/100$ for position of the yth percentile, so for the 10th percentile we have

$$L_{10} = (50 + 1)(10/100) = 5.1$$

L_{10} is between the fifth and sixth observations with values $X_5 = 0.26$ and $X_6 = 1.09$. The estimate of the 10th percentile (first decile) for dividend yield is

$$P_{10} \approx X_5 + (5.1 - 5)(X_6 - X_5) = 0.26 + 0.1(1.09 - 0.26)$$

$$= 0.26 + 0.1(0.83) = 0.34\%$$

For the 90th percentile,

$$L_{90} = (50 + 1)(90/100) = 45.9$$

L_{90} is between the 45th and 46th observations with values $X_{45} = 5.15$ and $X_{46} = 5.66$, respectively. The estimate of the 90th percentile (ninth decile) is

$$P_{90} \approx X_{45} + (45.9 - 45)(X_{46} - X_{45}) = 5.15 + 0.9(5.66 - 5.15)$$

$$= 5.15 + 0.9(0.51) = 5.61\%$$

Solution to 2: The first, second, and third quartiles correspond to $P_{25}, P_{50},$ and P_{75}, respectively.

$L_{25} = (51)(25/100) = 12.75$　　　L_{25} is between the 12th and 13th entries with values $X_{12} = 1.51$ and $X_{13} = 1.75$.

$$P_{25} = Q_1 \approx X_{12} + (12.75 - 12)(X_{13} - X_{12})$$

$$= 1.51 + 0.75(1.75 - 1.51)$$

$$= 1.51 + 0.75(0.24) = 1.69\%$$

$L_{50} = (51)(50/100) = 25.5$　　　L_{25} is between the 25th and 26th entries. But these entries share the same value, $X_{25} = X_{26} = 2.65$, so no interpolation is needed.

$$P_{50} = Q_2 = 2.65\%$$

$L_{75} = (51)(75/100) = 38.25$　　　L_{75} is between the 38th and 39th entries with values $X_{38} = 3.88$ and $X_{39} = 4.06$.

$$P_{75} = Q_3 \approx X_{38} + (38.25 - 38)(X_{39} - X_{38})$$

$$= 3.88 + 0.25(4.06 - 3.88)$$

$$= 3.88 + 0.25(0.18) = 3.93\%$$

Solution to 3: The median is the 50th percentile, 2.65 percent. This is the same value that we would obtain by taking the mean of the $n/2 = 50/2 = 25$th item and $(n + 2)/2 = 52/2 = 26$th item, consistent with the procedure given earlier for the median of an even-numbered sample.

Solution to 4: There are four quintiles, and they correspond to P_{20}, P_{40}, P_{60}, and P_{80}.

Solution to 5: The first quintile is P_{20}.

$$L_{20} = (50 + 1)(20/100) = 10.2 \quad L_{20} \text{ is between the 10th and 11th}$$
observations with values $X_{10} = 1.39$
and $X_{11} = 1.41$.

The estimate of the first quintile is

$$P_{20} \approx X_{10} + (10.2 - 10)(X_{11} - X_{10})$$

$$= 1.39 + 0.2(1.41 - 1.39)$$

$$= 1.39 + 0.2(0.02) = 1.394\% \text{ or } 1.39\%$$

6.2. Quantiles in Investment Practice

In this section, we discuss the use of quantiles in investments. Quantiles are used in portfolio performance evaluation as well as in investment strategy development and research.

Investment analysts use quantiles every day to rank performance—for example, the performance of portfolios. The performance of investment managers is often characterized in terms of the quartile in which they fall relative to the performance of their peer group of managers. The Morningstar mutual fund star rankings, for example, associates the number of stars with percentiles of performance relative to similar-style mutual funds.

Another key use of quantiles is in investment research. Analysts refer to a group defined by a particular quantile as that quantile. For example, analysts often refer to the set of companies with returns falling below the 10th percentile cutoff point as the bottom return decile. Dividing data into quantiles based on some characteristic allows analysts to evaluate the impact of that characteristic on a quantity of interest. For instance, empirical finance studies commonly rank companies based on the market value of their equity and then sort them into deciles. The 1st decile contains the portfolio of those companies with the smallest market values, and the 10th decile contains those companies with the largest market value. Ranking companies by decile allows analysts to compare the performance of small companies with large ones.

We can illustrate the use of quantiles, in particular quartiles, in investment research using the example of Bauman, Conover, and Miller (1998). That study compared the performance of international growth stocks to value stocks. Typically, value stocks are defined as those for which the market price is relatively low in relation to earnings per share, book value per share, or dividends per share. Growth stocks, on the other hand, have comparatively high prices in relation to those same measures. The Bauman et al. classification criteria were the following valuation measures: price-to-earnings (P/E), price-to-cash flow (P/CF), price-to-book value (P/B), and dividend yield (D/P). They assigned one-fourth of the total sample with the lowest P/E on 30 June of each year from 1986 to 1996 (the value group) to Quartile 1, and the one-fourth with the highest P/E of each year (the growth group) to Quartile 4. The stocks with the second-highest P/E formed Quartile 3, and the stocks with the second-lowest P/E, Quartile 2. The authors repeated this process for each of the four fundamental factors. Treating each

TABLE 3-18   Mean Annual Returns of Value and Growth Stocks Based on Selected Characteristics, 1986–1996

Selection Criteria	Total Observations	Q_1 (Value)	Q_2	Q_3	Q_4 (Growth)	Spread in Return, Q_1 to Q_4
Classification by P/E	28,463					
Median P/E		8.7	15.2	24.2	72.5	
Return		15.0%	13.6%	13.5%	10.6%	+4.4%
Standard deviation		46.5	38.3	42.5	50.4	
Classification by P/CF	30,240					
Median P/CF		4.4	8.2	13.3	34.2	
Return		15.5%	13.7%	12.9%	11.2%	+4.3%
Standard deviation		48.7	41.2	41.9	51.4	
Classification by P/B	32,265					
Median P/B		0.8	1.4	2.2	4.3	
Return		18.1%	14.4%	12.6%	12.4%	+5.7%
Standard deviation		69.6	45.9	45.1	57.0	
Classification by D/P	25,394					
Median D/P		5.6%	3.2%	1.9%	0.6%	
Return		14.1%	14.1%	12.5%	9.3%	+4.8%
Standard deviation		40.5	38.7	38.9	42.0	

Source: Bauman et al.

quartile group as a portfolio composed of equally weighted stocks, they were able to compare the performance of the various value/growth quartiles. Table 1 from their study is reproduced as Table 3-18.

Table 3-18 reports each valuation factor's median, mean return, and standard deviation for each quartile grouping. Moving from Quartile 1 to Quartile 4, P/E, P/CF, and P/B increase, but D/P decreases. Regardless of the selection criteria, international value stocks outperformed international growth stocks during the sample period.

Bauman, Conover, and Miller also divided companies into one of four quartiles based on market value of equity. Then they examined the returns to the stocks in the quartiles. Table 7 from their article is reproduced here as Table 3-19. As the table shows, the small-company portfolio had a median market value of $46.6 million and the large-company portfolio had a median value of $2,472.3 million. Large companies were more than 50 times larger than small companies, yet their mean stock returns were less than half those of the small companies (small, 22.0 percent; large, 10.8 percent). Overall, Bauman et al. found two effects. First, international value stocks (as the authors defined them) outperformed international growth stocks. Second, international small stocks outperformed international large stocks.

The authors' next step was to examine how value and growth stocks performed while controlling for size. This step involved constructing 16 different value/growth and size portfolios (4 × 4 = 16) and investigating the interaction between these two fundamental factors. They found that international value stocks outperformed international growth stocks except when market capitalization was very small. For portfolio managers, these findings suggest that value stocks offered investors relatively more favorable returns than did growth stocks in international markets during the specific time period studied.

TABLE 3-19   Mean Annual Returns of International Stocks Grouped by Market Capitalization, 1986–1996

Selection Criteria	Total Observations	Q_1 (Small)	Q_2	Q_3	Q_4 (Large)	Spread in Return, Q_1 to Q_4
Classification by size	32,555					
Median size (millions)		$46.6	$209.9	$583.7	$2,472.3	
Return		22.0%	13.6%	11.1%	10.8%	+11.2%
Standard deviation		87.8	45.2	39.5	34.0	

Source: Bauman et al.

7. MEASURES OF DISPERSION

As the well-known researcher Fischer Black has written, "[t]he key issue in investments is estimating expected return."[26] Few would disagree with the importance of expected return or mean return in investments: The mean return tells us where returns, and investment results, are centered. To completely understand an investment, however, we also need to know how returns are dispersed around the mean. **Dispersion** is the variability around the central tendency. If mean return addresses reward, dispersion addresses risk.

In this section, we examine the most common measures of dispersion: range, mean absolute deviation, variance, and standard deviation. These are all measures of **absolute dispersion**. Absolute dispersion is the amount of variability present without comparison to any reference point or benchmark.

These measures are used throughout investment practice. The variance or standard deviation of return is often used as a measure of risk pioneered by Nobel laureate Harry Markowitz. William Sharpe, another winner of the Nobel Prize in economics, developed the Sharpe ratio, a measure of risk-adjusted performance. That measure makes use of standard deviation of return. Other measures of dispersion, mean absolute deviation and range, are also useful in analyzing data.

7.1. The Range

We encountered range earlier when we discussed the construction of frequency distribution. The simplest of all the measures of dispersion, range can be computed with interval or ratio data.

- **Definition of Range.** The **range** is the difference between the maximum and minimum values in a dataset:

$$\text{Range} = \text{Maximum value} - \text{Minimum value} \tag{3-9}$$

---

[26] Black (1993).

As an illustration of range, the largest monthly return for the S&P 500 in the period from January 1926 to December 2002 is 42.56 percent (in April 1933) and the smallest is −29.73 percent (in September 1931). The range of returns is thus 72.29 percent [42.56 percent − (−29.73 percent)]. An alternative definition of range reports the maximum and minimum values. This alternative definition provides more information than does the range as defined in Equation 3-9. An alternative definition of range reports the maximum and minimum values. This alternative definition provides more information than does the range as defined in Equation 3-9.

One advantage of the range is ease of computation. A disadvantage is that the range uses only two pieces of information from the distribution. It cannot tell us how the data are distributed (that is, the shape of the distribution). Because the range is the difference between the maximum and minimum returns, it can reflect extremely large or small outcomes that may not be representative of the distribution.[27]

7.2. The Mean Absolute Deviation

Measures of dispersion can be computed using all the observations in the distribution rather than just the highest and lowest. The question is, how should we measure dispersion? Our previous discussion on properties of the arithmetic mean introduced the notion of distance or deviation from the mean $(X_i − \overline{X})$ as a fundamental piece of information used in statistics. We could compute measures of dispersion as the arithmetic average of the deviations around the mean, but we would encounter a problem: The deviations around the mean always sum to 0. If we computed the mean of the deviations, the result would also equal 0. Therefore, we need to find a way to address the problem of negative deviations canceling out positive deviation.

One solution is to examine the absolute deviations around the mean as in the mean absolute deviation.

- **Mean Absolute Deviation Formula**.   The **mean absolute deviation** (MAD) for a sample is

$$\text{MAD} = \frac{\sum_{i=1}^{n} |X_i − \overline{X}|}{n} \tag{3-10}$$

where $\overline{X}$ is the sample mean and n is the number of observations in the sample.

In calculating MAD, we ignore the signs of the deviations around the mean. For example, if $X_i = −11.0$ and $\overline{X} = 4.5$, the absolute value of the difference is $|−11.0 − 4.5| = |−15.5| = 15.5$. The mean absolute deviation uses all of the observations in the sample and is thus superior to the range as a measure of dispersion. One technical drawback of MAD is that it is difficult to manipulate mathematically compared with the next measure we will introduce, variance.[28] Example 3-10 illustrates the use of the range and the mean absolute deviation in evaluating risk.

---

[27]Another distance measure of dispersion that we may encounter, the interquartile range, focuses on the middle rather than the extremes. The **interquartile range** (IQR) is the difference between the third and first quartiles of a dataset: $IQR = Q_3 − Q_1$. The IQR represents the length of the interval containing the middle 50 percent of the data, with a larger interquartile range indicating greater dispersion, all else equal.

[28]In some analytic work such as optimization, the calculus operation of differentiation is important. Variance as a function can be differentiated, but absolute value cannot.

EXAMPLE 3-10   The Range and the Mean Absolute Deviation

Having calculated mean returns for the two mutual funds in Example 3-7, the analyst is now concerned with evaluating risk.

TABLE 3-15   (repeated) Total Returns for Two Mutual Funds, 1998–2002

Year	Selected American Shares (SLASX)	T. Rowe Price Equity Income (PRFDX)
1998	16.2%	9.2%
1999	20.3%	3.8%
2000	9.3%	13.1%
2001	−11.1%	1.6%
2002	−17.0%	−13.0%

Source: AAII.

Based on the data in Table 3-15 repeated above, answer the following:

1. Calculate the range of annual returns for (A) SLASX and (B) PRFDX, and state which mutual fund appears to be riskier based on these ranges.
2. Calculate the mean absolute deviation of returns on (A) SLASX and (B) PRFDX, and state which mutual fund appears to be riskier based on MAD.

Solutions to 1:

A. For SLASX, the largest return was 20.3 percent and the smallest was −17.0 percent. The range is thus $20.3 - (-17.0) = 37.3\%$.
B. For PFRDX, the range is $13.1 - (-13.0) = 26.1\%$. With a larger range of returns than PRFDX, SLASX appeared to be the riskier fund during the 1998–2002 period.

Solutions to 2:

A. The arithmetic mean return for SLASX as calculated in Example 3-7 is 3.54 percent. The MAD of SLASX returns is

$$\text{MAD} = \frac{|16.2 - 3.54| + |20.3 - 3.54| + |9.3 - 3.54| + |-11.1 - 3.54| + |-17.0 - 3.54|}{5}$$

$$= \frac{12.66 + 16.76 + 5.76 + 14.64 + 20.54}{5}$$

$$= \frac{70.36}{5} = 14.1\%$$

B. The arithmetic mean return for PRFDX as calculated in Example 3-7 is 2.94 percent. The MAD of PRFDX returns is

$$\text{MAD} = \frac{|9.2 - 2.94| + |3.8 - 2.94| + |13.1 - 2.94| + |1.6 - 2.94| + |-13.0 - 2.94|}{5}$$

$$= \frac{6.26 + 0.86 + 10.16 + 1.34 + 15.94}{5}$$

$$= \frac{34.56}{5} = 6.9\%$$

SLASX, with a MAD of 14.1 percent, appears to be much riskier than PRFDX, with a MAD of 6.9 percent.

7.3. Population Variance and Population Standard Deviation

The mean absolute deviation addressed the issue that the sum of deviations from the mean equals zero by taking the absolute value of the deviations. A second approach to the treatment of deviations is to square them. The variance and standard deviation, which are based on squared deviations, are the two most widely used measures of dispersion. **Variance** is defined as the average of the squared deviations around the mean. **Standard deviation** is the positive square root of the variance. The following discussion addresses the calculation and use of variance and standard deviation.

7.3.1. Population Variance
If we know every member of a population, we can compute the population variance. Denoted by the symbol σ^2, the population variance is the arithmetic average of the squared deviations around the mean.

- **Population Variance Formula.** The **population variance** is

$$\sigma^2 = \frac{\sum_{i=1}^{N}(X_i - \mu)^2}{N} \tag{3-11}$$

where μ is the population mean and N is the size of the population.

Given knowledge of the population mean, μ, we can use Equation 3-11 to calculate the sum of the squared differences from the mean, taking account of all N items in the population, and then to find the mean squared difference by dividing the sum by N. Whether a difference from the mean is positive or negative, squaring that difference results in a positive number. Thus variance takes care of the problem of negative deviations from the mean canceling out positive deviations by the operation of squaring those deviations. The P/Es for BJ, COST, and WMT were given earlier as 16.73, 22.02, and 29.30, respectively. We calculated the mean P/E as 22.68. Therefore, the population variance of the P/Es is $(1/3)[(16.73 - 22.68)^2 + (22.02 - 22.68)^2 + (29.30 - 22.68)^2] = (1/3)(-5.95^2 + -0.66^2 + 6.62^2) = (1/3)(35.4025 + 0.4356 + 43.8244) = (1/3)(79.6625) = 26.5542.$

7.3.2. Population Standard Deviation   Because the variance is measured in squared units, we need a way to return to the original units. We can solve this problem by using standard deviation, the square root of the variance. Standard deviation is more easily interpreted than the variance because standard deviation is expressed in the same unit of measurement as the observations.

- **Population Standard Deviation Formula**.   The **population standard deviation**, defined as the positive square root of the population variance, is

$$\sigma = \sqrt{\frac{\sum_{i=1}^{N}(X_i - \mu)^2}{N}} \qquad (3\text{-}12)$$

where μ is the population mean and N is the size of the population.

Using the example of the P/Es for BJ, COST, and WMT, according to Equation 3-12 we would calculate the variance, 26.5542, then take the square root: $\sqrt{26.5542} = 5.1531$ or approximately 5.2.

   Both the population variance and standard deviation are examples of parameters of a distribution. In later chapters, we will introduce the notion of variance and standard deviation as risk measures.

   In investments, we often do not know the mean of a population of interest, usually because we cannot practically identify or take measurements from each member of the population. We then estimate the population mean with the mean from a sample drawn from the population, and we calculate a sample variance or standard deviation using formulas different from Equations 3-11 and 3-12. We shall discuss these calculations in subsequent sections. However, in investments we sometimes have a defined group that we can consider to be a population. With well-defined populations, we use Equations 3-11 and 3-12, as in the following example.

EXAMPLE 3-11   Calculating the Population Standard Deviation

Table 3-20 gives the yearly portfolio turnover for the 10 U.S. equity funds that composed the 2002 Forbes Magazine Honor Roll.[29] Portfolio turnover, a measure of trading activity, is the lesser of the value of sales or purchases over a year divided by average net assets during the year. The number and identity of the funds on the Forbes Honor Roll changes from year to year.

---

[29] *Forbes* magazine annually selects U.S. equity mutual funds meeting certain criteria for its Honor Roll. The criteria relate to capital preservation (performance in bear markets), continuity of management (the fund must have a manager with at least six years' tenure), diversification, accessibility (disqualifying funds that are closed to new investors), and after-tax long-term performance.

TABLE 3-20   Portfolio Turnover: 2002 Forbes Honor Roll Mutual Funds

Fund	Yearly Portfolio Turnover
FPA Capital Fund (FPPTX)	23%
Mairs & Power Growth Fund (MPGFX)	8%
Muhlenkamp Fund (MUHLX)	11%
Longleaf Partners Fund (LLPFX)	18%
Heartland Value Fund (HRTVX)	56%
Scudder–Dreman High Return Equity-A (KDHAX)	29%
Clipper Fund (CFIMX)	23%
Weitz Value Fund (WVALX)	13%
Third Avenue Value Fund (TAVFX)	16%
Dodge & Cox Stock Fund (DODGX)	10%

Source: Forbes (2003).

Based on the data in Table 3-20, address the following:

1. Calculate the population mean portfolio turnover for the period used by *Forbes* for the ten 2002 Honor Roll funds.
2. Calculate the population variance and population standard deviation of portfolio turnover.
3. Explain the use of the population formulas in this example.

Solution to 1: $\mu = (23 + 8 + 11 + 18 + 56 + 29 + 23 + 13 + 16 + 10)/10 = 207/10 = 20.7$ percent

Solution to 2: Having established that $\mu = 20.7$, we can calculate $\sigma^2 = \dfrac{\sum_{i=1}^{N}(X_i - \mu)^2}{N}$ by first calculating the numerator in the expression and then dividing by $N = 10$. The numerator (the sum of the squared differences from the mean) is

$(23 - 20.7)^2 + (8 - 20.7)^2 + (11 - 20.7)^2 + (18 - 20.7)^2 + (56 - 20.7)^2 +$

$(29 - 20.7)^2 + (23 - 20.7)^2 + (13 - 20.7)^2 + (16 - 20.7)^2 +$

$(10 - 20.7)^2 = 1{,}784.1$

Thus $\sigma^2 = 1{,}784.1/10 = 178.41$.

To calculate standard deviation, $\sigma = \sqrt{178.41} = 13.357$ percent. (The unit of variance is percent squared, so the unit of standard deviation is percent.)

Solution to 3: If the population is clearly defined to be the Forbes Honor Roll funds in one specific year (2002), and if portfolio turnover is understood to refer to the specific one-year period reported upon by *Forbes,* the application of the population formulas to variance and standard deviation is appropriate. The results of 178.41 and 13.357 are, respectively, the cross-sectional variance and standard deviation in yearly portfolio turnover for the 2002 Forbes Honor Roll Funds.[30]

7.4. Sample Variance and Sample Standard Deviation

7.4.1. Sample Variance   In many instances in investment management, a subset or sample of the population is all that we can observe. When we deal with samples, the summary measures are called statistics. The statistic that measures the dispersion in a sample is called the sample variance.

- **Sample Variance Formula.**   The **sample variance** is

$$s^2 = \frac{\sum_{i=1}^{n}(X_i - \overline{X})^2}{n - 1} \tag{3-13}$$

where $\overline{X}$ is the sample mean and n is the number of observations in the sample.

Equation 3-13 tells us to take the following steps to compute the sample variance:

    i. Calculate the sample mean, $\overline{X}$.
    ii. Calculate each observation's squared deviation from the sample mean, $(X_i - \overline{X})^2$.
    iii. Sum the squared deviations from the mean: $\sum_{i=1}^{n}(X_i - \overline{X})^2$.
    iv. Divide the sum of squared deviations from the mean by $n - 1$: $\sum_{i=1}^{n}(X_i - \overline{X})^2/(n - 1)$.

We will illustrate the calculation of the sample variance and the sample standard deviation in Example 3-12.

    We use the notation s^2 for the sample variance to distinguish it from population variance, σ^2. The formula for sample variance is nearly the same as that for population variance except for the use of the sample mean, $\overline{X}$, in place of the population mean, μ, and a different divisor. In the case of the population variance, we divide by the size of the population, N. For the sample variance, however, we divide by the sample size minus 1, or $n - 1$. By using $n - 1$ (rather than n) as the divisor, we improve the statistical properties of the sample variance. In statistical terms, the sample variance defined in Equation 3-13 is an unbiased estimator of the population variance.[31] The quantity $n - 1$ is also known as the number of degrees of freedom in estimating the population variance. To estimate the population variance with s^2, we must first calculate the mean. Once we have computed the sample mean, there are only $n - 1$ independent deviations from it.

---

[30] In fact, we could not properly use the Honor Roll funds to estimate the population variance of portfolio turnover (for example) of any other differently defined population, because the Honor Roll funds are not a random sample from any larger population of U.S. equity mutual funds.
[31] We discuss this concept further in the chapter on sampling.

7.4.2. Sample Standard Deviation   Just as we computed a population standard deviation, we can compute a sample standard deviation by taking the positive square root of the sample variance.

- **Sample Standard Deviation Formula**.   The **sample standard deviation**, *s*, is

$$s = \sqrt{\dfrac{\displaystyle\sum_{i=1}^{n}(X_i - \overline{X})^2}{n-1}} \tag{3-14}$$

where $\overline{X}$ is the sample mean and *n* is the number of observations in the sample.

To calculate the sample standard deviation, we first compute the sample variance using the steps given. We then take the square root of the sample variance. Example 3-12 illustrates the calculation of the sample variance and standard deviation for the two mutual funds introduced earlier.

EXAMPLE 3-12   Calculating Sample Variance and Sample Standard Deviation

After calculating the geometric and arithmetic mean returns of two mutual funds in Example 3-7, we calculated two measures of dispersions for those funds, the range and mean absolute deviation of returns, in Example 3-10. We now calculate the sample variance and sample standard deviation of returns for those same two funds.

TABLE 3-15   (repeated) Total Returns for Two Mutual Funds, 1998–2002

Year	Selected American Shares (SLASX)	T. Rowe Price Equity Income (PRFDX)
1998	16.2%	9.2%
1999	20.3%	3.8%
2000	9.3%	13.1%
2001	−11.1%	1.6%
2002	−17.0%	−13.0%

Source: AAII.

Based on the data in Table 3-15 repeated above, answer the following:

1. Calculate the sample variance of return for (A) SLASX and (B) PRFDX.
2. Calculate sample standard deviation of return for (A) SLASX and (B) PRFDX.
3. Contrast the dispersion of returns as measured by standard deviation of return and mean absolute deviation of return for each of the two funds.

Solution to 1: To calculate the sample variance, we use Equation 3-13. (Deviation answers are all given in percent squared.)

A. SLASX

   i. The sample mean is $\overline{R} = (16.2 + 20.3 + 9.3 - 11.1 - 17.0)/5 = 17.7/5 = 3.54\%$.
   ii. The squared deviations from the mean are
       $(16.2 - 3.54)^2 = (12.66)^2 = 160.2756$
       $(20.3 - 3.54)^2 = (16.76)^2 = 280.8976$
       $(9.3 - 3.54)^2 = (5.76)^2 = 33.1776$
       $(-11.1 - 3.54)^2 = (-14.64)^2 = 214.3296$
       $(-17.0 - 3.54)^2 = (-20.54)^2 = 421.8916$
   iii. The sum of the squared deviations from the mean is $160.2756 + 280.8976 + 33.1776 + 214.3296 + 421.8916 = 1,110.5720$.
   iv. Divide the sum of the squared deviations from the mean by $n - 1$: $1,110.5720/(5 - 1) = 1,110.5720/4 = 277.6430$.

B. PRFDX

   i. The sample mean is $\overline{R} = (9.2 + 3.8 + 13.1 + 1.6 - 13.0)/5 = 14.7/5 = 2.94\%$.
   ii. The squared deviations from the mean are
       $(9.2 - 2.94)^2 = (6.26)^2 = 39.1876$
       $(3.8 - 2.94)^2 = (0.86)^2 = 0.7396$
       $(13.1 - 2.94)^2 = (10.16)^2 = 103.2256$
       $(1.6 - 2.94)^2 = (-1.34)^2 = 1.7956$
       $(-13.0 - 2.94)^2 = (-15.94)^2 = 254.0836$
   iii. The sum of the squared deviations from the mean is $39.1876 + 0.7396 + 103.2256 + 1.7956 + 254.0836 = 399.032$.
   iv. Divide the sum of the squared deviations from the mean by $n - 1$: $399.032/4 = 99.758$.

Solution to 2: To find the standard deviation, we take the positive square root of variance.

A. For SLASX, $\sigma = \sqrt{277.6430} = 16.66\%$ or 16.7 percent.
B. For PRFDX, $\sigma = \sqrt{99.758} = 9.99\%$ or 10.0 percent.

Solution to 3: Table 3-21 summarizes the results from Part 2 for standard deviation and incorporates the results for MAD from Example 3-10.

Note that the mean absolute deviation is less than the standard deviation. The mean absolute deviation will always be less than or equal to the standard deviation because the standard deviation gives more weight to large deviations than to small ones (remember, the deviations are squared).

TABLE 3-21   Two Mutual Funds: Comparison of Standard Deviation
and Mean Absolute Deviation

Fund	Standard Deviation	Mean Absolute Deviation
SLASX	16.7%	14.1%
PRFDX	10.0%	6.9%

Because the standard deviation is a measure of dispersion about the arithmetic mean, we usually present the arithmetic mean and standard deviation together when summarizing data. When we are dealing with data that represent a time series of percent changes, presenting the geometric mean—representing the compound rate of growth—is also very helpful. Table 3-22 presents the historical geometric and arithmetic mean returns, along with the historical standard deviation of returns, for various equity return series. We present these statistics for nominal (rather than inflation-adjusted) returns so we can observe the original magnitudes of the returns.

TABLE 3-22   Equity Market Returns: Means and
Standard Deviations

Return Series	Geometric Mean	Arithmetic Mean	Standard Deviation
I. Ibbotson Associates Series: 1926–2002			
S&P 500 (Annual)	10.20%	12.20%	20.49
S&P 500 (Monthly)	0.81%	0.97%	5.65
II. Dimson et al. (2002) Series (Annual): 1900–2000			
Australia	11.9%	13.3%	18.2%
Belgium	8.2%	10.5%	24.1%
Canada	9.7%	11.0%	16.6%
Denmark	8.9%	10.7%	21.7%
France	12.1%	14.5%	24.6%
Germany	9.7%	15.2%	36.4%
Ireland	9.5%	11.5%	22.8%
Italy	12.0%	16.1%	34.2%
Japan	12.5%	15.9%	29.5%
Netherlands	9.0%	11.0%	22.7%
South Africa	12.0%	14.2%	23.7%
Spain	10.0%	12.1%	22.8%
Sweden	11.6%	13.9%	23.5%
Switzerland	7.6%	9.3%	19.7%
United Kingdom	10.1%	11.9%	21.8%
United States	10.1%	12.0%	19.9%

Source: Ibbotson EnCorr Analyzer; Dimson et al.

7.5. Semivariance, Semideviation, and Related Concepts

An asset's variance or standard deviation of returns is often interpreted as a measure of the asset's risk. Variance and standard deviation of returns take account of returns above and below the mean, but investors are concerned only with downside risk, for example, returns below the mean. As a result, analysts have developed semivariance, semideviation, and related dispersion measures that focus on downside risk. **Semivariance** is defined as the average squared deviation below the mean. **Semideviation** (sometimes called semistandard deviation) is the positive square root of semivariance. To compute the sample semivariance, for example, we take the following steps:

    i. Calculate the sample mean.
    ii. Identify the observations that are smaller than the mean (discarding observations equal to and greater than the mean); suppose there are n^* observations smaller than the mean.
    iii. Compute the sum of the squared negative deviations from the mean (using the n^* observations that are smaller than the mean).
    iv. Divide the sum of the squared negative deviations from Step iii by $n^* - 1$. A formula for semivariance is

$$\sum_{\text{for all } X_i < \overline{X}} (X_i - \overline{X})^2 / (n^* - 1)$$

To take the case of Selected American Shares with returns (in percent) of 16.2, 20.3, 9.3, -11.1, and -17.0, we earlier calculated a mean return of 3.54 percent. Two returns, -11.1 and -17.0, are smaller than 3.54 ($n^* = 2$). We compute the sum of the squared negative deviations from the mean as $(-11.1 - 3.54)^2 + (-17.0 - 3.54)^2 = -14.64^2 + (-20.54)^2 = 214.3296 + 421.8916 = 636.2212$. With $n^* - 1 = 1$, we conclude that semivariance is $636.2212/1 = 636.2212$ and that semideviation is $\sqrt{636.2212} = 25.2$ percent, approximately. The semideviation of 25.2 percent is greater than the standard deviation of 16.7 percent. From this downside risk perspective, therefore, standard deviation understates risk.

    In practice, we may be concerned with values of return (or another variable) below some level other than the mean. For example, if our return objective is 10 percent annually, we may be concerned particularly with returns below 10 percent a year. We can call 10 percent the target. The name **target semivariance** has been given to average squared deviation below a stated target, and **target semideviation** is its positive square root. To calculate a sample target semivariance, we specify the target as a first step. After identifying observations below the target, we find the sum of the squared negative deviations from the target and divide that sum by the number of observations below the target minus 1. A formula for target semivariance is

$$\sum_{\text{for all } X_i < B} (X_i - B)^2 / (n^* - 1)$$

where B is the target and n^* is the number of observations below the target. With a target return of 10 percent, we find in the case of Selected American Shares that three returns (9.3, -11.1, and -17.0) were below the target. The target semivariance is $[(9.3 - 10.0)^2 + (-11.1 - 10.0)^2 + (-17.0 - 10.0)^2]/(3 - 1) = 587.35$, and the target semideviation is $\sqrt{587.35} = 24.24$ percent, approximately.

    When return distributions are symmetric, semivariance is a constant proportion (one-half) of variance and the two measures are effectively equivalent. For asymmetric distributions, variance and semivariance rank prospects' risk differently.[32] Semivariance (or semideviation) and target semivariance (or target semideviation) have intuitive appeal, but they are harder to work with mathematically than variance.[33] Variance or standard deviation enters into the definition of many of the most commonly used finance risk concepts, such as the Sharpe ratio and beta. Perhaps because of these reasons, variance (or standard deviation) is much more frequently used in investment practice.

7.6. Chebyshev's Inequality

The Russian mathematician Pafnuty Chebyshev developed an inequality using standard deviation as a measure of dispersion. The inequality gives the proportion of values within k standard deviations of the mean.

- **Definition of Chebyshev's Inequality**. According to Chebyshev's inequality, the proportion of the observations within k standard deviations of the arithmetic mean is at least $1 - 1/k^2$ for all $k > 1$.

Table 3-23 illustrates the proportion of the observations that must lie within a certain number of standard deviations around the sample mean.

When $k = 1.25$, for example, the inequality states that the minimum proportion of the observations that lie within $\pm 1.25s$ is $1 - 1/(1.25)^2 = 1 - 0.64 = 0.36$ or 36 percent.

The most frequently cited facts that result from Chebyshev's inequality are that a two-standard-deviation interval around the mean must contain at least 75 percent of the observations and a three-standard-deviation interval around the mean must contain at least 89 percent of the observations, no matter how the data are distributed.

The importance of Chebyshev's inequality stems from its generality. The inequality holds for samples and populations and for discrete and continuous data regardless of the shape of the distribution. As we shall see in the chapter on sampling, we can make much more precise interval statements if we can assume that the sample is drawn from a population that follows a specific distribution called the normal distribution. Frequently, however, we cannot confidently assume that distribution.

TABLE 3-23   Proportions from Chebyshev's Inequality

k	Interval Around the Sample Mean	Proportion
1.25	$\overline{X} \pm 1.25s$	36%
1.50	$\overline{X} \pm 1.50s$	56%
2.00	$\overline{X} \pm 2s$	75%
2.50	$\overline{X} \pm 2.50s$	84%
3.00	$\overline{X} \pm 3s$	89%
4.00	$\overline{X} \pm 4s$	94%

Note: Standard deviation is denoted as s.

---

[32] For negatively skewed returns, semivariance is greater than one-half variance; for positively skewed returns, semivariance is less than one-half variance. See Estrada (2003). We discuss skewness later in this chapter.

[33] As discussed in the chapter on probability concepts and the chapter on portfolio concepts, we can find a portfolio's variance as a straightforward function of the variances and correlations of the component securities. There is no similar procedure for semivariance and target semivariance. We also cannot take the derivative of semivariance or target semivariance.

The next example illustrates the use of Chebyshev's inequality.

EXAMPLE 3-13   Applying Chebyshev's Inequality

According to Table 3-22, the arithmetic mean monthly return and standard deviation of monthly returns on the S&P 500 were 0.97 percent and 5.65 percent, respectively, during the 1926–2002 period, totaling 924 monthly observations. Using this information, address the following:

1. Calculate the endpoints of the interval that must contain at least 75 percent of monthly returns according to Chebyshev's inequality.
2. What are the minimum and maximum number of observations that must lie in the interval computed in Part 1, according to Chebyshev's inequality?

Solution to 1: According to Chebyshev's inequality, at least 75 percent of the observations must lie within two standard deviations of the mean, $\overline{X} \pm 2s$. For the monthly S&P 500 return series, we have $0.97\% \pm 2(5.65\%) = 0.97\% \pm 11.30\%$. Thus the lower endpoint of the interval that must contain at least 75 percent of the observations is $0.97\% - 11.30\% = -10.33\%$, and the upper endpoint is $0.97\% + 11.30\% = 12.27\%$.

Solution to 2: For a sample size of 924, at least $0.75(924) = 693$ observations must lie in the interval from -10.33% to 12.27% that we computed in Part 1. Chebyshev's inequality gives the minimum percentage of observations that must fall within a given interval around the mean, but it does not give the maximum percentage. Table 3-4, which gave the frequency distribution of monthly returns on the S&P 500, is excerpted below. The data in the excerpted table are consistent with the prediction of Chebyshev's inequality. The set of intervals running from -10.0% to 12.0% is just slightly narrower than the two-standard-deviation interval -10.33% to 12.27%. A total of 886 observations (approximately 96 percent of observations) fall in the range from -10.0% to 12.0%.

TABLE 3-4   (Excerpt) Frequency Distribution for the Monthly Total Return on the S&P 500, January 1926 to December 2002

Return Interval	Absolute Frequency
-10.0% to -8.0%	20
-8.0% to -6.0%	30
-6.0% to -4.0%	54
-4.0% to -2.0%	90
-2.0% to 0.0%	138
0.0% to 2.0%	182
2.0% to 4.0%	153
4.0% to 6.0%	126
6.0% to 8.0%	58
8.0% to 10.0%	21
10.0% to 12.0%	14
	886

7.7. Coefficient of Variation

We noted earlier that standard deviation is more easily interpreted than variance because standard deviation uses the same units of measurement as the observations. We may sometimes find it difficult to interpret what standard deviation means in terms of the relative degree of variability of different sets of data, however, either because the datasets have markedly different means or because the datasets have different units of measurement. In this section we explain a measure of relative dispersion, the coefficient of variation that can be useful in such situations. **Relative dispersion** is the amount of dispersion relative to a reference value or benchmark.

We can illustrate the problem of interpreting the standard deviation of datasets with markedly different means using two hypothetical samples of companies. The first sample, composed of small companies, includes companies with 2003 sales of €50 million, €75 million, €65 million, and €90 million. The second sample, composed of large companies, includes companies with 2003 sales of €800 million, €825 million, €815 million, and €840 million. We can verify using Equation 3-14 that the standard deviation of sales in both samples is €16.8 million.[34] In the first sample, the largest observation, €90 million, is 80 percent larger than the smallest observation, €50 million. In the second sample, the largest observation is only 5 percent larger than the smallest observation. Informally, a standard deviation of €16.8 million represents a high degree of variability relative to the first sample, which reflects mean 2003 sales of €70 million, but a small degree of variability relative to the second sample, which reflects mean 2003 sales of €820 million.

The coefficient of variation is helpful in situations such as that just described.

- **Coefficient of Variation Formula.** The **coefficient of variation**, CV, is the ratio of the standard deviation of a set of observations to their mean value:[35]

$$CV = s/\overline{X} \qquad (3\text{-}15)$$

where s is the sample standard deviation and $\overline{X}$ is the sample mean.

When the observations are returns, for example, the coefficient of variation measures the amount of risk (standard deviation) per unit of mean return. Expressing the magnitude of variation among observations relative to their average size, the coefficient of variation permits direct comparisons of dispersion across different datasets. Reflecting the correction for scale, the coefficient of variation is a scale-free measure (that is, it has no units of measurement).

We can illustrate the application of the coefficient of variation using our earlier example of two samples of companies. The coefficient of variation for the first sample is (€16.8 million)/(€70 million) = 0.24; the coefficient of variation for the second sample is (€16.8 million)/(€820 million) = 0.02. This confirms our intuition that the first sample had much greater variability in sales than the second sample. Note that 0.24 and 0.02 are pure numbers in the sense that they are free of units of measurement (because we divided the standard deviation by the mean, which is measured in the same units as the standard deviation). If we need to compare the dispersion among data sets stated in different units of measurement, the coefficient of variation can be useful because it is free from units of measurement. Example 3-14 illustrates the calculation of the coefficient of variation.

---

[34]The second sample was created by adding €750 million to each observation in the first sample. Standard deviation (and variance) has the property of remaining unchanged if we add a constant amount to each observation.

[35]The reader will also encounter CV defined as $100(s/\overline{X})$, which states CV as a percentage.

EXAMPLE 3-14   Calculating the Coefficient of Variation

Table 3-24 summarizes annual mean returns and standard deviations for several major U.S. asset classes, using an option in Ibbotson EnCorr Analyzer to convert monthly return statistics to annual ones.

TABLE 3-24   Arithmetic Mean Annual Return and Standard Deviation of Returns, U.S. Asset Classes, 1926–2002

Asset Class	Arithmetic Mean Return	Standard Deviation of Return
S&P 500	12.3%	21.9%
U.S. small stock	16.9%	35.1%
U.S. long-term corporate	6.1%	7.2%
U.S. long-term government	5.8%	8.2%
U.S. 30-day T-bill	3.8%	0.9%

Source: Ibbotson EnCorr Analyzer.

Using the information in Table 3-24, address the following:

1. Calculate the coefficient of variation for each asset class given.
2. Rank the asset classes from most risky to least risky using CV as a measure of relative dispersion.
3. Determine whether there is more difference between the absolute or the relative riskiness of the S&P 500 and U.S. small stocks. Use the standard deviation as a measure of absolute risk and CV as a measure of relative risk.

Solution to 1:

S&P 500: CV = 21.9%/12.3% = 1.780

U.S. small stock: CV = 35.1%/16.9% = 2.077

U.S. long-term corporate: CV = 7.2%/6.1% = 1.180

U.S. long-term government: CV = 8.2%/5.8% = 1.414

U.S. 30-day T-bill: CV = 0.9%/3.8% = 0.237

Solution to 2:   Based on CV, the ranking is U.S. small stocks (most risky), S&P 500, U.S. long-term governments, U.S. long-term corporates, and U.S. 30-day T-bills (least risky).

Solution to 3:   As measured both by standard deviation and CV, U.S. small stocks were riskier than the S&P 500. However, the CVs reveal less difference between small stock and S&P 500 return variability than that suggested by the standard deviations alone. The standard deviation of small stock returns was (35.1 − 21.9)/21.9 = 0.603 or about 60 percent larger than S&P 500 returns, compared with a difference in the CV of (2.077 − 1.780)/1.780 = 0.167 or 17 percent.

7.8. The Sharpe Ratio

Although CV was designed as a measure of relative dispersion, its inverse reveals something about return per unit of risk because the standard deviation of returns is commonly used as a measure of investment risk. For example, a portfolio with a mean monthly return of 1.19 percent and a standard deviation of 4.42 percent has an inverse CV of $1.19\%/4.42\% = 0.27$. This result indicates that each unit of standard deviation represents a 0.27 percent return.

A more precise return–risk measure recognizes the existence of a risk-free return, a return for virtually zero standard deviation. With a risk-free asset, an investor can choose a risky portfolio, p, and then combine that portfolio with the risk-free asset to achieve any desired level of absolute risk as measured by standard deviation of return, s_p. Consider a graph with mean return on the vertical axis and standard deviation of return on the horizontal axis. Any combination of portfolio p and the risk-free asset lies on a ray (line) with slope equal to the quantity (Mean return − Risk-free return) divided by s_p. The ray giving investors choices offering the most reward (return in excess of the risk-free rate) per unit of risk is the one with the highest slope. The ratio of excess return to standard deviation of return for a portfolio p—the slope of the ray passing through p—is a single-number measure of a portfolio's performance known as the Sharpe ratio, after its developer, William F. Sharpe.

- **Sharpe Ratio Formula.**   The **Sharpe ratio** for a portfolio p, based on historical returns, is defined as

$$S_h = \frac{\overline{R}_p - \overline{R}_F}{s_p} \qquad (3\text{-}16)$$

where $\overline{R}_p$ is the mean return to the portfolio, $\overline{R}_F$ is the mean return to a risk-free asset, and s_p is the standard deviation of return on the portfolio.[36]

The numerator of the Sharpe measure is the portfolio's mean return minus the mean return on the risk-free asset over the sample period. The $\overline{R}_p - \overline{R}_F$ term measures the extra reward that investors receive for the added risk taken. We call this difference the **mean excess return** on portfolio p. Thus the Sharpe ratio measures the reward, in terms of mean excess return, per unit of risk, as measured by standard deviation of return. Those risk-averse investors who make decisions only in terms of mean return and standard deviation of return prefer portfolios with larger Sharpe ratios to those with smaller Sharpe ratios.

---

[36]The equation presents the *ex post* or historical Sharpe ratio. We can also think of the Sharpe ratio for a portfolio going forward based on our expectations for mean return, the risk-free return, and the standard deviation of return; this would be the *ex ante* Sharpe ratio. One may also encounter an alternative calculation for the Sharpe ratio in which the denominator is the standard deviation of the series (Portfolio return − Risk-free return) rather than the standard deviation of portfolio return; in practice, the two standard deviation calculations generally yield very similar results. For more information on the Sharpe ratio (which has also been called the Sharpe measure, the reward-to-variability ratio, and the excess return to variability measure), see Elton, Gruber, Brown, and Goetzmann (2003) and Sharpe (1994).

To illustrate the calculation of the Sharpe ratio, consider the performance of the S&P 500 and U.S. small stocks during the 1926–2002 period, as given previously in Table 3-24. Using the mean U.S. T-bill return to represent the risk-free rate, we find

$$\text{S\&P 500: } S_h = \frac{12.3 - 3.8}{21.9} = 0.39$$

$$\text{U.S. small stocks: } S_h = \frac{16.9 - 3.8}{35.1} = 0.37$$

Although U.S. small stocks earned higher mean returns, they performed slightly less well than the S&P 500, as measured by the Sharpe ratio.

The Sharpe ratio is a mainstay of performance evaluation. We must issue two cautions concerning its use, one related to interpreting negative Sharpe ratios and the other to conceptual limitations.

Finance theory tells us that in the long run, investors should be compensated with additional mean return above the risk-free rate for bearing additional risk, at least if the risky portfolio is well diversified. If investors are so compensated, the numerator of the Sharpe ratio will be positive. Nevertheless, we often find that portfolios exhibit negative Sharpe ratios when the ratio is calculated over periods in which bear markets for equities dominate. This raises a caution when dealing with negative Sharpe ratios. With positive Sharpe ratios, a portfolio's Sharpe ratio decreases if we increase risk, all else equal. That result is intuitive for a risk-adjusted performance measure. With negative Sharpe ratios, however, increasing risk results in a numerically larger Sharpe ratio (for example, doubling risk may increase the Sharpe ratio from -1 to -0.5). Therefore, in a comparison of portfolios with negative Sharpe ratios, we cannot generally interpret the larger Sharpe ratio (the one closer to zero) to mean better risk-adjusted performance.[37] Practically, to make an interpretable comparison in such cases using the Sharpe ratio, we may need to increase the evaluation period such that one or more of the Sharpe ratios becomes positive; we might also consider using a different performance evaluation metric.

The conceptual limitation of the Sharpe ratio is that it considers only one aspect of risk, standard deviation of return. Standard deviation is most appropriate as a risk measure for portfolio strategies with approximately symmetric return distributions. Strategies with option elements have asymmetric returns. Relatedly, an investment strategy may produce frequent small gains but have the potential for infrequent but extremely large losses.[38] Such a strategy is sometimes described as picking up coins in front of a bulldozer; for example, some hedge fund strategies tend to produce that return pattern. Calculated over a period in which the strategy is working (a large loss has not occurred), this type of strategy would have a high Sharpe ratio. In this case, the Sharpe ratio would give an overly optimistic picture of risk-adjusted performance because standard deviation would incompletely measure the risk assumed.[39] Therefore, before applying the Sharpe ratio to evaluate a manager, we should judge whether standard deviation adequately describes the risk of the manager's investment strategy.

---

[37] If the standard deviations are equal, however, the portfolio with the negative Sharpe ratio closer to zero is superior.

[38] This statement describes a return distribution with negative skewness. We discuss skewness later in this chapter.

[39] For more information, see Amin and Kat (2003).

Example 3-15 illustrates the calculation of the Sharpe ratio in a portfolio performance evaluation context.

EXAMPLE 3-15   Calculating the Sharpe Ratio

In earlier examples, we computed the various statistics for two mutual funds, Selected American Shares (SLASX) and T. Rowe Price Equity Income (PRFDX), for a five-year period ending in December 2002. Table 3-25 summarizes selected statistics for these two mutual funds for a longer period, the 10-year period ending in 2002.

TABLE 3-25   Mutual Fund Mean Return and Standard Deviation of Return, 1993–2002

Fund	Arithmetic Mean	Standard Deviation of Return
SLASX	12.58%	19.44%
PRFDX	11.64%	13.65%

Source: AAII.

The U.S. 30-day T-bill rate is frequently used as a proxy for the risk-free rate. Table 3-26 gives the annual return on T-bills for the 1993–2002 period.

TABLE 3-26   Annualized U.S. 30-Day T-Bill Rates of Return, 1993–2002

Year	Return
1993	2.90%
1994	3.90%
1995	5.60%
1996	5.21%
1997	5.26%
1998	4.86%
1999	4.68%
2000	5.89%
2001	3.83%
2002	1.65%

Source: Ibbotson Associates.

Using the information in Tables 3-25 and 3-26, address the following:

1. Calculate the Sharpe ratios for SLASX and PRFDX during the 1993–2002 period.

2. State which fund had superior risk-adjusted performance during this period, as measured by the Sharpe ratio.

Solution to 1: We already have in hand the means of the portfolio return and standard deviations of returns. The mean annual risk-free rate of return from 1993 to 2002, using U.S. T-bills as a proxy, is $(2.90 + 3.90 + 5.60 + 5.21 + 5.26 + 4.86 + 4.68 + 5.89 + 3.83 + 1.65)/10 = 43.78/10 = 4.38$ percent.

$$\text{SLASX: } S_{h,\text{SLASX}} = \frac{12.58 - 4.38}{19.44} = 0.42$$

$$\text{PRFDX: } S_{h,\text{PRFDX}} = \frac{11.64 - 4.38}{13.65} = 0.53$$

Solution to 2: PRFDX had a higher positive Sharpe ratio than SLASX during the period. As measured by the Sharpe ratio, PRFDX's performance was superior.

8. SYMMETRY AND SKEWNESS IN RETURN DISTRIBUTIONS

Mean and variance may not adequately describe an investment's distribution of returns. In calculations of variance, for example, the deviations around the mean are squared, so we do not know whether large deviations are likely to be positive or negative. We need to go beyond measures of central tendency and dispersion to reveal other important characteristics of the distribution. One important characteristic of interest to analysts is the degree of symmetry in return distributions.

If a return distribution is symmetrical about its mean, then each side of the distribution is a mirror image of the other. Thus equal loss and gain intervals exhibit the same frequencies. Losses from −5 percent to −3 percent, for example, occur with about the same frequency as gains from 3 percent to 5 percent.

One of the most important distributions is the normal distribution, depicted in Figure 3-6. This symmetrical, bell-shaped distribution plays a central role in the mean–variance model of portfolio selection; it is also used extensively in financial risk management. The normal distribution has the following characteristics:

- Its mean and median are equal.
- It is completely described by two parameters—its mean and variance.
- Roughly 68 percent of its observations lie between plus and minus one standard deviation from the mean; 95 percent lie between plus and minus two standard deviations; and 99 percent lie between plus and minus three standard deviations.

A distribution that is not symmetrical is called **skewed**. A return distribution with positive skew has frequent small losses and a few extreme gains. A return distribution with negative skew has frequent small gains and a few extreme losses. Figure 3-7 shows positively and negatively skewed distributions. The positively skewed distribution shown has a long tail on its

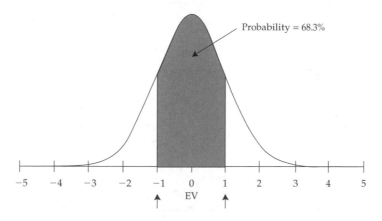

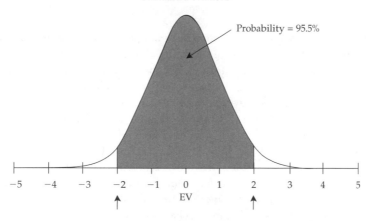

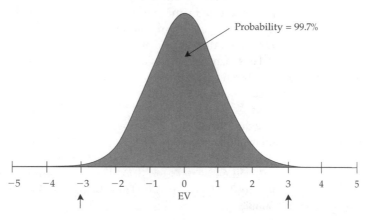

FIGURE 3-6   Properties of a Normal Distribution (EV = Expected Value)
Source: Reprinted with permission from *Fixed Income Readings for the Chartered Financial Analyst®
Program.* Copyright 2000, Frank J. Fabozzi Associates, New Hope, PA.

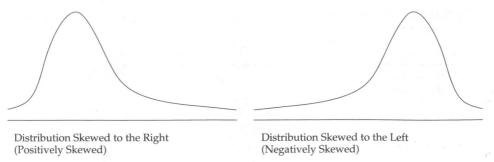

Distribution Skewed to the Right
(Positively Skewed)

Distribution Skewed to the Left
(Negatively Skewed)

FIGURE 3-7   Properties of a Skewed Distribution
Source: Reprinted with permission from *Fixed Income Readings for the Chartered Financial Analyst® Program.* Copyright 2000, Frank J. Fabozzi Associates, New Hope, PA.

right side; the negatively skewed distribution has a long tail on its left side. For the positively skewed unimodal distribution, the mode is less than the median, which is less than the mean. For the negatively skewed unimodal distribution, the mean is less than the median, which is less than the mode.[40] Investors should be attracted by a positive skew because the mean return falls above the median. Relative to the mean return, positive skew amounts to a limited, though frequent, downside compared with a somewhat unlimited, but less frequent, upside.

Skewness is the name given to a statistical measure of skew. (The word "skewness" is also sometimes used interchangeably for "skew.") Like variance, skewness is computed using each observation's deviation from its mean. **Skewness** (sometimes referred to as relative skewness) is computed as the average cubed deviation from the mean standardized by dividing by the standard deviation cubed to make the measure free of scale.[41] A symmetric distribution has skewness of 0, a positively skewed distribution has positive skewness, and a negatively skewed distribution has negative skewness, as given by this measure.

We can illustrate the principle behind the measure by focusing on the numerator. Cubing, unlike squaring, preserves the sign of the deviations from the mean. If a distribution is positively skewed with a mean greater than its median, then more than half of the deviations from the mean are negative and less than half are positive. In order for the sum to be positive, the losses must be small and likely, and the gains less likely but more extreme. Therefore, if skewness is positive, the average magnitude of positive deviations is larger than the average magnitude of negative deviations.

A simple example illustrates that a symmetrical distribution has a skewness measure equal to 0. Suppose we have the following data: 1, 2, 3, 4, 5, 6, 7, 8, and 9. The mean outcome is 5, and the deviations are $-4, -3, -2, -1, 0, 1, 2, 3$, and 4. Cubing the deviations yields $-64, -27, -8, -1, 0, 1, 8, 27$, and 64, with a sum of 0. The numerator of skewness (and so skewness itself) is thus equal to 0, supporting our claim. Below we give the formula for computing skewness from a sample.

---

[40] As a mnemonic, in this case the mean, median, and mode occur in the same order as they would be listed in a dictionary.

[41] We are discussing a moment coefficient of skewness. Some textbooks present the Pearson coefficient of skewness, equal to 3(Mean − Median)/Standard deviation, which has the drawback of involving the calculation of the median.

TABLE 3-27 S&P 500 Annual and Monthly Total Returns, 1926–2002: Summary Statistics

Return Series	Number of Periods	Arithmetic Mean	Standard Deviation	Skewness	Excess Kurtosis
S&P 500 (Annual)	77	12.20%	20.49%	−0.2943	−0.2207
S&P 500 (Monthly)	924	0.97%	5.65%	0.3964	9.4645

Source: Ibbotson EnCorr Analyzer.

- **Sample Skewness Formula.** **Sample skewness** (also called **sample relative skewness**), S_K, is

$$S_K = \left[\frac{n}{(n-1)(n-2)} \right] \frac{\sum_{i=1}^{n}(X_i - \overline{X})^3}{s^3} \tag{3-17}$$

where n is the number of observations in the sample and s is the sample standard deviation.[42]

The algebraic sign of Equation 3-17 indicates the direction of skew, with a negative S_K indicating a negatively skewed distribution and a positive S_K indicating a positively skewed distribution. Note that as n becomes large, the expression reduces to the mean cubed deviation,

$S_K \approx \left(\frac{1}{n} \right) \dfrac{\sum_{i=1}^{n}(X_i - \overline{X})^3}{s^3}$. As a frame of reference, for a sample size of 100 or larger taken from a normal distribution, a skewness coefficient of ± 0.5 would be considered unusually large.

Table 3-27 shows several summary statistics for the annual and monthly returns on the S&P 500. Earlier we discussed the arithmetic mean return and standard deviation of return, and we shall shortly discuss kurtosis.

Table 3-27 reveals that S&P 500 annual returns during this period were negatively skewed while monthly returns were positively skewed, and the magnitude of skewness was greater for the monthly series. We would find for other market series that the shape of the distribution of returns often depends on the holding period examined.

Some researchers believe that investors should prefer positive skewness, all else equal—that is, they should prefer portfolios with distributions offering a relatively large frequency of unusually large payoffs.[43] Different investment strategies may tend to introduce different types and amounts of skewness into returns. Example 3-16 illustrates the calculation of skewness for a managed portfolio.

EXAMPLE 3-16 Calculating Skewness for a Mutual Fund

Table 3-28 presents 10 years of annual returns on the T. Rowe Price Equity Income Fund (PRFDX).

---

[42]The term $n/[(n-1)(n-2)]$ in Equation 3-17 corrects for a downward bias in small samples.
[43]For more on the role of skewness in portfolio selection, see Reilly and Brown (2003) and Elton et al. (2003) and the references therein.

TABLE 3-28   Annual Rates
of Return: T. Rowe Price
Equity Income, 1993–2002

Year	Return
1993	14.8%
1994	4.5%
1995	33.3%
1996	20.3%
1997	28.8%
1998	9.2%
1999	3.8%
2000	13.1%
2001	1.6%
2002	−13.0%

Source: AAII.

Using the information in Table 3-28, address the following:

1. Calculate the skewness of PRFDX showing two decimal places.
2. Characterize the shape of the distribution of PRFDX returns based on your answer to Part 1.

Solution to 1:   To calculate skewness, we find the sum of the cubed deviations from the mean, divide by the standard deviation cubed, and then multiply that result by $n/[(n-1)(n-2)]$. Table 3-29 gives the calculations.

TABLE 3-29   Calculating Skewness for PRFDX

Year	R_t	$R_t - \overline{R}$	$(R_t - \overline{R})^3$
1993	14.8%	3.16	31.554
1994	4.5%	−7.14	−363.994
1995	33.3%	21.66	10,161.910
1996	20.3%	8.66	649.462
1997	28.8%	17.16	5,053.030
1998	9.2%	−2.44	−14.527
1999	3.8%	−7.84	−481.890
2000	13.1%	1.46	3.112
2001	1.6%	−10.04	−1,012.048
2002	−13.0%	−24.64	−14,959.673
$n =$	10		
$\overline{R} =$	11.64%		
		Sum =	−933.064
$s =$	13.65%	$s^3 =$	2,543.302
		Sum/s^3 =	−0.3669
		$n/[(n-1)(n-2)] =$	0.1389
		Skewness =	**−0.05**

Source: AAII.

Using Equation 3-17, the calculation is:

$$S_K = \left[\frac{10}{(9)(8)} \right] \frac{-933.064}{13.65^3} = -0.05$$

In this example, five deviations are negative and five are positive. Two large positive deviations, in 1995 and 1997, are more than offset by a very large negative deviation in 2002 and a moderately large negative deviation in 2001, both bear market years. The result is that skewness is a very small negative number.

Solution to 2: Based on this small sample, the distribution of annual returns for the fund appears to be approximately symmetric (or very slightly negatively skewed). The negative and positive deviations from the mean are equally frequent, and large positive deviations approximately offset large negative deviations.

9. KURTOSIS IN RETURN DISTRIBUTIONS

In the previous section, we discussed how to determine whether a return distribution deviates from a normal distribution because of skewness. One other way in which a return distribution might differ from a normal distribution is by having more returns clustered closely around the mean (being more peaked) and more returns with large deviations from the mean (having fatter tails). Relative to a normal distribution, such a distribution has a greater percentage of small deviations from the mean return (more small surprises) and a greater percentage of extremely large deviations from the mean return (more big surprises). Most investors would perceive a greater chance of extremely large deviations from the mean as increasing risk.

Kurtosis is the statistical measure that tells us when a distribution is more or less peaked than a normal distribution. A distribution that is more peaked than normal is called **leptokurtic** (*lepto* from the Greek word for slender); a distribution that is less peaked than normal is called **platykurtic** (*platy* from the Greek word for broad); and a distribution identical to the normal distribution in this respect is called **mesokurtic** (*meso* from the Greek word for middle). The situation of more-frequent extremely large surprises that we described is one of leptokurtosis.[44]

Figure 3-8 illustrates a leptokurtic distribution. It is more peaked and has fatter tails than the normal distribution.

The calculation for kurtosis involves finding the average of deviations from the mean raised to the fourth power and then standardizing that average by dividing by the standard deviation raised to the fourth power.[45] For all normal distributions, kurtosis is equal to 3. Many statistical packages report estimates of **excess kurtosis**, which is kurtosis minus 3.[46] Excess kurtosis thus characterizes kurtosis relative to the normal distribution. A normal or other mesokurtic distribution has excess kurtosis equal to 0. A leptokurtic distribution has

---

[44]Kurtosis has been described as an illness characterized by episodes of extremely rude behavior.

[45]This measure is free of scale. It is always positive because the deviations are raised to the fourth power.

[46]Ibbotson and some software packages, such as Microsoft Excel, label "excess kurtosis" as simply "kurtosis." This highlights the fact that one should familiarize oneself with the description of statistical quantities in any software packages that one uses.

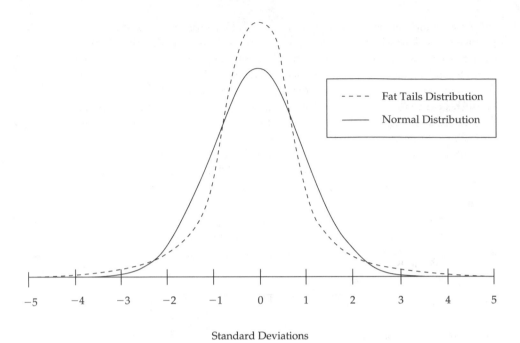

Standard Deviations

FIGURE 3-8   Leptokurtic: Fat Tailed
Source: Reprinted with permission from *Fixed Income Readings for the Chartered Financial Analyst® Program.* Copyright 2000, Frank J. Fabozzi Associates, New Hope, PA.

excess kurtosis greater than 0, and a platykurtic distribution has excess kurtosis less than 0. A return distribution with positive excess kurtosis—a leptokurtic return distribution—has more frequent extremely large deviations from the mean than a normal distribution. Below is the expression for computing kurtosis from a sample.

- **Sample Excess Kurtosis Formula.**   The **sample excess kurtosis** is

$$K_E = \left(\frac{n(n+1)}{(n-1)(n-2)(n-3)} \frac{\sum_{i=1}^{n}(X_i - \overline{X})^4}{s^4} \right) - \frac{3(n-1)^2}{(n-2)(n-3)} \tag{3-18}$$

where n is the sample size and s is the sample standard deviation.

In Equation 3-18, **sample kurtosis** is the first term. Note that as n becomes large, Equation 3-18 approximately equals $\dfrac{n^2}{n^3} \dfrac{\sum(X - \overline{X})^4}{s^4} - \dfrac{3n^2}{n^2} = \dfrac{1}{n} \dfrac{\sum(X - \overline{X})^4}{s^4} - 3$. For a sample of 100 or larger taken from a normal distribution, a sample excess kurtosis of 1.0 or larger would be considered unusually large.

Most equity return series have been found to be leptokurtic. If a return distribution has positive excess kurtosis (leptokurtosis) and we use statistical models that do not account for the fatter tails, we will underestimate the likelihood of very bad or very good outcomes. For example, the return on the S&P 500 for 19 October 1987 was 20 standard deviations away from the mean daily return. Such an outcome is possible with a normal distribution, but its likelihood is almost equal to 0. If daily returns are drawn from a normal distribution, a return four standard deviations or more away from the mean is expected once every 50 years; a return greater than five standard deviations away is expected once every 7,000 years. The return for October 1987 is more likely to have come from a distribution that had fatter tails than from a normal distribution. Looking at Table 3-27 given earlier, the monthly return series for the S&P 500 has very large excess kurtosis, approximately 9.5. It is extremely fat-tailed relative to the normal distribution. By contrast, the annual return series has very slightly negative excess kurtosis (roughly -0.2). The results for excess kurtosis in the table are consistent with research findings that the normal distribution is a better approximation for U.S. equity returns for annual holding periods than for shorter ones (such as monthly).[47]

The following example illustrates the calculations for sample excess kurtosis for one of the two mutual funds we have been examining.

EXAMPLE 3-17   Calculating Sample Excess Kurtosis

Having concluded in Example 3-16 that the annual returns on T. Rowe Price Equity Income Fund were approximately symmetrically distributed during the 1993–2002 period, what can we say about the kurtosis of the fund's return distribution? Table 3-28 (repeated below) recaps the annual returns for the fund.

TABLE 3-28   (repeated)
Annual Rates of Return:
T. Rowe Price Equity Income,
1993–2002

Year	Return
1993	14.8%
1994	4.5%
1995	33.3%
1996	20.3%
1997	28.8%
1998	9.2%
1999	3.8%
2000	13.1%
2001	1.6%
2002	−13.0%

Source: AAII.

---

[47] See Campbell, Lo, and MacKinlay (1997) for more details.

Using the information from Table 3-28 repeated above, address the following:

1. Calculate the sample excess kurtosis of PRFDX showing two decimal places.
2. Characterize the shape of the distribution of PRFDX returns based on your answer to Part 1 as leptokurtic, mesokurtic, or platykurtic.

Solution to 1: To calculate excess kurtosis, we find the sum of the deviations from the mean raised to the fourth power, divide by the standard deviation raised to the fourth power, and then multiply that result by $n(n + 1)/[(n - 1)(n - 2)(n - 3)]$. This calculation determines kurtosis. Excess kurtosis is kurtosis minus $3(n - 1)^2/[(n - 2)(n - 3)]$. Table 3-30 gives the calculations.

TABLE 3-30   Calculating Kurtosis for PRFDX

Year	R_t	$R_t - \overline{R}$	$(R_t - \overline{R})^4$
1993	14.8%	3.16	99.712
1994	4.5%	−7.14	2,598.920
1995	33.3%	21.66	220,106.977
1996	20.3%	8.66	5,624.340
1997	28.8%	17.16	86,709.990
1998	9.2%	−2.44	35.445
1999	3.8%	−7.84	3,778.020
2000	13.1%	1.46	4.544
2001	1.6%	−10.04	10,160.963
2002	−13.0%	−24.64	368,606.351
$n =$	10		
$\overline{R} =$	11.64%		
		Sum $=$	697,725.261
$s =$	13.65%	$s^4 =$	34,716.074
		Sum$/s^4 =$	20.098
		$n(n + 1)/[(n - 1)(n - 2)(n - 3)] =$	0.2183
		Kurtosis $=$	**4.39**
		$3(n - 1)^2/[(n - 2)(n - 3)] =$	4.34
		Excess Kurtosis $=$	**0.05**

Source: AAII.

Using Equation 3-18, the calculation is:

$$K_E = \left[\frac{110}{(9)(8)(7)} \frac{697,725.261}{13.65^4} \right] - \frac{3(9)^2}{(8)(7)}$$

$$= 4.39 - 4.34$$

$$= 0.05$$

Solution to 2: The distribution of PRFDX's annual returns appears to be mesokurtic, based on a sample excess kurtosis close to zero. With skewness and excess kurtosis both close to zero, PRFDX's annual returns appear to have been approximately normally distributed during the period.[48]

10. USING GEOMETRIC AND ARITHMETIC MEANS

With the concepts of descriptive statistics in hand, we will see why the geometric mean is appropriate for making investment statements about past performance. We will also explore why the arithmetic mean is appropriate for making investment statements in a forward-looking context.

For reporting historical returns, the geometric mean has considerable appeal because it is the rate of growth or return we would have had to earn each year to match the actual, cumulative investment performance. In our simplified Example 3-8, for instance, we purchased a stock for €100 and two years later it was worth €100, with an intervening year at €200. The geometric mean of 0 percent is clearly the compound rate of growth during the two years. Specifically, the ending amount is the beginning amount times $(1 + R_G)^2$. The geometric mean is an excellent measure of past performance.

Example 3-8 illustrated how the arithmetic mean can distort our assessment of historical performance. In that example, the total performance for the two-year period was unambiguously 0 percent. With a 100 percent return for the first year and −50 percent for the second, however, the arithmetic mean was 25 percent. As we noted previously, the arithmetic mean is always greater than or equal to the geometric mean. If we want to estimate the average return over a one-period horizon, we should use the arithmetic mean because the arithmetic mean is the average of one-period returns. If we want to estimate the average returns over more than one period, however, we should use the geometric mean of returns because the geometric mean captures how the total returns are linked over time.

As a corollary to using the geometric mean for performance reporting, the use of **semilogarithmic** rather than arithmetic scales is more appropriate when graphing past performance.[49] In the context of reporting performance, a semilogarithmic graph has an arithmetic scale on the horizontal axis for time and a logarithmic scale on the vertical axis for the value of the investment. The vertical axis values are spaced according to the differences between their logarithms. Suppose we want to represent £1, £10, £100, and £1,000 as values of an investment on the vertical axis. Note that each successive value represents a 10-fold increase over the previous value, and each will be equally spaced on the vertical axis because the difference in their logarithms is roughly 2.30; that is, $\ln 10 - \ln 1 = \ln 100 - \ln 10 = \ln 1,000 - \ln 100 = 2.30$. On a semilogarithmic scale, equal

---

[48] It is useful to know that we can conduct a Jarque-Bera (JB) statistical test of normality based on sample size n, sample skewness, and sample excess kurtosis. We can conclude that a distribution is not normal with no more than a 5 percent chance of being wrong if the quantity JB = $n[(S_K^2/6) + (K_E^2/24)]$ is 6 or greater for a sample with at least 30 observations. In this mutual fund example, we have only 10 observations and the test described is only correct based on large samples (as a guideline, for $n \geq 30$). Gujarati (2003) provides more details on this test.

[49] See Campbell (1974) for more information.

movements on the vertical axis reflect equal percentage changes, and growth at a constant compound rate plots as a straight line. A plot curving upward reflects increasing growth rates over time. The slopes of a plot at different points may be compared in order to judge relative growth rates.

In addition to reporting historical performance, financial analysts need to calculate expected equity risk premiums in a forward-looking context. For this purpose, the arithmetic mean is appropriate.

We can illustrate the use of the arithmetic mean in a forward-looking context with an example based on an investment's future cash flows. In contrasting the geometric and arithmetic means for discounting future cash flows, the essential issue concerns uncertainty. Suppose an investor with $100,000 faces an equal chance of a 100 percent return or a −50 percent return, represented on the tree diagram as a 50/50 chance of a 100 percent return or a −50 percent return per period. With 100 percent return in one period and −50 percent return in the other, the geometric mean return is $\sqrt{2(0.5)} - 1 = 0$.

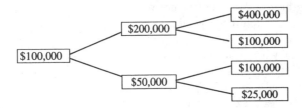

The geometric mean return of 0 percent gives the mode or median of ending wealth after two periods and thus accurately predicts the modal or median ending wealth of $100,000 in this example. Nevertheless, the arithmetic mean return better predicts the arithmetic mean ending wealth. With equal chances of 100 percent or −50 percent returns, consider the four equally likely outcomes of $400,000, $100,000, $100,000, and $25,000 as if they actually occurred. The arithmetic mean ending wealth would be $156,250 = ($400,000 + $100,000 + $100,000 + $25,000)/4. The actual returns would be 300 percent, 0 percent, 0 percent, and −75 percent for a two-period arithmetic mean return of (300 + 0 + 0 − 75)/4 = 56.25 percent. This arithmetic mean return predicts the arithmetic mean ending wealth of $100,000 × 1.5625 = $156,250. Noting that 56.25 percent for two periods is 25 percent per period, we then must discount the expected terminal wealth of $156,250 at the 25 percent arithmetic mean rate to reflect the uncertainty in the cash flows.

Uncertainty in cash flows or returns causes the arithmetic mean to be larger than the geometric mean. The more uncertain the returns, the more divergence exists between the arithmetic and geometric means. The geometric mean return approximately equals the arithmetic return minus half the variance of return.[50] Zero variance or zero uncertainty in returns would leave the geometric and arithmetic returns approximately equal, but real-world uncertainty presents an arithmetic mean return larger than the geometric. For example, Dimson et al. (2002) reported that from 1900 to 2000, U.S. equities had nominal annual returns with an arithmetic mean of 12 percent and standard deviation of 19.9 percent. They reported the geometric mean as 10.1 percent. We can see the geometric mean is approximately the arithmetic mean minus half of the variance of returns: $R_G \approx 0.12 - (1/2)(0.199^2) = 0.10$.

---

[50] See Bodie, Kane, and Marcus (2001).

CHAPTER 4

PROBABILITY CONCEPTS

1. INTRODUCTION

All investment decisions are made in an environment of risk. The tools that allow us to make decisions with consistency and logic in this setting come under the heading of probability. This chapter presents the essential probability tools needed to frame and address many real-world problems involving risk. We illustrate how these tools apply to such issues as predicting investment manager performance, forecasting financial variables, and pricing bonds so that they fairly compensate bondholders for default risk. Our focus is practical. We explore in detail the concepts that are most important to investment research and practice. One such concept is independence, as it relates to the predictability of returns and financial variables. Another is expectation, as analysts continually look to the future in their analyses and decisions. Analysts and investors must also cope with variability. We present variance, or dispersion around expectation, as a risk concept important in investments. The reader will acquire specific skills in using portfolio expected return and variance.

The basic tools of probability, including expected value and variance, are set out in Section 2 of this chapter. Section 3 introduces covariance and correlation (measures of relatedness between random quantities) and the principles for calculating portfolio expected return and variance. Two topics end the chapter: Bayes' formula and outcome counting. Bayes' formula is a procedure for updating beliefs based on new information. In several areas, including a widely used option-pricing model, the calculation of probabilities involves defining and counting outcomes. The chapter ends with a discussion of principles and shortcuts for counting.

2. PROBABILITY, EXPECTED VALUE, AND VARIANCE

The probability concepts and tools necessary for most of an analyst's work are relatively few and simple but require thought to apply. This section presents the essentials for working with probability, expectation, and variance, drawing on examples from equity and fixed income analysis.

An investor's concerns center on returns. The return on a risky asset is an example of a **random variable**, a quantity whose **outcomes** (possible values) are uncertain. For example, a portfolio may have a return objective of 10 percent a year. The portfolio manager's focus at the moment may be on the likelihood of earning a return that is less than 10 percent over the next year. Ten percent is a particular value or outcome of the random variable "portfolio return." Although we may be concerned about a single outcome, frequently our interest may be in a set of outcomes: The concept of "event" covers both.

- **Definition of Event.**   An **event** is a specified set of outcomes.

We may specify an event to be a single outcome—for example, *the portfolio earns a return of 10 percent.* (We use italics to highlight statements that define events.) We can capture the portfolio manager's concerns by defining the event as *the portfolio earns a return below 10 percent.* This second event, referring as it does to all possible returns greater than or equal to −100 percent (the worst possible return) but less than 10 percent, contains an infinite number of outcomes. To save words, it is common to use a capital letter in italics to represent a defined event. We could define $A =$ *the portfolio earns a return of 10 percent* and $B =$ *the portfolio earns a return below 10 percent.*

To return to the portfolio manager's concern, how likely is it that the portfolio will earn a return below 10 percent?

The answer to this question is a **probability**: a number between 0 and 1 that measures the chance that a stated event will occur. If the probability is 0.40 that the portfolio earns a return below 10 percent, there is a 40 percent chance of that event happening. If an event is impossible, it has a probability of 0. If an event is certain to happen, it has a probability of 1. If an event is impossible or a sure thing, it is not random at all. So, 0 and 1 bracket all the possible values of a probability.

Probability has two properties, which together constitute its definition.

- **Definition of Probability.**   The two defining properties of a probability are as follows:

  1. The probability of any event E is a number between 0 and 1: $0 \leq P(E) \leq 1$.
  2. The sum of the probabilities of any set of mutually exclusive and exhaustive events equals 1.

P followed by parentheses stands for "the probability of (the event in parentheses)," as in $P(E)$ for "the probability of event E." We can also think of P as a rule or function that assigns numerical values to events consistent with Properties 1 and 2.

In the above definition, the term **mutually exclusive** means that only one event can occur at a time; **exhaustive** means that the events cover all possible outcomes. The events $A =$ *the portfolio earns a return of 10 percent* and $B =$ *the portfolio earns a return below 10 percent* are mutually exclusive because A and B cannot both occur at the same time. For example, a return of 8.1 percent means that B has occurred and A has not occurred. Although events A and B are mutually exclusive, they are not exhaustive because they do not cover outcomes such as a return of 11 percent. Suppose we define a third event: $C =$ *the portfolio earns a return above 10 percent.* Clearly, A, B, and C are mutually exclusive and exhaustive events. Each of $P(A)$, $P(B)$, and $P(C)$ is a number between 0 and 1, and $P(A) + P(B) + P(C) = 1$.

The most basic kind of mutually exclusive and exhaustive events is the set of all the distinct possible outcomes of the random variable. If we know both that set and the assignment of probabilities to those outcomes—the probability distribution of the random variable—we have a complete description of the random variable, and we can assign a probability to any event that we might describe.[1] The probability of any event is the sum of the probabilities of the distinct outcomes included in the definition of the event. Suppose the event of interest is $D =$ *the portfolio earns a return above the risk-free rate,* and we know the probability distribution of portfolio returns. Assume the risk-free rate is 4 percent. To calculate $P(D)$, the probability

---

[1] In the chapter on common probability distributions, we describe some of the probability distributions most frequently used in investment applications.

of D, we would sum the probabilities of the outcomes that satisfy the definition of the event; that is, we would sum the probabilities of portfolio returns greater than 4 percent.

Earlier, to illustrate a concept, we assumed a probability of 0.40 for a portfolio earning less than 10 percent, without justifying the particular assumption. We also talked about using a probability distribution of outcomes to calculate the probability of events, without explaining how a probability distribution might be estimated. Making actual financial decisions using inaccurate probabilities might have grave consequences. How, in practice, do we estimate probabilities? This topic is a field of study in itself, but there are three broad approaches to estimating probabilities. In investments, we often estimate the probability of an event as a relative frequency of occurrence based on historical data. This method produces an **empirical probability**. For example, Amihud and Li (2002) report that of their sample of 16,189 dividend changes for NYSE and Amex stocks during the years 1962 to 2000, 14,911 were increases and 1,278 were decreases. The empirical probability that a dividend change is a dividend decrease for U.S. stocks is thus $1,278/16,189 = 0.08$, approximately. We will point out empirical probabilities in several places as they appear in this chapter.

Relationships must be stable through time for empirical probabilities to be accurate. We cannot calculate an empirical probability of an event not in the historical record or a reliable empirical probability for a very rare event. There are cases, then, in which we may adjust an empirical probability to account for perceptions of changing relationships. In other cases, we have no empirical probability to use at all. We may also make a personal assessment of probability without reference to any particular data. Each of these three types of probability is a **subjective probability**, one drawing on personal or subjective judgment. Subjective probabilities are of great importance in investments. Investors, in making buy and sell decisions that determine asset prices, often draw on subjective probabilities. Subjective probabilities appear in various places in this chapter, notably in our discussion of Bayes' formula.

In a more narrow range of well-defined problems, we can sometimes deduce probabilities by reasoning about the problem. The resulting probability is an **a priori probability**, one based on logical analysis rather than on observation or personal judgment. We will use this type of probability in Example 4-6. The counting methods we discuss later are particularly important in calculating an a priori probability. Because a priori and empirical probabilities generally do not vary from person to person, they are often grouped as **objective probabilities**.

In business and elsewhere, we often encounter probabilities stated in terms of odds—for instance, "the odds for E" or the "odds against E." For example, as of mid-2003, analysts' fiscal year 2004 EPS forecasts for one Toronto Stock Exchange—listed company ranged from C\$3.98 to C\$4.25. Nevertheless, one analyst asserts that the odds for the company beating the highest estimate, C\$4.25, are 1 to 7. A second analyst argues that the odds against that happening are 15 to 1. What do those statements imply about the probability of the company's EPS beating the highest estimate? We interpret probabilities stated in terms of odds as follows:

- **Probability Stated as Odds.**   Given a probability $P(E)$,

  1. Odds for $E = P(E)/[1 - P(E)]$. The odds for E are the probability of E divided by 1 minus the probability of E. Given odds for E of "a to b," the implied probability of E is $a/(a + b)$.

In the example, the statement that the odds for *the company's EPS for FY2004 beating C\$4.25* are 1 to 7 means that the speaker believes the probability of the event is $1/(1 + 7) = 1/8 = 0.125$.

  2. Odds against $E = [1 - P(E)]/P(E)$, the reciprocal of odds for E. Given odds against E of "a to b," the implied probability of E is $b/(a + b)$.

The statement that the odds against *the company's EPS for FY2004 beating C\$4.25* are 15 to 1 is consistent with a belief that the probability of the event is $1/(1 + 15) = 1/16 = 0.0625$.

To further explain odds for an event, if $P(E) = 1/8$, the odds for E are $(1/8)/(7/8) = (1/8)(8/7) = 1/7$, or "1 to 7." For each occurrence of E, we expect seven cases of nonoccurrence; out of eight cases in total, therefore, we expect E to happen once, and the probability of E is 1/8. In wagering, it is common to speak in terms of the odds against something, as in Statement 2. For odds of "15 to 1" against E (an implied probability of E of 1/16), a \$1 wager on E, if successful, returns \$15 in profits plus the \$1 staked in the wager. We can calculate the bet's anticipated profit as follows:

Win: Probability $= 1/16$; Profit $= \$15$

Loss: Probability $= 15/16$; Profit $= -\$1$

Anticipated profit $= (1/16)(\$15) + (15/16)(-\$1) = \$0$

Weighting each of the wager's two outcomes by the respective probability of the outcome, if the odds (probabilities) are accurate, the anticipated profit of the bet is \$0.

EXAMPLE 4-1 Profiting from Inconsistent Probabilities

You are examining the common stock of two companies in the same industry in which an important antitrust decision will be announced next week. The first company, SmithCo Corporation, will benefit from a governmental decision that there is no antitrust obstacle related to a merger in which it is involved. You believe that SmithCo's share price reflects a 0.85 probability of such a decision. A second company, Selbert Corporation, will equally benefit from a "go ahead" ruling. Surprisingly, you believe Selbert stock reflects only a 0.50 probability of a favorable decision. Assuming your analysis is correct, what investment strategy would profit from this pricing discrepancy?

Consider the logical possibilities. One is that the probability of 0.50 reflected in Selbert's share price is accurate. In that case, Selbert is fairly valued but SmithCo is overvalued, as its current share price overestimates the probability of a "go ahead" decision. The second possibility is that the probability of 0.85 is accurate. In that case, SmithCo shares are fairly valued, but Selbert shares, which build in a lower probability of a favorable decision, are undervalued. You diagram the situation as shown in Table 4-1.

TABLE 4-1   Worksheet for Investment Problem

	True Probability of a "Go Ahead" Decision	
	0.50	0.85
SmithCo	Shares Overvalued	Shares Fairly Valued
Selbert	Shares Fairly Valued	Shares Undervalued

The 0.50 probability column shows that Selbert shares are a better value than SmithCo shares. Selbert shares are also a better value if a 0.85 probability is accurate. Thus SmithCo shares are overvalued relative to Selbert shares.

Your investment actions depend on your confidence in your analysis and on any investment constraints you face (such as constraints on selling stock short).[2] A conservative strategy would be to buy Selbert shares and reduce or eliminate any current position in SmithCo. The most aggressive strategy is to short SmithCo stock (relatively overvalued) and simultaneously buy the stock of Selbert (relatively undervalued). This strategy is known as a **pairs arbitrage trade**: a trade in two closely related stocks involving the short sale of one and the purchase of the other.

The prices of SmithCo and Selbert shares reflect probabilities that are not **consistent**. According to one of the most important probability results for investments, the **Dutch Book Theorem**,[3] inconsistent probabilities create profit opportunities. In our example, investors, by their buy and sell decisions to exploit the inconsistent probabilities, should eliminate the profit opportunity and inconsistency.

To understand the meaning of a probability in investment contexts, we need to distinguish between two types of probability: unconditional and conditional. Both unconditional and conditional probabilities satisfy the definition of probability stated earlier, but they are calculated or estimated differently and have different interpretations. They provide answers to different questions.

The probability in answer to the straightforward question "What is the probability of this event *A*?" is an **unconditional probability**, denoted *P(A)*. Unconditional probabilities are also frequently referred to as **marginal probabilities**.[4]

Suppose the question is "What is the probability that *the stock earns a return above the risk-free rate* (event *A*)?" The answer is an unconditional probability that can be viewed as the ratio of two quantities. The numerator is the sum of the probabilities of stock returns above the risk-free rate. Suppose that sum is 0.70. The denominator is 1, the sum of the probabilities of all possible returns. The answer to the question is *P(A)* = 0.70.

Contrast the question "What is the probability of *A*?" with the question "What is the probability of *A*, given that *B* has occurred?" The probability in answer to this last question is a **conditional probability**, denoted *P(A | B)* (read: "the probability of *A* given *B*").

Suppose we want to know the probability that *the stock earns a return above the risk-free rate* (event *A*), given that *the stock earns a positive return* (event *B*). With the words "given that," we are restricting returns to those larger than 0 percent—a new element in contrast to the question that brought forth an unconditional probability. The conditional probability is calculated as the ratio of two quantities. The numerator is the sum of the probabilities of stock

---

[2] *Selling short* or *shorting stock* means selling borrowed shares in the hope of repurchasing them later at a lower price.

[3] The theorem's name comes from the terminology of wagering. Suppose someone places a $100 bet on *X* at odds of 10 to 1 against *X*, and later he is able to place a $600 bet against *X* at odds of 1 to 1 against *X*. Whatever the outcome of *X*, that person makes a riskless profit (equal to $400 if *X* occurs or $500 if *X* does not occur) because the implied probabilities are inconsistent. He is said to have made a *Dutch book* in *X*. Ramsey (1931) presented the problem of inconsistent probabilities. See also Lo (1999).

[4] In analyses of probabilities presented in tables, unconditional probabilities usually appear at the ends or *margins* of the table, hence the term *marginal probability*. Because of possible confusion with the way *marginal* is used in economics (roughly meaning *incremental*), we use the term *unconditional probability* throughout this discussion.

returns above the risk-free rate; in this particular case, the numerator is the same as it was in the unconditional case, which we gave as 0.70. The denominator, however, changes from 1 to the sum of the probabilities for all outcomes (returns) above 0 percent. Suppose that number is 0.80, a larger number than 0.70 because returns between 0 and the risk-free rate have some positive probability of occurring. Then $P(A \mid B) = 0.70/0.80 = 0.875$. If we observe that the stock earns a positive return, the probability of a return above the risk-free rate is greater than the unconditional probability, which is the probability of the event given no other information. The result is intuitive.[5] To review, an unconditional probability is the probability of an event without any restriction; it might even be thought of as a stand-alone probability. A conditional probability, in contrast, is a probability of an event given that another event has occurred.

In discussing approaches to calculating probability, we gave one empirical estimate of the probability that a change in dividends is a dividend decrease. That probability was an unconditional probability. Given additional information on company characteristics, could an investor refine that estimate? Investors continually seek an information edge that will help improve their forecasts. In mathematical terms, they are attempting to frame their view of the future using probabilities conditioned on relevant information or events. Investors do not ignore useful information; they adjust their probabilities to reflect it. Thus, the concepts of conditional probability (which we analyze in more detail below), as well as related concepts discussed further on, are extremely important in investment analysis and financial markets.

To state an exact definition of conditional probability, we first need to introduce the concept of joint probability. Suppose we ask the question "What is the probability of both A and B happening?" The answer to this question is a **joint probability**, denoted $P(AB)$ (read: "the probability of A and B"). If we think of the probability of A and the probability of B as sets built of the outcomes of one or more random variables, the joint probability of A and B is the sum of the probabilities of the outcomes they have in common. For example, consider two events: *the stock earns a return above the risk-free rate* (A) and *the stock earns a positive return* (B). The outcomes of A are contained within (a subset of) the outcomes of B, so $P(AB)$ equals $P(A)$. We can now state a formal definition of conditional probability that provides a formula for calculating it.

- **Definition of Conditional Probability**. The conditional probability of A given that B has occurred is equal to the joint probability of A and B divided by the probability of B (assumed not to equal 0).

$$P(A \mid B) = P(AB)/P(B), P(B) \neq 0 \qquad (4\text{-}1)$$

Sometimes we know the conditional probability $P(A \mid B)$ and we want to know the joint probability $P(AB)$. We can obtain the joint probability from the following **multiplication rule for probabilities**, which is Equation 4-1 rearranged.

- **Multiplication Rule for Probability**. The joint probability of A and B can be expressed as

$$P(AB) = P(A \mid B)P(B) \qquad (4\text{-}2)$$

---

[5] In this example, the conditional probability is greater than the unconditional probability. The conditional probability of an event may, however, be greater than, equal to, or less than the unconditional probability, depending on the facts. For instance, the probability that *the stock earns a return above the risk-free rate* given that *the stock earns a negative return* is 0.

Equation 4-2 states that the joint probability of A and B equals the probability of A given B times the probability of B. Because $P(AB) = P(BA)$, the expression $P(AB) = P(BA) = P(B \mid A)P(A)$ is equivalent to Equation 4-2.

EXAMPLE 4-2   Conditional Probabilities and Predictability of Mutual Fund Performance (1)

Kahn and Rudd (1995) examined whether historical performance predicts future performance for a sample of mutual funds that included 300 actively managed U.S. domestic equity funds. One approach they used involved calculating each fund's exposure to a set of style indexes (the term "style" captures the distinctions of growth/value and large-capitalization/mid-capitalization/small-capitalization). After establishing a style benchmark (a comparison portfolio matched to the fund's style) for each fund, Kahn and Rudd computed the fund's selection return for two periods. They defined selection return as fund return minus the fund's style-benchmark return. The first period was October 1990 to March 1992. The top 50 percent of funds by selection return for that period were labeled winners; the bottom 50 percent were labeled losers. Based on selection return in the next period, April 1992 to September 1993, the top 50 percent of funds were tagged as winners and the bottom 50 percent as losers for that period. An excerpt from their results is given in Table 4-2. The winner–winner entry, for example, shows that 79 of the 150 first-period winner funds were also winners in the second period (52.7% = 79/150). Note that the four entries in parentheses in the table can be viewed as conditional probabilities.

TABLE 4-2   Equity Selection Returns
Period 1: October 1990 to March 1992
Period 2: April 1992 to September 1993
Entries are number of funds (percent of row total in parentheses)

	Period 2 Winner	Period 2 Loser
Period 1 Winner	79 (52.7%)	71 (47.3%)
Period 1 Loser	71 (47.3%)	79 (52.7%)

Source: Kahn and Rudd (1995), Table 3.

Based on the data in Table 4-2, answer the following questions:

1. State the four events needed to define the four conditional probabilities.
2. State the four entries of the table as conditional probabilities using the form $P(this\ event \mid that\ event) =$ number.
3. Are the conditional probabilities in Part 2 empirical, a priori, or subjective probabilities?

4. Using information in the table, calculate the probability of the event a *fund is a loser in both Period 1 and Period 2*. (Note that because 50 percent of funds are categorized as losers in each period, the unconditional probability that a fund is labeled a loser in either period is 0.5.)

Solution to 1: The four events needed to define the conditional probabilities are as follows:

> *Fund is a Period 1 winner*
> *Fund is a Period 1 loser*
> *Fund is a Period 2 loser*
> *Fund is a Period 2 winner*

Solution to 2:
From Row 1:

> $P(fund\ is\ a\ Period\ 2\ winner\ |\ fund\ is\ a\ Period\ 1\ winner) = 0.527$
> $P(fund\ is\ a\ Period\ 2\ loser\ |\ fund\ is\ a\ Period\ 1\ winner) = 0.473$

From Row 2:

> $P(fund\ is\ a\ Period\ 2\ winner\ |\ fund\ is\ a\ Period\ 1\ loser) = 0.473$
> $P(fund\ is\ a\ Period\ 2\ loser\ |\ fund\ is\ a\ Period\ 1\ loser) = 0.527$

Solution to 3: These probabilities are calculated from data, so they are empirical probabilities.

Solution to 4: The estimated probability is 0.264. With A the event that a *fund is a Period 2 loser* and B the event that a *fund is a Period 1 loser*, AB is the event that a *fund is a loser in both Period 1 and Period 2*. From Table 4-2, $P(A\ |\ B) = 0.527$ and $P(B) = 0.50$. Thus, using Equation 4-2, we find that

$$P(AB) = P(A\ |\ B)P(B) = 0.527(0.50) = 0.2635$$

or a probability of approximately 0.264.

When we have two events, A and B, that we are interested in, we often want to know the probability that either A or B occurs. Here the word "or" is inclusive, meaning that either A or B occurs or that both A and B occur. Put another way, the probability of A or B is the probability that at least one of the two events occurs. Such probabilities are calculated using the **addition rule for probabilities**.

- **Addition Rule for Probabilities**. Given events A and B, the probability that A or B occurs, or both occur, is equal to the probability that A occurs, plus the probability that B occurs, minus the probability that both A and B occur.

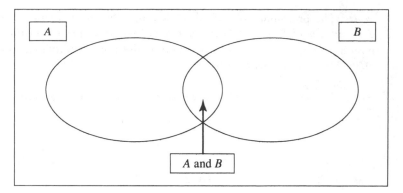

FIGURE 4-1   Addition Rule for Probabilities

$$P(A \text{ or } B) = P(A) + P(B) - P(AB) \tag{4-3}$$

If we think of the individual probabilities of A and B as sets built of outcomes of one or more random variables, the first step in calculating the probability of A or B is to sum the probabilities of the outcomes in A to obtain $P(A)$. If A and B share any outcomes, then if we now added $P(B)$ to $P(A)$, we would count twice the probabilities of those shared outcomes. So we add to $P(A)$ the quantity $[P(B) - P(AB)]$, which is the probability of outcomes in B net of the probability of any outcomes already counted when we computed $P(A)$. Figure 4-1 illustrates this process; we avoid double-counting the outcomes in the intersection of A and B by subtracting $P(AB)$. As an example of the calculation, if $P(A) = 0.50, P(B) = 0.40$, and $P(AB) = 0.20$, then $P(A \text{ or } B) = 0.50 + 0.40 - 0.20 = 0.70$. Only if the two events A and B were mutually exclusive, so that $P(AB) = 0$, would it be correct to state that $P(A \text{ or } B) = P(A) + P(B)$.

The next example shows how much useful information can be obtained using the few probability rules presented to this point.

EXAMPLE 4-3   Probability of a Limit Order Executing

You have two buy limit orders outstanding on the same stock. A limit order to buy stock at a stated price is an order to buy at that price or lower. A number of vendors, including an Internet service that you use, supply the estimated probability that a limit order will be filled within a stated time horizon, given the current stock price and the price limit. One buy order (Order 1) was placed at a price limit of $10. The probability that it will execute within one hour is 0.35. The second buy order (Order 2) was placed at a price limit of $9.75; it has a 0.25 probability of executing within the same one-hour time frame.

1. What is the probability that either Order 1 or Order 2 will execute?
2. What is the probability that Order 2 executes, given that Order 1 executes?

Solution to 1: The probability is 0.35. The two probabilities that are given are $P(Order\ 1\ executes) = 0.35$ and $P(Order\ 2\ executes) = 0.25$. Note that if Order 2 executes, it is certain that Order 1 also executes because the price must pass through $10 to reach $9.75. Thus,

$$P(Order\ 1\ executes\ |\ Order\ 2\ executes) = 1$$

and

$$P(Order\ 1\ executes\ and\ Order\ 2\ executes) = P(Order\ 1\ executes\ |\ Order\ 2\ executes)P(Order\ 2\ executes) = 1(0.25) = 0.25$$

To answer the question, we use the addition rule for probabilities:

$$P(Order\ 1\ executes\ or\ Order\ 2\ executes) = P(Order\ 1\ executes) + P(Order\ 2\ executes) - P(Order\ 1\ executes\ and\ Order\ 2\ executes) = 0.35 + 0.25 - 0.25 = 0.35$$

Note that the outcomes for which Order 2 executes are a subset of the outcomes for which Order 1 executes. After you count the probability that Order 1 executes, you have counted the probability of the outcomes for which Order 2 also executes. Therefore, the answer to the question is the probability that Order 1 executes, 0.35.

Solution to 2: If the first order executes, the probability that the second order executes is 0.714. In the solution to Part 1, you found that $P(Order\ 1\ executes\ and\ Order\ 2\ executes) = P(Order\ 1\ executes\ |\ Order\ 2\ executes)P(Order\ 2\ executes) = 1(0.25) = 0.25$. An equivalent way to state this joint probability is useful here:

$$P(Order\ 1\ executes\ and\ Order\ 2\ executes) = 0.25 =$$
$$P(Order\ 2\ executes\ |\ Order\ 1\ executes)P(Order\ 1\ executes)$$

Because $P(Order\ 1\ executes) = 0.35$ was a given, you have one equation with one unknown:

$$0.25 = P(Order\ 2\ executes\ |\ Order\ 1\ executes)(0.35)$$

You conclude that $P(Order\ 2\ executes\ |\ Order\ 1\ executes) = 0.25/0.35 = 5/7$, or about 0.714. You can also use Equation 4-1 to obtain this answer.

Of great interest to investment analysts are the concepts of independence and dependence. These concepts bear on such basic investment questions as which financial variables are useful for investment analysis, whether asset returns can be predicted, and whether superior investment managers can be selected based on their past records.

Two events are independent if the occurrence of one event does not affect the probability of occurrence of the other event.

- **Definition of Independent Events.**   Two events A and B are **independent** if and only if $P(A \mid B) = P(A)$ or, equivalently, $P(B \mid A) = P(B)$.

When two events are not independent, they are **dependent**: The probability of occurrence of one is related to the occurrence of the other. If we are trying to forecast one event, information about a dependent event may be useful, but information about an independent event will not be useful.

When two events are independent, the multiplication rule for probabilities, Equation 4-2, simplifies because $P(A \mid B)$ in that equation then equals $P(A)$.

- **Multiplication Rule for Independent Events.**   When two events are independent, the joint probability of A and B equals the product of the individual probabilities of A and B.

$$P(AB) = P(A)P(B) \tag{4-4}$$

Therefore, if we are interested in two independent events with probabilities of 0.75 and 0.50, respectively, the probability that both will occur is $0.375 = 0.75(0.50)$. The multiplication rule for independent events generalizes to more than two events; for example, if A, B, and C are independent events, then $P(ABC) = P(A)P(B)P(C)$.

EXAMPLE 4-4   BankCorp's Earnings per Share (1)

As part of your work as a banking industry analyst, you build models for forecasting earnings per share of the banks you cover. Today you are studying BankCorp. The historical record shows that in 55 percent of recent quarters BankCorp's EPS has increased sequentially, and in 45 percent of quarters EPS has decreased or remained unchanged sequentially.[6] At this point in your analysis, you are assuming that changes in sequential EPS are independent.

Earnings per share for 2Q:2004 (that is, EPS for the second quarter of 2004) were larger than EPS for 1Q:2004.

1. What is the probability that 3Q:2004 EPS will be larger than 2Q:2004 EPS (a positive change in sequential EPS)?
2. What is the probability that EPS decreases or remains unchanged in the next two quarters?

Solution to 1:   Under the assumption of independence, the probability that 3Q:2004 EPS will be larger than 2Q:2004 EPS is the unconditional probability of positive change, 0.55. The fact that 2Q:2004 EPS was larger than 1Q:2004 EPS is not useful information, as the next change in EPS is independent of the prior change.

Solution to 2:   The probability is $0.2025 = 0.45(0.45)$.

---

[6] *Sequential* comparisons of quarterly EPS are with the immediate prior quarter. A sequential comparison stands in contrast to a comparison with the same quarter one year ago (another frequent type of comparison).

The following example illustrates how difficult it is to satisfy a set of independent criteria even when each criterion by itself is not necessarily stringent.

EXAMPLE 4-5 Screening Stocks for Investment

You have developed a stock screen—a set of criteria for selecting stocks. Your investment universe (the set of securities from which you make your choices) is the Russell 1000 Index, an index of 1,000 large-capitalization U.S. equities. Your criteria capture different aspects of the selection problem; you believe that the criteria are independent of each other, to a close approximation.

Criterion	Fraction of Russell 1000 Stocks Meeting Criterion
First valuation criterion	0.50
Second valuation criterion	0.50
Analyst coverage criterion	0.25
Profitability criterion for company	0.55
Financial strength criterion for company	0.67

How many stocks do you expect to pass your screen?

Only 23 stocks out of 1,000 pass through your screen. If you define five events—*the stock passes the first valuation criterion, the stock passes the second valuation criterion, the stock passes the analyst coverage criterion, the company passes the profitability criterion, the company passes the financial strength criterion* (say events *A, B, C, D,* and *E,* respectively)—then the probability that a stock will pass all five criteria, under independence, is

$$P(ABCDE) = P(A)P(B)P(C)P(D)P(E) = (0.50)(0.50)(0.25)(0.55)(0.67)$$

$$= 0.023031$$

Although only one of the five criteria is even moderately strict (the strictest lets 25 percent of stocks through), the probability that a stock can pass all five is only 0.023031, or about 2 percent. The size of the list of candidate investments is $0.023031(1,000) = 23.031$, or 23 stocks.

An area of intense interest to investment managers and their clients is whether records of past performance are useful in identifying repeat winners and losers. The following example shows how this issue relates to the concept of independence.

EXAMPLE 4-6   Conditional Probabilities and Predictability of Mutual Fund Performance (2)

The purpose of the Kahn and Rudd (1995) study, introduced in Example 4-2, was to address the question of repeat mutual fund winners and losers. If the status of a fund as a winner or a loser in one period is independent of whether it is a winner in the next period, the practical value of performance ranking is questionable. Using the four events defined in Example 4-2 as building blocks, we can define the following events to address the issue of predictability of mutual fund performance:

> *Fund is a Period 1 winner* and *fund is a Period 2 winner*
> *Fund is a Period 1 winner* and *fund is a Period 2 loser*
> *Fund is a Period 1 loser* and *fund is a Period 2 winner*
> *Fund is a Period 1 loser* and *fund is a Period 2 loser*

In Part 4 of Example 4-2, you calculated that

$$P(\textit{fund is a Period 2 loser} \text{ and } \textit{fund is a Period 1 loser}) = 0.264$$

If the ranking in one period is independent of the ranking in the next period, what will you expect *P(fund is a Period 2 loser* and *fund is a Period 1 loser)* to be? Interpret the empirical probability 0.264.

By the multiplication rule for independent events, *P(fund is a Period 2 loser* and *fund is a Period 1 loser) = P(fund is a Period 2 loser)P(fund is a Period 1 loser)*. Because 50 percent of funds are categorized as losers in each period, the unconditional probability that a fund is labeled a loser in either period is 0.50. Thus *P(fund is a Period 2 loser)P(fund is a Period 1 loser)* = 0.50(0.50) = 0.25. If the status of a fund as a loser in one period is independent of whether it is a loser in the prior period, we conclude that *P(fund is a Period 2 loser* and *fund is a Period 1 loser)* = 0.25. This probability is a priori because it is obtained from reasoning about the problem. You could also reason that the four events described above define categories and that if funds are randomly assigned to the four categories, there is a 1/4 probability of *fund is a Period 1 loser* and *fund is a Period 2 loser*. If the classifications in Period 1 and Period 2 were dependent, then the assignment of funds to categories would not be random. The empirical probability of 0.264 is only slightly above 0.25. Is this apparent slight amount of predictability the result of chance? A test conducted by Kahn and Rudd indicated a 35.6 percent chance of observing the tabled data if the Period 1 and Period 2 rankings were independent.

In investments, the question of whether one event (or characteristic) provides information about another event (or characteristic) arises in both time-series settings (through time) and cross-sectional settings (among units at a given point in time). Examples 4-4 and 4-6 illustrated independence in a time-series setting. Example 4-5 illustrated independence in a cross-sectional setting. Independence/dependence relationships are often also explored in both settings using regression analysis, a technique we discuss in a later chapter.

In many practical problems, we logically analyze a problem as follows: We formulate scenarios that we think affect the likelihood of an event that interests us. We then estimate the probability of the event, given the scenario. When the scenarios (conditioning events) are mutually exclusive and exhaustive, no possible outcomes are left out. We can then analyze the event using the **total probability rule**. This rule explains the unconditional probability of the event in terms of probabilities conditional on the scenarios.

The total probability rule is stated below for two cases. Part 1 gives the simplest case, in which we have two scenarios. One new notation is introduced: If we have an event or scenario S, the event not-S, called the **complement** of S, is written S^C.[7] Note that $P(S) + P(S^C) = 1$, as either S or not-S must occur. Part 2 states the rule for the general case of n mutually exclusive and exhaustive events or scenarios.

- **The Total Probability Rule.**

  1. $P(A) = P(AS) + P(AS^C)$

  $$= P(A \mid S)P(S) + P(A \mid S^C)P(S^C) \qquad (4\text{-}5)$$

  2. $P(A) = P(AS_1) + P(AS_2) + \cdots + P(AS_n)$

  $$= P(A \mid S_1)P(S_1) + P(A \mid S_2)P(S_2) + \cdots + P(A \mid S_n)P(S_n) \qquad (4\text{-}6)$$

where $S_1, S_2, \ldots, S_n$ are mutually exclusive and exhaustive scenarios or events.

Equation 4-6 states the following: The probability of any event $[P(A)]$ can be expressed as a weighted average of the probabilities of the event, given scenarios [terms such $P(A \mid S_1)$]; the weights applied to these conditional probabilities are the respective probabilities of the scenarios [terms such as $P(S_1)$ multiplying $P(A \mid S_1)$], and the scenarios must be mutually exclusive and exhaustive. Among other applications, this rule is needed to understand Bayes' formula, which we discuss later in the chapter.

In the next example, we use the total probability rule to develop a consistent set of views about BankCorp's earnings per share.

EXAMPLE 4-7   BankCorp's Earnings per Share (2)

You are continuing your investigation into whether you can predict the direction of changes in BankCorp's quarterly EPS. You define four events:

Event	Probability
A = change in sequential EPS is positive next quarter	0.55
A^C = change in sequential EPS is 0 or negative next quarter	0.45
S = change in sequential EPS is positive in the prior quarter	0.55
S^C = change in sequential EPS is 0 or negative in the prior quarter	0.45

---

[7] For readers familiar with mathematical treatments of probability, S, a notation usually reserved for a concept called the sample space, is being appropriated to stand for *scenario*.

On inspecting the data, you observe some persistence in EPS changes: Increases tend to be followed by increases, and decreases by decreases. The first probability estimate you develop is *P(change in sequential EPS is positive next quarter | change in sequential EPS is 0 or negative in the prior quarter)* = $P(A \mid S^C) = 0.40$. The most recent quarter's EPS (2Q:2004) is announced, and the change is a positive sequential change (the event S). You are interested in forecasting EPS for 3Q:2004.

1. Write this statement in probability notation: "the probability that the change in sequential EPS is positive next quarter, given that the change in sequential EPS is positive the prior quarter."
2. Calculate the probability in Part 1. (Calculate the probability that is consistent with your other probabilities or beliefs.)

Solution to 1: In probability notation, this statement is written $P(A \mid S)$.

Solution to 2: The probability is 0.673 that the change in sequential EPS is positive for 3Q:2004, given the positive change in sequential EPS for 2Q:2004, as shown below.

According to Equation 4-5, $P(A) = P(A \mid S)P(S) + P(A \mid S^C)P(S^C)$. The values of the probabilities needed to calculate $P(A \mid S)$ are already known: $P(A) = 0.55$, $P(S) = 0.55$, $P(S^C) = 0.45$, and $P(A \mid S^C) = 0.40$. Substituting into Equation 4-5,

$$0.55 = P(A \mid S)(0.55) + 0.40(0.45)$$

Solving for the unknown, $P(A \mid S) = [0.55 - 0.40(0.45)]/0.55 = 0.672727$, or 0.673.

You conclude that *P(change in sequential EPS is positive next quarter | change in sequential EPS is positive the prior quarter)* = 0.673. Any other probability is not consistent with your other estimated probabilities. Reflecting the persistence in EPS changes, this conditional probability of a positive EPS change, 0.673, is greater than the unconditional probability of an EPS increase, 0.55.

In the chapter on statistical concepts and market returns, we discussed the concept of a weighted average or weighted mean. The example highlighted in that chapter was that portfolio return is a weighted average of the returns on the individual assets in the portfolio, where the weight applied to each asset's return is the fraction of the portfolio invested in that asset. The total probability rule, which is a rule for stating an unconditional probability in terms of conditional probabilities, is also a weighted average. In that formula, probabilities of scenarios are used as weights. Part of the definition of weighted average is that the weights sum to 1. The probabilities of mutually exclusive and exhaustive events do sum to 1 (this is part of the definition of probability). The next weighted average we discuss, the expected value of a random variable, also uses probabilities as weights.

The expected value of a random variable is an essential quantitative concept in investments. Investors continually make use of expected values—in estimating the rewards of alternative investments, in forecasting EPS and other corporate financial variables and ratios, and in assessing any other factor that may affect their financial position. The expected value of a random variable is defined as follows:

- **Definition of Expected Value.** The **expected value** of a random variable is the probability-weighted average of the possible outcomes of the random variable. For a random variable X, the expected value of X is denoted $E(X)$.

Expected value (for example, expected stock return) looks either to the future, as a forecast, or to the "true" value of the mean (the population mean, discussed in the chapter on statistical concepts and market returns). We should distinguish expected value from the concepts of historical or sample mean. The sample mean also summarizes in a single number a central value. However, the sample mean presents a central value for a particular set of observations as an equally weighted average of those observations. To summarize, the contrast is forecast versus historical, or population versus sample.

EXAMPLE 4-8 BankCorp's Earnings per Share (3)

You continue with your analysis of BankCorp's EPS. In Table 4-3, you have recorded a probability distribution for BankCorp's EPS for the current fiscal year.

TABLE 4-3 Probability Distribution for BankCorp's EPS

Probability	EPS
0.15	$2.60
0.45	$2.45
0.24	$2.20
0.16	$2.00
1.00	

What is the expected value of BankCorp's EPS for the current fiscal year?

Following the definition of expected value, list each outcome, weight it by its probability, and sum the terms.

$$E(\text{EPS}) = 0.15(\$2.60) + 0.45(\$2.45) + 0.24(\$2.20) + 0.16(\$2.00)$$
$$= \$2.3405$$

The expected value of EPS is $2.34.

An equation that summarizes your calculation in Example 4-8 is

$$E(X) = P(X_1)X_1 + P(X_2)X_2 + \cdots + P(X_n)X_n = \sum_{i=1}^{n} P(X_i)X_i \qquad (4\text{-}7)$$

where X_i is one of n possible outcomes of the random variable X.[8]

---

[8] For simplicity, we model all random variables in this chapter as discrete random variables, which have a countable set of outcomes. For continuous random variables, which are discussed along with discrete random variables in the chapter on common probability distributions, the operation corresponding to summation is integration.

The expected value is our forecast. Because we are discussing random quantities, we cannot count on an individual forecast being realized (although we hope that, on average, forecasts will be accurate). It is important, as a result, to measure the risk we face. Variance and standard deviation measure the dispersion of outcomes around the expected value or forecast.

- **Definition of Variance.**   The **variance** of a random variable is the expected value (the probability-weighted average) of squared deviations from the random variable's expected value:

$$\sigma^2(X) = E\{[X - E(X)]^2\} \qquad\qquad (4\text{-}8)$$

The two notations for variance are $\sigma^2(X)$ and $\text{Var}(X)$.

Variance is a number greater than or equal to 0 because it is the sum of squared terms. If variance is 0, there is no dispersion or risk. The outcome is certain, and the quantity X is not random at all. Variance greater than 0 indicates dispersion of outcomes. Increasing variance indicates increasing dispersion, all else equal. Variance of X is a quantity in the squared units of X. For example, if the random variable is return in percent, variance of return is in units of percent squared. Standard deviation is easier to interpret than variance, as it is in the same units as the random variable. If the random variable is return in percent, standard deviation of return is also in units of percent.

- **Definition of Standard Deviation.**   **Standard deviation** is the positive square root of variance.

The best way to become familiar with these concepts is to work examples.

EXAMPLE 4-9   BankCorp's Earnings per Share (4)

In Example 4-8, you calculated the expected value of BankCorp's EPS as $2.34, which is your forecast. Now you want to measure the dispersion around your forecast. Table 4-4 shows your view of the probability distribution of EPS for the current fiscal year.

TABLE 4-4   Probability Distribution for BankCorp's EPS

Probability	EPS
0.15	$2.60
0.45	$2.45
0.24	$2.20
0.16	$2.00
1.00	

What are the variance and standard deviation of BankCorp's EPS for the current fiscal year?

The order of calculation is always expected value, then variance, then standard deviation. Expected value has already been calculated. Following the definition of variance above, calculate the deviation of each outcome from the mean or expected value, square each deviation, weight (multiply) each squared deviation by its probability of occurrence, and then sum these terms.

$$\sigma^2(\text{EPS}) = P(\$2.60)[\$2.60 - E(\text{EPS})]^2 + P(\$2.45)[\$2.45 - E(\text{EPS})]^2$$
$$+ P(\$2.20)[\$2.20 - E(\text{EPS})]^2 + P(\$2.00)[\$2.00 - E(\text{EPS})]^2$$
$$= 0.15(2.60 - 2.34)^2 + 0.45(2.45 - 2.34)^2$$
$$+ 0.24(2.20 - 2.34)^2 + 0.16(2.00 - 2.34)^2$$
$$= 0.01014 + 0.005445 + 0.004704 + \$0.018496 = \$0.038785$$

Standard deviation is the positive square root of $0.038785:

$$\sigma(\text{EPS}) = \$0.038785^{1/2} = \$0.196939, \text{ or approximately } \$0.20.$$

An equation that summarizes your calculation of variance in Example 4-9 is

$$\sigma^2(X) = P(X_1)[X_1 - E(X)]^2 + P(X_2)[X_2 - E(X)]^2$$
$$+ \cdots + P(X_n)[X_n - E(X)]^2$$
$$= \sum_{i=1}^{n} P(X_i)[X_i - E(X)]^2 \tag{4-9}$$

where X_i is one of n possible outcomes of the random variable X.

In investments, we make use of any relevant information available in making our forecasts. When we refine our expectations or forecasts, we are typically making adjustments based on new information or events; in these cases we are using **conditional expected values**. The expected value of a random variable X given an event or scenario S is denoted $E(X \mid S)$. Suppose the random variable X can take on any one of n distinct outcomes $X_1, X_2, \ldots, X_n$ (these outcomes form a set of mutually exclusive and exhaustive events). The expected value of X conditional on S is the first outcome, X_1, times the probability of the first outcome given $S, P(X_1 \mid S)$, plus the second outcome, X_2, times the probability of the second outcome given $S, P(X_2 \mid S)$, and so forth.

$$E(X \mid S) = P(X_1 \mid S)X_1 + P(X_2 \mid S)X_2 + \cdots + P(X_n \mid S)X_n \tag{4-10}$$

We will illustrate this equation shortly.

Parallel to the total probability rule for stating unconditional probabilities in terms of conditional probabilities, there is a principle for stating (unconditional) expected values in terms of conditional expected values. This principle is the **total probability rule for expected value**.

- **The Total Probability Rule for Expected Value.**

  1. $E(X) = E(X \mid S)P(S) + E(X \mid S^C)P(S^C)$ (4-11)

  2. $E(X) = E(X \mid S_1)P(S_1) + E(X \mid S_2)P(S_2) + \cdots + E(X \mid S_n)P(S_n)$ (4-12)

where $S_1, S_2, \ldots, S_n$ are mutually exclusive and exhaustive scenarios or events.

The general case, Equation 4-12, states that the expected value of X equals the expected value of X given Scenario 1, $E(X \mid S_1)$, times the probability of Scenario 1, $P(S_1)$, plus the expected value of X given Scenario 2, $E(X \mid S_2)$, times the probability of Scenario 2, $P(S_2)$, and so forth.

    To use this principle, we formulate mutually exclusive and exhaustive scenarios that are useful for understanding the outcomes of the random variable. This approach was employed in developing the probability distribution of BankCorp's EPS in Examples 4-8 and 4-9, as we now discuss.

    The earnings of BankCorp are interest rate sensitive, benefiting from a declining interest rate environment. Suppose there is a 0.60 probability that BankCorp will operate in a *declining interest rate environment* in the current fiscal year and a 0.40 probability that it will operate in a *stable interest rate environment* (assessing the chance of an increasing interest rate environment as negligible). If a *declining interest rate environment* occurs, the probability that EPS will be $2.60 is estimated at 0.25, and the probability that EPS will be $2.45 is estimated at 0.75. Note that 0.60, the probability of *declining interest rate environment,* times 0.25, the probability of $2.60 EPS given a *declining interest rate environment,* equals 0.15, the (unconditional) probability of $2.60 given in the table in Examples 4-8 and 4-9 above. The probabilities are consistent. Also, 0.60(0.75) = 0.45, the probability of $2.45 EPS given in Tables 4-3 and 4-4. The **tree diagram** in Figure 4-2 shows the rest of the analysis.

    A declining interest rate environment points us to the node of the tree that branches off into outcomes of $2.60 and $2.45. We can find expected EPS given a declining interest rate environment as follows, using Equation 4-10:

$$E(\text{EPS} \mid \textit{declining interest rate environment}) = 0.25(\$2.60) + 0.75(\$2.45)$$

$$= \$2.4875$$

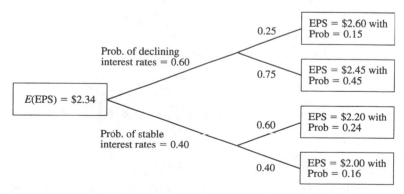

FIGURE 4-2   BankCorp's Forecasted EPS

If interest rates are stable,

$$E(\text{EPS} \mid \textit{stable interest rate environment}) = 0.60(\$2.20) + 0.40(\$2.00)$$
$$= \$2.12$$

Once we have the new piece of information that interest rates are stable, for example, we revise our original expectation of EPS from \$2.34 downward to \$2.12. Now using the total probability rule for expected value,

$$E(\text{EPS}) = E(\text{EPS} \mid \textit{declining interest rate environment})$$
$$P(\textit{declining interest rate environment})$$
$$+ E(\text{EPS} \mid \textit{stable interest rate environment})$$
$$P(\textit{stable interest rate environment})$$

So $E(\text{EPS}) = \$2.4875(0.60) + \$2.12(0.40) = \$2.3405$ or about \$2.34.

This amount is identical to the estimate of the expected value of EPS calculated directly from the probability distribution in Example 4-8. Just as our probabilities must be consistent, so must our expected values, unconditional and conditional; otherwise our investment actions may create profit opportunities for other investors at our expense.

To review, we first developed the factors or scenarios that influence the outcome of the event of interest. After assigning probabilities to these scenarios, we formed expectations conditioned on the different scenarios. Then we worked backward to formulate an expected value as of today. In the problem just worked, EPS was the event of interest, and the interest rate environment was the factor influencing EPS.

We can also calculate the variance of EPS given each scenario:

$$\sigma^2(\text{EPS} \mid \textit{declining interest rate environment})$$
$$= P(\$2.60 \mid \textit{declining interest rate environment})$$
$$\times [\$2.60 \mid E(\text{EPS} \mid \textit{declining interest rate environment})]^2$$
$$+ P(\$2.45 \mid \textit{declining interest rate environment})$$
$$\times [\$2.45 - E(\text{EPS} \mid \textit{declining interest rate environment})]^2$$
$$= 0.25(\$2.60 - \$2.4875)^2 + 0.75(\$2.45 - \$2.4875)^2$$
$$= 0.004219$$
$$\sigma^2(\text{EPS} \mid \textit{stable interest rate environment})$$
$$= P(\$2.20 \mid \textit{stable interest rate environment})$$
$$\times [\$2.20 - E(\text{EPS} \mid \textit{stable interest rate environment})]^2$$
$$+ P(\$2.00 \mid \textit{stable interest rate environment})$$
$$\times [\$2.00 - E(\text{EPS} \mid \textit{stable interest rate environment})]^2$$
$$= 0.60(\$2.20 - \$2.12)^2 + 0.40(\$2.00 - \$2.12)^2$$
$$= 0.0096$$

These are **conditional variances**, the variance of EPS given a *declining interest rate environment* and the variance of EPS given a *stable interest rate environment*. The relationship between unconditional variance and conditional variance is a relatively advanced topic.[9] The main points are 1) that variance, like expected value, has a conditional counterpart to the unconditional concept and 2) that we can use conditional variance to assess risk given a particular scenario.

EXAMPLE 4-10   BankCorp's Earnings per Share (5)

Continuing with BankCorp, you focus now on BankCorp's cost structure. One model you are researching for BankCorp's operating costs is

$$\hat{Y} = a + bX$$

where $\hat{Y}$ is a forecast of operating costs in millions of dollars and X is the number of branch offices. $\hat{Y}$ represents the expected value of Y given X, or $E(Y \mid X)$. ($\hat{Y}$ is a notation used in regression analysis, which we discuss in a later chapter.) You interpret the intercept a as fixed costs and b as variable costs. You estimate the equation as

$$\hat{Y} = 12.5 + 0.65X$$

BankCorp currently has 66 branch offices, and the equation estimates that $12.5 + 0.65(66) = \$55.4$ million. You have two scenarios for growth, pictured in the tree diagram in Figure 4-3.

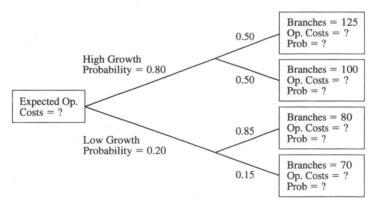

FIGURE 4-3   BankCorp's Forecasted Operating Costs

---

[9]The unconditional variance of EPS is the sum of two terms: (1) the expected value (probability-weighted average) of the conditional variances (parallel to the total probability rules) and (2) the variance of conditional expected values of EPS. The second term arises because the variability in conditional expected value is a source of risk. Term 1 is $\sigma^2(\text{EPS}) = P(declining\ interest\ rate\ environment)$ $\sigma^2(EPS \mid declining\ interest\ rate\ environment) + P(stable\ interest\ rate\ environment)\ \sigma^2(EPS \mid stable\ interest\ rate\ environment) = 0.60(0.004219) + 0.40(0.0096) = 0.006371$. Term 2 is $\sigma^2[E(EPS \mid interest\ rate\ environment)] = 0.60(\$2.4875 - \$2.34)^2 + 0.40(\$2.12 - \$2.34)^2 = 0.032414$. Summing the two terms, unconditional variance equals $0.006371 + 0.032414 = 0.038785$.

1. Compute the forecasted operating costs given the different levels of operating costs, using $\hat{Y} = 12.5 + 0.65X$. State the probability of each level of the number of branch offices. These are the answers to the questions in the terminal boxes of the tree diagram.
2. Compute the expected value of operating costs under the high growth scenario. Also calculate the expected value of operating costs under the low growth scenario.
3. Answer the question in the initial box of the tree: What are BankCorp's expected operating costs?

Solution to 1: Using $\hat{Y} = 12.5 + 0.65X$, from top to bottom, we have

Operating Costs	Probability
$\hat{Y} = 12.5 + 0.65(125) = \$93.75$ million	$0.80(0.50) = 0.40$
$\hat{Y} = 12.5 + 0.65(100) = \$77.50$ million	$0.80(0.50) = 0.40$
$\hat{Y} = 12.5 + 0.65(80) = \$64.50$ million	$0.20(0.85) = 0.17$
$\hat{Y} = 12.5 + 0.65(70) = \$58.00$ million	$0.20(0.15) = 0.03$
	Sum $= 1.00$

Solution to 2: Dollar amounts are in millions.

$$E(\text{operating costs} \mid \textit{high growth}) = 0.50(\$93.75) + 0.50(\$77.50)$$
$$= \$85.625$$
$$E(\text{operating costs} \mid \textit{low growth}) = 0.85(\$64.50) + 0.15(\$58.00)$$
$$= \$63.525$$

Solution to 3: Dollar amounts are in millions.

$$E(\text{operating costs}) = E(\text{operating costs} \mid \textit{high growth})P(\textit{high growth})$$
$$+ E(\text{operating costs} \mid \textit{low growth})P(\textit{low growth})$$
$$= \$85.625(0.80) + \$63.525(0.20)$$
$$= \$81.205$$

BankCorp's expected operating costs are $81.205 million.

We will see conditional probabilities again when we discuss Bayes' formula. This section has introduced a few problems that can be addressed using probability concepts. The following problem draws on these concepts, as well as on analytical skills.

EXAMPLE 4-11 The Default Risk Premium for a One-Period Debt Instrument

As the co-manager of a short-term bond portfolio, you are reviewing the pricing of a speculative-grade, one-year-maturity, zero-coupon bond. For this type of bond, the return is the difference between the amount paid and the principal value received at maturity. Your goal is to estimate an appropriate default risk premium for this bond. You define the default risk premium as the extra return above the risk-free return that will compensate investors for default risk. If R is the promised return (yield-to-maturity) on the debt instrument and R_F is the risk-free rate, the default risk premium is $R - R_F$. You assess the probability that the bond defaults as $P(\text{the bond defaults}) = 0.06$. Looking at current money market yields, you find that one-year U.S. Treasury bills (T-bills) are offering a return of 5.8 percent, an estimate of R_F. As a first step, you make the simplifying assumption that bondholders will recover nothing in the event of a default. What is the minimum default risk premium you should require for this instrument?

The challenge in this type of problem is to find a starting point. In many problems, including this one, an effective first step is to divide up the possible outcomes into mutually exclusive and exhaustive events in an economically logical way. Here, from the viewpoint of a bondholder, the two events that affect returns are *the bond defaults* and *the bond does not default*. These two events cover all outcomes. How do these events affect a bondholder's returns? A second step is to compute the value of the bond for the two events. We have no specifics on bond face value, but we can compute value per $1 or one unit of currency invested.

	The Bond Defaults	*The Bond Does Not Default*
Bond value	$0	$(1 + R)$

The third step is to find the expected value of the bond (per $1 invested).

$$E(\text{bond}) = \$0 \times P(\textit{the bond defaults})$$

$$+ \$(1 + R)[1 - P(\textit{the bond defaults})]$$

So $E(\text{bond}) = \$(1 + R)[1 - P(\textit{the bond defaults})]$. The expected value of the T-bill per $1 invested is $(1 + R_F)$. In fact, this value is certain because the T-bill is risk free. The next step requires economic reasoning. You want the default premium to be large enough so that you expect to at least break even compared with investing in the T-bill. This outcome will occur if the expected value of the bond equals the expected value of the T-bill per $1 invested.

$$\textit{Expected Value of Bond} = \textit{Expected Value of T-Bill}$$

$$\$(1 + R)[1 - P(\textit{the bond defaults})] = (1 + R_F)$$

Solving for the promised return on the bond, you find $R = \{(1 + R_F)/[1 - P(\textit{the bond defaults})]\} - 1$. Substituting in the values in the statement of the problem, $R = [1.058/(1 - 0.06)] - 1 = 1.12553 - 1 = 0.12553$ or about 12.55 percent, and default risk premium is $R - R_F = 12.55\% - 5.8\% = 6.75\%$.

You require a default risk premium of at least 675 basis points. You can state the matter as follows: If the bond is priced to yield 12.55 percent, you will earn a 675 basis-point spread and receive the bond principal with 94 percent probability. If the bond defaults, however, you will lose everything. With a premium of 675 basis points, you expect to just break even relative to an investment in T-bills. Because an investment in the zero-coupon bond has variability, if you are risk averse, you will demand that the premium be larger than 675 basis points.

This analysis is a starting point. Bondholders usually recover part of their investment after a default. A next step would be to incorporate a recovery rate.

In this section, we have treated random variables such as EPS as stand-alone quantities. We have not explored how descriptors such as expected value and variance of EPS may be functions of other random variables. Portfolio return is one random variable that is clearly a function of other random variables, the random returns on the individual securities in the portfolio. To analyze a portfolio's expected return and variance of return, we must understand these quantities are a function of characteristics of the individual securities' returns. Looking at the dispersion or variance of portfolio return, we see that the way individual security returns move together or covary is important. To understand the significance of these movements, we need to explore some new concepts, covariance and correlation. The next section, which deals with portfolio expected return and variance of return, introduces these concepts.

3. PORTFOLIO EXPECTED RETURN AND VARIANCE OF RETURN

Modern portfolio theory makes frequent use of the idea that investment opportunities can be evaluated using expected return as a measure of reward and variance of return as a measure of risk. The calculation and interpretation of portfolio expected return and variance of return are fundamental skills. In this section, we will develop an understanding of portfolio expected return and variance of return.[10] Portfolio return is determined by the returns on the individual holdings. As a result, the calculation of portfolio variance, as a function of the individual asset returns, is more complex than the variance calculations illustrated in the previous section.

We work with an example of a portfolio that is 50 percent invested in an S&P 500 Index fund, 25 percent invested in a U.S. long-term corporate bond fund, and 25 percent invested in a fund indexed to the MSCI EAFE Index (representing equity markets in Europe, Australasia, and the Far East). Table 4-5 shows these weights.

TABLE 4-5   Portfolio Weights

Asset Class	Weights
S&P 500	0.50
U.S. long-term corporate bonds	0.25
MSCI EAFE	0.25

---

[10]Although we outline a number of basic concepts in this section, we do not present mean−variance analysis per se. For a presentation of mean−variance analysis, see the chapter on portfolio concepts, as well as the extended treatments in standard investment textbooks such as Bodie, Kane, and Marcus (2001), Elton, Gruber, Brown, and Goetzmann (2003), Reilly and Brown (2003), and Sharpe, Alexander, and Bailey (1999).

We first address the calculation of the expected return on the portfolio. In the previous section, we defined the expected value of a random variable as the probability-weighted average of the possible outcomes. Portfolio return, we know, is a weighted average of the returns on the securities in the portfolio. Similarly, the expected return on a portfolio is a weighted average of the expected returns on the securities in the portfolio, using exactly the same weights. When we have estimated the expected returns on the individual securities, we immediately have portfolio expected return. This convenient fact follows from the properties of expected value.

- **Properties of Expected Value.**   Let w_i be any constant and R_i be a random variable.

  1. The expected value of a constant times a random variable equals the constant times the expected value of the random variable.

  $$E(w_i R_i) = w_i E(R_i)$$

  2. The expected value of a weighted sum of random variables equals the weighted sum of the expected values, using the same weights.

  $$E(w_1 R_1 + w_2 R_2 + \cdots + w_n R_n) = w_1 E(R_1) + w_2 E(R_2) + \cdots + w_n E(R_n) \quad (4\text{-}13)$$

Suppose we have a random variable with a given expected value. If we multiply each outcome by 2, for example, the random variable's expected value is multiplied by 2 as well. That is the meaning of Part 1. The second statement is the rule that directly leads to the expression for portfolio expected return. A portfolio with n securities is defined by its portfolio weights, $w_1, w_2, \ldots, w_n$, which sum to 1. So portfolio return, R_p, is $R_p = w_1 R_1 + w_2 R_2 + \cdots + w_n R_n$. We can state the following principle:

- **Calculation of Portfolio Expected Return.**   Given a portfolio with n securities, the expected return on the portfolio is a weighted average of the expected returns on the component securities:

  $$E(R_p) = E(w_1 R_1 + w_2 R_2 + \cdots + w_n R_n)$$
  $$= w_1 E(R_1) + w_2 E(R_2) + \cdots + w_n E(R_n)$$

Suppose we have estimated expected returns on the assets in the portfolio, as given in Table 4-6. We calculate the expected return on the portfolio as 11.75 percent:

$$E(R_p) = w_1 E(R_1) + w_2 E(R_2) + w_3 E(R_3)$$
$$= 0.50(13\%) + 0.25(6\%) + 0.25(15\%) = 11.75\%$$

TABLE 4-6   Weights and Expected Returns

Asset Class	Weight	Expected Return (%)
S&P 500	0.50	13
U.S. long-term corporate bonds	0.25	6
MSCI EAFE	0.25	15

In the previous section, we studied variance as a measure of dispersion of outcomes around the expected value. Here we are interested in portfolio variance of return as a measure of investment risk. Letting R_p stand for the return on the portfolio, portfolio variance is $\sigma^2(R_p) = E\{[R_p - E(R_p)]^2\}$ according to Equation 4-8. How do we implement this definition? In the chapter on statistical concepts and market returns, we learned how to calculate a historical or sample variance based on a sample of returns. Now we are considering variance in a forward-looking sense. We will use information about the individual assets in the portfolio to obtain portfolio variance of return. To avoid clutter in notation, we write ER_p for $E(R_p)$. We need the concept of covariance.

- **Definition of Covariance.** Given two random variables R_i and R_j, the covariance between R_i and R_j is

$$\text{Cov}(R_i, R_j) = E[(R_i - ER_i)(R_j - ER_j)] \tag{4-14}$$

Alternative notations are $\sigma(R_i, R_j)$ and σ_{ij}.

Equation 4-14 states that the covariance between two random variables is the probability-weighted average of the cross-products of each random variable's deviation from its own expected value. We will return to discuss covariance after we establish the need for the concept. Working from the definition of variance, we find

$$\sigma^2(R_p) = E[(R_p - ER_p)^2]$$
$$= E\{[w_1 R_1 + w_2 R_2 + w_3 R_3 - E(w_1 R_1 + w_2 R_2 + w_3 R_3)]^2\}$$
$$= E\{[w_1 R_1 + w_2 R_2 + w_3 R_3 - w_1 ER_1 - w_2 ER_2 - w_3 ER_3]^2\}$$

(using Equation 4−13)

$$= E\{[w_1(R_1 - ER_1) + w_2(R_2 - ER_2) + w_3(R_3 - ER_3)]^2\} \qquad \text{(rearranging)}$$
$$= E\{[w_1(R_1 - ER_1) + w_2(R_2 - ER_2) + w_3(R_3 - ER_3)]$$
$$\times [w_1(R_1 - ER_1) + w_2(R_2 - ER_2) + w_3(R_3 - ER_3)]\}$$

(what squaring means)

$$= E[w_1 w_1(R_1 - ER_1)(R_1 - ER_1) + w_1 w_2(R_1 - ER_1)(R_2 - ER_2)$$
$$+ w_1 w_3(R_1 - ER_1)(R_3 - ER_3) + w_2 w_1(R_2 - ER_2)(R_1 - ER_1)$$
$$+ w_2 w_2(R_2 - ER_2)(R_2 - ER_2) + w_2 w_3(R_2 - ER_2)(R_3 - ER_3)$$
$$+ w_3 w_1(R_3 - ER_3)(R_1 - ER_1) + w_3 w_2(R_3 - ER_3)(R_2 - ER_2)$$
$$+ w_3 w_3(R_3 - ER_3)(R_3 - ER_3)] \qquad \text{(doing the multiplication)}$$
$$= w_1^2 E[(R_1 - ER_1)^2] + w_1 w_2 E[(R_1 - ER_1)(R_2 - ER_2)]$$
$$+ w_1 w_3 E[(R_1 - ER_1)(R_3 - ER_3)] + w_2 w_1 E[(R_2 - ER_2)(R_1 - ER_1)]$$
$$+ w_2^2 E[(R_2 - ER_2)^2] + w_2 w_3 E[(R_2 - ER_2)(R_3 - ER_3)]$$
$$+ w_3 w_1 E[(R_3 - ER_3)(R_1 - ER_1)] + w_3 w_2 E[(R_3 - ER_3)(R_2 - ER_2)]$$

$$+w_3^2 E[(R_3 - ER_3)^2] \qquad \text{(recalling that the } w_i \text{ terms are constants)}$$

$$= w_1^2 \sigma^2(R_1) + w_1 w_2 \text{Cov}(R_1, R_2) + w_1 w_3 \text{Cov}(R_1, R_3)$$

$$+ w_1 w_2 Cov(R_1, R_2) + w_2^2 \sigma^2(R_2) + w_2 w_3 \text{Cov}(R_2, R_3)$$

$$+ w_1 w_3 Cov(R_1, R_3) + w_2 w_3 Cov(R_2, R_3) + w_3^2 \sigma^2(R_3) \qquad \text{(4-15)}$$

The last step follows from the definitions of variance and covariance.[11] For the italicized covariance terms in Equation 4-15, we used the fact that the order of variables in covariance does not matter: $\text{Cov}(R_2, R_1) = \text{Cov}(R_1, R_2)$, for example. As we will show, the diagonal variance terms $\sigma^2(R_1), \sigma^2(R_2)$, and $\sigma^2(R_3)$ can be expressed as $\text{Cov}(R_1, R_1), \text{Cov}(R_2, R_2)$, and $\text{Cov}(R_3, R_3)$, respectively. Using this fact, the most compact way to state Equation 4-15 is $\sigma^2(R_P) = \sum_{i=1}^{3} \sum_{j=1}^{3} w_i w_j \text{Cov}(R_i, R_j)$. The double summation signs say: "Set $i = 1$ and let j run from 1 to 3; then set $i = 2$ and let j run from 1 to 3; next set $i = 3$ and let j run from 1 to 3; finally, add the nine terms." This expression generalizes for a portfolio of any size n to

$$\sigma^2(R_p) = \sum_{i=1}^{n} \sum_{j=1}^{n} w_i w_j \text{Cov}(R_i, R_j) \qquad \text{(4-16)}$$

We see from Equation 4-15 that individual variances of return (the bolded diagonal terms) constitute part, but not all, of portfolio variance. The three variances are actually outnumbered by the six covariance terms off the diagonal. For three assets, the ratio is 1 to 2, or 50 percent. If there are 20 assets, there are 20 variance terms and $20(20) - 20 = 380$ off-diagonal covariance terms. The ratio of variance terms to off-diagonal covariance terms is less than 6 to 100, or 6 percent. A first observation, then, is that as the number of holdings increases, covariance[12] becomes increasingly important, all else equal.

What exactly is the effect of covariance on portfolio variance? The covariance terms capture how the co-movements of returns affect portfolio variance. For example, consider two stocks: One tends to have high returns (relative to its expected return) when the other has low returns (relative to its expected return). The returns on one stock tend to offset the returns on the other stock, lowering the variability or variance of returns on the portfolio. Like variance, the units of covariance are hard to interpret, and we will introduce a more intuitive concept shortly. Meanwhile, from the definition of covariance, we can establish two essential observations about covariance.

1. We can interpret the sign of covariance as follows:
    Covariance of returns is negative if, when the return on one asset is above its expected value, the return on the other asset tends to be below its expected value (an average inverse relationship between returns).
    Covariance of returns is 0 if returns on the assets are unrelated.

---

[11] Useful facts about variance and covariance include: 1) The variance of a constant *times* a random variable equals the constant squared times the variance of the random variable, or $\sigma^2(wR) = w^2 \sigma^2(R)$; 2) The variance of a constant *plus* a random variable equals the variance of the random variable, or $\sigma^2(w + R) = \sigma^2(R)$ because a constant has zero variance; 3) The covariance between a constant and a random variable is zero.

[12] When the meaning of covariance as "off-diagonal covariance" is obvious, as it is here, we omit the qualifying words. Covariance is usually used in this sense.

TABLE 4-7   Inputs to Portfolio Expected Return and Variance

A. Inputs to Portfolio Expected Return

Asset	A	B	C
	$E(R_A)$	$E(R_B)$	$E(R_C)$

B. Covariance Matrix: The Inputs to Portfolio Variance of Return

Asset	A	B	C
A	$\mathbf{Cov(R_A, R_A)}$	$Cov(R_A, R_B)$	$Cov(R_A, R_C)$
B	$Cov(R_B, R_A)$	$\mathbf{Cov(R_B, R_B)}$	$Cov(R_B, R_C)$
C	$Cov(R_C, R_A)$	$Cov(R_C, R_B)$	$\mathbf{Cov(R_C, R_C)}$

Covariance of returns is positive when the returns on both assets tend to be on the same side (above or below) their expected values at the same time (an average positive relationship between returns).

2. The covariance of a random variable with itself (*own covariance*) is its own variance: $Cov(R, R) = E\{[R - E(R)][R - E(R)]\} = E\{[R - E(R)]^2\} = \sigma^2(R)$.

A complete list of the covariances constitutes all the statistical data needed to compute portfolio variance of return. Covariances are often presented in a square format called a **covariance matrix**. Table 4-7 summarizes the inputs for portfolio expected return and variance of return.

With three assets, the covariance matrix has $3^2 = 3 \times 3 = 9$ entries, but it is customary to treat the diagonal terms, the variances, separately from the off-diagonal terms. These diagonal terms are bolded in Table 4-7. This distinction is natural, as security variance is a single-variable concept. So there are $9 - 3 = 6$ covariances, excluding variances. But $Cov(R_B, R_A) = Cov(R_A, R_B)$, $Cov(R_C, R_A) = Cov(R_A, R_C)$, and $Cov(R_C, R_B) = Cov(R_B, R_C)$. The covariance matrix below the diagonal is the mirror image of the covariance matrix above the diagonal. As a result, there are only $6/2 = 3$ distinct covariance terms to estimate. In general, for n securities, there are $n(n - 1)/2$ distinct covariances to estimate and n variances to estimate.

Suppose we have the covariance matrix shown in Table 4-8. Taking Equation 4-15 and grouping variance terms together produces the following:

$$\sigma^2(R_p) = w_1^2 \sigma^2(R_1) + w_2^2 \sigma^2(R_2) + w_3^2 \sigma^2(R_3) + 2w_1 w_2 Cov(R_1, R_2)$$

$$+ 2w_1 w_3 Cov(R_1, R_3) + 2w_2 w_3 Cov(R_2, R_3) \tag{4-17}$$

$$= (0.50)^2 (400) + (0.25)^2 (81) + (0.25)^2 (441) + 2(0.50)(0.25)(45)$$

$$+ 2(0.50)(0.25)(189) + 2(0.25)(0.25)(38)$$

$$= 100 + 5.0625 + 27.5625 + 11.25 + 47.25 + 4.75 = 195.875$$

The variance is 195.875. Standard deviation of return is $195.875^{1/2} = 14$ percent. To summarize, the portfolio has an expected annual return of 11.75 percent and a standard deviation of return of 14 percent.

Let us look at the first three terms in the calculation above. Their sum, $100 + 5.0625 + 27.5625 = 132.625$, is the contribution of the individual variances to portfolio variance. If the returns on the three assets were independent, covariances would be 0 and the standard

TABLE 4-8   Covariance Matrix

	S&P 500	U.S. Long-Term Corporate Bonds	MSCI EAFE
S&P 500	400	45	189
U.S. long-term corporate bonds	45	81	38
MSCI EAFE	189	38	441

deviation of portfolio return would be $132.625^{1/2} = 11.52$ percent as compared to 14 percent before. The portfolio would have less risk. Suppose the covariance terms were negative. Then a negative number would be added to 132.625, so portfolio variance and risk would be even smaller. At the same time, we have not changed expected return. For the same expected portfolio return, the portfolio has less risk. This risk reduction is a diversification benefit, meaning a risk-reduction benefit from holding a portfolio of assets. The diversification benefit increases with decreasing covariance. This observation is a key insight of modern portfolio theory. It is even more intuitively stated when we can use the concept of correlation. Then we can say that as long as security returns are not perfectly positively correlated, diversification benefits are possible. Furthermore, the smaller the correlation between security returns, the greater the cost of not diversifying (in terms of risk-reduction benefits forgone), all else equal.

- **Definition of Correlation.** The correlation between two random variables, R_i and R_j, is defined as $\rho(R_i, R_j) = \text{Cov}(R_i, R_j)/\sigma(R_i)\sigma(R_j)$. Alternative notations are $\text{Corr}(R_i, R_j)$ and ρ_{ij}.

Frequently, covariance is substituted out using the relationship $\text{Cov}(R_i, R_j) = \rho(R_i, R_j)\sigma(R_i)$ $\sigma(R_j)$. The division indicated in the definition makes correlation a pure number (one without a unit of measurement) and places bounds on its largest and smallest possible values. Using the above definition, we can state a correlation matrix from data in the covariance matrix alone. Table 4-9 shows the correlation matrix.

For example, the covariance between long-term bonds and MSCI EAFE is 38, from Table 4-8. The standard deviation of long-term bond returns is $81^{1/2} = 9$ percent, that of MSCI EAFE returns is $441^{1/2} = 21$ percent, from diagonal terms in Table 4-8. The correlation ρ(Return on long-term bonds, Return on EAFE) is $38/(9\%)(21\%) = 0.201$, rounded to 0.20. The correlation of the S&P 500 with itself equals 1: The calculation is own covariance divided by its standard deviation squared.

TABLE 4-9   Correlation Matrix of Returns

	S&P 500	U.S. Long-Term Corporate Bonds	MSCI EAFE
S&P 500	1.00	0.25	0.45
U.S. long-term corporate bonds	0.25	1.00	0.20
MSCI EAFE	0.45	0.20	1.00

- **Properties of Correlation**.

    1. Correlation is a number between -1 and $+1$ for two random variables, X and Y:

    $$-1 \leq \rho(X, Y) \leq +1$$

    2. A correlation of 0 (uncorrelated variables) indicates an absence of any linear (straight-line) relationship between the variables.[13] Increasingly positive correlation indicates an increasingly strong positive linear relationship (up to 1, which indicates a perfect linear relationship). Increasingly negative correlation indicates an increasingly strong negative (inverse) linear relationship (down to -1, which indicates a perfect inverse linear relationship).[14]

EXAMPLE 4-12   Portfolio Expected Return and Variance of Return

You have a portfolio of two mutual funds, A and B, 75 percent invested in A, as shown in Table 4-10.

TABLE 4-10   Mutual Fund Expected Returns, Return Variances, and Covariances

Fund	A	B
	$E(R_A) = 20\%$	$E(R_B) = 12\%$
	Covariance Matrix	
Fund	A	B
A	625	120
B	120	196

1. Calculate the expected return of the portfolio.
2. Calculate the correlation matrix for this problem. Carry out the answer to two decimal places.
3. Compute portfolio standard deviation of return.

Solution to 1: $E(R_p) = w_A E(R_A) + (1 - w_A)E(R_B) = 0.75(20\%) + 0.25(12\%) = 18\%$. Portfolio weights must sum to 1: $w_B = 1 - w_A$.

Solution to 2: $\sigma(R_A) = 625^{1/2} = 25$ percent $\sigma(R_B) = 196^{1/2} = 14$ percent. There is one distinct covariance and thus one distinct correlation:

$$\rho(R_A, R_B) = \text{Cov}(R_A, R_B)/\sigma(R_A)\sigma(R_B) = 120/25(14) = 0.342857, \text{ or } 0.34$$

---

[13] If the correlation is 0, $R_1 = a + bR_2 + \text{error}$, with $b = 0$.

[14] If the correlation is positive, $R_1 = a + bR_2 + \text{error}$, with $b > 0$. If the correlation is negative, $b < 0$.

Table 4-11 shows the correlation matrix.

TABLE 4-11   Correlation Matrix

	A	B
A	1.00	0.34
B	0.34	1.00

Diagonal terms are always equal to 1 in a correlation matrix.

Solution to 3:

$$\sigma^2(R_p) = w_A^2 \sigma^2(R_A) + w_B^2 \sigma^2(R_B) + 2w_A w_B \text{Cov}(R_A, R_B)$$

$$= (0.75)^2(625) + (0.25)^2(196) + 2(0.75)(0.25)(120)$$

$$= 351.5625 + 12.25 + 45 = 408.8125$$

$$\sigma(R_p) = 408.8125^{1/2} = 20.22 \text{ percent}$$

How do we estimate return covariance and correlation? Frequently, we make forecasts on the basis of historical covariance or use other methods based on historical return data, such as a market model regression.[15] We can also calculate covariance using the **joint probability function** of the random variables, if that can be estimated. The joint probability function of two random variables X and Y, denoted $P(X, Y)$, gives the probability of joint occurrences of values of X and Y. For example, $P(3, 2)$, is the probability that X equals 3 and Y equals 2.

Suppose that the joint probability function of the returns on BankCorp stock (R_A) and the returns on NewBank stock (R_B) has the simple structure given in Table 4-12.

TABLE 4-12   Joint Probability Function of BankCorp and NewBank Returns (Entries are joint probabilities)

	$R_B = 20\%$	$R_B = 16\%$	$R_B = 10\%$
$R_A = 25\%$	0.20	0	0
$R_A = 12\%$	0	0.50	0
$R_A = 10\%$	0	0	0.30

The expected return on BankCorp stock is $0.20(25\%) + 0.50(12\%) + 0.30(10\%) = 14\%$. The expected return on NewBank stock is $0.20(20\%) + 0.50(16\%) + 0.30(10\%) = 15\%$. The joint probability function above might reflect an analysis based on whether banking industry conditions are good, average, or poor. Table 4-13 presents the calculation of covariance.

---

[15] See any of the textbooks mentioned in Footnote 10.

TABLE 4-13   Covariance Calculations

Banking Industry Condition	Deviations BankCorp	Deviations NewBank	Product of Deviations	Probability of Condition	Probability-Weighted Product
Good	25−14	20−15	55	0.20	11
Average	12−14	16−15	−2	0.50	−1
Poor	10−14	10−15	20	0.30	6
					$\text{Cov}(R_A, R_B) = 16$

Note: Expected return for BankCorp is 14% and for NewBank, 15%.

The first and second columns of numbers show, respectively, the deviations of BankCorp and NewBank returns from their mean or expected value. The next column shows the product of the deviations. For example, for good industry conditions, $(25 - 14)(20 - 15) = 11(5) = 55$. Then 55 is multiplied or weighted by 0.20, the probability that banking industry conditions are good: $55(0.20) = 11$. The calculations for average and poor banking conditions follow the same pattern. Summing up these probability-weighted products, we find that $\text{Cov}(R_A, R_B) = 16$.

A formula for computing the covariance between random variables R_A and R_B is

$$\text{Cov}(R_A, R_B) = \sum_i \sum_j P(R_{A,i}, R_{B,j})(R_{A,i} - ER_A)(R_{B,j} - ER_B) \qquad (4\text{-}18)$$

The formula tells us to sum all possible deviation cross-products weighted by the appropriate joint probability. In the example we just worked, as Table 4-12 shows, only three joint probabilities are nonzero. Therefore, in computing the covariance of returns in this case, we need to consider only three cross-products:

$$\text{Cov}(R_A, R_B) = P(25, 20)[(25 - 14)(20 - 15)] + P(12, 16)[(12 - 14)(16 - 15)]$$

$$+ P(10, 10)[(10 - 14)(10 - 15)]$$

$$= 0.20(11)(5) + 0.50(-2)(1) + 0.30(-4)(-5)$$

$$= 11 - 1 + 6 = 16$$

One theme of this chapter has been independence. Two random variables are independent when every possible pair of events—one event corresponding to a value of X and another event corresponding to a value of Y—are independent events. When two random variables are independent, their joint probability function simplifies.

- **Definition of Independence for Random Variables.** Two random variables X and Y are independent if and only if $P(X, Y) = P(X)P(Y)$.

For example, given independence, $P(3, 2) = P(3)P(2)$. We multiply the individual probabilities to get the joint probabilities. *Independence* is a stronger property than *uncorrelatedness* because correlation addresses only linear relationships. The following condition holds for independent random variables and, therefore, also holds for uncorrelated random variables.

- **Multiplication Rule for Expected Value of the Product of Uncorrelated Random Variables**. The expected value of the product of uncorrelated random variables is the product of their expected values.

$$E(XY) = E(X)E(Y) \text{ if } X \text{ and } Y \text{ are uncorrelated.}$$

Many financial variables, such as revenue (price times quantity), are the product of random quantities. When applicable, the above rule simplifies calculating expected value of a product of random variables.[16]

4. TOPICS IN PROBABILITY

In the remainder of the chapter we discuss two topics that can be important in solving investment problems. We start with Bayes' formula: what probability theory has to say about learning from experience. Then we move to a discussion of shortcuts and principles for counting.

4.1. Bayes' Formula

When we make decisions involving investments, we often start with viewpoints based on our experience and knowledge. These viewpoints may be changed or confirmed by new knowledge and observations. Bayes' formula is a rational method for adjusting our viewpoints as we confront new information.[17] Bayes' formula and related concepts have been applied in many business and investment decision-making contexts, including the evaluation of mutual fund performance.[18]

Bayes' formula makes use of Equation 4-6, the total probability rule. To review, that rule expressed the probability of an event as a weighted average of the probabilities of the event, given a set of scenarios. Bayes' formula works in reverse; more precisely, it reverses the "given that" information. Bayes' formula uses the occurrence of the event to infer the probability of the scenario generating it. For that reason, Bayes' formula is sometimes called an inverse probability. In many applications, including the one illustrating its use in this section, an individual is updating his beliefs concerning the causes that may have produced a new observation.

- **Bayes' Formula**. Given a set of prior probabilities for an event of interest, if you receive new information, the rule for updating your probability of the event is

Updated probability of event given the new information =

$$\frac{\text{Probability of the new information given event}}{\text{Unconditional probability of the new information}} \times \text{Prior probability of event}$$

---

[16] Otherwise, the calculation depends on conditional expected value; the calculation can be expressed as $E(XY) = E(X)E(Y \mid X)$.

[17] Named after the Reverend Thomas Bayes (1702–61).

[18] See Baks, Metrick, and Wachter (2001).

In probability notation, this formula can be written concisely as:

$$P(\text{Event} \mid \text{Information}) = \frac{P(\text{Information} \mid \text{Event})}{P(\text{Information})} P(\text{Event})$$

To illustrate Bayes' formula, we work through an investment example that can be adapted to any actual problem. Suppose you are an investor in the stock of DriveMed, Inc. Positive earnings surprises relative to consensus EPS estimates often result in positive stock returns, and negative surprises often have the opposite effect. DriveMed is preparing to release last quarter's EPS result, and you are interested in which of these three events happened: *last quarter's EPS exceeded the consensus EPS estimate,* or *last quarter's EPS exactly met the consensus EPS estimate,* or *last quarter's EPS fell short of the consensus EPS estimate.* This list of the alternatives is mutually exclusive and exhaustive.

On the basis of your own research, you write down the following **prior probabilities** (or **priors**, for short) concerning these three events:

- *P(EPS exceeded consensus)* = 0.45
- *P(EPS met consensus)* = 0.30
- *P(EPS fell short of consensus)* = 0.25

These probabilities are "prior" in the sense that they reflect only what you know now, before the arrival of any new information.

The next day, DriveMed announces that it is expanding factory capacity in Singapore and Ireland to meet increased sales demand. You assess this new information. The decision to expand capacity relates not only to current demand but probably also to the prior quarter's sales demand. You know that sales demand is positively related to EPS. So now it appears more likely that last quarter's EPS will exceed the consensus.

The question you have is, "In light of the new information, what is the updated probability that the prior quarter's EPS exceeded the consensus estimate?"

Bayes' formula provides a rational method for accomplishing this updating. We can abbreviate the new information as *DriveMed expands*. The first step in applying Bayes' formula is to calculate the probability of the new information (here: *DriveMed expands*), given a list of events or scenarios that may have generated it. The list of events should cover all possibilities, as it does here. Formulating these conditional probabilities is the key step in the updating process. Suppose your view is

$$P(\textit{DriveMed expands} \mid \textit{EPS exceeded consensus}) = 0.75$$

$$P(\textit{DriveMed expands} \mid \textit{EPS met consensus}) = 0.20$$

$$P(\textit{DriveMed expands} \mid \textit{EPS fell short of consensus}) = 0.05$$

Conditional probabilities of an observation (here: *DriveMed expands*) are sometimes referred to as **likelihoods**. Again, likelihoods are required for updating the probability.

Next, you combine these conditional probabilities or likelihoods with your prior probabilities to get the unconditional probability for DriveMed expanding, $P(DriveMed\ expands)$, as follows:

$$
\begin{aligned}
P(DriveMed\ expands) = \ & P(DriveMed\ expands\mid EPS\ exceeded\ consensus) \\
& \times P(EPS\ exceeded\ consensus) \\
& + P(DriveMed\ expands\mid EPS\ met\ consensus) \\
& \times P(EPS\ met\ consensus) \\
& + P(DriveMed\ expands\mid EPS\ fell\ short\ of\ consensus) \\
& \times P(EPS\ fell\ short\ of\ consensus) \\
= \ & 0.75(0.45) + 0.20(0.30) + 0.05(0.25) = 0.41,\ \text{or } 41\%
\end{aligned}
$$

This is Equation 4-6, the total probability rule, in action. Now you can answer your question by applying Bayes' formula:

$$
\begin{aligned}
& P(EPS\ exceeded\ consensus\mid DriveMed\ expands) \\
& = \frac{P(DriveMed\ expands\mid EPS\ exceeded\ consensus)}{P(DriveMed\ expands)} P(EPS\ exceeded\ consensus) \\
& = (0.75/0.41)(0.45) = 1.829268(0.45) = 0.823171
\end{aligned}
$$

Prior to DriveMed's announcement, you thought the probability that DriveMed would beat consensus expectations was 45 percent. On the basis of your interpretation of the announcement, you update that probability to 82.3 percent. This updated probability is called your **posterior probability** because it reflects or comes after the new information.

The Bayes' calculation takes the prior probability, which was 45 percent, and multiplies it by a ratio—the first term on the right-hand side of the equal sign. The denominator of the ratio is the probability that DriveMed expands, as you view it without considering (conditioning on) anything else. Therefore, this probability is unconditional. The numerator is the probability that DriveMed expands, if last quarter's EPS actually exceeded the consensus estimate. This last probability is larger than unconditional probability in the denominator, so the ratio (1.83 roughly) is greater than 1. As a result, your updated or posterior probability is larger than your prior probability. Thus, the ratio reflects the impact of the new information on your prior beliefs.

EXAMPLE 4-13   Inferring Whether DriveMed's EPS Met Consensus EPS

You are still an investor in DriveMed stock. To review the givens, your prior probabilities are $P(EPS\ exceeded\ consensus) = 0.45$, $P(EPS\ met\ consensus) = 0.30$, and

$P(EPS\ fell\ short\ of\ consensus) = 0.25$. You also have the following conditional probabilities:

$$P(DriveMed\ expands\ |\ EPS\ exceeded\ consensus) = 0.75$$

$$P(DriveMed\ expands\ |\ EPS\ met\ consensus) = 0.20$$

$$P(DriveMed\ expands\ |\ EPS\ fell\ short\ of\ consensus) = 0.05$$

Recall that you updated your probability that last quarter's EPS exceeded the consensus estimate from 45 percent to 82.3 percent after DriveMed announced it would expand. Now you want to update your other priors.

1. Update your prior probability that DriveMed's EPS met consensus.
2. Update your prior probability that DriveMed's EPS fell short of consensus.
3. Show that the three updated probabilities sum to 1. (Carry each probability to four decimal places.)
4. Suppose, because of lack of prior beliefs about whether DriveMed would meet consensus, you updated on the basis of prior probabilities that all three possibilities were equally likely: $P(EPS\ exceeded\ consensus) = P(EPS\ met\ consensus) = P(EPS\ fell\ short\ of\ consensus) = 1/3$. What is your estimate of the probability $P(EPS\ exceeded\ consensus\ |\ DriveMed\ expands)$?

Solution to 1: The probability is

$$P(EPS\ met\ consensus\ |\ DriveMed\ expands)$$

$$= \frac{P(DriveMed\ expands\ |\ EPS\ met\ consensus)}{P(DriveMed\ expands)} P(EPS\ met\ consensus)$$

The probability $P(DriveMed\ expands)$ is found by taking each of the three conditional probabilities in the statement of the problem, such as $P(DriveMed\ expands\ |\ EPS\ exceeded\ consensus)$; multiplying each one by the prior probability of the conditioning event, such as $P(EPS\ exceeded\ consensus)$; then adding the three products. The calculation is unchanged from the problem in the text above: $P(DriveMed\ expands) = 0.75(0.45) + 0.20(0.30) + 0.05(0.25) = 0.41$, or 41 percent. The other probabilities needed, $P(DriveMed\ expands\ |\ EPS\ met\ consensus) = 0.20$ and $P(EPS\ met\ consensus) = 0.30$, are givens. So

$$P(EPS\ met\ consensus\ |\ DriveMed\ expands)$$

$$= [P(DriveMed\ expands\ |\ EPS\ met\ consensus)/$$

$$P(DriveMed\ expands)]P(EPS\ met\ consensus)$$

$$= (0.20/0.41)(0.30) = 0.487805(0.30) = 0.146341$$

After taking account of the announcement on expansion, your updated probability that last quarter's EPS for DriveMed just met consensus is 14.6 percent compared with your prior probability of 30 percent.

Solution to 2:   P(*DriveMed expands*) was already calculated as 41 percent. Recall that P(*DriveMed expands | EPS fell short of consensus*) = 0.05 and P(*EPS fell short of consensus*) = 0.25 are givens.

$$P(\text{EPS fell short of consensus } | \text{ DriveMed expands})$$

$$= [P(\text{DriveMed expands } | \text{ EPS fell short of consensus})/$$

$$P(\text{DriveMed expands})]P(\text{EPS fell short of consensus})$$

$$= (0.05/0.41)(0.25) = 0.121951(0.25) = 0.030488$$

As a result of the announcement, you have revised your probability that DriveMed's EPS fell short of consensus from 25 percent (your prior probability) to 3 percent.

Solution to 3:   The sum of the three updated probabilities is

$$P(\text{EPS exceeded consensus } | \text{ DriveMed expands}) + P(\text{EPS met consensus } |$$

$$\text{DriveMed expands}) + P(\text{EPS fell short of consensus } | \text{ DriveMed expands})$$

$$= 0.8232 + 0.1463 + 0.0305 = 1.0000$$

The three events (*EPS exceeded consensus, EPS met consensus, EPS fell short of consensus*) are mutually exclusive and exhaustive: One of these events or statements must be true, so the conditional probabilities must sum to 1. Whether we are talking about conditional or unconditional probabilities, whenever we have a complete set of the distinct possible events or outcomes, the probabilities must sum to 1. This calculation serves as a check on your work.

Solution to 4:   Using the probabilities given in the question,

$$P(\text{DriveMed expands}) =$$

$$P(\text{DriveMed expands } | \text{ EPS exceeded consensus})$$

$$P(\text{EPS exceeded consensus}) + P(\text{DriveMed expands } |$$

$$\text{EPS met consensus}) P(\text{EPS met consensus}) + P(\text{DriveMed expands } |$$

$$\text{EPS fell short of consensus}) P(\text{EPS fell short of consensus})$$

$$= 0.75(1/3) + 0.20(1/3) + 0.05(1/3) = 1/3$$

Not surprisingly, the probability of DriveMed expanding is 1/3 because the decision maker has no prior beliefs or views regarding how well EPS performed relative to the consensus estimate. Now we can use Bayes' formula to find P(*EPS exceeded consensus | DriveMed expands*) = [P(*DriveMed expands | EPS exceeded consensus*)/P(*DriveMed expands*)]P(*EPS exceeded consensus*) = [(0.75/(1/3)](1/3) = 0.75 or 75 percent. This probability is identical to your estimate of P(*DriveMed expands | EPS exceeded consensus*).

> When the prior probabilities are equal, the probability of information given an event equals the probability of the event given the information. When a decision-maker has equal prior probabilities (called **diffuse priors**), the probability of an event is determined by the information.

4.2. Principles of Counting

The first step in addressing a question often involves determining the different logical possibilities. We may also want to know the number of ways that each of these possibilities can happen. In the back of our mind is often a question about probability. How likely is it that I will observe this particular possibility? Records of success and failure are an example. When we evaluate a market timer's record, one well-known evaluation method uses counting methods presented in this section.[19] An important investment model, the binomial option pricing model, incorporates the combination formula that we will cover shortly. We can also use the methods in this section to calculate what we called a priori probabilities in Section 2. When we can assume that the possible outcomes of a random variable are equally likely, the probability of an event equals the number of possible outcomes favorable for the event divided by the total number of outcomes.

In counting, enumeration (counting the outcomes one by one) is of course the most basic resource. What we discuss in this section are shortcuts and principles. Without these shortcuts and principles, counting the total number of outcomes can be very difficult and prone to error. The first and basic principle of counting is the multiplication rule.

- **Multiplication Rule of Counting**. If one task can be done in n_1 ways, and a second task, given the first, can be done in n_2 ways, and a third task, given the first two tasks, can be done in n_3 ways, and so on for k tasks, then the number of ways the k tasks can be done is $(n_1)(n_2)(n_3)\ldots(n_k)$.

Suppose we have three steps in an investment decision process. The first step can be done in two ways, the second in four ways, and the third in three ways. Following the multiplication rule, there are $(2)(4)(3) = 24$ ways in which we can carry out the three steps.

Another illustration is the assignment of members of a group to an equal number of positions. For example, suppose you want to assign three security analysts to cover three different industries. In how many ways can the assignments be made? The first analyst may be assigned in three different ways. Then two industries remain. The second analyst can be assigned in two different ways. Then one industry remains. The third and last analyst can be assigned in only one way. The total number of different assignments equals $(3)(2)(1) = 6$. The compact notation for the multiplication we have just performed is 3! (read: 3 factorial). If we had n analysts, the number of ways we could assign them to n tasks would be

$$n! = n(n-1)(n-2)(n-3)\ldots 1$$

---

[19] Henriksson and Merton (1981).

or **n factorial**. (By convention, $0! = 1$.) To review, in this application we repeatedly carry out an operation (here, job assignment) until we use up all members of a group (here, three analysts). With n members in the group, the multiplication formula reduces to n factorial.[20]

The next type of counting problem can be called labeling problems.[21] We want to give each object in a group a label, to place it in a category. The following example illustrates this type of problem.

A mutual fund guide ranked 18 bond mutual funds by total returns for the year 2000. The guide also assigned each fund one of five risk labels: *high risk* (four funds), *above-average risk* (four funds), *average risk* (three funds), *below-average risk* (four funds), and *low risk* (three funds); as $4 + 4 + 3 + 4 + 3 = 18$, all the funds are accounted for. How many different ways can we take 18 mutual funds and label 4 of them high risk, 4 above-average risk, 3 average risk, 4 below-average risk, and 3 low risk, so that each fund is labeled?

The answer is close to 13 billion. We can label any of 18 funds *high risk* (the first slot), then any of 17 remaining funds, then any of 16 remaining funds, then any of 15 remaining funds (now we have 4 funds in the *high risk* group); then we can label any of 14 remaining funds *above-average risk*, then any of 13 remaining funds, and so forth. There are 18! possible sequences. However, order of assignment within a category does not matter. For example, whether a fund occupies the first or third slot of the four funds labeled *high risk*, the fund has the same label (*high risk*). Thus there are 4! ways to assign a given group of four funds to the four *high risk* slots. Making the same argument for the other categories, in total there are $(4!)(4!)(3!)(4!)(3!)$ equivalent sequences. To eliminate such redundancies from the 18! total, we divide 18! by $(4!)(4!)(3!)(4!)(3!)$. We have $18!/(4!)(4!)(3!)(4!)(3!) = 18!/(24)(24)(6)(24)(6) = 12,864,852,000$. This procedure generalizes as follows:

- **Multinomial Formula (General Formula for Labeling Problems).** The number of ways that n objects can be labeled with k different labels, with n_1 of the first type, n_2 of the second type, and so on, with $n_1 + n_2 + \cdots + n_k = n$, is given by

$$\frac{n!}{n_1! n_2! \ldots n_k!}$$

The multinomial formula with two different labels ($k = 2$) is especially important. This special case is called the combination formula. A **combination** is a listing in which the order of the listed items does not matter. We state the combination formula in a traditional way, but no new concepts are involved. Using the notation in the formula below, the number of objects with the first label is $r = n_1$ and the number with the second label is $n - r = n_2$ (there are just two categories, so $n_1 + n_2 = n$). Here is the formula.

- **Combination Formula (Binomial Formula).** The number of ways that we can choose r objects from a total of n objects, when the order in which the r objects are listed does not matter, is

$$_nC_r = \binom{n}{r} = \frac{n!}{(n-r)! r!}$$

---

[20]The shortest explanation of n factorial is that it is the number of ways to order n objects in a row. In all the problems to which we apply this counting method, we must use up all the members of a group (sampling without replacement).

[21]This discussion follows Kemeny, Schleifer, Snell, and Thompson (1972) in terminology and approach.

Here $_nC_r$ and $\binom{n}{r}$ are shorthand notations for $n!/(n-r)!r!$ (read: n choose r, or n combination r).

If we label the r objects as *belongs to the group* and the remaining objects as *does not belong to the group*, whatever the group of interest, the combination formula tells us how many ways we can select a group of size r. We can illustrate this formula with the binomial option pricing model. This model describes the movement of the underlying asset as a series of moves, price up (U) or price down (D). For example, two sequences of five moves containing three up moves, such as UUUDD and UDUUD, result in the same final stock price. At least for an option with a payoff dependent on final stock price, the number but not the order of up moves in a sequence matters. How many sequences of five moves *belong to the group with three up moves*? The answer is 10, calculated using the combination formula ("5 choose 3"):

$$_5C_3 = 5!/(5-3)!3!$$

$$= (5)(4)(3)(2)(1)/(2)(1)(3)(2)(1) = 120/12 = 10 \text{ ways}$$

A useful fact can be illustrated as follows: $_5C_3 = 5!/2!3!$ equals $_5C_2 = 5!/3!2!$, as $3 + 2 = 5$; $_5C_4 = 5!/1!4!$ equals $_5C_1 = 5!/4!1!$, as $4 + 1 = 5$. This symmetrical relationship can save work when we need to calculate many possible combinations.

Suppose jurors want to select three companies out of a group of five to receive the first-, second-, and third-place awards for the best annual report. In how many ways can the jurors make the three awards? Order does matter if we want to distinguish among the three awards (the rank within the group of three); clearly the question makes order important. On the other hand, if the question were "In how many ways can the jurors choose three winners, without regard to place of finish?" we would use the combination formula.

To address the first question above, we need to count ordered listings such as *first place, New Company; second place, Fir Company; third place, Well Company*. An ordered listing is known as a **permutation**, and the formula that counts the number of permutations is known as the permutation formula.[22]

- **Permutation Formula.** The number of ways that we can choose r objects from a total of n objects, when the order in which the r objects are listed does matter, is

$$_nP_r = \frac{n!}{(n-r)!}$$

So the jurors have $_5P_3 = 5!/(5-3)! = (5)(4)(3)(2)(1)/(2)(1) = 120/2 = 60$ ways in which they can make their awards. To see why this formula works, note that $(5)(4)(3)(2)(1)/(2)(1)$ reduces to $(5)(4)(3)$, after cancellation of terms. This calculation counts the number of ways to fill three slots choosing from a group of five people, according to the multiplication rule of counting. This number is naturally larger than it would be if order did not matter (compare 60 to the value of 10 for "5 choose 3" that we calculated above). For example, *first place, Well Company; second place, Fir Company; third place, New Company* contains the same three companies as *first place, New Company; second place, Fir Company; third place, Well Company*. If we were concerned only with award winners (without regard to

---

[22]A more formal definition states that a permutation is an ordered subset of n distinct objects.

place of finish), the two listings would count as one combination. But when we are concerned with the order of finish, the listings count as two permutations.

Answering the following questions may help you apply the counting methods we have presented in this section.

1. Does the task that I want to measure have a finite number of possible outcomes? If the answer is yes, you may be able to use a tool in this section, and you can go to the second question. If the answer is no, the number of outcomes is infinite, and the tools in this section do not apply.

2. Do I want to assign every member of a group of size n to one of n slots (or tasks)? If the answer is yes, use n factorial. If the answer is no, go to the third question.

3. Do I want to count the number of ways to apply one of three or more labels to each member of a group? If the answer is yes, use the multinomial formula. If the answer is no, go to the fourth question.

4. Do I want to count the number of ways that I can choose r objects from a total of n, when the order in which I list the r objects does not matter (can I give the r objects a label)? If the answer to these questions is yes, the combination formula applies. If the answer is no, go to the fifth question.

5. Do I want to count the number of ways I can choose r objects from a total of n, when the order in which I list the r objects is important? If the answer is yes, the permutation formula applies. If the answer is no, go to question 6.

6. Can the multiplication rule of counting be used? If it cannot, you may have to count the possibilities one by one, or use more advanced techniques than those presented here.[23]

---

[23]Feller (1957) contains a very full treatment of counting problems and solution methods.

CHAPTER 5

COMMON PROBABILITY DISTRIBUTIONS

1. INTRODUCTION

In nearly all investment decisions we work with random variables. The return on a stock and its earnings per share are familiar examples of random variables. To make probability statements about a random variable, we need to understand its probability distribution. A **probability distribution** specifies the probabilities of the possible outcomes of a random variable.

In this chapter, we present important facts about four probability distributions and their investment uses. These four distributions—the uniform, binomial, normal, and lognormal—are used extensively in investment analysis. They are used in such basic valuation models as the Black–Scholes–Merton option pricing model, the binomial option pricing model, and the capital asset pricing model. With the working knowledge of probability distributions provided in this chapter, you will also be better prepared to study and use other quantitative methods such as hypothesis testing, regression analysis, and time-series analysis.

After discussing probability distributions, we end the chapter with an introduction to Monte Carlo simulation, a computer-based tool for obtaining information on complex problems. For example, an investment analyst may want to experiment with an investment idea without actually implementing it. Or she may need to price a complex option for which no simple pricing formula exists. In these cases and many others, Monte Carlo simulation is an important resource. To conduct a Monte Carlo simulation, the analyst must identify risk factors associated with the problem and specify probability distributions for them. Hence, Monte Carlo simulation is a tool that requires an understanding of probability distributions.

Before we discuss specific probability distributions, we define basic concepts and terms. We then illustrate the operation of these concepts through the simplest distribution, the uniform distribution. That done, we address probability distributions that have more applications in investment work but also greater complexity.

2. DISCRETE RANDOM VARIABLES

A **random variable** is a quantity whose future outcomes are uncertain. The two basic types of random variables are discrete random variables and continuous random variables. A **discrete**

random variable can take on at most a countable number of possible values. For example, a discrete random variable X can take on a limited number of outcomes $x_1, x_2, \ldots, x_n$ (n possible outcomes), or a discrete random variable Y can take on an unlimited number of outcomes $y_1, y_2, \ldots$ (without end).[1] Because we can count all the possible outcomes of X and Y (even if we go on forever in the case of Y), both X and Y satisfy the definition of a discrete random variable. By contrast, we cannot count the outcomes of a **continuous random variable**. We cannot describe the possible outcomes of a continuous random variable Z with a list $z_1, z_2, \ldots$ because the outcome $(z_1 + z_2)/2$, not in the list, would always be possible. Rate of return is an example of a continuous random variable.

In working with a random variable, we need to understand its possible outcomes. For example, stocks traded on the New York Stock Exchange and Nasdaq are quoted in ticks of $0.01. Quoted stock price is thus a discrete random variable with possible values $0, $0.01, $0.02, \ldots But we can also model stock price as a continuous random variable (as a lognormal random variable, to look ahead). In many applications, we have a choice between using a discrete or a continuous distribution. We are usually guided by which distribution is most efficient for the task we face. This opportunity for choice is not surprising, as many discrete distributions can be approximated with a continuous distribution, and vice versa. In most practical cases, a probability distribution is only a mathematical idealization, or approximate model, of the relative frequencies of a random variable's possible outcomes.

EXAMPLE 5-1   The Distribution of Bond Price

You are researching a probability model for bond price, and you begin by thinking about the characteristics of bonds that affect price. What are the lowest and the highest possible values for bond price? Why? What are some other characteristics of bonds that may affect the distribution of bond price?

The lowest possible value of bond price is 0, when the bond is worthless. Identifying the highest possible value for bond price is more challenging. The promised payments on a coupon bond are the coupons (interest payments) plus the face amount (principal). The price of a bond is the present discounted value of these promised payments. Because investors require a return on their investments, 0 percent is the lower limit on the discount rate that investors would use to discount a bond's promised payments. At a discount rate of 0 percent, the price of a bond is the sum of the face value and the remaining coupons without any discounting. The discount rate thus places the upper limit on bond price. Suppose, for example, that face value is $1,000 and two $40 coupons remain; the interval $0 to $1,080 captures all possible values of the bond's price. This upper limit decreases through time as the number of remaining payments decreases.

---

[1] We follow the convention that an uppercase letter represents a random variable and a lowercase letter represents an outcome or specific value of the random variable. Thus X refers to the random variable, and x refers to an outcome of X. We subscript outcomes, as in x_1 and x_2, when we need to distinguish among different outcomes in a list of outcomes of a random variable.

> Other characteristics of a bond also affect its price distribution. Pull to par value is one such characteristic: As the maturity date approaches, the standard deviation of bond price tends to grow smaller as bond price converges to par value. Embedded options also affect bond price. For example, with bonds that are currently callable, the issuer may retire the bonds at a prespecified premium above par; this option of the issuer cuts off part of the bond's upside. Modeling bond price distribution is a challenging problem.

Every random variable is associated with a probability distribution that describes the variable completely. We can view a probability distribution in two ways. The basic view is the **probability function**, which specifies the probability that the random variable takes on a specific value: $P(X = x)$ is the probability that a random variable X takes on the value x. (Note that capital X represents the random variable and lowercase x represents a specific value that the random variable may take.) For a discrete random variable, the shorthand notation for the probability function is $p(x) = P(X = x)$. For continuous random variables, the probability function is denoted $f(x)$ and called the **probability density function** (pdf), or just the density.[2]

A probability function has two key properties (which we state, without loss of generality, using the notation for a discrete random variable):

- $0 \leq p(x) \leq 1$, because probability is a number between 0 and 1.
- The sum of the probabilities $p(x)$ over all values of X equals 1. If we add up the probabilities of all the distinct possible outcomes of a random variable, that sum must equal 1.

We are often interested in finding the probability of a range of outcomes rather than a specific outcome. In these cases, we take the second view of a probability distribution, the cumulative distribution function (cdf). The **cumulative distribution function**, or distribution function for short, gives the probability that a random variable X is less than or equal to a particular value x, $P(X \leq x)$. For both discrete and continuous random variables, the shorthand notation is $F(x) = P(X \leq x)$. How does the cumulative distribution function relate to the probability function? The word "cumulative" tells the story. To find $F(x)$, we sum up, or cumulate, values of the probability function for all outcomes less than or equal to x. The function of the cdf is parallel to that of cumulative relative frequency, which we discussed in the chapter on statistical concepts and market returns.

Next, we illustrate these concepts with examples and show how we use discrete and continuous distributions. We start with the simplest distribution, the discrete uniform.

2.1. The Discrete Uniform Distribution

The simplest of all probability distributions is the discrete uniform distribution. Suppose that the possible outcomes are the integers (whole numbers) 1 to 8, inclusive, and the probability that the random variable takes on any of these possible values is the same for all outcomes (that

---

[2]The technical term for the probability function of a discrete random variable, probability mass function (pmf), is used less frequently.

TABLE 5-1   Probability Function and Cumulative
Distribution Function for a Discrete Uniform Random Variable

$X = x$	Probability Function $p(x) = P(X = x)$	Cumulative Distribution Function $F(x) = P(X \leq x)$
1	0.125	0.125
2	0.125	0.250
3	0.125	0.375
4	0.125	0.500
5	0.125	0.625
6	0.125	0.750
7	0.125	0.875
8	0.125	1.000

is, it is uniform). With eight outcomes, $p(x) = 1/8$, or 0.125, for all value of X ($X = 1, 2, 3, 4,$ 5, 6, 7, 8); the statement just made is a complete description of this discrete uniform random variable. The distribution has a finite number of specified outcomes, and each outcome is equally likely. Table 5-1 summarizes the two views of this random variable, the probability function and the cumulative distribution function.

We can use Table 5-1 to find three probabilities: $P(X \leq 7)$, $P(4 \leq X \leq 6)$, and $P(4 < X \leq 6)$. The following examples illustrate how to use the cdf to find the probability that a random variable will fall in any interval (for any random variable, not only the uniform).

- The probability that X is less than or equal to 7, $P(X \leq 7)$, is the next-to-last entry in the third column, 0.875 or 87.5 percent.
- To find $P(4 \leq X \leq 6)$, we need to find the sum of three probabilities: $p(4)$, $p(5)$, and $p(6)$. We can find this sum in two ways. We can add $p(4)$, $p(5)$, and $p(6)$ from the second column. Or we can calculate the probability as the difference between two values of the cumulative distribution function:

$$F(6) = P(X \leq 6) = p(6) + p(5) + p(4) + p(3) + p(2) + p(1)$$
$$F(3) = P(X \leq 3) = p(3) + p(2) + p(1)$$

so

$$P(4 \leq X \leq 6) = F(6) - F(3) = p(6) + p(5) + p(4) = 3/8$$

So we calculate the second probability as $F(6) - F(3) = 3/8$.
- The third probability, $P(4 < X \leq 6)$, the probability that X is less than or equal to 6 but greater than 4, is $p(5) + p(6)$. We compute it as follows, using the cdf:

$$P(4 < X \leq 6) = P(X \leq 6) - P(X \leq 4) = F(6) - F(4) = p(6) + p(5) = 2/8$$

So we calculate the third probability as $F(6) - F(4) = 2/8$.

Suppose we want to check that the discrete uniform probability function satisfies the general properties of a probability function given earlier. The first property is $0 \leq p(x) \leq 1$. We see that $p(x) = 1/8$ for all x in the first column of the table. (Note that $p(x)$ equals 0 for numbers x such as -14 or 12.215 that are not in that column.) The first property is satisfied. The second property is that the probabilities sum to 1. The entries in the second column of Table 5-1 do sum to 1.

The cdf has two other characteristic properties:

- The cdf lies between 0 and 1 for any x: $0 \leq F(x) \leq 1$
- As we increase x, the cdf either increases or remains constant.

Check these statements by looking at the third column in Table 5-1.

We now have some experience working with probability functions and cdfs for discrete random variables. Later in this chapter, we will discuss Monte Carlo simulation, a methodology driven by random numbers. As we will see, the uniform distribution has an important technical use: It is the basis for generating random numbers, which in turn produce random observations for all other probability distributions.[3]

2.2. The Binomial Distribution

In many investment contexts, we view a result as either a success or a failure, or as binary (twofold) in some other way. When we make probability statements about a record of successes and failures, or about anything with binary outcomes, we often use the binomial distribution. What is a good model for how a stock price moves through time? Different models are appropriate for different uses. Cox, Ross, and Rubinstein (1979) developed an option pricing model based on binary moves, price up or price down, for the asset underlying the option. Their binomial option pricing model was the first of a class of related option pricing models that have played an important role in the development of the derivatives industry. That fact alone would be sufficient reason for studying the binomial distribution, but the binomial distribution has uses in decision-making as well.

The building block of the binomial distribution is the **Bernoulli random variable**, named after the Swiss probabilist Jakob Bernoulli (1654–1704). Suppose we have a trial (an event that may repeat) that produces one of two outcomes. Such a trial is a **Bernoulli trial**. If we let Y equal 1 when the outcome is success and Y equal 0 when the outcome is failure, then the probability function of the Bernoulli random variable Y is

$$p(1) = P(Y = 1) = p$$
$$p(0) = P(Y = 0) = 1 - p$$

where p is the probability that the trial is a success. Our next example is the very first step on the road to understanding the binomial option pricing model.

---

[3]See Hillier and Lieberman (2000). Random numbers initially generated by computers are usually random positive integer numbers that are converted to approximate continuous uniform random numbers between 0 and 1. Then the continuous uniform random numbers are used to produce random observations on other distributions, such as the normal, using various techniques. We will discuss random observation generation further in the section on Monte Carlo simulation.

EXAMPLE 5-2   One-Period Stock Price Movement as a Bernoulli Random Variable

Suppose we describe stock price movement in the following way. Stock price today is S. Next period stock price can move up or down. The probability of an up move is p, and the probability of a down move is $1 - p$. Thus, stock price is a Bernoulli random variable with probability of success (an up move) equal to p. When the stock moves up, ending price is uS, with u equal to 1 plus the rate of return if the stock moves up. For example, if the stock earns 0.01 or 1 percent on an up move, $u = 1.01$. When the stock moves down, ending price is dS, with d equal to 1 plus the rate of return if the stock moves down. For example, if the stock earns -0.01 or -1 percent on a down move, $d = 0.99$. Figure 5-1 shows a diagram of this model of stock price dynamics.

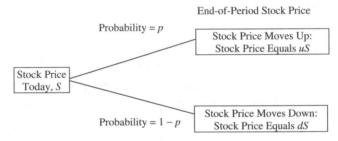

FIGURE 5-1   One-Period Stock Price as a Bernoulli Random Variable

---

We will continue with the above example later. In the model of stock price movement in Example 5-2, success and failure at a given trial relate to up moves and down moves, respectively. In the following example, success is a profitable trade and failure is an unprofitable one.

EXAMPLE 5-3   A Trading Desk Evaluates Block Brokers (1)

You work in equities trading at an institutional money manager that regularly trades with a number of block brokers. Blocks are orders to sell or buy that are too large for the liquidity ordinarily available in dealer networks or stock exchanges. Your firm has known interests in certain kinds of stock. Block brokers call your trading desk when they want to sell blocks of stocks that they think your firm may be interested in buying. You know that these transactions have definite risks. For example, if the broker's client (the seller of the shares) has unfavorable information on the stock, or if the total amount he is selling through all channels is not truthfully communicated to you, you may see an immediate loss on the trade. From time to time, your firm audits the performance of block brokers. Your firm calculates the post-trade, market-risk-adjusted dollar returns on stocks purchased from block brokers. On that basis, you classify each trade as unprofitable or profitable. You have summarized the performance of the brokers in a spreadsheet, excerpted in Table 5-2 for November 2003. (The broker names are coded BB001 and BB002.)

TABLE 5-2   Block Trading Gains and Losses

	November 2003	
	Profitable Trades	Losing Trades
BB001	3	9
BB002	5	3

View each trade as a Bernoulli trial. Calculate the percentage of profitable trades with the two block brokers for November 2003. These are estimates of p, the underlying probability of a successful (profitable) trade with each broker.

Your firm has logged $3 + 9 = 12$ trades (the row total) with block broker BB001. Because 3 of the 12 trades were profitable, the percentage of profitable trades was 3/12 or 25 percent. With broker BB002, the percentage of profitable trades was 5/8 or 62.5 percent. A trade is a Bernoulli trial, and the above calculations provide estimates of the underlying probability of a profitable trade (success) with the two brokers. For broker BB001, your estimate is $\hat{p} = 0.25$; for broker BB002, your estimate is $\hat{p} = 0.625$.[4]

In n Bernoulli trials, we can have 0 to n successes. If the outcome of an individual trial is random, the total number of successes in n trials is also random. A **binomial random variable** X is defined as the number of successes in n Bernoulli trials. A binomial random variable is the sum of Bernoulli random variables $Y_i, i = 1, 2, \ldots, n$:

$$X = Y_1 + Y_2 + \cdots + Y_n$$

where Y_i is the outcome on the ith trial (1 if a success, 0 if a failure). We know that a Bernoulli random variable is defined by the parameter p. The number of trials, n, is the second parameter of a binomial random variable. The binomial distribution makes these assumptions:

- The probability, p, of success is constant for all trials.
- The trials are independent.

---

[4]The "hat" over p indicates that it is an estimate of p, the underlying probability of a profitable trade with the broker.

The second assumption has great simplifying force. If individual trials were correlated, calculating the probability of a given number of successes in n trials would be much more complicated.

Under the above two assumptions, a binomial random variable is completely described by two parameters, n and p. We write

$$X \sim B(n, p)$$

which we read as "X has a binomial distribution with parameters n and p." You can see that a Bernoulli random variable is a binomial random variable with $n = 1$: $Y \sim B(1, p)$.

Now we can find the general expression for the probability that a binomial random variable shows x successes in n trials. We can think in terms of a model of stock price dynamics that can be generalized to allow any possible stock price movements if the periods are made extremely small. Each period is a Bernoulli trial: With probability p, the stock price moves up; with probability $1 - p$, the price moves down. A success is an up move, and x is the number of up moves or successes in n periods (trials). With each period's moves independent and p constant, the number of up moves in n periods is a binomial random variable. We now develop an expression for $P(X = x)$, the probability function for a binomial random variable.

Any sequence of n periods that shows exactly x up moves must show $n - x$ down moves. We have many different ways to order the up moves and down moves to get a total of x up moves, but given independent trials, any sequence with x up moves must occur with probability $p^x(1 - p)^{n-x}$. Now we need to multiply this probability by the number of different ways we can get a sequence with x up moves. Using a basic result in counting from the chapter on probability concepts, there are

$$\frac{n!}{(n - x)!x!}$$

different sequences in n trials that result in x up moves (or successes) and $n - x$ down moves (or failures). Recall from the chapter on probability concepts that n factorial ($n!$) is defined as $n(n - 1)(n - 2)\ldots 1$ (and $0! = 1$ by convention). For example, $5! = (5)(4)(3)(2)(1) = 120$. The combination formula $n!/[(n - x)!x!]$ is denoted by

$$\binom{n}{x}$$

(read "n combination x" or "n choose x"). For example, over three periods, exactly three different sequences have two up moves: UUD, UDU, and DUU. We confirm this by

$$\binom{3}{2} = \frac{3!}{(3 - 2)!2!} = \frac{(3)(2)(1)}{(1)(2)(1)} = 3$$

If, hypothetically, each sequence with two up moves had a probability of 0.15, then the total probability of two up moves in three periods would be $3 \times 0.15 = 0.45$. This example should persuade you that for X distributed $B(n, p)$, the probability of x successes in n trials is given by

$$p(x) = P(X = x) = \binom{n}{x} p^x(1 - p)^{n-x} = \frac{n!}{(n - x)!x!}p^x(1 - p)^{n-x} \qquad (5\text{-}1)$$

TABLE 5-3   Binomial Probabilities, $p = 0.50$ and $n = 5$

Number of Up Moves, x (1)	Number of Possible Ways to Reach x Up Moves (2)	Probability for Each Way (3)	Probability for x, $p(x)$ (4) = (2) × (3)	$F(x) = P(X \leq x)$ (5)
0	1	$0.50^0(1 - 0.50)^5 = 0.03125$	0.03125	0.03125
1	5	$0.50^1(1 - 0.50)^4 = 0.03125$	0.15625	0.18750
2	10	$0.50^2(1 - 0.50)^3 = 0.03125$	0.31250	0.50000
3	10	$0.50^3(1 - 0.50)^2 = 0.03125$	0.31250	0.81250
4	5	$0.50^4(1 - 0.50)^1 = 0.03125$	0.15625	0.96875
5	1	$0.50^5(1 - 0.50)^0 = 0.03125$	0.03125	1.00000

Some distributions are always symmetric, such as the normal, and others are always asymmetric or skewed, such as the lognormal. The binomial distribution is symmetric when the probability of success on a trial is 0.50, but it is asymmetric or skewed otherwise.

We illustrate Equation 5-1 (the probability function) and the cdf through the symmetrical case. Consider a random variable distributed $B(n = 5, p = 0.50)$. Table 5-3 contains a complete description of this random variable. The fourth column of Table 5-3 is Column 2, n combination x, times Column 3, $p^x(1 - p)^{n-x}$; Column 4 gives the probability for each value of the number of up moves from the first column. The fifth column, cumulating the entries in the fourth column, is the cumulative distribution function.

What would happen if we kept $n = 5$ but sharply lowered the probability of success on a trial to 10 percent? "Probability for Each Way" for $X = 0$ (no up moves) would then be about 59 percent: $0.10^0(1 - 0.10)^5 = 0.59049$. Because zero successes could still happen one way (Column 2), $p(0) = 59$ percent. You may want to check that given $p = 0.10, P(X \leq 2) = 99.14$ percent: The probability of two or fewer up moves would be more than 99 percent. The random variable's probability would be massed on 0, 1, and 2 up moves, and the probability of larger outcomes would be minute. The outcomes of 3 and larger would be the long right tail, and the distribution would be right skewed. On the other hand, if we set $p = 0.90$, we would have the mirror image of the distribution with $p = 0.10$. The distribution would be left skewed.

With an understanding of the binomial probability function in hand, we can continue with our example of block brokers.

EXAMPLE 5-4   A Trading Desk Evaluates Block Brokers (2)

You now want to evaluate the performance of the block brokers in Example 5-3. You begin with two questions:

1. If you are paying a fair price on average in your trades with a broker, what should be the probability of a profitable trade?

2. Did each broker meet or miss that expectation on probability?

You also realize that the brokers' performance has to be evaluated in light of the sample's size, and for that you need to use the binomial probability function (Equation 5-1). You thus address the following (referring to the data in Example 5-3):

3. Under the assumption that the prices of trades were fair,

    (a) calculate the probability of three or fewer profitable trades with broker BB001.
    (b) calculate the probability of five or more profitable trades with broker BB002.

Solutions to 1 and 2: If the price you trade at is fair, 50 percent of the trades you do with a broker should be profitable.[5] The rate of profitable trades with broker BB001 was 25 percent. Therefore, broker BB001 missed your performance expectation. Broker BB002, at 62.5 percent profitable trades, exceeded your expectation.

Solution to 3:
    A. For broker BB001, the number of trades (the trials) was $n = 12$, and 3 were profitable. You are asked to calculate the probability of three or fewer profitable trades, $F(3) = p(3) + p(2) + p(1) + p(0)$.
    Suppose the underlying probability of a profitable trade with BB001 is $p = 0.50$. With $n = 12$ and $p = 0.50$, according to Equation 5-1 the probability of three profitable trades is

$$p(3) = \binom{n}{x} p^x (1 - p)^{n-x} = \binom{12}{3} (0.50^3)(0.50^9)$$

$$= \frac{12!}{(12 - 3)!3!} 0.50^{12} = 220(0.000244) = 0.053711$$

The probability of exactly 3 profitable trades out of 12 is 5.4 percent if broker BB001 were giving you fair prices. Now you need to calculate the other probabilities:

$$p(2) = [12!/(12 - 2)!2!](0.50^2)(0.50^{10}) = 66(0.000244) = 0.016113$$

$$p(1) = [12!/(12 - 1)!1!](0.50^1)(0.50^{11}) = 12(0.000244) = 0.00293$$

$$p(0) = [12!/(12 - 0)!0!](0.50^0)(0.50^{12}) = 1(0.000244) = 0.000244$$

Adding all the probabilities, $F(3) = 0.053711 + 0.016113 + 0.00293 + 0.000244 = 0.072998$ or 7.3 percent. The probability of doing 3 or fewer profitable trades out of 12 would be 7.3 percent if your trading desk were getting fair prices from broker BB001.
    B. For broker BB002, you are assessing the probability that the underlying probability of a profitable trade with this broker was 50 percent, despite the good results. The question was framed as the probability of doing five or more profitable trades if the

---

[5] Of course, you need to adjust for the direction of the overall market after the trade (any broker's record will be helped by a bull market) and perhaps make other risk adjustments. Assume that these adjustments have been made.

underlying probability is 50 percent: $1 - F(4) = p(5) + p(6) + p(7) + p(8)$. You could calculate $F(4)$ and subtract it from 1, but you can also calculate $p(5) + p(6) + p(7) + p(8)$ directly.

You begin by calculating the probability that exactly 5 out of 8 trades would be profitable if BB002 were giving you fair prices:

$$p(5) = \binom{8}{5} (0.50^5)(0.50^3)$$

$$= 56(0.003906) = 0.21875$$

The probability is about 21.9 percent. The other probabilities are

$$p(6) = 28(0.003906) = 0.109375$$

$$p(7) = 8(0.003906) = 0.03125$$

$$p(8) = 1(0.003906) = 0.003906$$

So $p(5) + p(6) + p(7) + p(8) = 0.21875 + 0.109375 + 0.03125 + 0.003906 = 0.363281$ or 36.3 percent.[6] A 36.3 percent probability is substantial; the underlying probability of executing a fair trade with BB002 might well have been 0.50 despite your success with BB002 in November 2003. If one of the trades with BB002 had been reclassified from profitable to unprofitable, exactly half the trades would have been profitable. In summary, your trading desk is getting at least fair prices from BB002; you will probably want to accumulate additional evidence before concluding that you are trading at better-than-fair prices.

The magnitude of the profits and losses in these trades is another important consideration. If all profitable trades had small profits but all unprofitable trades had large losses, for example, you might lose money on your trades even if the majority of them were profitable.

In the next example, the binomial distribution helps in evaluating the performance of an investment manager.

EXAMPLE 5-5   Meeting a Tracking Error Objective

You work for a pension fund sponsor. You have assigned a new money manager to manage a $500 million portfolio indexed on the MSCI EAFE (Europe, Australasia, and Far East) Index, which is designed to measure developed-market equity performance

---

[6]In this example all calculations were worked through by hand, but binomial probability and cdf functions are also available in computer spreadsheet programs.

excluding the United States and Canada. After research, you believe it is reasonable to expect that the manager will keep tracking error within a band of 75 basis points (bps) of the benchmark's return, on a quarterly basis.[7] **Tracking error** is the total return on the portfolio (gross of fees) minus the total return on the benchmark index—here, the EAFE.[8] To quantify this expectation further, you will be satisfied if tracking error is within the 75 bps band 90 percent of the time. The manager meets the objective in six out of eight quarters. Of course, six out of eight quarters is a 75 percent success rate. But how does the manager's record precisely relate to your expectation of a 90 percent success rate and the sample size, 8 observations? To answer this question, you must find the probability that, given an assumed true or underlying success rate of 90 percent, performance could be as bad as or worse than that delivered. Calculate the probability (by hand or with a spreadsheet).

Specifically, you want to find the probability that tracking error is within the 75 bps band in six or fewer quarters out of the eight in the sample. With $n = 8$ and $p = 0.90$, this probability is $F(6) = p(6) + p(5) + p(4) + p(3) + p(2) + p(1) + p(0)$. Start with

$$p(6) = (8!/6!2!)(0.90^6)(0.10^2) = 28(0.005314) = 0.148803$$

and work through the other probabilities:

$$p(5) = (8!/5!3!)(0.90^5)(0.10^3) = 56(0.00059) = 0.033067$$

$$p(4) = (8!/4!4!)(0.90^4)(0.10^4) = 70(0.000066) = 0.004593$$

$$p(3) = (8!/3!5!)(0.90^3)(0.10^5) = 56(0.000007) = 0.000408$$

$$p(2) = (8!/2!6!)(0.90^2)(0.10^6) = 28(0.000001) = 0.000023$$

$$p(1) = (8!/1!7!)(0.90^1)(0.10^7) = 8(0.00000009) = 0.00000072$$

$$p(0) = (8!/0!8!)(0.90^0)(0.10^8) = 1(0.00000001) = 0.00000001$$

Summing all these probabilities, you conclude that $F(6) = 0.148803 + 0.033067 + 0.004593 + 0.000408 + 0.000023 + 0.00000072 + 0.00000001 = 0.186895$ or 18.7 percent. There is a moderate 18.7 percent probability that the manager would show the record he did (or a worse record) if he had the skill to meet your expectations 90 percent of the time.

You can use other evaluation concepts such as tracking risk, defined as the standard deviation of tracking error, to assess the manager's performance. The calculation above would be only one input into any conclusions that you reach concerning the manager's performance. But to answer problems involving success rates, you need to be skilled in using the binomial distribution.

---

[7]A basis point is one-hundredth of 1 percent (0.01 percent).
[8]Some practitioners use tracking error to describe what we later call tracking risk, the standard deviation of the differences between the portfolio's and benchmark's returns.

TABLE 5-4   Mean and Variance of
Binomial Random Variables

	Mean	Variance
Bernoulli, $B(1, p)$	p	$p(1 - p)$
Binomial, $B(n, p)$	np	$np(1 - p)$

Two descriptors of a distribution that are often used in investments are the mean and the variance (or the standard deviation, the positive square root of variance).[9] Table 5-4 gives the expressions for the mean and variance of binomial random variables.

Because a single Bernoulli random variable, $Y \sim B(1, p)$, takes on the value 1 with probability p and the value 0 with probability $1 - p$, its mean or weighted-average outcome is p. Its variance is $p(1 - p)$.[10] A general binomial random variable, $B(n, p)$, is the sum of n Bernoulli random variables, and so the mean of a $B(n, p)$ random variable is np. Given that a $B(1, p)$ variable has variance $p(1 - p)$, the variance of a $B(n, p)$ random variable is n times that value, or $np(1 - p)$, assuming that all the trials (Bernoulli random variables) are independent. We can illustrate the calculation for two binomial random variables with differing probabilities as follows:

Random Variable	Mean	Variance
$B(n = 5, \ p = 0.50)$	$2.50 = 5(0.50)$	$1.25 = 5(0.50)(0.50)$
$B(n = 5, \ p = 0.10)$	$0.50 = 5(0.10)$	$0.45 = 5(0.10)(0.90)$

For a $B(n = 5, \ p = 0.50)$ random variable, the expected number of successes is 2.5 with a standard deviation of $1.118 = (1.25)^{1/2}$; for a $B(n = 5, p = 0.10)$ random variable, the expected number of successes is 0.50 with a standard deviation of $0.67 = (0.45)^{1/2}$.

EXAMPLE 5-6   The Expected Number of Defaults in a Bond Portfolio

Suppose as a bond analyst you are asked to estimate the number of bond issues expected to default over the next year in an unmanaged high-yield bond portfolio with 25 U.S. issues from distinct issuers. The credit ratings of the bonds in the portfolio are tightly clustered around Moody's B2/Standard & Poor's B, meaning that the bonds

---

[9]The mean (or arithmetic mean) is the sum of all values in a distribution or dataset, divided by the number of values summed. The variance is a measure of dispersion about the mean. See the chapters on statistical concepts and market returns for further details on these concepts.

[10]We can show that $p(1 - p)$ is the variance of a Bernoulli random variable as follows, noting that a Bernoulli random variable can take on only one of two values, 1 or 0: $\sigma^2(Y) = E[(Y - EY)^2] = E[(Y - p)^2] = (1 - p)^2 p + (0 - p)^2 (1 - p) = (1 - p)[(1 - p)p + p^2] = p(1 - p)$.

are speculative with respect to the capacity to pay interest and repay principal. The estimated annual default rate for B2/B rated bonds is 10.7 percent.

1. Over the next year, what is the expected number of defaults in the portfolio, assuming a binomial model for defaults?
2. Estimate the standard deviation of the number of defaults over the coming year.
3. Critique the use of the binomial probability model in this context.

Solution to 1: For each bond, we can define a Bernoulli random variable equal to 1 if the bond defaults during the year and zero otherwise. With 25 bonds, the expected number of defaults over the year is $np = 25(0.107) = 2.675$ or approximately 3.

Solution to 2: The variance is $np(1 - p) = 25(0.107)(0.893) = 2.388775$. The standard deviation is $(2.388775)^{1/2} = 1.55$. Thus a two-standard-deviation confidence interval about the expected number of defaults would run from approximately 0 to approximately 6, for example.

Solution to 3: An assumption of the binomial model is that the trials are independent. In this context, a trial relates to whether an individual bond issue will default over the next year. Because the issuing companies probably share exposure to common economic factors, the trials may not be independent. Nevertheless, for a quick estimate of the expected number of defaults, the binomial model may be adequate.

Earlier, we looked at a simple one-period model for stock price movement. Now we extend the model to describe stock price movement on three consecutive days. Each day is an independent trial. The stock moves up with constant probability p (the **up transition probability**); if it moves up, u is 1 plus the rate of return for an up move. The stock moves down with constant probability $1 - p$ (the **down transition probability**); if it moves down, d is 1 plus the rate of return for a down move. We graph stock price movement in Figure 5-2, where we now associate each of the $n = 3$ stock price moves with time indexed by t. The shape of the graph suggests why it is called a **binomial tree**. Each boxed value from which successive moves or outcomes branch in the tree is called a **node**; in this example, a node is potential value for the stock price at a specified time.

We see from the tree that the stock price at $t = 3$ has four possible values: *uuuS, uudS, uddS,* and *dddS*. The probability that the stock price equals *any* one of these four values is given by the binomial distribution. For example, three sequences of moves result in a final stock price of *uudS*: These are *uud, udu,* and *duu*. These sequences have two up moves out of three moves in total; the combination formula confirms that the number of ways to get two up moves (successes) in three periods (trials) is $3!/(3 - 2)!2! = 3$. Next note that each of these sequences, *uud, udu,* and *duu*, has probability $p^2(1 - p)$. So $P(S_3 = uudS) = 3p^2(1 - p)$, where S_3 indicates the stock's price after three moves.

The binomial random variable in this application is the number of up moves. Final stock price distribution is a function of the initial stock price, the *number* of up moves, and the *size* of the up moves and down moves. We cannot say that stock price itself is a binomial random variable; rather, it is a function of a binomial random variable, as well as of u and d, and initial price. This richness is actually one key to why this way of modeling stock price is useful: It

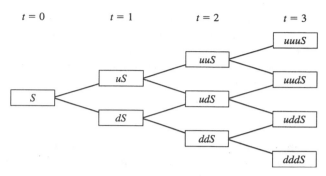

FIGURE 5-2   A Binomial Model of Stock Price Movement

allows us to choose values of these parameters to approximate various distributions for stock price (using a large number of time periods).[11] One distribution that can be approximated is the lognormal, an important continuous distribution model for stock price that we will discuss later. The flexibility extends further. In the tree shown above, the transition probabilities are the same at each node: p for an up move and $1 - p$ for a down move. That standard formula describes a process in which stock return volatility is constant through time. Option experts, however, sometimes model changing volatility through time using a binomial tree in which the probabilities for up and down moves differ at different nodes.

The binomial tree also supplies the possibility of testing a condition or contingency at any node. This flexibility is useful in investment applications such as option pricing. Consider an American call option on a dividend-paying stock. (Recall that an American option can be exercised at any time before expiration, at any node on the tree.) Just before an ex-dividend date, it may be optimal to exercise an American call option on stock to buy the stock and receive the dividend.[12] If we model stock price with a binomial tree, we can test, at each node, whether exercising the option is optimal. Also, if we know the value of the call at the four terminal nodes at $t = 3$ and we have a model for discounting values by one period, we can step backward one period to $t = 2$ to find the call's value at the three nodes there. Continuing back recursively, we can find the call's value today. This type of recursive operation is easily programmed on a computer. As a result, binomial trees can value options even more complex than American calls on stock.[13]

3. CONTINUOUS RANDOM VARIABLES

In the previous section, we considered discrete random variables (i.e., random variables whose set of possible outcomes is countable). In contrast, the possible outcomes of continuous random variables are never countable. If 1.250 is one possible value of a continuous random variable, for example, we cannot name the next higher or lower possible value. Technically, the

---

[11] For example, we can split 20 days into 100 subperiods, taking care to use compatible values for u and d.

[12] Cash dividends represent a reduction of a company's assets. Early exercise may be optimal because the exercise price of options is typically not reduced by the amount of cash dividends, so cash dividends negatively affect the position of an American call option holder.

[13] See Chance (2003) for more information on option pricing models.

range of possible outcomes of a continuous random variable is the real line (all real numbers between $-\infty$ and $+\infty$) or some subset of the real line.

In this section, we focus on the two most important continuous distributions in investment work, the normal and lognormal. As we did with discrete distributions, we introduce the topic through the uniform distribution.

3.1. Continuous Uniform Distribution

The continuous uniform distribution is the simplest continuous probability distribution. The uniform distribution has two main uses. As the basis of techniques for generating random numbers, the uniform distribution plays a role in Monte Carlo simulation. As the probability distribution that describes equally likely outcomes, the uniform distribution is an appropriate probability model to represent a particular kind of uncertainty in beliefs in which all outcomes appear equally likely.

The pdf for a uniform random variable is

$$f(x) = \begin{cases} \dfrac{1}{b-a} & \text{for } a < x < b \\ 0 & \text{otherwise} \end{cases}$$

For example, with $a = 0$ and $b = 8$, $f(x) = 1/8$ or 0.125. We graph this density in Figure 5-3. The graph of the density function plots as a horizontal line with a value of 0.125.

What is the probability that a uniform random variable with limits $a = 0$ and $b = 8$ is less than or equal to 3, or $F(3) = P(X \le 3)$? When we were working with the discrete uniform random variable with possible outcomes $1, 2, \ldots, 8$, we summed individual probabilities: $p(1) + p(2) + p(3) = 0.375$. In contrast, the probability that a continuous uniform random variable, or any continuous random variable, assumes any given fixed value is 0. To illustrate

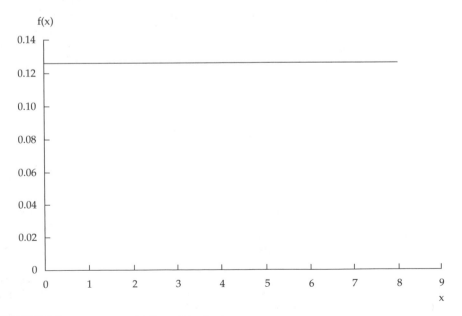

FIGURE 5-3   Continuous Uniform Distribution

this point, consider the narrow interval 2.510 to 2.511. Because that interval holds an infinity of possible values, the sum of the probabilities of values in that interval alone would be infinite if each individual value in it had a positive probability. To find the probability $F(3)$, we find the area under the curve graphing the pdf, between 0 to 3 on the x axis. In calculus, this operation is called integrating the probability function $f(x)$ from 0 to 3. This area under the curve is a rectangle with base $3 - 0 = 3$ and height 1/8. The area of this rectangle equals base times height: $3(1/8) = 3/8$ or 0.375. So $F(3) = 3/8$ or 0.375.

The interval from 0 to 3 is three-eighths of the total length between the limits of 0 and 8, and $F(3)$ is three-eighths of the total probability of 1. The middle line of the expression for the cdf captures this relationship.

$$F(x) = \begin{cases} 0 & \text{for } x \leq a \\[2mm] \dfrac{x - a}{b - a} & \text{for } a < x < b \\[2mm] 1 & \text{for } x \geq b \end{cases}$$

For our problem, $F(x) = 0$ for $x \leq 0$, $F(x) = x/8$ for $0 < x < 8$, and $F(x) = 1$ for $x \geq 8$. We graph this cdf in Figure 5-4.

The mathematical operation that corresponds to finding the area under the curve of a pdf $f(x)$ from a to b is the integral of $f(x)$ from a to b:

$$P(a \leq X \leq b) = \int_a^b f(x)\, dx \tag{5-2}$$

where $\int dx$ is the symbol for summing $\int$ over small changes dx, and the limits of integration (a and b) can be any real numbers or $-\infty$ and $+\infty$. All probabilities of continuous

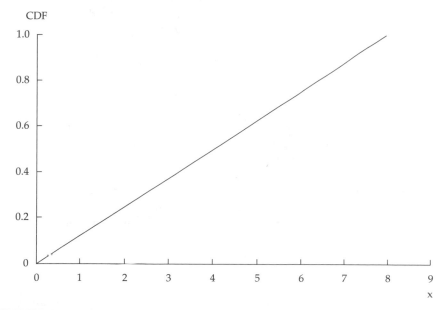

FIGURE 5-4   Continuous Uniform Cumulative Distribution

random variables can be computed using Equation 5-2. For the uniform distribution example considered above, $F(7)$ is Equation 5-2 with lower limit $a = 0$ and upper limit $b = 7$. The integral corresponding to the cdf of a uniform distribution reduces to the three-line expression given previously. To evaluate Equation 5-2 for nearly all other continuous distributions, including the normal and lognormal, we rely on spreadsheet functions, computer programs, or tables of values to calculate probabilities. Those tools use various numerical methods to evaluate the integral in Equation 5-2.

Recall that the probability of a continuous random variable equaling any fixed point is 0. This fact has an important consequence for working with the cumulative distribution function of a continuous random variable: For any continuous random variable X, $P(a \leq X \leq b) = P(a < X \leq b) = P(a \leq X < b) = P(a < X < b)$, because the probabilities at the endpoints a and b are 0. For discrete random variables, these relations of equality are not true, because probability accumulates at points.

EXAMPLE 5-7   Probability That a Lending Facility Covenant Is Breached

You are evaluating the bonds of a below-investment-grade borrower at a low point in its business cycle. You have many factors to consider, including the terms of the company's bank lending facilities. The contract creating a bank lending facility such as an unsecured line of credit typically has clauses known as covenants. These covenants place restrictions on what the borrower can do. The company will be in breach of a covenant in the lending facility if the interest coverage ratio, EBITDA/interest, calculated on EBITDA over the four trailing quarters, falls below 2.0. EBITDA is earnings before interest, taxes, depreciation, and amortization.[14] Compliance with the covenants will be checked at the end of the current quarter. If the covenant is breached, the bank can demand immediate repayment of all borrowings on the facility. That action would probably trigger a liquidity crisis for the company. With a high degree of confidence, you forecast interest charges of $25 million. Your estimate of EBITDA runs from $40 million on the low end to $60 million on the high end.

Address two questions (treating projected interest charges as a constant):

1. If the outcomes for EBITDA are equally likely, what is the probability that EBITDA/interest will fall below 2.0, breaching the covenant?
2. Estimate the mean and standard deviation of EBITDA/interest. For a continuous uniform random variable, the mean is given by $\mu = (a + b)/2$ and the variance is given by $\sigma^2 = (b - a)^2/12$.

Solution to 1:   EBITDA/interest is a continuous uniform random variable because all outcomes are equally likely. The ratio can take on values between $1.6 = (\$40$ million$)/(\$25$ million$)$ on the low end and $2.4 = (\$60$ million$/\$25$ million$)$ on the high end. The range of possible values is $2.4 - 1.6 = 0.8$. What fraction of the possible values

---

[14]For a detailed discussion on the use and misuse of EBITDA, see Moody's Investors Service Global Credit Research, *Putting EBITDA in Perspective* (June 2000).

falls below 2.0, the level that triggers default? The distance between 2.0 and 1.6 is 0.40; the value 0.40 is one-half the total length of 0.8, or $0.4/0.8 = 0.50$. So the probability that the covenant will be breached is 50 percent.

Solution to 2: In Solution 1, we found that the lower limit of EBITDA/interest is 1.6. This lower limit is *a*. We found that the upper limit is 2.4. This upper limit is *b*. Using the formula given above,

$$\mu = (a + b)/2 = (1.6 + 2.4)/2 = 2.0$$

The variance of the interest coverage ratio is

$$\sigma^2 = (b - a)^2/12 = (2.4 - 1.6)^2/12 = 0.053333$$

The standard deviation is the positive square root of the variance, $0.230940 = (0.053333)^{1/2}$. The standard deviation is not particularly useful as a risk measure for a uniform distribution, however. The probability that lies within various standard deviation bands around the mean is sensitive to different specifications of the upper and lower limits (although Chebyshev's inequality is always satisfied).[15] Here, a one-standard-deviation interval around the mean of 2.0 runs from 1.769 to 2.231 and captures $0.462/0.80 = 0.5775$ or 57.8 percent of the probability. A two-standard-deviation interval runs from 1.538 to 2.462, which extends past both the lower and upper limits of the random variable.

3.2. The Normal Distribution

The normal distribution may be the most extensively used probability distribution in quantitative work. It plays key roles in modern portfolio theory and in a number of risk management technologies. Because it has so many uses, the normal distribution must be thoroughly understood by investment professionals.

The role of the normal distribution in statistical inference and regression analysis is vastly extended by a crucial result known as the central limit theorem. The central limit theorem states that the sum (and mean) of a large number of independent random variables is approximately normally distributed.[16]

The French mathematician Abraham de Moivre (1667–1754) introduced the normal distribution in 1733 in developing a version of the central limit theorem. As Figure 5-5 shows, the normal distribution is symmetrical and bell-shaped.

The range of possible outcomes of the normal distribution is the entire real line: all real numbers lying between $-\infty$ and $+\infty$. The tails of the bell curve extend without limit to the left and to the right.

The defining characteristics of a normal distribution are as follows:

---

[15]Chebyshev's inequality is discussed in the chapter on statistical concepts and market returns.

[16]The central limit theorem is discussed further in the chapter on sampling.

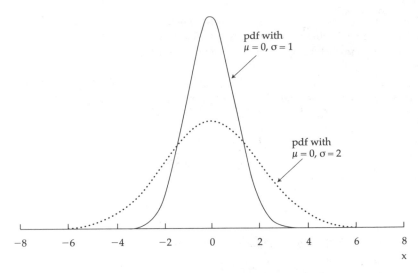

FIGURE 5-5   Two Normal Distributions

- The normal distribution is completely described by two parameters—its mean, μ, and variance, σ^2. We indicate this as $X \sim N(\mu, \sigma^2)$ (read "X follows a normal distribution with mean μ and variance σ^2"). We can also define a normal distribution in terms of the mean and the standard deviation, σ (this is often convenient because σ is measured in the same units as X and μ). As a consequence, we can answer any probability question about a normal random variable if we know its mean and variance (or standard deviation).
- The normal distribution has a skewness of 0 (it is symmetric). The normal distribution has a kurtosis (measure of peakedness) of 3; its excess kurtosis (kurtosis −3.0) equals 0.[17] As a consequence of symmetry, the mean, the median, and the mode are all equal for a normal random variable.
- A linear combination of two or more normal random variables is also normally distributed.

These bullet points concern a single variable or univariate normal distribution: the distribution of one normal random variable. A **univariate distribution** describes a single random variable. A **multivariate distribution** specifies the probabilities for a group of related random variables. You will encounter the **multivariate normal distribution** in investment work and reading and should know the following about it.

When we have a group of assets, we can model the distribution of returns on each asset individually, or the distribution of returns on the assets as a group. "As a group" means that we take account of all the statistical interrelationships among the return series. One model that has often been used for security returns is the multivariate normal distribution. A multivariate normal distribution for the returns on n stocks is completely defined by three lists of parameters:

---

[17] If we have a sample of size n from a normal distribution, we may want to know the possible variation in sample skewness and kurtosis. For a normal random variable, the standard deviation of sample skewness is $6/n$ and the standard deviation of sample kurtosis is $24/n$.

- the list of the mean returns on the individual securities (n means in total);
- the list of the securities' variances of return (n variances in total); and
- the list of all the distinct pairwise return correlations: $n(n-1)/2$ distinct correlations in total.[18]

The need to specify correlations is a distinguishing feature of the multivariate normal distribution in contrast to the univariate normal distribution.

The statement "assume returns are normally distributed" is sometimes used to mean a joint normal distribution. For a portfolio of 30 securities, for example, portfolio return is a weighted average of the returns on the 30 securities. A weighted average is a linear combination. Thus, portfolio return is normally distributed if the individual security returns are (joint) normally distributed. To review, in order to specify the normal distribution for portfolio return, we need the means, the variances, and the distinct pairwise correlations of the component securities.

With these concepts in mind, we can return to the normal distribution for one random variable. The curves graphed in Figure 5-5 are the normal density function:

$$f(x) = \frac{1}{\sigma\sqrt{2\pi}} \exp\left(\frac{-(x-\mu)^2}{2\sigma^2}\right) \text{ for } -\infty < x < +\infty \qquad (5\text{-}3)$$

The two densities graphed in Figure 5-5 correspond to a mean of $\mu = 0$ and standard deviations of $\sigma = 1$ and $\sigma = 2$. The normal density with $\mu = 0$ and $\sigma = 1$ is called the **standard normal distribution** (or **unit normal distribution**). Plotting two normal distributions with the same mean and different standard deviations helps us appreciate why standard deviation is a good measure of dispersion for the normal distribution: Observations are much more concentrated around the mean for the normal distribution with $\sigma = 1$ than for the normal distribution with $\sigma = 2$.

Although not literally accurate, the normal distribution can be considered an approximate model for returns. Nearly all the probability of a normal random variable is contained within three standard deviations of the mean. For realistic values of mean return and return standard deviation for many assets, the normal probability of outcomes below -100 percent is very small. Whether the approximation is useful in a given application is an empirical question. For example, the normal distribution is a closer fit for quarterly and yearly holding period returns on a diversified equity portfolio than it is for daily or weekly returns.[19] A persistent departure from normality in most equity return series is kurtosis greater than 3, the fat-tails problem. So when we approximate equity return distributions with the normal distribution, we should be aware that the normal distribution tends to underestimate the probability of extreme returns.[20] Option returns are skewed. Because the normal is a symmetrical distribution, we should be cautious in using the normal distribution to model the returns on portfolios containing significant positions in options.

---

[18] For example, a distribution with two stocks (a bivariate normal distribution) has two means, two variances, and one correlation: $2(2-1)/2$. A distribution with 30 stocks has 30 means, 30 variances, and 435 distinct correlations: $30(30-1)/2$. The return correlation of Dow Chemical with American Express stock is the same as the correlation of American Express with Dow Chemical stock, so these are counted as one distinct correlation.

[19] See Fama (1976) and Campbell, Lo, and MacKinlay (1997).

[20] Fat tails can be modeled by a mixture of normal random variables or by a Student's t-distribution with a relatively small number of degrees of freedom. See Kon (1984) and Campbell, Lo, and MacKinlay (1997). We discuss the Student's t-distribution in the chapter on sampling and estimation.

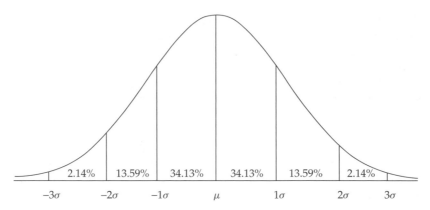

FIGURE 5-6   Units of Standard Deviation

The normal distribution, however, is less suitable as a model for asset prices than as a model for returns. A normal random variable has no lower limit. This characteristic has several implications for investment applications. An asset price can drop only to 0, at which point the asset becomes worthless. As a result, practitioners generally do not use the normal distribution to model the distribution of asset prices. Also note that moving from any level of asset price to 0 translates into a return of -100 percent. Because the normal distribution extends below 0 without limit, it cannot be literally accurate as a model for asset returns.

Having established that the normal distribution is the appropriate model for a variable of interest, we can use it to make the following probability statements:

- Approximately 50 percent of all observations fall in the interval $\mu \pm (2/3)\sigma$.
- Approximately 68 percent of all observations fall in the interval $\mu \pm \sigma$.
- Approximately 95 percent of all observations fall in the interval $\mu \pm 2\sigma$.
- Approximately 99 percent of all observations fall in the interval $\mu \pm 3\sigma$.

One, two, and three standard deviation intervals are illustrated in Figure 5-6. The intervals indicated are easy to remember but are only approximate for the stated probabilities. More-precise intervals are $\mu \pm 1.96\sigma$ for 95 percent of the observations and $\mu \pm 2.58\sigma$ for 99 percent of the observations.

In general, we do not observe the population mean or the population standard deviation of a distribution, so we need to estimate them.[21] We estimate the population mean, μ, using the sample mean, $\overline{X}$ (sometimes denoted as $\hat{\mu}$), and estimate the population standard deviation, σ, using the sample standard deviation, s (sometimes denoted as $\hat{\sigma}$). Using sample mean and the sample standard deviation to estimate the population mean and population standard deviation, respectively, we can make the following probability statements about a normally distributed random variable X, in which we use the more-precise numbers for standard deviation in stating intervals.

---

[21]A population is all members of a specified group, and the population mean is the arithmetic mean computed for the population. A sample is a subset of a population, and the sample mean is the arithmetic mean computed for the sample. For more information on these concepts, see the chapter on statistical concepts and market returns.

Confidence Intervals for Values of a Normal Random Variable X

- We expect 90 percent of the values of X to lie within the interval from $\overline{X} - 1.65s$ to $\overline{X} + 1.65s$. We call this interval a 90 percent confidence interval for X.
- We expect 95 percent of the values of X to lie within the interval from $\overline{X} - 1.96s$ to $\overline{X} + 1.96s$. We call this interval a 95 percent confidence interval for X.
- We expect 99 percent of the values of X to lie within the interval from $\overline{X} - 2.58s$ to $\overline{X} + 2.58s$. We call this interval a 99 percent confidence interval for X.

EXAMPLE 5-8 Probabilities for a Common Stock Portfolio (1)

You manage a U.S. core equity portfolio that is sector-neutral to the S&P 500 Index (its industry sector weights approximately match the S&P 500's). Taking a weighted average of the projected mean returns on the holdings, you forecast a portfolio return of 12 percent. You estimate a standard deviation of annual return of 22 percent, close to the long-run figure for the S&P 500. For the year-ahead return on the portfolio, you are asked to do the following:

1. Calculate and interpret a one-standard-deviation confidence interval for portfolio return, with a normality assumption for returns.
2. Calculate and interpret a 90 percent confidence interval for portfolio return, with a normality assumption for returns.
3. Calculate and interpret a 95 percent confidence interval for portfolio return, with a normality assumption for returns.

Solution to 1: A one-standard-deviation confidence interval is $\overline{X} \pm s$. With $\overline{X} = 12$ percent and $s = 22$ percent, the lower end of a one-standard-deviation interval is $-10\% = 12\% - 22\%$, and the upper end is $34\% = 12\% + 22\%$. The interval thus runs from -10 percent to 34 percent, and you expect approximately 68 percent of portfolio returns to lie within it, under normality. A compact notation for this one-standard-deviation confidence interval is $[-10\%, 34\%]$.

Solution to 2: A 90 percent confidence interval, with a normality assumption for returns, runs from $\overline{X} - 1.65s$ to $\overline{X} + 1.65s$. So the lower limit is $-24.3\% = 12\% - 1.65(22\%)$, and the upper limit is $48.3\% = 12\% + 1.65(22\%)$. Compactly, this interval is $[-24.3\%, 48.3\%]$.

Solution to 3: A 95 percent confidence interval, with a normality assumption for returns, goes from $\overline{X} - 1.96s$ to $\overline{X} + 1.96s$. So the lower limit is $-31.12\% = 12\% - 1.96(22\%)$, and the upper limit is $55.12\% = 12\% + 1.96(22\%)$. Compactly, this interval is $[-31.12\%, 55.12\%]$.

The 95 percent and 99 percent confidence intervals are probably the two most frequently used in practice. An approximate 95 percent confidence interval using 2 rather than 1.96 standard deviations as the multiplier gives a quick answer and thus is frequently used.

The calculation of the lower limit of −31.12 percent in Solution 3 illustrates an earlier point: For many realistic values of mean and standard deviation, the fact that the normal distribution extends to −∞ on the left may not be critical. For a normal distribution, only 2.5 percent of the total probability lies to the left of the mean minus 1.96 standard deviations (and 2.5 percent lies to the right of the mean plus 1.96 standard deviations). Figure 5-7 illustrates these probabilities by showing that 47.5 percent of the total probability lies between the mean and the mean plus (or minus) 1.96 standard deviations.

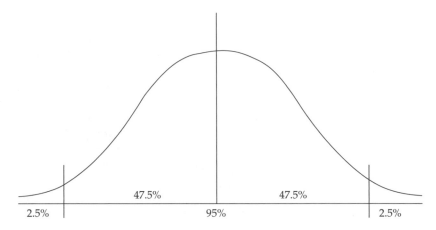

FIGURE 5-7   Tail Probabilities for a 95 Percent Confidence Interval

In working with confidence intervals, we specify the desired level of confidence and find the endpoints. We have given the formulas for important conventional intervals, but we may also have questions on other intervals, such as "How wide do I have to make the confidence interval to capture 75 percent of the returns on this portfolio?" We may also be interested in other probabilities. For example, we may ask, "What is the probability that the annual return on this equity index will be less than the one-year T-bill return?"

There are as many different normal distributions as there are choices for mean (μ) and variance (σ^2). We can answer all of the above questions in terms of any normal distribution. Spreadsheets, for example, have functions for the normal cdf for any specification of mean and variance. For the sake of efficiency, however, we would like to refer all probability statements to a single normal distribution. The standard normal distribution (the normal distribution with $\mu = 0$ and $\sigma = 1$) fills that role.

There are two steps in **standardizing** a random variable X: Subtract the mean of X from X, then divide that result by the standard deviation of X. If we have a list of observations on a normal random variable, X, we subtract the mean from each observation to get a list of deviations from the mean, then divide each deviation by the standard deviation. The result is the standard normal random variable, Z. (Z is the conventional symbol for a standard normal

TABLE 5-5 $P(Z \le x) = N(x)$ for $x \ge 0$ or $P(Z \le z) = N(z)$ for $z \ge 0$

x or z	0	0.01	0.02	0.03	0.04	0.05	0.06	0.07	0.08	0.09
0.00	0.5000	0.5040	0.5080	0.5120	0.5160	0.5199	0.5239	0.5279	0.5319	0.5359
0.10	0.5398	0.5438	0.5478	0.5517	0.5557	0.5596	0.5636	0.5675	0.5714	0.5753
0.20	0.5793	0.5832	0.5871	0.5910	0.5948	0.5987	0.6026	0.6064	0.6103	0.6141
0.30	0.6179	0.6217	0.6255	0.6293	0.6331	0.6368	0.6406	0.6443	0.6480	0.6517
0.40	0.6554	0.6591	0.6628	0.6664	0.6700	0.6736	0.6772	0.6808	0.6844	0.6879
0.50	0.6915	0.6950	0.6985	0.7019	0.7054	0.7088	0.7123	0.7157	0.7190	0.7224

random variable.) If we have $X \sim N(\mu, \sigma^2)$ (read "X follows the normal distribution with parameters μ and σ^2"), we standardize it using the formula

$$Z = (X - \mu)/\sigma \tag{5-4}$$

Suppose we have a normal random variable, X, with $\mu = 5$ and $\sigma = 1.5$. We standardize X with $Z = (X - 5)/1.5$. For example, a value $X = 9.5$ corresponds to a standardized value of 3, calculated as $Z = (9.5 - 5)/1.5 = 3$. The probability that we will observe a value as small as or smaller than 9.5 for $X \sim N(5, 1.5)$ is exactly the same as the probability that we will observe a value as small as or smaller than 3 for $Z \sim N(0, 1)$. We can answer all probability questions about X using standardized values and probability tables for Z. We generally do not know the population mean and standard deviation, so we often use the sample mean $\overline{X}$ for μ and the sample standard deviation s for σ.

Standard normal probabilities can also be computed with spreadsheets, statistical and econometric software, and programming languages. Tables of the cumulative distribution function for the standard normal random variable are in the back of this book. Table 5-5 shows an excerpt from those tables. $N(x)$ is a conventional notation for the cdf of a standard normal variable.[22]

To find the probability that a standard normal variable is less than or equal to 0.24, for example, locate the row that contains 0.20, look at the 0.04 column, and find the entry 0.5948. Thus, $P(Z \le 0.24) = 0.5948$ or 59.48 percent.

The following are some of the most frequently referenced values in the standard normal table:

- The 90th percentile point is 1.282: $P(Z \le 1.282) = N(1.282) = 0.90$ or 90 percent, and 10 percent of values remain in the right tail.
- The 95th percentile point is 1.65: $P(Z \le 1.65) = N(1.65) = 0.95$ or 95 percent, and 5 percent of values remain in the right tail. Note the difference between the use of a percentile point when dealing with one tail rather than two tails. Earlier, we used 1.65 standard deviations for the 90 percent confidence interval, where 5 percent of values lie outside that interval on each of the two sides. Here we use 1.65 because we are concerned with the 5 percent of values that lie only on one side, the right tail.
- The 99th percentile point is 2.327: $P(Z \le 2.327) = N(2.327) = 0.99$ or 99 percent, and 1 percent of values remain in the right tail.

---

[22]Another often-seen notation for the cdf of a standard normal variable is $\Phi(x)$.

The tables that we give for the normal cdf include probabilities for $x \leq 0$. Many sources, however, give tables only for $x \geq 0$. How would one use such tables to find a normal probability? Because of the symmetry of the normal distribution, we can find all probabilities using tables of the cdf of the standard normal random variable, $P(Z \leq x) = N(x)$, for $x \geq 0$. The relations below are helpful for using tables for $x \geq 0$, as well as in other uses:

- For a non-negative number x, use $N(x)$ from the table. Note that for the probability to the right of x, we have $P(Z \geq x) = 1.0 - N(x)$.
- For a negative number $-x$, $N(-x) = 1.0 - N(x)$: Find $N(x)$ and subtract it from 1. All the area under the normal curve to the left of x is $N(x)$. The balance, $1.0 - N(x)$, is the area and probability to the right of x. By the symmetry of the normal distribution around its mean, the area and the probability to the right of x are equal to the area and the probability to the left of $-x$, $N(-x)$.
- For the probability to the right of $-x$, $P(Z \geq -x) = N(x)$.

EXAMPLE 5-9   Probabilities for a Common Stock Portfolio (2)

Recall that in Example 5-8, the portfolio mean return estimate was 12 percent and the standard deviation of return estimate was 22 percent per year.

Using these estimates, you want to calculate the following probabilities, assuming that a normal distribution describes returns. (You can use the excerpt from the table of normal probabilities to answer these questions.)

1. What is the probability that portfolio return will exceed 20 percent?
2. What is the probability that portfolio return will be between 12 percent and 20 percent? In other words, what is $P(12\% \leq \text{Portfolio return} \leq 20\%)$?
3. You can buy a one-year T-bill that yields 5.5 percent. This yield is effectively a one-year risk-free interest rate. What is the probability that your portfolio's return will be equal to or less than the risk-free rate?

If X is portfolio return, standardized portfolio return is $Z = (X - \overline{X})/s = (X - 12\%)/22\%$. We use this expression throughout the solutions.

Solution to 1: For $X = 20\%$, $Z = (20\% - 12\%)/22\% = 0.363636$. You want to find $P(Z > 0.363636)$. First note that $P(Z > x) = P(Z \geq x)$ because the normal is a continuous distribution. Recall that $P(Z \geq x) = 1.0 - P(Z \leq x)$ or $1 - N(x)$. Rounding 0.363636 to 0.36, according to the table, $N(0.36) = 0.6406$. Thus, $1 - 0.6406 = 0.3594$. The probability that portfolio return will exceed 20 percent is about 36 percent if your normality assumption is accurate.

Solution to 2: $P(12\% \leq \text{Portfolio return} \leq 20\%) = N(Z \text{ corresponding to } 20\%) - N(Z \text{ corresponding to } 12\%)$. For the first term, $Z = (20\% - 12\%)/22\% = 0.36$

approximately, and $N(0.36) = 0.6406$ (as in Solution 1). To get the second term immediately, note that 12 percent is the mean, and for the normal distribution 50 percent of the probability lies on either side of the mean. Therefore, $N(Z$ corresponding to 12%) must equal 50 percent. So $P(12\% \leq$ Portfolio return $\leq 20\%) = 0.6406 - 0.50 = 0.1406$ or approximately 14 percent.

Solution to 3: If X is portfolio return, then we want to find P(Portfolio return $\leq 5.5\%$). This question is more challenging than Parts 1 or 2, but when you have studied the solution below, you will have a useful pattern for calculating other shortfall probabilities.

There are three steps, which involve standardizing the portfolio return: First, subtract the portfolio mean return from each side of the inequality: P(Portfolio return $- 12\% \leq 5.5\% - 12\%$). Second, divide each side of the inequality by the standard deviation of portfolio return: $P[$(Portfolio return $- 12\%)/22\% \leq (5.5\% - 12\%)/22\%] = P(Z \leq -0.295455) = N(-0.295455)$. Third, recognize that on the left-hand side we have a standard normal variable, denoted by Z. As we pointed out above, $N(-x) = 1 - N(x)$. Rounding -0.29545 to -0.30 for use with the excerpted table, we have $N(-0.30) = 1 - N(0.30) = 1 - 0.6179 = 0.3821$, roughly 38 percent. The probability that your portfolio will underperform the one-year risk-free rate is about 38 percent.

We can get the answer above quickly by subtracting the mean portfolio return from 5.5 percent, dividing by the standard deviation of portfolio return, and evaluating the result (-0.295455) with the standard normal cdf.

3.3. Applications of the Normal Distribution

Modern portfolio theory (MPT) makes wide use of the idea that the value of investment opportunities can be meaningfully measured in terms of mean return and variance of return. In economic theory, **mean–variance analysis** holds exactly when investors are risk averse; when they choose investments so as to maximize expected utility, or satisfaction; and when either (1) returns are normally distributed or (2) investors have quadratic utility functions.[23] Mean–variance analysis can still be useful, however—that is, it can hold approximately—when either assumption (1) or (2) is violated. Because practitioners prefer to work with observables such as returns, the proposition that returns are at least approximately normally distributed has played a key role in much of MPT.

Mean–variance analysis generally considers risk symmetrically in the sense that standard deviation captures variability both above and below the mean.[24] An alternative approach evaluates only downside risk. We discuss one such approach, safety-first rules, as it provides an excellent illustration of the application of normal distribution theory to practical investment problems. **Safety-first rules** focus on **shortfall risk**, the risk that portfolio value will fall below some minimum acceptable level over some time horizon. The risk that the assets in a defined benefit plan will fall below plan liabilities is an example of a shortfall risk.

Suppose an investor views any return below a level of R_L as unacceptable. Roy's safety-first criterion states that the optimal portfolio minimizes the probability that portfolio return, R_P,

---

[23] Utility functions are mathematical representations of attitudes toward risk and return.

[24] We shall discuss mean–variance analysis in detail in the chapter on portfolio concepts.

falls below the threshold level, R_L.[25] In symbols, the investor's objective is to choose a portfolio that minimizes $P(R_P < R_L)$. When portfolio returns are normally distributed, we can calculate $P(R_P < R_L)$ using the number of standard deviations that R_L lies below the expected portfolio return, $E(R_P)$. The portfolio for which $E(R_P) - R_L$ is largest relative to standard deviation minimizes $P(R_P < R_L)$. Therefore, if returns are normally distributed, the safety-first optimal portfolio *maximizes* the safety-first ratio (SFRatio):

$$\text{SFRatio} = [E(R_P) - R_L]/\sigma_P$$

The quantity $E(R_P) - R_L$ is the distance from the mean return to the shortfall level. Dividing this distance by σ_P gives the distance in units of standard deviation. There are two steps in choosing among portfolios using Roy's criterion (assuming normality):[26]

1. Calculate each portfolio's SFRatio.
2. Choose the portfolio with the highest SFRatio.

For a portfolio with a given safety-first ratio, the probability that its return will be less than R_L is $N(-\text{SFRatio})$, and the safety-first optimal portfolio has the lowest such probability. For example, suppose an investor's threshold return, R_L, is 2 percent. He is presented with two portfolios. Portfolio 1 has an expected return of 12 percent with a standard deviation of 15 percent. Portfolio 2 has an expected return of 14 percent with a standard deviation of 16 percent. The SFRatios are $0.667 = (12 - 2)/15$ and $0.75 = (14 - 2)/16$ for Portfolios 1 and 2, respectively. For the superior Portfolio 2, the probability that portfolio return will be less than 2 percent is $N(-0.75) = 1 - N(0.75) = 1 - 0.7734 = 0.227$ or about 23 percent, assuming that portfolio returns are normally distributed.

You may have noticed the similarity of SFRatio to the Sharpe ratio. If we substitute the risk-free rate, R_F, for the critical level R_L, the SFRatio becomes the Sharpe ratio. The safety-first approach provides a new perspective on the Sharpe ratio: When we evaluate portfolios using the Sharpe ratio, the portfolio with the highest Sharpe ratio is the one that minimizes the probability that portfolio return will be less than the risk-free rate (given a normality assumption).

EXAMPLE 5-10   The Safety-First Optimal Portfolio for a Client

You are researching asset allocations for a client with an $800,000 portfolio. Although her investment objective is long-term growth, at the end of a year she may want to liquidate $30,000 of the portfolio to fund educational expenses. If that need arises, she

---

[25] A.D. Roy (1952) introduced this criterion.

[26] If there is an asset offering a risk-free return over the time horizon being considered, and if R_L is less than or equal to that risk-free rate, then it is optimal to be fully invested in the risk-free asset. Holding the risk-free asset in this case eliminates the chance that the threshold return is not met.

would like to be able to take out the $30,000 without invading the initial capital of $800,000. Table 5-6 shows three alternative allocations.

TABLE 5-6   Mean and Standard Deviation for
Three Allocations (in percent)

	A	B	C
Expected annual return	25	11	14
Standard deviation of return	27	8	20

Address these questions (assume normality for Parts 2 and 3):

1. Given the client's desire not to invade the $800,000 principal, what is the shortfall level, R_L? Use this shortfall level to answer Part 2.
2. According to the safety-first criterion, which of the three allocations is the best?
3. What is the probability that the return on the safety-first optimal portfolio will be less than the shortfall level?

Solution to 1:   Because $30,000/$800,000 is 3.75 percent, for any return less than 3.75 percent the client will need to invade principal if she takes out $30,000. So $R_L = 3.75$ percent.

Solution to 2:   To decide which of the three allocations is safety-first optimal, select the alternative with the highest ratio $[E(R_P) - R_L]/\sigma_P$:

Allocation A: $0.787037 = (25 - 3.75)/27$

Allocation B: $0.90625 = (11 - 3.75)/8$

Allocation C: $0.5125 = (14 - 3.75)/20$

Allocation B, with the largest ratio (0.90625), is the best alternative according to the safety-first criterion.

Solution to 3:   To answer this question, note that $P(R_B < 3.75) = N(-0.90625)$. We can round 0.90625 to 0.91 for use with tables of the standard normal cdf. First, we calculate $N(-0.91) = 1 - N(0.91) = 1 - 0.8186 = 0.1814$ or about 18.1 percent. Using a spreadsheet function for the standard normal cdf on -0.90625 without rounding, we get 18.24 percent or about 18.2 percent. The safety-first optimal portfolio has a roughly 18 percent chance of not meeting a 3.75 percent return threshold.

Several points are worth noting. First, if the inputs were even slightly different, we could get a different ranking. For example, if the mean return on B were 10 rather than 11 percent, A would be superior to B. Second, if meeting the 3.75 percent return threshold were a necessity rather than a wish, $830,000 in one year could be modeled as a liability. Fixed income strategies such as cash flow matching could be used to offset or immunize the $830,000 quasi-liability.

Roy's safety-first rule was the earliest approach to addressing shortfall risk. The standard mean–variance portfolio selection process can also accommodate a shortfall risk constraint.[27]

In many investment contexts besides Roy's safety-first criterion, we use the normal distribution to estimate a probability. For example, Kolb, Gay, and Hunter (1985) developed an expression based on the standard normal distribution for the probability that a futures trader will exhaust his liquidity because of losses in a futures contract. Another arena in which the normal distribution plays an important role is financial risk management. Financial institutions such as investment banks, security dealers, and commercial banks have formal systems to measure and control financial risk at various levels, from trading positions to the overall risk for the firm.[28] Two mainstays in managing financial risk are Value at Risk (VAR) and stress testing/scenario analysis. **Stress testing/scenario analysis**, a complement to VAR, refers to a set of techniques for estimating losses in extremely unfavorable combinations of events or scenarios. **Value at Risk (VAR)** is a money measure of the minimum value of losses expected over a specified time period (for example, a day, a quarter, or a year) at a given level of probability (often 0.05 or 0.01). Suppose we specify a one-day time horizon and a level of probability of 0.05, which would be called a 95 percent one-day VAR.[29] If this VAR equaled €5 million for a portfolio, there would be a 0.05 probability that the portfolio would lose €5 million or more in a single day (assuming our assumptions were correct). One of the basic approaches to estimating VAR, the variance–covariance or analytical method, assumes that returns follow a normal distribution. For more information on VAR, see Chance (2003).

3.4. The Lognormal Distribution

Closely related to the normal distribution, the lognormal distribution is widely used for modeling the probability distribution of share and other asset prices. For example, the lognormal appears in the Black–Scholes–Merton option pricing model. The Black–Scholes–Merton model assumes that the price of the asset underlying the option is lognormally distributed.

A random variable Y follows a lognormal distribution if its natural logarithm, $\ln Y$, is normally distributed. The reverse is also true: If the natural logarithm of random variable $Y, \ln Y$, is normally distributed, then Y follows a lognormal distribution. If you think of the term lognormal as "the log is normal," you will have no trouble remembering this relationship.

The two most noteworthy observations about the lognormal distribution are that it is bounded below by 0 and it is skewed to the right (it has a long right tail). Note these two properties in the graphs of the pdfs of two lognormal distributions in Figure 5-8. Asset prices are bounded from below by 0. In practice, the lognormal distribution has been found to be

---

[27] See Leibowitz and Henriksson (1989), for example.

[28] **Financial risk** is risk relating to asset prices and other financial variables. The contrast is to other, nonfinancial risks (for example, relating to operations and technology), which require different tools to manage.

[29] In 95 percent one-day VAR, the 95 percent refers to the confidence in the value of VAR and is equal to $1 - 0.05$; this is a traditional way to state VAR.

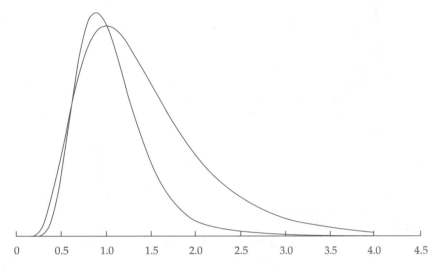

FIGURE 5-8   Two Lognormal Distributions

a usefully accurate description of the distribution of prices for many financial assets. On the other hand, the normal distribution is often a good approximation for returns. For this reason, both distributions are very important for finance professionals.

Like the normal distribution, the lognormal distribution is completely described by two parameters. Unlike the other distributions we have considered, a lognormal distribution is defined in terms of the parameters of a *different* distribution. The two parameters of a lognormal distribution are the mean and standard deviation (or variance) of its associated normal distribution: the mean and variance of ln Y, given that Y is lognormal. Remember, we must keep track of two sets of means and standard deviations (or variances): the mean and standard deviation (or variance) of the associated normal distribution (these are the parameters), and the mean and standard deviation (or variance) of the lognormal variable itself.

The expressions for the mean and variance of the lognormal variable itself are challenging. Suppose a normal random variable X has expected value μ and variance σ^2. Define $Y = \exp(X)$. Remember that the operation indicated by $\exp(X)$ or e^X is the opposite operation from taking logs.[30] Because ln $Y = \ln[\exp(X)] = X$ is normal (we assume X is normal), Y is lognormal. What is the expected value of $Y = \exp(X)$? A guess might be that the expected value of Y is $\exp(\mu)$. The expected value is actually $\exp(\mu + 0.50\sigma^2)$, which is larger than $\exp(\mu)$ by a factor of $\exp(0.50\sigma^2) > 1$.[31] To get some insight into this concept, think of what happens if we increase σ^2. The distribution spreads out; it can spread upward, but it cannot spread downward past 0. As a result, the center of its distribution is pushed to the right—the distribution's mean increases.[32]

The expressions for the mean and variance of a lognormal variable are summarized below, where μ and σ^2 are the mean and variance of the associated normal distribution (refer to these expressions as needed, rather than memorizing them):

---

[30]The quantity $e \approx 2.7182818$.
[31]Note that $\exp(0.50\sigma^2) > 1$ because $\sigma^2 > 0$.
[32]Luenberger (1998) is the source of this explanation.

- Mean (μ_L) of a lognormal random variable $= \exp(\mu + 0.50\sigma^2)$
- Variance (σ_L^2) of a lognormal random variable $= \exp(2\mu + \sigma^2) \times [\exp(\sigma^2) - 1]$

We now explore the relationship between the distribution of stock return and stock price. In the following we show that if a stock's continuously compounded return is normally distributed, then future stock price is necessarily lognormally distributed.[33] Furthermore, we show that stock price may be well described by the lognormal distribution even when continuously compounded returns do not follow a normal distribution. These results provide the theoretical foundation for using the lognormal distribution to model prices.

To outline the presentation that follows, we first show that the stock price at some future time T, S_T, equals the current stock price, S_0, multiplied by e raised to power $r_{0,T}$, the continuously compounded return from 0 to T; this relationship is expressed as $S_T = S_0 \exp(r_{0,T})$. We then show that we can write $r_{0,T}$ as the sum of shorter-term continuously compounded returns and that if these shorter-period returns are normally distributed, then $r_{0,T}$ is normally distributed (given certain assumptions) or approximately normally distributed (not making those assumptions). As S_T is proportional to the log of a normal random variable, S_T is lognormal.

To supply a framework for our discussion, suppose we have a series of equally spaced observations on stock price: $S_0, S_1, S_2, \ldots, S_T$. Current stock price, S_0, is a known quantity and so is nonrandom. The future prices (such as S_1), however, are random variables. The **price relative**, S_1/S_0, is an ending price, S_1, over a beginning price, S_0; it is equal to 1 plus the holding period return on the stock from $t = 0$ to $t = 1$:

$$S_1/S_0 = 1 + R_{0,1}$$

For example, if $S_0 = \$30$ and $S_1 = \$34.50$, then $S_1/S_0 = \$34.50/\$30 = 1.15$. Therefore, $R_{0,1} = 0.15$ or 15 percent. In general, price relatives have the form

$$S_{t+1}/S_t = 1 + R_{t,t+1}$$

where $R_{t,t+1}$ is the rate of return from t to $t + 1$.

An important concept is the continuously compounded return associated with a holding period return such as $R_{0,1}$. The **continuously compounded return** associated with a holding period is the natural logarithm of 1 plus that holding period return, or equivalently, the natural logarithm of the ending price over the beginning price (the price relative).[34] For example, if we observe a one-week holding period return of 0.04, the equivalent continuously compounded return, called the one-week continuously compounded return, is $\ln(1.04) = 0.039221$; €1.00 invested for one week at 0.039221 continuously compounded gives €1.04, equivalent to a 4 percent one-week holding period return. The continuously compounded return from t to $t + 1$ is

$$r_{t,t+1} = \ln(S_{t+1}/S_t) = \ln(1 + R_{t,t+1}) \tag{5-5}$$

---

[33] Continuous compounding treats time as essentially continuous or unbroken, in contrast to discrete compounding, which treats time as advancing in discrete finite intervals. Continuously compounded returns are the model for returns in so-called continuous time finance models such as the Black–Scholes–Merton option pricing model. See the chapter on the time value of money for more information on compounding.

[34] In this chapter only, we use lowercase r to refer specifically to continuously compounded returns.

For our example, $r_{0,1} = \ln(S_1/S_0) = \ln(1+R_{0,1}) = \ln(\$34.50/\$30) = \ln(1.15) = 0.139762$. Thus, 13.98 percent is the continuously compounded return from $t = 0$ to $t = 1$. The continuously compounded return is smaller than the associated holding period return. If our investment horizon extends from $t = 0$ to $t = T$, then the continuously compounded return to T is

$$r_{0,T} = \ln(S_T/S_0)$$

Applying the function exp to both sides of the equation, we have $\exp(r_{0,T}) = \exp[\ln(S_T/S_0)] = S_T/S_0$, so

$$S_T = S_0 \exp(r_{0,T})$$

We can also express S_T/S_0 as the product of price relatives:

$$S_T/S_0 = (S_T/S_{T-1})(S_{T-1}/S_{T-2})\ldots(S_1/S_0)$$

Taking logs of both sides of this equation, we find that continuously compounded return to time T is the sum of the one-period continuously compounded returns:

$$r_{0,T} = r_{T-1,T} + r_{T-2,T-1} + \cdots + r_{0,1} \tag{5-6}$$

Using holding period returns to find the ending value of a \$1 investment involves the multiplication of quantities (1 + holding period return). Using continuously compounded returns involves addition.

A key assumption in many investment applications is that returns are **independently and identically distributed** (IID). Independence captures the proposition that investors cannot predict future returns using past returns (i.e., weak-form market efficiency). Identical distribution captures the assumption of stationarity, to which we will return in the chapter on time-series analysis.[35]

Assume that the one-period continuously compounded returns (such as $r_{0,1}$) are IID random variables with mean μ and variance σ^2 (but making no normality or other distributional assumption). Then

$$E(r_{0,T}) = E(r_{T-1,T}) + E(r_{T-2,T-1}) + \cdots + E(r_{0,1}) = \mu T \tag{5-7}$$

(we add up μ for a total of T times) and

$$\sigma^2(r_{0,T}) = \sigma^2 T \tag{5-8}$$

(as a consequence of the independence assumption). The variance of the T holding period continuously compounded return is T multiplied by the variance of the one-period continuously compounded return; also, $\sigma(r_{0,T}) = \sigma\sqrt{T}$. If the one-period continuously compounded returns on the right-hand side of Equation 5-6 are normally distributed, then the T holding

---

[35] Stationarity implies that the mean and variance of return do not change from period to period.

period continuously compounded return, $r_{0,T}$, is also normally distributed with mean μT and variance $\sigma^2 T$. This relationship is so because a linear combination of normal random variables is also normal. But even if the one-period continuously compounded returns are not normal, their sum, $r_{0,T}$, is approximately normal according to a result in statistics known as the central limit theorem.[36] Now compare $S_T = S_0 \exp(r_{0,T})$ to $Y = \exp(X)$, where X is normal and Y is lognormal (as we discussed above). Clearly, we can model future stock price S_T as a lognormal random variable because $r_{0,T}$ should be at least approximately normal. This assumption of normally distributed returns is the basis in theory for the lognormal distribution as a model for the distribution of prices of shares and other assets.

Continuously compounded returns play a role in many option pricing models, as mentioned earlier. An estimate of volatility is crucial for using option pricing models such as the Black–Scholes–Merton model. **Volatility** measures the standard deviation of the continuously compounded returns on the underlying asset.[37] In practice, we very often estimate volatility using a historical series of continuously compounded daily returns. We gather a set of daily holding period returns and then use Equation 5-5 to convert them into continuously compounded daily returns. We then compute the standard deviation of the continuously compounded daily returns and annualize that number using Equation 5-8.[38] (By convention, volatility is stated as an annualized measure.)[39] Example 5-11 illustrates the estimation of volatility for the shares of Michelin.

EXAMPLE 5-11   Volatility as Used in Option Pricing Models

Suppose you are researching Michelin (Euronext: MICP.PA) and are interested in Michelin's price action in a week in which a number of international events affected stock markets. You decide to use volatility as a measure of the variability of Michelin shares during that week. Table 5-7 shows closing prices during that week.

---

[36]We mentioned the central limit theorem earlier in our discussion of the normal distribution. To give a somewhat fuller statement of it, according to the central limit theorem the sum (as well as the mean) of a set of independent, identically distributed random variables with finite variances is normally distributed, whatever distribution the random variables follow. We discuss the central limit theorem in the chapter on sampling.

[37]Volatility is also called the instantaneous standard deviation, and as such is denoted σ. The underlying asset, or simply the underlying, is the asset underlying the option. For more information on these concepts, see Chance (2003).

[38]To compute the standard deviation of a set or sample of n returns, we sum the squared deviation of each return from the mean return and then divide that sum by $n - 1$. The result is the sample variance. Taking the square root of the sample variance gives the sample standard deviation. To review the calculation of standard deviation, see the chapter on statistical concepts and market returns.

[39]Annualizing is often done on the basis of 250 days in a year, the approximate number of days markets are open for trading. The 250-day number may lead to a better estimate of volatility than the 365-day number. Thus if daily volatility were 0.01, we would state volatility (on an annual basis) as $0.01\sqrt{250} = 0.1581$.

TABLE 5-7   Michelin Daily
Closing Prices

Date	Closing Price
31 March 2003	€25.20
01 April 2003	€25.21
02 April 2003	€25.52
03 April 2003	€26.10
04 April 2003	€26.14

Source: http://fr.finance.yahoo.com.

Use the data in Table 5-7 to do the following:

1. Estimate the volatility of Michelin shares. (Annualize volatility based on 250 days in a year.)
2. Identify the probability distribution for Michelin share prices if continuously compounded daily returns follow the normal distribution.

Solution to 1: First, use Equation 5-5 to calculate the continuously compounded daily returns; then find their standard deviation in the usual way. (In the calculation of sample variance to get sample standard deviation, use a divisor of 1 less than the sample size.)

$$\ln(25.21/25.20) = 0.000397, \quad \ln(25.52/25.21) = 0.012222$$

$$\ln(26.10/25.52) = 0.022473, \quad \ln(26.14/26.10) = 0.001531$$

$$\text{Sum} = 0.036623, \quad \text{Mean} = 0.009156, \quad \text{Variance} = 0.000107,$$

$$\text{Standard Deviation} = 0.010354$$

The standard deviation of continuously compounded daily returns is 0.010354. Equation 5-8 states that $\hat{\sigma}(r_{0,T}) = \hat{\sigma}\sqrt{T}$. In this example, $\hat{\sigma}$ is the sample standard deviation of one-period continuously compounded returns. Thus, $\hat{\sigma}$ refers to 0.010354. We want to annualize, so the horizon T corresponds to one year. As $\hat{\sigma}$ is in days, we set T equal to the number of trading days in a year (250).

We find that annualized volatility for Michelin stock that week was 16.4 percent, calculated as $0.010354\sqrt{250} = 0.163711$.

Note that the sample mean, 0.009156, is a possible estimate of the mean, μ, of the continuously compounded one-period or daily returns. The sample mean can be translated into an estimate of the expected continuously compounded annual return using Equation 5-7: $\hat{\mu}T = 0.009156(250)$ (using 250 to be consistent with the calculation of volatility). But four observations are far too few to estimate expected returns. The variability in the daily returns overwhelms any information about expected return in a series this short.

Solution to 2: Michelin share prices should follow the lognormal distribution if the continuously compounded daily returns on Michelin shares follow the normal distribution.

We have shown that the distribution of stock price is lognormal, given certain assumptions. What are the mean and variance of S_T if S_T follows the lognormal distribution? Earlier in this section, we gave bullet-point expressions for the mean and variance of a lognormal random variable. In the bullet-point expressions, the $\hat{\mu}$ and $\hat{\sigma}^2$ would refer, in the context of this discussion, to the mean and variance of the T horizon (not the one-period) continuously compounded returns (assumed to follow a normal distribution), compatible with the horizon of S_T.[40] Related to the use of mean and variance (or standard deviation), earlier in this chapter we used those quantities to construct intervals in which we expect to find a certain percentage of the observations of a normally distributed random variable. Those intervals were symmetric about the mean. Can we state similar, symmetric intervals for a lognormal random variable? Unfortunately, we cannot. Because the lognormal distribution is not symmetric, such intervals are more complicated than for the normal distribution, and we will not discuss this specialist topic here.[41]

Finally, we have presented the relation between the mean and variance of continuously compounded returns associated with different time horizons (see Equations 5-7 and 5-8), but how are the means and variances of holding period returns and continuously compounded returns related? As analysts, we typically think in terms of holding period returns rather than continuously compounded returns, and we may desire to convert means and standard deviations of holding period returns to means and standard deviations of continuously compounded returns for an option application, for example. To effect such conversions (and those in the other direction, from a continuous compounding to a holding period basis), we can use the expressions in Ferguson (1993).

4. MONTE CARLO SIMULATION

With an understanding of probability distributions, we are now prepared to learn about a computer-based technique in which probability distributions play an integral role. The technique is called Monte Carlo simulation. **Monte Carlo simulation** in finance involves the use of a computer to represent the operation of a complex financial system. A characteristic feature of Monte Carlo simulation is the generation of a large number of random samples from a specified probability distribution or distributions to represent the role of risk in the system.

Monte Carlo simulation has several quite distinct uses. One use is in planning. Stanford University researcher Sam Savage provided the following neat picture of that role: "What is the last thing you do before you climb on a ladder? You shake it, and that is Monte Carlo simulation."[42] Just as shaking a ladder helps us assess the risks in climbing it, Monte Carlo simulation allows us to experiment with a proposed policy before actually implementing it. For example, investment performance can be evaluated with reference to a benchmark or a liability. Defined benefit pension plans often invest assets with reference to plan liabilities. Pension liabilities are a complex random process. In a Monte Carlo asset–liability financial planning study, the functioning of pension assets and liabilities is simulated over time, given assumptions

---

[40]The expression for the mean is $E(S_T) = S_0 \exp[E(r_{0,T}) + 0.5\sigma^2(r_{0,T})]$, for example.

[41]See Hull (2003) for a discussion of lognormal confidence intervals.

[42]*Business Week*, 22 January 2001.

about how assets are invested, the work force, and other variables. A key specification in this and all Monte Carlo simulations is the probability distributions of the various sources of risk (including interest rates and security market returns, in this case). The implications of different investment policy decisions on the plan's funded status can be assessed through simulated time. The experiment can be repeated for another set of assumptions. We can view Example 5-12 below as coming under this heading. In that example, market return series are not long enough to address researchers' questions on stock market timing, so the researchers simulate market returns to find answers to their questions.

Monte Carlo simulation is also widely used to develop estimates of VAR. In this application, we simulate the portfolio's profit and loss performance for a specified time horizon. Repeated trials within the simulation (each trial involving a draw of random observations from a probability distribution) produce a frequency distribution for changes in portfolio value. The point that defines the cutoff for the least favorable 5 percent of simulated changes is an estimate of 95 percent VAR, for example.

In an extremely important use, Monte Carlo simulation is a tool for valuing complex securities, particularly European-style options, for which no analytic pricing formula is available.[43] For other securities, such as mortgage-backed securities with complex embedded options, Monte Carlo simulation is also an important modeling resource.

Researchers use Monte Carlo simulation to test their models and tools. How critical is a particular assumption to the performance of a model? Because we control the assumptions when we do a simulation, we can run the model through a Monte Carlo simulation to examine a model's sensitivity to a change in our assumptions.

To understand the technique of Monte Carlo simulation, let us present the process as a series of steps.[44] To illustrate the steps, we take the case of using Monte Carlo simulation to value a type of option for which no analytic pricing formula is available, an Asian call option on a stock. An **Asian call option** is a European-style option with a value at maturity equal to the difference between the stock price at maturity and the average stock price during the life of the option, or $0, whichever is greater. For instance, if the final stock price is $34 with an average value of $31 over the life of the option, the value of the option at maturity is $3 (the greater of $34 − $31 = $3 and $0). Steps 1 through 3 of the process describe specifying the simulation; Steps 4 through 7 describe running the simulation.

1. Specify the quantities of interest (option value, for example, or the funded status of a pension plan) in terms of underlying variables. The underlying variable or variables could be stock price for an equity option, the market value of pension assets, or other variables relating to the pension benefit obligation for a pension plan. Specify the starting values of the underlying variables.

   To illustrate the steps, we are using the case of valuing an Asian call option on stock. We use C_{iT} to represent the value of the option at maturity T. The subscript i in C_{iT} indicates that C_{iT} is a value resulting from the ith **simulation trial**, each simulation trial involving a drawing of random values (an iteration of Step 4 below).

---

[43]A **European-style option** or **European option** is an option exercisable only at maturity.

[44]The steps should be viewed as providing an overview of Monte Carlo simulation rather than as a detailed recipe for implementing a Monte Carlo simulation in its many varied applications.

2. Specify a time grid. Take the horizon in terms of calendar time and split it into a number of subperiods, say K in total. Calendar time divided by the number of subperiods, K, is the time increment, Δt.

3. Specify distributional assumptions for the risk factors that drive the underlying variables. For example, stock price is the underlying variable for the Asian call, so we need a model for stock price movement. Say we choose the following model for changes in stock price, where Z_k stands for the standard normal random variable:

$$\Delta(\text{Stock price}) = (\mu \times \text{Prior stock price} \times \Delta t) + (\sigma \times \text{Prior stock price} \times Z_k)$$

In the way that we are using the term, Z_k is a risk factor in the simulation. Through our choice of μ and σ, we control the distribution of stock price. Although this example has one risk factor, a given simulation may have multiple risk factors.

4. Using a computer program or spreadsheet function, draw K random values of each risk factor. In our example, the spreadsheet function would produce a draw of K values of the standard normal variable Z_k: $Z_1, Z_2, Z_3, \ldots, Z_K$.

5. Calculate the underlying variables using the random observations generated in Step 4. Using the above model of stock price dynamics, the result is K observations on changes in stock price. An additional calculation is needed to convert those changes into K stock prices (using initial stock price, which is given). Another calculation produces the average stock price during the life of the option (the sum of K stock prices divided by K).

6. Compute the quantities of interest. In our example, the first calculation is the value of an Asian call at maturity, C_{iT}. A second calculation discounts this terminal value back to the present to get the call value as of today, C_{i0}. We have completed one simulation trial. (The subscript i in C_{i0} stands for the ith simulation trial, as it does in C_{iT}.) In a Monte Carlo simulation, a running tabulation is kept of statistics relating to the distribution of the quantities of interest, including their mean value and standard deviation, over the simulation trials to that point.

7. Iteratively go back to Step 4 until a specified number of trials, I, is completed. Finally, produce statistics for the simulation. The key value for our example is the mean value of C_{i0} for the total number of simulation trials. This mean value is the Monte Carlo estimate of the value of the Asian call.

How many simulation trials should be specified? In general, we need to increase the number of trials by a factor of 100 to get each extra digit of accuracy. Depending on the problem, tens of thousands of trials may be needed to obtain accuracy to two decimal places (as required for option value, for example). Conducting a large number of trials is not necessarily a problem, given today's computing power. The number of trials needed can be reduced using variance reduction procedures, a topic outside the scope of this book.[45]

In Step 4 of our example, a computer function produced a set of random observations on a standard normal random variable. Recall that for a uniform distribution, all possible numbers are equally likely. The term **random number generator** refers to an algorithm that produces uniformly distributed random numbers between 0 and 1. In the context of computer

---

[45] For details on this and other technical aspects of Monte Carlo simulation, see Hillier and Lieberman (2000).

simulations, the term **random number** refers to an observation drawn from a uniform distribution.[46] For other distributions, the term "random observation" is used in this context.

It is a remarkable fact that random observations from any distribution can be produced using the uniform random variable with endpoints 0 and 1. To see why this is so, consider the inverse transformation method of producing random observations. Suppose we are interested in obtaining random observations for a random variable, X, with cumulative distribution function $F(x)$. Recall that $F(x)$ evaluated at x is a number between 0 and 1. Suppose a random outcome of this random variable is 3.21 and that $F(3.21) = 0.25$ or 25 percent. Define an inverse of F, call it F^{-1}, that can do the following: Substitute the probability 0.25 into F^{-1} and it returns the random outcome 3.21. In other words, $F^{-1}(0.25) = 3.21$. To generate random observations on X, the steps are (1) generate a uniform random number, r, between 0 and 1 using the random number generator and (2) evaluate $F^{-1}(r)$ to obtain a random observation on X. Random observation generation is a field of study in itself, and we have briefly discussed the inverse transformation method here just to illustrate a point. As a generalist you do not need to address the technical details of converting random numbers into random observations, but you do need to know that random observations from any distribution can be generated using a uniform random variable.

In Examples 5-12 and 5-13, we give an application of Monte Carlo simulation to a question of great interest to investment practice: the potential gains from market timing.

EXAMPLE 5-12   Potential Gains from Market Timing: A Monte Carlo Simulation (1)

All active investors want to achieve superior performance. One possible source of superior performance is market timing ability. How accurate does an investor need to be as a bull- and bear-market forecaster for market timing to be profitable? What size gains compared with a buy-and-hold strategy accrue to a given level of accuracy? Because of the variability in asset returns, a huge amount of return data is needed to find statistically reliable answers to these questions. Chua, Woodward, and To (1987) thus selected Monte Carlo simulation to address the potential gains from market timing. They were interested in the perspective of a Canadian investor.

To understand their study, suppose that at the beginning of a year, an investor predicts that the next year will see either a bull market or bear market. If the prediction is *bull market,* the investor puts all her money in stocks and earns the market return for that year. On the other hand, if the prediction is *bear market,* the investor holds T-bills and earns the T-bill return. After the fact, a market is categorized as *bull market* if the stock market return, R_{Mt}, minus T-bill return, R_{Ft}, is positive for the year; otherwise, the market is classed as *bear market.* The investment results of a market timer can be

---

[46]The numbers that random number generators produce depend on a seed or initial value. If the same seed is fed to the same generator, it will produce the same sequence. All sequences eventually repeat. Because of this predictability, the technically correct name for the numbers produced by random number generators is **pseudo-random numbers**. Pseudo-random numbers have sufficient qualities of randomness for most practical purposes.

compared with those of a buy-and-hold investor. A buy-and-hold investor earns the market return every year. For Chua et al., one quantity of interest was the gain from market timing. They defined this quantity as the market timer's average return minus the average return to a buy-and-hold investor.

To simulate market returns, Chua et al. generated 10,000 random standard normal observations, Z_t. At the time of the study, Canadian stocks had a historical mean annual return of 12.95 percent with a standard deviation of 18.30 percent. To reflect these parameters, the simulated market returns are $R_{Mt} = 0.1830Z_t + 0.1295, t = 1, 2, \ldots, 10,000$. Using a second set of 10,000 random standard normal observations, historical return parameters for Canadian T-bills, as well as the historical correlation of T-bill and stock returns, the authors generated 10,000 T-bill returns.

An investor can have different skills in forecasting bull and bear markets. Chua et al. characterized market timers by accuracy in forecasting bull markets and accuracy in forecasting bear markets. For example, bull market forecasting accuracy of 50 percent means that when the timer forecasts *bull market* for the next year, she is right just half the time, indicating no skill. Suppose an investor has 60 percent accuracy in forecasting *bull market* and 80 percent accuracy in forecasting *bear market* (a 60–80 timer). We can simulate how an investor would fare. After generating the first observation on $R_{Mt} - R_{Ft}$, we know whether that observation is a bull or bear market. If the observation is *bull market,* then 0.60 (forecast accuracy for bull markets) is compared with a random number (between 0 and 1). If the random number is less than 0.60, which occurs with a 60 percent probability, then the market timer is assumed to have correctly predicted *bull market* and her return for that first observation is the market return. If the random number is greater than 0.60, then the market timer is assumed to have made an error and predicted *bear market;* her return for that observation is the risk-free rate. In a similar fashion, if that first observation is *bear market,* the timer has an 80 percent chance of being right in forecasting *bear market* based on a random number draw. In either case, her return is compared with the market return to record her gain versus a buy-and-hold strategy. That process is one simulation trial. The simulated mean return earned by the timer is the average return earned by the timer over all trials in the simulation.

To increase our understanding of the process, consider a hypothetical Monte Carlo simulation with four trials for the 60–80 timer (who, to reiterate, has 60 percent accuracy in forecasting bull markets and 80 percent accuracy in forecasting bear markets). Table 5-8 gives data for the simulation. Let us look at Trials 1 and 2. In Trial 1, the first random number drawn leads to a market return of 0.121. Because the market return, 0.121, exceeded the T-bill return, 0.050, we have a bull market. We generate a random number, 0.531, which we then compare with the timer's bull market accuracy, 0.60. Because 0.531 is less than 0.60, the timer is assumed to have made a correct bull market forecast and thus to have invested in stocks. Thus the timer earns the stock market return, 0.121, for that trial. In the second trial we observe another bull market, but because the random number 0.725 is greater than 0.60, the timer is assumed to have made an error and predicted a bear market; therefore, the timer earned the T-bill return, 0.081, rather than the higher stock market return.

TABLE 5-8   Hypothetical Simulation for a 60–80 Market Timer

	After Draws for Z_t and for the T-bill Return			Simulation Results		
Trial	R_{Mt}	R_{Ft}	Bull or Bear Market?	Value of X	Timer's Prediction Correct?	Return Earned by Timer
1	0.121	0.050	Bull	0.531	Yes	0.121
2	0.092	0.081	Bull	0.725	No	0.081
3	−0.020	0.034	Bear	0.786	Yes	0.034
4	0.052	0.055	*A*	0.901	*B*	*C*
						$\overline{R} = D$

Note: $\overline{R}$ is the mean return earned by the timer over the four simulation trials.

Using the data in Table 5-8, determine the values of A, B, C, and D.

Solution: The value of A is *Bear* because the stock market return was less than the T-bill return in Trial 4. The value of B is *No*. Because we observe a bear market, we compare the random number 0.901 with 0.80, the timer's bear-market forecasting accuracy. Because 0.901 is greater than 0.8, the timer is assumed to have made an error. The value of C is 0.052, the return on the stock market, because the timer made an error and invested in the stock market and earned 0.052 rather than the higher T-bill return of 0.055. The value of D is $\overline{R} = (0.121 + 0.081 + 0.034 + 0.052) = 0.288/4 = 0.072$. Note that we could calculate other statistics besides the mean, such as the standard deviation of the returns earned by the timer over the four trials in the simulation.

EXAMPLE 5-13   Potential Gains from Market Timing: A Monte Carlo Simulation (2)

Having discussed the plan of the Chua et al. study and illustrated the method for a hypothetical Monte Carlo simulation with four trials, we conclude our presentation of the study.

The hypothetical simulation in Example 5-12 had four trials, far too few to reach statistically precise conclusions. The simulation of Chua et al. incorporated 10,000 trials. Chua et al. specified bull- and bear-market prediction skill levels of 50, 60, 70, 80, 90, and 100 percent. Table 5-9 presents a very small excerpt from their simulation results for the no transaction costs case (transaction costs were also examined). Reading across the row, the timer with 60 percent bull market and 80 percent bear market forecasting accuracy had a mean annual gain from market timing of −1.12 percent per year. On average, the buy-and-hold investor out-earned this skillful timer by 1.12

percentage points. There was substantial variability in gains across the simulation trials, however: The standard deviation of the gain was 14.77 percent, so in many trials (but not on average) the gain was positive. Row 3 (win/loss) is the ratio of profitable switches between stocks and T-bills to unprofitable switches. This ratio was a favorable 1.2070 for the 60–80 timer. (When transaction costs were considered, however, fewer switches are profitable: The win/loss ratio was 0.5832 for the 60–80 timer.)

TABLE 5-9   Gains from Stock Market Timing (No Transaction Costs)

Bull Market Accuracy (%)		Bear Market Accuracy (%)					
		50	60	70	80	90	100
60	Mean (%)	−2.50	−1.99	−1.57	−1.12	−0.68	−0.22
	S.D. (%)	13.65	14.11	14.45	14.77	15.08	15.42
	Win/Loss	0.7418	0.9062	1.0503	1.2070	1.3496	1.4986

Source: Chua, Woodward, and To (1987), Table II (excerpt).

The authors concluded that the cost of not being invested in the market during bull market years is high. Because a buy-and-hold investor never misses a bull market year, she has 100 percent forecast accuracy for bull markets (at the cost of 0 percent accuracy for bear markets). Given their definitions and assumptions, the authors also concluded that successful market timing requires a minimum accuracy of 80 percent in forecasting both bull and bear markets. Market timing is a continuing area of interest and study, and other perspectives exist. However, this example illustrates how Monte Carlo simulation is used to address important investment issues.

The analyst chooses the probability distributions in Monte Carlo simulation. By contrast, **historical simulation** samples from a historical record of returns (or other underlying variables) to simulate a process. The concept underlying historical simulation (also called **back simulation**) is that the historical record provides the most direct evidence on distributions (and that the past applies to the future). For example, refer back to Step 2 in the outline of Monte Carlo simulation above and suppose the time increment is one day. Further, suppose we base the simulation on the record of daily stock returns over the last five years. In one type of historical simulation, we randomly draw K returns from that record to generate one simulation trial. We put back the observations into the sample, and in the next trial we again randomly sample with replacement. The simulation results directly reflect frequencies in the data. A drawback of this approach is that any risk not represented in the time period selected (for example, a stock market crash) will not be reflected in the simulation. Compared with Monte Carlo simulation, historical simulation does not lend itself to "what if" analyses. Nevertheless, historic simulation is an established alternative simulation methodology.

Monte Carlo simulation is a complement to analytical methods. It provides only statistical estimates, not exact results. Analytical methods, where available, provide more insight into cause-and-effect relationships. For example, the Black–Scholes–Merton option pricing model for the value of a European call option is an analytical method, expressed as a formula. It is a much more efficient method for valuing such a call than is Monte Carlo simulation. As an analytical expression, the Black–Scholes–Merton model permits the analyst to quickly gauge the sensitivity of call value to changes in current stock price and the other variables that determine call value. In contrast, Monte Carlo simulations do not directly provide such precise insights. However, only some types of options can be priced with analytical expressions. As financial product innovations proceed, the field of applications for Monte Carlo simulation continues to grow.

CHAPTER 6

SAMPLING AND ESTIMATION

1. INTRODUCTION

Each day, we observe the high, low, and close of stock market indexes from around the world. Indexes such as the S&P 500 Index and the Nikkei–Dow Jones Average are samples of stocks. Although the S&P 500 and the Nikkei do not represent the populations of U.S. or Japanese stocks, we view them as valid indicators of the whole population's behavior. As analysts, we are accustomed to using this sample information to assess how various markets from around the world are performing. Any statistics that we compute with sample information, however, are only estimates of the underlying population parameters. A sample, then, is a subset of the population—a subset studied to infer conclusions about the population itself.

This chapter explores how we sample and use sample information to estimate population parameters. In the next section, we discuss **sampling**—the process of obtaining a sample. In investments, we continually make use of the mean as a measure of central tendency of random variables, such as return and earnings per share. Even when the probability distribution of the random variable is unknown, we can make probability statements about the population mean using the central limit theorem. In Section 3, we discuss and illustrate this key result. Following that discussion, we turn to statistical estimation. Estimation seeks precise answers to the question "What is this parameter's value?"

The central limit theorem and estimation are the core of the body of methods presented in this chapter. In investments, we apply these and other statistical techniques to financial data; we often interpret the results for the purpose of deciding what works and what does not work in investments. We end this chapter with a discussion of the interpretation of statistical results based on financial data and the possible pitfalls in this process.

2. SAMPLING

In this section, we present the various methods for obtaining information on a population (all members of a specified group) through samples (part of the population). The information on a population that we try to obtain usually concerns the value of a **parameter**, a quantity computed from or used to describe a population of data. When we use a sample to estimate a parameter, we make use of sample statistics (statistics, for short). A **statistic** is a quantity computed from or used to describe a sample of data.

We take samples for one of two reasons. In some cases, we cannot possibly examine every member of the population. In other cases, examining every member of the population would not be economically efficient. Thus, savings of time and money are two primary factors that cause an analyst to use sampling to answer a question about a population. In this section, we discuss two methods of random sampling: simple random sampling and stratified random sampling. We then define and illustrate the two types of data an analyst uses: cross-sectional data and time-series data.

2.1. Simple Random Sampling

Suppose a telecommunications equipment analyst wants to know how much major customers will spend on average for equipment during the coming year. One strategy is to survey the population of telecom equipment customers and inquire what their purchasing plans are. In statistical terms, the characteristics of the population of customers' planned expenditures would then usually be expressed by descriptive measures such as the mean and variance. Surveying all companies, however, would be very costly in terms of time and money.

Alternatively, the analyst can collect a representative sample of companies and survey them about upcoming telecom equipment expenditures. In this case, the analyst will compute the sample mean expenditure, $\overline{X}$, a statistic. This strategy has a substantial advantage over polling the whole population because it can be accomplished more quickly and at lower cost.

Sampling, however, introduces error. The error arises because not all the companies in the population are surveyed. The analyst who decides to sample is trading time and money for sampling error.

When an analyst chooses to sample, he must formulate a sampling plan. A **sampling plan** is the set of rules used to select a sample. The basic type of sample from which we can draw statistically sound conclusions about a population is the **simple random sample** (random sample, for short).

- **Definition of Simple Random Sample**. A simple random sample is a subset of a larger population created in such a way that each element of the population has an equal probability of being selected to the subset.

The procedure of drawing a sample to satisfy the definition of a simple random sample is called **simple random sampling**. How is simple random sampling carried out? We need a method that ensures randomness—the lack of any pattern—in the selection of the sample. For a finite (limited) population, the most common method for obtaining a random sample involves the use of random numbers (numbers with assured properties of randomness). First, we number the members of the population in sequence. For example, if the population contains 500 members, we number them in sequence with three digits, starting with 001 and ending with 500. Suppose we want a simple random sample of size 50. In that case, using a computer random-number generator or a table of random numbers, we generate a series of three-digit random numbers. We then match these random numbers with the number codes of the population members until we have selected a sample of size 50.

Sometimes we cannot code (or even identify) all the members of a population. We often use **systematic sampling** in such cases. With systematic sampling, we select every kth member until we have a sample of the desired size. The sample that results from this procedure should be approximately random. Real sampling situations may require that we take an approximately random sample.

Suppose the telecommunications equipment analyst polls a random sample of telecom equipment customers to determine the average equipment expenditure. The sample mean will provide the analyst with an estimate of the population mean expenditure. Any difference between the sample mean and the population mean is called **sampling error**.

- **Definition of Sampling Error.**   Sampling error is the difference between the observed value of a statistic and the quantity it is intended to estimate.

A random sample reflects the properties of the population in an unbiased way, and sample statistics, such as the sample mean, computed on the basis of a random sample are valid estimates of the underlying population parameters.

A sample statistic is a random variable. In other words, not only do the original data from the population have a distribution but so does the sample statistic. This distribution is the statistic's sampling distribution.

- **Definition of Sampling Distribution of a Statistic.**   The sampling distribution of a statistic is the distribution of all the distinct possible values that the statistic can assume when computed from samples of the same size randomly drawn from the same population.

In the case of the sample mean, for example, we refer to the "sampling distribution of the sample mean" or the distribution of the sample mean. We will have more to say about sampling distributions later in this chapter. Next, however, we look at another sampling method that is useful in investment analysis.

2.2. Stratified Random Sampling

The simple random sampling method just discussed may not be the best approach in all situations. One frequently used alternative is stratified random sampling.

- **Definition of Stratified Random Sampling.**   In stratified random sampling, the population is divided into subpopulations (strata) based on one or more classification criteria. Simple random samples are then drawn from each stratum in sizes proportional to the relative size of each stratum in the population. These samples are then pooled to form a stratified random sample.

In contrast to simple random sampling, stratified random sampling guarantees that population subdivisions of interest are represented in the sample. Another advantage is that estimates of parameters produced from stratified sampling have greater precision—that is, smaller variance or dispersion—than estimates obtained from simple random sampling.

Bond indexing is one area in which stratified sampling is frequently applied. **Indexing** is an investment strategy in which an investor constructs a portfolio to mirror the performance of a specified index. In pure bond indexing, also called the full-replication approach, the investor attempts to fully replicate an index by owning all the bonds in the index in proportion to their market value weights. Many bond indexes consist of thousands of issues, however, so pure bond indexing is difficult to implement. In addition, transaction costs would be high because many bonds do not have liquid markets. Although a simple random sample could be a solution to the cost problem, the sample would probably not match the index's major risk factors—interest rate sensitivity, for example. Because the major risk factors of fixed-income portfolios are well known and quantifiable, stratified sampling offers a more effective approach. In this approach, we divide the population of index bonds into groups of similar duration (interest rate sensitivity), cash flow distribution, sector, credit quality, and call exposure. We refer to each group as a stratum or cell (a term frequently used in this context).[1] Then, we choose a sample from each stratum proportional to the relative market weighting of the stratum in the index to be replicated.

EXAMPLE 6-1   Bond Indexes and Stratified Sampling

Suppose you are the manager of a mutual fund indexed to the Lehman Brothers Government Index. You are exploring several approaches to indexing, including a stratified sampling approach. You first distinguish agency bonds from U.S. Treasury bonds. For each of these two groups, you define 10 maturity intervals—1 to 2 years, 2 to 3 years, 3 to 4 years, 4 to 6 years, 6 to 8 years, 8 to 10 years, 10 to 12 years, 12 to 15 years, 15 to 20 years, and 20 to 30 years—and also separate the bonds with coupons (annual interest rates) of 6 percent or less from the bonds with coupons of more than 6 percent.

1. How many cells or strata does this sampling plan entail?
2. If you use this sampling plan, what is the minimum number of issues the indexed portfolio can have?
3. Suppose that in selecting among the securities that qualify for selection within each cell, you apply a criterion concerning the liquidity of the security's market. Is the sample obtained random? Explain your answer.

Solution to 1: We have 2 issuer classifications, 10 maturity classifications, and 2 coupon classifications. So, in total, this plan entails $2(10)(2) = 40$ different strata or cells. (This answer is an application of the multiplication rule of counting discussed in the chapter on probability concepts.)

Solution to 2: You cannot have fewer than one issue for each cell, so the portfolio must include at least 40 issues.

Solution to 3: If you apply any additional criteria to the selection of securities for the cells, not every security that might be included has an equal probability of being selected. As a result, the sampling is not random. In practice, indexing using stratified sampling usually does not strictly involve random sampling because the selection of bond issues within cells is subject to various additional criteria. Because the purpose of sampling in this application is not to make an inference about a population parameter but rather to index a portfolio, lack of randomness is not in itself a problem in this application of stratified sampling.

---

[1] See Fabozzi (2004b).

In the next section, we discuss the kinds of data used by financial analysts in sampling and practical issues that arise in selecting samples.

2.3. Time-Series and Cross-Sectional Data

Investment analysts commonly work with both time-series and cross-sectional data. A time series is a sequence of returns collected at discrete and equally spaced intervals of time (such as a historical series of monthly stock returns). Cross-sectional data are data on some characteristic of individuals, groups, geographical regions, or companies at a single point in time. The 2003 year-end book value per share for all New York Stock Exchange–listed companies is an example of cross-sectional data.

Economic or financial theory offers no basis for determining whether a long or short time period should be selected to collect a sample. As analysts, we might have to look for subtle clues. For example, combining data from a period of fixed exchange rates with data from a period of floating exchange rates would be inappropriate. The variance of exchange rates when exchange rates were fixed would certainly be less than when rates were allowed to float. As a consequence, we would not be sampling from a population described by a single set of parameters.[2] Tight versus loose monetary policy also influences the distribution of returns to stocks; thus, combining data from tight-money and loose-money periods would be inappropriate. Example 6-2 illustrates the problems that can arise when sampling from more than one distribution.

EXAMPLE 6-2   Calculating Sharpe Ratios: One or Two Years of Quarterly Data?

Analysts often use the Sharpe ratio to evaluate the performance of a managed portfolio. The **Sharpe ratio** is the average return in excess of the risk-free rate divided by the standard deviation of returns. This ratio measures the excess return earned per unit of standard deviation of return.

To compute the Sharpe ratio, suppose that an analyst collects eight quarterly excess returns (i.e., total return in excess of the risk-free rate). During the first year, the investment manager of the portfolio followed a low-risk strategy, and during the second year, the manager followed a high-risk strategy. For each of these years, the analyst also tracks the quarterly excess returns of some benchmark against which the manager will be evaluated. For each of the two years, the Sharpe ratio for the benchmark is 0.21. Table 6-1 gives the calculation of the Sharpe ratio of the portfolio.

For the first year, during which the manager followed a low-risk strategy, the average quarterly return in excess of the risk-free rate was 1 percent with a standard deviation of 4.62 percent. The Sharpe ratio is thus $1/4.62 = 0.22$. The second year's results mirror the first year except for the higher average return and volatility. The Sharpe ratio for the second year is $4/18.48 = 0.22$. The Sharpe ratio for the benchmark is 0.21 during

---

[2]When the mean or variance of a time series is not constant through time, the time series is not stationary. We discuss stationarity in more detail in the chapter on time-series analysis.

TABLE 6-1   Calculation of Sharpe Ratios: Low-Risk and High-Risk Strategies

Quarter/Measure	Year 1 Excess Returns	Year 2 Excess Returns
Quarter 1	−3%	−12%
Quarter 2	5	20
Quarter 3	−3	−12
Quarter 4	5	20
Quarterly average	1%	4%
Quarterly standard deviation	4.62%	18.48%
Sharpe ratio = 0.22 = 1/4.62 = 4/18.48		

the first and second years. Because larger Sharpe ratios are better than smaller ones (providing more return per unit of risk), the manager appears to have outperformed the benchmark.

Now, suppose the analyst believes a larger sample to be superior to a small one. She thus decides to pool the two years together and calculate a Sharpe ratio based on eight quarterly observations. The average quarterly excess return for the two years is the average of each year's average excess return. For the two-year period, the average excess return is $(1 + 4)/2 = 2.5$ percent per quarter. The standard deviation for all eight quarters measured from the sample mean of 2.5 percent is 12.57 percent. The portfolio's Sharpe ratio for the two-year period is now $2.5/12.57 = 0.199$; the Sharpe ratio for the benchmark remains 0.21. Thus, when returns for the two-year period are pooled, the manager appears to have provided less return per unit of risk than the benchmark and less when compared with the separate yearly results.

The problem with using eight quarters of return data is that the analyst has violated the assumption that the sampled returns come from the same population. As a result of the change in the manager's investment strategy, returns in Year 2 followed a different distribution than returns in Year 1. Clearly, during Year 1, returns were generated by an underlying population with lower mean and variance than the population of the second year. Combining the results for the first and second years yielded a sample that was representative of no population. Because the larger sample did not satisfy model assumptions, any conclusions the analyst reached based on the larger sample are incorrect. For this example, she was better off using a smaller sample than a larger sample because the smaller sample represented a more homogeneous distribution of returns.

The second basic type of data is cross-sectional data.[3] With cross-sectional data, the observations in the sample represent a characteristic of individuals, groups, geographical

---

[3] The reader may also encounter two types of datasets that have both time-series and cross-sectional aspects. **Panel data** consist of observations through time on a single characteristic of multiple observational units. For example, the annual inflation rate of the Eurozone countries over a five-year period would represent panel data. **Longitudinal data** consist of observations on characteristic(s) of the same observational unit through time. Observations on a set of financial ratios for a single company over a 10-year period would be an example of longitudinal data. Both panel and longitudinal data may be represented by arrays (matrixes) in which successive rows represent the observations for successive time periods.

regions, or companies at a single point in time. The telecommunications analyst discussed previously is essentially collecting a cross-section of planned capital expenditures for the coming year.

Whenever we sample cross-sectionally, certain assumptions must be met if we wish to summarize the data in a meaningful way. Again, a useful approach is to think of the observation of interest as a random variable that comes from some underlying population with a given mean and variance. As we collect our sample and begin to summarize the data, we must be sure that all the data do, in fact, come from the same underlying population. For example, an analyst might be interested in how efficiently companies use their inventory assets. Some companies, however, turn over their inventory more quickly than others because of differences in their operating environments (e.g., grocery stores turn over inventory more quickly than automobile manufacturers, in general). So the distribution of inventory turnover rates may not be characterized by a single distribution with a given mean and variance. Therefore, summarizing inventory turnover across all companies might be inappropriate. If random variables are generated by different underlying distributions, the sample statistics computed from combined samples are not related to one underlying population parameter. The size of the sampling error in such cases is unknown.

In instances such as these, analysts often summarize company-level data by industry. Attempting to summarize by industry partially addresses the problem of differing underlying distributions, but large corporations are likely to be in more than one industrial sector, so analysts should be sure they understand how companies are assigned to the industry groups.

Whether we deal with time-series data or cross-sectional data, we must be sure to have a random sample that is representative of the population we wish to study. With the objective of inferring information from representative samples, we now turn to the next part of this chapter, which focuses on the central limit theorem as well as point and interval estimates of the population mean.

3. DISTRIBUTION OF THE SAMPLE MEAN

Earlier in this chapter, we presented a telecommunications equipment analyst who decided to sample in order to estimate mean planned capital expenditures by his customers. Supposing that the sample is representative of the underlying population, how can the analyst assess the sampling error in estimating the population mean? Viewed as a formula that takes a function of the random outcomes of a random variable, the sample mean is itself a random variable with a probability distribution. That probability distribution is called the statistic's sampling distribution.[4] To estimate how closely the sample mean can be expected to match the underlying population mean, the analyst needs to understand the sampling distribution of the mean. Fortunately, we have a result, the central limit theorem, that helps us understand the sampling distribution of the mean for many of the estimation problems we face.

---

[4]Sometimes confusion arises because "sample mean" is also used in another sense. When we calculate the sample mean for a particular sample, we obtain a definite number, say 8. If we state that "the sample mean is 8," we are using "sample mean" in the sense of a particular outcome of sample mean as a random variable. The number 8 is of course a constant and does not have a probability distribution. In this discussion, we are not referring to "sample mean" in the sense of a constant number related to a particular sample.

3.1. The Central Limit Theorem

One of the most practically useful theorems in probability theory, the central limit theorem has important implications for how we construct confidence intervals and test hypotheses. Formally, it is stated as follows:

- **The Central Limit Theorem**. Given a population described by any probability distribution having mean μ and finite variance σ^2, the sampling distribution of the sample mean $\overline{X}$ computed from samples of size n from this population will be approximately normal with mean μ (the population mean) and variance σ^2/n (the population variance divided by n) when the sample size n is large.

The central limit theorem allows us to make quite precise probability statements about the population mean by using the sample mean, *whatever the distribution of the population*, because the sample mean follows an approximate normal distribution for large-size samples. The obvious question is, "When is a sample's size large enough that we can assume the sample mean is normally distributed?" In general, when sample size n is greater than or equal to 30, we can assume that the sample mean is approximately normally distributed.[5]

The central limit theorem states that the variance of the distribution of the sample mean is σ^2/C. The positive square root of variance is standard deviation. The standard deviation of a sample statistic is known as the standard error of the statistic. The standard error of the sample mean is an important quantity in applying the central limit theorem in practice.

- **Definition of the Standard Error of the Sample Mean**. For sample mean $\overline{X}$ calculated from a sample generated by a population with standard deviation σ, the standard error of the sample mean is given by one of two expressions:

$$\sigma_{\overline{X}} = \frac{\sigma}{\sqrt{n}} \qquad (6\text{-}1)$$

when we know σ, the population standard deviation, or by

$$s_{\overline{X}} = \frac{s}{\sqrt{n}} \qquad (6\text{-}2)$$

when we do not know the population standard deviation and need to use the sample standard deviation, s, to estimate it.[6]

---

[5]When the underlying population is very nonnormal, a sample size well in excess of 30 may be required for the normal distribution to be a good description of the sampling distribution of the mean.

[6]We need to note a technical point: When we take a sample of size n from a finite population of size N, we apply a shrinkage factor to the estimate of the standard error of the sample mean that is called the finite population correction factor (fpc). The fpc is equal to $[(N - n)/(N - 1)]^{1/2}$. Thus, if $N = 100$ and $n = 20$, $[(100 - 20)/(100 - 1)]^{1/2} = 0.898933$. If we have estimated a standard error of, say, 20, according to Equation 6-1 or Equation 6-2, the new estimate is $20(0.898933) = 17.978663$. The fpc applies only when we sample from a finite population without replacement; most practitioners also do not apply the fpc if sample size n is very small relative to N (say, less than 5 percent of N). For more information on the finite population correction factor, see Daniel and Terrell (1995).

In practice, we almost always need to use Equation 6-2. The estimate of s is given by the square root of the sample variance, s^2, calculated as follows:

$$s^2 = \frac{\sum_{i=1}^{n}(X_i - \overline{X})^2}{n - 1} \tag{6-3}$$

We will soon see how we can use the sample mean and its standard error to make probability statements about the population mean by using the technique of confidence intervals. First, however, we provide an illustration of the central limit theorem's force.

EXAMPLE 6-3   The Central Limit Theorem

It is remarkable that the sample mean for large sample sizes will be distributed normally regardless of the distribution of the underlying population. To illustrate the central limit theorem in action, we specify in this example a distinctly nonnormal distribution and use it to generate a large number of random samples of size 100. We then calculate the sample mean for each sample. The frequency distribution of the calculated sample means is an approximation of the sampling distribution of the sample mean for that sample size. Does that sampling distribution look like a normal distribution?

We return to the telecommunications analyst studying the capital expenditure plans of telecom businesses. Suppose that capital expenditures for communications equipment form a continuous uniform random variable with a lower bound equal to $0 and an upper bound equal to $100—for short, call this a uniform (0, 100) random variable. The probability function of this continuous uniform random variable has a rather simple shape that is anything but normal. It is a horizontal line with a vertical intercept equal to 1/100. Unlike a normal random variable, for which outcomes close to the mean are most likely, all possible outcomes are equally likely for a uniform random variable.

To illustrate the power of the central limit theorem, we conduct a Monte Carlo simulation to study the capital expenditure plans of telecom businesses.[7] In this simulation, we collect 200 random samples of the capital expenditures of 100 companies (200 random draws, each consisting of the capital expenditures of 100 companies with $n = 100$). In each simulation trial, 100 values for capital expenditure are generated from the uniform (0, 100) distribution. For each random sample, we then compute the sample mean. We conduct 200 simulation trials in total. Because we have specified the distribution generating the samples, we know that the population mean capital expenditure is equal to ($0 + $100 million)/2 = $50 million; the population variance of capital expenditures is equal to $(100 - 0)^2/12 = 833.33$; thus, the standard deviation

---

[7]Monte Carlo simulation involves the use of a computer to represent the operation of a system subject to risk. An integral part of Monte Carlo simulation is the generation of a large number of random samples from a specified probability distribution or distributions.

is $28.87 million and the standard error is $28.87/\sqrt{100} = 2.887$ under the central limit theorem.[8]

The results of this Monte Carlo experiment are tabulated in Table 6-2 in the form of a frequency distribution. This distribution is the estimated sampling distribution of the sample mean.

The frequency distribution can be described as bell-shaped and centered close to the population mean of 50. The most frequent, or modal, range, with 41 observations, is 48.5 to 50. The overall average of the sample means is $49.92, with a standard error equal to $2.80. The calculated standard error is close to the value of 2.887 given by the central limit theorem. The discrepancy between calculated and expected values of the mean and standard deviation under the central limit theorem is a result of random chance (sampling error).

TABLE 6-2   Frequency Distribution: 200 Random Samples
of a Uniform (0,100) Random Variable

Range of Sample Means ($ million)	Absolute Frequency
$42.5 \leq \overline{X} < 44$	1
$44 \leq \overline{X} < 45.5$	6
$45.5 \leq \overline{X} < 47$	22
$47 \leq \overline{X} < 48.5$	39
$48.5 \leq \overline{X} < 50$	41
$50 \leq \overline{X} < 51.5$	39
$51.5 \leq \overline{X} < 53$	23
$53 \leq \overline{X} < 54.5$	12
$54.5 \leq \overline{X} < 56$	12
$56 \leq \overline{X} < 57.5$	5

Note: $\overline{X}$ is the mean capital expenditure for each sample.

In summary, although the distribution of the underlying population is very nonnormal, the simulation has shown that a normal distribution well describes the estimated sampling distribution of the sample mean, with mean and standard error consistent with the values predicted by the central limit theorem.

To summarize, according to the central limit theorem, when we sample from any distribution, the distribution of the sample mean will have the following properties as long as our sample size is large:

- The distribution of the sample mean $\overline{X}$ will be approximately normal.
- The mean of the distribution of $\overline{X}$ will be equal to the mean of the population from which the samples are drawn.

---

[8]If a is the lower limit of a uniform random variable and b is the upper limit, then the random variable's mean is given by $(a + b)/2$ and its variance is given by $(b - a)^2/12$. The chapter on common probability distributions fully describes continuous uniform random variables.

- The variance of the distribution of $\overline{X}$ will be equal to the variance of the population divided by the sample size.

With the central limit theorem in hand, we next discuss the concepts and tools related to estimating the population parameters, with a special focus on the population mean. We focus on the population because analysts are more likely to meet interval estimates for the population mean than any other type of interval estimate.

4. POINT AND INTERVAL ESTIMATES OF THE POPULATION MEAN

Statistical inference traditionally consists of two branches, hypothesis testing and estimation. Hypothesis testing addresses the question "Is the value of this parameter (say, a population mean) equal to some specific value (0, for example)?" In this process, we have a hypothesis concerning the value of a parameter, and we seek to determine whether the evidence from a sample supports or does not support that hypothesis. We discuss hypothesis testing in detail in the chapter on hypothesis testing.

The second branch of statistical inference, and the focus of this chapter, is estimation. Estimation seeks an answer to the question "What is this parameter's (for example, the population mean's) value?" In estimating, unlike in hypothesis testing, we do not start with a hypothesis about a parameter's value and seek to test it. Rather, we try to make the best use of the information in a sample to form one of several types of estimates of the parameter's value. With estimation, we are interested in arriving at a rule for best calculating a single number to estimate the unknown population parameter (a point estimate). Together with calculating a point estimate, we may also be interested in calculating a range of values that brackets the unknown population parameter with some specified level of probability (a confidence interval). In Section 4.1, we discuss point estimates of parameters and then, in Section 4.2, the formulation of confidence intervals for the population mean.

4.1. Point Estimators

An important concept introduced in this chapter is that sample statistics viewed as formulas involving random outcomes are random variables. The formulas that we use to compute the sample mean and all the other sample statistics are examples of estimation formulas or **estimators**. The particular value that we calculate from sample observations using an estimator is called an **estimate**. An estimator has a sampling distribution; an estimate is a fixed number pertaining to a given sample and thus has no sampling distribution. To take the example of the mean, the calculated value of the sample mean in a given sample, used as an estimate of the population mean, is called a **point estimate** of the population mean. As Example 6-3 illustrated, the formula for the sample mean can and will yield different results in repeated samples as different samples are drawn from the population.

In many applications, we have a choice among a number of possible estimators for estimating a given parameter. How do we make our choice? We often select estimators because they have one or more desirable statistical properties. Following is a brief description of three desirable properties of estimators: unbiasedness (lack of bias), efficiency, and consistency.[9]

---

[9]See Daniel and Terrell (1995) or Greene (2003) for a thorough treatment of the properties of estimators.

- **Definition of Unbiasedness.** An unbiased estimator is one whose expected value (the mean of its sampling distribution) equals the parameter it is intended to estimate.

For example, the expected value of the sample mean, $\overline{X}$, equals μ, the population mean, so we say that the sample mean is an unbiased estimator (of the population mean). The sample variance, s^2, which is calculated using a divisor of $n - 1$ (Equation 6-3), is an unbiased estimator of the population variance, σ^2. If we were to calculate the sample variance using a divisor of n, the estimator would be biased: Its expected value would be smaller than the population variance. We would say that sample variance calculated with a divisor of n is a biased estimator of the population variance.

Whenever one unbiased estimator of a parameter can be found, we can usually find a large number of other unbiased estimators. How do we choose among alternative unbiased estimators? The criterion of efficiency provides a way to select from among unbiased estimators of a parameter.

- **Definition of Efficiency.** An unbiased estimator is efficient if no other unbiased estimator of the same parameter has a sampling distribution with smaller variance.

To explain the definition, in repeated samples we expect the estimates from an efficient estimator to be more tightly grouped around the mean than estimates from other unbiased estimators. Efficiency is an important property of an estimator.[10] Sample mean $\overline{X}$ is an efficient estimator of the population mean; sample variance s^2 is an efficient estimator of σ^2.

Recall that a statistic's sampling distribution is defined for a given sample size. Different sample sizes define different sampling distributions. For example, the variance of sampling distribution of the sample mean is smaller for larger sample sizes. Unbiasedness and efficiency are properties of an estimator's sampling distribution that hold for any size sample. An unbiased estimator is unbiased equally in a sample of size 10 and in a sample of size 1,000. In some problems, however, we cannot find estimators that have such desirable properties as unbiasedness in small samples.[11] In this case, statisticians may justify the choice of an estimator based on the properties of the estimator's sampling distribution in extremely large samples, the estimator's so-called asymptotic properties. Among such properties, the most important is consistency.

- **Definition of Consistency.** A consistent estimator is one for which the probability of estimates close to the value of the population parameter increases as sample size increases.

Somewhat more technically, we can define a consistent estimator as an estimator whose sampling distribution becomes concentrated on the value of the parameter it is intended to estimate as the sample size approaches infinity. The sample mean, in addition to being an efficient estimator, is also a consistent estimator of the population mean: As sample size n goes to infinity, its standard error, $\sigma/\sqrt{n}$, goes to 0 and its sampling distribution becomes concentrated right over the value of population mean, μ. To summarize, we can think of a consistent estimator as one that tends to produce more and more accurate estimates of the population parameter as we increase the sample's size. If an estimator is consistent, we may attempt to increase the accuracy of estimates of a population parameter by calculating

---

[10]An efficient estimator is sometimes referred to as the best unbiased estimator.

[11]Such problems frequently arise in regression and time-series analyses, which we discuss in later chapters.

estimates using a larger sample. For an inconsistent estimator, however, increasing sample size does not help to increase the probability of accurate estimates.

4.2. Confidence Intervals for the Population Mean

When we need a single number as an estimate of a population parameter, we make use of a point estimate. However, because of sampling error, the point estimate is not likely to equal the population parameter in any given sample. Often, a more useful approach than finding a point estimate is to find a range of values that we expect to bracket the parameter with a specified level of probability—an interval estimate of the parameter. A confidence interval fulfills this role.

- **Definition of Confidence Interval**. A confidence interval is a range for which one can assert with a given probability $1 - \alpha$, called the **degree of confidence**, that it will contain the parameter it is intended to estimate. This interval is often referred to as the $(1 - \alpha)\%$ confidence interval for the parameter.

The endpoints of a confidence limit are referred to as the lower and upper confidence limits. In this chapter, we are concerned only with two-sided confidence intervals—confidence intervals for which we calculate both lower and upper limits.[12]

Confidence intervals are frequently given either a probabilistic interpretation or a practical interpretation. In the probabilistic interpretation, we interpret a 95 percent confidence interval for the population mean as follows: In repeated sampling, 95 percent of such confidence intervals will, in the long run, include or bracket the population mean. For example, suppose we sample from the population 1,000 times, and based on each sample, we construct a 95 percent confidence interval using the calculated sample mean. Because of random chance, these confidence intervals will vary from each other, but we expect 95 percent, or 950, of these intervals to include the unknown value of the population mean. In practice, we generally do not carry out such repeated sampling. Therefore, in the practical interpretation, we assert that we are 95 percent confident that a single 95 percent confidence interval contains the population mean. We are justified in making this statement because we know that 95 percent of all possible confidence intervals constructed in the same manner will contain the population mean. The confidence intervals that we discuss in this chapter have structures similar to the following basic structure:

- **Construction of Confidence Intervals**. A $(1 - \alpha)\%$ confidence interval for a parameter has the following structure:

$$\text{Point estimate} \pm \text{Reliability factor} \times \text{Standard error}$$

---

[12]It is also possible to define two types of one-sided confidence intervals for a population parameter. A lower one-sided confidence interval establishes a lower limit only. Associated with such an interval is an assertion that with a specified degree of confidence the population parameter equals or exceeds the lower limit. An upper one-sided confidence interval establishes an upper limit only; the related assertion is that the population parameter is less than or equal to that upper limit, with a specified degree of confidence. Investment researchers rarely present one-sided confidence intervals, however.

where

Point estimate = a point estimate of the parameter (a value of a sample statistic)

Reliability factor = a number based on the assumed distribution of the point estimate and the degree of confidence $(1 - \alpha)$ for the confidence interval

Standard error = the standard error of the sample statistic providing the point estimate[13]

The most basic confidence interval for the population mean arises when we are sampling from a normal distribution with known variance. The reliability factor in this case is based on the standard normal distribution, which has a mean of 0 and a variance of 1. A standard normal random variable is conventionally denoted by Z. The notation z_α denotes the point of the standard normal distribution such that α of the probability remains in the right tail. For example, 0.05 or 5 percent of the possible values of a standard normal random variable are larger than $z_{0.05} = 1.65$.

Suppose we want to construct a 95 percent confidence interval for the population mean and, for this purpose, we have taken a sample of size 100 from a normally distributed population with known variance of $\sigma^2 = 400$ (so, $\sigma = 20$). We calculate a sample mean of $\overline{X} = 25$. Our point estimate of the population mean is, therefore, 25. If we move 1.96 standard deviations above the mean of a normal distribution, 0.025 or 2.5 percent of the probability remains in the right tail; by symmetry of the normal distribution, if we move 1.96 standard deviations below the mean, 0.025 or 2.5 percent of the probability remains in the left tail. In total, 0.05 or 5 percent of the probability is in the two tails and 0.95 or 95 percent lies in between. So, $z_{0.025} = 1.96$ is the reliability factor for this 95 percent confidence interval. Note the relationship $(1 - \alpha)\%$ for the confidence interval and the $z_{\alpha/2}$ for the reliability factor. The standard error of the sample mean, given by Equation 6-1, is $\sigma_{\overline{X}} = 20/\sqrt{100} = 2$. The confidence interval, therefore, has a lower limit of $\overline{X} - 1.96\sigma_{\overline{X}} = 25 - 1.96(2) = 25 - 3.92 = 21.08$. The upper limit of the confidence interval is $\overline{X} + 1.96\sigma_{\overline{X}} = 25 + 1.96(2) = 25 + 3.92 = 28.92$. The 95 percent confidence interval for the population mean spans 21.08 to 28.92.

- **Confidence Intervals for the Population Mean (Normally Distributed Population with Known Variance).** A $(1 - \alpha)\%$ confidence interval for population mean μ when we are sampling from a normal distribution with known variance σ^2 is given by

$$\overline{X} \pm z_{\alpha/2} \frac{\sigma}{\sqrt{n}} \qquad (6\text{-}4)$$

The reliability factors for the most frequently used confidence intervals are as follows:

- **Reliability Factors for Confidence Intervals Based on the Standard Normal Distribution.** We use the following reliability factors when we construct confidence intervals based on the standard normal distribution:[14]

---

[13]The quantity (Reliability factor) × (Standard error) is sometimes called the precision of the estimator; larger values of the product imply lower precision in estimating the population parameter.

[14]Most practitioners use values for $z_{0.05}$ and $z_{0.005}$ that are carried to two decimal places. For reference, more exact values for $z_{0.05}$ and $z_{0.005}$ are 1.645 and 2.575, respectively. For a quick calculation of a 95 percent confidence interval, $z_{0.025}$ is sometimes rounded from 1.96 to 2.

- 90 percent confidence intervals: Use $z_{0.05} = 1.65$
- 95 percent confidence intervals: Use $z_{0.025} = 1.96$
- 99 percent confidence intervals: Use $z_{0.005} = 2.58$

These reliability factors highlight an important fact about all confidence intervals. As we increase the degree of confidence, the confidence interval becomes wider and gives us less precise information about the quantity we want to estimate. "The surer we want to be, the less we have to be sure of."[15]

In practice, the assumption that the sampling distribution of the sample mean is at least approximately normal is frequently reasonable, either because the underlying distribution is approximately normal or because we have a large sample and the central limit theorem applies. However, rarely do we know the population variance in practice. When the population variance is unknown but the sample mean is at least approximately normally distributed, we have two acceptable ways to calculate the confidence interval for the population mean. We will soon discuss the more conservative approach, which is based on Student's *t*-distribution (the *t*-distribution, for short).[16] In investment literature, it is the most frequently used approach in both estimation and hypothesis tests concerning the mean when the population variance is not known, whether sample size is small or large.

A second approach to confidence intervals for the population mean, based on the standard normal distribution, is the *z*-alternative. It can be used only when sample size is large. (In general, a sample size of 30 or larger may be considered large.) In contrast to the confidence interval given in Equation 6-4, this confidence interval uses the sample standard deviation, *s*, in computing the standard error of the sample mean (Equation 6-2).

- **Confidence Intervals for the Population Mean—The *z*-Alternative (Large Sample, Population Variance Unknown).**   A $(1 - \alpha)\%$ confidence interval for population mean μ when sampling from any distribution with unknown variance and when sample size is large is given by

$$\overline{X} \pm z_{\alpha/2}\frac{s}{\sqrt{n}} \qquad (6\text{-}5)$$

Because this type of confidence interval appears quite often, we illustrate its calculation in Example 6-4.

EXAMPLE 6-4   Confidence Interval for the Population Mean of Sharpe Ratios—*z*-Statistic

Suppose an investment analyst takes a random sample of U.S. equity mutual funds and calculates the average Sharpe ratio. The sample size is 100, and the average Sharpe ratio is 0.45. The sample has a standard deviation of 0.30. Calculate and interpret the 90

---

[15]Freund and Williams (1977), p. 266.
[16]The distribution of the statistic *t* is called Student's *t*-distribution after the pen name "Student" used by W. S. Gosset, who published his work in 1908.

percent confidence interval for the population mean of all U.S. equity mutual funds by using a reliability factor based on the standard normal distribution.

The reliability factor for a 90 percent confidence interval, as given earlier, is $z_{0.05} = 1.65$. The confidence interval will be

$$\overline{X} \pm z_{0.05}\frac{s}{\sqrt{n}} = 0.45 \pm 1.65\frac{0.30}{\sqrt{100}} = 0.45 \pm 1.65(0.03) = 0.45 \pm 0.0495$$

The confidence interval spans 0.4005 to 0.4995, or 0.40 to 0.50, carrying two decimal places. The analyst can say with 90 percent confidence that the interval includes the population mean.

In this example, the analyst makes no specific assumption about the probability distribution describing the population. Rather, the analyst relies on the central limit theorem to produce an approximate normal distribution for the sample mean.

As Example 6-4 shows, even if we are unsure of the underlying population distribution, we can still construct confidence intervals for the population mean as long as the sample size is large because we can apply the central limit theorem.

We now turn to the conservative alternative, using the t-distribution, for constructing confidence intervals for the population mean when the population variance is not known. For confidence intervals based on samples from normally distributed populations with unknown variance, the theoretically correct reliability factor is based on the t-distribution. Using a reliability factor based on the t-distribution is essential for a small sample size. Using a t reliability factor is appropriate when the population variance is unknown, even when we have a large sample and could use the central limit theorem to justify using a z reliability factor. In this large sample case, the t-distribution provides more-conservative (wider) confidence intervals.

The t-distribution is a symmetrical probability distribution defined by a single parameter known as **degrees of freedom** (df). Each value for the number of degrees of freedom defines one distribution in this family of distributions. We will shortly compare t-distributions with the standard normal distribution, but first we need to understand the concept of degrees of freedom. We can do so by examining the calculation of the sample variance.

Equation 6-3 gives the unbiased estimator of the sample variance that we use. The term in the denominator, $n - 1$, which is the sample size minus 1, is the number of degrees of freedom in estimating the population variance when using Equation 6-3. We also use $n - 1$ as the number of degrees of freedom for determining reliability factors based on the t-distribution. The term "degrees of freedom" is used because in a random sample, we assume that observations are selected independently of each other. The numerator of the sample variance, however, uses the sample mean. How does the use of the sample mean affect the number of observations collected independently for the sample variance formula? With a sample of size 10 and a mean of 10 percent, for example, we can freely select only 9 observations. Regardless of the 9 observations selected, we can always find the value for the 10th observation that gives a mean equal to 10 percent. From the standpoint of the sample variance formula, then, there are 9 degrees of freedom. Given that we must first compute the sample mean from the total of n independent observations, only $n - 1$ observations can be chosen independently for the calculation of the sample variance. The concept of degrees of freedom comes up frequently in statistics, and you will see it often in later chapters.

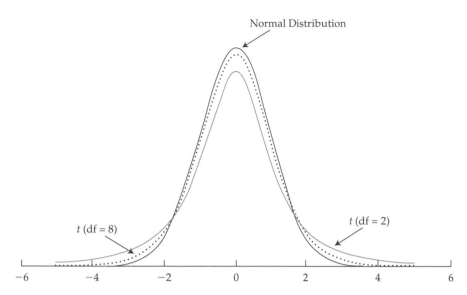

FIGURE 6-1 Student's *t*-Distribution Versus the Standard Normal Distribution

Suppose we sample from a normal distribution. The ratio $z = (\overline{X} - \mu)/(\sigma/\sqrt{n})$ is distributed normally with a mean of 0 and standard deviation of 1; however, the ratio $t = (\overline{X} - \mu)/(s/\sqrt{n})$ follows the *t*-distribution with a mean of 0 and $n - 1$ degrees of freedom. The ratio represented by *t* is not normal because *t* is the ratio of two random variables, the sample mean and the sample standard deviation. The definition of the standard normal random variable involves only one random variable, the sample mean. As degrees of freedom increase, however, the *t*-distribution approaches the standard normal distribution. Figure 6-1 shows the standard normal distribution and two *t*-distributions, one with df = 2 and one with df = 8.

Of the three distributions shown in Figure 6-1, the standard normal distribution is clearly the most peaked; it has tails that approach zero faster than the tails of the two *t*-distributions. The *t*-distribution is also symmetrically distributed around its mean value of zero, just like the normal distribution. The *t*-distribution with df = 2 is the least peaked of the three distributions, and its tails lie above the tails for the normal and *t* with df = 8. The *t*-distribution with df = 8 has an intermediate degree of peakedness, and its tails lie above the tails for the normal but below those for *t* with df = 2. As the degrees of freedom increase, the *t*-distribution approaches the standard normal. The *t*-distribution with df = 8 is closer to the standard normal than the *t*-distribution with df = 2.

Beyond plus and minus four standard deviations from the mean, the area under the standard normal distribution appears to approach 0; both *t*-distributions continue to show some area under each curve beyond four standard deviations, however. The *t*-distributions have fatter tails, but the tails of the *t*-distribution with df = 8 more closely resemble the normal distribution's tails. As the degrees of freedom increase, the tails of the *t*-distribution become less fat.

Frequently referred to values for the *t*-distribution are presented in tables at the end of the book. For each degree of freedom, five values are given: $t_{0.10}$, $t_{0.05}$, $t_{0.025}$, $t_{0.01}$, and $t_{0.005}$. The values for $t_{0.10}$, $t_{0.05}$, $t_{0.025}$, $t_{0.01}$, and $t_{0.005}$ are such that, respectively, 0.10, 0.05, 0.025, 0.01, and 0.005 of the probability remains in the right tail, for the specified number of degrees of freedom.[17] For example, for df $= 30$, $t_{0.10} = 1.310$, $t_{0.05} = 1.697$, $t_{0.025} = 2.042$, $t_{0.01} = 2.457$, and $t_{0.005} = 2.750$.

We now give the form of confidence intervals for the population mean using the t-distribution.

- **Confidence Intervals for the Population Mean (Population Variance Unknown)—** **t-Distribution.** If we are sampling from a population with unknown variance and either of the conditions below holds:

  - the sample is large, or
  - the sample is small but the population is normally distributed, or approximately normally distributed,

  then a $(1 - \alpha)\%$ confidence interval for the population mean μ is given by

  $$\overline{X} \pm t_{\alpha/2}\frac{s}{\sqrt{n}} \tag{6-6}$$

  where the number of degrees of freedom for $t_{\alpha/2}$ is $n - 1$ and n is the sample size.

Example 6-5 reprises the data of Example 6-4 but uses the t-statistic rather than the z-statistic to calculate a confidence interval for the population mean of Sharpe ratios.

EXAMPLE 6-5   Confidence Interval for the Population Mean of Sharpe Ratios—t-Statistic

As in Example 6-4, an investment analyst seeks to calculate a 90 percent confidence interval for the population mean Sharpe ratio of U.S. equity mutual funds based on a random sample of 100 U.S. equity mutual funds. The sample mean Sharpe ratio is 0.45, and the sample standard deviation of the Sharpe ratios is 0.30. Now recognizing that the population variance of the distribution of Sharpe ratios is unknown, the analyst decides to calculate the confidence interval using the theoretically correct t-statistic.

Because the sample size is 100, df $= 99$. In the tables in the back of the book, the closest value is df $= 100$. Using df $= 100$ and reading down the 0.05 column, we find that $t_{0.05} = 1.66$. This reliability factor is slightly larger than the reliability factor $z_{0.05} = 1.65$ that was used in Example 6-4. The confidence interval will be

$$\overline{X} \pm t_{0.05}\frac{s}{\sqrt{n}} = 0.45 \pm 1.66\frac{0.30}{\sqrt{100}} = 0.45 \pm 1.66(0.03) = 0.45 \pm 0.0498$$

---

[17]The values $t_{0.10}$, $t_{0.05}$, $t_{0.025}$, $t_{0.01}$, and $t_{0.005}$ are also referred to as one-sided critical values of t at the 0.10, 0.05, 0.025, 0.01, and 0.005 significance levels, for the specified number of degrees of freedom.

The confidence interval spans 0.4002 to 0.4998, or 0.40 to 0.50, carrying two decimal places. To two decimal places, the confidence interval is unchanged from the one computed in Example 6-4.

Table 6-3 summarizes the various reliability factors that we have used.

TABLE 6-3   Basis of Computing Reliability Factors

Sampling from:	Statistic for Small Sample Size	Statistic for Large Sample Size
Normal distribution with known variance	z	z
Normal distribution with unknown variance	t	t *
Nonnormal distribution with known variance	not available	z
Nonnormal distribution with unknown variance	not available	t *

*Use of z also acceptable.

4.3. Selection of Sample Size

What choices affect the width of a confidence interval? To this point we have discussed two factors that affect width: the choice of statistic (t or z) and the choice of degree of confidence (affecting which specific value of t or z we use). These two choices determine the reliability factor. (Recall that a confidence interval has the structure Point estimate ± Reliability factor × Standard error.)

The choice of sample size also affects the width of a confidence interval. All else equal, a larger sample size decreases the width of a confidence interval. Recall the expression for the standard error of the sample mean:

$$\text{Standard error of the sample mean} = \frac{\text{Sample standard deviation}}{\sqrt{\text{Sample size}}}$$

We see that the standard error varies inversely with the square root of sample size. As we increase sample size, the standard error decreases and consequently the width of the confidence interval also decreases. The larger the sample size, the greater precision with which we can estimate the population parameter.[18] All else equal, larger samples are good, in that sense. In practice, however, two considerations may operate against increasing sample size. First, as we saw in Example 6-2 concerning the Sharpe ratio, increasing the size of a sample may result in sampling from more than one population. Second, increasing sample size may involve additional expenses that outweigh the value of additional precision. Thus three issues that the analyst should weigh in selecting sample size are the need for precision, the risk of sampling from more than one population, and the expenses of different sample sizes.

---

[18]A formula exists for determining the sample size needed to obtain a desired width for a confidence interval. Define E = Reliability factor × Standard error. The smaller E is, the smaller the width of the confidence interval, because $2E$ is the confidence interval's width. The sample size to obtain a desired value of E at a given degree of confidence $(1 - \alpha)$ is $n = [(t_{\alpha/2}s)/E]^2$.

EXAMPLE 6-6   A Money Manager Estimates Net Client Inflows

A money manager wants to obtain a 95 percent confidence interval for fund inflows and outflows over the next six months for his existing clients. He begins by calling a random sample of 10 clients and inquiring about their planned additions to and withdrawals from the fund. The manager then computes the change in cash flow for each client sampled as a percentage change in total funds placed with the manager. A positive percentage change indicates a net cash inflow to the client's account, and a negative percentage change indicates a net cash outflow from the client's account. The manager weights each response by the relative size of the account within the sample and then computes a weighted average.

As a result of this process, the money manager computes a weighted average of 5.5 percent. Thus, a point estimate is that the total amount of funds under management will increase by 5.5 percent in the next six months. The standard deviation of the observations in the sample is 10 percent. A histogram of past data looks fairly close to normal, so the manager assumes the population is normal.

1. Calculate a 95 percent confidence interval for the population mean and interpret your findings.

The manager decides to see what the confidence interval would look like if he had used a sample size of 20 or 30 and found the same mean (5.5 percent) and standard deviation (10 percent).

2. Using the sample mean of 5.5 percent and standard deviation of 10 percent, compute the confidence interval for sample sizes of 20 and 30. For the sample size of 30, use Equation 6-6.
3. Interpret your results from Parts 1 and 2.

Solution to 1: Because the population is unknown and the sample size is small, the manager must use the t-statistic in Equation 6-6 to calculate the confidence interval. Based on the sample size of 10, df $= n - 1 = 10 - 1 = 9$. For a 95 percent confidence interval, he needs to use the value of $t_{0.025}$ for df $= 9$. According to the tables in the back of the book, this value is 2.262. Therefore, a 95 percent confidence interval for the population mean is

$$\overline{X} \pm t_{0.025} \frac{s}{\sqrt{n}} = 5.5\% \pm 2.262 \frac{10\%}{\sqrt{10}}$$

$$= 5.5\% \pm 2.262(3.162)$$

$$= 5.5\% \pm 7.15\%$$

The confidence interval for the population mean spans −1.65 percent to +12.65 percent.[19] The manager can be confident at the 95 percent level that this range includes the population mean.

Solution to 2: Table 6-4 gives the calculations for the three sample sizes.

TABLE 6-4   The 95 Percent Confidence Interval for Three Sample Sizes

Distribution	95% Confidence Interval	Lower Bound	Upper Bound	Relative Size
$t(n = 10)$	5.5% ± 2.262(3.162)	−1.65%	12.65%	100.0%
$t(n = 20)$	5.5% ± 2.093(2.236)	0.82%	10.18%	65.5%
$t(n = 30)$	5.5% ± 2.045(1.826)	1.77%	9.23%	52.2%

Solution to 3: The width of the confidence interval decreases as we increase the sample size. This decrease is a function of the standard error becoming smaller as n increases. The reliability factor also becomes smaller as the number of degrees of freedom increases. The last column of Table 6-4 shows the relative size of the width of confidence intervals based on $n = 10$ to be 100 percent. Using a sample size of 20 reduces the confidence interval's width to 65.5 percent of the interval width for a sample size of 10. Using a sample size of 30 cuts the width of the interval almost in half. Comparing these choices, the money manager would obtain the most precise results using a sample of 30.

Having covered many of the fundamental concepts of sampling and estimation, we are in a good position to focus on sampling issues of special concern to analysts. The quality of inferences depends on the quality of the data as well as on the quality of the sampling plan used. Financial data pose special problems, and sampling plans frequently reflect one or more biases. The next section of this chapter discusses these issues.

5. MORE ON SAMPLING

We have already seen that the selection of sample period length may raise the issue of sampling from more than one population. There are, in fact, a range of challenges to valid sampling that arise in working with financial data. In this section we discuss four such sampling-related issues: data-mining bias, sample selection bias, look-ahead bias, and time-period bias. All of these issues are important for point and interval estimation and hypothesis testing. As we will see, if the sample is biased in any way, then point and interval estimates and any other conclusions that we draw from the sample will be in error.

---

[19] We assumed in this example that sample size is sufficiently small compared with the size of the client base that we can disregard the finite population correction factor (mentioned in Footnote 6).

5.1. Data-Mining Bias

Data mining relates to overuse of the same or related data in ways that we shall describe shortly. Data-mining bias refers to the errors that arise from such misuse of data. Investment strategies that reflect data-mining biases are often not successful in the future. Nevertheless, both investment practitioners and researchers have frequently engaged in data mining. Analysts thus need to understand and guard against this problem.

Data-mining is the practice of determining a model by extensive searching through a dataset for statistically significant patterns (that is, repeatedly "drilling" in the same data until finding something that appears to work).[20] In exercises involving statistical significance we set a significance level, which is the probability of rejecting the hypothesis we are testing when the hypothesis is in fact correct.[21] Because rejecting a true hypothesis is undesirable, the investigator often sets the significance level at a relatively small number such as 0.05 or 5 percent.[22] Suppose we test the hypothesis that a variable does not predict stock returns, and we test in turn 100 different variables. Let us also suppose that in truth none of the 100 variables has the ability to predict stock returns. Using a 5 percent significance level in our tests, we would still expect that 5 out of 100 variables would appear to be significant predictors of stock returns because of random chance alone. We have mined the data to find some apparently significant variables. In essence, we have explored the same data again and again until we found some after-the-fact pattern or patterns in the dataset. This is the sense in which data mining involves overuse of data. If we were to just report the significant variables, without also reporting the total number of variables that we tested that were unsuccessful as predictors, we would be presenting a very misleading picture of our findings. Our results would appear to be far more significant than they actually were, because a series of tests such as the one just described invalidates the conventional interpretation of a given significance level (such as 5 percent), according to the theory of inference.

How can we investigate the presence of data-mining bias? With most financial data, the most ready means is to conduct out-of-sample tests of the proposed variable or strategy. An **out-of-sample test** uses a sample that does not overlap the time period(s) of the sample(s) on which a variable, strategy, or model, was developed. If a variable or investment strategy is the result of data mining, it should generally not be significant in out-of-sample tests. A variable or investment strategy that is statistically and economically significant in out-of-sample tests, and that has a plausible economic basis, may be the basis for a valid investment strategy. Caution is still warranted, however. The most crucial out-of-sample test is future investment success. If the strategy becomes known to other investors, prices may adjust so that the strategy, however well tested, does not work in the future. To summarize, the analyst should be aware that many apparently profitable investment strategies may reflect data-mining bias and thus should be cautious about the future applicability of published investment research results.

Untangling the extent of data mining can be complex. To assess the significance of an investment strategy, we need to know how many unsuccessful strategies were tried not only

---

[20]Some researchers use the term "data snooping" instead of data mining.

[21]To convey an understanding of data mining, it is very helpful to introduce some basic concepts related to hypothesis testing. The chapter on hypothesis testing contains further discussion of significance levels and tests of significance.

[22]In terms of our previous discussion of confidence intervals, significance at the 5 percent level corresponds to a hypothesized value for a population statistic falling outside a 95 percent confidence interval based on an appropriate sample statistic (e.g., the sample mean, when the hypothesis concerns the population mean).

by the current investigator but also by *previous* investigators using the same or related datasets. Much research, in practice, closely builds on what other investigators have done, and so reflects intergenerational data mining, to use the terminology of McQueen and Thorley (1999). **Intergenerational data mining** involves using information developed by previous researchers using a dataset to guide current research using the same or a related dataset.[23] Analysts have accumulated many observations about the peculiarities of many financial datasets, and other analysts may develop models or investment strategies that will tend to be supported within a dataset based on their familiarity with the prior experience of other analysts. As a consequence, the importance of those new results may be overstated. Research has suggested that the magnitude of this type of data-mining bias may be considerable.[24]

With the background of the above definitions and explanations, we can understand McQueen and Thorley's (1999) cogent exploration of data mining in the context of the popular Motley Fool "Foolish Four" investment strategy. The Foolish Four strategy, first presented in 1996, was a version of the Dow Dividend Strategy that was tuned by its developers to exhibit an even higher arithmetic mean return than the Dow Dividend Strategy over 1973 to 1993.[25] From 1973 to 1993, the Foolish Four portfolio had an average annual return of 25 percent, and the claim was made in print that the strategy should have similar returns in the future. As McQueen and Thorley discussed, however, the Foolish Four strategy was very much subject to data-mining bias, including bias from intergenerational data mining, as the strategy's developers exploited observations about the dataset made by earlier workers. McQueen and Thorley highlighted the data-mining issues by taking the Foolish Four portfolio one step further. They mined the data to create a "Fractured Four" portfolio that earned nearly 35 percent over 1973 to 1996, beating the Foolish Four strategy by almost 8 percentage points. Observing that all of the Foolish Four stocks did well in even years but not odd years and that the second-to-lowest-priced high-yielding stock was relatively the best performing stock in odd years, the strategy of the Fractured Four portfolio was to hold the Foolish Four stocks with equal weights in even years and hold only the second-to-lowest-priced stock in odd years. How likely is it that a performance difference between even and odd years reflected underlying economic forces, rather than a chance pattern of the data over the particular time period? Probably, very unlikely. Unless an investment strategy reflected underlying economic forces, we would not expect it to have any value in a forward-looking sense. Because the Foolish Four strategy also partook of data mining, the same issues applied to it. McQueen and Thorley found that in an out-of-sample test over the 1949–72 period, the Foolish Four strategy had about the same mean return as buying and holding the DJIA, but with higher

---

[23] The term "intergenerational" comes from viewing each round of researchers as a generation. Campbell, Lo, and MacKinlay (1997) have called intergenerational data mining "data snooping." The latter phrase, however, is commonly used as a synonym of data mining; thus McQueen and Thorley's terminology is less ambiguous. The term "intragenerational data mining" is available when we want to highlight that the reference is to an investigator's new or independent data mining.

[24] For example, Lo and MacKinlay (1990) concluded that the magnitude of this type of bias on tests of the capital asset pricing model was considerable.

[25] The Dow Dividend Strategy, also known as Dogs of the Dow Strategy, consists of holding an equally weighted portfolio of the 10 highest-yielding DJIA stocks as of the beginning of a year. At the time of McQueen and Thorley's research, the Foolish Four strategy was as follows: At the beginning of each year, the Foolish Four portfolio purchases a 4-stock portfolio from the 5 lowest-priced stocks of the 10 highest-yielding DJIA stocks. The lowest-priced stock of the 5 is excluded, and 40 percent is invested in the second-to-lowest-priced stock, with 20 percent weights in the remaining 3.

risk. If the higher taxes and transaction costs of the Foolish Four strategy were accounted for, the comparison would have been even more unfavorable.

McQueen and Thorley presented two signs that can warn analysts about the potential existence of data mining:

- **Too much digging/too little confidence.** The testing of many variables by the researcher is the "too much digging" warning sign of a data-mining problem. Unfortunately, many researchers do not disclose the number of variables examined in developing a model. Although the number of variables examined may not be reported, we should look closely for verbal hints that the researcher searched over many variables. The use of terms such as "we noticed (or noted) that" or "someone noticed (or noted) that," with respect to a pattern in a dataset, should raise suspicions that the researchers were trying out variables based on their own or others' observations of the data.
- **No story/no future.** The absence of an explicit economic rationale for a variable or trading strategy is the "no story" warning sign of a data-mining problem. Without a plausible economic rationale or story for why a variable should work, the variable is unlikely to have predictive power. In a demonstration exercise using an extensive search of variables in an international financial database, Leinweber (1997) found that butter production in a particular country remote from the United States explained 75 percent of the variation in U.S. stock returns as represented by the S&P 500. Such a pattern, with no plausible economic rationale, is highly likely to be a random pattern particular to a specific time period.[26] What if we do have a plausible economic explanation for a significant variable? McQueen and Thorley caution that a plausible economic rationale is a necessary but not a sufficient condition for a trading strategy to have value. As we mentioned earlier, if the strategy is publicized, market prices may adjust to reflect the new information as traders seek to exploit it; as a result, the strategy may no longer work.

5.2. Sample Selection Bias

When researchers look into questions of interest to analysts or portfolio managers, they may exclude certain stocks, bonds, portfolios, or time periods from the analysis for various reasons—perhaps because of data availability. When data availability leads to certain assets being excluded from the analysis, we call the resulting problem **sample selection bias**. For example, you might sample from a database that tracks only companies currently in existence. Many mutual fund databases, for instance, provide historical information about only those funds that currently exist. Databases that report historical balance sheet and income statement information suffer from the same sort of bias as the mutual fund databases: Funds or companies that are no longer in business do not appear there. So, a study that uses these types of databases suffers from a type of sample selection bias known as **survivorship bias**.

Dimson, Marsh, and Staunton (2002) raised the issue of survivorship bias in international indexes:

> An issue that has achieved prominence is the impact of market survival on estimated long-run returns. Markets can experience not only disappointing performance but also total loss of value through confiscation, hyperinflation, nationalization, and

---

[26]In the finance literature, such a random but irrelevant-to-the-future pattern is sometimes called an artifact of the dataset.

market failure. By measuring the performance of markets that survive over long intervals, we draw inferences that are conditioned on survival. Yet, as pointed out by Brown, Goetzmann, and Ross (1995) and Jorion and Goetzmann (1999), one cannot determine in advance which markets will survive and which will perish. (p. 41)

Survivorship bias sometimes appears when we use both stock price and accounting data. For example, many studies in finance have used the ratio of a company's market price to book equity per share (i.e., the price-to-book ratio, P/B) and found that P/B is inversely related to a company's returns [see Fama and French (1992, 1993)]. P/B is also used to create many popular value and growth indexes. If the database that we use to collect accounting data excludes failing companies, however, a survivorship bias might result. Kothari, Shanken, and Sloan (1995) investigated just this question and argued that failing stocks would be expected to have low returns and low P/Bs. If we exclude failing stocks, then those stocks with low P/Bs that are included will have returns that are higher on average than if all stocks with low P/Bs were included. Kothari, Shanken, and Sloan suggested that this bias is responsible for the previous findings of an inverse relationship between average return and P/B.[27] The only advice we can offer at this point is to be aware of any biases potentially inherent in a sample. Clearly, sample selection biases can cloud the results of any study.

A sample can also be biased because of the removal (or delisting) of a company's stock from an exchange.[28] For example, the Center for Research in Security Prices at the University of Chicago is a major provider of return data used in academic research. When a delisting occurs, CRSP attempts to collect returns for the delisted company, but many times, it cannot do so because of the difficulty involved; CRSP must simply list delisted company returns as missing. A study in the *Journal of Finance* by Shumway and Warther (1999) documented the bias caused by delisting for CRSP Nasdaq return data. The authors showed that delistings associated with poor company performance (e.g., bankruptcy) are missed more often than delistings associated with good or neutral company performance (e.g., merger or moving to another exchange). In addition, delistings occur more frequently for small companies.

Sample selection bias occurs even in markets where the quality and consistency of the data are quite high. Newer asset classes such as hedge funds may present even greater problems of sample selection bias. Hedge funds are a heterogeneous group of investment vehicles typically organized so as to be free from regulatory oversight. In general, hedge funds are not required to publicly disclose performance (in contrast to, say, mutual funds). Hedge funds themselves decide whether they want to be included in one of the various databases of hedge fund performance. Hedge funds with poor track records clearly may not wish to make their records public, creating a problem of self-selection bias in hedge fund databases. Further, as pointed out by Fung and Hsieh (2002), because only hedge funds with good records will volunteer to enter a database, in general, overall past hedge fund industry performance will tend to appear better than it really is. Furthermore, many hedge fund databases drop funds that go out of business, creating survivorship bias in the database. Even if the database does not drop defunct

---

[27] See Fama and French (1996, p. 80) for discussion of data snooping and survivorship bias in their tests.
[28] Delistings occur for a variety of reasons: merger, bankruptcy, liquidation, or migration to another exchange.

hedge funds, in the attempt to eliminate survivorship bias, the problem remains of hedge funds that stop reporting performance because of poor results.[29]

5.3. Look-Ahead Bias

A test design is subject to **look-ahead bias** if it uses information that was not available on the test date. For example, tests of trading rules that use stock market returns and accounting balance sheet data must account for look-ahead bias. In such tests, a company's book value per share is commonly used to construct the P/B variable. Although the market price of a stock is available for all market participants at the same point in time, fiscal year-end book equity per share might not become publicly available until sometime in the following quarter.

5.4. Time-Period Bias

A test design is subject to **time-period bias** if it is based on a time period that may make the results time-period specific. A short time series is likely to give period-specific results that may not reflect a longer period. A long time series may give a more accurate picture of true investment performance; its disadvantage lies in the potential for a structural change occurring during the time frame that would result in two different return distributions. In this situation, the distribution that would reflect conditions before the change differs from the distribution that would describe conditions after the change.

EXAMPLE 6-7 Biases in Investment Research

An analyst is reviewing the empirical evidence on historical U.S. equity returns. She finds that value stocks (i.e., those with low P/Bs) outperformed growth stocks (i.e., those with high P/Bs) in some recent time periods. After reviewing the U.S. market, the analyst wonders whether value stocks might be attractive in the United Kingdom. She investigates the performance of value and growth stocks in the U.K. market from January 1990 to December 2003. To conduct this research, the analyst does the following:

- obtains the current composition of the Financial Times Stock Exchange (FTSE) All Share Index, which is a market-capitalization-weighted index;
- eliminates the few companies that do not have December fiscal year-ends;
- uses year-end book values and market prices to rank the remaining universe of companies by P/Bs at the end of the year;
- based on these rankings, divides the universe into 10 portfolios, each of which contains an equal number of stocks;
- calculates the equal-weighted return of each portfolio and the return for the FTSE All Share Index for the 12 months following the date each ranking was made; and

---

[29] See Ackerman, McEnally, and Ravenscraft (1999) and Fung and Hsieh (2002) for more details on the problems of interpreting hedge fund performance. Note that an offsetting type of bias may occur if successful funds stop reporting performance because they no longer want new cash inflows.

- subtracts the FTSE returns from each portfolio's returns to derive excess returns for each portfolio.

Describe and discuss each of the following biases introduced by the analyst's research design:

- survivorship bias,
- look-ahead bias, and
- time-period bias.

Survivorship bias. A test design is subject to survivorship bias if it fails to account for companies that have gone bankrupt, merged, or otherwise departed the database. In this example, the analyst used the current list of FTSE stocks rather than the actual list of stocks that existed at the start of each year. To the extent that the computation of returns excluded companies removed from the index, the performance of the portfolios with the lowest P/B is subject to survivorship bias and may be overstated. At some time during the testing period, those companies not currently in existence were eliminated from testing. They would probably have had low prices (and low P/Bs) and poor returns.

Look-ahead bias. A test design is subject to look-ahead bias if it uses information unavailable on the test date. In this example, the analyst conducted the test under the assumption that the necessary accounting information was available at the end of the fiscal year. For example, the analyst assumed that book value per share for fiscal 1990 was available on 31 December 1990. Because this information is not released until several months after the close of a fiscal year, the test may have contained look-ahead bias. This bias would make a strategy based on the information appear successful, but it assumes perfect forecasting ability.

Time-period bias. A test design is subject to time-period bias if it is based on a time period that may make the results time-period specific. Although the test covered a period extending more than 10 years, that period may be too short for testing an anomaly. Ideally, an analyst should test market anomalies over several business cycles to ensure that results are not period specific. This bias can favor a proposed strategy if the time period chosen was favorable to the strategy.

CHAPTER 7

HYPOTHESIS TESTING

1. INTRODUCTION

Analysts often confront competing ideas about how financial markets work. Some of these ideas develop through personal research or experience with markets; others come from interactions with colleagues; and many others appear in the professional literature on finance and investments. In general, how can an analyst decide whether statements about the financial world are probably true or probably false?

When we can reduce an idea or assertion to a definite statement about the value of a quantity, such as an underlying or population mean, the idea becomes a statistically testable statement or hypothesis. The analyst may want to explore questions such as the following:

- Is the underlying mean return on this mutual fund different from the underlying mean return on its benchmark?
- Did the volatility of returns on this stock change after the stock was added to a stock market index?
- Are a security's bid-ask spreads related to the number of dealers making a market in the security?
- Do data from a national bond market support a prediction of an economic theory about the term structure of interest rates (the relationship between yield and maturity)?

To address these questions, we use the concepts and tools of hypothesis testing. Hypothesis testing is part of statistical inference, the process of making judgments about a larger group (a population) on the basis of a smaller group actually observed (a sample). The concepts and tools of hypothesis testing provide an objective means to gauge whether the available evidence supports the hypothesis. After a statistical test of a hypothesis we should have a clearer idea of the probability that a hypothesis is true or not, although our conclusion always stops short of certainty. Hypothesis testing has been a powerful tool in the advancement of investment knowledge and science. As Robert L. Kahn of the Institute for Social Research (Ann Arbor, Michigan) has written, "The mill of science grinds only when hypothesis and data are in continuous and abrasive contact."

The main emphases of this chapter are the framework of hypothesis testing and tests concerning mean and variance, two quantities frequently used in investments. We give an overview of the procedure of hypothesis testing in the next section. We then address testing hypotheses about the mean and hypotheses about the differences between means. In the fourth section of this chapter, we address testing hypotheses about a single variance and hypotheses about the differences between variances. We end the chapter with an overview of some other important issues and techniques in statistical inference.

2. HYPOTHESIS TESTING

Hypothesis testing, as we have mentioned, is part of the branch of statistics known as statistical inference. Traditionally, the field of statistical inference has two subdivisions: **estimation** and **hypothesis testing**. Estimation addresses the question "What is this parameter's (e.g., the population mean's) value?" The answer is in the form of a confidence interval built around a point estimate. Take the case of the mean: We build a confidence interval for the population mean around the sample mean as a point estimate. For the sake of specificity, suppose the sample mean is 50 and a 95 percent confidence interval for the population mean is 50 ± 10 (the confidence interval runs from 40 to 60). If this confidence interval has been properly constructed, there is a 95 percent probability that the interval from 40 to 60 contains the population mean's value.[1] The second branch of statistical inference, hypothesis testing, has a somewhat different focus. A hypothesis testing question is "Is the value of the parameter (say, the population mean) 45 (or some other specific value)?" The assertion "the population mean is 45" is a hypothesis. A **hypothesis** is defined as a statement about one or more populations.

This section focuses on the concepts of hypothesis testing. The process of hypothesis testing is part of a rigorous approach to acquiring knowledge known as the scientific method. The scientific method starts with observation and the formulation of a theory to organize and explain observations. We judge the correctness of the theory by its ability to make accurate predictions—for example, to predict the results of new observations.[2] If the predictions are correct, we continue to maintain the theory as a possibly correct explanation of our observations. When risk plays a role in the outcomes of observations, as in finance, we can only try to make unbiased, probability-based judgments about whether the new data support the predictions. Statistical hypothesis testing fills that key role of testing hypotheses when chance plays a role. In an analyst's day-to-day work, he may address questions to which he might give answers of varying quality. When an analyst correctly formulates the question into a testable hypothesis and carries out and reports on a hypothesis test, he has provided an element of support to his answer consistent with the standards of the scientific method. Of course, the analyst's logic, economic reasoning, information sources, and perhaps other factors also play a role in our assessment of the answer's quality.[3]

We organize this introduction to hypothesis testing around the following list of seven steps.

- **Steps in Hypothesis Testing**.   The steps in testing a hypothesis are as follows:[4]

    1. Stating the hypotheses.
    2. Identifying the appropriate test statistic and its probability distribution.
    3. Specifying the significance level.
    4. Stating the decision rule.
    5. Collecting the data and calculating the test statistic.
    6. Making the statistical decision.
    7. Making the economic or investment decision.

---

[1] We discussed the construction and interpretation of confidence intervals in the chapter on sampling.
[2] To be testable, a theory must be capable of making predictions that can be shown to be wrong.
[3] See Freeley and Steinberg (1999) for a discussion of critical thinking applied to reasoned decision making.
[4] This list is based on one in Daniel and Terrell (1986).

We will explain each of these steps using as illustration a hypothesis test concerning the sign of the risk premium on Canadian stocks. The steps above constitute a traditional approach to hypothesis testing. We will end the section with a frequently used alternative to those steps, the *p*-value approach.

   The first step in hypothesis testing is stating the hypotheses. We always state two hypotheses: the null hypothesis (or null), designated H_0, and the alternative hypothesis, designated H_a.

- **Definition of Null Hypothesis**.   The null hypothesis is the hypothesis to be tested. For example, we could hypothesize that the population mean risk premium for Canadian equities is less than or equal to zero.

The null hypothesis is a proposition that is considered true unless the sample we use to conduct the hypothesis test gives convincing evidence that the null hypothesis is false. When such evidence is present, we are led to the alternative hypothesis.

- **Definition of Alternative Hypothesis**.   The alternative hypothesis is the hypothesis accepted when the null hypothesis is rejected. Our alternative hypothesis is that the population mean risk premium for Canadian equities is greater than zero.

Suppose our question concerns the value of a population parameter, θ, in relation to one possible value of the parameter, θ_0 (these are read, respectively, "theta" and "theta sub zero").[5] Examples of a population parameter include the population mean, μ, and the population variance, σ^2. We can formulate three different sets of hypotheses, which we label according to the assertion made by the alternative hypothesis.

- **Formulations of Hypotheses**.   We can formulate the null and alternative hypotheses in three different ways:

   1. $H_0\colon \theta = \theta_0$ versus $H_a\colon \theta \neq \theta_0$ (a "not equal to" alternative hypothesis)
   2. $H_0\colon \theta \leq \theta_0$ versus $H_a\colon \theta > \theta_0$ (a "greater than" alternative hypothesis)
   3. $H_0\colon \theta \geq \theta_0$ versus $H_a\colon \theta < \theta_0$ (a "less than" alternative hypothesis)

In our Canadian example, $\theta = \mu_{RP}$ and represents the population mean risk premium on Canadian equities. Also, $\theta_0 = 0$ and we are using the second of the above three formulations.

   The first formulation is a **two-sided hypothesis test** (or **two-tailed hypothesis test**): We reject the null in favor of the alternative if the evidence indicates that the population parameter is either smaller or larger than θ_0. In contrast, Formulations 2 and 3 are each a **one-sided hypothesis test** (or **one-tailed hypothesis test**). For Formulations 2 and 3, we reject the null only if the evidence indicates that the population parameter is respectively greater than or less than θ_0. The alternative hypothesis has one side.

   Notice that in each case above, we state the null and alternative hypotheses such that they account for all possible values of the parameter. With Formulation 1, for example, the parameter is either equal to the hypothesized value θ_0 (under the null hypothesis) or not equal to the hypothesized value θ_0 (under the alternative hypothesis). Those two statements logically exhaust all possible values of the parameter.

---

[5]Greek letters, such as σ, are reserved for population parameters; Roman letters in italics, such as *s*, are used for sample statistics.

Despite the different ways to formulate hypotheses, we always conduct a test of the null hypothesis at the point of equality, $\theta = \theta_0$. Whether the null is H_0: $\theta = \theta_0$, H_0: $\theta \leq \theta_0$, or H_0: $\theta \geq \theta_0$, we actually test $\theta = \theta_0$. The reasoning is straightforward. Suppose the hypothesized value of the parameter is 5. Consider H_0: $\theta \leq 5$, with a "greater than" alternative hypothesis, H_a: $\theta > 5$. If we have enough evidence to reject H_0: $\theta = 5$ in favor of H_a: $\theta > 5$, we definitely also have enough evidence to reject the hypothesis that the parameter, θ, is some smaller value, such as 4.5 or 4. To review, the calculation to test the null hypothesis is the same for all three formulations. What is different for the three formulations, we will see shortly, is how the calculation is evaluated to decide whether or not to reject the null.

How do we choose the null and alternative hypotheses? Probably most common are "not equal to" alternative hypotheses. We reject the null because the evidence indicates that the parameter is either larger or smaller than θ_0. Sometimes, however, we may have a "suspected" or "hoped for" condition for which we want to find supportive evidence.[6] In that case, we can formulate the alternative hypothesis as the statement that this condition is true; the null hypothesis that we test is the statement that this condition is not true. If the evidence supports rejecting the null and accepting the alternative, we have statistically confirmed what we thought was true. For example, economic theory suggests that investors require a positive risk premium on stocks (the **risk premium** is defined as the expected return on stocks minus the risk-free rate). Following the principle of stating the alternative as the "hoped for" condition, we formulate the following hypotheses:

H_0: The population mean risk premium on Canadian stocks is less than or equal to 0.

H_a: The population mean risk premium on Canadian stocks is positive.

Note that "greater than" and "less than" alternative hypotheses reflect the beliefs of the researcher more strongly than a "not equal to" alternative hypothesis. To emphasize an attitude of neutrality, the researcher may sometimes select a "not equal to" alternative hypothesis when a one-sided alternative hypothesis is also reasonable.

The second step in hypothesis testing is identifying the appropriate test statistic and its probability distribution.

- **Definition of Test Statistic.**   A test statistic is a quantity, calculated based on a sample, whose value is the basis for deciding whether or not to reject the null hypothesis.

The focal point of our statistical decision is the value of the test statistic. Frequently (in all the cases that we examine in this chapter), the test statistic has the form

$$\text{Test statistic} = \frac{\text{Sample statistic} - \text{Value of the population parameter under } H_0}{\text{Standard error of the sample statistic}} \qquad (7\text{-}1)$$

For our risk premium example, the population parameter of interest is the population mean risk premium, μ_{RP}. We label the hypothesized value of the population mean under H_0 as μ_0. Restating the hypotheses using symbols, we test H_0: $\mu_{RP} \leq \mu_0$ versus H_a: $\mu_{RP} > \mu_0$. However, because under the null we are testing $\mu_0 = 0$, we write H_0: $\mu_{RP} \leq 0$ versus H_a: $\mu_{RP} > 0$.

---

[6]Part of this discussion of the selection of hypotheses follows Bowerman and O'Connell (1997, p. 386).

The sample mean provides an estimate of the population mean. Therefore, we can use the sample mean risk premium calculated from historical data, $\overline{X}_{RP}$, as the sample statistic in Equation 7-1. The standard deviation of the sample statistic, known as the "standard error" of the statistic, is the denominator in Equation 7-1. For this example, the sample statistic is a sample mean. For a sample mean, $\overline{X}$, calculated from a sample generated by a population with standard deviation σ, the standard error is given by one of two expressions:

$$\sigma_{\overline{X}} = \frac{\sigma}{\sqrt{n}} \tag{7-2}$$

when we know σ (the population standard deviation), or

$$s_{\overline{X}} = \frac{s}{\sqrt{n}} \tag{7-3}$$

when we do not know the population standard deviation and need to use the sample standard deviation s to estimate it. For this example, because we do not know the population standard deviation of the process generating the return, we use Equation 7-3. The test statistic is thus

$$\frac{\overline{X}_{RP} - \mu_0}{s_{\overline{X}}} = \frac{\overline{X}_{RP} - 0}{s/\sqrt{n}}$$

In making the substitution of 0 for μ_0, we use the fact already highlighted that we test any null hypothesis at the point of equality, as well as the fact that $\mu_0 = 0$ here.

We have identified a test statistic to test the null hypothesis. What probability distribution does it follow? We will encounter four distributions for test statistics in this chapter:

- the t-distribution (for a t-test),
- the standard normal or z-distribution (for a z-test),
- the chi-square (χ^2) distribution (for a chi-square test), and
- the F-distribution (for an F-test).

We will discuss the details later, but assume we can conduct a z-test based on the cen-tral limit theorem because our Canadian sample has many observations.[7] To summarize, the test statistic for the hypothesis test concerning the mean risk premium is $\overline{X}_{RP}/s_{\overline{X}}$. We can conduct a z-test because we can plausibly assume that the test statistic follows a standard normal distribution.

The third step in hypothesis testing is specifying the significance level. When the test statistic has been calculated, two actions are possible: (1) We reject the null hypothesis or (2) we do not reject the null hypothesis. The action we take is based on comparing the calculated test statistic to a specified possible value or values. The comparison values we choose are based on the level of significance selected. The level of significance reflects how much sample evidence we require to reject the null. Analogous to its counterpart in a court of law, the required standard of proof can change according to the nature of the hypotheses and the seriousness of the consequences of making a mistake. There are four possible outcomes when we test a null hypothesis:

---

[7]The central limit theorem says that the sampling distribution of the sample mean will be approximately normal with mean μ and variance σ^2/n when the sample size is large. The sample we will use for this example has 103 observations.

TABLE 7-1   Type I and Type II Errors in Hypothesis Testing

	True Situation	
Decision	H_0 True	H_0 False
Do not reject H_0	Correct Decision	Type II Error
Reject H_0 (accept H_a)	Type I Error	Correct Decision

1. We reject a false null hypothesis. This is a correct decision.
2. We reject a true null hypothesis. This is called a **Type I error**.
3. We do not reject a false null hypothesis. This is called a **Type II error**.
4. We do not reject a true null hypothesis. This is a correct decision.

We illustrate these outcomes in Table 7-1.

When we make a decision in a hypothesis test, we run the risk of making either a Type I or a Type II error. These are mutually exclusive errors: If we mistakenly reject the null, we can only be making a Type I error; if we mistakenly fail to reject the null, we can only be making a Type II error.

The probability of a Type I error in testing a hypothesis is denoted by the Greek letter alpha, α. This probability is also known as the **level of significance** of the test. For example, a level of significance of 0.05 for a test means that there is a 5 percent probability of rejecting a true null hypothesis. The probability of a Type II error is denoted by the Greek letter beta, β.

Controlling the probabilities of the two types of errors involves a trade-off. All else equal, if we decrease the probability of a Type I error by specifying a smaller significance level (say, 0.01 rather than 0.05), we increase the probability of making a Type II error because we will reject the null less frequently, including when it is false. The only way to reduce the probabilities of both types of errors simultaneously is to increase the sample size, n.

Quantifying the trade-off between the two types of error in practice is usually impossible because the probability of a Type II error is itself hard to quantify. Consider H_0: $\theta \leq 5$ versus H_a: $\theta > 5$. Because every true value of θ greater than 5 makes the null hypothesis false, each value of θ greater than 5 has a different β (Type II error probability). In contrast, it is sufficient to state a Type I error probability for $\theta = 5$, the point at which we conduct the test of the null hypothesis. Thus, in general, we specify only α, the probability of a Type I error, when we conduct a hypothesis test. Whereas the significance level of a test is the probability of incorrectly rejecting the null, the **power of a test** is the probability of *correctly* rejecting the null—that is, the probability of rejecting the null when it is false.[8] When more than one test statistic is available to conduct a hypothesis test, we should prefer the most powerful, all else equal.[9]

To summarize, the standard approach to hypothesis testing involves specifying a level of significance (probability of Type I error) only. It is most appropriate to specify this significance level prior to calculating the test statistic. If we specify it after calculating the test statistic, we may be influenced by the result of the calculation, which detracts from the objectivity of the test.

We can use three conventional significance levels to conduct hypothesis tests: 0.10, 0.05, and 0.01. Qualitatively, if we can reject a null hypothesis at the 0.10 level of significance, we have *some evidence* that the null hypothesis is false. If we can reject a null hypothesis at the

---

[8] The power of a test is, in fact, 1 minus the probability of a Type II error.

[9] We do not always have information on the relative power of the test for competing test statistics, however.

0.05 level, we have *strong evidence* that the null hypothesis is false. And if we can reject a null hypothesis at the 0.01 level, we have *very strong evidence* that the null hypothesis is false. For the risk premium example, we will specify a 0.05 significance level.

The fourth step in hypothesis testing is stating the decision rule. The general principle is simply stated. When we test the null hypothesis, if we find that the calculated value of the test statistic is as extreme or more extreme than a given value or values determined by the specified level of significance, α, we reject the null hypothesis. We say the result is **statistically significant**. Otherwise, we do not reject the null hypothesis and we say the result is **not statistically significant**. The value or values with which we compare the calculated test statistic to make our decision are the rejection points (critical values) for the test.[10]

- **Definition of a Rejection Point (Critical Value) for the Test Statistic.** A rejection point (critical value) for a test statistic is a value with which the computed test statistic is compared to decide whether to reject or not reject the null hypothesis.

For a one-tailed test, we indicate a rejection point using the symbol for the test statistic with a subscript indicating the specified probability of a Type I error, α; for example, z_α. For a two-tailed test, we indicate $z_{\alpha/2}$. To illustrate the use of rejection points, suppose we are using a z-test and have chosen a 0.05 level of significance.

- For a test of H_0: $\theta = \theta_0$ versus H_a: $\theta \neq \theta_0$, two rejection points exist, one negative and one positive. For a two-sided test at the 0.05 level, the total probability of a Type I error must sum to 0.05. Thus, $0.05/2 = 0.025$ of the probability should be in each tail of the distribution of the test statistic under the null. Consequently, the two rejection points are $z_{0.025} = 1.96$ and $-z_{0.025} = -1.96$. Let z represent the calculated value of the test statistic. We reject the null if we find that $z < -1.96$ or $z > 1.96$. We do not reject if $-1.96 \leq z \leq 1.96$.
- For a test of H_0: $\theta \leq \theta_0$ versus H_a: $\theta > \theta_0$ at the 0.05 level of significance, the rejection point is $z_{0.05} = 1.645$. We reject the null hypothesis if $z > 1.645$. The value of the standard normal distribution such that 5 percent of the outcomes lie to the right is $z_{0.05} = 1.645$.
- For a test of H_0: $\theta \geq \theta_0$ versus H_a: $\theta < \theta_0$, the rejection point is $-z_{0.05} = -1.645$. We reject the null hypothesis if $z < -1.645$.

Figure 7-1 illustrates a test H_0: $\mu = \mu_0$ versus H_a: $\mu \neq \mu_0$ at the 0.05 significance level using a z-test. The "acceptance region" is the traditional name for the set of values of the test statistic for which we do not reject the null hypothesis. (The traditional name, however, is inaccurate. We should avoid using phrases such as "accept the null hypothesis" because such a statement implies a greater degree of conviction about the null than is warranted when we fail to reject it.[11]) On either side of the acceptance region is a rejection region (or critical region). If the null hypothesis that $\mu = \mu_0$ is true, the test statistic has a 2.5 percent chance of falling in the left rejection region and a 2.5 percent chance of falling in the right rejection region. Any calculated value of the test statistic that falls in either of these two regions causes us to reject the null hypothesis at the 0.05 significance level. The rejection points

---

[10]"Rejection point" is a descriptive synonym for the more traditional term "critical value."
[11]The analogy in some courts of law (for example, in the United States) is that if a jury does not return a verdict of guilty (the alternative hypothesis), it is most accurate to say that the jury has failed to reject the null hypothesis, namely, that the defendant is innocent.

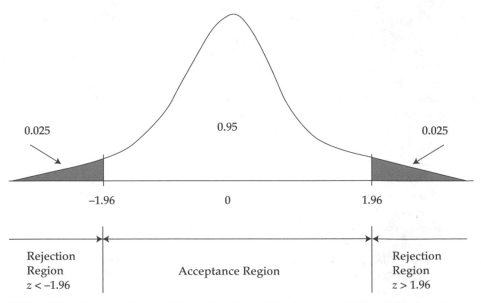

FIGURE 7-1   Rejection Points (Critical Values), 0.05 Significance Level, Two-Sided Test of the Population Mean Using a z-Test

of 1.96 and -1.96 are seen to be the dividing lines between the acceptance and rejection regions.

Figure 7-1 affords a good opportunity to highlight the relationship between confidence intervals and hypothesis tests. A 95 percent confidence interval for the population mean, μ, based on sample mean, $\overline{X}$, is given by $\overline{X} - 1.96\,s_{\overline{X}}$ to $\overline{X} + 1.96\,s_{\overline{X}}$, where $s_{\overline{X}}$ is the standard error of the sample mean (Equation 7-3).[12]

Now consider one of the conditions for rejecting the null hypothesis:

$$\frac{\overline{X} - \mu_0}{s_{\overline{X}}} > 1.96$$

Here, μ_0 is the hypothesized value of the population mean. The condition states that rejection is warranted if the test statistic exceeds 1.96. Multiplying both sides by $s_{\overline{X}}$, we have $\overline{X} - \mu_0 > 1.96\,s_{\overline{X}}$ or, after rearranging, $\overline{X} - 1.96\,s_{\overline{X}} > \mu_0$, which we can also write as $\mu_0 < \overline{X} - 1.96\,s_{\overline{X}}$. This expression says that if the hypothesized population mean, μ_0, is less than the lower limit of the 95 percent confidence interval based on the sample mean, we must reject the null hypothesis at the 5 percent significance level (the test statistic falls in the rejection region to the right).

Now, we can take the other condition for rejecting the null hypothesis

$$\frac{\overline{X} - \mu_0}{s_{\overline{X}}} < -1.96$$

---

[12]Just as with the hypothesis test, we can use this confidence interval, based on the standard normal distribution, when we have large samples. An alternative hypothesis test and confidence interval uses the t-distribution, which requires concepts that we introduce in the next section.

and, using algebra as before, rewrite it as $\mu_0 > \overline{X} + 1.96\, s_{\overline{X}}$. If the hypothesized population mean is larger than the upper limit of the 95 percent confidence interval, we reject the null hypothesis at the 5 percent level (the test statistic falls in the rejection region to the left). Thus, an α significance level in a two-sided hypothesis test can be interpreted in exactly the same way as a $(1 - \alpha)$ confidence interval.

In summary, when the hypothesized value of the population parameter under the null is outside the corresponding confidence interval, the null hypothesis is rejected. We could use confidence intervals to test hypotheses; practitioners, however, usually do not. Computing a test statistic (one number, versus two numbers for the usual confidence interval) is more efficient. Also, analysts encounter actual cases of one-sided confidence intervals only rarely. Furthermore, only when we compute a test statistic can we obtain a *p*-value, a useful quantity relating to the significance of our results (we will discuss *p*-values shortly).

To return to our risk premium test, we stated hypotheses $H_0: \mu_{\mathrm{RP}} \leq 0$ versus $H_a: \mu_{\mathrm{RP}} > 0$. We identified the test statistic as $\overline{X}_{\mathrm{RP}}/s_{\overline{X}}$ and stated that it follows a standard normal distribution. We are, therefore, conducting a one-sided *z*-test. We specified a 0.05 significance level. For this one-sided *z*-test, the rejection point at the 0.05 level of significance is 1.645. We will reject the null if the calculated *z*-statistic is larger than 1.645. Figure 7-2 illustrates this test.

The fifth step in hypothesis testing is collecting the data and calculating the test statistic. The quality of our conclusions depends not only on the appropriateness of the statistical model but also on the quality of the data we use in conducting the test. We first need to check for measurement errors in the recorded data. Some other issues to be aware of include sample selection bias and time-period bias. Sample selection bias refers to bias introduced by systematically excluding some members of the population according to a particular attribute. One type of sample selection bias is survivorship bias. For example, if we define our sample as U.S. bond mutual funds currently operating and we collect returns for just these funds, we will systematically exclude funds that have not survived to the present date. Nonsurviving funds

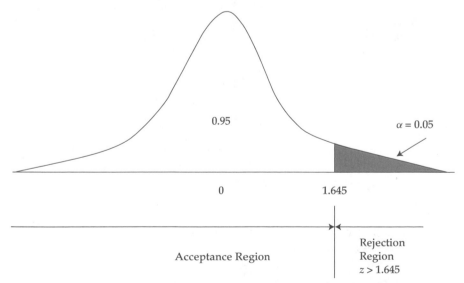

FIGURE 7-2   Rejection Point (Critical Value), 0.05 Significance Level, One-Sided Test of the Population Mean Using a *z*-Test

are likely to have underperformed surviving funds, on average; as a result the performance reflected in the sample may be biased upward. Time-period bias refers to the possibility that when we use a time-series sample, our statistical conclusion may be sensitive to the starting and ending dates of the sample.[13]

To continue with the risk premium hypothesis, we focus on Canadian equities. According to Dimson, Marsh, and Staunton (2002) as updated to the end of 2002,[14] for the period 1900 to 2002 inclusive (103 annual observations), the arithmetic mean equity risk premium for Canadian stocks relative to bond returns, $\overline{X}_{RP}$, was 5.1 percent per year. The sample standard deviation of the annual risk premiums was 18.6 percent. Using Equation 7-3, the standard error of the sample mean is $s_{\overline{X}} = s/\sqrt{n} = 18.6\%/\sqrt{103} = 1.833\%$. The test statistic is $z = \overline{X}_{RP}/s_{\overline{X}} = 5.1\%/1.833\% = 2.78$.

The sixth step in hypothesis testing is making the statistical decision. For our example, because the test statistic $z = 2.78$ is larger than the rejection point of 1.645, we reject the null hypothesis in favor of the alternative hypothesis that the risk premium on Canadian stocks is positive. The first six steps are the statistical steps. The final decision concerns our use of the statistical decision.

The seventh and final step in hypothesis testing is making the economic or investment decision. The economic or investment decision takes into consideration not only the statistical decision but also all pertinent economic issues. In the sixth step, we found strong statistical evidence that the Canadian risk premium is positive. The magnitude of the estimated risk premium, 5.1 percent a year, is economically very meaningful as well. Based on these considerations, an investor might decide to commit funds to Canadian equities. A range of nonstatistical considerations, such as the investor's tolerance for risk and financial position, might also enter the decision-making process.

The preceding discussion raises an issue that often arises in this decision-making step. We frequently find that slight differences between a variable and its hypothesized value are statistically significant but not economically meaningful. For example, we may be testing an investment strategy and reject a null hypothesis that the mean return to the strategy is zero based on a large sample. Equation 7-1 shows that the smaller the standard error of the sample statistic (the divisor in the formula), the larger the value of the test statistic and the greater the chance the null will be rejected, all else equal. The standard error decreases as the sample size, n, increases, so that for very large samples, we can reject the null for small departures from it. We may find that although a strategy provides a statistically significant positive mean return, the results are not economically significant when we account for transaction costs, taxes, and risk. Even if we conclude that a strategy's results are economically meaningful, we should explore the logic of why the strategy might work in the future before actually implementing it. Such considerations cannot be incorporated into a hypothesis test.

Before leaving the subject of the process of hypothesis testing, we should discuss an important alternative approach called the *p*-value approach to hypothesis testing. Analysts and researchers often report the *p*-value (also called the marginal significance level) associated with hypothesis tests.

- **Definition of *p*-Value.** The *p*-value is the smallest level of significance at which the null hypothesis can be rejected.

---

[13]These issues are discussed further in the chapter on sampling.

[14]Updated by communication dated 19 May 2003 to the authors.

For the value of the test statistic of 2.78 in the risk premium hypothesis test, using a spreadsheet function for the standard normal distribution, we calculate a p-value of 0.002718. We can reject the null hypothesis at that level of significance. The smaller the p-value, the stronger the evidence against the null hypothesis and in favor of the alternative hypothesis. The p-value for a two-sided test that a parameter equals zero is frequently generated automatically by statistical and econometric software programs.[15]

We can use p-values in the hypothesis testing framework presented above as an alternative to using rejection points. If the p-value is less than our specified level of significance, we reject the null hypothesis. Otherwise, we do not reject the null hypothesis. Using the p-value in this fashion, we reach the same conclusion as we do using rejection points. For example, because 0.002718 is less than 0.05, we would reject the null hypothesis in the risk premium test. The p-value, however, provides more precise information on the strength of the evidence than does the rejection points approach. The p-value of 0.002718 indicates that the null is rejected at a far smaller level of significance than 0.05.

If one researcher examines a question using a 0.05 significance level and another researcher uses a 0.01 significance level, the reader may have trouble comparing the findings. This concern has given rise to an approach to presenting the results of hypothesis tests that features p-values and omits specification of the significance level (Step 3). The interpretation of the statistical results is left to the consumer of the research. This has sometimes been called the p-value approach to hypothesis testing.[16]

3. HYPOTHESIS TESTS CONCERNING THE MEAN

Hypothesis tests concerning the mean are among the most common in practice. In this section we discuss such tests for several distinct types of problems. In one type (discussed in Section 3.1), we test whether the population mean of a single population is equal to (or greater or less than) some hypothesized value. Then, in Sections 3.2 and 3.3, we address inference on means based on two samples. Is an observed difference between two sample means due to chance or to different underlying (population) means? When we have two random samples that are independent of each other—no relationship exists between the measurements in one sample and the measurements in the other—the techniques of Section 3.2 apply. When the samples are dependent, the methods of Section 3.3 are appropriate.[17]

---

[15]We can use spreadsheets to calculate p-values as well. In Microsoft Excel, for example, we may use the worksheet functions TTEST, NORMSDIST, CHIDIST, and FDIST to calculate p-values for t-tests, z-tests, chi-square tests, and F-tests, respectively.

[16]Davidson and MacKinnon (1993) argued the merits of this approach: "The P value approach does not necessarily force us to make a decision about the null hypothesis. If we obtain a P value of, say, 0.000001, we will almost certainly want to reject the null. But if we obtain a P value of, say, 0.04, or even 0.004, we are not *obliged* to reject it. We may simply file the result away as information that casts some doubt on the null hypothesis, but that is not, by itself, conclusive. We believe that this somewhat agnostic attitude toward test statistics, in which they are merely regarded as pieces of information that we may or may not want to act upon, is usually the most sensible one to take." (p. 80).

[17]When we want to test whether the population means of more than two populations are equal, we use analysis of variance (ANOVA). We introduce ANOVA in its most common application, regression analysis, in the chapter on correlation and regression analysis.

3.1. Tests Concerning a Single Mean

An analyst who wants to test a hypothesis concerning the value of an underlying or population mean will conduct a *t*-test in the great majority of cases. A **t-test** is a hypothesis test using a statistic (*t*-statistic) that follows a *t*-distribution. The *t*-distribution is a probability distribution defined by a single parameter known as degrees of freedom (df). Each value of degrees of freedom defines one distribution in this family of distributions. The *t*-distribution is closely related to the standard normal distribution. Like the standard normal distribution, a *t*-distribution is symmetrical with a mean of zero. However, the *t*-distribution is more spread out: It has a standard deviation greater than 1 (compared to 1 for the standard normal)[18] and more probability for outcomes distant from the mean (it has fatter tails than the standard normal distribution). As the number of degrees of freedom increases with sample size, the spread decreases and the *t*-distribution approaches the standard normal distribution as a limit.

Why is the *t*-distribution the focus for the hypothesis tests of this section? In practice, investment analysts need to estimate the population standard deviation by calculating a sample standard deviation; that is, the population variance (or standard deviation) is unknown. For hypothesis tests concerning the population mean of a normally distributed population with unknown variance, the theoretically correct test statistic is the *t*-statistic. What if a normal distribution does not describe the population? The *t*-test is **robust** to moderate departures from normality, except for outliers and strong skewness.[19] When we have large samples, departures of the underlying distribution from the normal are of increasingly less concern. The sample mean is approximately normally distributed in large samples according to the central limit theorem, whatever the distribution describing the population. In general, a sample size of 30 or more usually can be treated as a large sample and a sample size of 29 or less is treated as a small sample.[20]

- **Test Statistic for Hypothesis Tests of the Population Mean (Practical Case—Population Variance Unknown).** If the population sampled has unknown variance and either of the conditions below holds:

  1. the sample is large, or
  2. the sample is small but the population sampled is normally distributed, or approximately normally distributed,

  then the test statistic for hypothesis tests concerning a single population mean, μ, is

  $$t_{n-1} = \frac{\overline{X} - \mu_0}{s/\sqrt{n}} \tag{7-4}$$

  where

  $$t_{n-1} = t\text{-statistic with } n - 1 \text{ degrees of freedom (} n \text{ is the sample size)}$$
  $$\overline{X} = \text{the sample mean}$$

---

[18] The formula for the variance of a *t*-distribution is $df/(df - 2)$.

[19] See Moore and McCabe (1998). A statistic is robust if the required probability calculations are insensitive to violations of the assumptions.

[20] Although this generalization is useful, we caution that the sample size needed to obtain an approximately normal sampling distribution for the sample mean depends on how nonnormal the original population is. For some populations, "large" may be a sample size well in excess of 30.

μ_0 = the hypothesized value of the population mean

s = the sample standard deviation

The denominator of the t-statistic is an estimate of the sample mean standard error, $s_{\overline{X}} = s/\sqrt{n}$.[21]

In Example 7-1, because the sample size is small, the test is called a small sample test concerning the population mean.

EXAMPLE 7-1 Risk and Return Characteristics of an Equity Mutual Fund (1)

You are analyzing Sendar Equity Fund, a midcap growth fund that has been in existence for 24 months. During this period, it has achieved a mean monthly return of 1.50 percent with a sample standard deviation of monthly returns of 3.60 percent. Given its level of systematic (market) risk and according to a pricing model, this mutual fund was expected to have earned a 1.10 percent mean monthly return during that time period. Assuming returns are normally distributed, are the actual results consistent with an underlying or population mean monthly return of 1.10 percent?

1. Formulate null and alternative hypotheses consistent with the verbal description of the research goal.
2. Identify the test statistic for conducting a test of the hypotheses in Part 1.
3. Identify the rejection point or points for the hypothesis tested in Part 1 at the 0.10 level of significance.
4. Determine whether the null hypothesis is rejected or not rejected at the 0.10 level of significance. (Use the tables in the back of this book.)

Solution to 1: We have a "not equal to" alternative hypothesis, where μ is the underlying mean return on Sendar Equity Fund—H_0: $\mu = 1.10$ versus H_a: $\mu \neq 1.10$.

Solution to 2: Because the population variance is not known, we use a t-test with $24 - 1 = 23$ degrees of freedom.

Solution to 3: Because this is a two-tailed test, we have the rejection point $t_{\alpha/2, n-1} = t_{0.05, 23}$. In the table for the t-distribution, we look across the row for 23 degrees of freedom to the 0.05 column, to find 1.714. The two rejection points for this two-sided

---

[21]A technical note, for reference, is required. When the sample comes from a finite population, estimates of the standard error of the mean, whether from Equation 7-2 or Equation 7-3, overestimate the true standard error. To address this, the computed standard error is multiplied by a shrinkage factor called the finite population correction factor (fpc), equal to $\sqrt{(N - n)/(N - 1)}$, where N is the population size and n is the sample size. When the sample size is small relative to the population size (less than 5 percent of the population size), the fpc is usually ignored. The overestimation problem arises only in the usual situation of sampling without replacement (after an item is selected, it cannot be picked again), as opposed to sampling with replacement.

test are 1.714 and −1.714. We will reject the null if we find that $t > 1.714$ or $t < -1.714$.

Solution to 4:

$$t_{23} = \frac{1.50 - 1.10}{3.60/\sqrt{24}} = \frac{0.40}{0.734847} = 0.544331 \text{ or } 0.544$$

Because 0.544 does not satisfy either $t > 1.714$ or $t < -1.714$, we do not reject the null hypothesis.

   The confidence interval approach provides another perspective on this hypothesis test. The theoretically correct $100(1 - \alpha)\%$ confidence interval for the population mean of a normal distribution with unknown variance, based on a sample of size n, is

$$\overline{X} - t_{\alpha/2}\, s_{\overline{X}} \quad \text{to} \quad \overline{X} + t_{\alpha/2}\, s_{\overline{X}}$$

where $t_{\alpha/2}$ is the value of t such that $\alpha/2$ of the probability remains in the right tail and where $-t_{\alpha/2}$ is the value of t such that $\alpha/2$ of the probability remains in the left tail, for $n - 1$ degrees of freedom. Here, the 90 percent confidence interval runs from $1.5 - (1.714)(0.734847) = 0.240$ to $1.5 + (1.714)(0.734847) = 2.760$, compactly [0.240, 2.760]. The hypothesized value of mean return, 1.10, falls within this confidence interval, and we see from this perspective also that the null hypothesis is not rejected. At a 10 percent level of significance, we conclude that a population mean monthly return of 1.10 percent is consistent with the 24-month observed data series. Note that 10 percent is a relatively high probability of rejecting the hypothesis of a 1.10 percent population mean monthly return when it is true.

EXAMPLE 7-2   A Slowdown in Payments of Receivables

FashionDesigns, a supplier of casual clothing to retail chains, is concerned about a possible slowdown in payments from its customers. The controller's office measures the rate of payment by the average number of days in receivables.[22] FashionDesigns has generally maintained an average of 45 days in receivables. Because it would be too costly to analyze all of the company's receivables frequently, the controller's office uses sampling to track customers' payment rates. A random sample of 50 accounts shows a mean number of days in receivables of 49 with a standard deviation of 8 days.

1. Formulate null and alternative hypotheses consistent with determining whether the evidence supports the suspected condition that customer payments have slowed.
2. Identify the test statistic for conducting a test of the hypotheses in Part 1.

---

[22]This measure represents the average length of time that the business must wait after making a sale before receiving payment. The calculation is (Accounts receivable)/(Average sales per day).

3. Identify the rejection point or points for the hypothesis tested in Part 1 at the 0.05 and 0.01 levels of significance.
4. Determine whether the null hypothesis is rejected or not rejected at the 0.05 and 0.01 levels of significance.

Solution to 1: The suspected condition is that the number of days in receivables has increased relative to the historical rate of 45 days, which suggests a "greater than" alternative hypothesis. With μ as the population mean number of days in receivables, the hypotheses are H_0: $\mu \leq 45$ versus H_a: $\mu > 45$.

Solution to 2: Because the population variance is not known, we use a *t*-test with $50 - 1 = 49$ degrees of freedom.

Solution to 3: The rejection point is found across the row for degrees of freedom of 49. To find the one-tailed rejection point for a 0.05 significance level, we use the 0.05 column: The value is 1.677. To find the one-tailed rejection point for a 0.01 level of significance, we use the 0.01 column: The value is 2.405. To summarize, at a 0.05 significance level, we reject the null if we find that $t > 1.677$; at a 0.01 significance level, we reject the null if we find that $t > 2.405$.

Solution to 4: $t_{49} = \dfrac{49 - 45}{8/\sqrt{50}} = \dfrac{4}{1.131371} = 3.536$

Because $3.536 > 1.677$, the null hypothesis is rejected at the 0.05 level. Because $3.536 > 2.405$, the null hypothesis is also rejected at the 0.01 level. We can say with a high level of confidence that FashionDesigns has experienced a slowdown in customer payments. The level of significance, 0.01, is a relatively low probability of rejecting the hypothesized mean of 45 days or less. Rejection gives us confidence that the mean has increased above 45 days.

We stated above that when population variance is not known, we use a *t*-test for tests concerning a single population mean. Given at least approximate normality, the *t*-test is always called for when we deal with small samples and do not know the population variance. For large samples, the central limit theorem states that the sample mean is approximately normally distributed, whatever the distribution of the population. So the *t*-test is still appropriate, but an alternative test may be more useful when sample size is large.

For large samples, practitioners sometimes use a *z*-test in place of a *t*-test for tests concerning a mean.[23] The justification for using the *z*-test in this context is twofold. First, in large samples, the sample mean should follow the normal distribution at least approximately, as we have already stated, fulfilling the normality assumption of the *z*-test. Second, the difference between the rejection points for the *t*-test and *z*-test becomes quite small when sample size is large. For a two-sided test at the 0.05 level of significance, the rejection points for a *z*-test are 1.96 and -1.96. For a *t*-test, the rejection points are 2.045 and -2.045 for df $= 29$ (about a 4 percent difference between the *z* and *t* rejection points) and 2.009 and -2.009

---

[23]These practitioners choose between *t*-tests and *z*-tests based on sample size. For small samples ($n < 30$), they use a *t*-test, and for large samples, a *z*-test.

for df = 50 (about a 2.5 percent difference between the z and t rejection points). Because the t-test is readily available as statistical program output and theoretically correct for unknown population variance, we present it as the test of choice.

In a very limited number of cases, we may know the population variance; in such cases, the z-test is theoretically correct.[24]

- **The z-Test Alternative.**

  1. If the population sampled is normally distributed with known variance σ^2, then the test statistic for a hypothesis test concerning a single population mean, μ, is

$$z = \frac{\overline{X} - \mu_0}{\sigma/\sqrt{n}} \qquad (7\text{-}5)$$

  2. If the population sampled has unknown variance and the sample is large, in place of a t-test, an alternative test statistic (relying on the central limit theorem) is

$$z = \frac{\overline{X} - \mu_0}{s/\sqrt{n}} \qquad (7\text{-}6)$$

In the above equations,

σ = the known population standard deviation
s = the sample standard deviation
μ_0 = the hypothesized value of the population mean

When we use a z-test, we most frequently refer to a rejection point in the list below.

- **Rejection Points for a z-Test.**

  A. Significance level of $\alpha = 0.10$.

  1. H_0: $\theta = \theta_0$ versus H_a: $\theta \neq \theta_0$. The rejection points are $z_{0.05} = 1.645$ and $-z_{0.05} = -1.645$.
     Reject the null hypothesis if $z > 1.645$ or if $z < -1.645$.
  2. H_0: $\theta \leq \theta_0$ versus H_a: $\theta > \theta_0$. The rejection point is $z_{0.10} = 1.28$.
     Reject the null hypothesis if $z > 1.28$.
  3. H_0: $\theta \geq \theta_0$ versus H_a: $\theta < \theta_0$. The rejection point is $-z_{0.10} = -1.28$.
     Reject the null hypothesis if $z < -1.28$.

  B. Significance level of $\alpha = 0.05$.

  1. H_0: $\theta = \theta_0$ versus H_a: $\theta \neq \theta_0$. The rejection points are $z_{0.025} = 1.96$ and $-z_{0.025} = -1.96$.
     Reject the null hypothesis if $z > 1.96$ or if $z < -1.96$.

---

[24] For example, in Monte Carlo simulation, we prespecify the probability distributions for the risk factors. If we use a normal distribution, we know the true values of mean and variance. Monte Carlo simulation involves the use of a computer to represent the operation of a system subject to risk; we discuss Monte Carlo simulation in the chapter on common probability distributions.

2. H_0: $\theta \leq \theta_0$ versus H_a: $\theta > \theta_0$. The rejection point is $z_{0.05} = 1.645$. Reject the null hypothesis if $z > 1.645$.

3. H_0: $\theta \geq \theta_0$ versus H_a: $\theta < \theta_0$. The rejection point is $-z_{0.05} = -1.645$. Reject the null hypothesis if $z < -1.645$.

C. Significance level of $\alpha = 0.01$.

1. H_0: $\theta = \theta_0$ versus H_a: $\theta \neq \theta_0$. The rejection points are $z_{0.005} = 2.575$ and $-z_{0.005} = -2.575$. Reject the null hypothesis if $z > 2.575$ or if $z < -2.575$.

2. H_0: $\theta \leq \theta_0$ versus H_a: $\theta > \theta_0$. The rejection point is $z_{0.01} = 2.33$. Reject the null hypothesis if $z > 2.33$.

3. H_0: $\theta \geq \theta_0$ versus H_a: $\theta < \theta_0$. The rejection point is $-z_{0.01} = -2.33$. Reject the null hypothesis if $z < -2.33$.

EXAMPLE 7-3   The Effect of Commercial Paper Issuance on Stock Prices

Commercial paper (CP) is unsecured short-term corporate debt that, like U.S. Treasury bills, is characterized by a single payment at maturity. When a company enters the CP market for the first time, how do stock market participants react to the announcement of the CP ratings?

Nayar and Rozeff (1994) addressed this question using data for the period October 1981 to December 1985. During this period, 132 CP issues (96 industrial and 36 non-industrial) received an initial rating in Standard & Poor's *CreditWeek* or Moody's Investors Service *Bond Survey*. Nayar and Rozeff categorized ratings as superior or inferior. Superior CP ratings were A1+ or A1 from Standard & Poor's and Prime-1 (P1) from Moody's. Inferior CP ratings were A2 or lower from Standard & Poor's and Prime-2 (P2) or lower from Moody's. The publication day of the initial ratings was designated $t = 0$. The researchers found, however, that companies themselves often disseminate the rating information prior to publication in *CreditWeek* or the *Bond Survey*. The reaction of stock price was studied on the day before publication, $t - 1$, because that date was closer to the actual date of information release.

If CP ratings provide *new* information useful for equity valuation, the information should cause a change in stock prices and returns once it is available. Only one component of stock returns is of interest: the return in excess of that predicted given a stock's market risk or beta, called the abnormal return. Positive (negative) abnormal returns indicate that investors perceive favorable (unfavorable) corporate news in the ratings announcement. Although Nayar and Rozeff examined abnormal returns for various time horizons or event windows, we report a selection of their findings for the day prior to rating publication ($t - 1$):

All CP Issues ($n = 132$ issues). The null hypothesis was that the average abnormal stock return on day $t - 1$ was 0. The null would be true if stock investors did not find either positive or negative information in the announcement.

Mean abnormal return = 0.39 percent

Sample standard error of the mean of abnormal returns = 0.1336 percent[25]

Industrial CP Issues with Superior Ratings ($n = 72$ issues). The null hypothesis was that the average abnormal stock return on day $t - 1$ was 0. The null would be true if stock investors did not find either positive or negative information in the announcement.

Mean abnormal return = 0.79 percent

Sample standard error of the mean of abnormal returns = 0.197 percent

Industrial CP Issues with Inferior Ratings ($n = 24$ issues). The null hypothesis was that the average abnormal stock return on day $t - 1$ was 0. The null would be true if stock investors did not find either positive or negative information in the announcement.

Mean abnormal return = −0.57 percent

Sample standard error of the mean of abnormal returns = 0.38 percent

The researchers chose to use z-tests.

1. With respect to each of the three cases, suppose that the null hypothesis reflects the belief that investors do not, on average, perceive either positive or negative information in initial ratings. State one set of hypotheses (a null hypothesis and an alternative hypothesis) that covers all three cases.
2. Determine whether the null hypothesis formulated in Part 1 is rejected or not rejected at the 0.05 and 0.01 levels of significance for the *All CP Issues* case. Interpret the results.
3. Determine whether the null hypothesis formulated in Part 1 is rejected or not rejected at the 0.05 and 0.01 levels of significance for the *Industrial CP Issues with Superior Ratings* case. Interpret the results.
4. Determine whether the null hypothesis formulated in Part 1 is rejected or not rejected at the 0.05 and 0.01 levels of significance for the *Industrial CP Issues with Inferior Ratings* case. Interpret the results.

Solution to 1: A set of hypotheses consistent with no information in CP credit ratings relevant to stock investors is

H_0: The population mean abnormal return on day $t - 1$ equals 0

H_a: The population mean abnormal return on day $t - 1$ does not equal 0

Solution to 2: From the information on rejection points for z-tests, we know that we reject the null hypothesis at the 0.05 significance level if $z > 1.96$ or if $z < -1.96$, and at the 0.01 significance level if $z > 2.575$ or if $z < -2.575$. Using the z-test, $z = (0.39\% - 0\%)/0.1336\% = 2.92$ is significant at the 0.05 and 0.01 levels. The null is rejected. The fact of CP issuance itself appears to be viewed as favorable news.

Because it is possible that significant results could be due to outliers, the researchers also reported the number of cases of positive and negative abnormal returns. The ratio of cases of positive to negative abnormal returns was 80:52, which tends to support the conclusion of positive abnormal returns from the z-test.

---

[25] This standard error was calculated as a sample standard deviation over the 132 issues (a cross-sectional standard deviation) divided by the square root of 132. Other standard errors were calculated similarly.

Solution to 3: Using the z-test, $z = (0.79\% - 0\%)/0.197\% = 4.01$ is significant at the 0.05 and 0.01 levels. Stocks earned clearly positive abnormal returns in response to the news of a superior initial CP rating. Investors may view rating agencies as certifying through a superior rating that a company's future prospects are strong.

The ratio of cases of positive to negative abnormal returns was 48:24, which tends to support the conclusion of positive abnormal returns from the z-test.

Solution to 4: Using the z-test, $z = (-0.57\% - 0\%)/0.38\% = -1.50$ is not significant at either the 0.01 or 0.05 levels. In the case of inferior ratings, we cannot conclude that investors found either positive or negative information in the announcements of initial CP ratings.

The ratio of cases of positive to negative abnormal returns was 11:13 and tends to support the conclusion of the z-test, which did not reject the null hypothesis.

Nearly all practical situations involve an unknown population variance. Table 7-2 summarizes our discussion for tests concerning the population mean when the population variance is unknown.

TABLE 7-2   Test Concerning the Population Mean
(Population Variance Unknown)

	Large Sample ($n \geq 30$)	Small Sample ($n < 30$)
Population normal	t-Test (z-Test alternative)	t-Test
Population nonnormal	t-Test (z-Test alternative)	Not Available

3.2. Tests Concerning Differences between Means

We often want to know whether a mean value—for example, a mean return—differs between two groups. Is an observed difference due to chance or to different underlying values for the mean? We have two samples, one for each group. When it is reasonable to believe that the samples are from populations at least approximately normally distributed and that the samples are also independent of each other, the techniques of this section apply. We discuss two t-tests for a test concerning differences between the means of two populations. In one case, the population variances, although unknown, can be assumed to be equal. Then, we efficiently combine the observations from both samples to obtain a pooled estimate of the common but unknown population variance. A **pooled** estimate is an estimate drawn from the combination of two different samples. In the second case, we do not assume that the unknown population variances are equal, and an approximate t-test is then available. Letting μ_1 and μ_2 stand, respectively, for the population means of the first and second populations, we most often want to test whether the population means are equal or whether one is larger than the other. Thus we usually formulate the following hypotheses:

1. $H_0: \mu_1 - \mu_2 = 0$ versus $H_a: \mu_1 - \mu_2 \neq 0$ (the alternative is that $\mu_1 \neq \mu_2$)
2. $H_0: \mu_1 - \mu_2 \leq 0$ versus $H_a: \mu_1 - \mu_2 > 0$ (the alternative is that $\mu_1 > \mu_2$)
3. $H_0: \mu_1 - \mu_2 \geq 0$ versus $H_a: \mu_1 - \mu_2 < 0$ (the alternative is that $\mu_1 < \mu_2$)

We can, however, formulate other hypotheses, such as $H_0: \mu_1 - \mu_2 = 2$ versus $H_a: \mu_1 - \mu_2 \neq 2$. The procedure is the same.

The definition of the t-test follows.

- **Test Statistic for a Test of the Difference between Two Population Means (Normally Distributed Populations, Population Variances Unknown but Assumed Equal).** When we can assume that the two populations are normally distributed and that the unknown population variances are equal, a t-test based on independent random samples is given by

$$t = \frac{(\overline{X}_1 - \overline{X}_2) - (\mu_1 - \mu_2)}{\left(\dfrac{s_p^2}{n_1} + \dfrac{s_p^2}{n_2}\right)^{1/2}} \tag{7-7}$$

where $s_p^2 = \dfrac{(n_1 - 1)s_1^2 + (n_2 - 1)s_2^2}{n_1 + n_2 - 2}$ is a pooled estimator of the common variance.
The number of degrees of freedom is $n_1 + n_2 - 2$.

EXAMPLE 7-4   Mean Returns on the S&P 500: A Test of Equality across Decades

The realized mean monthly return on the S&P 500 Index in the 1980s appears to have been substantially different from the mean return in the 1970s. Was the difference statistically significant? The data, shown in Table 7-3, indicate that assuming equal population variances for returns in the two decades is not unreasonable.

TABLE 7-3   S&P 500 Monthly Return and Standard Deviation for Two Decades

Decade	Number of Months (n)	Mean Monthly Return (%)	Standard Deviation
1970s	120	0.580	4.598
1980s	120	1.470	4.738

1. Formulate null and alternative hypotheses consistent with a two-sided hypothesis test.
2. Identify the test statistic for conducting a test of the hypotheses in Part 1.
3. Identify the rejection point or points for the hypothesis tested in Part 1 at the 0.10, 0.05, and 0.01 levels of significance.
4. Determine whether the null hypothesis is rejected or not rejected at the 0.10, 0.05, and 0.01 levels of significance.

Solution to 1: Letting μ_1 stand for the population mean return for the 1970s and μ_2 stand for the population mean return for the 1980s, we formulate the following hypotheses:

$$H_0: \mu_1 - \mu_2 = 0 \text{ versus } H_a: \mu_1 - \mu_2 \neq 0$$

Solution to 2: Because the two samples are drawn from different decades, they are independent samples. The population variances are not known but can be assumed to be equal. Given all these considerations, the *t*-test given in Equation 7-7 has $120 + 120 - 2 = 238$ degrees of freedom.

Solution to 3:   In the tables (Appendix B), the closest degree of freedom to 238 is 200. For a two-sided test, the rejection points are $\pm 1.653, \pm 1.972$, and ± 2.601 for, respectively, the 0.10, 0.05, and 0.01 levels for df = 200. To summarize, at the 0.10 level, we will reject the null if $t < -1.653$ or $t > 1.653$; at the 0.05 level, we will reject the null if $t < -1.972$ or $t > 1.972$; and at the 0.01 level, we will reject the null if $t < -2.601$ or $t > 2.601$.

Solution to 4:   In calculating the test statistic, the first step is to calculate the pooled estimate of variance:

$$s_p^2 = \frac{(n_1 - 1)s_1^2 + (n_2 - 1)s_2^2}{n_1 + n_2 - 2} = \frac{(120 - 1)(4.598)^2 + (120 - 1)(4.738)^2}{120 + 120 - 2}$$

$$= \frac{5{,}187.239512}{238} = 21.795124$$

$$t = \frac{(\overline{X}_1 - \overline{X}_2) - (\mu_1 - \mu_2)}{\left(\dfrac{s_p^2}{n_1} + \dfrac{s_p^2}{n_2}\right)^{1/2}} = \frac{(0.580 - 1.470) - 0}{\left(\dfrac{21.795124}{120} + \dfrac{21.795124}{120}\right)^{1/2}}$$

$$= \frac{-0.89}{0.602704} = -1.477$$

The *t* value of -1.477 is not significant at the 0.10 level, so it is also not significant at the 0.05 and 0.01 levels. Therefore, we do not reject the null hypothesis at any of the three levels.

In many cases of practical interest, we cannot assume that population variances are equal. The following test statistic is often used in the investment literature in such cases:

- **Test Statistic for a Test of the Difference between Two Population Means (Normally Distributed Populations, Unequal and Unknown Population Variances).** When we can assume that the two populations are normally distributed but do not know the population variances and cannot assume that they are equal, an approximate *t*-test based on independent random samples is given by

$$t = \frac{(\overline{X}_1 - \overline{X}_2) - (\mu_1 - \mu_2)}{\left(\dfrac{s_1^2}{n_1} + \dfrac{s_2^2}{n_2}\right)^{1/2}} \tag{7-8}$$

where we use tables of the *t*-distribution using "modified" degrees of freedom computed with the formula

$$df = \frac{\left(\dfrac{s_1^2}{n_1} + \dfrac{s_2^2}{n_2}\right)^2}{\dfrac{(s_1^2/n_1)^2}{n_1} + \dfrac{(s_2^2/n_2)^2}{n_2}} \tag{7-9}$$

A practical tip is to compute the t-statistic before computing the degrees of freedom. Whether or not the t-statistic is significant will sometimes be obvious.

EXAMPLE 7-5   Recovery Rates on Defaulted Bonds: A Hypothesis Test

How are the required yields on risky corporate bonds determined? Two key factors are the expected probability of default and the expected amount that will be recovered in the event of default, or the recovery rate. Altman and Kishore (1996) documented for the first time the average recovery rates on defaulted bonds stratified by industry and seniority. For their study period, 1971 to 1995, Altman and Kishore discovered that defaulted bonds of public utilities and chemicals, petroleum, and plastics manufacturers experienced much higher recovery rates than did other industrial sectors. Could the differences be explained by a greater preponderance of senior debt in the higher-recovery sectors? They studied this by examining recovery rates stratified by seniority. We discuss their results for senior secured bonds. With μ_1 denoting the population mean recovery rate for the senior secured bonds of utilities and μ_2 denoting the population mean recovery rate for the senior secured bonds of other sectors (non-utilities), the hypotheses are H_0: $\mu_1 - \mu_2 = 0$ versus H_a: $\mu_1 - \mu_2 \neq 0$.

Table 7-4 excerpts from their findings.

TABLE 7-4   Recovery Rates by Seniority

Industry Group/ Seniority	Industry Group			Ex-Utilities Sample		
	Number of Observations	Average Price*	Standard Deviation	Number of Observations	Average Price*	Standard Deviation
Public Utilities Senior Secured	21	$64.42	$14.03	64	$55.75	$25.17

Source: Altman and Kishore (1996), Table 5.
*This is the average price at default and is a measure of recovery rate.

Following the researchers, assume that the populations (recovery rates of utilities, recovery rates of non-utilities) are normally distributed and that the samples are independent. Based on the data in the table, address the following:

1. Discuss why Altman and Kishore would choose a test based on Equation 7-8 rather than Equation 7-7.
2. Calculate the test statistic to test the null hypothesis given above.
3. What is the value of the test's modified degrees of freedom?
4. Determine whether to reject the null hypothesis at the 0.10 level.

Solution to 1: The sample standard deviation for the recovery rate on the senior secured bonds of utilities ($14.03) appears much smaller than the sample standard deviation of the comparable bonds for non-utilities ($25.17). Properly choosing not to assume equal variances, Altman and Kishore employed the approximate *t*-test given in Equation 7-8.

Solution to 2:   The test statistic is

$$t = \frac{(\overline{X}_1 - \overline{X}_2)}{\left(\dfrac{s_1^2}{n_1} + \dfrac{s_2^2}{n_2}\right)^{1/2}}$$

where

$\overline{X}_1$ = sample mean recovery rate for utilities = 64.42
$\overline{X}_2$ = sample mean recovery rate for non-utility sectors = 55.75
s_1^2 = sample variance for utilities = 14.03^2 = 196.8409
s_2^2 = sample variance for non-utilities = 25.17^2 = 633.5289
n_1 = sample size of the utility sample = 21
n_2 = sample size of the non-utility sample = 64

Thus, $t = (64.42 - 55.75)/[(196.8409/21) + (633.5289/64)]^{1/2} = 8.67/(9.373376 + 9.898889)^{1/2} = 8.67/4.390019 = 1.975$. The calculated *t*-statistic is thus 1.975.

Solution to 3:

$$df = \frac{\left(\dfrac{s_1^2}{n_1} + \dfrac{s_2^2}{n_2}\right)^2}{\dfrac{(s_1^2/n_1)^2}{n_1} + \dfrac{(s_2^2/n_2)^2}{n_2}} = \frac{\left(\dfrac{196.8409}{21} + \dfrac{633.5289}{64}\right)^2}{\dfrac{(196.8409/21)^2}{21} + \dfrac{(633.5289/64)^2}{64}}$$

$$= \frac{371.420208}{5.714881} = 64.99 \text{ or } 65 \text{ degrees of freedom}$$

Solution to 4:   The closest entry to df = 65 in the tables for the *t*-distribution is df = 60. For $\alpha = 0.10$, we find $t_{\alpha/2} = 1.671$. Thus, we reject the null if $t < -1.671$ or $t > 1.671$. Based on the computed value of 1.975, we reject the null hypothesis at the 0.10 level. Some evidence exists that recovery rates differ between utilities and other industries. Why? Altman and Kishore suggest that the differing nature of the companies' assets and industry competitive structures may explain the different recovery rates.

3.3. Tests Concerning Mean Differences

In the previous section, we presented two *t*-tests for discerning differences between population means. The tests were based on two samples. An assumption for those tests' validity was that the samples were independent—that is, unrelated to each other. When we want to conduct tests on two means based on samples that we believe are dependent, the methods of this section apply.

The *t*-test in this section is based on data arranged in **paired observations**, and the test itself is sometimes called a **paired comparisons test**. Paired observations are observations that are dependent because they have something in common. A paired comparisons test is a statistical test for differences in dependent items. For example, we may be concerned with the dividend policy of companies before and after a change in the tax law affecting the taxation of dividends. We then have pairs of "before" and "after" observations for the same companies. We may test a hypothesis about the mean of the differences (mean differences) that we observe across companies. In other cases, the paired observations are not on the same units. For example, we may be testing whether the mean returns earned by two investment strategies were equal over a study period. The observations here are dependent in the sense that there is one observation for each strategy in each month, and both observations depend on underlying market risk factors. Because the returns to both strategies are likely to be related to some common risk factors, such as the market return, the samples are dependent. By calculating a standard error based on differences, the t-test presented below takes account of correlation between the observations.

Letting A represent "after" and B "before," suppose we have observations for the random variables X_A and X_B and that the samples are dependent. We arrange the observations in pairs. Let d_i denote the difference between two paired observations. We can use the notation $d_i = x_{Ai} - x_{Bi}$, where x_{Ai} and x_{Bi} are the ith pair of observations, $i = 1, 2, \ldots, n$ on the two variables. Let μ_d stand for the population mean difference. We can formulate the following hypotheses, where μ_{d0} is a hypothesized value for the population mean difference:

1. $H_0: \mu_d = \mu_{d0}$ versus $H_a: \mu_d \neq \mu_{d0}$
2. $H_0: \mu_d \leq \mu_{d0}$ versus $H_a: \mu_d > \mu_{d0}$
3. $H_0: \mu_d \geq \mu_{d0}$ versus $H_a: \mu_d < \mu_{d0}$

In practice, the most commonly used value for μ_{d0} is 0.

As usual, we are concerned with the case of normally distributed populations with unknown population variances, and we will formulate a t-test. To calculate the t-statistic, we first need to find the sample mean difference:

$$\overline{d} = \frac{1}{n} \sum_{i=1}^{n} d_i \tag{7-10}$$

where n is the number of pairs of observations. The sample variance, denoted by s_d^2, is

$$s_d^2 = \frac{\sum_{i=1}^{n} (d_i - \overline{d})^2}{n - 1} \tag{7-11}$$

Taking the square root of this quantity, we have the sample standard deviation, s_d, which then allows us to calculate the standard error of the mean difference as follows:[26]

$$s_{\overline{d}} = \frac{s_d}{\sqrt{n}} \tag{7-12}$$

- **Test Statistic for a Test of Mean Differences (Normally Distributed Populations, Unknown Population Variances).** When we have data consisting of paired observations

---

[26] We can also use the following equivalent expression, which makes use of the correlation between the two variables: $s_{\overline{d}} = \sqrt{s_A^2 + s_B^2 - 2r(X_A, X_B)s_A s_B}$, where s_A^2 is the sample variance of X_A, s_B^2 is the sample variance of X_B, and $r(X_A, X_B)$ is the sample correlation between X_A and X_B.

from samples generated by normally distributed populations with unknown variances, a
t-test is based on

$$t = \frac{\bar{d} - \mu_{d0}}{s_{\bar{d}}} \qquad (7\text{-}13)$$

with $n - 1$ degrees of freedom, where n is the number of paired observations, $\bar{d}$ is the
sample mean difference (as given by Equation 7-10), and $s_{\bar{d}}$ is the standard error of $\bar{d}$ (as
given by Equation 7-12).

Table 7-5 reports the quarterly returns from 1997 to 2002 for two managed portfolios
specializing in precious metals. The two portfolios were closely similar in risk (as measured
by standard deviation of return and other measures) and had nearly identical expense ratios.
A major investment services company rated Portfolio B more highly than Portfolio A in
early 2003. In investigating the portfolios' relative performance, suppose we want to test
the hypothesis that the mean quarterly return on Portfolio A equaled the mean quarterly
return on Portfolio B from 1997 to 2002. Because the two portfolios shared essentially the
same set of risk factors, their returns were not independent, so a paired comparisons test is
appropriate. Let μ_d stand for the population mean value of difference between the returns

TABLE 7-5   Quarterly Returns on Two Managed Portfolios: 1997–2002

Quarter	Portfolio A (%)	Portfolio B (%)	Difference (Portfolio A − Portfolio B)
4Q:2002	11.40	14.64	−3.24
3Q:2002	−2.17	0.44	−2.61
2Q:2002	10.72	19.51	−8.79
1Q:2002	38.91	50.40	−11.49
4Q:2001	4.36	1.01	3.35
3Q:2001	5.13	10.18	−5.05
2Q:2001	26.36	17.77	8.59
1Q:2001	−5.53	4.76	−10.29
4Q:2000	5.27	−5.36	10.63
3Q:2000	−7.82	−1.54	−6.28
2Q:2000	2.34	0.19	2.15
1Q:2000	−14.38	−12.07	−2.31
4Q:1999	−9.80	−9.98	0.18
3Q:1999	19.03	26.18	−7.15
2Q:1999	4.11	−2.39	6.50
1Q:1999	−4.12	−2.51	−1.61
4Q:1998	−0.53	−11.32	10.79
3Q:1998	5.06	0.46	4.60
2Q:1998	−14.01	−11.56	−2.45
1Q:1998	12.50	3.52	8.98
4Q:1997	−29.05	−22.45	−6.60
3Q:1997	3.60	0.10	3.50
2Q:1997	−7.97	−8.96	0.99
1Q:1997	−8.62	−0.66	−7.96
Mean	1.87	2.52	−0.65

Sample standard deviation of differences = 6.71

on the two portfolios during this period. We test H_0: $\mu_d = 0$ versus H_a: $\mu_d \neq 0$ at a 0.05 significance level.

The sample mean difference, $\bar{d}$, between Portfolio A and Portfolio B is -0.65 percent per quarter. The standard error of the sample mean difference is $s_{\bar{d}} = 6.71/\sqrt{24} = 1.369673$. The calculated test statistic is $t = (-0.65 - 0)/1.369673 = -0.475$ with $n - 1 = 24 - 1 = 23$ degrees of freedom. At the 0.05 significance level, we reject the null if $t > 2.069$ or if $t < -2.069$. Because -0.475 is not less than -2.069, we fail to reject the null. At the 0.10 significance level, we reject the null if $t > 1.714$ or if $t < -1.714$. Thus the difference in mean quarterly returns is not significant at any conventional significance level.

The following example illustrates the application of this test to evaluate two competing investment strategies.

EXAMPLE 7-6   The Dow-10 Investment Strategy

McQueen, Shields, and Thorley (1997) examined the popular investment strategy of investing in the 10 stocks with the highest yields (rebalancing annually) in the Dow Jones Industrial Average, compared with a buy-and-hold strategy in all 30 stocks of the DJIA. Their study period was the 50 years from 1946 to 1995.

From Table 7-6 we have $\bar{d} = 3.06\%$ and $s_d = 6.62\%$.

TABLE 7-6   Annual Return Summary for Dow-10 and Dow-30 Portfolios: 1946 to 1995 ($n = 50$)

Strategy	Mean Return	Standard Deviation
Dow-10	16.77%	19.10%
Dow-30	13.71	16.64
Difference	3.06	6.62*

Source: McQueen, Shields, and Thorley (1997), Table 1.
*Sample standard deviation of differences.

1. Formulate null and alternative hypotheses consistent with a two-sided test that the mean difference between the Dow-10 and Dow-30 strategies equals 0.
2. Identify the test statistic for conducting a test of the hypotheses in Part 1.
3. Identify the rejection point or points for the hypothesis tested in Part 1 at the 0.01 level of significance.
4. Determine whether the null hypothesis is rejected or not rejected at the 0.01 level of significance. (Use the tables in the back of this book.)
5. Discuss the choice of a paired comparisons test.

Solution to 1: With μ_d as the underlying mean difference between the Dow-10 and Dow-30 strategies, we have H_0: $\mu_d = 0$ versus H_a: $\mu_d \neq 0$.

Solution to 2: Because the population variance is unknown, the test statistic is a t-test with $50 - 1 = 49$ degrees of freedom.

Solution to 3: In the table for the *t*-distribution, we look across the row for 49 degrees of freedom to the 0.005 column, to find 2.68. We will reject the null if we find that $t > 2.68$ or $t < -2.68$.

Solution to 4:

$$t_{49} = \frac{3.06}{6.62/\sqrt{50}} = \frac{3.06}{0.936209} = 3.2685 \text{ or } 3.27$$

Because $3.27 > 2.68$, we reject the null hypothesis. The authors concluded that the difference in mean returns was clearly statistically significant. However, after adjusting for the Dow-10's higher risk, extra transaction costs, and unfavorable tax treatment, they found that the Dow-10 portfolio did not beat the Dow-30 economically.

Solution to 5: The Dow-30 includes the Dow-10. As a result, they are not independent samples; in general, the correlation of returns on the Dow-10 and Dow-30 should be positive. Because the samples are dependent, a paired comparisons test was appropriate.

4. HYPOTHESIS TESTS CONCERNING VARIANCE

Because variance and standard deviation are widely used quantitative measures of risk in investments, analysts should be familiar with hypothesis tests concerning variance. The tests discussed in this section make regular appearances in investment literature. We examine two types: tests concerning the value of a single population variance and tests concerning the differences between two population variances.

4.1. Tests Concerning a Single Variance

In this section, we discuss testing hypotheses about the value of the variance, σ^2, of a single population. We use σ_0^2 to denote the hypothesized value of σ^2. We can formulate hypotheses as follows:

1. H_0: $\sigma^2 = \sigma_0^2$ versus H_a: $\sigma^2 \neq \sigma_0^2$ (a "not equal to" alternative hypothesis)
2. H_0: $\sigma^2 \leq \sigma_0^2$ versus H_a: $\sigma^2 > \sigma_0^2$ (a "greater than" alternative hypothesis)
3. H_0: $\sigma^2 \geq \sigma_0^2$ versus H_a: $\sigma^2 < \sigma_0^2$ (a "less than" alternative hypothesis)

In tests concerning the variance of a single normally distributed population, we make use of a chi-square test statistic, denoted χ^2. The chi-square distribution, unlike the normal and *t*-distributions, is asymmetrical. Like the *t*-distribution, the chi-square distribution is a family of distributions. A different distribution exists for each possible value of degrees of freedom, $n - 1$ (*n* is sample size). Unlike the *t*-distribution, the chi-square distribution is bounded below by 0; χ^2 does not take on negative values.

- **Test Statistic for Tests Concerning the Value of a Population Variance (Normal Population).** If we have n independent observations from a normally distributed population, the appropriate test statistic is

$$\chi^2 = \frac{(n-1)s^2}{\sigma_0^2} \qquad (7\text{-}14)$$

with $n-1$ degrees of freedom. In the numerator of the expression is the sample variance, calculated as

$$s^2 = \frac{\sum_{i=1}^{n}(X_i - \overline{X})^2}{n-1} \qquad (7\text{-}15)$$

In contrast to the t-test, for example, the chi-square test is sensitive to violations of its assumptions. If the sample is not actually random or if it does not come from a normally distributed population, inferences based on a chi-square test are likely to be faulty.

If we choose a level of significance, α, the rejection points for the three kinds of hypotheses are as follows:

- **Rejection Points for Hypothesis Tests on the Population Variance.**

1. "Not equal to" H_a: Reject the null hypothesis if the test statistic is greater than the upper $\alpha/2$ point (denoted $\chi^2_{\alpha/2}$) or less than the lower $\alpha/2$ point (denoted $\chi^2_{1-\alpha/2}$) of the chi-square distribution with df $= n - 1$.[27]
2. "Greater than" H_a: Reject the null hypothesis if the test statistic is greater than the upper α point of the chi-square distribution with df $= n - 1$.
3. "Less than" H_a: Reject the null hypothesis if the test statistic is less than the lower α point of the chi-square distribution with df $= n - 1$.

EXAMPLE 7-7 Risk and Return Characteristics of an Equity Mutual Fund (2)

You continue with your analysis of Sendar Equity Fund, a midcap growth fund that has been in existence for only 24 months. Recall that during this period, Sendar Equity achieved a sample standard deviation of monthly returns of 3.60 percent. You now want to test a claim that the particular investment disciplines followed by Sendar result in a standard deviation of monthly returns of less than 4 percent.

1. Formulate null and alternative hypotheses consistent with the verbal description of the research goal.

---

[27]Just as with other hypothesis tests, the chi-square test can be given a confidence interval interpretation. Unlike confidence intervals based on z- or t-statistics, however, chi-square confidence intervals for variance are asymmetric. A two-sided confidence interval for population variance, based on a sample of size n, has a lower limit $L = (n-1)s^2/\chi^2_{\alpha/2}$ and an upper limit $U = (n-1)s^2/\chi^2_{1-\alpha/2}$. Under the null hypothesis, the hypothesized value of the population variance should fall within these two limits.

2. Identify the test statistic for conducting a test of the hypotheses in Part 1.
3. Identify the rejection point or points for the hypothesis tested in Part 1 at the 0.05 level of significance.
4. Determine whether the null hypothesis is rejected or not rejected at the 0.05 level of significance. (Use the tables in the back of this book.)

Solution to 1: We have a "less than" alternative hypothesis, where σ is the underlying standard deviation of return on Sendar Equity Fund. Being careful to square standard deviation to obtain a test in terms of variance, the hypotheses are H_0: $\sigma^2 \geq 16.0$ versus H_a: $\sigma^2 < 16.0$.

Solution to 2: The test statistic is chi-square with $24 - 1 = 23$ degrees of freedom.

Solution to 3: The lower 0.05 rejection point is found on the line for df = 23, under the 0.95 column (95 percent probability in the right tail, to give 0.95 probability of getting a test statistic this large or larger). The rejection point is 13.091. We will reject the null if we find that chi-square is less than 13.091.

Solution to 4:

$$\chi^2 = \frac{(n-1)s^2}{\sigma_0^2} = \frac{23 \times 3.60^2}{4^2} = \frac{298.08}{16} = 18.63$$

Because 18.63 (the calculated value of the test statistic) is not less than 13.091, we do not reject the null hypothesis. We cannot conclude that Sendar's investment disciplines result in a standard deviation of monthly returns of less than 4 percent.

4.2. Tests Concerning the Equality (Inequality) of Two Variances

Suppose we have a hypothesis about the relative values of the variances of two normally distributed populations with means μ_1 and μ_2 and variances σ_1^2 and σ_2^2. We can formulate all hypotheses as one of the choices below:

1. H_0: $\sigma_1^2 = \sigma_2^2$ versus H_a: $\sigma_1^2 \neq \sigma_2^2$
2. H_0: $\sigma_1^2 \leq \sigma_2^2$ versus H_a: $\sigma_1^2 > \sigma_2^2$
3. H_0: $\sigma_1^2 \geq \sigma_2^2$ versus H_a: $\sigma_1^2 < \sigma_2^2$

Note that at the point of equality, the null hypothesis $\sigma_1^2 = \sigma_2^2$ implies that the ratio of population variances equals 1: $\sigma_1^2/\sigma_2^2 = 1$. Given independent random samples from these populations, tests related to these hypotheses are based on an F-test, which is the ratio of sample variances. Suppose we use n_1 observations in calculating the sample variance s_1^2 and n_2 observations in calculating the sample variance s_2^2. Tests concerning the difference between the variances of two populations make use of the F-distribution. Like the chi-square distribution, the F-distribution is a family of asymmetrical distributions bounded from below by 0. Each F-distribution is defined by two values of degrees of freedom, called the numerator and denominator degrees of freedom.[28] The F-test, like the chi-square test, is not robust to violations of its assumptions.

- **Test Statistic for Tests Concerning Differences between the Variances of Two Populations (Normally Distributed Populations).** Suppose we have two samples, the first with n_1 observations and sample variance s_1^2, the second with n_2 observations and sample variance s_2^2. The samples are random, independent of each other, and generated by normally distributed populations. A test concerning differences between the variances of the two populations is based on the ratio of sample variances

$$F = \frac{s_1^2}{s_2^2} \tag{7-16}$$

with $df_1 = n_1 - 1$ numerator degrees of freedom and $df_2 = n_2 - 1$ denominator degrees of freedom. Note that df_1 and df_2 are the divisors used in calculating s_1^2 and s_2^2, respectively.

A convention, or usual practice, is to use the larger of the two ratios s_1^2/s_2^2 or s_2^2/s_1^2 as the actual test statistic. When we follow this convention, the value of the test statistic is always greater than or equal to 1; tables of critical values of F then need include only values greater than or equal to 1. Under this convention, the rejection point for any formulation of hypotheses is a single value in the right-hand side of the relevant F-distribution. Note that the labeling of populations as "1" or "2" is arbitrary in any case.

- **Rejection Points for Hypothesis Tests on the Relative Values of Two Population Variances.** Follow the convention of using the larger of the two ratios s_1^2/s_2^2 and s_2^2/s_1^2 and consider two cases:

  1. A "not equal to" alternative hypothesis: Reject the null hypothesis at the α significance level if the test statistic is greater than the upper $\alpha/2$ point of the F-distribution with the specified numerator and denominator degrees of freedom.
  2. A "greater than" or "less than" alternative hypothesis: Reject the null hypothesis at the α significance level if the test statistic is greater than the upper α point of the F-distribution with the specified number of numerator and denominator degrees of freedom.

Thus, if we conduct a two-sided test at the $\alpha = 0.01$ level of significance, we need to find the rejection point in F-tables at the $\alpha/2 = 0.01/2 = 0.005$ significance level for a one-sided test (Case 1). But a one-sided test at 0.01 uses rejection points in F-tables for $\alpha = 0.01$ (Case 2). As an example, suppose we are conducting a two-sided test at the 0.05 significance level. We calculate a value of F of 2.77 with 12 numerator and 19 denominator degrees of freedom. Using the F-tables for $0.05/2 = 0.025$ in the back of the book, we find that the rejection point is 2.72. Because the value 2.77 is greater than 2.72, we reject the null hypothesis at the 0.05 significance level.

If the convention stated above is not followed and we are given a calculated value of F less than 1, can we still use F-tables? The answer is yes; using a reciprocal property of F-statistics, we can calculate the needed value. The easiest way to present this property is to

---

[28]The relationship between the chi-square and F-distributions is as follows: If χ_1^2 is one chi-square random variable with m degrees of freedom and χ_2^2 is another chi-square random variable with n degrees of freedom, then $F = (\chi_1^2/m)/(\chi_2^2/n)$ follows an F-distribution with m numerator and n denominator degrees of freedom.

show a calculation. Suppose our chosen level of significance is 0.05 for a two-tailed test and we have a value of F of 0.11, with 7 numerator degrees of freedom and 9 denominator degrees of freedom. We take the reciprocal, $1/0.11 = 9.09$. Then we look up this value in the F-tables for 0.025 (because it is a two-tailed test) with degrees of freedom reversed: F for 9 numerator and 7 denominator degrees of freedom. In other words, $F_{9,7} = 1/F_{7,9}$ and 9.09 exceeds the critical value of 4.82, so $F_{7,9} = 0.11$ is significant at the 0.05 level.

EXAMPLE 7-8 Volatility and the Crash of 1987

You are investigating whether the population variance of returns on the S&P 500 changed subsequent to the October 1987 market crash. You gather the data in Table 7-7 for 120 months of returns before October 1987 and 120 months of returns after October 1987. You have specified a 0.01 level of significance.

TABLE 7-7   S&P 500 Returns and Variance before and after October 1987

	n	Mean Monthly Return (%)	Variance of Returns
Before October 1987	120	1.498	18.776
After October 1987	120	1.392	13.097

1. Formulate null and alternative hypotheses consistent with the verbal description of the research goal.
2. Identify the test statistic for conducting a test of the hypotheses in Part 1.
3. Determine whether or not to reject the null hypothesis at the 0.01 level of significance. (Use the F-tables in the back of this book.)

Solution to 1: We have a "not equal to" alternative hypothesis:

$$H_0: \sigma^2_{\text{Before}} = \sigma^2_{\text{After}} \text{ versus } H_a: \sigma^2_{\text{Before}} \neq \sigma^2_{\text{After}}$$

Solution to 2: To test a null hypothesis of the equality of two variances, we use $F = s_1^2/s_2^2$ with $120 - 1 = 119$ numerator and denominator degrees of freedom.

Solution to 3: The "before" sample variance is larger, so following a convention for calculating F-statistics, the "before" sample variance goes in the numerator: $F = 18.776/13.097 = 1.434$. Because this is a two-tailed test, we use F-tables for the 0.005 level ($= 0.01/2$) to give a 0.01 significance level. In the tables in the back of the book, the closest value to 119 degrees of freedom is 120 degrees of freedom. At the 0.01 level, the rejection point is 1.61. Because 1.434 is less than the critical value 1.61, we cannot reject the null hypothesis that the population variance of returns is the same in the pre- and postcrash periods.

EXAMPLE 7-9   The Volatility of Derivatives Expiration Days

In the 1980s concern arose in the United States about the triple occurrence of stock option, index option, and futures expirations on the same day during four months of the year. Such days were known as "triple witching days." Table 7-8 presents evidence on the daily standard deviation of return for normal days and options/futures expiration days during the period 1 July 1983 to 24 October 1986. The tabled data refer to options and futures on the S&P 100, a subset of the S&P 500 that includes 100 of the most liquid S&P 500 stocks on which there are traded options.

TABLE 7-8   Standard Deviation of Return: 1 July 1983 to 24 October 1986

Type of Day	n	Standard Deviation (%)
Normal trading	115	0.786
Options/futures expiration	12	1.178

Source: Based on Edwards (1988), Table I.

1. Formulate null and alternative hypotheses consistent with the belief that triple witching days displayed above-normal volatility.
2. Identify the test statistic for conducting a test of the hypotheses in Part 1.
3. Determine whether or not to reject the null hypothesis at the 0.05 level of significance. (Use the F-tables in the back of this book.)

Solution to 1: We have a "greater than" alternative hypothesis:

$$H_0: \sigma^2_{\text{Expirations}} \leq \sigma^2_{\text{Normal}} \text{ versus } H_a: \sigma^2_{\text{Expirations}} > \sigma^2_{\text{Normal}}$$

Solution to 2: Let σ^2_1 represent the variance of triple witching days, and σ^2_2 represent the variance of normal days, following the convention for the selection of the numerator and the denominator stated earlier. To test the null hypothesis, we use $F = s^2_1/s^2_2$ with $12 - 1 = 11$ numerator and $115 - 1 = 114$ denominator degrees of freedom.

Solution to 3: $F = (1.178)^2/(0.786)^2 = 1.388/0.618 = 2.25$. Because this is a one-tailed test at the 0.05 significance level, we use F-tables for the 0.05 level directly. In the tables in the back of the book, the closest value to 114 degrees of freedom is 120 degrees of freedom. At the 0.05 level, the rejection point is 1.87. Because 2.25 is greater than 1.87, we reject the null hypothesis. It appears that triple witching days had above-normal volatility.

5. OTHER ISSUES: NONPARAMETRIC INFERENCE

The hypothesis-testing procedures we have discussed to this point have two characteristics in common. First, they are concerned with parameters, and second, their validity depends on a definite set of assumptions. Mean and variance, for example, are two parameters, or defining quantities, of a normal distribution. The tests also make specific assumptions—in particular, assumptions about the distribution of the population producing the sample. Any test or procedure with either of the above two characteristics is a **parametric test** or procedure. In some cases, however, we are concerned about quantities other than parameters of distributions. In other cases, we may believe that the assumptions of parametric tests do not hold for the particular data we have. In such cases, a nonparametric test or procedure can be useful. A **nonparametric test** is a test that is not concerned with a parameter, or a test that makes minimal assumptions about the population from which the sample comes.[29]

We primarily use nonparametric procedures in three situations: when the data we use do not meet distributional assumptions, when the data are given in ranks, or when the hypothesis we are addressing does not concern a parameter.

The first situation occurs when the data available for analysis suggest that the distributional assumptions of the parametric test are not satisfied. For example, we may want to test a hypothesis concerning the mean of a population but believe that neither a *t*-test nor a *z*-test is appropriate because the sample is small and may come from a markedly nonnormally distributed population. In that case, we may use a nonparametric test. The nonparametric test will frequently involve the conversion of observations (or a function of observations) into ranks according to magnitude, and sometimes it will involve working with only "greater than" or "less than" relationships (using the signs + and − to denote those relationships). Characteristically, one must refer to specialized statistical tables to determine the rejection points of the test statistic, at least for small samples.[30] Such tests, then, typically interpret the null hypothesis as a thesis about ranks or signs. In Table 7-9, we give examples of nonparametric alternatives to the parametric tests we have discussed in this chapter.[31] The reader should consult a comprehensive business statistics textbook for an introduction to such tests and a specialist textbook for details.[32]

We pointed out that when we use nonparametric tests, we often convert the original data into ranks. In some cases, the original data are already ranked. In those cases, we also use nonparametric tests because parametric tests generally require a stronger measurement scale than ranks. For example, if our data were the rankings of investment managers, hypotheses concerning those rankings would be tested using nonparametric procedures. Ranked data also appear in many other finance contexts. For example, Heaney, Koga, Oliver, and Tran (1999) studied the relationship between the size of Japanese companies (as measured by revenue) and their use of derivatives. The companies studied used derivatives to hedge one or more

---

[29] Some writers make a distinction between "nonparametric" and "distribution-free" tests. They refer to procedures that do not concern the parameters of a distribution as nonparametric and to procedures that make minimal assumptions about the underlying distribution as distribution free. We follow a commonly accepted, inclusive usage of the term nonparametric.

[30] For large samples, there is often a transformation of the test statistic that permits the use of tables for the standard normal or *t*-distribution.

[31] In some cases, there are several nonparametric alternatives to a parametric test.

[32] See, for example, Hettmansperger and McKean (1998) or Siegel (1956).

TABLE 7-9   Nonparametric Alternatives to Parametric Tests

	Parametric	Nonparametric
Tests concerning a single mean	t-Test	Wilcoxon signed-rank test
	z-Test	
Tests concerning differences between means	t-Test Approximate t-test	Mann–Whitney U test
Tests concerning mean differences (paired comparisons tests)	t-Test	Wilcoxon signed-rank test Sign test

of five types of risk exposure: interest rate risk, foreign exchange risk, commodity price risk, marketable security price risk, and credit risk. The researchers gave a "perceived scope of risk exposure" score to each company that was equal to the number of types of risk exposure that the company reported hedging. Although revenue is measured on a strong scale (a ratio scale), scope of risk exposure is measured on only an ordinal scale.[33] The researchers thus employed nonparametric statistics to explore the relationship between derivatives usage and size.

A third situation in which we use nonparametric procedures occurs when our question does not concern a parameter. For example, if the question concerns whether a sample is random or not, we use the appropriate nonparametric test (a so-called runs test). Another type of question nonparametrics can address is whether a sample came from a population following a particular probability distribution (using the Kolmogorov–Smirnov test, for example).

We end this chapter by describing in some detail a nonparametric statistic that has often been used in investment research, the Spearman rank correlation.

5.1. Tests Concerning Correlation: The Spearman Rank Correlation Coefficient

In many contexts in investments, we want to assess the strength of the linear relationship between two variables—the correlation between them. In a majority of cases, we use the correlation coefficient described in the chapters on probability concepts and on correlation and regression. However, the t-test of the hypothesis that two variables are uncorrelated, based on the correlation coefficient, relies on fairly stringent assumptions.[34] When we believe that the population under consideration meaningfully departs from those assumptions, we can employ a test based on the **Spearman rank correlation coefficient**, r_S. The Spearman rank correlation coefficient is essentially equivalent to the usual correlation coefficient calculated on the *ranks* of the two variables (say, X and Y) within their respective samples. Thus it is a number between -1 and $+1$, where -1 $(+1)$ denotes a perfect inverse (positive) straight-line

---

[33] We discussed scales of measurement in the chapter on statistical concepts and market returns.

[34] The t-test is described in the chapter on correlation and regression. The assumption of the test is that each observation (x, y) on the two variables (X, Y) is a random observation from a bivariate normal distribution. Informally, in a bivariate or two-variable normal distribution, each individual variable is normally distributed and their joint relationship is completely described by the correlation, ρ, between them. For more details, see, for example, Daniel and Terrell (1986).

relationship between the variables and 0 represents the absence of any straight-line relationship (no correlation). The calculation of r_S requires the following steps:

1. Rank the observations on X from largest to smallest. Assign the number 1 to the observation with the largest value, the number 2 to the observation with second-largest value, and so on. In case of ties, we assign to each tied observation the average of the ranks that they jointly occupy. For example, if the third- and fourth-largest values are tied, we assign both observations the rank of 3.5 (the average of 3 and 4). Perform the same procedure for the observations on Y.
2. Calculate the difference, d_i, between the ranks of each pair of observations on X and Y.
3. Then, with n the sample size, the Spearman rank correlation is given by[35]

$$r_S = 1 - \frac{6\sum_{i=1}^{n} d_i^2}{n(n^2 - 1)} \tag{7-17}$$

Suppose an investor wants to invest in a U.S. large-cap growth mutual fund. He has narrowed the field to 10 funds. In examining the funds, a question arises as to whether the funds' reported three-year Sharpe ratios are related to their most recent reported expense ratios. Because the assumptions of the t-test on the correlation coefficient may not be met, it is appropriate to conduct a test on the rank correlation coefficient.[36] Table 7-10 presents the calculation of r_S.[37]

The first two rows contain the original data. The row of X ranks converts the Sharpe ratios to ranks; the row of Y ranks converts the expense ratios to ranks. We want to test H_0: $\rho = 0$ versus H_a: $\rho \neq 0$, where ρ is defined in this context as the population correlation of X and Y after ranking. For small samples, the rejection points for the test based on r_S must be looked up in Table 7-11. For large samples (say, $n > 30$), we can conduct a t-test using

$$t = \frac{(n-2)^{1/2}r_s}{(1 - r_s^2)^{1/2}} \tag{7-18}$$

based on $n - 2$ degrees of freedom.

In the example at hand, a two-tailed test with a 0.05 significance level, Table 7-11 gives the upper-tail rejection point for $n = 10$ as 0.6364 (we use the 0.025 column for a two-tailed test at a 0.05 significance level). Accordingly, we reject the null hypothesis if r_S is less than -0.6364 or greater than 0.6364. With r_S equal to 0.2545, we do not reject the null hypothesis.

In the mutual fund example, we converted observations on two variables into ranks. If one or both of the original variables were in the form of ranks, we would need to use r_S to investigate correlation.

---

[35] Calculating the usual correlation coefficient on the ranks would yield approximately the same result as Equation 7-17.

[36] The expense ratio (the ratio of a fund's operating expenses to average net assets) is bounded both from below (by zero) and from above. The Sharpe ratio is also observed within a limited range, in practice. Thus neither variable can be normally distributed, and hence jointly they cannot follow a bivariate normal distribution. In short, the assumptions of a t-test are not met.

[37] The data for the table are based on statistics reported in Standard & Poor's Mutual Fund Reports for actual large-cap growth funds for the three-year period ending in the first quarter of 2003. The negative Sharpe ratios reflect in part declining U.S. equity markets during this period.

TABLE 7-10   The Spearman Rank Correlation: An Example

	Mutual Fund									
	1	2	3	4	5	6	7	8	9	10
Sharpe Ratio (X)	-1.08	-0.96	-1.13	-1.16	-0.91	-1.08	-1.18	-1.00	-1.06	-1.00
Expense Ratio (Y)	1.34	0.92	1.02	1.45	1.35	0.50	1.00	1.50	1.45	1.50
X Rank	6.5	2	8	9	1	6.5	10	3.5	5	3.5
Y Rank	6	9	7	3.5	5	10	8	1.5	3.5	1.5
d_i	0.5	-7	1	5.5	-4	-3.5	2	2	1.5	2
d_i^2	0.25	49	1	30.25	16	12.25	4	4	2.25	4

$$r_S = 1 - \frac{6\Sigma d_i^2}{n(n^2 - 1)} = 1 - \frac{6(123)}{10(100 - 1)} = 0.2545$$

TABLE 7-11   Spearman Rank Correlation
Distribution Approximate Upper-Tail
Rejection Points

Sample size: n	$\alpha = 0.05$	$\alpha = 0.025$	$\alpha = 0.01$
5	0.8000	0.9000	0.9000
6	0.7714	0.8286	0.8857
7	0.6786	0.7450	0.8571
8	0.6190	0.7143	0.8095
9	0.5833	0.6833	0.7667
10	0.5515	0.6364	0.7333
11	0.5273	0.6091	0.7000
12	0.4965	0.5804	0.6713
13	0.4780	0.5549	0.6429
14	0.4593	0.5341	0.6220
15	0.4429	0.5179	0.6000
16	0.4265	0.5000	0.5824
17	0.4118	0.4853	0.5637
18	0.3994	0.4716	0.5480
19	0.3895	0.4579	0.5333
20	0.3789	0.4451	0.5203
21	0.3688	0.4351	0.5078
22	0.3597	0.4241	0.4963
23	0.3518	0.4150	0.4852
24	0.3435	0.4061	0.4748
25	0.3362	0.3977	0.4654
26	0.3299	0.3894	0.4564
27	0.3236	0.3822	0.4481
28	0.3175	0.3749	0.4401
29	0.3113	0.3685	0.4320
30	0.3059	0.3620	0.4251

Note: The corresponding lower tail critical value
is obtained by changing the sign of the upper-tail
critical value.

5.2. Nonparametric Inference: Summary

Nonparametric statistical procedures extend the reach of inference because they make few assumptions, can be used on ranked data, and may address questions unrelated to parameters. Quite frequently, nonparametric tests are reported alongside parametric tests. The reader can then assess how sensitive the statistical conclusion is to the assumptions underlying the parametric test. However, if the assumptions of the parametric test are met, the parametric test (where available) is generally preferred to the nonparametric test because the parametric test usually permits us to draw sharper conclusions.[38] For complete coverage of all the nonparametric procedures that may be encountered in the finance and investment literature, it is best to consult a specialist textbook.[39]

---

[38] To use a concept introduced in an earlier section, the parametric test is often more powerful.

[39] See, for example, Hettmansperger and McKean (1998) or Siegel (1956).

CHAPTER 8

CORRELATION AND REGRESSION

1. INTRODUCTION

As a financial analyst, you will often need to examine the relationship between two or more financial variables. For example, you might want to know whether returns to different stock market indexes are related and, if so, in what way. Or you might hypothesize that the spread between a company's return on invested capital and its cost of capital helps to explain the company's value in the marketplace. Correlation and regression analysis are tools for examining these issues.

This chapter is organized as follows. In Section 2, we present correlation analysis, a basic tool in measuring how two variables vary in relation to each other. Topics covered include the calculation, interpretation, uses, limitations, and statistical testing of correlations. Section 3 introduces basic concepts in regression analysis, a powerful technique for examining the ability of one or more variables (independent variables) to explain or predict another variable (the dependent variable).

2. CORRELATION ANALYSIS

We have many ways to examine how two sets of data are related. Two of the most useful methods are scatter plots and correlation analysis. We examine scatter plots first.

2.1. Scatter Plots

A **scatter plot** is a graph that shows the relationship between the observations for two data series in two dimensions. Suppose, for example, that we want to graph the relationship between long-term money growth and long-term inflation in six industrialized countries to see how strongly the two variables are related. Table 8-1 shows the average annual growth rate in the money supply and the average annual inflation rate from 1970 to 2001 for the six countries.

To translate the data in Table 8-1 into a scatter plot, we use the data for each country to mark a point on a graph. For each point, the x-axis coordinate is the country's annual average money supply growth from 1970–2001 and the y-axis coordinate is the country's annual average inflation rate from 1970–2001. Figure 8-1 shows a scatter plot of the data in Table 8-1.

TABLE 8-1   Annual Money Supply Growth Rate and
Inflation Rate by Country, 1970–2001

Country	Money Supply Growth Rate	Inflation Rate
Australia	11.66%	6.76%
Canada	9.15%	5.19%
New Zealand	10.60%	8.15%
Switzerland	5.75%	3.39%
United Kingdom	12.58%	7.58%
United States	6.34%	5.09%
Average	9.35%	6.03%

Source: International Monetary Fund.

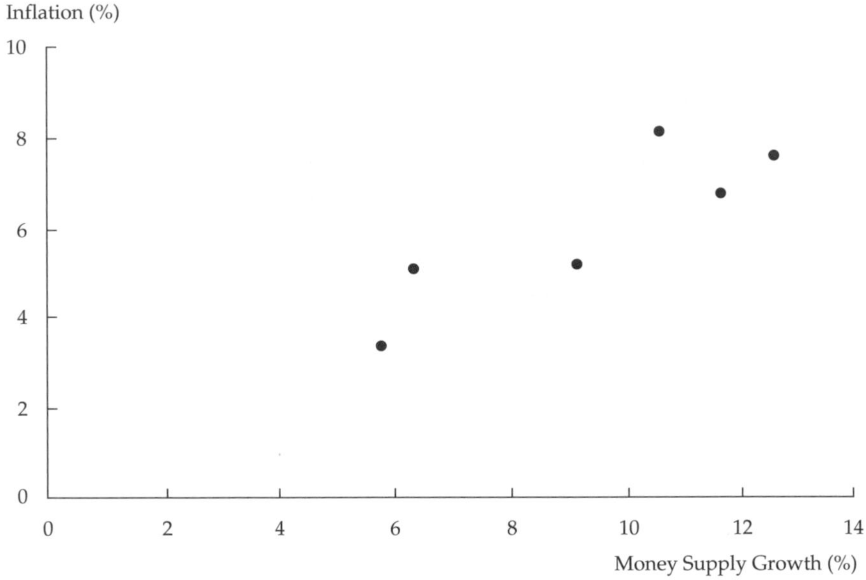

FIGURE 8-1   Scatter Plot of Annual Money Supply Growth Rate and Inflation Rate by Country:
1970–2001
Source: International Monetary Fund.

Note that each observation in the scatter plot is represented as a point, and the points are not connected. The scatter plot does not show which observation comes from which country; it shows only the actual observations of both data series plotted as pairs. For example, the rightmost point shows the data for the United Kingdom. The data plotted in Figure 8-1 show a fairly strong linear relationship with a positive slope. Next we examine how to quantify this linear relationship.

2.2. Correlation Analysis

In contrast to a scatter plot, which graphically depicts the relationship between two data series, **correlation analysis** expresses this same relationship using a single number. The correlation coefficient is a measure of how closely related two data series are. In particular, the correlation

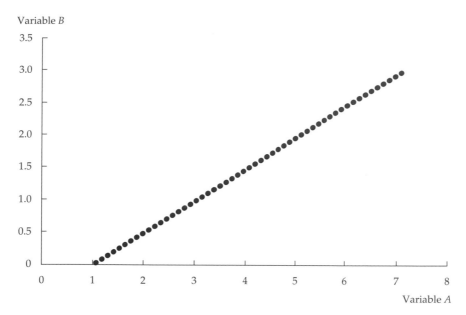

FIGURE 8-2   Variables with a Correlation of 1

coefficient measures the direction and extent of **linear association** between two variables. A correlation coefficient can have a maximum value of 1 and a minimum value of -1. A correlation coefficient greater than 0 indicates a positive linear association between the two variables: When one variable increases (or decreases), the other also tends to increase (or decrease). A correlation coefficient less than 0 indicates a negative linear association between the two variables: When one increases (or decreases), the other tends to decrease (or increase). A correlation coefficient of 0 indicates no linear relation between the two variables.[1] Figure 8-2 shows the scatter plot of two variables with a correlation of 1.

Note that all the points on the scatter plot in Figure 8-2 lie on a straight line with a positive slope. Whenever variable A increases by one unit, variable B increases by half a unit. Because all of the points in the graph lie on a straight line, an increase of one unit in A is associated with exactly the same half-unit increase in B, regardless of the level of A. Even if the slope of the line in the figure were different (but positive), the correlation between the two variables would be 1 as long as all the points lie on that straight line.

Figure 8-3 shows a scatter plot for two variables with a correlation coefficient of -1. Once again, the plotted observations fall on a straight line. In this graph, however, the line has a negative slope. As A increases by one unit, B decreases by half a unit, regardless of the initial value of A.

Figure 8-4 shows a scatter plot of two variables with a correlation of 0; they have no linear relation. This graph shows that the value of A tells us absolutely nothing about the value of B.

2.3. Calculating and Interpreting the Correlation Coefficient

To define and calculate the correlation coefficient, we need another measure of linear association: covariance. In the chapter on probability concepts, we defined covariance as the

---

[1]Later, we show that variables with a correlation of 0 can have a strong nonlinear relation.

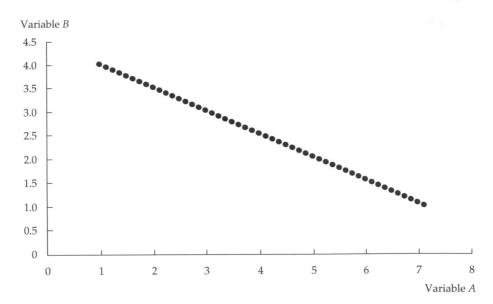

FIGURE 8-3   Variables with a Correlation of -1

expected value of the product of the deviations of two random variables from their respective population means. That was the definition of population covariance, which we would also use in a forward-looking sense. To study historical or sample correlations, we need to use sample covariance. The sample covariance of X and Y, for a sample of size n, is

$$\text{Cov}\,(X, Y) = \sum_{i=1}^{n}(X_i - \overline{X})(Y_i - \overline{Y})/(n - 1) \qquad (8\text{-}1)$$

The sample covariance is the average value of the product of the deviations of observations on two random variables from their sample means.[2] If the random variables are returns, the unit of covariance would be returns squared.

The sample correlation coefficient is much easier to explain than the sample covariance. To understand the sample correlation coefficient, we need the expression for the sample standard deviation of a random variable X. We need to calculate the sample variance of X to obtain its sample standard deviation. The variance of a random variable is simply the covariance of the random variable with itself. The expression for the sample variance of X, s_X^2, is

$$s_X^2 = \sum_{i=1}^{n}(X_i - \overline{X})^2/(n - 1)$$

The sample standard deviation is the positive square root of the sample variance:

$$s_X = \sqrt{s_X^2}$$

[2]The use of $n - 1$ in the denominator is a technical point; it ensures that the sample covariance is an unbiased estimate of population covariance.

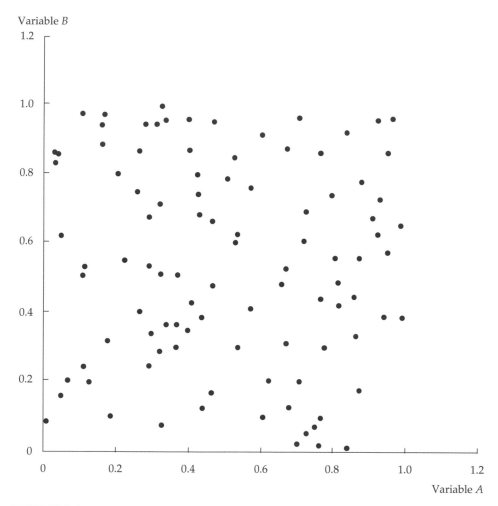

Variable *B*

Variable *A*

FIGURE 8-4   Variables with a Correlation of 0

Both the sample variance and the sample standard deviation are measures of the dispersion of observations about the sample mean. Standard deviation uses the same units as the random variable; variance is measured in the units squared.

The formula for computing the sample correlation coefficient is

$$r = \frac{\text{Cov}(X, Y)}{s_X s_Y} \qquad (8\text{-}2)$$

The correlation coefficient is the covariance of two variables (X and Y) divided by the product of their sample standard deviations (s_X and s_Y). Like covariance, the correlation coefficient is a measure of linear association. The correlation coefficient, however, has the advantage of being a simple number, with no unit of measurement attached. It has no units because it results from dividing the covariance by the product of the standard deviations. Because we will be using sample variance, standard deviation, and covariance in this chapter, we will repeat the calculations for these statistics.

TABLE 8-2   Sample Covariance and Sample Standard Deviations: Annual Money Supply Growth Rate and Inflation Rate by Country, 1970–2001

Country	Money Supply Growth Rate X_i	Inflation Rate Y_i	Cross-Product $(X_i - \overline{X})(Y_i - \overline{Y})$	Squared Deviations $(X_i - \overline{X})^2$	Squared Deviations $(Y_i - \overline{Y})^2$
Australia	0.1166	0.0676	0.000169	0.000534	0.000053
Canada	0.0915	0.0519	0.000017	0.000004	0.000071
New Zealand	0.1060	0.0815	0.000265	0.000156	0.000449
Switzerland	0.0575	0.0339	0.000950	0.001296	0.000697
United Kingdom	0.1258	0.0758	0.000501	0.001043	0.000240
United States	0.0634	0.0509	0.000283	0.000906	0.000088
Sum	0.5608	0.3616	0.002185	0.003939	0.001598
Average	0.0935	0.0603			
Covariance			0.000437		
Variance				0.000788	0.000320
Standard deviation				0.028071	0.017889

Source: International Monetary Fund.
Notes:
1. Divide the cross-product sum by $n - 1$ (with $n = 6$) to obtain the covariance of X and Y.
2. Divide the squared deviations sums by $n - 1$ (with $n = 6$) to obtain the variances of X and Y.

Table 8-2 shows how to compute the various components of the correlation equation (Equation 8-2) from the data in Table 8-1.[3] The individual observations on countries' annual average money supply growth from 1970–2001 are denoted X_i, and individual observations on countries' annual average inflation rate from 1970–2001 are denoted Y_i. The remaining columns show the calculations for the inputs to correlation: the sample covariance and the sample standard deviations.

Using the data shown in Table 8-2, we can compute the sample correlation coefficient for these two variables as follows:

$$ r = \frac{\text{Cov}(X, Y)}{s_X s_Y} = \frac{0.000437}{(0.028071)(0.017889)} = 0.8702 $$

The correlation coefficient of approximately 0.87 indicates a strong linear association between long-term money supply growth and long-term inflation for the countries in the sample. The correlation coefficient captures this strong association numerically, whereas the scatter plot in Figure 8-1 shows the information graphically.

What assumptions are necessary to compute the correlation coefficient? Correlation coefficients can be computed validly if the means and variances of X and Y, as well as the covariance of X and Y, are finite and constant. Later, we will show that when these

---

[3]We have not used full precision in the table's calculations. We used the average value of the money supply growth rate of $0.5608/6 = 0.0935$, rounded to four decimal places, in the cross-product and squared deviation calculations, and similarly, we used the mean inflation rate as rounded to 0.0603 in those calculations. We computed standard deviation as the square root of variance rounded to six decimal places, as shown in the table. Had we used full precision in all calculations, some of the table's entries would be different and the computed value of correlation would be 0.8709 rather than 0.8702, not materially affecting our conclusions.

assumptions are not true, correlations between two different variables can depend greatly on the sample that is used.

2.4. Limitations of Correlation Analysis

Correlation measures the linear association between two variables, but it may not always be reliable. Two variables can have a strong **nonlinear relation** and still have a very low correlation. For example, the relation $B = (A - 4)^2$ is a nonlinear relation contrasted to the linear relation $B = 2A - 4$. The nonlinear relation between variables A and B is shown in Figure 8-5. Below a level of 4 for A, variable B decreases with increasing values of A. When A

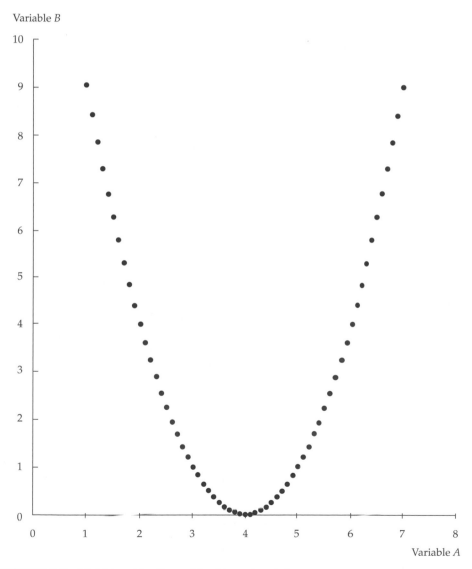

FIGURE 8-5   Variables with a Strong Non-Linear Association

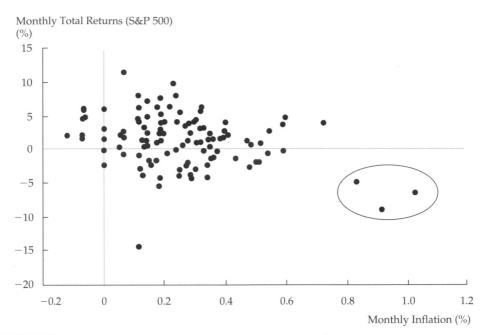

FIGURE 8-6   U.S. Inflation and Stock Returns in the 1990s
Source: Ibbotson Associates.

is 4 or greater, however, *B* increases whenever *A* increases. Even though these two variables are perfectly associated, the correlation between them is 0.[4]

Correlation also may be an unreliable measure when outliers are present in one or both of the series. Outliers are small numbers of observations at either extreme (small or large) of a sample. Figure 8-6 shows a scatter plot of the monthly returns to the Standard & Poor's 500 Index and the monthly inflation rate in the United States during the 1990s (January 1990 through December 1999).

In the scatter plot in Figure 8-6, most of the data lie clustered together with little discernible relation between the two variables. In three cases, however (the three circled observations), inflation was greater than 0.8 percent in a particular month and stock returns were strongly negative. These observations are outliers. If we compute the correlation coefficient for the entire data sample, that correlation is −0.2997. If we eliminate the three outliers, however, the correlation is −0.1347.

The correlation in Figure 8-6 is quite sensitive to excluding only three observations. Does it make sense to exclude those observations? Are they noise or news? One possible partial explanation of Figure 8-6 is that during the 1990s, whenever inflation was very high during a month, market participants became concerned that the Federal Reserve would raise interest rates, which would cause the value of stocks to decline. This story offers one plausible explanation for how investors reacted to large inflation announcements. Consequently, the outliers may provide important information about market reactions during this period. Therefore, the correlation that includes the outliers may make more sense than the correlation that excludes them.

---

[4]The perfect association is the quadratic relationship $B = (A - 4)^2$.

As a general rule, we must determine whether a computed sample correlation changes greatly by removing a few outliers. But we must also use judgment to determine whether those outliers contain information about the two variables' relationship (and should thus be included in the correlation analysis) or contain no information (and should thus be excluded).

Keep in mind that correlation does not imply causation. Even if two variables are highly correlated, one does not necessarily cause the other in the sense that certain values of one variable bring about the occurrence of certain values of the other. Furthermore, correlations can be spurious in the sense of misleadingly pointing towards associations between variables.

The term **spurious correlation** has been used to refer to (1) correlation between two variables that reflects chance relationships in a particular data set, (2) correlation induced by a calculation that mixes each of two variables with a third, and (3) correlation between two variables arising not from a direct relation between them but from their relation to a third variable. As an example of the second kind of spurious correlation, two variables that are uncorrelated may be correlated if divided by a third variable. As an example of the third kind of spurious correlation, height may be positively correlated with the extent of a person's vocabulary, but the underlying relationships are between age and height and between age and vocabulary. Investment professionals must be cautious in basing investment strategies on high correlations. Spurious correlation may suggest investment strategies that appear profitable but actually would not be so, if implemented.

2.5. Uses of Correlation Analysis

In this section, we give examples of correlation analysis for investment. Because investors' expectations about inflation are important in determining asset prices, inflation forecast accuracy will serve as our first example.

EXAMPLE 8-1 Evaluating Economic Forecasts (1)

Investors closely watch economists' forecasts of inflation, but do these forecasts contain useful information? In the United States, the Survey of Professional Forecasters (SPF) gathers professional forecasters' predictions about many economic variables.[5] Since the early 1980s, SPF has gathered predictions on the U.S. inflation rate using the change in the U.S. consumer price index (CPI) for all urban consumers and all items to measure inflation. If these forecasts of inflation could perfectly predict actual inflation, the correlation between forecasts and inflation would be 1; that is, predicted and actual inflation would always be the same.

Figure 8-7 shows a scatter plot of the mean forecast of current-quarter percentage change in CPI from previous quarter and actual percentage change in CPI, on an

---

[5]The survey was originally developed by Victor Zarnowitz for the American Statistical Association and the National Bureau of Economic Research. Starting in 1990, the survey has been directed by Dean Croushire of the Federal Reserve Bank of Philadelphia.

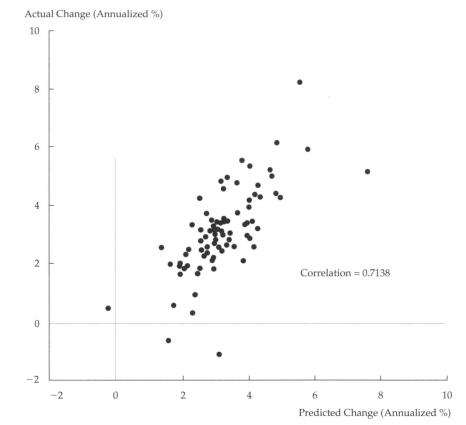

FIGURE 8-7   Actual Change in CPI vs. Predicted Change
Source: Federal Reserve Banks of Philadelphia and St. Louis.

annualized basis, from the first quarter of 1983 to the last quarter of 2002.[6] In this scatter plot, the forecast for each quarter is plotted on the *x*-axis and the actual change in the CPI is plotted on the *y*-axis.

As Figure 8-7 shows, a fairly strong linear association exists between the forecast and the actual inflation rate, suggesting that professional forecasts of inflation might be useful in investment decision-making. In fact, the correlation between the two series is 0.7138. Although there is no causal relation here, there is a direct relation because forecasters assimilate information to forecast inflation.

One important issue in evaluating a portfolio manager's performance is determining an appropriate benchmark for the manager. In recent years, style analysis has been an important component of benchmark selection.[7]

---

[6]In this scatter plot, the actual change in CPI is from the Federal Reserve's economic and financial database, available at the Web site of the Federal Reserve Bank of St. Louis.
[7]See, for example, Sharpe (1992) and Buetow, Johnson, and Runkle (2000).

EXAMPLE 8-2   Style Analysis Correlations

Suppose a portfolio manager uses small-cap stocks in an investment portfolio. By applying style analysis, we can try to determine whether the portfolio manager uses a small-cap growth style or a small-cap value style.

In the United States, the Russell 2000 Growth Index and the Russell 2000 Value Index are often used as benchmarks for small-cap growth and small-cap value managers, respectively. Correlation analysis shows, however, that the returns to these two indexes are very closely associated with each other. For the 20 years ending in 2002 (January 1983 to December 2002), the correlation between the monthly returns to the Russell 2000 Growth Index and the Russell 2000 Value Index was 0.8526.

If the correlation between the returns to the two indexes were 1, there would be absolutely no difference in equity management style between small-cap value and small-cap growth. If we knew the return to one style, we could be certain about the return to the other style. Because the returns to the two indexes are highly correlated, we can say that very little difference exists between the two return series, and therefore, we may not be able to justify distinguishing between small-cap growth and small-cap value as different investment styles.

The previous examples in this chapter have examined the correlation between two variables. Often, however, investment managers need to understand the correlations among many asset returns. For example, investors who have any exposure to movements in exchange rates must understand the correlations of the returns to different foreign currencies and other assets in order to determine their optimal portfolios and hedging strategies.[8] In the following example, we see how a correlation matrix shows correlation between pairs of variables when we have more than two variables. We also see one of the main challenges to investment managers: Investment return correlations can change substantially over time.

EXAMPLE 8-3   Exchange Rate Return Correlations

The exchange rate return measures the periodic domestic currency return to holding foreign currency. Suppose a change in inflation rates in the United Kingdom and the United States results in the U.S. dollar price of a pound changing from $1.50 to $1.25. If this change occurred in one month, the return in that month to holding pounds would be $(1.25 - 1.50)/1.50 = -16.67$ percent, in terms of dollars.

Table 8-3 shows a correlation matrix of monthly returns in U.S. dollars to holding Canadian, Japanese, Swedish, or British currencies.[9] To interpret a correlation matrix, we first examine the top panel of this table. The first column of numbers of that panel

---

[8]See, for example, Clarke and Kritzman (1996).

[9]Data for the 1980s run from January 1980 through December 1989. Data for the 1990s run from January 1990 through December 1999.

shows the correlations between USD returns to holding the Canadian dollar and USD returns to holding Canadian, Japanese, Swedish, and British currencies. Of course, any variable is perfectly correlated with itself, and so the correlation between USD returns to holding the Canadian dollar and USD returns to holding the Canadian dollar is 1. The second row of this column shows that the correlation between USD returns to holding the Canadian dollar and USD returns to holding the Japanese yen was 0.2593 from 1980 to 1989. The remaining correlations in the panel show how the USD returns to other combinations of currency holdings were correlated during this period.

Note that Table 8-3 omits many of the correlations. For example, Column 2 of the panel omits the correlation between USD returns to holding yen and USD returns

TABLE 8-3   Correlations of Monthly U.S. Dollar Returns to Selected Foreign Currency Returns

1980–1989	Canada	Japan	Sweden	United Kingdom
Canada	1.0000			
Japan	0.2593	1.0000		
Sweden	0.2834	0.6576	1.0000	
United Kingdom	0.3925	0.6068	0.6840	1.0000
1990–1999	Canada	Japan	Sweden	United Kingdom
Canada	1.0000			
Japan	−0.0734	1.0000		
Sweden	0.1640	0.2860	1.0000	
United Kingdom	0.0475	0.2906	0.6444	1.0000

Source: Ibbotson Associates.

to holding Canadian dollars. This correlation is omitted because it is identical to the correlation between USD returns to holding Canadian dollars and USD returns to holding yen shown in Row 2 of Column 1. Other omitted correlations would also have been duplicative. In fact, correlations are always symmetrical: The correlation between X and Y is always the same as the correlation between Y and X.

If you compare the two panels of this table, you will find that many of the currency return correlations changed dramatically between the 1980s and the 1990s. In the 1980s, for example, the correlation between the return to holding Japanese yen and the return to holding either Swedish kronor (0.6576) or British pounds (0.6068) was almost as high as the correlation between the return to holding kronor and the return to holding pounds (0.6840). In the 1990s, however, the correlation between yen returns and either krona or pound returns dropped by more than half (to 0.2860 and 0.2906, respectively), but the correlation between krona and pound returns hardly changed at all (0.6444). Some of the correlations between returns to the Canadian dollar and returns to other currencies dropped even more dramatically. In the 1980s, the correlation between Canadian dollar returns and Japanese yen returns was 0.2593. By the 1990s, that correlation actually became negative (−0.0734). The correlation between the Canadian dollar returns and British pound returns dropped from 0.3925 in the 1980s to 0.0475 in the 1990s.

Optimal asset allocation depends on expectations of future correlations. With less than perfect positive correlation between two assets' returns, there are potential risk-reduction benefits to holding both assets. Expectations of future correlation may be based on historical sample correlations, but the variability in historical sample correlations poses challenges. We discuss these issues in detail in the chapter on portfolio concepts.

In the next example, we extend the discussion of the correlations of stock market indexes begun in Example 8-2 to indexes representing large-cap, small-cap, and broad-market returns. This type of analysis has serious diversification and asset allocation consequences because the strength of the correlations among the assets tells us how successfully the assets can be combined to diversify risk.

EXAMPLE 8-4   Correlations among Stock Return Series

Table 8-4 shows the correlation matrix of monthly returns to three U.S. stock indexes during the period January 1971 to December 1999 and in three subperiods (the 1970s, 1980s, and 1990s).[10] The large-cap style is represented by the return to the S&P 500 Index, the small-cap style is represented by the return to the Dimensional Fund Advisors U.S. Small-Stock Index, and the broad-market returns are represented by the return to the Wilshire 5000 Index.

TABLE 8-4   Correlations of Monthly Returns to Various U.S. Stock Indexes

1971–1999	S&P 500	U.S. Small-Stock	Wilshire 5000
S&P 500	1.0000		
U.S. Small-Stock	0.7615	1.0000	
Wilshire 5000	0.9894	0.8298	1.0000
1971–1979	**S&P 500**	**U.S. Small-Stock**	**Wilshire 5000**
S&P 500	1.0000		
U.S. Small-Stock	0.7753	1.0000	
Wilshire 5000	0.9906	0.8375	1.0000
1980–1989	**S&P 500**	**U.S. Small-Stock**	**Wilshire 5000**
S&P 500	1.0000		
U.S. Small-Stock	0.8440	1.0000	
Wilshire 5000	0.9914	0.8951	1.0000

(continued)

---

[10]The 1970s data have an initiation date of January 1971 because that is the starting date of the Wilshire 5000 total return series.

TABLE 8-4   (*continued*)

1990–1999	S&P 500	U.S. Small-Stock	Wilshire 5000
S&P 500	1.0000		
U.S. Small-Stock	0.6843	1.0000	
Wilshire 5000	0.9858	0.7768	1.0000

Source: Ibbotson Associates.

The first column of numbers in the top panel of Table 8-4 shows nearly perfect positive correlation between returns to the S&P 500 and returns to the Wilshire 5000: The correlation between the two return series is 0.9894. This result should not be surprising, because both the S&P 500 and the Wilshire 5000 are value-weighted indexes, and large-cap stock returns receive most of the weight in both indexes. In fact, the companies that make up the S&P 500 have about 80 percent of the total market value of all companies included in the Wilshire 5000.

Small stocks also have a reasonably high correlation with large stocks. In the total sample, the correlation between the S&P 500 returns and the U.S. Small-Stock returns is 0.7615. The correlation between U.S. Small-Stock returns and returns to the Wilshire 5000 is slightly higher (0.8298). This result is also not too surprising because the Wilshire 5000 contains small-cap stocks and the S&P 500 does not. The second, third, and fourth panels of Table 8-4 show that correlations among the various stock market return series show some variation from decade to decade. For example, the correlation between returns to the S&P 500 and U.S. small-cap stocks dropped from 0.8440 in the 1980s to 0.6843 in the 1990s.[11]

For asset allocation purposes, correlations among asset classes are studied carefully with a view towards maintaining appropriate diversification based on forecasted correlations.

EXAMPLE 8-5   Correlations of Debt and Equity Returns

Table 8-5 shows the correlation matrix for various U.S. debt returns and S&P 500 returns using monthly data from January 1926 to December 2002.

The first column of numbers, in particular, shows the correlations of S&P 500 returns with various debt returns. Note that S&P 500 returns are almost completely uncorrelated (−0.0174) with 30-day Treasury bill returns for this period. Long-term corporate debt returns are somewhat more correlated (0.2143) with S&P 500 returns. Returns on high-yield corporate bonds have the highest correlation (0.6471) with S&P 500 total returns. This high correlation is understandable; high-yield debt securities behave partially as equities because of their high default risk. If a company defaults, holders of high-yield debt typically lose most of their investment.

---

[11] The correlation coefficient for the 1990s was less than that for the 1980s at the 0.01 significance level. A test for this type of hypothesis on the correlation coefficient can be conducted using Fisher's *z*-transformation. See Daniel and Terrell (1995) for information on this method.

TABLE 8-5   Correlations among U.S. Stock and
Debt Returns, 1926–2002

All	S&P 500	U.S. Long-Term Corp.	U.S. Long-Term Govt.	U.S. 30-Day T-Bill	High-Yield Corp.
S&P 500	1.0000				
U.S. Long-Term Corp.	0.2143	1.0000			
U.S. Long-Term Govt.	0.1466	0.8480	1.0000		
U.S. 30-Day T-bill	−0.0174	0.0970	0.1119	1.0000	
High-Yield Corp.	0.6471	0.4274	0.3131	0.0174	1.0000

Source: Ibbotson Associates.

Long-term government bonds, however, have a low correlation (0.1466) with S&P 500 returns. We expect some correlation between these variables because interest rate increases reduce the present value of future cash flows for both bonds and stocks. The relatively low correlation between these two return series, however, shows that other factors affect the returns on stocks besides interest rates. Without these other factors, the correlation between bond and stock returns would be higher.

The second column of numbers in Table 8-5 shows that the correlation between long-term government bond and corporate bond returns is quite high (0.8480) for this time period. Although this correlation is the highest in the entire matrix, it is not 1. The correlation is less than 1 because the default premium for long-term corporate bonds changes, whereas U.S. government bonds do not incorporate a default premium. As a result, changes in required yields for government bonds have a correlation less than 1 with changes in required yields for corporate bonds, and return correlations between government bonds and corporate bonds are also below 1. Note also that the correlation of high-yield corporate bond returns with long-term government bond returns (0.3131), indicated in the third column of numbers, is less than half the correlation of high-yield corporate bond returns with S&P 500 returns. This relatively low correlation is another indicator that high-yield bond returns behave more similarly to equity returns than to debt returns.

Note finally that 30-day T-bill returns have a very low correlation with all other return series. In fact, the correlations between T-bill returns and other return series are lower than any of the other correlations in this table.

In the final example of this section, correlation is used in a financial statement setting to show that net income is an inadequate proxy for cash flow.

EXAMPLE 8-6   Correlations among Net Income, Cash Flow from Operations, and Free Cash Flow to the Firm

Net income (NI), cash flow from operations (CFO), and free cash flow to the firm (FCFF) are three measures of company performance that analysts often use to value companies.

Differences in these measures for given companies would not cause differences in the relative valuation if the measures were highly correlated.

CFO equals net income plus the net noncash charges that were subtracted to obtain net income, minus the company's investment in working capital during the same time period. FCFF equals CFO plus net-of-tax interest expense, minus the company's investment in fixed capital over the time period. FCFF may be interpreted as the cash flow available to the company's suppliers of capital (debtholders and shareholders) after all operating expenses have been paid and necessary investments in working and fixed capital have been made.[12]

Some analysts base their valuations only on NI, ignoring CFO and FCFF. If the correlations among NI, CFO, and FCFF were very high, then an analyst's decision to ignore CFO and FCFF would be easy to understand because NI would then appear to capture everything one needs to know about cash flow.

TABLE 8-6   Correlations among Performance Measures: U.S. Women's Clothing Stores, 2001

	NI	CFO	FCFF
NI	1.0000		
CFO	0.6959	1.0000	
FCFF	0.4045	0.8217	1.0000

Source: Compustat.

Table 8-6 shows the correlations among NI, CFO, and FCFF for a group of six publicly traded U.S. companies involved in retailing women's clothing for 2001. Before computing the correlations, we normalized all of the data by dividing each company's three performance measures by the company's revenue for the year.[13]

Because CFO and FCFF include NI as a component (in the sense that CFO and FCFF can be obtained by adding and subtracting various quantities from NI), we might expect that the correlations between NI and CFO and between NI and FCFF would be positive. Table 8-6 supports that conclusion. These correlations with NI, however, are much smaller than the correlation between CFO and FCFF (0.8217). The lowest correlation in the table is between NI and FCFF (0.4045). This relatively low correlation shows that NI contained some but far from all the information in FCFF for these companies in 2001. Later in this chapter, we will test whether the correlation between NI and FCFF is significantly different from zero.

---

[12]For more on these three measures and their use in equity valuation, see Stowe, Robinson, Pinto, and McLeavey (2002). The statements in the footnoted paragraph explain the relationships among these measures according to U.S. GAAP. Stowe et al. also discuss the relationships among these measures according to international accounting standards.

[13]The results in this table are based on data for all women's clothing stores (U.S. Occupational Health and Safety Administration Standard Industrial Classification 5621) with a market capitalization of more than $250 million at the end of 2001. The market-cap criterion was used to eliminate microcap firms, whose performance-measure correlations may be different from those of higher-valued firms. We will discuss in detail the data normalization used in this example (dividing by firm revenue) in the section on misspecified regressions in Chapter 9.

2.6. Testing the Significance of the Correlation Coefficient

Significance tests allow us to assess whether apparent relationships between random variables are the result of chance. If we decide that the relationships do not result from chance, we will be inclined to use this information in predictions because a good prediction of one variable will help us predict the other variable. Using the data in Table 8-2, we calculated 0.8702 as the sample correlation between long-term money growth and long-term inflation in six industrialized countries between 1970 and 2001. That estimated correlation seems high, but is it significantly different from 0? Before we can answer this question, we must know some details about the distribution of the underlying variables themselves. For purposes of simplicity, let us assume that both of the variables are normally distributed.[14]

We propose two hypotheses: the null hypothesis, H_0, that the correlation in the population is 0 ($\rho = 0$); and the alternative hypothesis, H_a, that the correlation in the population is different from 0 ($\rho \neq 0$).

The alternative hypothesis is a test that the correlation is not equal to 0; therefore, a two-tailed test is appropriate.[15] As long as the two variables are distributed normally, we can test to determine whether the null hypothesis should be rejected using the sample correlation, r. The formula for the t-test is

$$t = \frac{r\sqrt{n-2}}{\sqrt{1-r^2}} \qquad (8\text{-}3)$$

This test statistic has a t-distribution with $n-2$ degrees of freedom if the null hypothesis is true. One practical observation concerning Equation 8-3 is that the magnitude of r needed to reject the null hypothesis H_0: $\rho = 0$ decreases as sample size n increases, for two reasons. First, as n increases, the number of degrees of freedom increases and the absolute value of the critical value t_c decreases. Second, the absolute value of the numerator increases with larger n, resulting in larger-magnitude t-values. For example, with sample size $n = 12$, $r = 0.58$ results in a t-statistic of 2.252 that is just significant at the 0.05 level ($t_c = 2.228$). With a sample size $n = 32$, a smaller sample correlation $r = 0.35$ yields a t-statistic of 2.046 that is just significant at the 0.05 level ($t_c = 2.042$); the $r = 0.35$ would not be significant with a sample size of 12 even at the 0.10 significance level. Another way to make this point is that sampling from the same population, a false null hypothesis H_0: $\rho = 0$ is more likely to be rejected as we increase sample size, all else equal.

EXAMPLE 8-7   Testing the Correlation between Money Supply Growth and Inflation

Earlier in this chapter, we showed that the sample correlation between long-term money supply growth and long-term inflation in six industrialized countries was 0.8702 during

---

[14] Actually, we must assume that the variables come from a bivariate normal distribution. If two variables, X and Y, come from a bivariate normal distribution, then for each value of X the distribution of Y is normal. See, for example, Ross (1997) or Greene (2003).

[15] See the chapter on hypothesis testing for a more in-depth discussion of two-tailed tests.

the 1970–2001 period. Suppose we want to test the null hypothesis, H_0, that the true correlation in the population is 0 ($\rho = 0$) against the alternative hypothesis, H_a, that the correlation in the population is different from 0 ($\rho \neq 0$).

Recalling that this sample has six observations, we can compute the statistic for testing the null hypothesis as follows:

$$t = \frac{0.8702\sqrt{6-2}}{\sqrt{1-0.8702^2}} = 3.532$$

The value of the test statistic is 3.532. As the table of critical values of the t-distribution for a two-tailed test shows, for a t-distribution with $n - 2 = 6 - 2 = 4$ degrees of freedom at the 0.05 level of significance, we can reject the null hypothesis (that the population correlation is equal to 0) if the value of the test statistic is greater than 2.776 or less than -2.776. The fact that we can reject the null hypothesis of no correlation based on only six observations is quite unusual; it further demonstrates the strong relation between long-term money supply growth and long-term inflation in these six countries.

EXAMPLE 8-8   Testing the Krona–Yen Return Correlation

The data in Table 8-3 showed that the sample correlation between the USD monthly returns to Swedish kronor and Japanese yen was 0.2860 for the period from January 1990 through December 1999. If we observe this sample correlation, can we reject a null hypothesis that the underlying or population correlation equals 0?

With 120 months from January 1990 through December 1999, we use the following statistic to test the null hypothesis, H_0, that the true correlation in the population is 0, against the alternative hypothesis, H_a, that the correlation in the population is different from 0:

$$t = \frac{0.2860\sqrt{120-2}}{\sqrt{1-0.2860^2}} = 3.242$$

At the 0.05 significance level, the critical level for this test statistic is 1.98 ($n = 120$, degrees of freedom $= 118$). When the test statistic is either larger than 1.98 or smaller than -1.98, we can reject the hypothesis that the correlation in the population is 0. The test statistic is 3.242, so we can reject the null hypothesis.

Note that the sample correlation coefficient in this case is significantly different from 0 at the 0.05 level, even though the coefficient is much smaller than that in the previous example. The correlation coefficient, though smaller, is still significant because the sample is much larger (120 observations instead of 6 observations).

The above example shows the importance of sample size in tests of the significance of the correlation coefficient. The following example also shows the importance of sample size and examines the relationship at the 0.01 level of significance as well as at the 0.05 level.

EXAMPLE 8-9   The Correlation Between Bond Returns and T-Bill Returns

Table 8-5 showed that the sample correlation between monthly returns to U.S. government bonds and monthly returns to 30-day T-bills was 0.1119 from January 1926 through December 2002. Suppose we want to test whether the correlation coefficient is statistically significantly different from zero. There are 924 months during the period January 1926 to December 2002. Therefore, to test the null hypothesis, H_0 (that the true correlation in the population is 0), against the alternative hypothesis, H_a (that the correlation in the population is different from 0), we use the following test statistic:

$$t = \frac{0.1119\sqrt{924 - 2}}{\sqrt{1 - 0.1119^2}} = 3.4193$$

At the 0.05 significance level, the critical value for the test statistic is approximately 1.96. At the 0.01 significance level, the critical value for the test statistic is approximately 2.58. The test statistic is 3.4193, so we can reject the null hypothesis of no correlation in the population at both the 0.05 and 0.01 levels. This example shows that, in large samples, even relatively small correlation coefficients can be significantly different from zero.

In the final example of this section, we explore another situation of small sample size.

EXAMPLE 8-10   Testing the Correlation Between Net Income and Free Cash Flow to the Firm

Earlier in this chapter, we showed that the sample correlation between NI and FCFF for six women's clothing stores was 0.4045 in 2001. Suppose we want to test the null hypothesis, H_0, that the true correlation in the population is 0 ($\rho = 0$) against the alternative hypothesis, H_a, that the correlation in the population is different from 0 ($\rho \neq 0$). Recalling that this sample has six observations, we can compute the statistic for testing the null hypothesis as follows:

$$t = \frac{0.4045\sqrt{6 - 2}}{\sqrt{1 - 0.4045^2}} = 0.8846$$

With $n - 2 = 6 - 2 = 4$ degrees of freedom and a 0.05 significance level, we reject the null hypothesis that the population correlation equals 0 for values of the test statistic greater than 2.776 or less than −2.776. In this case, however, the t-statistic is 0.8846, so we cannot reject the null hypothesis. Therefore, for this sample of women's clothing stores, there is no statistically significant correlation between NI and FCFF, when each is normalized by dividing by sales for the company.[16]

The scatter plot creates a visual picture of the relationship between two variables, while the correlation coefficient quantifies the existence of any linear relationship. Large absolute values of the correlation coefficient indicate strong linear relationships. Positive coefficients indicate a positive relationship and negative coefficients indicate a negative relationship between two data sets. In Examples 8-8 and 8-9, we saw that relatively small sample correlation coefficients (0.2860 and 0.1119) can be statistically significant and thus might provide valuable information about the behavior of economic variables.

Next we will introduce linear regression, another tool useful in examining the relationship between two variables.

3. LINEAR REGRESSION

3.1. Linear Regression with One Independent Variable

As a financial analyst, you will often want to understand the relationship between financial or economic variables, or to predict the value of one variable using information about the value of another variable. For example, you may want to know the impact of changes in the 10-year Treasury bond yield on the earnings yield of the S&P 500 (the earnings yield is the reciprocal of the price-to-earnings ratio). If the relationship between those two variables is linear, you can use linear regression to summarize it.

Linear regression allows us to use one variable to make predictions about another, test hypotheses about the relation between two variables, and quantify the strength of the relationship between the two variables. The remainder of this chapter focuses on linear regression with a single independent variable. In the next chapter, we will examine regression with more than one independent variable.

Regression analysis begins with the dependent variable (denoted Y), the variable that you are seeking to explain. The independent variable (denoted X) is the variable you are using to explain changes in the dependent variable. For example, you might try to explain small-stock returns (the dependent variable) based on returns to the S&P 500 (the independent variable). Or you might try to explain inflation (the dependent variable) as a function of growth in a country's money supply (the independent variable).

Linear regression assumes a linear relationship between the dependent and the independent variables. The following regression equation describes that relation:

$$Y_i = b_0 + b_1 X_i + \varepsilon_i, i = 1, \ldots, n \tag{8-4}$$

---

[16]It is worth repeating that the smaller the sample, the greater the evidence in terms of the magnitude of the sample correlation needed to reject the null hypothesis of zero correlation. With a sample size of 6, the absolute value of the sample correlation would need to be greater than 0.81 (carrying two decimal places) for us to reject the null hypothesis. Viewed another way, the value of 0.4045 in the text would be significant if the sample size were 24, because $0.4045(24 - 2)^{1/2}/(1 - 0.4045^2)^{1/2} = 2.075$, which is greater than the critical t-value of 2.074 at the 0.05 significance level with 22 degrees of freedom.

This equation states that the **dependent variable**, Y, is equal to the intercept, b_0, plus a slope coefficient, b_1, times the **independent variable**, X, plus an **error term**, ε. The error term represents the portion of the dependent variable that cannot be explained by the independent variable. We refer to the intercept b_0 and the slope coefficient b_1 as the **regression coefficients**.

Regression analysis uses two principal types of data: cross-sectional and time series. Cross-sectional data involve many observations on X and Y for the same time period. Those observations could come from different companies, asset classes, investment funds, people, countries, or other entities, depending on the regression model. For example, a cross-sectional model might use data from many companies to test whether predicted earnings-per-share growth explains differences in price-to-earnings ratios (P/Es) during a specific time period. The word "explain" is frequently used in describing regression relationships. One estimate of a company's P/E that does not depend on any other variable is the average P/E. If a regression of a P/E on an independent variable tends to give more-accurate estimates of P/E than just assuming that the company's P/E equals the average P/E, we say that the independent variable helps *explain* P/Es because using that independent variable improves our estimates. Finally, note that if we use cross-sectional observations in a regression, we usually denote the observations as $i = 1, 2, \ldots, n$.

Time-series data use many observations from different time periods for the same company, asset class, investment fund, person, country, or other entity, depending on the regression model. For example, a time-series model might use monthly data from many years to test whether U.S. inflation rates determine U.S. short-term interest rates.[17] If we use time-series data in a regression, we usually denote the observations as $t = 1, 2, \ldots, T$.[18]

Exactly how does linear regression estimate b_0 and b_1? Linear regression, also known as linear least squares, computes a line that best fits the observations; it chooses values for the intercept, b_0, and slope, b_1, that minimize the sum of the squared vertical distances between the observations and the regression line. Linear regression chooses the **estimated** or **fitted parameters** $\hat{b}_0$ and $\hat{b}_1$ in Equation 8-4 to minimize[19]

$$\sum_{i=1}^{n}(Y_i - \hat{b}_0 - \hat{b}_1 X_i)^2 \tag{8-5}$$

In this equation, the term $(Y_i - \hat{b}_0 - \hat{b}_1 X_i)^2$ means (Dependent variable–Predicted value of dependent variable)^2. Using this method to estimate the values of $\hat{b}_0$ and $\hat{b}_1$, we can fit a line through the observations on X and Y that best explains the value that Y takes for any particular value of X.[20]

Note that we never observe the population parameter values b_0 and b_1 in a regression model. Instead, we observe only $\hat{b}_0$ and $\hat{b}_1$, which are estimates of the population parameter values. Thus predictions must be based on the parameters' estimated values, and testing is based on estimated values in relation to the hypothesized population values.

---

[17] A mix of time-series and cross-sectional data, also known as panel data, is now frequently used in financial analysis. The analysis of panel data is an advanced topic that Greene (2003) discusses in detail.

[18] In this chapter, we primarily use the notation $i = 1, 2, \ldots, n$ even for time series to prevent confusion that would be caused by switching back and forth between different notations.

[19] Hats over the symbols for coefficients indicate estimated values.

[20] For a discussion of the precise statistical sense in which the estimates of b_0 and b_1 are optimal, see Greene (2003).

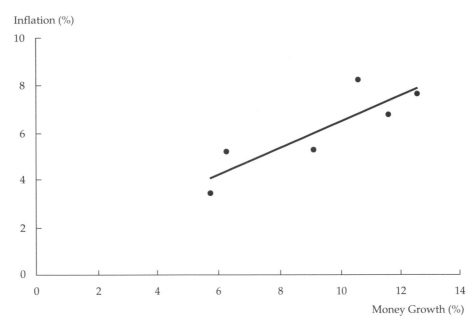

FIGURE 8-8   Fitted Regression Line Explaining the Inflation Rate Using Growth in the Money
Supply by Country: 1970–2001
Source: International Monetary Fund.

Figure 8-8 gives a visual example of how linear regression works. The figure shows the
linear regression that results from estimating the regression relation between the annual rate
of inflation (the dependent variable) and annual rate of money supply growth (the independent variable) for six industrialized countries from 1970 to 2001 ($n = 6$).[21] The equation
to be estimated is Long-term rate of inflation $= b_0 + b_1$ (Long-term rate of money supply
growth) $+\varepsilon$.

The distance from each of the six data points to the fitted regression line is the regression
residual, which is the difference between the actual value of the dependent variable and the
predicted value of the dependent variable made by the regression equation. Linear regression
chooses the estimated coefficients $\hat{b}_0$ and $\hat{b}_1$ in Equation 8-4 such that the sum of the
squared vertical distances is minimized. The estimated regression equation is Long-term
inflation $= 0.0084 + 0.5545$ (Long-term money supply growth).[22]

According to this regression equation, if the long-term money supply growth is 0 for
any particular country, the long-term rate of inflation in that country will be 0.84 percent.
For every 1-percentage-point increase in the long-term rate of money supply growth for a
country, the long-term inflation rate is predicted to increase by 0.5545 percentage points. In
a regression such as this one, which contains one independent variable, the slope coefficient
equals $\text{Cov}(Y,X)/\text{Var}(X)$. We can solve for the slope coefficient using data from Table 8-2,
excerpted here:

---

[21] These data appear in Table 8-2.
[22] We entered the monthly returns as decimals.

TABLE 8-2   (excerpted)

	Money Supply Growth Rate X_i	Inflation Rate Y_i	Cross-Product $(X_i - \overline{X})(Y_i - \overline{Y})$	Squared Deviations $(X_i - \overline{X})^2$	Squared Deviations $(Y_i - \overline{Y})^2$
Sum	0.5608	0.3616	0.002185	0.003939	0.001598
Average	0.0935	0.0603			
Covariance			**0.000437**		
Variance				**0.000788**	0.000320
Standard deviation				0.028071	0.017889

$$\text{Cov}\,(Y, X) = 0.000437$$

$$\text{Var}\,(X) = 0.000788$$

$$\text{Cov}\,(Y, X)/\text{Var}\,(X) = 0.000437/0.000788$$

$$\hat{b}_1 = 0.5545$$

In a linear regression, the regression line fits through the point corresponding to the means of the dependent and the independent variables. As shown in Table 8-1 (excerpted below), from 1970 to 2001, the mean long-term growth rate of the money supply for these six countries was 9.35 percent, whereas the mean long-term inflation rate was 6.03 percent.

TABLE 8-1   (excerpted)

	Money Supply Growth Rate	Inflation Rate
Average	9.35%	6.03%

Because the point (9.35, 6.03) lies on the regression line $\hat{b}_0 = \overline{Y} - \hat{b}_1 \overline{X}$, we can solve for the intercept using this point as follows:

$$\hat{b}_0 = 0.0603 - 0.5545(0.0935) = 0.0084$$

We are showing how to solve the linear regression equation step by step to make the source of the numbers clear. Typically, an analyst will use the data analysis function on a spreadsheet or a statistical package to perform linear regression analysis. Later, we will discuss how to use regression residuals to quantify the uncertainty in a regression model.

3.2. Assumptions of the Linear Regression Model

We have discussed how to interpret the coefficients in a linear regression model. Now we turn to the statistical assumptions underlying this model. Suppose that we have n observations on both the dependent variable, Y, and the independent variable, X, and we want to estimate Equation 8-4:

$$Y_i = b_0 + b_1 X_i + \varepsilon_i, i = 1, \ldots, n$$

To be able to draw valid conclusions from a linear regression model with a single independent variable, we need to make the following six assumptions, known as the classic normal linear regression model assumptions:

1. The relationship between the dependent variable, Y, and the independent variable, X is linear in the parameters b_0 and b_1. This requirement means that b_0 and b_1 are raised to the first power only and that neither b_0 nor b_1 is multiplied or divided by another regression parameter (as in b_0/b_1, for example). The requirement does not exclude X from being raised to a power other than 1.
2. The independent variable, X, is not random.[23]
3. The expected value of the error term is 0: $E(\varepsilon) = 0$.
4. The variance of the error term is the same for all observations: $E(\varepsilon_i^2) = \sigma_\varepsilon^2, i = 1, \ldots, n$.
5. The error term, ε, is uncorrelated across observations. Consequently, $E(\varepsilon_i \varepsilon_j) = 0$ for all i not equal to j.[24]
6. The error term, ε, is normally distributed.[25]

Now we can take a closer look at each of these assumptions.

Assumption 1 is critical for a valid linear regression. If the relationship between the independent and dependent variables is nonlinear in the parameters, then estimating that relation with a linear regression model will produce invalid results. For example, $Y_i = b_0 e^{b_1 X_i} + \varepsilon_i$ is nonlinear in b_1, so we could not apply the linear regression model to it.[26]

Even if the dependent variable is nonlinear, linear regression can be used as long as the regression is linear in the parameters. So, for example, linear regression can be used to estimate the equation $Y_i = b_0 + b_1 X_i^2 + \varepsilon_i$.

Assumptions 2 and 3 ensure that linear regression produces the correct estimates of b_0 and b_1.

Assumptions 4, 5, and 6 let us use the linear regression model to determine the distribution of the estimated parameters $\hat{b}_0$ and $\hat{b}_1$ and thus test whether those coefficients have a particular value.

- Assumption 4, that the variance of the error term is the same for all observations, is also known as the homoskedasticity assumption. The chapter on regression analysis discusses how to test for and correct violations of this assumption.

---

[23]Although we assume that the independent variable in the regression model is not random, that assumption is clearly often not true. For example, it is unrealistic to assume that the monthly returns to the S&P 500 are not random. If the independent variable is random, then is the regression model incorrect? Fortunately, no. Econometricians have shown that even if the independent variable is random, we can still rely on the results of regression models given the crucial assumption that the error term is uncorrelated with the independent variable. The mathematics underlying this reliability demonstration, however, are quite difficult. See, for example, Greene (2003) or Goldberger (1998).

[24]$\mathrm{Var}(\varepsilon_i) = E[\varepsilon_i - E(\varepsilon_i)]^2 = E(\varepsilon_i - 0)^2 = E(\varepsilon_i)^2$. $\mathrm{Cov}(\varepsilon_i, \varepsilon_j) = E\{[\varepsilon_i - E(\varepsilon_i)][\varepsilon_j - E(\varepsilon_j)]\} = E[(\varepsilon_i - 0)(\varepsilon_j - 0)] = E(\varepsilon_i \varepsilon_j) = 0$.

[25]If the regression errors are not normally distributed, we can still use regression analysis. Econometricians who dispense with the normality assumption use chi-square tests of hypotheses rather than F-tests. This difference usually does not affect whether the test will result in a particular null hypothesis being rejected.

[26]For more information on nonlinearity in the parameters, see Gujarati (2003).

- Assumption 5, that the errors are uncorrelated across observations, is also necessary for correctly estimating the variances of the estimated parameters $\hat{b}_0$ and $\hat{b}_1$. The chapter on multiple regression discusses violations of this assumption.
- Assumption 6, that the error term is normally distributed, allows us to easily test a particular hypothesis about a linear regression model.[27]

EXAMPLE 8-11   Evaluating Economic Forecasts (2)

If economic forecasts were completely accurate, every prediction of change in an economic variable in a quarter would exactly match the actual change that occurs in that quarter. Even though forecasts can be inaccurate, we hope at least that they are unbiased—that is, that the expected value of the forecast error is zero. An unbiased forecast can be expressed as E(Actual change − Predicted change) = 0. In fact, most evaluations of forecast accuracy test whether forecasts are unbiased.[28]

Figure 8-9 repeats Figure 8-7 in showing a scatter plot of the mean forecast of current-quarter percentage change in CPI from the previous quarter and actual percentage change in CPI, on an annualized basis, from the first quarter of 1983 to the last quarter of 2002, but it adds the fitted regression line for the equation Actual percentage change = $b_0 + b_1$ (Predicted percentage change) + ε. If the forecasts are unbiased, the intercept, b_0, should be 0 and the slope, b_1, should be 1. We should also find E(Actual change − Predicted change) = 0. If forecasts are actually unbiased, as long as $b_0 = 0$ and $b_1 = 1$, the error term [Actual change − b_0 − b_1(Predicted change)] will have an expected value of 0, as required by Assumption 3 of the linear regression model. With unbiased forecasts, any other values of b_0 and b_1 would yield an error term with an expected value different from 0.

If $b_0 = 0$ and $b_1 = 1$, our best guess of actual change in CPI would be 0 if professional forecasters' predictions of change in CPI were 0. For every 1-percentage-point increase in the prediction of change by the professional forecasters, the regression model would predict a 1-percentage-point increase in actual change.

The fitted regression line in Figure 8-9 comes from the equation Actual change = $-0.0140 + 0.9637$(Predicted change). Note that the estimated values of both b_0 and b_1 are close to the values $b_0 = 0$ and $b_1 = 1$ that are consistent with unbiased forecasts. Later in this chapter, we discuss how to test the hypotheses that $b_0 = 0$ and $b_1 = 1$.

---

[27] For large sample sizes, we may be able to drop the assumption of normality by appeal to the central limit theorem, which was discussed in the chapter on sampling; see Greene (2003). Asymptotic theory shows that, in many cases, the test statistics produced by standard regression programs are valid even if the error term is not normally distributed. As illustrated in the chapter on statistical concepts and market returns, however, non-normality of some financial time series can be quite severe. With severe non-normality, even with a relatively large number of observations, invoking asymptotic theory to justify using test statistics from linear regression models may be inappropriate.

[28] See, for example, Keane and Runkle (1990).

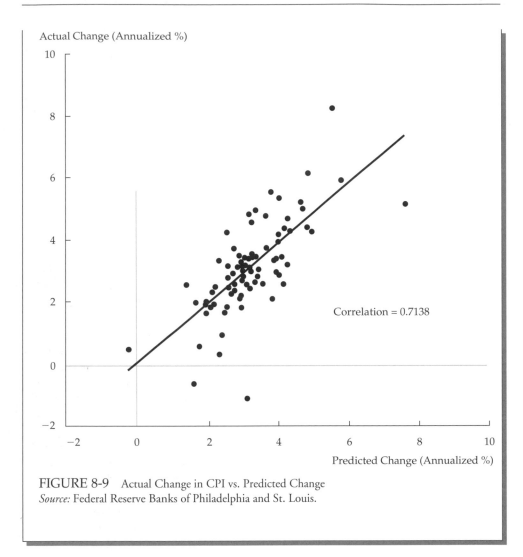

FIGURE 8-9   Actual Change in CPI vs. Predicted Change
Source: Federal Reserve Banks of Philadelphia and St. Louis.

3.3. The Standard Error of Estimate

The linear regression model sometimes describes the relationship between two variables quite well, but sometimes it does not. We must be able to distinguish between these two cases in order to use regression analysis effectively. Therefore, in this section and the next, we discuss statistics that measure how well a given linear regression model captures the relationship between the dependent and independent variables.

Figure 8-9, for example, shows a strong relation between predicted inflation and actual inflation. If we knew professional forecasters' predictions for inflation in a particular quarter, we would be reasonably certain that we could use this regression model to forecast actual inflation relatively accurately.

In other cases, however, the relation between the dependent and independent variables is not strong. Figure 8-10 adds a fitted regression line to the data on inflation and stock returns in the 1990s from Figure 8-6. In this figure, the actual observations are generally much farther from the fitted regression line than in Figure 8-9. Using the estimated regression equation to predict monthly stock returns assuming a particular level of inflation might result in an inaccurate forecast.

As noted, the regression relation in Figure 8-10 is less precise than that in Figure 8-9. The standard error of estimate (sometimes called the standard error of the regression) measures this uncertainty. This statistic is very much like the standard deviation for a single variable, except that it measures the standard deviation of $\hat{\varepsilon}_i$, the residual term in the regression.

The formula for the standard error of estimate (SEE) for a linear regression model with one independent variable is

$$\text{SEE} = \left(\sum_{i=1}^{n} \frac{(Y_i - \hat{b}_0 - \hat{b}_1 X_i)^2}{n-2} \right)^{1/2} = \left(\sum_{i=1}^{n} \frac{(\hat{\varepsilon}_i)^2}{n-2} \right)^{1/2} \qquad (8\text{-}6)$$

In the numerator of this equation, we are computing the difference between the dependent variable's actual value for each observation and its predicted value $(\hat{b}_0 + \hat{b}_1 X_i)$ for each observation. The difference between the actual and predicted values of the dependent variable is the regression residual, $\hat{\varepsilon}_i$.

Equation 8-6 looks very much like the formula for computing a standard deviation, except that $n - 2$ appears in the denominator instead of $n - 1$. We use $n - 2$ because the sample includes n observations and the linear regression model estimates two parameters ($\hat{b}_0$ and $\hat{b}_1$); the difference between the number of observations and the number of parameters is $n - 2$. This difference is also called the degrees of freedom; it is the denominator needed to ensure that the estimated standard error of estimate is unbiased.

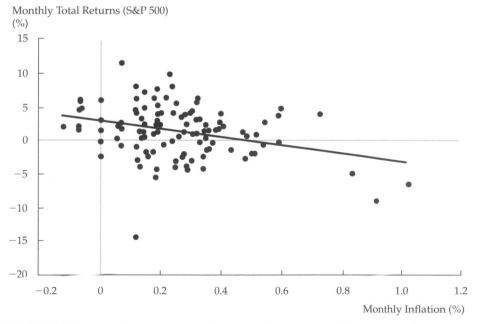

FIGURE 8-10   Fitted Regression Line Explaining Stock Returns by Inflation During the 1990s
Source: Ibbotson Associates.

EXAMPLE 8-12   Computing the Standard Error of Estimate

Recall that the estimated regression equation for the inflation and money supply growth data shown in Figure 8-8 was $Y_i = 0.0084 + 0.5545X_i$. Table 8-7 uses this estimated equation to compute the data needed for the standard error of estimate.

TABLE 8-7   Computing the Standard Error of Estimate

Country	Money Supply Growth Rate X_i	Inflation Rate Y_i	Predicted Inflation Rate $\hat{Y}_i$	Regression Residual $Y_i - \hat{Y}_i$	Squared Residual $(Y_i - \hat{Y}_i)^2$
Australia	0.1166	0.0676	0.0731	−0.0055	0.000030
Canada	0.0915	0.0519	0.0591	−0.0072	0.000052
New Zealand	0.1060	0.0815	0.0672	0.0143	0.000204
Switzerland	0.0575	0.0339	0.0403	−0.0064	0.000041
United Kingdom	0.1258	0.0758	0.0782	−0.0024	0.000006
United States	0.0634	0.0509	0.0436	0.0073	0.000053
Sum					0.000386

Source: International Monetary Fund.

The first and second columns of numbers in Table 8-7 show the long-term money supply growth rates, X_i, and long-term inflations rates, Y_i, for the six countries. The third column of numbers shows the predicted value of the dependent variable from the fitted regression equation for each observation. For the United States, for example, the predicted value of long-term inflation is $0.0084 + 0.5545(0.0634) = 0.0436$ or 4.36 percent. The next-to-last column contains the regression residual, which is the difference between the actual value of the dependent variable, Y_i, and the predicted value of the dependent variable, $(\hat{Y}_i = \hat{b}_0 + \hat{b}_1 X_i)$. So for the United States, the residual is equal to $0.0509 - 0.0436 = 0.0073$ or 0.73 percent. The last column contains the squared regression residual. The sum of the squared residuals is 0.000386. Applying the formula for the standard error of estimate, we obtain

$$\left(\frac{0.000386}{6 - 2}\right)^{1/2} = 0.009823$$

Thus the standard error of estimate is about 0.98 percent.

Later, we will combine this estimate with estimates of the uncertainty about the parameters in this regression to determine confidence intervals for predicting inflation rates from money supply growth. We will see that smaller standard errors result in more-accurate predictions.

3.4. The Coefficient of Determination

Although the standard error of estimate gives some indication of how certain we can be about a particular prediction of Y using the regression equation, it still does not tell us how well the independent variable explains variation in the dependent variable. The coefficient of determination does exactly this: It measures the fraction of the total variation in the de-pendent variable that is explained by the independent variable.

We can compute the coefficient of determination in two ways. The simpler method, which can be used in a linear regression with one independent variable, is to square the correlation coefficient between the dependent and independent variables. For example, recall that the correlation coefficient between the long-term rate of money growth and the long-term rate of inflation between 1970 and 2001 for six industrialized countries was 0.8702. Thus the coefficient of determination in the regression shown in Figure 8-8 is $(0.8702)^2 = 0.7572$. So in this regression, the long-term rate of money supply growth explains approximately 76 percent of the variation in the long-term rate of inflation across the countries between 1970 and 2001.

The problem with this method is that it cannot be used when we have more than one independent variable.[29] Therefore, we need an alternative method of computing the coefficient of determination for multiple independent variables. We now present the logic behind that alternative.

If we did not know the regression relationship, our best guess for the value of any particular observation of the dependent variable would simply be $\overline{Y}$, the mean of the dependent variable. One measure of accuracy in predicting Y_i based on $\overline{Y}$ is the sample variance of Y_i, $\sum_{i=1}^{n} \frac{(Y_i - \overline{Y})^2}{n-1}$. An alternative to using $\overline{Y}$ to predict a particular observation Y_i is using the regression relationship to make that prediction. In that case, our predicted value would be $\hat{Y}_i = \hat{b}_0 + \hat{b}_1 X_i$. If the regression relationship works well, the error in predicting Y_i using $\hat{Y}_i$ should be much smaller than the error in predicting Y_i using $\overline{Y}$. If we call $\sum_{i=1}^{n}(Y_i - \overline{Y})^2$ the total variation of Y and $\sum_{i=1}^{n}(Y_i - \hat{Y}_i)^2$ the unexplained variation from the regression, then we can measure the explained variation from the regression using the following equation:

$$\text{Total variation} = \text{Unexplained variation} + \text{Explained variation} \qquad (8\text{-}7)$$

The coefficient of determination is the fraction of the total variation that is explained by the regression. This gives us the relationship

$$R^2 = \frac{\text{Explained variation}}{\text{Total variation}} = \frac{\text{Total variation} - \text{Unexplained variation}}{\text{Total variation}} \qquad (8\text{-}8)$$

$$= 1 - \frac{\text{Unexplained variation}}{\text{Total variation}}$$

Note that total variation equals explained variation plus unexplained variation, as shown in Equation 8-7. Most regression programs report the coefficient of determination as R^2.[30]

---

[29] We will discuss such models in the chapter on multiple regression.

[30] As we illustrate in the tables of regression output later in this chapter, regression programs also report **multiple R**, which is the correlation between the actual values and the forecast values of Y. The coefficient of determination is the square of multiple R.

EXAMPLE 8-13   Inflation Rate and Growth in the Money Supply

Using the data in Table 8-7, we can see that the unexplained variation from the regression, which is the sum of the squared residuals, equals 0.000386. Table 8-8 shows the computation of total variation in the dependent variable, the long-term rate of inflation.

TABLE 8-8   Computing Total Variation

Country	Money Supply Growth Rate X_i	Inflation Rate Y_i	Deviation from Mean $Y_i - \overline{Y}$	Squared Deviation $(Y_i - \overline{Y})^2$
Australia	0.1166	0.0676	0.0073	0.000053
Canada	0.0915	0.0519	−0.0084	0.000071
New Zealand	0.1060	0.0815	0.0212	0.000449
Switzerland	0.0575	0.0339	−0.0264	0.000697
United Kingdom	0.1258	0.0758	0.0155	0.000240
United States	0.0634	0.0509	−0.0094	0.000088
	Average:	0.0603	Sum:	0.001598

Source: International Monetary Fund.

The average inflation rate for this period is 6.03 percent. The next-to-last column shows the amount each country's long-term inflation rate deviates from that average; the last column shows the square of that deviation. The sum of those squared deviations is the total variation in Y for the sample (0.001598), shown in Table 8-8.

The coefficient of determination for the regression is

$$\frac{\text{Total variation} - \text{Unexplained variation}}{\text{Total variation}} = \frac{0.001598 - 0.000386}{0.001598} = 0.7584$$

Note that this method gives the same result rounded to two decimal places, 0.76, that we obtained earlier (the difference at greater decimal places results from rounding). We will use this method again in the chapter on multiple regression; when we have more than one independent variable, this method is the only way to compute the coefficient of determination.

3.5. Hypothesis Testing

In this section, we address testing hypotheses concerning the population values of the intercept or slope coefficient of a regression model. This topic is critical in practice. For example, we may want to check a stock's valuation using the capital asset pricing model; we hypothesize that the stock has a market-average beta or level of systematic risk. Or we may want to test the hypothesis that economists' forecasts of the inflation rate are unbiased (not overestimates or underestimates, on average). In each case, does the evidence support the hypothesis? Questions such as these can be addressed with hypothesis tests within a regression model. Such tests are often t-tests of the value of the intercept or slope coefficient(s). To understand the concepts involved in this test, it is useful to first review a simple, equivalent approach based on confidence intervals.

We can perform a hypothesis test using the confidence interval approach if we know three things: (1) the estimated parameter value, $\hat{b}_0$ or $\hat{b}_1$, (2) the hypothesized value of the parameter, b_0 or b_1, and (3) a confidence interval around the estimated parameter. A confidence interval is an interval of values that we believe includes the true parameter value, b_1, with a given degree of confidence. To compute a confidence interval, we must select the significance level for the test and know the standard error of the estimated coefficient.

Suppose we regress a stock's returns on a stock market index's returns and find that the slope coefficient ($\hat{b}_1$) is 1.5 with a standard error ($s_{\hat{b}_1}$) of 0.200. Assume we used 62 monthly observations in our regression analysis. The hypothesized value of the parameter (b_1) is 1.0, the market average slope coefficient. The estimated and the population slope coefficients are often called beta, because the population coefficient is often represented by the Greek symbol beta (β) rather than the b_1 we use in this text. Our null hypothesis is that $b_1 = 1.0$ and $\hat{b}_1$ is the estimate for b_1. We will use a 95 percent confidence interval for our test, or we could say that the test has a significance level of 0.05.

Our confidence interval will span the range $\hat{b}_1 - t_c s_{\hat{b}_1}$ to $\hat{b}_1 + t_c s_{\hat{b}_1}$, or

$$\hat{b}_1 \pm t_c s_{\hat{b}_1} \tag{8-9}$$

where t_c is the critical t value.[31] The critical value for the test depends on the number of degrees of freedom for the t-distribution under the null hypothesis. The number of degrees of freedom equals the number of observations minus the number of parameters estimated. In a regression with one independent variable, there are two estimated parameters, the intercept term and the coefficient on the independent variable. For 62 observations and two parameters estimated in this example, we have 60 degrees of freedom ($62 - 2$). For 60 degrees of freedom, the table of critical values in the back of the book shows that the critical t-value at the 0.05 significance level is 2.00. Substituting the values from our example into Equation 8-9 gives us the interval

$$\hat{b}_1 \pm t_c s_{\hat{b}_1} = 1.5 \pm 2.00(0.200)$$

$$= 1.5 \pm 0.400$$

$$= 1.10 \text{ to } 1.90$$

Under the null hypothesis, the probability that the confidence interval includes b_1 is 95 percent. Because we are testing $b_1 = 1.0$ and because our confidence interval does not include 1.0, we can reject the null hypothesis. Therefore, we can be 95 percent confident that the stock's beta is different from 1.0.

---

[31] We use the t-distribution for this test because we are using a sample estimate of the standard error, s_b, rather than its true (population) value. In the chapter on sampling and estimation, we discussed the concept of degrees of freedom.

In practice, the most common way to test a hypothesis using a regression model is with a t-test of significance. To test the hypothesis, we can compute the statistic

$$t = \frac{\hat{b}_1 - b_1}{s_{\hat{b}_1}} \qquad (8\text{-}10)$$

This test statistic has a t-distribution with $n - 2$ degrees of freedom because two parameters were estimated in the regression. We compare the absolute value of the t-statistic to t_c. If the absolute value of t is greater than t_c, then we can reject the null hypothesis. Substituting the values from the above example into this relationship gives the t-statistic associated with the probability that the stock's beta equals 1.0 ($b_1 = 1.0$).

$$t = \frac{\hat{b}_1 - b_1}{s_{\hat{b}_1}}$$
$$= (1.5 - 1.0)/0.200$$
$$= 2.50$$

Because $t > t_c$, we reject the null hypothesis that $b_1 = 1.0$.

The t-statistic in the example above is 2.50, and at the 0.05 significance level, $t_c = 2.00$; thus we reject the null hypothesis because $t > t_c$. This statement is equivalent to saying that we are 95 percent confident that the interval for the slope coefficient does not contain the value 1.0. If we were performing this test at the 0.01 level, however, t_c would be 2.66 and we would not reject the hypothesis because t would not be greater than t_c at this significance level. A 99 percent confidence interval for the slope coefficient does contain the value 1.0.

The choice of significance level is always a matter of judgment. When we use higher levels of confidence, the t_c increases. This choice leads to wider confidence intervals and to a decreased likelihood of rejecting the null hypothesis. Analysts often choose the 0.05 level of significance, which indicates a 5 percent chance of rejecting the null hypothesis when, in fact, it is true (a Type I error). Of course, decreasing the level of significance from 0.05 to 0.01 decreases the probability of Type I error, but it increases the probability of Type II error—failing to reject the null hypothesis when, in fact, it is false.[32]

Often, financial analysts do not simply report whether or not their tests reject a particular hypothesis about a regression parameter. Instead, they report the p-value or probability value for a particular hypothesis. The p-value is the smallest level of significance at which the null hypothesis can be rejected. It allows the reader to interpret the results rather than be told that a certain hypothesis has been rejected or accepted. In most regression software packages, the p-values printed for regression coefficients apply to a test of null hypothesis that the true parameter is equal to 0 against the alternative that the parameter is not equal to 0, given the estimated coefficient and the standard error for that coefficient. For example, if the p-value is 0.005, we can reject the hypothesis that the true parameter is equal to 0 at the 0.5 percent significance level (99.5 percent confidence).

The standard error of the estimated coefficient is an important input for a hypothesis test concerning the regression coefficient (and for a confidence interval for the estimated coefficient). Stronger regression results lead to smaller standard errors of an estimated parameter and result

---

[32] For a full discussion of Type I and Type II errors, see the chapter on hypothesis testing.

in tighter confidence intervals. If the standard error $(s_{\hat{b}_1})$ in the above example were 0.100 instead of 0.200, the confidence interval range would be half as large and the t-statistic twice as large. With a standard error this small, we would reject the null hypothesis even at the 0.01 significance level because we would have $t = (1.5 - 1)/0.1 = 5.00$ and $t_c = 2.66$.

With this background, we can turn to hypothesis tests using actual regression results. The next three examples illustrate hypothesis tests in a variety of typical investment contexts.

EXAMPLE 8-14   Estimating Beta for General Motors Stock

You are an investor in General Motors stock and want an estimate of its beta. As in the text example, you hypothesize that GM has an average level of market risk and that its required return in excess of the risk-free rate is the same as the market's required excess return. One regression that summarizes these statements is

$$(R - R_F) = \alpha + \beta(R_M - R_F) + \varepsilon \qquad (8\text{-}11)$$

where R_F is the periodic risk-free rate of return (known at the beginning of the period), R_M is the periodic return on the market, R is the periodic return to the stock of the company, and β is the covariance of stock and market return divided by the variance of the market return, $\text{Cov}(R, R_M)/\sigma_M^2$. Estimating this equation with linear regression provides an estimate of β, $\hat{\beta}$, which tells us the size of the required return premium for the security, given expectations about market returns.[33]

Suppose we want to test the null hypothesis, H_0, that $\beta = 1$ for GM stock to see whether GM stock has the same required return premium as the market as a whole. We need data on returns to GM stock, a risk-free interest rate, and the returns to the market index. For this example, we use data from January 1998 through December 2002 ($n = 60$). The return to GM stock is R. The monthly return to 30-day Treasury bills is R_F. The return to the S&P 500 is R_M.[34] We are estimating two parameters, so the number of degrees of freedom is $n - 2 = 60 - 2 = 58$. Table 8-9 shows the results from the regression $(R - R_F) = \alpha + \beta(R_M - R_F) + \varepsilon$.

We are testing the null hypothesis, H_0, that β for GM equals 1 ($\beta = 1$) against the alternative hypothesis that β does not equal 1 ($\beta \neq 1$). The estimated $\hat{\beta}$ from the regression is 1.1958. The estimated standard error for that coefficient in the regression, $s_{\hat{\beta}}$ is 0.2354. The regression equation has 58 degrees of freedom ($60 - 2$), so the critical value for the test statistic is approximately $t_c = 2.00$ at the 0.05 significance

---

[33]Beta (β) is typically estimated using 60 months of historical data, but the data-sample length sometimes varies. Although monthly data is typically used, some financial analysts estimate β using daily data. For more information on methods of estimating β, see Reilly and Brown (2003). The expected excess return for GM stock above the risk-free rate $(R - R_F)$ is $\beta(R_M - R_F)$, given a particular excess return to the market above the risk-free rate $(R_M - R_F)$. This result holds because we regress $(R - R_F)$ against $(R_M - R_F)$. For example, if a stock's beta is 1.5, its expected excess return is 1.5 times that of the market portfolio.

[34]Data on GM stock returns came from Bloomberg. Data on T-bill returns and S&P 500 returns came from Ibbotson Associates.

level. Therefore, the 95 percent confidence interval for the data for any particular hypothesized value of β is shown by the range

$$\hat{\beta} \pm t_c s_{\hat{\beta}}$$

$$1.1958 \pm 2.00(0.2354)$$

$$0.7250 \text{ to } 1.6666$$

In this case, the hypothesized parameter value is $\beta = 1$, and the value 1 falls inside this confidence interval, so we cannot reject the hypothesis at the 0.05 significance level. This means that we cannot reject the hypothesis that GM stock has the same systematic risk as the market as a whole.

TABLE 8-9   Estimating Beta for GM Stock

Regression Statistics			
Multiple R	0.5549		
R-squared	0.3079		
Standard error of estimate	0.0985		
Observations	60		
	Coefficients	Standard Error	t-Statistic
Alpha	0.0036	0.0127	0.2840
Beta	1.1958	0.2354	5.0795

Source: Ibbotson Associates and Bloomberg L.P.

Another way of looking at this issue is to compute the t-statistic for the GM beta hypothesized parameter using Equation 8-10:

$$t = \frac{\hat{\beta} - \beta}{s_{\hat{\beta}}} = \frac{1.1958 - 1.0}{0.2354} = 0.8318$$

This t-statistic is less than the critical t-value of 2.00. Therefore, neither approach allows us to reject the null hypothesis. Note that the t-statistic associated with $\hat{\beta}$ in the regression results in Table 8-9 is 5.0795. Given the significance level we are using, we cannot reject the null hypothesis that $\beta = 1$, but we can reject the hypothesis that $\beta = 0$.[35]

Note also that the R^2 in this regression is only 0.3079. This result suggests that only about 31 percent of the total variation in the excess return to GM stock (the return to GM above the risk-free rate) can be explained by excess return to the market portfolio. The remaining 69 percent of GM stock's excess return variation is the nonsystematic component, which can be attributed to company-specific risk.

---

[35] The t-statistics for a coefficient automatically reported by statistical software programs assume that the null hypothesis states that the coefficient is equal to 0. If you have a different null hypothesis, as we do in this example ($\beta = 1$), then you must either construct the correct test statistic yourself or instruct the program to compute it.

In the next example, we show a regression hypothesis test with a one-sided alternative.

EXAMPLE 8-15   Explaining Company Value Based on Returns to Invested Capital

Some financial analysts have argued that one good way to measure a company's ability to create wealth is to compare the company's return on invested capital (ROIC) to its weighted-average cost of capital (WACC). If a company has an ROIC greater than its cost of capital, the company is creating wealth; if its ROIC is less than its cost of capital, it is destroying wealth.[36]

Enterprise value (EV) is a market-price-based measure of company value defined as the market value of equity and debt minus the value of cash and investments. Invested capital (IC) is an accounting measure of company value defined as the sum of the book values of equity and debt. Higher ratios of EV to IC should reflect greater success at wealth creation in general. Mauboussin (1996) argued that the spread between ROIC and WACC helps explains the ratio of EV to IC. Using data on companies in the food-processing industry, we can test the relationship between EV/IC and (ROIC−WACC) using the regression model given in Equation 8-12.

$$\text{EV}_i/\text{IC}_i = b_0 + b_1(\text{ROIC}_i - \text{WACC}_i) + \varepsilon_i \qquad (8\text{-}12)$$

where the subscript i is an index to identify the company. Our null hypothesis is $H_0: b_1 \le 0$, and we specify a significance level of 0.05. If we reject the null hypothesis, we have evidence of a statistically significant relationship between EV/IC and (ROIC−WACC). We estimate Equation 8-12 using data from nine food-processing companies for 2001.[37] The results of this regression are displayed in Table 8-10 and Figure 8-11.

TABLE 8-10   Explaining Enterprise Value/Invested Capital by the ROIC−WACC Spread

Regression Statistics			
Multiple R	0.9469		
R-squared	0.8966		
Standard error of estimate	0.7422		
Observations	9		

	Coefficients	Standard Error	t-Statistic
Intercept	1.3478	0.3511	3.8391
Spread	30.0169	3.8519	7.7928

Source: Nelson (2003).

---

[36] See, for example, Stewart (1991) and Mauboussin (1996).

[37] Our data come from Nelson (2003). Many sell-side analysts use this type of regression. It is one of the most frequently used cross-sectional regressions in published analyst reports.

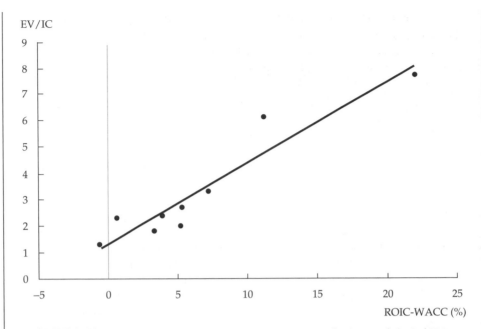

FIGURE 8-11   Fitted Regression Line Explaining Enterprise Value/Invested Capital Using
ROIC–WACC Spread for the Food Industry
Source: CSFB Food Investors Handbook 2003.

We reject the null hypothesis based on the *t*-statistic of approximately 7.79 on
estimated slope coefficient. There is a strong positive relationship between the return
spread (ROIC–WACC) and the ratio of EV to IC in our sample of companies.
Figure 8-11 illustrates the strong positive relationship. The R^2 of 0.8966 indicates
that the return spread explains about 90 percent of the variation in the ratio of EV
to IC among the food-processing companies in the sample in 2001. The coefficient
on the return spread of 30.0169 implies that the predicted increase in EV/IC is
0.01(30.0169) = 0.3002 or about 30 percent for a 1-percentage-point increase in the
return spread, for our sample of companies.

In the final example of this section, we show that the null hypothesis can involve a slope
coefficient of 1 just as well as a slope of 0.

EXAMPLE 8-16   Testing Whether Inflation Forecasts Are Unbiased

Example 8-11 introduced the concept of testing for bias in forecasts. That example
showed that if a forecast is unbiased, its expected error is 0. We can examine whether a
time-series of forecasts for a particular economic variable is unbiased by comparing the
forecast at each date with the actual value of the economic variable announced after the
forecast. If the forecasts are unbiased, then, by definition, the average realized forecast

error should be close to 0. In that case, the value of b_0 (the intercept) should be 0 and the value of b_1 (the slope) should be 1, as discussed in Example 8-11.

Refer once again to Figure 8-9, which shows the current-quarter predictions of percentage change in CPI made by professional economic forecasters and the actual percentage change from the first quarter of 1983 through the fourth quarter of 2002 ($n = 80$). To test whether the forecasts are unbiased, we must estimate the regression shown in Example 8-11. We report the results of this regression in Table 8-11. The equation to be estimated is

$$\text{Actual percentage change in CPI}_t = b_0 + b_1(\text{Predicted change}_t) + \varepsilon_t$$

This regression estimates two parameters (the intercept and the slope); therefore, the regression has $n - 2 = 80 - 2 = 78$ degrees of freedom.

TABLE 8-11   Testing Whether Forecasts of CPI Are Unbiased
(Dependent Variable: CPI Change Expressed in Percent)

Regression Statistics			
Multiple R	0.7138		
R-squared	0.5095		
Standard error of estimate	1.0322		
Observations	80		

	Coefficients	Standard Error	t-Statistic
Intercept	−0.0140	0.3657	−0.0384
Forecast (slope)	0.9637	0.1071	9.0008

Sources: Federal Reserve Banks of Philadelphia and St. Louis.

We can now test two null hypotheses about the parameters in this regression. Our first null hypothesis is that the intercept in this regression is 0 (H_0: $b_0 = 0$). The alternative hypothesis is that the intercept does not equal 0 (H_a: $b_0 \neq 0$). Our second null hypothesis is that the slope coefficient in this regression is 1 (H_0: $b_1 = 1$). The alternative hypothesis is that the slope coefficient does not equal 1 (H_a: $b_1 \neq 1$).

To test the hypotheses about b_0 and b_1, we must first decide on a critical value based on a particular significance level and then construct the confidence intervals for each parameter. If we choose the 0.05 significance level, with 78 degrees of freedom, the critical value, t_c, is approximately 1.99. The estimated value of the parameter $\hat{b}_0$ is −0.0140, and the estimated value of the standard error for $\hat{b}_0 (s_{\hat{b}_0})$ is 0.3657. Let B_0 stand for any particular hypothesized value. Therefore, under the null hypothesis that $b_0 = B_0$, a 95 percent confidence interval for b_0 is

$$\hat{b}_0 \pm t_c s_{\hat{b}_0}$$

$$-0.0140 \pm 1.99(0.3657)$$

$$-0.7417 \text{ to } 0.7137$$

In this case, B_0 is 0. The value of 0 falls within this confidence interval, so we cannot reject the first null hypothesis that $b_0 = 0$. We will explain how to interpret this result shortly.

Our second null hypothesis is based on the same sample as our first null hypothesis. Therefore, the critical value for testing that hypothesis is the same as the critical value for testing the first hypothesis ($t_c = 1.99$). The estimated value of the parameter $\hat{b}_1$ is 0.9637, and the estimated value of the standard error for $\hat{b}_1$, $s_{\hat{b}_1}$, is 0.1071. Therefore, the 95 percent confidence interval for any particular hypothesized value of b_1 can be constructed as follows:

$$\hat{b}_1 \pm t_c s_{\hat{b}_1}$$

$$0.9637 \pm 1.99(0.1071)$$

$$0.7506 \text{ to } 1.1768$$

In this case, our hypothesized value of b_1 is 1. The value 1 falls within this confidence interval, so we cannot reject the null hypothesis that $b_1 = 1$ at the 0.05 significance level. Because we did not reject either of the null hypotheses ($b_0 = 0, b_1 = 1$) about the parameters in this model, we cannot reject the hypothesis that the forecasts of CPI change were unbiased.[38]

As an analyst, you often will need forecasts of economic growth to help you make recommendations about asset allocation, expected returns, and other investment decisions. The hypothesis tests just conducted suggest that you cannot reject the hypothesis that the CPI predictions in the Survey of Professional Forecasters are unbiased. If you need an unbiased forecast of future percentage change in CPI for your asset-allocation decision, you might want to use these forecasts.

3.6. Analysis of Variance in a Regression with One Independent Variable

Analysis of variance (ANOVA) is a statistical procedure for dividing the total variability of a variable into components that can be attributed to different sources.[39] In regression analysis, we use ANOVA to determine the usefulness of the independent variable or variables in explaining variation in the dependent variable. An important statistical test conducted in analysis of variance is the F-test. The F-statistic tests whether all the slope coefficients in a linear regression are equal to 0. In a regression with one independent variable, this is a test of the null hypothesis H_0: $b_1 = 0$ against the alternative hypothesis H_a: $b_1 \neq 0$.

To correctly determine the test statistic for the null hypothesis that the slope coefficient equals 0, we need to know the following:

---

[38] Jointly testing the hypothesis $b_0 = 0$ and $b_1 = 1$ would require us to take into account the covariance of $\hat{b}_0$ and $\hat{b}_1$. For information on testing joint hypotheses of this type, see Greene (2003).

[39] In this chapter, we focus on regression applications of ANOVA, the most common context in which financial analysts will encounter this tool. In this context, ANOVA is used to test whether all the regression slope coefficients are equal to 0. Analysts also use ANOVA to test a hypothesis that the means of two or more populations are equal. See Daniel and Terrell (1995) for details.

- the total number of observations (n);
- the total number of parameters to be estimated (in a one-independent-variable regression, this number is two: the intercept and the slope coefficient);
- the sum of squared errors or residuals, $\sum_{i=1}^{n}(Y_i - \hat{Y}_i)^2$, abbreviated SSE. This value is also known as the residual sum of squares; and
- the regression sum of squares, $\sum_{i=1}^{n}(\hat{Y}_i - \overline{Y})^2$, abbreviated RSS. This value is the amount of total variation in Y that is explained in the regression equation. Total variation (TSS) is the sum of SSE and RSS.

The F-test for determining whether the slope coefficient equals 0 is based on an F-statistic, constructed using these four values. The F-statistic measures how well the regression equation explains the variation in the dependent variable. The F-statistic is the ratio of the average regression sum of squares to the average sum of the squared errors. The average regression sum of squares is computed by dividing the regression sum of squares by the number of slope parameters estimated (in this case, one). The average sum of squared errors is computed by dividing the sum of squared errors by the number of observations, n, minus the total number of parameters estimated (in this case, two: the intercept and the slope). These two divisors are the degrees of freedom for an F-test. If there are n observations, the F-test for the null hypothesis that the slope coefficient is equal to 0 is here denoted $F_{\#\text{ slope parameters, }n-\#\text{ parameters}} = F_{1,n-2}$, and the test has 1 and $n - 2$ degrees of freedom.

Suppose, for example, that the independent variable in a regression model explains none of the variation in the dependent variable. Then the predicted value for the regression model, $\hat{Y}_i$, is the average value of the dependent variable $\overline{Y}$. In this case, the regression sum of squares $\sum_{i=1}^{n}(\hat{Y}_i - \overline{Y})^2$ is 0. Therefore, the F-statistic is 0. If the independent variable explains little of the variation in the dependent variable, the value of the F-statistic will be very small.

The formula for the F-statistic in a regression with one independent variable is

$$F = \frac{\text{RSS}/1}{\text{SSE}/(n-2)} = \frac{\text{Mean regression sum of squares}}{\text{Mean squared error}} \tag{8-13}$$

If the regression model does a good job of explaining variation in the dependent variable, then this ratio should be high. The explained regression sum of squares per estimated parameter will be high relative to the unexplained variation for each degree of freedom. A table of critical values for this F-statistic is given in the back of this book.

Even though the F-statistic is commonly computed by regression software packages, analysts typically do not use ANOVA and F-tests in regressions with just one independent variable. Why not? In such regressions, the F-statistic is the square of the t-statistic for the slope coefficient. Therefore, the F-test duplicates the t-test for the significance of the slope coefficient. This relation is not true for regressions with two or more slope coefficients. Nevertheless, the one-slope coefficient case gives a foundation for understanding the multiple-slope coefficient cases.

Often, mutual fund performance is evaluated based on whether the fund has positive alpha—significantly positive excess risk-adjusted returns.[40] One commonly used

---

[40]Note that the Greek letter alpha, α, is traditionally used to represent the intercept in Equation 8-14 and should not be confused with another traditional usage of α to represent a significance level.

method of risk adjustment is based on the capital asset pricing model. Consider the regression

$$(R_i - R_F) = \alpha_i + \beta_i(R_M - R_F) + \varepsilon_i \qquad (8\text{-}14)$$

where R_F is the periodic risk-free rate of return (known at the beginning of the period), R_M is the periodic return on the market, R_i is the periodic return to Mutual Fund i, and β_i is the fund's beta. A fund has zero risk-adjusted excess return if $\alpha_i = 0$. If $\alpha_i = 0$, then $(R_i - R_F) = \beta_i(R_M - R_F) + \varepsilon_i$ and taking expectations, $E(R_i) = R_F + \beta_i(R_M - R_F)$, implying that β_i completely explains the fund's mean excess returns. If, for example, $\alpha_i > 0$, the fund is earning higher returns than expected given its beta.

In summary, to test whether a fund has a positive alpha, we must test the null hypothesis that the fund has no risk-adjusted excess returns (H_0: $\alpha = 0$) against the alternative hypothesis of nonzero risk-adjusted returns (H_a: $\alpha \neq 0$).

EXAMPLE 8-17   Performance Evaluation: The Dreyfus Appreciation Fund

Table 8-12 presents results evaluating the excess return to the Dreyfus Appreciation Fund from January 1998 through December 2002. Note that the estimated beta in this regression, $\hat{\beta}_i$, is 0.7902. The Dreyfus Appreciation Fund was estimated to be about 0.8 times as risky as the market as a whole.

TABLE 8-12   Performance Evaluation of Dreyfus Appreciation Fund, January 1998 to December 2002

Regression Statistics				
Multiple R		0.9280		
R-squared		0.8611		
Standard error of estimate		0.0174		
Observations		60		

ANOVA	Degrees of Freedom (df)	Sum of Squares (SS)	Mean Sum of Squares (MSS)	F
Regression	1	0.1093	0.1093	359.64
Residual	58	0.0176	0.0003	
Total	59	0.1269		

	Coefficients	Standard Error	t-Statistic
Alpha	0.0009	0.0023	0.4036
Beta	0.7902	0.0417	18.9655

Source: Center for Research in Security Prices, University of Chicago.

Note also that the estimated alpha ($\hat{\alpha}$) in this regression is positive (0.0009). The value of the coefficient is only a little more than one-third the size of the standard error for that coefficient (0.0023), so the t-statistic for the coefficient is only 0.4036. Therefore, we cannot reject the null hypothesis ($\alpha = 0$) that the fund did not have a significant excess return beyond the return associated with the market risk of the fund. This result means that the returns to the fund were explained by the market risk of the fund and there was no additional statistical significance to the excess returns to the fund during this period.[41]

Because the t-statistic for the slope coefficient in this regression is 18.9655, the p-value for that coefficient is less than 0.0001 and is approximately zero. Therefore, the probability that the true value of this coefficient is actually 0 is microscopic.

How can we use an F-test to determine whether the slope coefficient in this regression is equal to 0? The ANOVA portion of Table 8-12 provides the data we need. In this case,

- the total number of observations (n) is 60;
- the total number of parameters to be estimated is 2 (intercept and slope);
- the sum of squared errors or residuals, SSE, is 0.0176; and
- the regression sum of squares, RSS, is 0.1093.

Therefore, the F-statistic to test whether the slope coefficient is equal to 0 is

$$\frac{0.1093/1}{0.0176/(60-2)} = 360.19$$

(The slight difference from the F-statistic in Table 8-12 is due to rounding.) The ANOVA output would show that the p-value for this F-statistic is less than 0.0001 and is exactly the same as the p-value for the t-statistic for the slope coefficient. Therefore, the F-test tells us nothing more than we already knew from the t-test. Note also that the F-statistic (359.64) is the square of the t-statistic (18.9655).

3.7. Prediction Intervals

Financial analysts often want to use regression results to make predictions about a dependent variable. For example, we might ask, "How fast will the sales of XYZ Corporation grow this year if real GDP grows by 4 percent?" But we are not merely interested in making these forecasts; we also want to know how certain we should be about the forecasts' results. For example, if we predicted that sales for XYZ Corporation would grow by 6 percent this year, our prediction would mean more if we were 95 percent confident that sales growth would fall in the interval from 5 percent to 7 percent, rather than only 25 percent confident that this outcome would occur. Therefore, we need to understand how to compute confidence intervals around regression forecasts.

We must take into account two sources of uncertainty when using the regression model $Y_i = b_0 + b_1 X_i + \varepsilon_i, i = 1, \ldots, n$ and the estimated parameters, $\hat{b}_0$ and $\hat{b}_1$, to make a

---

[41]This example introduces a well known investment use of regression involving the capital asset pricing model. Researchers, however, recognize qualifications to the interpretation of alpha from a linear regression. The systematic risk of a managed portfolio is controlled by the portfolio manager. If, as a consequence, portfolio beta is correlated with the return on the market (as could result from market timing), inferences on alpha based on least-squares beta, as here, can be mistaken. This advanced subject is discussed in Dybvig and Ross (1985a) and (1985b).

prediction. First, the error term itself contains uncertainty. The standard deviation of the error term, σ_ε, can be estimated from the standard error of estimate for the regression equation. A second source of uncertainty in making predictions about Y, however, comes from uncertainty in the estimated parameters $\hat{b}_0$ and $\hat{b}_1$.

If we knew the true values of the regression parameters, b_0 and b_1, then the variance of our prediction of Y, given any particular predicted (or assumed) value of X, would simply be s^2, the squared standard error of estimate. The variance would be s^2 because the prediction, $\hat{Y}$, would come from the equation $\hat{Y} = b_0 + b_1 X$ and $(Y - \hat{Y}) = \varepsilon$.

Because we must estimate the regression parameters $\hat{b}_0$ and $\hat{b}_1$ however, our prediction of Y, $\hat{Y}$, given any particular predicted value of X, is actually $\hat{Y} = \hat{b}_0 + \hat{b}_1 X$. The estimated variance of the prediction error, s_f^2 of Y, given X, is

$$s_f^2 = s^2 \left[1 + \frac{1}{n} + \frac{(X - \overline{X})^2}{(n-1)s_x^2} \right] \tag{8-15}$$

This estimated variance depends on

- the squared standard error of estimate, s^2;
- the number of observations, n;
- the value of the independent variable, X, used to predict the dependent variable;
- the estimated mean, $\overline{X}$; and
- variance, s_x^2 of the independent variable.[42]

Once we have this estimate of the variance of the prediction error, determining a prediction interval around the prediction is very similar to estimating a confidence interval around an estimated parameter, as shown earlier in this chapter. We need to take the following four steps to determine the prediction interval for the prediction:

1. Make the prediction.
2. Compute the variance of the prediction error using Equation 8-15.
3. Choose a significance level, α, for the forecast. For example, the 0.05 level, given the degrees of freedom in the regression, determines the critical value for the forecast interval, t_c.
4. Compute the $(1 - \alpha)$ percent prediction interval for the prediction, namely $\hat{Y} \pm t_c s_f$.

EXAMPLE 8-18 Predicting the Ratio of Enterprise Value to Invested Capital

We continue with the example of explaining the ratio of enterprise value to invested capital among food-processing companies by the spread between the return to invested capital and the weighted-average cost of capital (ROIC–WAAC). In Example 8-15, we estimated the regression given in Table 8-10.

[42]For a derivation of this equation, see Pindyck and Rubinfeld (1998).

You are interested in predicting the ratio of enterprise value to invested capital for a company if the return spread between ROIC and WACC is 10 percentage points.

TABLE 8-10   (repeated) Explaining Enterprise Value/Invested Capital by the ROIC–WACC Spread

Regression Statistics			
Multiple *R*		0.9469	
R-squared		0.8966	
Standard error of estimate		0.7422	
Observations		9	
	Coefficients	Standard Error	*t*-Statistic
Intercept	1.3478	0.3511	3.8391
Spread	30.0169	3.8519	7.7928

Source: Nelson (2003).

What is the 95 percent confidence interval for the ratio of enterprise value to invested capital for that company?

Using the data provided in Table 8-10, take the following steps:

1. Make the prediction: Expected EV/IC $= 1.3478 + 30.0169(0.10) = 4.3495$. This regression suggests that if the return spread between ROIC and WACC (X_i) is 10 percent, the EV/IC ratio will be 4.3495.
2. Compute the variance of the prediction error. To compute the variance of the forecast error, we must know

   - the standard error of the estimate of the equation, $s = 0.7422$ (as shown in Table 8-10);
   - the mean return spread, $\overline{X} = 0.0647$ (this computation is not shown in the table); and
   - the variance of the mean return spread in the sample, $s_x^2 = 0.004641$ (this computation is not shown in the table).

   Using these data, you can compute the variance of the forecast error (s_f^2) for predicting EV/IC for a company with a 10 percent spread between ROIC and WACC.

$$s_f^2 = 0.7422^2 \left[1 + \frac{1}{9} + \frac{(0.10 - 0.0647)^2}{(9-1)0.004641} \right]$$
$$= 0.630556$$

In this example, the variance of the forecast error is 0.630556, and the standard deviation of the forecast error is $s_f = (0.630556)^{1/2} = 0.7941$.

3. Determine the critical value of the t-statistic. Given a 95 percent confidence interval and $9 - 2 = 7$ degrees of freedom, the critical value of the t-statistic, t_c, is 2.365 using the tables in the back of the book.
4. Compute the prediction interval. The 95 percent confidence interval for EV/IC extends from $4.3495 - 2.365(0.7941)$ to $4.3495 + 2.365(0.7941)$, or 2.4715 to 6.2275.

In summary, if the spread between the ROIC and the WACC is 10 percent, the 95 percent prediction interval for EV/IC will extend from 2.4715 to 6.2275. The small sample size is reflected in the relatively large prediction interval.

3.8. Limitations of Regression Analysis

Although this chapter has shown many of the uses of regression models for financial analysis, regression models do have limitations. First, regression relations can change over time, just as correlations can. This fact is known as the issue of **parameter instability**, and its existence should not be surprising as the economic, tax, regulatory, political, and institutional contexts in which financial markets operate change. Whether considering cross-sectional or time-series regression, the analyst will probably face this issue. As one example, cross-sectional regression relationships between stock characteristics may differ between growth-led and value-led markets. As a second example, the time-series regression estimating the beta often yields significantly different estimated betas depending on the time period selected. In both cross-sectional and time-series contexts, the most common problem is sampling from more than one population, with the challenge of identifying when doing so is an issue.

A second limitation to the use of regression results specific to investment contexts is that public knowledge of regression relationships may negate their future usefulness. Suppose, for example, an analyst discovers that stocks with a certain characteristic have had historically very high returns. If other analysts discover and act upon this relationship, then the prices of stocks with that characteristic will be bid up. The knowledge of the relationship may result in the relation no longer holding in the future.

Finally, if the regression assumptions listed in Section 3.2 are violated, hypothesis tests and predictions based on linear regression will not be valid. Although there are tests for violations of regression assumptions, often uncertainty exists as to whether an assumption has been violated. This limitation will be discussed in detail in the chapter on multiple regression.

CHAPTER 9

MULTIPLE REGRESSION AND ISSUES IN REGRESSION ANALYSIS

1. INTRODUCTION

As financial analysts, we often need to use more-sophisticated statistical methods than correlation analysis or regression involving a single independent variable. For example, a trading desk interested in the costs of trading Nasdaq stocks might want information on the determinants of the bid–ask spread on the Nasdaq. A mutual fund analyst might want to know whether returns to a technology mutual fund behaved more like the returns to a growth stock index or like the returns to a value stock index. An investor might be interested in the factors that determine whether analysts cover a stock. We can answer these questions using linear regression with more than one independent variable—multiple linear regression.

In Sections 2 and 3, we introduce and illustrate the basic concepts and models of multiple regression analysis. These models rest on assumptions that are sometimes violated in practice. In Section 4, we discuss three major violations of a regression assumption. We address practical concerns such as how to diagnose an assumption violation and what remedial steps to take when a model assumption has been violated. Section 5 outlines some guidelines for building good regression models and discusses ways that analysts sometimes go wrong in this endeavor. In a number of investment applications, we are in-terested in the probability that one of two outcomes occurs: For example, we may be interested in whether a stock has analyst coverage or not. Section 6 discusses a class of models, qualitative dependent variable models, that addresses such questions.

2. MULTIPLE LINEAR REGRESSION

As investment analysts, we often hypothesize that more than one variable explains the behavior of a variable in which we are interested. The variable we seek to explain is called the dependent variable. The variables that we believe explain the dependent variable are called the independent variables.[1] A tool that permits us to examine the relationship (if any) between the two types of variables is multiple linear regression. **Multiple linear regression** allows us to determine the effect of more than one independent variable on a particular dependent variable.

---

[1] Independent variables are also called explanatory variables or regressors.

To give an example of how we might use this tool, suppose we want to know whether the bid–ask spread for stocks trading in a dealer market is affected by the number of market makers (dealers) for that stock and the market capitalization of the stock. We can address this question using the following multiple linear regression model:

$$Y_i = b_0 + b_1 X_{1i} + b_2 X_{2i} + \epsilon_i$$

where

> Y_i = the natural logarithm of the bid-ask spread for stock i (the dependent variable)
> X_{1i} = the natural logarithm of the number of market makers for stock i
> X_{2i} = the natural logarithm of the market capitalization of company i
> ϵ_i = the error term

Of course, linear regression models can use more than two independent variables to explain the dependent variable. A **multiple linear regression model** has the general form

$$Y_i = b_0 + b_1 X_{1i} + b_2 X_{2i} + \cdots + b_k X_{ki} + \epsilon_i, i = 1, 2, \ldots, n \qquad (9\text{-}1)$$

where

> Y_i = the ith observation of the dependent variable Y
> X_{ji} = the ith observation of the independent variable $X_j, j = 1, 2, \ldots, k$
> b_0 = the intercept of the equation
> $b_1, \ldots, b_k$ = the slope coefficients for each of the independent variables
> ϵ_i = the error term
> n = the number of observations

A slope coefficient, b_j, measures how much the dependent variable, Y, changes when the independent variable, X_j, changes by one unit, holding all other independent variables constant. For example, if $b_1 = 1$ and all of the other independent variables remain constant, then we predict that if X_1 increases by one unit, Y will also increase by one unit. If $b_1 = -1$ and all of the other independent variables are held constant, then we predict that if X_1 increases by one unit, Y will decrease by one unit. Multiple linear regression estimates $b_0, \ldots, b_k$. In this chapter, we will refer to both the intercept, b_0, and the slope co-efficients, $b_1, \ldots, b_k$, as **regression coefficients**. As we proceed with our discussion, keep in mind that a regression equation has k slope coefficients and $k + 1$ regression coefficients.

In practice, we use software to estimate a multiple regression model. Example 9-1 presents an application of multiple regression analysis in investment practice. In the course of discussing a hypothesis test, Example 9-1 presents typical regression output and its interpretation.

EXAMPLE 9-1   Explaining the Bid–Ask Spread

As the manager of the trading desk at an investment management firm, you have noticed that the average bid–ask spreads of different Nasdaq-listed stocks can vary widely.

When the ratio of a stock's bid–ask spread to its price is higher than for another stock, your firm's costs of trading in that stock tend to be higher. You have formulated the hypothesis that Nasdaq stocks' percentage bid–ask spreads are related to the number of market makers and the company's stock market capitalization. You have decided to investigate your hypothesis using multiple regression analysis.

You specify a regression model in which the dependent variable measures the percentage bid–ask spread and the independent variables measure the number of market makers and the company's stock market capitalization. The regression is estimated using data from December 2002 for 1,819 Nasdaq-listed stocks. Based on earlier published research exploring bid–ask spreads, you express the dependent and independent variables as natural logarithms, a so-called **log-log regression model**. A log-log regression model may be appropriate when one believes that proportional changes in the dependent variable bear a constant relationship to proportional changes in the independent variable(s), as we illustrate below. You formulate the multiple regression:

$$Y_i = b_0 + b_1 X_{1i} + b_2 X_{2i} + \epsilon_i \qquad (9\text{-}2)$$

where

Y_i = the natural logarithm of (bid–ask spread/stock price) for stock i

X_{1i} = the natural logarithm of the number of Nasdaq market makers for stock i

X_{2i} = the natural logarithm of the market capitalization (measured in millions of dollars) of company i

In a log-log regression such as Equation 9-2, the slope coefficients are interpreted as elasticities, assumed to be constant. For example, $b_2 = -0.75$ means that for a 1 percent increase in the market capitalization, we expect bid–ask spread/stock price to decrease by 0.75 percent, holding all other independent variables constant.[2]

Reasoning that greater competition tends to lower costs, you suspect that the greater the number of market makers, the smaller the percentage bid–ask spread. Therefore, you formulate a first null hypothesis and alternative hypothesis:

$$H_0 : b_1 \geq 0$$

$$H_a : b_1 < 0$$

The null hypothesis is the hypothesis that the "suspected" condition is not true. If the evidence supports rejecting the null hypothesis and accepting the alternative hypothesis, you have statistically confirmed your suspicion.[3]

You also believe that the stocks of companies with higher market capitalization may have more-liquid markets, tending to lower percentage bid–ask spreads. Therefore, you formulate a second null hypothesis and alternative hypothesis:

---

[2] Note that $\Delta(\ln X) \approx \Delta X / X$, where Δ represents "change in" and $\Delta X / X$ is a proportional change in X. We discuss the model further in Example 9-11.

[3] An alternative valid formulation is a two-sided test $H_0 : b_1 = 0$, versus $H_a : b_1 \neq 0$ which reflects the beliefs of the researcher less strongly. See the chapter on hypothesis testing. A two-sided test could also be conducted for the hypothesis on market capitalization that we discuss next.

$$H_0: b_2 \geq 0$$

$$H_a: b_2 < 0$$

For both tests, we use a t-test, rather than a z-test, because we do not know the population variance of b_1 and b_2.[4] Suppose that you choose a 0.01 significance level for both tests. Table 9-1 shows the results of estimating this linear regression using data from December 2002.

TABLE 9-1   Results from Regressing ln(Bid−Ask Spread/Price) on ln(Number of Market Makers) and ln(Market Cap)

			Coefficient	Standard Error	t-Statistic
Intercept			−0.7586	0.1369	−5.5416
ln(Number of Nasdaq market makers)			−0.2790	0.0673	−4.1427
ln(Company's market cap)			−0.6635	0.0246	−27.0087
ANOVA	df	SS	MSS	F	Significance F
Regression	2	2,681.6482	1,340.8241	1,088.8325	0.00
Residual	1,816	2,236.2820	1.2314		
Total	1,818	4,917.9302			
Residual standard error		1.1097			
Multiple R-squared		0.5453			
Observations		1,819			

Source: FactSet, Nasdaq.

If the regression result is not significant, we follow the useful principle of not proceeding to interpret the individual regression coefficients. Thus the analyst might look first at the ANOVA section, which addresses the regression's overall significance.

- The ANOVA (analysis of variance) section reports quantities related to the overall explanatory power and significance of the regression. SS stands for sum of squares, and MSS stands for mean sum of squares (SS divided by df). The F-test reports the overall significance of the regression. For example, an entry of 0.01 for the significance of F means that the regression is significant at the 0.01 level. In Table 9-1, the regression is even more significant becausethe significance of F is 0 at two decimal places. Later in the chapter, we will present more information on the F-test.

Having ascertained that the overall regression is highly significant, an analyst might turn to the first listed column in the first section of the regression output.

---

[4]The use of t-tests and z-tests is discussed in the chapter on hypothesis testing.

- The Coefficients column gives the estimates of the intercept, b_0, and the slope coefficients, b_1 and b_2. These estimates are all negative, but are they significantly negative? The Standard Error column gives the standard error (the standard deviation) of the estimated regression coefficients. The test statistic for hypotheses concerning the population value of a regression coefficient has the form (Estimated regression coefficient—Hypothesized population value of the regression coefficient)/(Standard error of the regression coefficient). This is a *t*-test. Under the null hypothesis, the hypothesized population value of the regression coefficient is 0. Thus (Estimated regression coefficient)/(Standard error of the regression coefficient) is the *t*-statistic given in the third column. For example, the *t*-statistic for the intercept is $-0.7586/0.1369 = -5.5416$, ignoring the effects of rounding errors. To evaluate the significance of the *t*-statistic we need to determine a quantity called degrees of freedom (df).[5] The calculation is Degrees of freedom = Number of observations—(Number of independent variables + 1) = $n - (k + 1)$.
- The final section of Table 9-1 presents two measures of how well the estimated regression fits or explains the data. The first is the standard deviation of the regression residual, the residual standard error. This standard deviation is called the standard error of estimate (SEE). The second measure quantifies the degree of linear association between the dependent variable and all of the independent variables jointly. This measure is known as multiple R^2 or simply R^2 (the square of the correlation between predicted and actual values of the dependent variable).[6] A value of 0 for R^2 indicates no linear association; a value of 1 indicates perfect linear association. The final item in Table 9-1 is the number of observations in the sample (1,819).

Having reviewed the meaning of typical regression output, we can return to complete the hypothesis tests.

The estimated regression supports the hypothesis that the greater the number of market makers, the smaller the percentage bid–ask spread: We reject $H_0 : b_1 \geq 0$ in favor of $H_a : b_1 < 0$. The results also support the belief that the stocks of companies with higher market capitalization have lower percentage bid–ask spreads: We reject $H_0 : b_2 \geq 0$ in favor of $H_a : b_2 < 0$. To see that the null hypothesis is rejected for both tests, we can use tables in the back of the book.[7] For both tests, df $= 1,819 - 3 = 1,816$. The tables do not give critical values for degrees of freedom that large. The critical value for a one-tailed test with df $= 200$ at the 0.01 significance level is 2.345; for a larger number of degrees of freedom, the critical value would be even smaller in magnitude. Therefore, in our one-sided tests, we reject the null hypothesis in favor of the alternative hypothesis if

$$t = \frac{\hat{b}_j - b_j}{s_{\hat{b}_j}} = \frac{\hat{b}_j - 0}{s_{\hat{b}_j}} < -2.345$$

---

[5] To calculate the degrees of freedom lost in the regression, we add 1 to the number of independent variables to account for the intercept term. The *t*-test and the concept of degrees of freedom are discussed in the chapter on sampling.

[6] Multiple R^2 is also known as the multiple coefficient of determination, or simply the coefficient of determination.

[7] See Appendix B for *t*-test values.

where

$\hat{b}_j$ = the regression estimate of $b_j, j = 1, 2$

b_j = the hypothesized value[8] of the coefficient (0)

$s_{\hat{b}_j}$ = the estimated standard error of $\hat{b}_j$

The t-values of -4.1427 and -27.0087 for the estimates of b_1 and b_2, respectively, are both less than -2.345.

Before proceeding further, we should address the interpretation of a prediction stated in natural logarithm terms. We can convert a natural logarithm to the original units by taking the antilogarithm. To illustrate this conversion, suppose that a particular stock has five Nasdaq market makers and a market capitalization of $100 million. The natural logarithm of the number of Nasdaq market makers is equal to ln $5 = 1.6094$, and the natural logarithm of the company's market cap (in millions) is equal to ln $100 = 4.6052$. With these values, the regression model predicts that the natural log of the ratio of the bid–ask spread to the stock price will be $-0.7586 + (-0.2790 \times 1.6094) + (-0.6635 \times 4.6052) = -4.2632$. We take the antilogarithm of -4.2632 by raising e to that power: $e^{-4.2632} = 0.0141$. The predicted bid–ask spread will be 1.41 percent of the stock price.[9] Later we state the assumptions of the multiple regression model; before using an estimated regression to make predictions in actual practice, we should assure ourselves that those assumptions are satisfied.

In Table 9-1, we presented output common to most regression software programs. Many software programs also report p-values for the regression coefficients.[10] For each regression coefficient, the p-value would be the smallest level of significance at which we can reject a null hypothesis that the population value of the coefficient is 0, in a two-sided test. The lower the p-value, the stronger the evidence against that null hypothesis. A p-value quickly allows us to determine if an independent variable is significant at a conventional significance level such as 0.05, or at any other standard we believe is appropriate.

Having estimated Equation 9-1, we can write

$$\hat{Y}_i = \hat{b}_0 + \hat{b}_1 X_{1i} + \hat{b}_2 X_{2i}$$

$$= -0.7586 - 0.2790 X_{1i} - 0.6635 X_{2i}$$

where $\hat{Y}_i$ stands for the predicted value of Y_i, and $\hat{b}_0$, $\hat{b}_1$, and $\hat{b}_2$, stand for the estimated values of b_0, b_1, and b_2, respectively. How should we interpret the estimated slope coefficients -0.2790 and -0.6635?

Interpreting the slope coefficients in a multiple linear regression model is different than doing so in the one-independent-variable regressions explored in the chapter on correlation

---

[8]To economize on notation in stating test statistics, in this context we use b_j to represent the hypothesized value of the parameter (elsewhere we use it to represent the unknown population parameter).

[9]The operation illustrated (taking the antilogarithm) recovers the value of a variable in the original units as $e^{\ln X} = X$.

[10]The entry 0.00 for the significance of F was a p-value for the F-test. See the chapter on hypothesis testing for more information on the p-value.

and regression. Suppose we have a one-independent-variable regression that we estimate as $\hat{Y}_i = 0.50 + 0.75X_{1i}$. The interpretation of the slope estimate 0.75 is that for every 1 unit increase in X_1, we expect Y to increase by 0.75 units. If we were to add a second independent variable to the equation, we would generally find that the estimated coefficient on X_1 is *not* 0.75 unless the second independent variable were uncorrelated with X_1. The slope coefficients in a multiple regression are known as **partial regression coefficients** or **partial slope coefficients** and need to be interpreted with care.[11] Suppose the coefficient on X_1 in a regression with the second independent variable was 0.60. Can we say that for every 1-unit increase in X_1, we expect Y to increase by 0.60 units? Not without qualification. For every 1-unit increase in X_1, we still expect Y to increase by 0.75 units when X_2 is not held constant. We would interpret 0.60 as the expected increase in Y for a 1-unit increase X_1 *holding the second independent variable constant*.

To explain what the shorthand reference "holding the second independent constant" refers to, if we were to regress X_1 on X_2, the residuals from that regression would represent the part of X_1 that is uncorrelated with X_2. We could then regress Y on those residuals in a 1-independent-variable regression. We would find that the slope coefficient on the residuals would be 0.60; by construction, 0.60 would represent the expected effect on Y of a 1-unit increase in X_1 after removing the part of X_1 that is correlated with X_2. Consistent with this explanation, we can view 0.60 as the expected net effect on Y of a 1-unit increase in X_1, after accounting for any effects of the other independent variables on the expected value of Y. To reiterate, a partial regression coefficient measures the expected change in the dependent variable for a one-unit increase in an independent variable, holding all the other independent variables constant.

To apply this process to the regression in Table 9-1, we see that the estimated coefficient on the natural logarithm of market capitalization is -0.6635. Therefore, the model predicts that an increase of 1 in the natural logarithm of the company's market capitalization is associated with a -0.6635 change in the natural logarithm of the ratio of the bid–ask spread to the stock price, holding the natural logarithm of the number of market makers constant. We need to be careful not to expect that the natural logarithm of the ratio of the bid-ask spread to the stock price would differ by -0.6635 if we compared two stocks for which the natural logarithm of the company's market capitalization differed by 1, because in all likelihood the number of market makers for the two stocks would differ as well, which would affect the dependent variable. The value -0.6635 is the expected net effect of difference in log market capitalizations, net of the effect of the log number of market makers on the expected value of the dependent variable.

2.1. Assumptions of the Multiple Linear Regression Model

Before we can conduct correct statistical inference on a multiple linear regression model (a model with more than one independent variable estimated using ordinary least squares), we need to know the assumptions underlying that model.[12] Suppose we have n observations on

---

[11] The terminology comes from the fact that they correspond to the partial derivatives of Y with respect to the independent variables. Note that in this usage, the term "regression coefficients" refers just to the slope coefficients.

[12] **Ordinary least squares** (OLS) is an estimation method based on the criterion of minimizing the sum of the squared residuals of a regression.

the dependent variable, Y, and the independent variables, $X_1, X_2, \ldots, X_k$, and we want to estimate the equation $Y_i = b_0 + b_1 X_{1i} + b_2 X_{2i} + \cdots + b_k X_{ki} + \epsilon_i$.

In order to make a valid inference from a multiple linear regression model, we need to make the following six assumptions, which as a group define the classical normal multiple linear regression model:

1. The relationship between the dependent variable, Y, and the independent variables, $X_1, X_2, \ldots, X_k$, is linear as described in Equation 9-1.
2. The independent variables $(X_1, X_2, \ldots, X_k)$ are not random.[13] Also, no exact linear relation exists between two or more of the independent variables.[14]
3. The expected value of the error term, conditioned on the independent variables, is 0: $E(\epsilon | X_1, X_2, \ldots, X_k) = 0$.
4. The variance of the error term is the same for all observations:[15] $E(\epsilon_i{}^2) = \sigma_\epsilon^2$.
5. The error term is uncorrelated across observations: $E(\epsilon_i \epsilon_j) = 0$, $j \neq i$.
6. The error term is normally distributed.

Note that these assumptions are almost exactly the same as those for the single-variable linear regression model presented in the chapter on linear regression. Assumption 2 is modified such that no exact linear relation exists between two or more independent variables or combinations of independent variables. If this part of Assumption 2 is violated, then we cannot compute linear regression estimates.[16] Also, even if no exact linear relationship exists between two or more independent variables, or combinations of independent variables, linear regression may encounter problems if two or more of the independent variables or combinations thereof are highly correlated. Such a high correlation is known as multicollinearity, which we will discuss later in this chapter. We will also discuss the consequences of supposing that Assumptions 4 and 5 are met if, in fact, they are violated.

Although Equation 9-1 may seem to apply only to cross-sectional data because the notation for the observations is the same ($i = 1, \ldots, n$), all of these results apply to time-series data as well. For example, if we analyze data from many time periods for one company, we would typically use the notation $Y_t, X_{1t}, X_{2t}, \ldots, X_{kt}$, in which the first subscript denotes the variable and the second denotes the tth time period.

---

[13] As discussed in the chapter on correlation and regression, even though we assume that independent variables in the regression model are not random, often that assumption is clearly not true. For example, the monthly returns to the S&P 500 are not random. If the independent variable is random, then is the regression model incorrect? Fortunately, no. Even if the independent variable is random but uncorrelated with the error term, we can still rely on the results of regression models. See, for example, Greene (2003) or Goldberger (1998).

[14] No independent variable can be expressed as a linear combination of any set of the other independent variables. Technically, a constant equal to 1 is included as an independent variable associated with the intercept in this condition.

[15] $\text{Var}(\epsilon) = E(\epsilon^2)$ and $\text{Cov}(\epsilon_i \epsilon_j) = E(\epsilon_i \epsilon_j)$ because $E(\epsilon) = 0$.

[16] When we encounter this kind of linear relationship (called **perfect collinearity**), we cannot compute the matrix inverse needed to compute the linear regression estimates. See Greene (2003) for a further description of this issue.

EXAMPLE 9-2   Factors Explaining Pension Fund Performance

Ambachtsheer, Capelle, and Scheibelhut (1998) tested to see which factors affect the performance of pension funds. Specifically, they wanted to know whether the risk-adjusted net value added (RANVA) of 80 U.S. and Canadian pension funds depended on the size of the individual fund and the proportion of the fund's assets that were passively managed (indexed). Using data from 80 funds for four years (1993 to 1996), the authors regressed RANVA on the size of the pension fund and the fraction of pension fund assets that were passively managed.[17] They used the equation

$$\text{RANVA}_i = b_0 + b_1 \text{Size}_i + b_2 \text{Passive}_i + \epsilon_i$$

where

RANVA_i = the average RANVA (in percent) for fund i from 1993 to 1996
Size_i = the $\log_{10}$ of average assets under management for fund i
Passive_i = the fraction (decimal) of passively managed assets in fund i

Table 9-2 shows the results of their analysis.[18]

TABLE 9-2   Results from Regressing RANVA on Size and Passive Management

	Coefficients	Standard Error	t-Statistic
Intercept	−2.1	0.45	−4.7
Size	0.4	0.14	2.8
Passive management	0.8	0.42	1.9

Source: Ambachtsheer, Capelle, and Scheibelhut (1998).

Suppose we use the results in Table 9-2 to test the null hypothesis that a pension fund's size had no effect on its RANVA. Our null hypothesis is that the coefficient on the size variable equals 0 ($H_0: b_1 = 0$), and our alternative hypothesis is that the coefficient does not equal 0 ($H_a: b_1 \neq 0$). The t-statistic for testing that hypothesis is

$$\frac{\hat{b}_1 - b_1}{s_{\hat{b}_1}} = \frac{0.4 - 0}{0.14} = 2.8$$

---

[17] As mentioned in an earlier footnote, technically a constant equal to 1 is included as an independent variable associated with the intercept term in a regression. Because all the regressions reported in this chapter include an intercept term, we will not separately mention a constant as an independent variable in the remainder of this chapter.

[18] Size is the log base 10 of average assets. A log transformation is commonly used for independent variables that can take a wide range of values; company size and fund size are two such variables. One reason to use the log transformation is to improve the statistical properties of the residuals. If the authors had not taken the log of assets and instead used assets as the independent variable, the regression model probably would not have explained RANVA as well.

With 80 observations and three coefficients, the t-statistic has $80 - 3 = 77$ degrees of freedom. At the 0.05 significance level, the critical value for t is about 1.99. The computed t-statistic on the size coefficient is 2.8, which suggests strongly that we can reject the null hypothesis that size is unrelated to RANVA. The estimated coefficient of 0.4 implies that every 10-fold increase in fund size (an increase of 1 in $Size_i$) is associated with an expected 0.4 percentage point increase (40 basis points) in RANVA, *holding constant the fraction of passively managed assets*. Because $Size_i$ is the base 10 log of average assets, an increase of 1 in Size is the same as a 10-fold increase in fund assets.

Of course, no causal relation between size and RANVA is clear: Funds that are more successful may attract more assets. This regression equation is consistent with that result, as well as the result that larger funds perform better. On one hand, we could argue that larger funds are more successful. On the other hand, we could argue that more successful funds attract more assets and become larger.

Now suppose we want to test the null hypothesis that passive management is not related to RANVA; we want to test whether the coefficient on the fraction of assets under passive management equals 0 ($H_0: b_2 = 0$) against the alternative hypothesis that the coefficient on the fraction of assets under passive management does not equal 0 ($H_a: b_2 \neq 0$). The t-statistic to test this hypothesis is

$$\frac{\hat{b}_2 - b_2}{s_{\hat{b}_2}} = \frac{0.8 - 0}{0.42} = 1.9$$

The critical value of the t-test is 1.99 at the 0.05 significance level and about 1.66 at the 0.10 level. Therefore, at the 0.10 significance level, we can reject the null hypothesis that passive management has no effect on fund returns; however, we cannot do so at the 0.05 significance level. Although researchers typically use a significance level of 0.05 or smaller, these results and others like them are strong enough that many pension plan sponsors have increased the use of passive management for pension fund assets. We can interpret the coefficient on passive man-agement of 0.8 as implying that an increase of 0.10 in the proportion of a fund's passively managed assets is associated with an expected 0.08 percentage point increase (8 basis points) in RANVA for the fund, holding Size constant.

EXAMPLE 9-3   Explaining Returns to the Fidelity Select Technology Fund

Suppose you are considering an investment in the Fidelity Select Technology Fund (FSPTX), a U.S. mutual fund specializing in technology stocks. You want to know whether the fund behaves more like a large-cap growth fund or a large-cap value fund.[19] You decide to estimate the regression

---

[19] This regression is related to return-based style analysis, one of the most frequent applications of regression analysis in the investment profession. For more information, see Sharpe (1988), who pioneered this field, and Buetow, Johnson, and Runkle (2000).

$$Y_t = b_0 + b_1 X_{1t} + b_2 X_{2t} + \epsilon_t$$

where

Y_t = the monthly return to the FSPTX
X_{1t} = the monthly return to the S&P 500/BARRA Growth Index
X_{2t} = the monthly return to the S&P 500/BARRA Value Index

The S&P 500/BARRA Growth and Value indexes represent predominantly large-cap growth and value stocks, respectively.

Table 9-3 shows the results of this linear regression using monthly data from January 1998 through December 2002. The estimated intercept in the regression is 0.0079. Thus, if both the return to the S&P 500/BARRA Growth Index and the return to the S&P 500/BARRA Value Index equal 0 in a specific month, the regression model predicts that the return to the FSPTX will be 0.79 percent. The coefficient on the large-cap growth index is 2.2308, and the coefficient on the large-cap value index return is −0.4143. Therefore, if in a given month the return to the S&P 500/BARRA Growth Index was 1 percent and the return to the S&P 500/BARRA Value Index was −2 percent, the model predicts that the return to the FSPTX would be $0.0079 + 2.2308(0.01) - 0.4143(-0.02) = 3.85$ percent.

TABLE 9-3   Results from Regressing the FSPTX Returns on the S&P 500/BARRA Growth and Value Indexes

	Coefficient	Standard Error	*t*-Statistic
Intercept	0.0079	0.0091	0.8635
S&P 500/BARRA Growth Index	2.2308	0.2299	9.7034
S&P 500/BARRA Value Index	−0.4143	0.2597	−1.5953

ANOVA	df	SS	MSS	F	Significance *F*
Regression	2	0.8649	0.4324	86.4483	5.48E-18
Residual	57	0.2851	0.0050		
Total	59	1.1500			

Residual standard error	0.0707			
Multiple *R*-squared	0.7521			
Observations	60			

Source: Ibbotson Associates.

We may want to know whether the coefficient on the returns to the S&P 500/BARRA Value Index is statistically significant. Our null hypothesis states that the coefficient equals 0 (H_0: $b_2 = 0$); our alternative hypothesis states that the coefficient does not equal 0 (H_a: $b_2 \neq 0$).

Our test of the null hypothesis uses a *t*-test constructed as follows:

$$t = \frac{\hat{b}_2 - b_2}{s_{\hat{b}_2}} = \frac{-0.4143 - 0}{0.2597} = -1.5953$$

where

$\hat{b}_2 =$ the regression estimate of b_2

$b_2 =$ the hypothesized value[20] of the coefficient (0)

$s_{\hat{b}_2} =$ the estimated standard error of $\hat{b}_2$

This regression has 60 observations and three coefficients (two independent variables and the intercept); therefore, the t-test has $60 - 3 = 57$ degrees of freedom. At the 0.05 significance level, the critical value for the test statistic is about 2.00.[21] The absolute value of the test statistic is 1.5953. Because the test statistic's absolute value is less than the critical value ($1.5953 < 2.00$), we fail to reject the null hypothesis that $b_2 = 0$. (Note that the t-tests reported in Table 9-3, as well as the other regression tables, are tests of the null hypothesis that the population value of a regression coefficient equals 0.)

Similar analysis shows that at the 0.05 significance level, we cannot reject the null hypothesis that the intercept equals 0 (H_0: $b_0 = 0$) in favor of the alternative hypothesis that the intercept does not equal 0 (H_a: $b_0 \neq 0$). Table 9-3 shows that the t-statistic for testing that hypothesis is 0.8635, a result smaller in absolute value than the critical value of 2.00. However, at the 0.05 significance level we *can* reject the null hypothesis that the coefficient on the S&P 500/BARRA Growth Index equals 0 (H_0: $b_1 = 0$) in favor of the alternative hypothesis that the coefficient does not equal 0 (H_a: $b_1 \neq 0$). As Table 9-3 shows, the t-statistic for testing that hypothesis is 9.70, a result far above the critical value of 2.00. Thus multiple regression analysis suggests that returns to the FSPTX are very closely associated with the returns to the S&P 500/BARRA Growth Index, but they are not related to S&P 500/BARRA Value Index (the t-statistic of -1.60 is not statistically significant).

2.2. Predicting the Dependent Variable in a Multiple Regression Model

Financial analysts often want to predict the value of the dependent variable in a multiple regression based on assumed values of the independent variables. We have previously discussed how to make such a prediction in the case of only one independent variable. The process for making that prediction with multiple linear regression is very similar.

To predict the value of a dependent variable using a multiple linear regression model, we follow these three steps:

1. Obtain estimates $\hat{b}_0, \hat{b}_1, \hat{b}_2, \ldots, \hat{b}_k$ of the regression parameters $b_0, b_1, b_2, \ldots, b_k$.
2. Determine the assumed values of the independent variables, $\hat{X}_{1i}, \hat{X}_{2i}, \ldots, \hat{X}_{ki}$.
3. Compute the predicted value of the dependent variable, $\hat{Y}_i$, using the equation

$$\hat{Y}_i = \hat{b}_0 + \hat{b}_1 \hat{X}_{1i} + \hat{b}_2 \hat{X}_{2i} + \cdots + \hat{b}_k \hat{X}_{ki} \qquad (9\text{-}3)$$

Two practical points concerning using an estimated regression to predict the dependent variable are in order. First, we should be confident that the assumptions of the regression

---

[20] To economize on notation in stating test statistics, in this context we use b_2 to represent the hypothesized value of the parameter (elsewhere we use it to represent the unknown population parameter).

[21] See Appendix B for t-test values.

model are met. Second, we should be cautious about predictions based on values of the independent variables that are outside the range of the data on which the model was estimated; such predictions are often unreliable.

EXAMPLE 9-4   Predicting a Pension Fund's RANVA

In Example 9-2, we explained the RANVA for U.S. and Canadian pension funds based on the log base 10 of the assets under management for a fund ($Size_i$) and the fraction of assets in the fund that were passively managed ($Passive_i$).

$$RANVA_i = b_0 + b_1 Size_i + b_2 Passive_i + \epsilon_i$$

Now we can use the results of the regression reported in Table 9-2 (excerpted here) to predict the performance (RANVA) for a pension fund.

TABLE 9-2   (excerpt)

	Coefficients
Intercept	−2.1
Size	0.4
Passive management	0.8

Suppose that a particular fund has assets under management of $10 million, and 25 percent of the assets are passively managed. The log base 10 of the assets under management equals $\log(10,000,000) = 7$. The fraction of assets in the fund that are passively managed is 0.25. Accordingly, the predicted RANVA for that fund, based on the regression, is $-2.1 + (0.4 \times 7) + (0.8 \times 0.25) = 0.9$ percent (90 basis points). The regression predicts that the RANVA will be 90 basis points for a pension fund with assets under management of $10 million, 25 percent of which are passively managed.

When predicting the dependent variable using a linear regression model, we encounter two types of uncertainty: uncertainty in the regression model itself, as reflected in the standard error of estimate, and uncertainty about the estimates of the regression model's parameters. In the chapter on correlation and regression, we presented procedures for constructing a prediction interval for linear regression with one independent variable. For multiple regression, however, computing a prediction interval to properly incorporate both types of uncertainty requires matrix algebra, which is outside the scope of this book.[22]

---

[22]For more information, see Greene (2003).

2.3. Testing Whether All Population Regression Coefficients Equal Zero

Earlier, we illustrated how to conduct hypothesis tests on regression coefficients individually. But what about the significance of the regression as a whole? As a group, do the independent variables help explain the dependent variable? To address this question, we test the null hypothesis that all the slope coefficients in a regression are simultaneously equal to 0. In this section, we discuss **analysis of variance (ANOVA)**, which provides information about a regression's explanatory power and the inputs for an F-test of the above null hypothesis.

If none of the independent variables in a regression model helps explain the dependent variable, the slope coefficients should all equal 0. In a multiple regression, however, we cannot test the null hypothesis that *all* slope coefficients equal 0 based on t-tests that *each individual* slope coefficient equals 0, because the individual tests do not account for the effects of interactions among the independent variables. For example, a classic symptom of multicollinearity is that we can reject the hypothesis that all the slope coefficients equal 0 even though none of the t-statistics for the individual estimated slope coefficients is significant. Conversely, we can construct unusual examples in which the estimated slope coefficients are significantly different from 0 although jointly they are not.

To test the null hypothesis that all of the slope coefficients in the multiple regression model are jointly equal to 0 ($H_0: b_1 = b_2 = \cdots = b_k = 0$) against the alternative hypothesis that at least one slope coefficient is not equal to 0 we must use an F-test. The F-test is viewed as a test of the regression's overall significance.

To correctly calculate the test statistic for the null hypothesis, we need four inputs:

- total number of observations, n;
- total number of regression coefficients to be estimated, $k + 1$, where k is the number of slope coefficients;
- sum of squared errors or residuals, $\sum_{i=1}^{n}(Y_i - \hat{Y}_i)^2 = \sum_{i=1}^{n}\hat{\epsilon}_i^2$, abbreviated SSE, also known as the residual sum of squares (unexplained variation);[23] and
- regression sum of squares, $\sum_{i=1}^{n}(\hat{Y}_i - \overline{Y})^2$, abbreviated RSS.[24] This amount is the variation in Y from its mean that the regression equation explains (explained variation).

The F-test for determining whether the slope coefficients equal 0 is based on an F-statistic calculated using the four values listed above.[25] The F-statistic measures how well the regression equation explains the variation in the dependent variable; it is the ratio of the mean regression sum of squares to the mean squared error.

We compute the mean regression sum of squares by dividing the regression sum of squares by the number of slope coefficients estimated, k. We compute the mean squared error by dividing the sum of squared errors by the number of observations, n, minus $(k + 1)$. The two divisors in these computations are the degrees of freedom for calculating an F-statistic. For n observations and k slope coefficients, the F-test for the null hypothesis that the slope coefficients are all equal to 0 is denoted $F_{k,n-(k+1)}$. The subscript indicates that the test should have k degrees of freedom in the numerator (numerator degrees of freedom) and $n - (k + 1)$ degrees of freedom in the denominator (denominator degrees of freedom).

---

[23] In a table of regression output, this is the number under the "SS" column in the row "Residual."

[24] In a table of regression output, this is the number under the "SS" column in the row "Regression."

[25] F-tests are described in further detail in the chapter on hypothesis testing.

The formula for the F-statistic is

$$F = \frac{\frac{\text{RSS}}{k}}{\frac{\text{SSE}}{[n-(k+1)]}} = \frac{\text{Mean regression sum of squares}}{\text{Mean squared error}} = \frac{\text{MSR}}{\text{MSE}} \qquad (9\text{-}4)$$

where MSR is the mean regression sum of squares and MSE is the mean squared error. In our regression output tables, MSR and MSE are the first and second quantities under the MSS (mean sum of squares) column in the ANOVA section of the output. If the regression model does a good job of explaining variation in the dependent variable, then the ratio MSR/MSE will be large.

What does this F-test tell us when the independent variables in a regression model explain none of the variation in the dependent variable? In this case, each predicted value in the regression model, $\hat{Y}_i$, has the average value of the dependent variable, $\overline{Y}$, and the regression sum of squares, $\sum_{i=1}^{n}(\hat{Y}_i - \overline{Y})^2$ is 0. Therefore, the F-statistic for testing the null hypothesis (that all the slope coefficients are equal to 0) has a value of 0 when the independent variables do not explain the dependent variable at all.

To specify the details of making the statistical decision when we have calculated F, we reject the null hypothesis at the α significance level if the calculated value of F is greater than the upper α critical value of the F distribution with the specified numerator and denominator degrees of freedom. Note that we use a one-tailed F-test.[26] Appendix D provides the critical values for the F-test.

We can illustrate the test using Example 9-1, in which we investigated whether the natural log of the number of Nasdaq market makers and the natural log of the stock's market capitalization explained the natural log of the bid–ask spread divided by price. Assume that we set the significance level for this test to $\alpha = 0.05$ (i.e., a 5 percent probabilitythat we will mistakenly reject the null hypothesis if it is true). Table 9-1 (excerpted here) presents the results of variance computations for this regression.

TABLE 9-1   (excerpt)

ANOVA	df	SS	MSS	F	Significance F
Regression	2	2,681.6482	1,340.8241	1,088.8325	0.00
Residual	1,816	2,236.2820	1.2314		
Total	1,818	4,917.9302			

This model has two slope coefficients ($k = 2$), so there are two degrees of freedom in the numerator of this F-test. With 1,819 observations in the sample, the number of degrees of freedom in the denominator of the F-test is $n - (k + 1) = 1,819 - 3 = 1,816$. The sum of the squared errors is 2,236.2820. The regression sum of squares is 2,681.6482. Therefore, the F-test for the null hypothesis that the two slope coefficients in this model equal 0 is

$$\frac{2681.6482/2}{2236.2820/1,816} = 1,088.8325$$

This test statistic is distributed as an $F_{2,1,816}$ random variable under the null hypothesis that the slope coefficients are equal to 0. In the table for the 0.05 significance level, we look at the

---

[26]We use a one-tailed test because MSR necessarily increases relative to MSE as the explanatory power of the regression increases.

second column, which shows F-distributions with two degrees of freedom in the numerator. Near the bottom of the column, we find that the critical value of the F-test needed to reject the null hypothesis is between 3.00 and 3.07.[27] The actual value of the F-test statistic at 1,088.83 is much greater, so we reject the null hypothesis that coefficients of both independent variables equal 0. In fact, Table 9-1, under "Significance F," reports a p-value of 0. This p-value means that the smallest level of significance at which the null hypothesis can be rejected is practically 0. The large value for this F-statistic implies a minuscule probability of incorrectly rejecting the null hypothesis (a mistake known as a Type I error).

2.4. Adjusted R^2

In the chapter on correlation and regression, we presented the coefficient of variation, R^2, as a measure of the goodness of fit of an estimated regression to the data. In a multiple linear regression, however, R^2 is less appropriate as a measure of whether a regression model fits the data well (goodness of fit). Recall that R^2 is defined as

$$\frac{\text{Total variation} - \text{Unexplained variation}}{\text{Total variation}}$$

The numerator equals the regression sum of squares, RSS. Thus R^2 states RSS as a fraction of the total sum of squares, $\sum_{i=1}^{n}(Y_i - \overline{Y})^2$. If we add regression variables to the model, the amount of unexplained variation will decrease, and RSS will increase, if the new independent variable explains any of the unexplained variation in the model. Such a reduction occurs when the new independent variable is even slightly correlated with the dependent variable and is not a linear combination of other independent variables in the regression.[28] Consequently, we can increase R^2 simply by including many additional independent variables that explain even a slight amount of the previously unexplained variation, even if the amount they explain is not statistically significant.

Some financial analysts use an alternative measure of goodness of fit called **adjusted R^2**, or $\overline{R}^2$. This measure of fit does not automatically increase when another variable is added to a regression; it is adjusted for degrees of freedom. Adjusted R^2 is typically part of the multiple regression output produced by statistical software packages.

The relation between R^2 and $\overline{R}^2$ is

$$\overline{R}^2 = 1 - \left(\frac{n-1}{n-k-1}\right)(1 - R^2)$$

where n is the number of observations and k is the number of independent variables (the number of slope coefficients). Note that if $k \geq 1$, then R^2 is strictly greater than adjusted R^2. When a new independent variable is added, $\overline{R}^2$ can decrease if adding that variable results in only a small increase in R^2. In fact, $\overline{R}^2$ can be negative, although R^2 is always nonnegative.[29] If we use $\overline{R}^2$ to compare regression models, it is important that the dependent variable be defined the same way in both models and that the sample sizes used to estimate the models are the same.[30]

---

[27]We see a range of values because the denominator has more than 120 degrees of freedom but less than an infinite number of degrees of freedom.

[28]We say that variable y is a linear combination of variables x and z if $y = ax + bz$ for some constants a and b. A variable can also be a linear combination of more than two variables.

[29]When $\overline{R}^2$ is negative, we can effectively consider its value to be 0.

[30]See Gujarati (2003). The value of adjusted R^2 depends on sample size. These points hold if we are using R^2 to compare two regression models.

For example, it makes a difference for the value of $\overline{R}^2$ if the dependent variable is GDP (gross domestic product) or ln(GDP), even if the independent variables are identical. Furthermore, we should be aware that a high $\overline{R}^2$ does not necessarily indicate that the regression is well specified in the sense of including the correct set of variables.[31] One reason for caution is that a high $\overline{R}^2$ may reflect peculiarities of the dataset used to estimate the regression. To evaluate a regression model, we need to take many other factors into account, as we discuss in Section 5.1.

3. USING DUMMY VARIABLES IN REGRESSIONS

Often, financial analysts need to use qualitative variables as independent variables in a regression. One type of qualitative variable, called a **dummy variable**, takes on a value of 1 if a particular condition is true and 0 if that condition is false.[32] For example, suppose we want to test whether stock returns were different in January than during the remaining months of a particular year. We include one independent variable in the regression, X_{1t}, that has a value of 1 for each January and a value of 0 for every other month of the year. We estimate the regression model

$$Y_t = b_0 + b_1 X_{1t} + \epsilon_t$$

In this equation, the coefficient b_0 is the average value of Y_t in months other than January, and b_1 is the difference between the average value of Y_t in January and the average value of Y_t in months other than January.

We need to exercise care in choosing the number of dummy variables in a regression. The rule is that if we want to distinguish among n categories, we need $n - 1$ dummy variables. For example, to distinguish between *during January* and *not during January* above ($n = 2$ categories), we used one dummy variable ($n - 1 = 2 - 1 = 1$). If we want to distinguish between each of the four quarters in a year, we would include dummy variables for three of the four quarters in a year. If we make the mistake of including dummy variables for four rather than three quarters, we have violated Assumption 2 of the multiple regression model and cannot estimate the regression. The next example illustrates the use of dummy variables in a regression with monthly data.

EXAMPLE 9-5   Month-of-the-Year Effects on Small-Stock Returns

For many years, financial analysts have been concerned about seasonality in stock returns.[33] In particular, analysts have researched whether returns to small stocks differ during various months of the year. Suppose we want to test whether total

---

[31] See Mayer (1975, 1980).

[32] Not all qualitative variables are simple dummy variables. For example, in a trinomial choice model (a model with three choices), a qualitative variable might have the value 0, 1, or 2.

[33] For a discussion of this issue, see Siegel (1998).

returns to one small-stock index, the Russell 2000 Index, differ by month. Using data from January 1979 (the first available date for the Russell 2000 data) through the end of 2002, we can estimate a regression including an intercept and 11 dummy variables, one for each of the first 11 months of the year. The equation that we estimate is

$$\text{Returns}_t = b_0 + b_1 \text{Jan}_t + b_2 \text{Feb}_t + \cdots + b_{11} \text{Nov}_t + \epsilon_t$$

where each monthly dummy variable has a value of 1 when the month occurs (e.g., $\text{Jan}_1 = \text{Jan}_{13} = 1$, as the first observation is a January) and a value of 0 for the other months. Table 9-4 shows the results of this regression.

TABLE 9-4   Results from Regressing Russell 2000 Returns on Monthly Dummy Variables

	Coefficient	Standard Error	t-Statistic
Intercept	0.0301	0.0116	2.5902
January	0.0003	0.0164	0.0176
February	−0.0111	0.0164	−0.6753
March	−0.0211	0.0164	−1.2846
April	−0.0141	0.0164	−0.8568
May	−0.0137	0.0164	−0.8320
June	−0.0200	0.0164	−1.2164
July	−0.0405	0.0164	−2.4686
August	−0.0230	0.0164	−1.4025
September	−0.0375	0.0164	−2.2864
October	−0.0393	0.0164	−2.3966
November	−0.0059	0.0164	−0.3565

ANOVA	df	SS	MSS	F	Significance F
Regression	11	0.0543	0.0049	1.5270	0.1213
Residual	276	0.8924	0.0032		
Total	287	0.9467			

Residual standard error	0.0569		
Multiple R-squared	0.0574		
Observations	288		

Source: Ibbotson Associates.

The intercept, b_0, measures the average return for stocks in December because there is no dummy variable for December.[34] This equation estimates that the average return in December is 3.01 percent ($\hat{b}_0 = 0.0301$). Each of the estimated coefficients for the dummy variables shows the estimated difference between returns in that month and returns for December. So, for example, the estimated additional return in January is 0.03 percent higher than December ($\hat{b}_1 = 0.0003$). This gives a January return prediction of 3.04 percent (3.01 December + 0.03 additional).

---

[34]When $\text{Jan}_t = \text{Feb}_t = \cdots = \text{Nov}_t = 0$, the return is not associated with January through November so the month is December and the regression equation simplifies to $\text{Returns}_t = b_0 + \epsilon_t$. Because $E(\text{Returns}_t) = b_0 + E(\epsilon_t) = b_0$, the intercept b_0 represents the mean return for December.

The low R^2 in this regression (0.0574), however, suggests that a month-of-the-year effect in small-stock returns may not be very important for explaining small-stock returns. We can use the F-test to analyze the null hypothesis that jointly, the monthly dummy variables all equal 0 (H_0: $b_1 = b_2 = \cdots = b_{11} = 0$). We are testing for significant monthly variation in small-stock returns. Table 9-4 shows the data needed to perform an analysis of variance. The number of degrees of freedom in the numerator of the F-test is 11; the number of degrees of freedom in the denominator is $[288 - (11 + 1)] = 276$. The regression sum of squares equals 0.0543, and the sum of squared errors equals 0.8924. Therefore, the F-statistic to determine whether all of the regression slope coefficients are jointly equal to 0 is

$$\frac{0.0543/11}{0.8924/276} = 1.53$$

Appendix D shows the critical values for this F-test. If we choose a significance level of 0.05 and look in Column 11 (because the numerator has 11 degrees of freedom), we see that the critical value is 1.87 when the denominator has 120 degrees of freedom. The denominator actually has 276 degrees of freedom, so the critical value of the F-statistic is smaller than 1.87 (for df $= 120$) but larger than 1.79 (for an infinite number of degrees of freedom). The value of the test statistic is 1.53, so we clearly cannot reject the null hypothesis that all of the coefficients jointly are equal to 0.

The p-value of 0.1213 shown for the F-test in Table 9-4 means that the smallest level of significance at which we can reject the null hypothesis is roughly 0.12, or 12 percent—above the conventional level of 5 percent. Among the 11 monthly dummy variables, July, September, and October have a t-statistic with an absolute value greater than 2. Although the coefficients for these dummy variables are statistically significant, we have so many insignificant estimated coefficients that we cannot reject the null hypothesis that returns are equal across the months. This test suggests that the significance of a few coefficients in this regression model may be the result of random variation. We may thus want to avoid portfolio strategies calling for differing investment weights for small stocks in different months.

EXAMPLE 9-6   Determinants of Spreads on New High-Yield Bonds

Fridson and Garman (1998) used data from 1995 and 1996 to examine variables that may explain the initial yield spread between a newly issued high-yield bond and a Treasury bond with similar maturity. They built a model of yield spreads using variables that affect the creditworthiness and interest-rate risk of the bond. Their model included the following factors:

- Rating: Moody's senior-equivalent rating
- Zero-coupon status: Dummy variable ($0 = $ no, $1 = $ yes)
- BB-B spread: Yield differential (Merrill Lynch Single-B Index minus Double-B Index, in basis points)

- Seniority: Dummy variable (0 = senior, 1 = subordinated)
- Callability: Dummy variable (0 = noncallable, 1 = callable)
- Term: Maturity (years)
- First-time issuer: Dummy variable (0 = no, 1 = yes)
- Underwriter type: Dummy variable (0 = investment bank, 1 = commercial bank)
- Interest rate change

Table 9-5 shows the authors' results.

TABLE 9-5   Multiple Regression Model of New
High-Yield Issue Spread, 1995–96

	Coefficient	Standard Error	t-Statistic
Intercept	−213.67	63.03	−3.39
Rating	66.19	4.13	16.02
Zero-coupon status	136.54	32.82	4.16
BB-B spread	95.31	24.82	3.84
Seniority	41.46	11.95	3.47
Callability	51.65	15.42	3.35
Term	−8.51	2.71	−3.14
First-time issuer	25.23	10.97	2.30
Underwriter type	28.13	12.67	2.22
Interest rate change	40.44	19.08	2.12
R-squared	0.56		
Observations	428		

Source: Fridson and Garman (1998).

We can summarize Fridson and Garman's findings as follows:

- Bond rating has the highest significance level of any coefficient in the regression. This result should not be surprising, because the rating captures rating agencies' estimates of the risk involved with the bond.
- Zero-coupon status increases the yield spread because zero-coupon bonds have more interest rate risk than coupon bonds of a similar maturity.
- The BB-B spread affects yields because it captures the market's evaluation of how much influence rating differentials have on credit risk.
- Seniority affects yields because subordinated debt has a much lower recovery rate in the case of default.
- Callability increases yields because it limits upside potential on the bond if yields decline.
- Term actually reduces the yield spread. Perhaps term enters with a negative coefficient because the market is willing to buy long-term debt only from high-quality companies; lower-quality companies must issue shorter-term debt.
- First-time issuers must pay a premium because the market does not know much about them.
- Bonds underwritten by commercial banks have a premium over bonds underwritten by investment banks, most likely because the market believes that investment banks have a competitive edge in attracting high-quality corporate clients.

> - Interest-rate increases in Treasuries during the previous month cause yield spreads to widen, presumably because the market believes that increasing interest rates will worsen the economic prospects of companies issuing high-yield debt.
>
> Note that all of the coefficients in this regression model are statistically significant at the 0.05 level. The smallest absolute value of a *t*-statistic in this table is 2.12.

4. VIOLATIONS OF REGRESSION ASSUMPTIONS

In Section 2.1, we presented the assumptions of the multiple linear regression model. Inference based on an estimated regression model rests on those assumptions being satisfied. In applying regression analysis to financial data, analysts need to be able to diagnose violations of regression assumptions, understand the consequences of violations, and know the remedial steps to take. In the following sections we discuss three regression violations: heteroskedasticity, serial correlation, and multicollinearity.

4.1. Heteroskedasticity

So far, we have made an important assumption that the variance of error in a regression is constant across observations. In statistical terms, we assumed that the errors were homoskedastic. Errors in financial data, however, are often **heteroskedastic**: the variance of the errors differs across observations. In this section, we discuss how heteroskedasticity affects statistical analysis, how to test for heteroskedasticity, and how to correct for it.

We can see the difference between homoskedastic and heteroskedastic errors by comparing two graphs. Figure 9-1 shows the values of the dependent and independent variables and a fitted regression line for a model with homoskedastic errors. There is no systematic relationship between the value of the independent variable and the regression residuals (the vertical distance between a plotted point and the fitted regression line). Figure 9-2 shows the values of the dependent and independent variables and a fitted regression line for a model with heteroskedastic errors. Here, a systematic relationship is visually apparent: On average, the regression residuals grow much larger as the size of the independent variable increases.

4.1.1. The Consequences of Heteroskedasticity
What are the consequences when the assumption of constant error variance is violated? Although heteroskedasticity does not affect the **consistency**[35] of the regression parameter estimators, it can lead to mistakes in inference.

---

[35] Informally, an estimator of a regression parameter is consistent if the probability that estimates of a regression parameter differ from the true value of the parameter decreases as the number of observations used in the regression increases. The regression parameter estimates from ordinary least squares are consistent regardless of whether the errors are heteroskedastic or homoskedastic. See the chapter on sampling and, for a more advanced discussion, see Greene (2003).

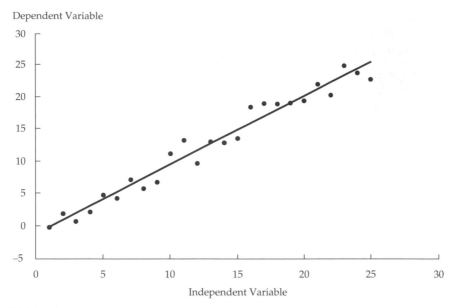

FIGURE 9-1   Regression with Homoskedasticity

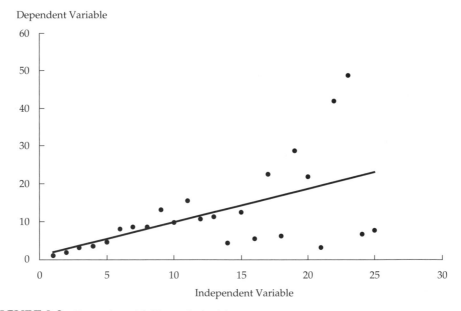

FIGURE 9-2   Regression with Heteroskedasticity

When errors are heteroskedastic, the F-test for the overall significance of the regression is unreliable.[36] Furthermore, t-tests for the significance of individual regression coefficients are unreliable because heteroskedasticity introduces bias into estimators of the standard error of regression coefficients. If a regression shows significant heteroskedasticity, the standard errors

---

[36]This unreliability occurs because the mean squared error is a biased estimator of the true population variance given heteroskedasticity.

and test statistics computed by regression programs will be incorrect unless they are adjusted for heteroskedasticity.

In regressions with financial data, the most likely result of heteroskedasticity is that the estimated standard errors will be underestimated and the t-statistics will be inflated. When we ignore heteroskedasticity, we tend to find significant relationships where none actually exist.[37] The consequences in practice may be serious if we are using regression analysis in the development of investment strategies. As Example 9-7 shows, the issue impinges even on our understanding of financial models.

EXAMPLE 9-7   Heteroskedasticity and Tests of an Asset Pricing Model

MacKinlay and Richardson (1991) examined how heteroskedasticity affects tests of the capital asset pricing model (CAPM).[38] These authors argued that if the CAPM is correct, they should find no significant differences between the risk-adjusted returns for holding small stocks versus large stocks. To implement their test, MacKinlay and Richardson grouped all stocks on the New York and American exchanges by market-value decile with annual reassignment. They then tested for systematic differences in risk-adjusted returns across market-capitalization-based stock portfolios. They estimated the following regression:

$$r_{i,t} = \alpha_i + \beta_i r_{m,t} + \epsilon_{i,t}$$

where
$r_{i,t}$ = excess return (return above the risk-free rate) to portfolio i in period t
$r_{m,t}$ = excess return to the market as a whole in period t

The CAPM formulation hypothesizes that excess returns on a portfolio are explained by excess returns on the market as a whole. That hypothesis implies that $\alpha_i = 0$ for every i; on average, no excess return accrues to any portfolio after taking into account its systematic (market) risk.

Using data from January 1926 to December 1988 and a market index based on equal-weighted returns, MacKinlay and Richardson failed to reject the CAPM at the 0.05 level when they assumed that the errors in the regression model are normally distributed and homoskedastic. They found, however, that they could reject the CAPM when they corrected their test statistics to account for heteroskedasticity. They rejected the hypothesis that there are no size-based, risk-adjusted excess returns in historical data.[39]

We have stated that effects of heteroskedasticity on statistical inference can be severe. To be more precise about this concept, we should distinguish between two broad kinds of heteroskedasticity, unconditional and conditional.

---

[37] Sometimes, however, failure to adjust for heteroskedasticity results in standard errors that are too large (and t-statistics that are too small).

[38] For more on the CAPM, see Bodie, Kane, and Marcus (2001), for example.

[39] MacKinlay and Richardson also show that when using value-weighted returns, one can reject the CAPM whether or not one assumes normally distributed returns and homoskedasticity.

Unconditional heteroskedasticity occurs when heteroskedasticity of the error variance is not correlated with the independent variables in the multiple regression. Although this form of heteroskedasticity violates Assumption 4 of the linear regression model, it creates no major problems for statistical inference.

The type of heteroskedasticity that causes the most problems for statistical inference is **conditional heteroskedasticity**—heteroskedasticity in the error variance that is correlated with (conditional on) the values of the independent variables in the regression. Fortunately, many statistical software packages easily test and correct for conditional heteroskedasticity.

4.1.2. Testing for Heteroskedasticity   Because of conditional heteroskedasticity's consequences on inference, the analyst must be able to diagnose its presence. The Breusch–Pagan test is widely used in finance research because of its generality.[40]

Breusch and Pagan (1979) suggested the following test for conditional heteroskedasticity: Regress the squared residuals from the estimated regression equation on the independent variables in the regression. If no conditional heteroskedasticity exists, the independent variables will not explain much of the variation in the squared residuals. If conditional heteroskedasticity is present in the original regression, however, the independent variables will explain a significant portion of the variation in the squared residuals. The independent variables can explain the variation because each observation's squared residual will be correlated with the independent variables if the independent variables affect the variance of the errors.

Breusch and Pagan showed that under the null hypothesis of no conditional heteroskedasticity, nR^2 (from the regression of the squared residuals on the independent variables from the original regression) will be a χ^2 random variable with the number of degrees of freedom equal to the number of independent variables in the regression.[41] Therefore, the null hypothesis states that the regression's squared error term is uncorrelated with the independent variables. The alternative hypothesis states that the squared error term is correlated with the independent variables. Example 9-8 illustrates the Breusch–Pagan test for conditional heteroskedasticity.

EXAMPLE 9-8   Testing for Conditional Heteroskedasticity in the Relation between Interest Rates and Expected Inflation

Suppose an analyst wants to know how closely nominal interest rates are related to expected inflation to determine how to allocate assets in a fixed income portfolio. The analyst wants to test the Fisher effect, the hypothesis suggested by Irving Fisher that nominal interest rates increase by 1 percentage point for every 1 percentage point increase in expected inflation.[42] The Fisher effect assumes the following relation between nominal interest rates, real interest rates, and expected inflation:

---

[40] Some other tests require more-specific assumptions about the functional form of the heteroskedasticity. For more information, see Greene (2003).

[41] The Breusch–Pagan test is distributed as a χ^2 random variable in large samples. The constant 1 technically associated with the intercept term in a regression is not counted here in computing the number of independent variables. For more on the Breusch–Pagan test, see Greene (2003).

[42] For more on the Fisher effect, see, for example, Mankiw (2000).

$$i = r + \pi^e$$

where

i = the nominal interest rate

r = the real interest rate (assumed constant)

π^e = the expected rate of inflation

To test the Fisher effect using time-series data, we could specify the following regression model for the nominal interest rate:

$$i_t = b_0 + b_1 \pi_t^e + \epsilon_t \qquad (9\text{-}5)$$

Noting that the Fisher effect predicts that the coefficient on the inflation variable is 1, we can state the null and alternative hypotheses as

$$H_0: \ b_1 = 1$$

$$H_a: \ b_1 \neq 1$$

We might also specify a 0.05 significance level for the test. Before we estimate Equation 9-5, we must decide how to measure expected inflation (π_t^e) and the nominal interest rate (i_t).

The Survey of Professional Forecasters (SPF) has compiled data on the quarterly inflation expectations of professional forecasters.[43] We use those data as our measure of expected inflation. We use three-month Treasury bill returns as our measure of the (risk-free) nominal interest rate.[44] We use quarterly data from the fourth quarter of 1968 to the fourth quarter of 2002 to estimate Equation 9-5. Table 9-6 shows the regression results.

TABLE 9-6   Results from Regressing T-Bill Returns on Predicted Inflation

	Coefficient	Standard Error	t-Statistic
Intercept	0.0304	0.0040	7.6887
Inflation prediction	0.8774	0.0812	10.8096
Residual standard error		0.0220	
Multiple R-squared		0.4640	
Observations		137	
Durbin–Watson statistic		0.4673	

Source: Federal Reserve Bank of Philadelphia, U.S. Department of Commerce.

---

[43] For this example, we use the annualized median SPF prediction of current-quarter growth in the GDP deflator (GNP deflator before 1992).

[44] Our data on Treasury bill returns are based on three-month T-bill yields in the secondary market. Because those yields are stated on a discount basis, we convert them to a compounded annual rate so they will be measured on the same basis as our data on inflation expectations. These returns are risk-free because they are known at the beginning of the quarter and there is no default risk.

To make the statistical decision on whether the data support the Fisher effect, we calculate the following t-statistic, which we then compare to its critical value.

$$t = \frac{\hat{b}_1 - b_1}{s_{\hat{b}_1}} = \frac{0.8774 - 1}{0.0812} = -1.5099$$

With a t-statistic of -1.5099 and $137 - 2 = 135$ degrees of freedom, the critical t-value is about 1.98. If we have conducted a valid test, we cannot reject at the 0.05 significance level the hypothesis that the true coefficient in this regression is 1 and that the Fisher effect holds. The t-test assumes that the errors are homoskedastic. Before we accept the validity of the t-test, therefore, we should test whether the errors are conditionally heteroskedastic. If those errors prove to be conditionally heteroskedastic, then the test is invalid.

We can perform the **Breusch–Pagan test** for conditional heteroskedasticity on the squared residuals from the Fisher effect regression. The test regresses the squared residuals on the predicted inflation rate. The R^2 in the squared residuals regression (not shown here) is 0.1651. The test statistic from this regression, nR^2, is $137 \times 0.1651 = 22.619$. Under the null hypothesis of no conditional heteroskedasticity, this test statistic is a χ^2 random variable with one degree of freedom (because there is only one independent variable).

We should be concerned about heteroskedasticity only for large values of the test statistic. Therefore, we should use a one-tailed test to determine whether we can reject the null hypothesis. Appendix C shows that the critical value of the test statistic for a variable from a χ^2 distribution with one degree of freedom at the 0.05 significance level is 3.84. The test statistic from the Breusch–Pagan test is 22.619, so we can reject the hypothesis of no conditional heteroskedasticity at the 0.05 level. In fact, we can even reject the hypothesis of no conditional heteroskedasticity at the 0.01 significance level, because the critical value of the test statistic in that case is 6.63. As a result, we conclude that the error term in the Fisher effect regression is conditionally heteroskedastic. The standard errors computed in the original regression are not correct, because they do not account for heteroskedasticity. Therefore, we cannot accept the t-test as valid.

In Example 9-8, we concluded that a t-test that we might use to test the Fisher effect was not valid. Does that mean that we cannot use a regression model to investigate the Fisher effect? Fortunately, no. A methodology is available to adjust regression coefficients' standard error to correct for heteroskedasticity. Using an adjusted standard error for $\hat{b}_1$, we can reconduct the t-test. As we shall see in the next section, using this valid t-test we still do not reject the null hypothesis in Example 9-8.

4.1.3. Correcting for Heteroskedasticity   Financial analysts need to know how to correct for heteroskedasticity, because such a correction may reverse the conclusions about a particular hypothesis test—and thus affect a particular investment decision. (In Example 9-7, for instance, MacKinlay and Richardson reversed their investment conclusions after correcting their model's significance tests for heteroskedasticity.)

We can use two different methods to correct the effects of conditional heteroskedasticity in linear regression models. The first method, computing **robust standard errors**, corrects the standard errors of the linear regression model's estimated coefficients to account for the conditional heteroskedasticity. The second method, **generalized least squares**, modifies the original equation in an attempt to eliminate the heteroskedasticity. The new, modified regression equation is then estimated under the assumption that heteroskedasticity is no longer a problem.[45] The technical details behind these two methods of correcting for conditional heteroskedasticity are outside the scope of this book.[46] Many statistical software packages can easily compute robust standard errors, however, and we recommend using them.[47]

Returning to the subject of Example 9-8 concerning the Fisher effect, recall that we concluded that the error variance was heteroskedastic. If we correct the regression coefficients' standard errors for conditional heteroskedasticity, we get the results shown in Table 9-7. In comparing the standard errors in Table 9-7 with those in Table 9-6, we see that the standard error for the intercept changes very little but the standard error for the coefficient on predicted inflation (the slope coefficient) increases by about 25.5 percent (from 0.0812 to 0.1019). Note also that the regression coefficients are the same in both tables, because the results in Table 9-7 correct only the standard errors in Table 9-6.

TABLE 9-7   Results from Regressing T-Bill Returns on Predicted Inflation (Standard Errors Corrected for Conditional Heteroskedasticity)

	Coefficients	Standard Error	*t*-Statistics
Intercept	0.0304	0.0038	8.0740
Inflation prediction	0.8774	0.1019	8.6083
Residual standard error		0.0220	
Multiple *R*-squared		0.4640	
Observations		137	

Source: Federal Reserve Bank of Philadelphia, U.S. Department of Commerce.

We can now conduct a valid *t*-test of the null hypothesis that the slope coefficient has a true value of 1, using the robust standard error for $\hat{b}_1$. We find that $t = (0.8774 - 1)/0.1019 = -1.2031$. In absolute value, this number is still much smaller than the critical value of 1.98 needed to reject the null hypothesis that the slope equals 1.[48] Thus, in this particular example, even though conditional heteroskedasticity was statistically significant, correcting for it had no effect on the result of the hypothesis test about the slope of the predicted inflation coefficient. In other cases, however, our statistical decision might change based on using robust standard errors in the *t*-test. Example 9-7 concerning tests of the CAPM is a case in point.

4.2. Serial Correlation

A more common—and potentially more serious—problem than violation of the homoskedasticity assumption is the violation of the assumption that regression errors are uncorrelated

---

[45]Generalized least squares requires econometric expertise to implement correctly on financial data. See Greene (2003), Hansen (1982), and Keane and Runkle (1998).

[46]For more details on both methods, see Greene (2003).

[47]Robust standard errors are also known as **heteroskedasticity-consistent standard errors** or **White-corrected standard errors**.

[48]Remember, this is a two-tailed test.

across observations. Trying to explain a particular financial relation over a number of periods is risky, because errors in financial regression models are often correlated through time.

When regression errors are correlated across observations, we say that they are **serially correlated** (or autocorrelated). Serial correlation most typically arises in time-series regressions. In this section, we discuss three aspects of serial correlation: its effect on statistical inference, tests for it, and methods to correct for it.

4.2.1. The Consequences of Serial Correlation

As with heteroskedasticity, the principal problem caused by serial correlation in a linear regression is an incorrect estimate of the regression coefficient standard errors computed by statistical software packages. As long as none of the independent variables is a lagged value of the dependent variable (a value of the dependent variable from a previous period), then the estimated parameters themselves will be consistent and need not be adjusted for the effects of serial correlation. If, however, one of the independent variables is a lagged value of the dependent variable—for example, if the T-bill return from the previous month was an independent variable in the Fisher effect regression—then serial correlation in the error term will cause all the parameter estimates from linear regression to be inconsistent and they will not be valid estimates of the true parameters.[49]

In this chapter, we assume that none of the independent variables is a lagged value of the dependent variable. When that is the case, the effect of serial correlation appears in the regression coefficient standard errors. We will examine it here for the positive serial correlation case, because that case is so common. **Positive serial correlation** is serial correlation in which a positive error for one observation increases the chance of a positive error for another observation. Positive serial correlation also means that a negative error for one observation increases the chance of a negative error for another observation.[50] In examining positive serial correlation, we make the common assumption that serial correlation takes the form of **first-order serial correlation**, or serial correlation between adjacent observations. In a time-series context, that assumption means the sign of the error term tends to persist from one period to the next.

Although positive serial correlation does not affect the consistency of the estimated regression coefficients, it does affect our ability to conduct valid statistical tests. First, the F-statistic to test for overall significance of the regression may be inflated because the mean squared error (MSE) will tend to underestimate the population error variance. Second, positive serial correlation typically causes the ordinary least squares (OLS)standard errors for the regression coefficients to underestimate the true standard errors. As a consequence, if positive serial correlation is present in the regression, standard linear regression analysis will typically lead us to compute artificially small standard errors for the regression coefficient. These small standard errors will cause the estimated t-statistics to be inflated, suggesting significance where perhaps there is none. The inflated t-statistics may, in turn, lead us to incorrectly reject null hypotheses about population values of the parameters of the regression model more often than we would if the standard errors were correctly estimated. This Type I error could lead to improper investment recommendations.[51]

---

[49] We address this issue in the chapter on time-series analysis.

[50] In contrast, with **negative serial correlation**, a positive error for one observation increases the chance of a negative error for another observation, and a negative error for one observation increases the chance of a positive error for another.

[51] OLS standard errors need not be underestimates of actual standard errors if negative serial correlation is present in the regression.

4.2.2. Testing for Serial Correlation We can choose from a variety of tests for serial correlation in a regression model,[52] but the most common is based on a statistic developed by Durbin and Watson (1951); in fact, many statistical software packages compute the Durbin–Watson statistic automatically. The equation for the Durbin–Watson test statistic is

$$\text{DW} = \frac{\sum_{t=2}^{T}(\hat{\epsilon}_t - \hat{\epsilon}_{t-1})^2}{\sum_{t=1}^{T}\hat{\epsilon}_t^2} \tag{9-6}$$

where $\hat{\epsilon}_t$ is the regression residual for period t. We can rewrite this equation as

$$\frac{\frac{1}{T-1}\sum_{t=2}^{T}(\hat{\epsilon}_t^2 - 2\hat{\epsilon}_t\hat{\epsilon}_{t-1} + \hat{\epsilon}_{t-1}^2)}{\frac{1}{T-1}\sum_{t=1}^{T}\hat{\epsilon}_2^t}$$

$$\approx \frac{\text{Var}(\hat{\epsilon}_t) - 2\,\text{Cov}(\hat{\epsilon}_t, \hat{\epsilon}_{t-1}) + \text{Var}(\hat{\epsilon}_{t-1})}{\text{Var}(\hat{\epsilon}_t)}$$

If the variance of the error is constant through time, then we expect $\text{Var}(\hat{\epsilon}_t) = \hat{\sigma}_\epsilon^2$ for all t, where we use σ_ϵ^2 to represent the estimate of the constant error variance. If, in addition, the errors are also not serially correlated, then we expect $\text{Cov}(\hat{\epsilon}_t, \hat{\epsilon}_{t-1}) = 0$. In that case, the Durbin–Watson statistic is approximately equal to

$$\frac{\hat{\sigma}_\epsilon^2 - 0 + \hat{\sigma}_\epsilon^2}{\hat{\sigma}_\epsilon^2} = 2$$

This equation tells us that if the errors are homoskedastic and not serially correlated, then the Durbin–Watson statistic will be close to 2. Therefore, we can test the null hypothesis that the errors are not serially correlated by testing whether the Durbin–Watson statistic differs significantly from 2.

If the sample is very large, the Durbin–Watson statistic will be approximately equal to $2(1 - r)$, where r is the sample correlation between the regression residuals from one period and those from the previous period. This approximation is useful because it shows the value of the Durbin–Watson statistic for differing levels of serial correlation. The Durbin–Watson statistic can take on values ranging from 0 (in the case of serial correlation of +1) to 4 (in the case of serial correlation of −1):

- If the regression has no serial correlation, then the regression residuals will be uncorrelated through time and the value of the Durbin–Watson statistic will be equal to $2(1 - 0) = 2$.
- If the regression residuals are positively serially correlated, then the Durbin–Watson statistic will be less than 2. For example, if the serial correlation of the errors is 1, then the value of the Durbin–Watson statistic will be 0.
- If the regression residuals are negatively serially correlated, then the Durbin–Watson statistic will be greater than 2. For example, if the serial correlation of the errors is −1, then the value of the Durbin–Watson statistic will be 4.

---

[52]See Greene (2003) for a detailed discussion of tests of serial correlation.

Returning to Example 9-8, which explored the Fisher effect, as shown in Table 9-6 the Durbin–Watson statistic for the OLS regression is 0.4673. This result means that the regression residuals are positively serially correlated:

$$DW = 0.4673$$

$$\approx 2(1 - r)$$

$$r \approx 1 - DW/2$$

$$= 1 - 0.4673/2$$

$$= 0.766$$

This outcome raises the concern that OLS standard errors may be incorrect because of positive serial correlation. Does the observed Durbin–Watson statistic (0.4673) provide enough evidence to warrant rejecting the null hypothesis of no positive serial correlation?

We should reject the null hypothesis of no serial correlation if the Durbin–Watson statistic is below a critical value, d^*. Unfortunately, Durbin and Watson also showed that, for a given sample, we cannot know the true critical value, d^*. Instead, we can determine only that d^* lies either between two values, d_u (an upper value) and d_l (a lower value), or outside those values.[53] Figure 9-3 depicts the upper and lower values of d^* as they relate to the results of the Durbin–Watson statistic.

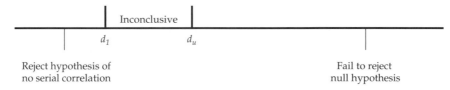

FIGURE 9-3   Value of the Durbin–Watson Statistic

From Figure 9-3, we learn the following:

- When the Durbin–Watson (DW) statistic is less than d_l, we reject the null hypothesis of no positive serial correlation.
- When the DW statistic falls between d_l and d_u, the test results are inconclusive.
- When the DW statistic is greater than d_u, we fail to reject the null hypothesis of no positive serial correlation.[54]

Returning to Example 9-8, the Fisher effect regression has one independent variable and 137 observations. The Durbin–Watson statistic is 0.4673. If we look at Appendix E in the column marked $k = 1$, we see that we can reject the null hypothesis of no correlation in favor of the alternative hypothesis of positive serial correlation at the 0.05 level because the Durbin–Watson statistic is far below d_l for $k = 1$ and $n = 100$ (1.65). The level of d_l would

---

[53]Appendix E tabulates the 0.05 significance levels of d_u and d_l for differing numbers of estimated parameters ($k = 1, 2, \ldots, 5$) and time periods between 15 and 100.

[54]Of course, sometimes serial correlation in a regression model is negative rather than positive. For a null hypothesis of no serial correlation, the null hypothesis is rejected if $DW < d_l$ (indicating significant positive serial correlation) or if $DW > 4 - d_l$ (indicating significant negative serial correlation).

be even higher for a sample of 137 observations. This finding of significant positive serial correlation suggests that the OLS standard errors in this regression probably significantly underestimate the true standard errors.

4.2.3. Correcting for Serial Correlation
We have two alternative remedial steps when a regression has significant serial correlation. First, we can adjust the coefficient standard errors for the linear regression parameter estimates to account for the serial correlation. Second, we can modify the regression equation itself to eliminate the serial correlation. We recommend using the first method for dealing with serial correlation; the second method may result in inconsistent parameter estimates unless implemented with extreme care.

The most prevalent method for adjusting standard errors was developed by Hansen (1982) and is a standard feature in many statistical software packages.[55] An additional advantage of Hansen's method is that it simultaneously corrects for conditional heteroskedasticity.[56]

Table 9-8 shows the results of correcting the standard errors from Table 9-6 for serial correlation and heteroskedasticity using Hansen's method. Note that the coefficients for both the intercept and the slope are exactly the same as in the original regression. The robust standard errors are now much larger, however—about twice the OLS standard errors. Because of the severe serial correlation in the regression error, OLS greatly underestimates the uncertainty about the estimated parameters in the regression.

Note also that the Durbin–Watson statistic has not changed from Table 9-6. The serial correlation has not been eliminated, but the standard error has been corrected to account for the serial correlation.

TABLE 9-8 Results from Regressing T-Bill Returns on Predicted Inflation (Standard Errors Corrected for Conditional Heteroskedasticity and Serial Correlation)

	Coefficient	Standard Error	*t*-Statistic
Intercept	0.0304	0.0069	4.4106
Inflation prediction	0.8774	0.1729	5.0730
Residual standard error		0.0220	
Multiple *R*-squared		0.4640	
Observations		137	
Durbin–Watson statistic		0.4673	

Source: Federal Reserve Bank of Philadelphia, U.S. Department of Commerce.

Now suppose we want to test our original null hypothesis (the Fisher effect) that the coefficient on the predicted inflation term equals 1 ($H_0: b_1 = 1$) against the alternative that the coefficient on the inflation term is not equal to 1 ($H_a: b_1 \neq 1$). With the corrected standard errors, the value of the test statistic for this null hypothesis is

---

[55]This correction is known by various names, including serial-correlation consistent standard errors, serial correlation and heteroskedasticity adjusted standard errors, robust standard errors, and Hansen–White standard errors. Analysts may also say that they use the Newey–West method for computing robust standard errors.

[56]We do not always use Hansen's method to correct for serial correlation and heteroskedasticity because sometimes the errors of a regression are not serially correlated.

$$\frac{\hat{b}_1 - b_1}{s_{\hat{b}_1}} = \frac{0.8774 - 1}{0.1729} = -0.7091$$

The critical values for both the 0.05 and 0.01 significance level are much larger than 0.7091 (absolute value of the t-test statistic), so we cannot reject the null hypothesis.

In this particular case, our conclusion about the Fisher effect was not affected by serial correlation, but the standard error on the slope coefficient after taking into account serial correlation and conditional heteroskedasticity (0.1729) is more than double the OLS standard error (0.0812). Therefore, for some hypotheses, serial correlation and conditional heteroskedasticity could have had a big effect on whether we accepted or rejected those hypotheses.[57]

4.3. Multicollinearity

The second assumption of the multiple linear regression model is that no exact linear relationship exists between two or more of the independent variables. When one of the independent variables is an exact linear combination of other independent variables, it becomes mechanically impossible to estimate the regression. That case, known as perfect collinearity, is much less of a practical concern than multicollinearity.[58] **Multicollinearity** occurs when two or more independent variables (or combinations of independent variables) are highly (but not perfectly) correlated with each other. With multicollinearity we can estimate the regression, but the interpretation of the regression output becomes problematic. Multicollinearity is a serious practical concern because approximate linear relationships among financial variables are common.

4.3.1. The Consequences of Multicollinearity
Although the presence of multi-collinearity does not affect the consistency of the OLS estimates of the regression coefficients, the estimates become extremely imprecise and unreliable. Furthermore, it becomes practically impossible to distinguish the individual impacts of the independent variables on the dependent variable. These consequences are reflected in inflated OLS standard errors for the regression coefficients. With inflated standard errors, t-tests on the coefficients have little power (ability to reject the null hypothesis).

4.3.2. Detecting Multicollinearity
In contrast to the cases of heteroskedasticity and serial correlation, we shall not provide a formal statistical test for multicollinearity. In practice, multicollinearity is often a matter of degree rather than of absence or presence.[59]

The analyst should be aware that using the magnitude of pairwise correlations among the independent variables to assess multicollinearity, as has occasionally been suggested, is generally not adequate. Although very high pairwise correlations among independent variables can indicate multicollinearity, it is not necessary for such pairwise correlations to be high for

---

[57] Serial correlation can also affect forecast accuracy. We discuss this issue in the chapter on time series.

[58] To give an example of perfect collinearity, suppose we tried to explain a company's credit ratings with a regression that included net sales, cost of goods sold, and gross profit as independent variables. Because Gross profit = Net sales − Cost of goods sold by definition, there is an exact linear relationship between these variables. This type of blunder is relatively obvious (and easy to avoid).

[59] See Kmenta (1986).

there to be a problem of multicollinearity.[60] Stated another way, high pairwise correlations among the independent variables are not a necessary condition for multicollinearity, and low pairwise correlations do not mean that multicollinearity is not a problem. The only case in which correlation between independent variables may be a reasonable indicator of multicollinearity occurs in a regression with exactly two independent variables.

The classic symptom of multicollinearity is a high R^2 (and significant F-statistic) even though the t-statistics on the estimated slope coefficients are not significant. The insignificant t-statistics reflect inflated standard errors. Although the coefficients might be estimated with great imprecision, as reflected in low t-statistics, the independent variables *as a group* may do a good job of explaining the dependent variable, and a high R^2 would reflect this effectiveness. Example 9-9 illustrates this diagnostic.

EXAMPLE 9-9   Multicollinearity in Explaining Returns to the Fidelity Select Technology Fund

In Example 9-3 we regressed returns to the Fidelity Select Technology Fund (FSPTX) on returns to the S&P 500/BARRA Growth Index and the S&P 500/BARRA Value Index. Table 9-9 shows the results of our regression, which uses data from January 1998 through December 2002. The t-statistic of 9.7034 on the growth index return is greater than 2.0, indicating that the coefficient on the growth index differs significantly from 0 at standard significance levels. On the other hand, the t-statistic on the value index return is -1.5953 and thus is not statistically significant. This result suggests that the returns to the FSPTX are linked to the returns to the growth index and not closely associated with the returns to the value index. The coefficient on the growth index, however, is 2.23. This result implies that returns on the FSPTX are more volatile than are returns on the growth index.

TABLE 9-9   Results from Regressing the FSPTX Returns on the S&P 500/BARRA Growth and Value Indexes

	Coefficient	Standard Error	t-Statistic
Intercept	0.0079	0.0091	0.8635
S&P 500/BARRA Growth Index	2.2308	0.2299	9.7034
S&P 500/BARRA Value Index	−0.4143	0.2597	−1.5953

ANOVA	df	SS	MSS	F	Significance F
Regression	2	0.8649	0.4324	86.4483	5.48E-18
Residual	57	0.2851	0.0050		
Total	59	1.1500			

Residual standard error	0.0707
Multiple R-squared	0.7521
Observations	60

Source: Ibbotson Associates.

---

[60]Even if pairs of independent variables have low correlation, there may be linear combinations of the independent variables that are very highly correlated, creating a multicollinearity problem.

Note also that this regression explains a significant amount of the variation in the returns to the FSPTX. Specifically, the R^2 from this regression is 0.7521. Thus approximately 75 percent of the variation in the returns to the FSPTX is explained by returns to the S&P 500/BARRA growth and value indexes.

Now suppose we run another linear regression that adds returns to the S&P 500 itself to the returns to the S&P 500/BARRA Growth and Value indexes. The S&P 500 includes the component stocks of these two style indexes, so we are introducing a severe multicollinearity problem.

Table 9-10 shows the results of that regression. Note that the R^2 in this regression has changed almost imperceptibly from the R^2 in the previous regression (increasing from 0.7521 to 0.7539), but now the standard errors of the coefficients are much larger. Adding the return to the S&P 500 to the previous regression does not explain any more of the variance in the returns to the FSPTX than the previous regression did, but now none of the coefficients is statistically significant. This is the classic case of multicollinearity mentioned in the text.

TABLE 9-10   Results from Regressing the FSPTX Returns on Returns to the S&P 500/BARRA Growth and Value Indexes and the S&P 500 Index

	Coefficient	Standard Error	t-Statistic
Intercept	0.0072	0.0092	0.7761
S&P 500/BARRA Growth Index	−1.1324	5.2443	−0.2159
S&P 500/BARRA Value Index	−3.4912	4.8004	−0.7273
S&P 500 Index	6.4436	10.0380	0.6419

ANOVA	df	SS	MSS	F	Significance F
Regression	3	0.8670	0.2890	57.1751	4.73E-17
Residual	56	0.2830	0.0051		
Total	59	1.1500			

Residual standard error	0.0711
Multiple R-squared	0.7539
Observations	60

Source: Ibbotson Associates.

Multicollinearity may be a problem even when we do not observe the classic symptom of insignificant t-statistics but a highly significant F-test. Advanced textbooks provide further tools to help diagnose multicollinearity.[61]

4.3.3. Correcting for Multicollinearity

The most direct solution to multicollinearity is excluding one or more of the regression variables. In the example above, we can see that the S&P 500 total returns should not be included if both the S&P 500/BARRA Growth and Value Indexes are included, because the returns to the entire S&P 500 Index are a weighted average of the return to growth stocks and value stocks. In many cases, however, no easy solution is

---

[61] See Greene (2003).

available to the problem of multicollinearity, and you will need to experiment with including or excluding different independent variables to determine the source of multicollinearity.

4.4. Heteroskedasticity, Serial Correlation, Multicollinearity: Summarizing the Issues

We have discussed some of the problems that heteroskedasticity, serial correlation, and multicollinearity may cause in interpreting regression results. These violations of regression assumptions, we have noted, all lead to problems in making valid inferences. The analyst should check that model assumptions are fulfilled before interpreting statistical tests.

Table 9-11 gives a summary of these problems, the effect they have on the linear regression results (an analyst can see these effects using regression software), and the solutions to these problems.

TABLE 9-11   Problems in Linear Regression and Their Solutions

Problem	Effect	Solution
Heteroskedasticity	Incorrect standard errors	Use robust standard errors (corrected for conditional heteroskedasticity)
Serial Correlation	Incorrect standard errors (additional problems if a lagged value of the dependent variable is used as an independent variable)	Use robust standard errors (corrected for serial correlation)
Multicollinearity	High R^2 and low t-statistics	Remove one or more independent variables; often no solution based in theory

5. MODEL SPECIFICATION AND ERRORS IN SPECIFICATION

Until now, we have assumed that whatever regression model we estimate is correctly specified. **Model specification** refers to the set of variables included in the regression and the regression equation's functional form. In the following, we first give some broad guidelines for correctly specifying a regression. Then we turn to three types of model misspecification: misspecified functional form, regressors that are correlated with the error term, and additional time-series misspecification. Each of these types of misspecification invalidates statistical inference using OLS; most of these misspecifications will cause the estimated regression coefficients to be inconsistent.

5.1. Principles of Model Specification

In discussing the principles of model specification, we need to acknowledge that there are competing philosophies about how to approach model specification. Furthermore, our purpose for using regression analysis may affect the specification we choose. The following principles have fairly broad application, however.

- *The model should be grounded in cogent economic reasoning.* We should be able to supply the economic reasoning behind the choice of variables, and the reasoning should make sense. When this condition is fulfilled, we increase the chance that the model will have predictive value with new data. This approach contrasts to thevariable-selection process known as data mining, discussed in the chapter on sampling. With data mining, the investigator essentially develops a model that maximally exploits the characteristics of a specific dataset.
- *The functional form chosen for the variables in the regression should be appropriate given the nature of the variables.* As one illustration, consider studying mutual fund market timing based on fund and market returns alone. One might reason that for a successful timer, a plot of mutual fund returns against market returns would show curvature, because a successful timer would tend to increase (decrease) beta when market returns were high (low). The model specification should reflect the expected nonlinear relationship.[62] In other cases, we may transform the data such that a regression assumption is better satisfied.
- *The model should be parsimonious.* In this context, "parsimonious" means accomplishing a lot with a little. We should expect each variable included in a regression to play an essential role.
- *The model should be examined for violations of regression assumptions before being accepted.* We have already discussed detecting the presence of heteroskedasticity, serial correlation, and multicollinearity. As a result of such diagnostics, we may conclude that we need to revise the set of included variables and/or their functional form.
- *The model should be tested and be found useful out of sample before being accepted.* The term "out of sample" refers to observations outside the dataset on which the model was estimated. A plausible model may not perform well out of sample because economic relationships have changed since the sample period. That possibility is itself useful to know. A second explanation, however, may be that relationships have not changed but that the model explains only a specific dataset.

Having given some broad guidance on model specification, we turn to a discussion of specific model specification errors. Understanding these errors will help an analyst develop better models and be a more informed consumer of investment research.

5.2. Misspecified Functional Form

Whenever we estimate a regression, we must assume that the regression has the correct functional form. This assumption can fail in several ways:

- One or more important variables could be omitted from regression.
- One or more of the regression variables may need to be transformed (for example, by taking the natural logarithm of the variable) before estimating the regression.
- The regression model pools data from different samples that should not be pooled.

First, consider the effects of omitting an important independent variable from a regression (omitted variable bias). If the true regression model was

---

[62]This example is based on Treynor and Mazuy (1966), an early regression study of mutual fund timing. To capture curvature, they included a term in the squared market excess return, which does not violate the assumption of the multiple linear regression model that relationship between the dependent and independent variables is linear *in the coefficients*.

$$Y_i = b_0 + b_1 X_{1i} + b_2 X_{2i} + \epsilon_i \tag{9-7}$$

but we estimate the model[63]

$$Y_i = a_0 + a_1 X_{1i} + \epsilon_i$$

then our regression model would be misspecified. What is wrong with the model?

If the omitted variable (X_2) is correlated with the remaining variable (X_1), then the error term in the model will be correlated with (X_1), and the estimated values of the regression coefficients a_0 and a_1 would be biased and inconsistent. In addition, the estimates of the standard errors of those coefficients will also be inconsistent, so we can use neither the coefficients estimates nor the estimated standard errors to make statistical tests.

EXAMPLE 9-10   Omitted Variable Bias and the Bid–Ask Spread

In this example, we extend our examination of the bid–ask spread to show the effect of omitting an important variable from a regression. In Example 9-1, we showed that the natural logarithm of the ratio [(Bid–ask spread)/Price] was significantly related to both the natural logarithm of the number of market makers and the natural logarithm of the market capitalization of the company. We repeat Table 9-1 from Example 9-1 below.

TABLE 9-1   (repeated) Results from Regressing ln(Bid–Ask Spread/Price) on ln(Number of Market Makers) and ln(Market Cap)

	Coefficients	Standard Error	t-Statistic
Intercept	−0.7586	0.1369	−5.5416
ln(Number of Nasdaq market makers)	−0.2790	0.0673	−4.1427
ln(Company's market cap)	−0.6635	0.0246	−27.0087

ANOVA	df	SS	MSS	F	Significance F
Regression	2	2,681.6482	1,340.8241	1,088.8325	0.00
Residual	1,816	2,236.2820	1,2314		
Total	1,818	4,917.9302			

Residual standard error	1.1097	
Multiple R-squared	0.5453	
Observations	1,819	

Source: FactSet, Nasdaq.

If we did not include the natural log of market capitalization as an independent variable in the regression, and we regressed the natural logarithm of the ratio [(Bid–ask spread)/Price] only on the natural logarithm of the number of market makers for the stock, the results would be as shown in Table 9-12.

---

[63]We use a different regression coefficient notation when X_{2i} is omitted, because the intercept term and slope coefficient on X_{1i} will generally not be the same as when X_{2i} is included.

TABLE 9-12   Results from Regressing ln(Bid–Ask Spread/Price) on ln (Number of Market Makers)

	Coefficients	Standard Error	t-Statistic
Intercept	−0.1229	0.1596	−0.7698
ln(Number of Nasdaq market makers)	−1.6629	0.0517	−32.1519

ANOVA	df	SS	MSS	F	Significance F
Regression	1	1,783.3549	1,783.3549	1,033.7464	0.00
Residual	1,817	3,134.5753	1.7251		
Total	1,818	4,917.9302			

Residual standard error	1.3134
Multiple R-squared	0.3626
Observations	1,819

Source: FactSet, Nasdaq.

Note that the coefficient on ln(Number of Nasdaq market makers) fell from −0.2790 in the original (correctly specified) regression to −1.6629 in the misspecified regression. Also, the intercept rose from −0.7586 in the correctly specified regression to −0.1229 in the misspecified regression. These results illustrate that omitting an independent variable that should be in the regression can cause the remaining regression coefficients to be inconsistent.

A second common cause of misspecification in regression models is the use of the wrong form of the data in a regression, when a transformed version of the data is appropriate. For example, sometimes analysts fail to account for curvature or nonlinearity in the relationship between the dependent variable and one or more of the independent variables, instead specifying a linear relation among variables. When we are specifying a regression model, we should consider whether economic theory suggests a nonlinear relation. We can often confirm the nonlinearity by plotting the data, as we will illustrate in Example 9-11 below. If the relationship between the variables becomes linear when one or more of the variables is represented as a proportional change in the variable, we may be able to correct the misspecification by taking the natural logarithm of the variable(s) we want to represent as a proportional change. Other times, analysts use unscaled data in regressions, when scaled data (such as dividing net income or cash flow by sales) are more appropriate. In Example 9-1, we scaled the bid–ask spread by stock price because what a given bid–ask spread means in terms of transactions costs for a given size investment depends on the price of the stock; if we had not scaled the bid–ask spread, the regression would have been misspecified.

EXAMPLE 9-11   Nonlinearity and the Bid–Ask Spread

In Example 9-1, we showed that the natural logarithm of the ratio [(Bid–ask spread)/ Price] was significantly related to both the natural logarithm of the number of market makers and the natural logarithm of the company's market capitalization. But why did we take the natural logarithm of each of the variables in the regression? We began a discussion of this question in Example 9-1, which we continue now.

What does theory suggest about the nature of the relationship between the ratio (Bid–ask spread)/Price, or the percentage bid–ask spread, and its determinants (the independent variables)? Stoll (1978) builds a theoretical model of the determinants of percentage bid–ask spread in a dealer market. In his model, the determinants enter multiplicatively in a particular fashion. In terms of the independent variables introduced in Example 9-1, the functional form assumed is

$$[(\text{Bid-ask spread})/\text{Price}]_i = c(\text{Number of market makers})_i^{b_1}$$

$$\times (\text{Market capitalization})_i^{b_2}$$

where c is a constant. The relationship of the percentage bid–ask spread with the number of market makers and market capitalization is not linear in the original variables.[64] If we take natural log of both sides of the above model, however, we have a log-log regression that is linear in the transformed variables:[65]

$$Y_i = b_0 + b_1 X_{1i} + b_2 X_{2i} + \epsilon_i$$

where

    Y_i = the natural logarithm of the ratio (Bid-ask spread)/Price for stock i
    b_0 = a constant that equals $\ln(c)$
    X_{1i} = the natural logarithm of the number of market makers for stock i
    X_{2i} = the natural logarithm of the market capitalization of company i
    ϵ_i = the error term

As mentioned in Example 9-1, a slope coefficient in the log-log model is interpreted as an elasticity, precisely, the partial elasticity of the dependent variable with respect to the independent variable ("partial" means holding the other independent variables constant).

We can plot the data to assess whether the variables are linearly related after the logarithmic transformation. For example, Figure 9-4 shows a scatterplot of the natural logarithm of the number of market makers for a stock (on the X axis) and the natural logarithm of (Bid–ask spread)/Price (on the Y axis), as well as a regression line showing the linear relation between the two transformed variables. The relation between the two transformed variables is clearly linear.

If we do not take log of the ratio (Bid–ask spread)/Price, the plot is not linear. Figure 9-5 shows a plot of the natural logarithm of the number of market makers for a stock (on the X axis) and the ratio (Bid–ask spread)/Price (on the Y axis), as well as a regression line that attempts to show a linear relation between the two variables. We see that the relation between the two variables is very nonlinear.[66] Consequently, we should not estimate a regression with (Bid–ask spread)/Price as the dependent

---

[64] The form of the model is analogous to the Cobb–Douglas production function in economics.
[65] We have added an error term to the model.
[66] The relation between (Bid–ask spread)/Price and ln(Market cap) is also nonlinear, while the relation between ln(Bid–ask spread)/Price and ln(Market cap) is linear. We omit these scatterplots to save space.

variable. Consideration of the need to assure that predicted bid–ask spreads are positive would also lead us to not use (Bid–ask spread)/Price as the dependent variable. If we use the nontransformed ratio (Bid–ask spread)/Price as the dependent variable, the estimated model could predict negative values of the bid–ask spread. This result would be nonsensical; in reality, no bid–ask spread is negative (it is hard to motivate traders to simultaneously buy high and sell low), so a model that predicts negative bid–ask spreads is certainly misspecified.[67] We illustrate the problem of negative values of the predicted bid–ask spreads now.

Table 9-13 shows the results of a regression with (Bid–ask spread)/Price as the dependent variable and the natural logarithm of the number of market makers and the natural logarithm of the company's market capitalization as the independent variables.

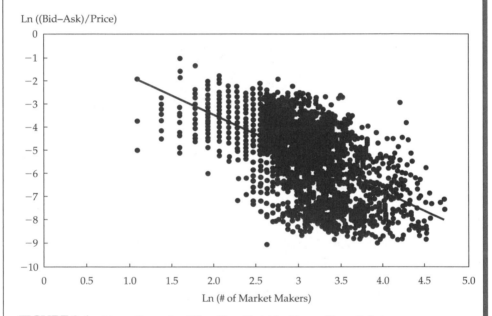

FIGURE 9-4   Linear Regression When Two Variables Have a Linear Relation

Suppose that for a particular Nasdaq-listed stock, the number of market makers is 20 and the market capitalization is $5 billion. Therefore, the natural log of the number of market makers equals ln 20 = 2.9957 and the natural log of the stock's market capitalization (in millions) is ln 5,000 = 8.5172. In this case, the predicted ratio of bid–ask spread to price is 0.0658 + (2.9957 × −0.0045) + (−0.0068 × 8.5172) = −0.0056. Therefore, the model predicts that the ratio of bid–ask spread to stock price is −0.0056 or −0.56 percent of the stock price. Thus the predicted bid–ask spread is negative, which does not make economic sense. This problem could be avoided by using log of (Bid–ask spread)/Price as the dependent variable.[68]

---

[67]In our data sample, the bid–ask spread for each of the 1,819 companies is positive.
[68]Whether the natural log of the percentage bid–ask spread, Y, is positive or negative, the percentage bid–ask spread found as e^Y is positive, because a positive number raised to any power is positive. The constant e is positive ($e \approx 2.7183$).

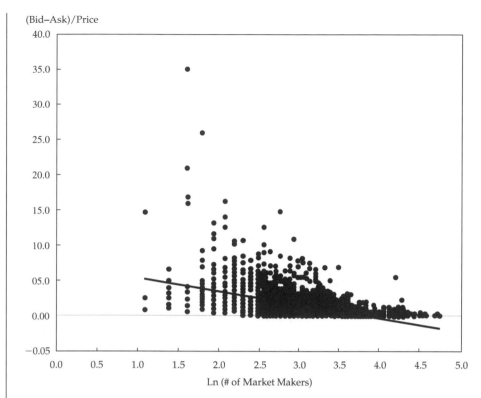

FIGURE 9-5   Linear Regression When Two Variables Have a Nonlinear Relation

TABLE 9-13   Results from Regressing Bid–Ask Spread/Price on
ln(Number of Market Makers) and ln(Market Cap)

	Coefficient	Standard Error	t-Statistic
Intercept	0.0658	0.0024	27.6430
ln(Number of Nasdaq market makers)	−0.0045	0.0012	−3.8714
ln(Company's market cap)	−0.0068	0.0004	−15.8679

ANOVA	df	SS	MSS	F	Significance F
Regression	2	0.3185	0.1592	427.8174	0.00
Residual	1816	0.6760	0.0004		
Total	1818	0.9944			

Residual standard error	0.0193
Multiple R-squared	0.3203
Observations	1,819

Source: FactSet, Nasdaq.

Often, analysts must decide whether to scale variables before they compare data across companies. For example, in financial statement analysis, analysts often compare companies using **common size statements**. In a common size income statement, all the line items in a company's income statement are divided by the company's revenues.[69] Common size statements make comparability across companies much easier. An analyst can use common size statements to quickly compare trends in gross margins (or other income statement variables) for a group of companies.

Issues of comparability also appear for analysts who want to use regression analysis to compare the performance of a group of companies. Example 9-12 illustrates this issue.

EXAMPLE 9-12 Scaling and the Relation between Cash Flow from Operations and Free Cash Flow

Suppose an analyst wants to explain free cash flow to the firm as a function of cash flow from operations in 2001 for 11 family clothing stores in the United States with market capitalizations of more than $100 million as of the end of 2001.

To investigate this issue, the analyst might use free cash flow as the dependent variable and cash flow from operations as the independent variable in single-independent-variable linear regression. Table 9-14 shows the results of that regression. Note that the t-statistic for the slope coefficient for cash flow from operations is quite high (6.5288), the significance level for the F-statistic for the regression is very low (0.0001), and the R-squared is quite high. We might be tempted to believe that this regression is a success and that for a family clothing store, if cash flow from operations increased by $1.00, we could confidently predict that free cash flow to the firm would increase by $0.3579.

TABLE 9-14   Results from Regressing the Free Cash Flow on Cash Flow from Operations for Family Clothing Stores

		Coefficient	Standard Error	t-Statistic
Intercept		0.7295	27.7302	0.0263
Cash flow from operations		0.3579	0.0548	6.5288

ANOVA	df	SS	MSS	F	Significance F
Regression	1	245,093.7836	245,093.7836	42.6247	0.0001
Residual	9	51,750.3139	5,750.0349		
Total	10	296,844.0975			

Residual standard error	75.8290
Multiple R-squared	0.8257
Observations	11

Source: Compustat.

But is this specification correct? The regression does not account for size differences among the companies in the sample.

---

[69] For more on common size statements, see White, Sondhi, and Fried (2003). Free cash flow and cash flow from operations are discussed in Stowe, Robinson, Pinto, and McLeavey (2002).

We can account for size differences by using common size cash flow results across companies. We scale the variables by dividing cash flow from operations and free cash flow to the firm by the company's sales before using regression analysis. We will use (Free cash flow to the firm/Sales) as the dependent variable and (Cash flow from operations/Sales) as the independent variable. Table 9-15 shows the results of this regression. Note that the t-statistic for the slope coefficient on (Cash flow from operations/Sales) is 1.6262, so it is not significant at the 0.05 level. Note also that the significance level of the F-statistic is 0.1383, so we cannot reject at the 0.05 level the hypothesis that the regression does not explain variation in (Free cash flow/Sales) among family clothing stores. Finally, note that the R-squared in this regression is much lower than that of the previous regression.

TABLE 9-15   Results from Regressing the Free Cash Flow/Sales on Cash Flow from Operations/Sales for Family Clothing Stores

	Coefficient	Standard Error	t-Statistic
Intercept	−0.0121	0.0221	−0.5497
Cash flow from operations/Sales	0.4749	0.2920	1.6262

ANOVA	df	SS	MSS	F	Significance F
Regression	1	0.0030	0.0030	2.6447	0.1383
Residual	9	0.0102	0.0011		
Total	10	0.0131			

Residual standard error	0.0336
Multiple R-squared	0.2271
Observations	11

Source: Compustat.

Which regression makes more sense? Usually, the scaled regression makes more sense. We want to know what happens to free cash flow (as a fraction of sales) if a change occurs in cash flow from operations (as a fraction of sales). Without scaling, the results of the regression can be based solely on scale differences across companies, rather than based on the companies' underlying economics.

A third common form of misspecification in regression models is pooling data from different samples that should not be pooled. This type of misspecification can best be illustrated graphically. Figure 9-6 shows two clusters of data on variables X and Y, with a fitted regression line. The data could represent the relationship between two financial variables at two stages of a company's growth, for example.

In each cluster of data on X and Y, the correlation between the two variables is virtually 0. Because the means of both X and Y are different for the two clusters of data in the combined sample, X and Y are highly correlated. The correlation is spurious (misleading), however, because it reflects scale differences across companies.

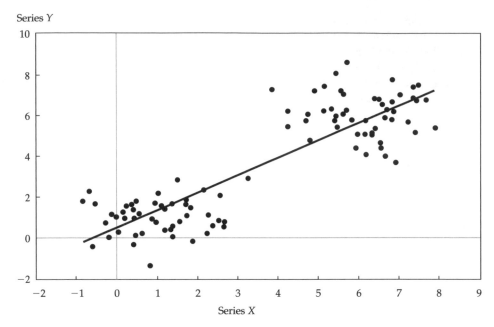

FIGURE 9-6   Plot of Two Series with Changing Means

5.3. Time-Series Misspecification (Independent Variables Correlated with Errors)

In the previous section, we discussed the misspecification that arises when a relevant independent variable is omitted from a regression. In this section, we discuss problems that arise from the kinds of variables included in the regression, particularly in a time-series context. In models that use time-series data to explain the relations among different variables, it is particularly easy to violate Regression Assumption 3, that the error term has mean 0, conditioned on the independent variables. If this assumption is violated, the estimated regression coefficients will be biased and inconsistent.

   Three common problems that create this type of time-series misspecification are

- including lagged dependent variables as independent variables in regressions with serially correlated errors,
- including a function of a dependent variable as an independent variable, sometimes as a result of the incorrect dating of variables, and
- independent variables that are measured with error.

The next examples demonstrate these problems.

   Suppose that an analyst has estimated a linear regression with significant serial correlation in the errors. That serial correlation could be corrected by the methods discussed previously in this chapter. Nevertheless, suppose that the analyst includes as an additional independent variable the first lagged value of the dependent variable. For example, the analyst might use the regression equation

$$Y_t = b_0 + b_1 X_{1t} + b_2 Y_{t-1} + \epsilon_t \qquad (9\text{-}8)$$

Because we assume that the error term is serially correlated, by definition the error term is correlated with the dependent variable. Consequently, the lagged dependent variable, Y_{t-1}, will be correlated with the error term, violating the assumption that the independent variables are uncorrelated with the error term. As a result, the estimates of the regression coefficients will be biased and inconsistent.

EXAMPLE 9-13   Fisher Effect with a Lagged Dependent Variable

In our discussion of serial correlation, we concluded from a test using the Durbin–Watson test that the error term in the Fisher effect equation (Equation 9-5) showed-positive (first-order) serial correlation, using three-month T-bill returns as the dependent variable and inflation expectations of professional forecasters as the independent variable. Observations on the dependent and independent variables were quarterly. Table 9-16 modifies that regression by including the previous quarter's three-month T-bill returns as an additional independent variable.

TABLE 9-16   Results from Regressing T-Bill Returns on Predicted Inflation and Lagged T-Bill Returns

	Coefficient	Standard Error	*t*-Statistic
Intercept	0.0046	0.0040	1.5718
Inflation prediction	0.2753	0.0631	4.3610
Lagged T-bill return	0.7553	0.0495	15.2510
Residual standard error		0.0134	
Multiple *R*-squared		0.8041	
Observations		137	

Source: Federal Reserve Bank of Philadelphia, U.S. Department of Commerce.

At first glance, these regression results look very interesting—the coefficient on the lagged T-bill return appears to be highly significant. But on closer consideration, we must ignore these regression results, because the regression is fundamentally misspecified. As long as the error term is serially correlated, including lagged T-bill returns as an independent variable in the regression will cause all the coefficient estimates to be biased and inconsistent. Therefore, this regression is not useable for either testing a hypothesis or for forecasting.

A second common time-series misspecification in investment analysis is to forecast the past. What does that mean? If we forecast the future (say we predict at time t the value of variable Y in period $t + 1$), we must base our predictions on information we knew at time t. We could use a regression to make that forecast using the equation

$$Y_{t+1} = b_0 + b_1 X_{1t} + \epsilon_{t+1} \tag{9-9}$$

In this equation, we predict the value of Y in time $t + 1$ using the value of X in time t. The error term, ϵ_{t+1}, is unknown at time t and thus should be uncorrelated with X_{1t}.

Unfortunately, analysts sometimes use regressions that try to forecast the value of a dependent variable at time $t + 1$ based on independent variable(s) that are functions of the value of the dependent variable at time $t + 1$. In such a model, the independent variable(s) would be correlated with the error term, so the equation would be misspecified. As an example, an analyst may try to explain the cross-sectional returns for a group of companies during a particular year using the market-to-book ratio and the market capitalization for those companies at the end of the year.[70] If the analyst believes that such a regression predicts whether companies with high market-to-book ratios or high market capitalizations will have high returns, the analyst is mistaken. For any given period, the higher the return during the period, the higher the market capitalization at the end of the period. It is also true that the higher the return during the period, the higher the market-to-book ratio at the end of the period. So in this case, if all the cross-sectional data come from period $t + 1$, a high value of the dependent variable (returns) actually causes a high value of the independent variables (market cap and market-to-book), rather than the other way around. In this type of misspecification, the regression model effectively includes the dependent variable on both the right- and left-hand sides of the regression equation.

The third common time-series misspecification arises when an independent variable is measured with error. Suppose a financial theory tells us that a particular variable X_t, such as expected inflation, should be included in the regression model. We do not observe X_t; instead, we observe actual inflation, $Z_t = X_t + u_t$, where u_t is an error term that is uncorrelated with X_t. Even in this best of circumstances, using Z_t in the regression instead of X_t will cause the regression coefficient estimates to be biased and inconsistent. Let's see why. If we want to estimate the regression

$$Y_t = b_0 + b_1 X_t + \epsilon_t$$

but we observe Z_t not X_t, then we would estimate

$$Y_t = b_0 + b_1 Z_t + (-b_1 u_t + \epsilon_t)$$

But because $Z_t = X_t + u_t$, Z_t is correlated with the error term $(-b_1 u_t + \epsilon_t)$. Therefore, our estimated model violates the assumption that the error term is uncorrelated with the independent variable. Consequently, the estimated regression coefficients will be biased and inconsistent.

EXAMPLE 9-14   The Fisher Effect with Measurement Error

Recall from Example 9-8 on the Fisher effect that we could not reject the hypothesis that three-month T-bill returns moved one-for-one with expected inflation.

---

[70]"Market-to-book ratio" is the ratio of price per share divided by book value per share.

TABLE 9-16   (repeated) Results from Regressing T-Bill Returns on Predicted Inflation

	Coefficient	Standard Error	*t*-Statistic
Intercept	0.0304	0.0040	7.6887
Inflation prediction	0.8774	0.0812	10.8096
Residual standard error		0.0220	
Multiple *R*-squared		0.4640	
Observations		137	
Durbin–Watson statistic		0.4673	

Source: Federal Reserve Bank of Philadelphia, U.S. Department of Commerce.

What if we used actual inflation instead of expected inflation as the independent variable? Note first that

$$\pi = \pi^e + v$$

where

π = actual rate of inflation

π^e = expected rate of inflation

v = the difference between actual and expected inflation

Because actual inflation measures expected inflation with error, the estimators of the regression coefficients using T-bill yields as the dependent variable and actual inflation as the dependent variable will not be consistent.[71]

Table 9-17 shows the results of using actual inflation as the independent variable. The estimates in this table are quite different from those presented in the previous table. Note that the slope coefficient on actual inflation is much lower than the slope coefficient on predicted inflation in the previous regression. This result is an illustration of a general proposition: In a single-independent-variable regression, if we select a version of that independent variable that is measured with error, the estimated slope coefficient on that variable will be biased toward 0.[72]

TABLE 9-17   Results from Regressing T-Bill Returns on Actual Inflation

	Coefficient	Standard Error	*t*-Statistic
Intercept	0.0432	0.0034	12.7340
Actual inflation	0.5066	0.0556	9.1151
Residual standard error		0.0237	
Multiple *R*-squared		0.3810	
Observations		137	

Source: Federal Reserve Bank of Philadelphia, U.S. Department of Commerce.

---

[71]A consistent estimator is one for which the probability of estimates close to the value of the population parameter increases as sample size increases.

[72]This proposition does not generalize to regressions with more than one independent variable. Of course, we ignore serially-correlated errors in this example, but because the regression coefficients are inconsistent (due to measurement error), testing or correcting for serial correlation is not worthwhile.

5.4. Other Types of Time-Series Misspecification

By far the most frequent source of misspecification in linear regressions that use time series from two or more different variables is nonstationarity. Very roughly, **nonstationarity** means that a variable's properties, such as mean and variance, are not constant through time. We will postpone our discussion about stationarity until Chapter 10, but we can list some examples in which we need to use stationarity tests before we use regression statistical inference.[73]

- Relations among time series with trends (for example, the relation between consumption and GDP).
- Relations among time series that may be **random walks** (time series for which the best predictor of next period's value is this period's value). Exchange rates are often random walks.

The time-series examples in this chapter were carefully chosen such that nonstationarity was unlikely to be an issue for any of them. But nonstationarity can be a very severe problem for analyzing the relations among two or more time series in practice. Analysts must understand these issues before they apply linear regression to analyzing the relations among time series. Otherwise, they may rely on invalid statistical inference.

6. MODELS WITH QUALITATIVE DEPENDENT VARIABLES

Financial analysts often need to be able to explain the outcomes of a qualitative dependent variable. **Qualitative dependent variables** are dummy variables used as dependent variables instead of as independent variables.

For example, to predict whether or not a company will go bankrupt, we need to use a qualitative dependent variable (bankrupt or not) as the dependent variable and use data on the company's financial performance (e.g., return on equity, debt-to-equity ratio, or debt rating) as independent variables. Unfortunately, linear regression is not the best statistical method to use for estimating such a model. If we use the qualitative dependent variable bankrupt (1) or not bankrupt (0) as the dependent variable in a regression with financial variables as the independent variables, the predicted value of the dependent variable could be much greater than 1 or much lower than 0. Of course, these results would be invalid. The probability of bankruptcy (or of anything, for that matter) cannot be greater than 100 percent or less than 0 percent. Instead of a linear regression model, we should use probit, logit, or discriminant analysis for this kind of estimation.

Probit and **logit models** estimate the probability of a discrete outcome given the values of the independent variables used to explain that outcome. The probit model, which is based on the normal distribution, estimates the probability that $Y = 1$ (a condition is fulfilled) given the value of the independent variable X. The logit model is identical, except that it is based on the logistic distribution rather than the normal distribution.[74] Both models must be estimated using maximum likelihood methods.[75]

---

[73]We include both unit root tests and tests for cointegration in the term "stationarity tests." These tests will be discussed in Chapter 10.

[74]The logistic distribution $e^{(b_0+b_1X)}/[1 + e^{(b_0+b_1X)}]$ is easier to compute than the cumulative normal distribution. Consequently, logit models gained popularity when computing power was expensive.

[75]For more on probit and logit models, see Greene (2003).

Another technique to handle qualitative dependent variables is **discriminant analysis**. In his Z-score and Zeta analysis, Altman (1968, 1977) reported on the results of discriminant analysis. Altman uses financial ratios to predict the qualitative dependent variable bankruptcy. Discriminant analysis yields a linear function, similar to a regression equation, which can then be used to create an overall score. Based on the score, an observation can be classified into the bankrupt or not bankrupt category.

Qualitative dependent variable models can be useful not only for portfolio management but also for business management. For example, we might want to predict whether a client is likely to continue investing in a company or to withdraw assets from the company. We might also want to explain how particular demographic characteristics might affect the probability that a potential investor will sign on as a new client, or evaluate the effectiveness of a particular direct-mail advertising campaign based on the demographic characteristics of the target audience. These issues can be analyzed with either probit or logit models.

EXAMPLE 9-15   Explaining Analyst Coverage

Suppose we want to investigate what factors determine whether at least one analyst covers a company. We can employ a probit model to address the question. The sample consists of 2,047 observations on public companies in 1999. All data comefrom Disclosure, Inc. The analyst coverage data on Disclosure come from I/B/E/S.

The variables in the probit model are as follows:

> ANALYSTS = the discrete dependent variable, which takes on a value
> of 1 if at least one analyst covers the company and a
> value of 0 if no analysts cover the company
> LNVOLUME = the natural log of trading volume in the most recent week
> LNMV = the natural log of market value
> ESTABLISHED = a dummy independent variable that takes on a value of 1
> if the company's financial data has been audited for at
> least five years
> LNTA = the natural log of total assets(book value)
> LNSALES = the natural log of net sales

In this attempt to explain analyst coverage, the market (volume and value) and the book (value and sales) variables might be expected to explain coverage through various dimensions of size and, hence, importance.[76] The audit history variable reflects a possible comfort level that analysts could be expected to have with audited statements. The model includes three variables (LNMV, LNTA, and LNSALES) that we may expect

---

[76]For more information on tests of multicollinearity, see Greene (2003).

to be correlated. Based on analysis not shown here, our probit regression did not exhibit the classic symptom of multicollinearity. Table 9-18 shows the results of the probit estimation.

TABLE 9-18   Explaining Analyst Coverage Using a Probit Model

	Coefficient	Standard Error	t-Statistic
Intercept	−7.9738	0.4362	−18.2815
LNVOLUME	0.1574	0.0158	9.9482
LNMV	0.4442	0.0369	12.0268
ESTABLISHED	0.3168	0.1045	3.0320
LNTA	0.0548	0.0296	1.8494
LNSALES	0.0507	0.0266	1.9059
Percent correctly predicted		73.67	

Source: Disclosure, Inc.

As Table 9-18 shows, three coefficients (besides the intercept) have t-statistics with an absolute value greater than 2.0. The coefficient on LNVOLUME has a t-statistic of 9.95. That value is far above the critical value at the 0.05 level for the t-statistic (1.96), so we can reject at the 0.05 level of significance the null hypothesis that the coefficient on LNVOLUME equals 0, in favor of the alternative hypothesis that the coefficient is not equal to 0. The second coefficient with an absolute value greater than 2 is LNMV, which has a t-statistic of 12.03. We can also reject at the 0.05 level of significance the null hypothesis that the coefficient on LNMV is equal to 0, in favor of the alternative hypothesis that the coefficient is not equalto 0. Finally, the coefficient on ESTABLISHED has a t-statistic of 3.03. We can reject at the 0.05 level of significance the null hypothesis that the coefficient on ESTABLISHED is equal to 0.

Neither of the two remaining independent variables is statistically significant at the 0.05 level in this probit analysis. Neither of the t-statistics on these two variables is larger in absolute value than 1.91, so neither one reaches the critical value of 1.96 needed to reject the null hypothesis (that the associated coefficient is significantly different from 0). This result shows that once we take into account a company's market value, trading volume, and the existence of a five-year audit history, the other factors—book value of assets and value of sales—have no power to explain whether at least one analyst will cover the company.

CHAPTER 10

TIME-SERIES ANALYSIS

1. INTRODUCTION

As financial analysts, we often use time-series data to make investment decisions. A **time series** is a set of observations on a variable's outcomes in different time periods: the quarterly sales for a particular company during the past five years, for example, or the daily returns on a traded security. In this chapter, we explore the two chief uses of time-series models: to explain the past and to predict the future of a time series. We also discuss how to estimate time-series models, and we examine how a model describing a particular time series can change over time. The following two examples illustrate the kinds of questions we might want to ask about time series.

Suppose it is the beginning of 2003 and we are managing a U.S.-based investment portfolio that includes Swiss stocks. Because the value of this portfolio would decrease if the Swiss franc depreciates with respect to the dollar, and vice-versa, holding all else constant, we are considering whether to hedge the portfolio's exposure to changes in the value of the franc. To help us in making this decision, we decide to model the time series of the franc/dollar exchange rate. Figure 10-1 shows monthly data on the franc/dollar exchange rate. (The data are monthly averages of daily exchange rates.) Has the exchange rate been more stable since 1987 than it was in previous years? Has the exchange rate shown a long-term trend? How can we best use past exchange rates to predict future exchange rates?

As another example, suppose it is the beginning of 2001. We cover retail stores for a sell-side firm and want to predict retail sales for the coming year. Figure 10-2 shows monthly data on U.S. real retail sales. The data are inflation adjusted but not seasonally adjusted, hence the spikes around the holiday season at the turn of each year. Because the reported sales in the stores financial statements are not seasonally adjusted, we model seasonally unadjusted retail sales. How can we model the trend in retail sales? How can we adjust for the extreme seasonality reflected in the peaks and troughs occurring at regular intervals? How can we best use past retail sales to predict future retail sales?

Some fundamental questions arise in time-series analysis: How do we model trends? How do we predict the future value of a time series based on its past values? How do we model seasonality? How do we choose among time-series models? And how do we model changes in the variance of time series over time? We address each of these issues in this chapter.

2. CHALLENGES OF WORKING WITH TIME SERIES

Throughout the chapter, our objective will be to apply linear regression to a given time series. Unfortunately, in working with time series we often find that the assumptions of the

Swiss Franc/U.S. Dollar

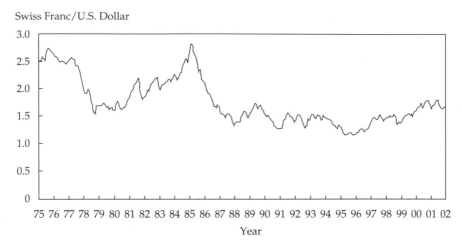

FIGURE 10-1   Swiss Franc/U.S. Dollar Exchange Rate, Monthly Average of Daily Data
Source: Board of Governors of the Federal Reserve System.

$ Millions

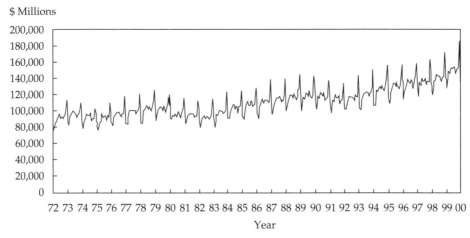

FIGURE 10-2   Monthly U.S. Real Retail Sales
Source: U.S. Department of Commerce, Census Bureau.

linear regression model are not satisfied. To apply time-series analysis, we need to assure ourselves that the linear regression model assumptions are met. When those assumptions are not satisfied, in many cases we can transform the time series, or specify the regression model differently, so that the assumptions of the linear regression model are met.

    We can illustrate assumption difficulties in the context of a common time-series model, an autoregressive model. Informally, an autoregressive model is one in which the independent variable is a lagged (that is, past) value of the dependent variable, such as the model $x_t = b_0 + b_1 x_{t-1} + \epsilon_t$.[1] Specific problems that we often encounter in dealing with time series include the following:

---

[1] We could also write the equation as $y_t = b_0 + b_1 y_{t-1} + \epsilon_t$.

- The residual errors are correlated instead of being uncorrelated.

  In the calculated regression, the difference between x_t and $b_0 + b_1 x_{t-1}$ is called the residual error. The linear regression assumes that this error term is not correlated across observations. The violation of that assumption is frequently more critical in terms of its consequences in the case of time-series models involving past values of the time series as independent variables than for other models (such as cross-sectional) in which the dependent and independent variables are distinct. As we discussed in the chapter on multiple regression, in a regression in which the dependent and independent variables are distinct, serial correlation of the errors in this model does not affect the consistency of our estimates of intercept or slope coefficients. By contrast, in an autoregressive time-series regression such as $x_t = b_0 + b_1 x_{t-1} + \epsilon_t$, serial correlation in the error term causes estimates of the intercept (b_0) and slope coefficient (b_1) to be inconsistent.

- The mean and/or variance of the time series changes over time.

  Regression results are invalid if we estimate an autoregressive model for a time series with mean and/or variance that changes over time.

Before we try to use time series for forecasting, we may need to transform the time-series model so that it is well specified for linear regression. With this objective in mind, you will observe that time-series analysis is relatively straightforward and logical.

3. TREND MODELS

Estimating a trend in a time series and using that trend to predict future values of the time series is the simplest method of forecasting. For example, we saw in Figure 10-2 that monthly U.S. real retail sales show a long-term pattern of upward movement—that is, a **trend**. In this section, we examine two types of trends, linear trends and log-linear trends, and discuss how to choose between them.

3.1. Linear Trend Models

The simplest type of trend is a **linear trend**, one in which the dependent variable changes at a constant rate with time. If a time series, y_t, has a linear trend, then we can model the series using the following regression equation:

$$y_t = b_0 + b_1 t + \epsilon_t, \quad t = 1, 2, \ldots, T \tag{10-1}$$

where

  y_t = the value of the time series at time t (value of the dependent variable)
  b_0 = the y-intercept term
  b_1 = the slope coefficient
  t = time, the independent or explanatory variable
  ϵ_t = a random-error term

In Equation 10-1, the trend line, $b_0 + b_1 t$, predicts the value of the time series at time t (where t takes on a value of 1 in the first period of the sample and increases by 1 in each subsequent period). Because the coefficient b_1 is the slope of the trend line, we refer to b_1 as the trend coefficient. We can estimate the two coefficients, b_0 and b_1, using ordinary least squares, denoting the estimated coefficients as $\hat{b}_0$ and $\hat{b}_1$.[2]

---

[2] Recall that ordinary least squares is an estimation method based on the criterion of minimizing the sum of a regression's squared residuals.

Now we demonstrate how to use these estimates to predict the value of the time series in a particular period. Recall that t takes on a value of 1 in Period 1. Therefore, the predicted or fitted value of y_t in Period 1 is $\hat{y}_1 = \hat{b}_0 + \hat{b}_1(1)$. Similarly, in a subsequent period, say the sixth period, the fitted value is $\hat{y}_6 = \hat{b}_0 + \hat{b}_1(6)$. Now suppose that we want to predict the value of the time series for a period outside the sample, say period $T + 1$. The predicted value of y_t for period $T + 1$ is $\hat{y}_{T+1} = \hat{b}_0 + \hat{b}_1(T + 1)$. For example, if $\hat{b}_0$ is 5.1 and $\hat{b}_1$ is 2, then at $t = 5$ the predicted value of y_5 is 15.1 and at $t = 6$ the predicted value of y_6 is 17.1. Note that each consecutive observation in this time series increases by $\hat{b}_1 = 2$ irrespective of the level of the series in the previous period.

EXAMPLE 10-1   The Trend in the U.S. Consumer Price Index

It is January 2001. As a fixed income analyst in the trust department of a bank, Lisette Miller is concerned about the future level of inflation and how it might affect portfolio value. Therefore, she wants to predict future inflation rates. For this purpose, she first needs to estimate the linear trend in inflation. To do so, she uses the monthly U.S. Consumer Price Index (CPI) inflation data, expressed as an annual percentage rate,[3] shown in Figure 10-3. The data include 192 months from January 1985 to December 2000, and the model to be estimated is $y_t = b_0 + b_1 t + \epsilon_t, t = 1, 2, \ldots, 192$. Table 10-1 shows the results of estimating this equation. With 192 observations and two parameters, this model has 190 degrees of freedom. At the 0.05 significance level, the critical value for a t-statistic is 1.97. Both the intercept ($\hat{b}_0 = 4.1342$) and the trend coefficient ($\hat{b}_1 = -0.0095$) are statistically significant because the absolute values of t-statistics for both coefficients are well above the critical value. The estimated regression equation can be written as

$$y_t = 4.1342 - 0.0095t$$

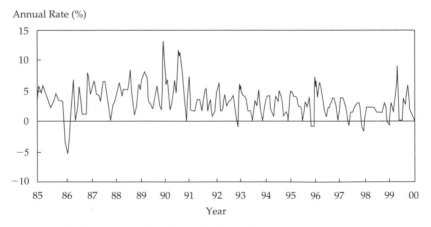

FIGURE 10-3   Monthly CPI Inflation, Not Seasonally Adjusted
Source: Bureau of Labor Statistics.

---

[3] In these data, 1 percent is represented as 1.0.

TABLE 10-1   Estimating a Linear Trend in Inflation
Monthly Observations, January 1985–December 2000

Regression Statistics		
R-squared	0.0408	
Standard error	2.5544	
Observations	192	
Durbin–Watson	1.38	

	Coefficient	Standard Error	t-Statistic
Intercept	4.1342	0.3701	11.1693
Trend	−0.0095	0.0033	−2.8445

Source: U.S. Bureau of Labor Statistics.

Because the trend line slope is estimated to be −0.0095, Miller concludes that the linear trend model's best estimate is that the annualized rate of inflation declined at a rate of about one one-hundredth of a percentage point per month during the sample time period.

In January 1985, the first month of the sample, the predicted value of inflation is $\hat{y}_1 = 4.1342 - 0.0095(1) = 4.1247$ percent. In December 2000, the 192nd or last month of the sample, the predicted value of inflation is $\hat{y}_{192} = 4.1342 - 0.0095(192) = 2.3177$ percent.[4] Note, though, that these predicted values are for in-sample periods. A comparison of these values with the actual values indicates how well Miller's model fits the data; however, a main purpose of the estimated model is to predict the level of inflation for out-of-sample periods. For example, for December 2001 (12 months after the end of the sample), $t = 192 + 12 = 204$, and the predicted level of inflation is $\hat{y}_{204} = 4.1342 - 0.0095(204) = 2.2041$ percent.

Annual Rate (%)

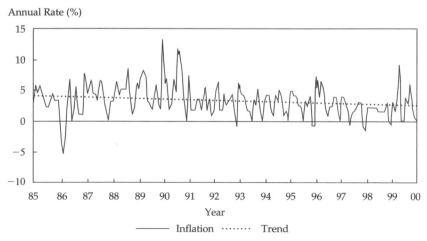

FIGURE 10-4   Monthly CPI Inflation with Trend
Source: U.S. Bureau of Labor Statistics.

---

[4]In reporting the final result (here, 2.3177), we use estimated regression coefficients without rounding; in stating the calculation, we use the regression coefficients with rounding, so carrying out the calculation with the rounded coefficients often results in slightly different answers.

Figure 10-4 shows the inflation data along with the fitted trend. Note that inflation does not appear to be above or below the trend line for a long period of time. No persistent differences exist between the trend and actual inflation. The residuals (actual minus trend values) appear to be unpredictable and uncorrelated in time. Therefore, it is reasonable to use a linear trend line to model inflation rates from 1985 through 2000. Furthermore, we can conclude that inflation has been steadily decreasing during that time period. Note also that the R^2 in this model is quite low, indicating great uncertainty in the inflation forecasts from this model. In fact, the trend explains only 4.08 percent of the variation in monthly inflation. Later in this chapter, we will examine whether we can build a better model of inflation than a model that uses only a trend line.

3.2. Log-Linear Trend Models

Sometimes a linear trend does not correctly model the growth of a time series. In those cases, we often find that fitting a linear trend to a time series leads to persistent rather than uncorrelated errors. If the residuals from a linear trend model are persistent, we then need to employ an alternative model satisfying the conditions of linear regression. For financial time series, an important alternative to a linear trend is a log-linear trend. Log-linear trends work well in fitting time series that have exponential growth.

Exponential growth means constant growth at a particular rate. So, annual growth at a constant rate of 5 percent is exponential because the series continues to increase without an upper bound. How does exponential growth work? Suppose we describe a time series by the following equation:

$$y_t = e^{b_0 + b_1 t}, \quad t = 1, 2, \ldots, T \tag{10-2}$$

Exponential growth is growth at a constant rate ($e^{b_1} - 1$) with continuous compounding. For instance, consider values of the time series in two consecutive periods. In Period 1, the time series has the value $y_1 = e^{b_0 + b_1(1)}$, and in Period 2, it has the value $y_2 = e^{b_0 + b_1(2)}$. The resulting ratio of the values of the time series in the first two periods is $y_2/y_1 = (e^{b_0 + b_1(2)})/(e^{b_0 + b_1(1)}) = e^{b_1(1)}$. Generally, in any period t, the time series has the value $y_t = e^{b_0 + b_1(t)}$. In period $t + 1$, the time series has the value $y_{t+1} = e^{b_0 + b_1(t+1)}$. The ratio of the values in the periods $(t + 1)$ and t is $y_{t+1}/y_t = e^{b_0 + b_1(t+1)}/e^{b_0 + b_1(t)} = e^{b_1(1)}$. Thus, the proportional rate of growth in the time series over two consecutive periods is always the same: $(y_{t+1} - y_t)/y_t = y_{t+1}/y_t - 1 = e^{b_1} - 1$.[5] Therefore, exponential growth is growth at a constant rate. Continuous compounding is a mathematical convenience that allows us to restate the equation in a form that is easy to estimate.

If we take the natural log of both sides of Equation 10-2, the result is the following equation:

$$\ln y_t = b_0 + b_1 t, \quad t = 1, 2, \ldots, T$$

Therefore, if a time series grows at an exponential rate, we can model the natural log of that series using a linear trend.[6] Of course, no time series grows exactly at an exponential rate.

---

[5]For example, if we use annual periods and $e^{b_1} = 1.04$ for a particular series, then that series grows by $1.04 - 1 = 0.04$, or 4 percent a year.

[6]An exponential growth rate is a compound growth rate with continuous compounding. We discussed continuous compounding in the chapter on the time value of money.

Consequently, if we want to use a **log-linear model**, we must estimate the following equation:

$$\ln y_t = b_0 + b_1 t + \epsilon_t, \quad t = 1, 2, \ldots, T \tag{10-3}$$

Note that this equation is linear in the coefficients b_0 and b_1. In contrast to a linear trend model, in which the predicted trend value of y_t is $\hat{b}_0 + \hat{b}_1 t$, the predicted trend value of y_t in a log-linear trend model is $e^{\hat{b}_0 + \hat{b}_1 t}$ because $e^{\ln y_t} = y_t$.

Examining Equation 10-3, we see that a log-linear model predicts that $\ln y_t$ will increase by b_1 from one time period to the next. The model predicts a constant growth rate in y_t of $e^{b_1} - 1$. For example, if $b_1 = 0.05$, then the predicted growth rate of y_t in each period is $e^{0.05} - 1 = 0.051271$ or 5.13 percent. In contrast, the linear trend model (Equation 10-1) predicts that y_t grows by a constant amount from one period to the next.

Example 10-2 illustrates the problem of nonrandom residuals in a linear trend model, and Example 10-3 shows a log-linear regression specification fit to the same data.

EXAMPLE 10-2   A Linear Trend Regression for Quarterly Sales at Intel

In January 2000, technology analyst Ray Benedict wants to use Equation 10-1 to fit the data on quarterly sales for Intel Corporation shown in Figure 10-5. He uses 60 observations on Intel's sales from the first quarter of 1985 to the fourth quarter of 1999 to estimate the linear trend regression model $y_t = b_0 + b_1 t + \epsilon_t, t = 1, 2, \ldots, 60$. Table 10-2 shows the results of estimating this equation.

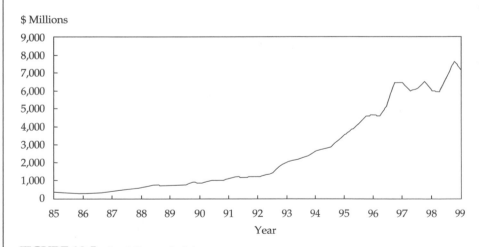

FIGURE 10-5   Intel Quarterly Sales
Source: Compustat.

At first glance, the results shown in Table 10-2 seem quite reasonable: Both the intercept and the trend coefficient are highly statistically significant. When Benedict plots the data on Intel's sales and the trend line, however, he sees a different picture. As Figure 10-6 shows, before 1989 the trend line is persistently below sales. Between 1989 and 1996, the trend line is persistently above sales, but after 1996, the trend line is once again persistently below sales.

TABLE 10-2   Estimating a Linear Trend in Intel Sales

Regression Statistics		
R-squared	0.8774	
Standard error	871.6858	
Observations	60	
Durbin–Watson	0.13	
	Coefficient	Standard Error	t-Statistic
Intercept	−1,318.7729	227.9585	−5.7852
Trend	132.4005	6.4994	20.3712

Source: Compustat.

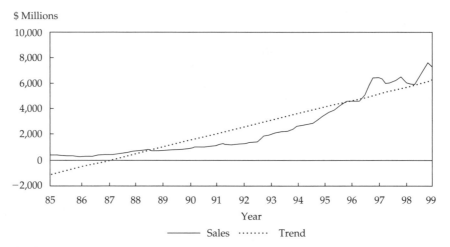

FIGURE 10-6   Intel Quarterly Sales with Trend
Source: Compustat.

Recall a key assumption underlying the regression model: that the regression errors are not correlated across observations. If a trend is persistently above or below the value of the time series, however, the residuals (the difference between the time series and the trend) are serially correlated. Figure 10-7 shows the residuals (the difference between sales and the trend) from estimating a linear trend model with the raw sales data. The figure shows that the residuals are persistent. Because of this persistent serial correlation in the errors of the trend model, using a linear trend to fit sales at Intel would be inappropriate, even though the R^2 of the equation is high (0.88). The assumption of uncorrelated residual errors has been violated. Because the dependent and independent variables are not distinct, as in cross-sectional regressions, this assumption violation is serious and causes us to search for a better model.

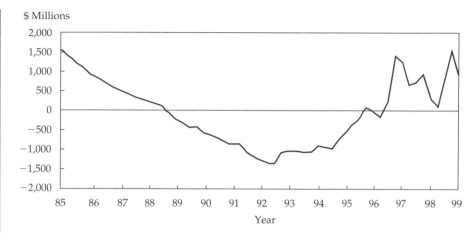

FIGURE 10-7   Residual from Predicting Intel Sales with a Trend
Source: Compustat.

EXAMPLE 10-3   A Log-Linear Regression for Quarterly Sales at Intel

Having rejected a linear trend model in Example 10-2, technology analyst Benedict now tries a different model for the quarterly sales for Intel Corporation from the first quarter of 1985 to the fourth quarter of 1999. The curvature in the data plot shown in Figure 10-5 is a hint that an exponential curve may fit the data. Consequently, he estimates the following linear equation:

$$\ln y_t = b_0 + b_1 t + \epsilon_t, \quad t = 1, 2, \ldots, 60$$

This equation seems to fit the sales data much better than did Equation 10-1. As Table 10-3 shows, the R^2 for this equation is 0.98 (the R^2 with Equation 10-1 was 0.88). An R^2 of 0.98 means that 98 percent of the variation in the natural log of Intel's sales is explained solely by a linear trend.

Figure 10-8 shows how well a linear trend fits the natural log of Intel's sales. The natural logs of the sales data lie very close to the linear trend during the sample period, and log sales are not above or below the trend for long periods of time. Thus, a log-linear trend model seems much better suited for modeling Intel's sales than does a linear trend model.

How can Benedict use the results of estimating Equation 10-3 to predict Intel's sales in the future? Suppose Benedict wants to predict Intel's sales for the first quarter of 2000 ($t = 61$). The estimated value $\hat{b}_0$ is 5.5529, and the estimated value $\hat{b}_1$ is 0.0609.

Therefore, the estimated model predicts that $\ln \hat{y}_{61} = 5.5529 + 0.0609(61) = 9.2673$ and that predicted sales are $\hat{y}_{61} = e^{\ln \hat{y}_{61}} = e^{9.2673} = \$10,585.63$ million.[7]

TABLE 10-3   Estimating a Linear Trend in Lognormal Intel Sales

Regression Statistics		
R-squared	0.9831	
Standard error	0.1407	
Observations	60	
Durbin–Watson	0.30	

	Coefficient	Standard Error	t-Statistic
Intercept	5.5529	0.0368	150.9809
Trend	0.0609	0.0010	58.0680

Source: Compustat.

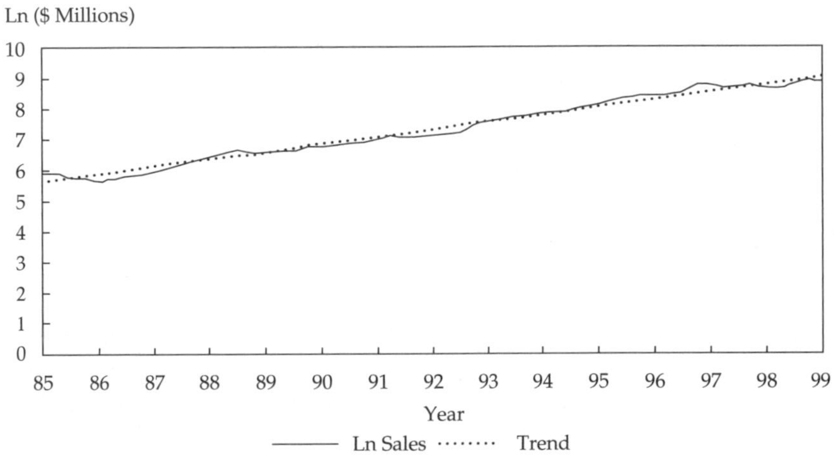

Ln ($ Millions)

FIGURE 10-8   Natural Log of Intel Quarterly Sales
Source: Compustat.

How much different is this forecast from the prediction of the linear trend model? Table 10-2 showed that for the linear trend model, the estimated value of $\hat{b}_0$ is -1318.7729 and the estimated value of $\hat{b}_1$ is 132.4005. Thus, if we predict Intel's sales for the first quarter of 2000 ($t = 61$) using the linear trend model, the forecast is $\hat{y}_{61} = -1318.7729 + 132.4005(61) = \$6,757.66$ million. This forecast is far below the prediction made by the log-linear regression model. Later in this chapter, we will examine whether we can build a better model of Intel's quarterly sales than a model that uses only a log-linear trend.

---

[7] Note that $\hat{b}_1 = 0.0609$ implies that the exponential growth rate per quarter in Intel's sales will be 6.28 percent ($e^{0.0609} - 1 = 0.062793$).

3.3. Trend Models and Testing for Correlated Errors

Both the linear trend model and the log-linear trend model are single-variable regression models. If they are to be correctly specified, the regression-model assumptions must be satisfied. In particular, the regression error for one period must be uncorrelated with the regression error for all other periods.[8] In Example 10-2 in the previous section, we could infer an obvious violation of that assumption from a visual inspection of a plot of residuals (Figure 10-7). The log-linear trend model of Example 10-3 appeared to fit the data much better, but we still need to confirm that the uncorrelated errors assumption is satisfied. To address that question formally, we must carry out a Durbin–Watson test on the residuals.

In the chapter on regression analysis, we showed how to test whether regression errors are serially correlated using the Durbin–Watson statistic. For example, if the trend models shown in Examples 10-1 and 10-3 really capture the time-series behavior of inflation and the log of Intel's sales, then the Durbin–Watson statistic for both of those models should not differ significantly from 2.0. Otherwise, the errors in the model are either positively or negatively serially correlated, and that correlation can be used to build a better forecasting model for those time series.

In Example 10-1, estimating a linear trend in the monthly CPI inflation yielded a Durbin–Watson statistic of 1.38. Is this result significantly different from 2.0? To find out, we need to test the null hypothesis of no positive serial correlation. For a sample with 192 observations and one independent variable, the critical value, d_l, for the Durbin–Watson test statistic at the 0.05 significance level is above 1.65. Because the value of the Durbin–Watson statistic (1.38) is below this critical value, we can reject the hypothesis of no positive serial correlation in the errors. We can conclude that a regression equation that uses a linear trend to model inflation has positive serial correlation in the errors.[9] We will need a different kind of regression model because this one violates the least-squares assumption of no serial correlation in the errors.

In Example 10-3, estimating a linear trend with the natural logarithm of sales for the Intel example yielded a Durbin–Watson statistic of 0.30. Suppose we wish to test the null hypothesis of no positive serial correlation. The critical value, d_l, is 1.55 at the 0.05 significance level. The value of the Durbin–Watson statistic (0.30) is below this critical value, so we can reject the null hypothesis of no positive serial correlation in the errors. We can conclude that a regression equation that uses a trend to model the log of Intel's quarterly sales has positive serial correlation in the errors. So, for this series as well, we need to build a different kind of model.

Overall, we conclude that the trend models sometimes have the limitation that errors are serially correlated. Existence of serial correlation suggests that we can build better forecasting models for such time series than trend models.

---

[8]Note that time-series observations, in contrast to cross-sectional observations, have a logical ordering: They must be processed in chronological order of the time periods involved. For example, we should not make a prediction of the inflation rate using a CPI series in which the order of the observations had been scrambled, because time patterns such as growth in the independent variables can negatively affect the statistical properties of the estimated regression coefficients.

[9]Significantly small values of the Durbin–Watson statistic indicate positive serial correlation; significantly large values point to negative serial correlation. Here the DW statistic of 1.38 indicates positive serial correlation. For more information, see the chapter on regression analysis.

4. AUTOREGRESSIVE (AR)
TIME-SERIES MODELS

A key feature of the log-linear model's depiction of time series and a key feature of time series in general is that current-period values are related to previous-period values. For example, Intel's sales for the current period are related to its sales in the previous period. An **autoregressive model** (AR), a time series regressed on its own past values, represents this relationship effectively. When we use this model, we can drop the normal notation of y as the dependent variable and x as the independent variable because we no longer have that distinction to make. Here we simply use x_t. For example, Equation 10-4 shows a first-order autoregression, AR(1), for the variable x_t:

$$x_t = b_0 + b_1 x_{t-1} + \epsilon_t \qquad (10\text{-}4)$$

Thus, in an AR(1) model, we use only the most recent past value of x_t to predict the current value of x_t. In general, a pth-order autoregression, AR(p), for the variable x_t is shown by

$$x_t = b_0 + b_1 x_{t-1} + b_2 x_{t-2} + \cdots + b_p x_{t-p} + \epsilon_t \qquad (10\text{-}5)$$

In this equation, p past values of x_t are used to predict the current value of x_t. In the next section we discuss a key assumption of time-series models that include lagged values of the dependent variable as independent variables.

4.1. Covariance-Stationary Series

Note that the independent variable (x_{t-1}) in Equation 10-4 is a random variable. This fact may seem like a mathematical subtlety, but it is not. If we use ordinary least squares to estimate Equation 10-4 when we have a randomly distributed independent variable that is a lagged value of the dependent variable, our statistical inference may be invalid. To conduct valid statistical inference, we must make a key assumption in time-series analysis: We must assume that the time series we are modeling is **covariance stationary**.[10]

What does it mean for a time series to be covariance stationary? The basic idea is that a time series is covariance stationary if its properties, such as mean and variance, do not change over time. A covariance stationary series must satisfy three principal requirements.[11] First, the expected value of the time series must be constant and finite in all periods: $E(y_t) = \mu$ and $|\mu| < \infty, t = 1, 2, \ldots, T$. Second, the variance of the time series must be constant and finite in all periods. Third, the covariance of the time series with itself for a fixed number of periods in the past or future must be constant and finite in all periods. The second and third requirements can be summarized as follows:[12]

$$\text{Cov}(y_t, y_{t-s}) = \lambda, |\lambda| < \infty, \quad t = 1, 2, \ldots, T; \quad s = 0, \pm 1, \pm 2, \ldots, \pm T$$

---

[10]"Weakly stationary" is a synonym for covariance stationary. Note that the terms "stationary" or "stationarity" are often used to mean "covariance stationary" or "covariance stationarity," respectively. You may also encounter the more restrictive concept of "strictly" stationary, which has little practical application. For details, see Diebold (2004).

[11]In the first requirement, we will use the absolute value to rule out the case in which the mean is negative without limit (minus infinity).

[12]When s in this equation equals 0, then this equation imposes the condition that the variance of the time series is finite. This is so because the covariance of a random variable with itself is its variance: $\text{Cov}(y_t, y_t) = \text{Var}(y_t)$.

where λ signifies a constant. What happens if a time series is not covariance stationary but we model it using Equation 10-4? The estimation results will have no economic meaning. For a non-covariance-stationary time series, estimating the regression in Equation 10-4 will yield spurious results. In particular, the estimate of b_1 will be biased and any hypothesis tests will be invalid.

How can we tell if a time series is covariance stationary? We can often answer this question by looking at a plot of the time series. If the plot shows roughly the same mean and variance through time without any significant seasonality, then we may want to assume that the time series is covariance stationary.

Some of the time series we looked at in Figures 10-1 to 10-4 appear to be covariance stationary. For example, the inflation data shown in Figure 10-3 appear to have roughly the same mean and variance over the sample period. Many of the time series one encounters in business and investments, however, are not covariance stationary. For example, many time series appear to grow (or decline) steadily through time and so have a mean that is nonconstant, which implies that they are nonstationary. As an example, the time series of Intel's quarterly sales in Figure 10-5 clearly shows the mean increasing as time passes. Thus Intel's quarterly sales are not covariance stationary.[13] Macroeconomic time series such as those relating to income and consumption are often strongly trending as well. A time series with seasonality (regular patterns of movement with the year) also has a nonconstant mean, as do other types of time series that we discuss later.[14]

Figure 10-2 showed that monthly retail sales (not seasonally adjusted) are also not covariance stationary. Sales in December are always much higher than sales in other months (these are the regular large peaks), and sales in January are always much lower (these are the regular large drops after the December peaks). On average, sales also increase over time, so the mean of sales is not constant.

Later in the chapter, we will show that we can often transform a nonstationary time series into a stationary time series. But whether a stationary time series is original or transformed, a caution applies: Stationarity in the past does not guarantee stationarity in the future. There is always the possibility that a well-specified model will fail when the state of the world changes and yields a different underlying model that generates the time series.

4.2. Detecting Serially Correlated Errors in an Autoregressive Model

We can estimate an autoregressive model using ordinary least squares if the time series is covariance stationary and the errors are uncorrelated. Unfortunately, our previous test for serial correlation, the Durbin–Watson statistic, is invalid when the independent variables include past values of the dependent variable. Therefore, for most time-series models, we cannot use the Durbin–Watson statistic. Fortunately, we can use other tests to determine whether the errors in a time-series model are serially correlated. One such test reveals whether the autocorrelations of the error term are significantly different from 0. This test is a *t*-test involving a residual autocorrelation and the standard error of the residual autocorrelation. As background for the test, we next discuss autocorrelation in general before moving to residual autocorrelation.

The **autocorrelations** of a time series are the correlations of that series with its own past values. The order of the correlation is given by k where k represents the number of periods

---

[13]In general, any time series accurately described with a linear or log-linear trend model is not covariance stationary, although a transformation of the original series might be covariance stationary.

[14]In particular, random walks are not covariance stationary.

lagged. When $k = 1$, the autocorrelation shows the correlation of the variable in one period to its occurrence in the previous period. For example, the **kth order autocorrelation (ρ_k)** is

$$\rho_k = \frac{\text{Cov}(x_t, x_{t-k})}{\sigma_x^2} = \frac{E(x_t - \mu)(x_{t-k} - \mu)]}{\sigma_x^2}$$

Note that we have the relationship $\text{Cov}(x_t, x_{t-k}) \leq \text{Var}(x_t)$ with equality holding when $k = 0$. This means that the absolute value of ρ_k is less than or equal to 1.

Of course, we can never directly observe the autocorrelations, ρ_k. Instead, we must estimate them. Thus we replace the expected value of x_t, μ, with its estimated value, $\bar{x}$, to compute the estimated autocorrelations. The kth order estimated autocorrelation of the time series x_t, which we denote $\hat{\rho}_k$, is

$$\hat{\rho}_k = \frac{\displaystyle\sum_{t=k+1}^{T} [(x_t - \bar{x})(x_{t-k} - \bar{x})]}{\displaystyle\sum_{t=1}^{T} (x_t - \bar{x})^2}$$

Analogous to the definition of autocorrelations for a time series, we can define the autocorrelations of the error term for a time-series model as[15]

$$\rho_{\epsilon,k} = \frac{\text{Cov}(\epsilon_t, \epsilon_{t-k})}{\sigma_\epsilon^2}$$

$$= \frac{E[(\epsilon_t - 0)(\epsilon_{t-k} - 0)]}{\sigma_\epsilon^2}$$

$$= \frac{E(\epsilon_t \epsilon_{t-k})}{\sigma_\epsilon^2}$$

where E stands for the expected value. We assume that the expected value of the error term in a time-series model is 0.[16]

We can determine whether we are using the correct time-series model by testing whether the autocorrelations of the error term (**error autocorrelations**) differ significantly from 0. If they do, the model is not specified correctly. We estimate the error autocorrelation using the sample autocorrelations of the residuals (**residual autocorrelations**) and their sample variance.

A test of the null hypothesis that an error autocorrelation at a specified lag equals 0 is based on the residual autocorrelation for that lag and the standard error of the residual correlation, which is equal to $1/\sqrt{T}$, where T is the number of observations in the time series.[17] Thus, if we have 100 observations in a time series, the standard error for each of the estimated autocorrelations is 0.1. We can compute the t-test of the null hypothesis that the error correlation at a particular lag equals 0, by dividing the residual autocorrelation at that lag by its standard error ($1/\sqrt{T}$).

---

[15]Whenever we refer to autocorrelation without qualification, we mean autocorrelation of the time series itself rather than autocorrelation of the error term or residuals.

[16]This assumption is similar to the one made in the previous two chapters about the expected value of the error term.

[17]This calculation is derived in Diebold (2004).

How can we use information about the error autocorrelations to determine whether an autoregressive time-series model is correctly specified? We can use a simple three-step method. First, estimate a particular autoregressive model, say an AR(1) model. Second, compute the autocorrelations of the residuals from the model.[18] Third, test to see whether the residual autocorrelations differ significantly from 0. If significance tests show that the residual autocorrelations differ significantly from 0, the model is not correctly specified; we may need to modify it in ways that we will discuss shortly.[19] We now present an example to demonstrate how this three-step method works.

EXAMPLE 10-4   Predicting Gross Margins for Intel Corporation

Having investigated the time-series modeling of Intel Corporation's sales, analyst Ray Benedict decides to use a time-series model to predict Intel's gross margin [(Sales − Cost of goods sold)/Sales]. His observations on the dependent variable are 2Q:1985 through 4Q:1999. He does not know the best model for gross margin but believes that the current-period value will be related to the previous-period value. He decides to start out with a first-order autoregressive model, AR(1): Gross margin$_t = b_0 + b_1$(Gross margin$_{t-1}$) $+ \epsilon_t$. Table 10-4 shows the results of estimating this AR(1) model, along with the autocorrelations of the residuals from that model.

The first thing to note about Table 10-4 is that both the intercept ($\hat{b}_0 = 0.0834$) and the coefficient on the first lag ($\hat{b}_1 = 0.8665$) of the gross margin are highly significant in the regression equation.[20] The t-statistic for the intercept is about 2.3, whereas the t-statistic for the first lag of the gross margin is more than 14. With 59 observations and two parameters, this model has 57 degrees of freedom. At the 0.05 significance level, the critical value for a t-statistic is about 2.0. Therefore, Benedict must reject the null hypotheses that the intercept is equal to 0 ($b_0 = 0$) and the coefficient on the first lag is equal to 0 ($b_1 = 0$) in favor of the alternative hypothesis that the coefficients, individually, are not equal to 0. But are these statistics valid? We will know when we test whether the residuals from this model are serially correlated.

At the bottom of Table 10-4, the first four autocorrelations of the residual are displayed along with the standard error and the t-statistic for each of those autocorrelations.[21] The sample has 59 observations, so the standard error for each of the

---

[18]We can compute these residual autocorrelations easily with most statistical software packages. In Microsoft Excel, for example, to compute the first-order residual autocorrelation, we compute the correlation of the residuals from observations 1 through $T - 1$ with the residuals from observations 2 through T.

[19]Often, econometricians use additional tests for the significance of residual autocorrelations. For example, the Box–Pierce Q-statistic is frequently used to test the joint hypothesis that all autocorrelations of the residuals are equal to 0. For further discussion, see Diebold (2004).

[20]The first lag of a time series is the value of the time series in the previous period.

[21]For seasonally unadjusted data, analysts often compute the same number of autocorrelations as there are observations in a year (for example, four for quarterly data). The number of autocorrelations computed also often depends on sample size, as discussed in Diebold (2004).

autocorrelations is $1/\sqrt{59} = 0.1302$. Table 10-4 shows that none of the first four auto-correlations has a t-statistic larger than 1.50 in absolute value. Therefore, Benedict can conclude that none of these autocorrelations differs significantly from 0. Consequently, he can assume that the residuals are not serially correlated and that the model is correctly specified, and he can validly use ordinary least squares to estimate the parameters and the parameters' standard errors in the autoregressive model.[22]

Now that Benedict has concluded that this model is correctly specified, how can he use it to predict Intel's gross margin in the next period? The estimated equation is Gross margin$_t = 0.0834 + 0.8665$(Gross margin$_{t-1}$) $+ \epsilon_t$. The expected value of the error term is 0 in any period. Therefore, this model predicts that gross margin in period $t + 1$ will be Gross margin$_{t+1} = 0.0834 + 0.8665$(Gross margin$_t$). For example, if gross margin is 55 percent in this quarter (0.55), the model predicts that in the next quarter gross margin will increase to $0.0834 + 0.8665(0.55) = 0.5600$ or 56.0 percent. On the other hand, if gross margin is currently 65 percent (0.65), the model predicts that in the next quarter, gross margin will fall to $0.0834 + 0.8665(0.65) = 0.6467$ or 64.67 percent. As we show in the following section, the model predicts that gross margin will increase if it is below a certain level (62.50 percent) and decrease if it is above that level.

TABLE 10-4　Autoregression: AR(1) Model Gross Margin of Intel Quarterly Observations, April 1985–December 1999

Regression Statistics			
R-squared	0.7784		
Standard error	0.0402		
Observations	59		
Durbin–Watson	1.8446		
	Coefficient	Standard Error	t-Statistic
Intercept	0.0834	0.0367	2.2705
Lag 1	0.8665	0.0612	14.1493
Autocorrelations of the Residual			
Lag	Autocorrelation	Standard Error	t-Statistic
1	0.0677	0.1302	0.5197
2	−0.1929	0.1302	−1.4814
3	0.0541	0.1302	0.4152
4	−0.1498	0.1302	−1.1507

Source: Compustat.

---

[22]Statisticians have many other tests for serial correlation of the residuals in a time-series model. For details, see Diebold (2004).

4.3. Mean Reversion

We say that a time series shows **mean reversion** if it tends to fall when its level is above its mean and rise when its level is below its mean. Much like the temperature in a room controlled by a thermostat, a mean-reverting time series tends to return to its long-term mean. How can we determine the value that the time series tends toward? If a time series is currently at its mean-reverting level, then the model predicts that the value of the time series will be the same in the next period. At its mean-reverting level, we have the relationship $x_{t+1} = x_t$. For an AR(1) model $(x_{t+1} = b_0 + b_1 x_t)$, the equality $x_{t+1} = x_t$ implies the level $x_t = b_0 + b_1 x_t$, or that the mean-reverting level, x_t, is given by

$$x_t = \frac{b_0}{1 - b_1}$$

So the AR(1) model predicts that the time series will stay the same if its current value is $b_0/(1 - b_1)$, increase if its current value is below $b_0/(1 - b_1)$, and decrease if its current value is above $b_0/(1 - b_1)$.

In the case of gross margins for Intel, the mean-reverting level for the model shown in Table 10-4 is $0.0834/(1 - 0.8665) = 0.6250$. If the current gross margin is above 0.6250, the model predicts that the gross margin will fall in the next period. If the current gross margin is below 0.6250, the model predicts that the gross margin will rise in the next period. As we will discuss later, all covariance-stationary time series have a finite mean-reverting level.

4.4. Multiperiod Forecasts and the Chain Rule of Forecasting

Often, financial analysts want to make forecasts for more than one period. For example, we might want to use a quarterly sales model to predict sales for a company for each of the next four quarters. To use a time-series model to make forecasts for more than one period, we must examine how to make multiperiod forecasts using an AR(1) model. The one-period-ahead forecast of x_t from an AR(1) model is as follows:

$$\hat{x}_{t+1} = \hat{b}_0 + \hat{b}_1 x_t \tag{10-6}$$

If we want to forecast x_{t+2} using an AR(1) model, our forecast will be based on

$$\hat{x}_{t+2} = \hat{b}_0 + \hat{b}_1 x_{t+1} \tag{10-7}$$

Unfortunately, we do not know x_{t+1} in period t, so we cannot use Equation 10-7 directly to make a two-period-ahead forecast. We can, however, use our forecast of x_{t+1} and the AR(1) model to make a prediction of x_{t+2}. The **chain rule of forecasting** is a process in which the next period's value, predicted by the forecasting equation, is substituted into the equation to give a predicted value two periods ahead. Using the chain rule of forecasting, we can substitute the predicted value of x_{t+1} into Equation 10-7 to get $\hat{x}_{t+2} = \hat{b}_0 + \hat{b}_1 \hat{x}_{t+1}$. We already know $\hat{x}_{t+1}$ from our one-period-ahead forecast in Equation 10-6. Now we have a simple way of predicting x_{t+2}.

Multiperiod forecasts are more uncertain than single-period forecasts because each forecast period has uncertainty. For example, in forecasting x_{t+2}, we first have the uncertainty associated with forecasting x_{t+1} using x_t, and then we have the uncertainty associated with forecasting

x_{t+2} using the forecast of x_{t+1}. In general, the more periods a forecast has, the more uncertain it is.[23]

EXAMPLE 10-5   Multiperiod Prediction of Intel's Gross Margin

Suppose that at the beginning of 2000, we want to predict Intel's gross margin in two periods using the model shown in Table 10-4. Assume that Intel's gross margin in the current period is 65 percent. The one-period-ahead forecast of Intel's gross margin from this model is $0.6467 = 0.0834 + 0.8665(0.65)$. By substituting the one-period-ahead forecast, 0.6467, back into the regression equation, we can derive the following two-period-ahead forecast: $0.6438 = 0.0834 + 0.8665(0.6467)$. Therefore, if the current gross margin for Intel is 65 percent, the model predicts that Intel's gross margin in two quarters will be 64.38 percent.

EXAMPLE 10-6   Modeling U.S. CPI Inflation

Analyst Lisette Miller has been directed to build a time-series model for monthly U.S. inflation. Inflation and expectations about inflation, of course, have a significant effect on bond returns. Beginning with January 1971, she selects as data the annualized monthly percentage change in the CPI. Which model should Miller use?

The process of model selection parallels that of Example 10-4 relating to Intel's gross margins. The first model Miller estimates is an AR(1) model, using the previous month's inflation rate as the independent variable: Inflation$_t = b_0 + b_1$ Inflation$_{t-1} + \epsilon_t, t = 1, 2, \ldots, 359$. To estimate this model, she uses monthly CPI inflation data from January 1971 to December 2000 ($t = 1$ denotes February 1971). Table 10-5 shows the results of estimating this model.

As Table 10-5 shows, both the intercept ($\hat{b}_0 = 1.9658$) and the coefficient on the first lagged value of inflation ($\hat{b}_1 = 0.6175$) are highly statistically significant, with large t-statistics. With 359 observations and two parameters, this model has 357 degrees of freedom. The critical value for a t-statistic at the 0.05 significance level is about 1.97. Therefore, Miller can reject the individual null hypotheses that the intercept is equal to 0 ($b_0 = 0$) and the coefficient on the first lag is equal to 0 ($b_1 = 0$) in favor of the alternative hypothesis that the coefficients, individually, are not equal to 0.

Are these statistics valid? Miller will know when she tests whether the residuals from this model are serially correlated. With 359 observations in this sample, the

---

[23]If a forecasting model is well specified, the prediction errors from the model will not be serially correlated. If the prediction errors for each period are not serially correlated, then the variance of a multiperiod forecast will be higher than the variance of a single-period forecast.

TABLE 10-5   Monthly CPI Inflation at an Annual Rate: AR(1) Model
Monthly Observations, February 1971–December 2000

Regression Statistics			
R-squared	0.3808		
Standard error	3.4239		
Observations	359		
Durbin–Watson	2.3059		

	Coefficient	Standard Error	t-Statistic
Intercept	1.9658	0.2803	7.0119
Lag 1	0.6175	0.0417	14.8185

Autocorrelations of the Residual			
Lag	Autocorrelation	Standard Error	t-Statistic
1	−0.1538	0.0528	−2.9142
2	0.1097	0.0528	2.0782
3	0.0657	0.0528	1.2442
4	0.0920	0.0528	1.7434

Source: U.S. Bureau of Labor Statistics.

standard error for each of the estimated autocorrelations is $1/\sqrt{359} = 0.0528$. The critical value for the *t*-statistic is 1.97. Because both the first and the second estimated autocorrelation have *t*-statistics larger than 1.97 in absolute value, Miller concludes that the autocorrelations are significantly different from 0. This model is thus misspecified because the residuals are serially correlated.

If the residuals in an autoregressive model are serially correlated, Miller can eliminate the correlation by estimating an autoregressive model with more lags of the dependent variable as explanatory variables. Table 10-6 shows the result of estimating a second time-series model, an AR(2) model using the same data as in the analysis shown in Table 10-5.[24] With 358 observations and three parameters, this model has 355 degrees of freedom. Because the degrees of freedom are almost the same as those for the estimates shown in Table 10-5, the critical value of the *t*-statistic at the 0.05 significance level also is almost the same (1.97). If she estimates the equation with two lags, $\text{Inflation}_t = b_0 + b_1 \text{Inflation}_{t-1} + b_2 \text{Inflation}_{t-2} + \epsilon_t$, Miller finds that all three of the coefficients in the regression model (an intercept and the coefficients on two lags of the dependent variable) differ significantly from 0. The bottom portion of Table 10-6 shows that none of the first four autocorrelations of the residual has a *t*-statistic greater in absolute value than the critical value of 1.97. Therefore, Miller fails to reject the hypothesis that the individual autocorrelations of the residual are significantly different from 0. She concludes that this model is correctly specified because she finds no evidence of serial correlation in the residuals.

---

[24]Note that Table 10-6 shows only 358 observations in the regression because the extra lag of inflation requires the estimation sample to start one month later than the regression in Table 10-5. (With two lags, inflation for January and February 1971 must be known in order to estimate the equation starting in March 1971.)

TABLE 10-6   Monthly CPI Inflation at an Annual Rate: AR(2) Model
Monthly Observations, March 1971–December 2000

Regression Statistics		
Multiple R	0.6479	
R-squared	0.4197	
Standard error	3.3228	
Observations	358	
Durbin–Watson	2.0582	

	Coefficient	Standard Error	t-Statistic
Intercept	1.4609	0.2913	5.0147
Lag 1	0.4634	0.0514	9.0117
Lag 2	0.2515	0.0514	4.8924

Autocorrelations of the Residual			
Lag	Autocorrelation	Standard Error	t-Statistic
1	−0.0320	0.0529	−0.6048
2	−0.0982	0.0529	−1.8574
3	−0.0114	0.0529	−0.2150
4	0.0320	0.0529	0.6053

Source: U.S. Bureau of Labor Statistics.

In the previous example, the analyst selected an AR(2) model because the residuals from the AR(1) model were serially correlated. Suppose that in a given month, inflation had been 4 percent at an annual rate in the previous month and 3 percent in the month before that. The AR(1) model shown in Table 10-5 predicted that inflation in the next month would be $1.9658 + 0.6175(4) = 4.44$ percent approximately, whereas the AR(2) model shown in Table 10-6 predicts that inflation in the next month will be $1.4609 + 0.4634(4) + 0.2515(3) = 4.07$ percent approximately. If the analyst had used the incorrect AR(1) model, she would have predicted inflation to be 37 basis points higher (4.44 percent versus 4.07 percent) than using the AR(2) model. This incorrect forecast could have adversely affected the quality of her company's investment choices.

4.5. Comparing Forecast Model Performance

One way to compare the forecast performance of two models is to compare the variance of the forecast errors that the two models make. The model with the smaller forecast error variance will be the more accurate model, and it will also have the smaller standard error of the time-series regression. (This standard error usually is reported directly in the output for the time-series regression.)

In comparing forecast accuracy among models, we must distinguish between in-sample forecast errors and out-of-sample forecast errors. **In-sample forecast errors** are the residuals from a fitted time-series model. For example, when we estimated a linear trend with raw inflation data from January 1971 to December 2000, the in-sample forecast errors were the residuals from January 1971 to December 2000. If we use this model to predict inflation outside this period, the differences between actual and predicted inflation are **out-of-sample forecast errors**.

EXAMPLE 10-7   In-Sample Forecast Comparisons of U.S. CPI Inflation

In Example 10-6, the analyst compared an AR(1) forecasting model of monthly U.S. inflation with an AR(2) model of monthly U.S. inflation and decided that the AR(2) model was preferable. Table 10-5 showed that the standard error from the AR(1) model of inflation is 3.4239, and Table 10-6 showed that the standard error from the AR(2) model is 3.3228. Therefore, the AR(2) model had a lower in-sample forecast error variance than the AR(1) model, which is consistent with our belief that the AR(2) model was preferable. Its standard error is 3.3228/3.4239 = 97.05 percent of the forecast error of the AR(1) model.

Often, we want to compare the forecasting accuracy of different models after the sample period for which they were estimated. We wish to compare the out-of-sample forecast accuracy of the models. Out-of-sample forecast accuracy is important because the future is always out of sample. Although professional forecasters distinguish between out-of-sample and in-sample forecasting performance, many articles that analysts read contain only in-sample forecast evaluations. Analysts should be aware that out-of-sample performance is critical for evaluating a forecasting model's real-world contribution.

Typically, we compare the out-of-sample forecasting performance of forecasting models by comparing their **root mean squared error** (RMSE), which is the square root of the average squared error. The model with the smallest RMSE is judged most accurate. The following example illustrates the computation and use of RMSE in comparing forecasting models.

EXAMPLE 10-8   Out-of-Sample Forecast Comparisons of U.S. CPI Inflation

Suppose we want to compare the forecasting accuracy of the AR(1) and AR(2) models of U.S. inflation estimated over 1971 to 2000, using data on U.S. inflation from January 2001 to December 2002.

For each month from January 2001 to December 2002, the first column of numbers in Table 10-7 shows the actual annualized inflation rate during the month. The second and third columns show the rate of inflation in the previous two months. The fourth column shows the out-of-sample errors from the AR(1) model shown in Table 10-5. The fifth column shows the squared errors from the AR(1) model. The sixth column shows the out-of-sample errors from the AR(2) model shown in Table 10-6. The final

TABLE 10-7 Out-of-Sample Forecast Error Comparisons: January 2001–December 2002 U.S. CPI Inflation (annualized)

Date	Infl(t)	Infl(t − 1)	Infl(t − 2)	AR(1) Error	Squared Error	AR(2) Error	Squared Error
2001							
January	7.8556	−0.6871	0.6918	6.3141	39.8681	6.5392	42.7611
February	4.9042	7.8556	−0.6871	−1.9122	3.6564	−0.0242	0.0006
March	2.7648	4.9042	7.8556	−2.2291	4.9689	−2.9440	8.6669
April	4.8729	2.7648	4.9042	1.1999	1.4399	0.8976	0.8058
May	5.5638	4.8729	2.7648	0.5892	0.3472	1.1497	1.3217
June	2.0448	5.5638	4.8729	−3.3564	11.2656	−3.2196	10.3660
July	−3.3192	2.0448	5.5638	−6.5475	42.8703	−7.1267	50.7892
August	0.0000	−3.3192	2.0448	0.0837	0.0070	−0.4369	0.1909
September	5.5446	0.0000	−3.3192	3.5788	12.8078	4.9183	24.1899
October	−3.9642	5.5446	0.0000	−9.3536	87.4891	−7.9944	63.9110
November	−2.0072	−3.9642	5.5446	−1.5252	2.3261	−3.0252	9.1519
December	−4.6336	−2.0072	−3.9642	−5.3600	28.7299	−4.1675	17.3685
2002							
January	2.7505	−4.6336	−2.0072	3.6459	13.2927	3.9416	15.5365
February	4.8476	2.7505	−4.6336	1.1834	1.4005	3.2772	10.7404
March	6.9619	4.8476	2.7505	2.0029	4.0118	2.5630	6.5692
April	6.9218	6.9619	4.8476	0.6573	0.4320	1.0158	1.0319
May	0.0000	6.9218	6.9619	−6.2397	38.9339	−6.4190	41.2034
June	0.6695	0.0000	6.9218	−1.2963	1.6804	−2.5319	6.4105
July	1.3423	0.6695	0.0000	−1.0369	1.0751	−0.4288	0.1839
August	4.0719	1.3423	0.6695	1.2773	1.6315	1.8207	3.3148
September	2.0105	4.0719	1.3423	−2.4694	6.0981	−1.6747	2.8047
October	2.0072	2.0105	4.0719	−1.2000	1.4400	−1.4092	1.9860
November	0.0000	2.0072	2.0105	−3.2051	10.2728	−2.8965	8.3900
December	−2.6157	0.0000	2.0072	−4.5814	20.9893	−4.5812	20.9876
				Average	14.0431	Average	14.5284
				RMSE	3.7474	RMSE	3.8116

Source: U.S. Bureau of Labor Statistics.

column shows the squared errors from the AR(2) model. The bottom of the table displays the average squared error and the RMSE. According to these measures, the AR(1) model was slightly more accurate than the AR(2) model in its out-of-sample forecasts of inflation from January 2001 to December 2002. The RMSE from the AR(1) model was only $3.7474/3.8116 = 98.32$ percent as large as the RMSE from the AR(2) model. Therefore, even though the AR(2) model was more accurate in-sample, the AR(1) model was slightly more accurate out of sample. Of course, this was a small sample to use in evaluating out-of-sample forecasting performance. Although we seem to have conflicting information about whether to choose an AR(1) or an AR(2) model here, we must also consider regression coefficient stability. We will continue the comparison between these two models in the following section.

4.6. Instability of Regression Coefficients

One of the important issues an analyst faces in modeling a time series is the sample period to use. The estimates of regression coefficients of the time-series model can change substantially across different sample periods used for estimating the model. Often, the regression coefficient estimates of a time-series model estimated using an earlier sample period can be quite different from those of a model estimated using a later sample period. Similarly, the estimates can be different between models estimated using relatively shorter and longer sample periods. Further, the choice of model for a particular time series can also depend on the sample period. For example, an AR(1) model may be appropriate for the sales of a company in one particular sample period, but an AR(2) model may be necessary for an earlier or later sample period (or for a longer or shorter sample period). Thus the choice of a sample period is an important decision in modeling a financial time series.

Unfortunately, there is usually no clear-cut basis in economic or financial theory for determining whether to use data from a longer or shorter sample period to estimate a time-series model. We can get some guidance, however, if we remember that our models are valid only for covariance-stationary time series. For example, we should not combine data from a period when exchange rates were fixed with data from a period when exchange rates were floating. The exchange rates in these two periods would not likely have the same variance because exchange rates are usually much more volatile under a floating-rate regime than when rates are fixed. Similarly, many U.S. analysts consider it inappropriate to model U.S. inflation or interest-rate behavior since the 1960s as a part of one sample period, because the Federal Reserve had distinct policy regimes during this period. The best way to determine appropriate samples for time-series estimation is to look at graphs of the data to see if the time series looks stationary before estimation begins. If we know that a government policy changed on a specific date, we might also test whether the time-series relation was the same before and after that date.

In the following example, we illustrate how the choice of a longer versus a shorter period can affect the decision of whether to use, for example, a first- or second-order time-series model. We then show how the choice of the time-series model (and the associated regression coefficients) affects our forecast. Finally, we discuss which sample period, and accordingly which model and corresponding forecast, is appropriate for the time series analyzed in the example.

EXAMPLE 10-9   Instability in Time-Series Models of U.S. Inflation

In Example 10-6, analyst Lisette Miller concluded that U.S. CPI inflation should be modeled as an AR(2) time series. A colleague examined her results and questioned estimating one time-series model for inflation in the United States since 1971, given that Federal Reserve policy changed dramatically in the late 1970s and early 1980s. He argues that the inflation time series from 1971 to 2000 has two **regimes** or underlying models generating the time series: one running from 1971 through 1984, and another starting in 1985. Therefore, the colleague suggests that Miller estimate a new time-series model for U.S. inflation starting in 1985. Because of his suggestion, Miller first estimates an AR(1) model for inflation using data for a shorter sample period from 1985 to 2000. Table 10-8 shows her AR(1) estimates.

The bottom part of Table 10-8 shows that the first four autocorrelations of the residuals from the AR(1) model are quite small. None of these autocorrelations has a t-statistic larger than 1.97, the critical value for significance. Consequently, Miller cannot reject the null hypothesis that the residuals are serially uncorrelated. The AR(1) model is correctly specified for the sample period from 1985 to 2000, so there is no need to estimate the AR(2) model. This conclusion is very different from that reached in Example 10-6 using data from 1971 to 2000. In that example, Miller initially rejected the AR(1) model because its residuals exhibited serial correlation. When she used a larger sample, an AR(2) model initially appeared to fit the data much better than did an AR(1) model.

TABLE 10-8   Autoregression: AR(1) Model Monthly CPI Inflation at an Annual Rate February 1985–December 2000

Regression Statistics			
R-squared	0.1540		
Standard error	2.4641		
Observations	191		
Durbin–Watson	1.9182		

	Coefficient	Standard Error	t-Statistic
Intercept	2.1371	0.2859	7.4747
Lag 1	0.3359	0.0690	4.8716

Autocorrelations of the Residual			
Lag	Autocorrelation	Standard Error	t-Statistic
1	0.0284	0.0724	0.3922
2	−0.0900	0.0724	−1.2426
3	−0.0141	0.0724	−0.1955
4	−0.0297	0.0724	−0.4103

Source: U.S. Bureau of Labor Statistics.

How deeply does our choice of sample period affect our forecast of future inflation? Suppose that in a given month, inflation was 4 percent at an annual rate, and the month before that it was 3 percent. The AR(1) model shown in Table 10-8 predicts that inflation in the next month will be $2.1371 + 0.3359(4) =$ approximately 3.48 percent. Therefore, the forecast of the next month's inflation using the 1985 to 2000 sample is 3.48 percent. Remember from the analysis following Example 10-6 that the AR(2) model for the 1971 to 2000 sample predicts inflation of 4.07 percent in the next month. Thus, using the correctly specified model for the shorter sample produces an inflation forecast almost 0.6 percentage points below the forecast made from the correctly specified model for the longer sample period. Such a difference might substantially affect a particular investment decision.

Which model is correct? Figure 10-9 suggests an answer. Monthly U.S. inflation was, on average, so much higher and so much more volatile during the mid-1970s to early 1980s than it was after 1984 that inflation is probably not a covariance-stationary time series from 1971 to 2000. Therefore, we can reasonably believe that the data have more than one regime and Miller should estimate a separate model for inflation from 1985 to 2000, as shown above. As the example shows, judgment and experience (such as knowledge of government policy changes) play a vital role in determining how to model a time series. Simply relying on autocorrelations of the residuals from a time-series model cannot tell us the correct sample period for our analysis.

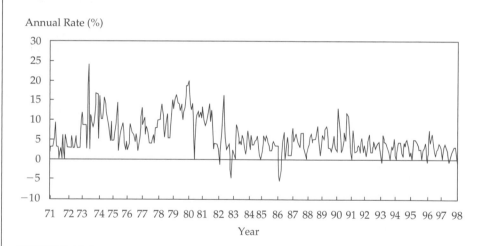

FIGURE 10-9   Monthly CPI Inflation
Source: U.S. Bureau of Labor Statistics.

5. RANDOM WALKS AND UNIT ROOTS

So far, we have examined those time series in which the time series has a tendency to revert to its mean level as the change in a variable from one period to the next follows a mean-reverting pattern. In contrast, there are many financial time series in which the changes follow a random pattern. We discuss these "random walks" in the following section.

5.1. Random Walks

A random walk is one of the most widely studied time-series models for financial data. A **random walk** is a time series in which the value of the series in one period is the value of the series in the previous period plus an unpredictable random error. A random walk can be described by the following equation:

$$x_t = x_{t-1} + \epsilon_t, E(\epsilon_t) = 0, E(\epsilon_t^2) = \sigma^2, E(\epsilon_t \epsilon_s) = 0 \text{ if } t \neq s \qquad (10\text{-}8)$$

Equation 10-8 means that the time series x_t is in every period equal to its value in the previous period plus an error term, ϵ_t, that has constant variance and is uncorrelated with the error term in previous periods. Note two important points. First, this equation is a special case of an AR(1) model with $b_0 = 0$ and $b_1 = 1$.[25] Second, the expected value of ϵ_t is zero. Therefore, the best forecast of x_t that can be made in period $t - 1$ is x_{t-1}. In fact, in this model, x_{t-1} is the best forecast of x in every period after $t - 1$.

Random walks are quite common in financial time series. For example, many studies have tested and found that currency exchange rates follow a random walk. Consistent with the second point made above, some studies have found that sophisticated exchange rate forecasting models cannot outperform forecasts made using the random walk model, and that the best forecast of the future exchange rate is the current exchange rate.

Unfortunately, we cannot use the regression methods we have discussed so far to estimate an AR(1) model on a time series that is actually a random walk. To see why this is so, we must determine why a random walk has no finite mean-reverting level or finite variance. Recall that if x_t is at its mean-reverting level, then $x_t = b_0 + b_1 x_t$, or $x_t = b_0/(1 - b_1)$. In a random walk, however, $b_0 = 0$ and $b_1 = 1$, so $b_0/(1 - b_1) = 0/0$. Therefore, a random walk has an undefined mean-reverting level.

What is the variance of a random walk? Suppose that in Period 1, the value of x_1 is 0. Then we know that $x_2 = 0 + \epsilon_2$. Therefore, the variance of $x_2 = \text{Var}(\epsilon_2) = \sigma^2$. Now $x_3 = x_2 + \epsilon_3 = \epsilon_2 + \epsilon_3$. Because the error term in each period is assumed to be uncorrelated with the error terms in all other periods, the variance of $x_3 = \text{Var}(\epsilon_2) + \text{Var}(\epsilon_3) = 2\sigma^2$. By a similar argument, we can show that for any period t, the variance of $x_t = (t - 1)\sigma^2$. But this means that as t grows large, the variance of x_t grows without an upper bound: It approaches infinity. This lack of upper bound, in turn, means that a random walk is not a covariance-stationary time series, because a covariance-stationary time series must have a finite variance.

What is the practical implication of these issues? *We cannot use standard regression analysis on a time series that is a random walk.* We can, however, attempt to convert the data to a covariance-stationary time series if we suspect that the time series is a random walk. In statistical terms, we can difference it.

We difference a time series by creating a new time series, say y_t, that in each period is equal to the difference between x_t and x_{t-1}. This transformation is called **first-differencing** because it subtracts the value of the time series in the first prior period from the current value of the time series. Sometimes the first difference of x_t is written as $\Delta x_t = x_t - x_{t-1}$. Note that the first difference of the random walk in Equation 10-8 yields

$$y_t = x_t - x_{t-1} = \epsilon_t, \quad E(\epsilon_t) = 0, \quad E(\epsilon_t^2) = \sigma^2, \quad E(\epsilon_t \epsilon_s) = 0 \text{ for } t \neq s$$

---

[25]Equation 10-8 with a nonzero intercept added (as in Equation 10-9 given later) is sometimes referred to as a random walk with drift.

The expected value of ϵ_t is 0. Therefore, the best forecast of y_t that can be made in period $t - 1$ is 0. This implies that the best forecast is that there will be no change in the value of the current time series, x_{t-1}.

The first-differenced variable, y_t, is covariance stationary. How is this so? First, note that this model ($y_t = \epsilon_t$) is an AR(1) model with $b_0 = 0$ and $b_1 = 0$. We can compute the mean-reverting level of the first-differenced model as $b_0/(1 - b_1) = 0/1 = 0$. Therefore, a first-differenced random walk has a mean-reverting level of 0. Note also that the variance of y_t in each period is $\text{Var}(\epsilon_t) = \sigma^2$. Because the variance and the mean of y_t are constant and finite in each period, y_t is a covariance-stationary time series and we can model it using linear regression.[26] Of course, modeling the first-differenced series with an AR(1) model does not help us predict the future, as $b_0 = 0$ and $b_1 = 0$. We simply conclude that the original time series is, in fact, a random walk.

Had we tried to estimate an AR(1) model for a time series that was a random walk, our statistical conclusions would have been incorrect because AR models cannot be used to estimate random walks or any time series that is not covariance stationary. The following example illustrates this issue with exchange rates.

EXAMPLE 10-10   The Yen/U.S. Dollar Exchange Rate

Financial analysts often assume that exchange rates are random walks. Consider an AR(1) model for the Japanese yen/U.S. dollar exchange rate. Table 10-9 shows the results of estimating the model using month-end observations from January 1975 to December 2002.

The results in Table 10-9 suggest that the yen/U.S. dollar exchange rate is a random walk because the estimated intercept does not appear to be significantly different from 0 and the estimated coefficient on the first lag of the exchange rate is very close to 1. Can we use the *t*-statistics in Table 10-9 to test whether the exchange rate is a random walk? Unfortunately, no, because the standard errors in an AR model are invalid if the model is estimated on a random walk (remember, a random walk is not covariance stationary). If the exchange rate is, in fact, a random walk, we might come to an incorrect conclusion based on faulty statistical tests and then invest incorrectly. We can use a test presented in the next section to test whether the time-series is a random walk.

Suppose the exchange rate is a random walk, as we now suspect. If so, the first-differenced series, $y_t = x_t - x_{t-1}$, will be covariance stationary. We present the results from estimating $y_t = b_0 + b_1 y_{t-1} + \epsilon_t$ in Table 10-10. If the exchange rate is a random walk, then $b_0 = 0$ and $b_1 = 0$ and the error term will not be serially correlated.

In Table 10-10, neither the intercept nor the coefficient on the first lag of the first-differenced exchange rate differs significantly from 0, and no residual autocorrelations differ significantly from 0.[27] These findings are consistent with the yen/U.S. dollar exchange rate being a random walk.

---

[26] All the covariances are finite, for two reasons: The variance is finite, and the covariance of a time series with its own past value can be no greater than the variance of the series.

[27] See Greene (2003) for a test of the joint hypothesis that both regression coefficients are equal to 0.

TABLE 10-9   Yen/U.S. Dollar Exchange Rate: AR(1) Model
Month-End Observations, January 1975–December 2002

Regression Statistics		
R-squared	0.9914	
Standard error	5.9006	
Observations	336	
Durbin–Watson	1.8492	

	Coefficient	Standard Error	t-Statistic
Intercept	1.0223	0.9268	1.1092
Lag 1	0.9910	0.0050	196.4517

Autocorrelations of the Residual			
Lag	Autocorrelation	Standard Error	t-Statistic
1	0.0706	0.0546	1.2930
2	0.0364	0.0546	0.6667
3	0.0864	0.0546	1.5824
4	0.0566	0.0546	1.0366

Source: U.S. Federal Reserve Board of Governors.

TABLE 10-10   First-Differenced Yen/U.S. Dollar
Exchange Rate: AR(1) Model
Month-End Observations, January 1975–December 2002

Regression Statistics		
R-squared	0.0053	
Standard error	5.9133	
Observations	336	
Durbin–Watson	1.9980	

	Coefficient	Standard Error	t-Statistic
Intercept	−0.4963	0.3244	−1.5301
Lag 1	0.0726	0.0547	1.3282

Autocorrelations of the Residual			
Lag	Autocorrelation	Standard Error	t-Statistic
1	−0.0045	0.0546	−0.0824
2	0.0259	0.0546	0.4744
3	0.0807	0.0546	1.4780
4	0.0488	0.0546	0.8938

Source: U.S. Federal Reserve Board of Governors.

We have concluded that the differenced regression is the model to choose. Now we can see that we would have been seriously misled if we had based our model choice on an R^2 comparison. In Table 10-9, the R^2 is 0.9914, whereas in Table 10-10 the R^2

is 0.0053. How can this be, if we just concluded that the model in Table 10-10 is the one that we should use? In Table 10-9, the R^2 measures how well the exchange rate in one period predicts the exchange rate in the next period. If the exchange rate is a random walk, its current value will be an extremely good predictor of its value in the next period, and thus the R^2 will be extremely high. At the same time, if the exchange rate is a random walk, then changes in the exchange rate should be completely unpredictable. Table 10-10 estimates whether changes in the exchange rate from one month to the next can be predicted by changes in the exchange rate over the previous month. If they cannot be predicted, the R^2 in Table 10-10 should be very low. In fact, it is low (0.0053). This comparison provides a good example of the general rule that we cannot necessarily choose which model is correct solely by comparing the R^2 from the two models.

The exchange rate is a random walk, and changes in a random walk are by definition unpredictable. Therefore, we cannot profit from an investment strategy that predicts changes in the exchange rate.

To this point, we have discussed only simple random walks; that is, random walks without drift. In a random walk without drift, the best predictor of the time series in the next period is its current value. A random walk with drift, however, should increase or decrease by a constant amount in each period. The equation describing a random walk with drift is a special case of the AR(1) model:

$$x_t = b_0 + b_1 x_{t-1} + \epsilon_t$$

$$b_1 = 1, b_0 \neq 0, \text{ or}$$

$$x_t = b_0 + x_{t-1} + \epsilon_t, E(\epsilon_t) = 0 \qquad (10\text{-}9)$$

A random walk with drift has $b_0 \neq 0$ compared to a simple random walk, which has $b_0 = 0$.

We have already seen that $b_1 = 1$ implies an undefined mean-reversion level and thus nonstationarity. Consequently, we cannot use an AR model to analyze a time series that is a random walk with drift until we transform the time series by taking first differences. If we first-difference Equation 10-9, the result is $y_t = x_t - x_{t-1}, y_t = b_0 + \epsilon_t, b_0 \neq 0$.

5.2. The Unit Root Test of Nonstationarity

In this section, we discuss how to use random walk concepts to determine whether a time series is covariance stationary. This approach focuses on the slope coefficient in the random-walk-with-drift case of an AR(1) model in contrast with the traditional autocorrelation approach which we discuss first.

The examination of the autocorrelations of a time series at various lags is a well-known prescription for inferring whether or not a time-series is stationary. Typically, for a stationary time series, either autocorrelations at all lags are statistically indistinguishable from zero, or the autocorrelations drop off rapidly to zero as the number of lags becomes large. Conversely, the autocorrelations of a nonstationary time series do not exhibit those characteristics. However, this approach is less definite than a currently more popular test for nonstationarity known as the Dickey–Fuller test for a unit root.

We can explain what is known as the unit root problem in the context of an AR(1) model. If a time series comes from an AR(1) model, then to be covariance stationary the absolute value of the lag coefficient, b_1, must be less than 1.0. We could not rely on the statistical results of an AR(1) model if the absolute value of the lag coefficient were greater than or equal to 1.0 because the time series would not be covariance stationary. If the lag coefficient is equal to 1.0, the time series has a **unit root**: It is a random walk and is not covariance stationary.[28] By definition, all random walks, with or without a drift term, have unit roots.

How do we test for unit roots in a time series? If we believed that a time series, x_t, was a random walk with drift, it would be tempting to estimate the parameters of the AR(1) model $x_t = b_0 + b_1 x_{t-1} + \epsilon_t$ using linear regression and conduct a t-test of the hypothesis that $b_1 = 1$. Unfortunately, if $b_1 = 1$, then x_t is not covariance stationary and the t-value of the estimated coefficient, $\hat{b}_1$, does not actually follow the t-distribution; consequently, a t-test would be invalid.

Dickey and Fuller (1979) developed a regression-based unit root test based on a transformed version of the AR(1) model $x_t = b_0 + b_1 x_{t-1} + \epsilon_t$. Subtracting x_{t-1} from both sides of the AR(1) model produces

$$x_t - x_{t-1} = b_0 + (b_1 - 1)x_{t-1} + \epsilon_t$$

or

$$x_t - x_{t-1} = b_0 + g_1 x_{t-1} + \epsilon_t, E(\epsilon_t) = 0 \qquad (10\text{-}10)$$

where $g_1 = (b_1 - 1)$. If $b_1 = 1$, then $g_1 = 0$ and thus a test of $g_1 = 0$ is a test of $b_1 = 1$. If there is a unit root in the AR(1) model, then g_1 will be 0 in a regression where the dependent variable is the first difference of the time series and the independent variable is the first lag of the time series. The null hypothesis of the Dickey–Fuller test is $H_0: g_1 = 0$—that is, that the time series has a unit root and is nonstationary—and the alternative hypothesis is $H_a: g_1 \neq 0$, that the time series does not have a unit root and is stationary. To conduct the test, one calculates a t-statistic in the conventional manner for g_1 but instead of using conventional critical values for a t-test, one uses a revised set of values computed by Dickey and Fuller; the revised set of critical values are larger in absolute value than the conventional critical values. A number of software packages incorporate Dickey–Fuller tests.[29]

EXAMPLE 10-11   Intel's Quarterly Sales (1)

Earlier, we concluded that we could not model the log of Intel's quarterly sales using only a time-trend line (as shown in Example 10-3). Recall that the Durbin–Watson statistic from the log-linear regression caused us to reject the hypothesis that the errors in the regression were serially uncorrelated. Suppose, instead, that the analyst

---

[28] When b_1 is greater than 1 in absolute value, we say that there is an explosive root. For details, see Diebold (2004).

[29] Dickey and Fuller developed three separate tests of the hypothesis that $g_1 = 0$ assuming the following models: random walk, random walk with drift, or random walk with drift and trend. The critical values for the Dickey–Fuller tests for the three models are different. For more on this topic, see Greene (2003) or Hamilton (1994).

decides to model the log of Intel's quarterly sales using an AR(1) model. He uses ln Sales$_t = b_0 + b_1 \ln$ Sales$_{t-1} + \epsilon_t$.

Before he estimates this regression, the analyst should use the Dickey–Fuller test to determine whether there is a unit root in the log of Intel's quarterly sales. If he uses the sample of quarterly data on Intel's sales from the first quarter of 1985 through the fourth quarter of 1999, takes the natural log of each observation, and computes the Dickey–Fuller t-test statistic, the value of that statistic might cause him to fail to reject the null hypothesis that there is a unit root in the log of Intel's quarterly sales.

If a time series appears to have a unit root, how should we model it? One method that is often successful is to first-difference the time series (as discussed previously) and try to model the first-differenced series as an autoregressive time series. The following example demonstrates this method.

EXAMPLE 10-12   Intel's Quarterly Sales (2)

Suppose you are convinced—from looking at the plot of the time series—that the log of Intel's quarterly sales is not covariance stationary (it has a unit root). So you create a new series, y_t, that is the first difference of the log of Intel's quarterly sales. Figure 10-10 shows that series.

If you compare Figure 10-10 to Figures 10-6 and 10-8, you will see that first-differencing the log of Intel's quarterly sales eliminates the strong upward trend that was present in both Intel's sales and the log of Intel's sales. Because the first-differenced series has no strong trend, you are better off assuming that the differenced series is covariance stationary rather than assuming that Intel's sales or the log of Intel's sales is a covariance-stationary time series.

Now suppose you decide to model the new series using an AR(1) model. You use ln (Sales$_t$) − ln (Sales$_{t-1}$) = $b_0 + b_1$[ln (Sales$_{t-1}$) − ln (Sales$_{t-2}$)] + ϵ_t. Table 10-11 shows the results of that regression.

The lower part of Table 10-11 shows that the first four autocorrelations of residuals in this model are quite small. With 60 observations and two parameters, this model has 58 degrees of freedom. The critical value for a t-statistic in this model is about 2.0 at the 0.05 significance level. None of the t-statistics for these autocorrelations has an absolute value larger than 2.0. Therefore, we fail to reject the null hypotheses that each of these autocorrelations is equal to 0 and conclude instead that no significant autocorrelation is present in the residuals.

This result suggests that the model is well specified and that we could use the estimates. Both the intercept ($\hat{b}_0 = 0.0352$) and the coefficient ($\hat{b}_1 = 0.3064$) on the first lag of the new first-differenced series are statistically significant. How can we interpret the estimated coefficients in the model? The value of the intercept (0.0352) implies that if sales have not changed in the current quarter ($y_t = \ln$ Sales$_t - \ln$ Sales$_{t-1} = 0$), sales will grow by 3.52 percent next quarter.[30] If sales have changed during this quarter, however, the model predicts that sales will grow by 3.52 percent plus 0.3064 times the sales growth in this quarter.

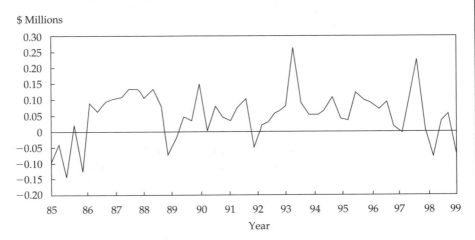

$ Millions

FIGURE 10-10   Log Difference, Intel Quarterly Sales
Source: Compustat.

Suppose we wanted to use this model at the end of the fourth quarter of 1999 to predict Intel's sales for the first quarter of 2000. Let us say that t is the fourth quarter of 1999, so $t - 1$ is the third quarter of 1999 and $t + 1$ is the first quarter of 2000. Then we would have to compute $\hat{y}_{t+1} = 0.0352 + 0.3064\,y_t$. To compute $\hat{y}_{t+1}$, we need to know $y_t = \ln \text{Sales}_t - \ln \text{Sales}_{t-1}$. In the third quarter of 1999, Intel's sales were \$7,328 million, so $\ln(\text{Sales}_{t-1}) = \ln 7,328 = 8.8995$. In the fourth quarter of 1999, Intel's sales were \$8,212 million, so $\ln(\text{Sales}_t) = \ln 8,212 = 9.0134$. Thus $y_t = 9.0134 - 8.8995 = 0.1139$. Therefore, $\hat{y}_{t+1} = 0.0352 + 0.3064(0.1139) = 0.0701$. If $\hat{y}_{t+1} = 0.0701$, then $0.0701 = \ln(\text{Sales}_{t+1}) - \ln(\text{Sales}_t) = \ln(\text{Sales}_{t+1}/\text{Sales}_t)$. If we exponentiate both sides of this equation, the result is

$$e^{0.0701} = (\text{Sales}_{t+1}/\text{Sales}_t)$$

$$\text{Sales}_{t+1} = \text{Sales}_t e^{0.0701}$$

$$= \$8,212 \text{ million} \times 1.0726$$

$$= \$8,808 \text{ million}$$

---

[30]Note that 3.52 percent is the exponential growth rate, not [(Current quarter sales/Previous quarter sales) − 1]. The difference between these two methods of computing growth is usually small.

Thus, in the fourth quarter of 1999, this model would have predicted that Intel's sales in the first quarter of 2000 would be $8,808 million. This sales forecast might have affected our decision to buy Intel's stock at the time.

TABLE 10-11   Log Differenced Sales: AR(1) Model Intel Corporation Quarterly Observations, January 1985–December 1999

Regression Statistics			
R-squared	0.0946		
Standard error	0.0758		
Observations	60		
Durbin–Watson	1.9709		

	Coefficient	Standard Error	*t*-Statistic
Intercept	0.0352	0.0114	3.0875
Lag 1	0.3064	0.1244	2.4620

Autocorrelations of the Residual			
Lag	Autocorrelation	Standard Error	*t*-Statistic
1	−0.0140	0.1291	−0.1088
2	−0.0855	0.1291	−0.6624
3	−0.0582	0.1291	−0.4506
4	0.2125	0.1291	1.6463

Source: Compustat.

6. MOVING-AVERAGE TIME-SERIES MODELS

So far, many of the forecasting models we have used have been autoregressive models. Because most financial time series have the qualities of an autoregressive process, auto-regressive time-series models are probably the most frequently used time-series models in financial forecasting. Some financial time series, however, seem to follow more closely another kind of time-series model called a moving-average model. For example, as we will see later, returns on the Standard & Poor's 500 Index can be better modeled as a moving-average process than as an autoregressive process.

   In this section, we present the fundamentals of moving-average models so that you can ask the right questions when presented with them. We first discuss how to smooth past values with a moving average and then how to forecast a time series using a moving-average model. Even though both methods include the words "moving average" in the name, they are very different.

6.1. Smoothing Past Values with an *n*-Period Moving Average

Suppose you are analyzing the long-term trend in the past sales of a company. In order to focus on the trend, you may find it useful to remove short-term fluctuations or noise by smoothing out the time series of sales. One technique to smooth out period-to-period fluctuations in the value of a time series is an **n-period moving average**. An n-period moving average of the current and past $n - 1$ values of a time series, x_t, is calculated as

$$\frac{x_t + x_{t-1} + \cdots + x_{t-(n-1)}}{n} \tag{10-11}$$

The following example demonstrates how to compute a moving average of Intel's quarterly sales.

EXAMPLE 10-13   Intel's Quarterly Sales (3)

Suppose we want to compute the four-quarter moving average of Intel's sales at the end of the fourth quarter of 1999. Intel's sales in the previous four quarters were 1Q:1999, $7,103 million; 2Q:1999, $6,746 million; 3Q:1999, $7,328 million; and 4Q:1999, $8,212 million. The four-quarter moving average of sales as of the first quarter of 2000 is thus $(7,103 + 6,746 + 7,328 + 8,212)/4 = \$7,347.25$ million.

We often plot the moving average of a series with large fluctuations to help discern any patterns in the data. Figure 10-11 shows monthly real (inflation-adjusted) retail sales for the United States from January 1972 to December 2000, along with a 12-month moving average of the data.[31]

As Figure 10-11 shows, each year has a very strong peak in retail sales (December) followed by a sharp drop in sales (January). Because of the extreme seasonality in the data, a 12-month moving average can help us focus on the long-term movements in retail sales instead of seasonal fluctuations. Note that the moving average does not have the sharp seasonal fluctuations of the original retail sales data. Rather, the moving average of retail sales grows steadily, for example, from 1985 through 1990, then declines until 1993, and grows steadily thereafter. We can see that trend more easily by looking at a 12-month moving average than by looking at the time series itself.

Figure 10-12 shows monthly crude oil prices in the United States along with a 12-month moving average of oil prices. Although these data do not have the same sharp regular seasonality displayed in the retail sales data in Figure 10-11, the moving average smoothes out the monthly fluctuations in oil prices to show the longer-term movements.

Figure 10-12 also shows one weakness with a moving average: It always lags large movements in the actual data. For example, when oil prices fell sharply in late 1985 and remained relatively low, the moving average fell only gradually. When oil prices rose quickly in 1999, the moving average also lagged. Consequently, a simple moving average of the recent past, though often useful in smoothing out a time series, may not be the best predictor of the future. A main reason for this is that a simple moving average gives equal weight to all

---

[31]A 12-month moving average is the average value of a time series over each of the last 12 months. Although the sample period starts in 1972, data from 1971 are used to compute the 12-month moving average for the months of 1972.

$ Millions

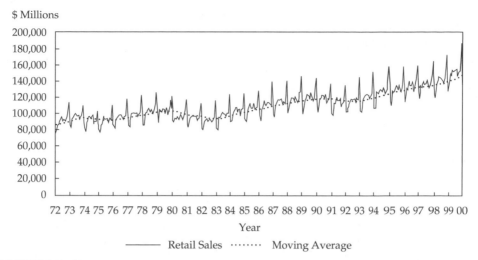

FIGURE 10-11   Monthly U.S. Real Retail Sales and a 12-Month Moving Average of Retail Sales
Source: U.S. Department of Commerce, Census Bureau.

U.S. Dollars per Barrel

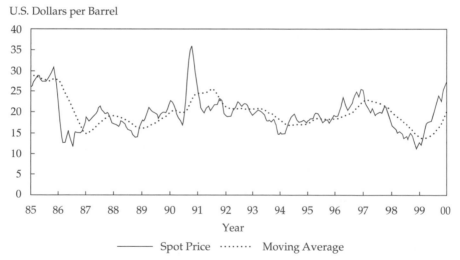

FIGURE 10-12   Monthly Oil Price and 12-Month Moving Average of Prices
Source: Dow Jones Energy Service.

the periods in the moving average. In order to forecast the future values of a time series, it is often better to use a more sophisticated moving-average time-series model. We discuss such models below.

6.2. Moving-Average Time-Series Models for Forecasting

Suppose that a time series, x_t, is consistent with the following model:

$$x_t = \epsilon_t + \theta\epsilon_{t-1}, E(\epsilon_t) = 0, E(\epsilon_t{}^2) = \sigma^2, E(\epsilon_t\epsilon_s) = 0 \text{ for } t \neq s \qquad (10\text{-}12)$$

This equation is called a moving-average model of order 1, or simply an MA(1) model. Theta (θ) is the parameter of the MA(1) model.[32]

Equation 10-12 is a moving-average model because in each period, x_t is a moving average of ϵ_t and ϵ_{t-1}, two uncorrelated random variables that each have an expected value of zero. Unlike the simple moving-average model of Equation 10-11, this moving-average model places different weights on the two terms in the moving average (1 on ϵ_t, and θ on ϵ_{t-1}).

We can see if a time series fits an MA(1) model by looking at its autocorrelations to determine whether x_t is correlated only with its preceding and following values. First, we examine the variance of x_t in Equation 10-12 and its first two autocorrelations. Because the expected value of x_t is 0 in all periods and ϵ_t is uncorrelated with its own past values, the first autocorrelation is not equal to 0, but the second and higher autocorrelations are equal to 0. Further analysis shows that all autocorrelations except for the first will be equal to 0 in an MA(1) model. Thus for an MA(1) process, any value x_t is correlated with x_{t-1} and x_{t+1} but with no other time-series values; we could say that an MA(1) model has a memory of one period.

Of course, an MA(1) model is not the most complex moving-average model. A qth order moving-average model, denoted MA(q) and with varying weights on lagged terms, can be written as

$$x_t = \epsilon_t + \theta_1\epsilon_{t-1} + \ldots + \theta_q\epsilon_{t-q}, E(\epsilon_t) = 0, E(\epsilon_t^2) = \sigma^2, \qquad (10\text{-}13)$$

$$E(\epsilon_t\epsilon_s) = 0 \text{ for } t \neq s$$

How can we tell whether an MA(q) model fits a time series? We examine the autocorrelations. For an MA(q) model, the first q autocorrelations will be significantly different from 0, and all autocorrelations beyond that will be equal to 0; an MA(q) model has a memory of q periods. This result is critical for choosing the right value of q for an MA model. We discussed this result above for the specific case of $q = 1$ that all autocorrelations except for the first will be equal to 0 in an MA(1) model.

How can we distinguish an autoregressive time series from a moving-average time series? Once again, we do so by examining the autocorrelations of the time series itself. The autocorrelations of most autoregressive time series start large and decline gradually, whereas the autocorrelations of an MA(q) time series suddenly drop to 0 after the first q autocorrelations. We are unlikely to know in advance whether a time series is autoregressive or moving average. Therefore, the autocorrelations give us our best clue about how to model the time series. Most time series, however, are best modeled with an autoregressive model.

EXAMPLE 10-14   A Time-Series Model for Monthly Returns on the S&P 500

Are monthly returns on the S&P autocorrelated? If so, we may be able to devise an investment strategy to exploit the autocorrelation. What is an appropriate time-series model for S&P 500 monthly returns?

---

[32]Note that a moving-average time-series model is very different from a simple moving average, as discussed in Section 6.1. The simple moving average is based on observed values of a time series. In a moving-average time-series model, we never directly observe ϵ_t or any other ϵ_{t-j}, but we can infer how a particular moving-average model will imply a particular pattern of serial correlation for a time series, as we discuss below.

Table 10-12 shows the first six autocorrelations of returns to the S&P 500 using monthly data from January 1991 to December 2002. Note that all of the autocorrelations are quite small. Do they reach significance? With 144 observations, the critical value for a *t*-statistic in this model is about 1.98 at the 0.05 significance level. None of the autocorrelations has a *t*-statistic larger in absolute value than the critical value of 1.98. Consequently, we fail to reject the null hypothesis that those autocorrelations, individually, do not differ significantly from 0.

TABLE 10-12   Annualized Monthly Returns to the S&P 500, January 1991–December 2002

| | Autocorrelations | | |
Lag	Autocorrelation	Standard Error	*t*-Statistic
1	−0.0090	0.0833	−0.1083
2	−0.0207	0.0833	−0.2481
3	0.0020	0.0833	0.0240
4	−0.0730	0.0833	−0.8756
5	0.1143	0.0833	1.3717
6	−0.0007	0.0833	−0.0082
Observations	144		

Source: Ibbotson Associates.

If returns on the S&P 500 were an MA(q) time series, then the first q autocorrelations would differ significantly from 0. None of the autocorrelations is statistically significant, however, so returns to the S&P 500 appear to come from an MA(0) time series. An MA(0) time series in which we allow the mean to be nonzero takes the following form:[33]

$$x_t = \mu + \epsilon_t, E(\epsilon_t) = 0, E(\epsilon_t^2) = \sigma^2, E(\epsilon_t\epsilon_s) = 0 \text{ for } t \neq s \qquad (10\text{-}14)$$

which means that the time series is not predictable. This result should not be too surprising, as most research suggests that short-term returns to stock indexes are difficult to predict.

We can see from this example how examining the autocorrelations allowed us to choose between the AR and MA models. If returns to the S&P 500 had come from an AR(1) time series, the first autocorrelation would have differed significantly from 0 and the autocorrelations would have declined gradually. Not even the first autocorrelation is significantly different from 0, however. Therefore, we can be sure that returns to the S&P 500 do not come from an AR(1) model—or from any higher-order AR model, for that matter. This finding is consistent with our conclusion that the S&P 500 series is MA(0).

---

[33]On the basis of investment theory and evidence, we expect that the mean monthly return on the S&P 500 is positive ($\mu > 0$). We can also generalize Equation 10-13 for an MA(q) time series by adding a constant term, μ. Including a constant term in a moving-average model does not change the expressions for the variance and autocovariances of the time series. A number of early studies of weak-form market efficiency used Equation 10-14 as the model for stock returns. See Garbade (1982).

7. SEASONALITY IN TIME-SERIES MODELS

As we analyze the results of the time-series models in this chapter, we encounter complications. One common complication is significant seasonality, a case in which the series shows regular patterns of movement within the year. At first glance, seasonality might appear to rule out using autoregressive time-series models. After all, autocorrelations will differ by season. This problem can often be solved, however, by using seasonal lags in an autoregressive model.

A seasonal lag is usually the value of the time series one year before the current period, included as an extra term in an autoregressive model. Suppose, for example, that we model a particular quarterly time series using an AR(1) model, $x_t = b_0 + b_1 x_{t-1} + \epsilon_t$. If the time series had significant seasonality, this model would not be correctly specified. The seasonality would be easy to detect because the seasonal autocorrelation (in the case of quarterly data, the fourth autocorrelation) of the error term would differ significantly from 0. Suppose this quarterly model has significant seasonality. In this case, we might include a seasonal lag in the autoregressive model and estimate

$$x_t = b_0 + b_1 x_{t-1} + b_2 x_{t-4} + \epsilon_t \qquad (10\text{-}15)$$

to test whether including the seasonal lag would eliminate statistically significant autocorrelation in the error term.

In Examples 10-15 and 10-16, we illustrate how to test and adjust for seasonality in a time-series model. We also illustrate how to compute a forecast using an autoregressive model with a seasonal lag.

EXAMPLE 10-15 Seasonality in Sales at Medtronic

We want to predict sales for Medtronic, Inc. Based on the previous results in this chapter, we determine that the first difference of the log of sales is probably covariance stationary. Using quarterly data from the first quarter of 1985 to the last quarter of 2001, we estimate an AR(1) model using ordinary least squares on the first-differenced data. We estimate the following equation: $(\ln \text{Sales}_t - \ln \text{Sales}_{t-1}) = b_0 + b_1 (\ln \text{Sales}_{t-1} - \ln \text{Sales}_{t-2}) + \epsilon_t$. Table 10-13 shows the results of the regression.

The first thing to note in Table 10-13 is the strong seasonal autocorrelation of the residuals. The bottom portion of the table shows that the fourth autocorrelation has a value of 0.4072 and a t-statistic of 3.36. With 68 observations and two parameters, this model has 66 degrees of freedom.[34] The critical value for a t-statistic is about 2.0 at the 0.05 significance level. Given this value of the t-statistic, we must reject the null hypothesis that the fourth autocorrelation is equal to 0 because the t-statistic is larger than the critical value of 2.0.

---

[34]Although the sample period begins in 1985, we use prior observations for the lags. Otherwise, the model would have fewer degrees of freedom because the sample size would be reduced with each increase in the number of lags.

In this model, the fourth autocorrelation is the seasonal autocorrelation because this AR(1) model is estimated with quarterly data. Table 10-13 shows the strong and statistically significant seasonal autocorrelation that occurs when a time series with strong seasonality is modeled without taking the seasonality into account. Therefore, the AR(1) model is misspecified, and we should not use it for forecasting.

TABLE 10-13   Log Differenced Sales: AR(1) Model Medtronic, Inc. Quarterly Observations, January 1985–December 2001

Regression Statistics			
R-squared		0.1619	
Standard error		0.0693	
Observations		68	
Durbin–Watson		2.0588	

	Coefficient	Standard Error	*t*-Statistic
Intercept	0.0597	0.0091	6.5411
Lag 1	−0.4026	0.1128	−3.5704

Autocorrelations of the Residual			
Lag	Autocorrelation	Standard Error	*t*-Statistic
1	−0.0299	0.1213	−0.2463
2	−0.1950	0.1213	−1.6077
3	−0.1138	0.1213	−0.9381
4	0.4072	0.1213	3.3581

Source: Compustat.

Suppose we decide to use an autoregressive model with a seasonal lag because of the seasonal autocorrelation. We are modeling quarterly data, so we estimate Equation 10-15: $(\ln \text{Sales}_t - \ln \text{Sales}_{t-1}) = b_0 + b_1(\ln \text{Sales}_{t-1} - \ln \text{Sales}_{t-2}) + b_2(\ln \text{Sales}_{t-4} - \ln \text{Sales}_{t-5}) + \epsilon_t$. The estimates of this equation appear in Table 10-14.

Note the autocorrelations of the residual shown at the bottom of Table 10-14. When we include a seasonal lag in the regression, none of the *t*-statistics on the first four autocorrelations remains significant.

Now that we know that the residuals of this model do not have significant serial correlation, we can assume that the model is correctly specified. How can we interpret the coefficients in this model? To predict the current quarter's sales growth at Medtronic, we need to know two things: sales growth in the previous quarter and sales growth four quarters ago. If sales remained constant in each of those two quarters, the model in Table 10-14 predicts that sales will grow by 0.0403 (4.03 percent) in the current quarter. If sales grew by 1 percent last quarter and by 2 percent four quarters ago, then the model predicts that sales growth this quarter will be $0.0403 - 0.2955(0.01) + 0.3896(0.02) = 0.0451$ or 4.51 percent.[35] Notice also that the R^2 in the model with the seasonal lag (0.3219 in Table 10-14) was almost two times

---

[35] Note that all of these growth rates are exponential growth rates.

higher than the R^2 in the model without the seasonal lag (0.1619 in Table 10-13). Again, the seasonal lag model does a much better job of explaining the data.

TABLE 10-14   Log Differenced Sales: AR(1) Model with Seasonal Lag Medtronic, Inc. Quarterly Observations, January 1985–December 2001

Regression Statistics		
R-squared	0.3219	
Standard error	0.0580	
Observations	68	
Durbin–Watson	2.0208	

	Coefficient	Standard Error	t-Statistic
Intercept	0.0403	0.0096	4.1855
Lag 1	−0.2955	0.1058	−2.7927
Lag 4	0.3896	0.0995	3.9159

Autocorrelations of the Residual			
Lag	Autocorrelation	Standard Error	t-Statistic
1	−0.0108	0.1213	−0.0889
2	−0.0957	0.1213	−0.7889
3	0.0075	0.1213	0.0621
4	−0.0340	0.1213	−0.2801

Source: Compustat.

EXAMPLE 10-16   Retail Sales Growth

We want to predict the growth in U.S. monthly retail sales so that we can decide whether to recommend discount store stocks. We decide to use non-seasonally adjusted data on retail sales, adjusted for inflation. To begin with, we estimate an AR(1) model with observations on the annualized monthly growth in real retail sales from February 1972 to December 2000. We estimate the following equation: Sales growth$_t = b_0 + b_1$ Sales growth$_{t-1} + \epsilon_t$. Table 10-15 shows the results from this model.

The autocorrelations of the residuals from this model, shown at the bottom of Table 10-15, indicate that seasonality is extremely significant in this model. With 347 observations and two parameters, this model has 345 degrees of freedom. At the 0.05 significance level, the critical value for a t-statistic is about 1.97. The 12th-lag autocorrelation (the seasonal autocorrelation, because we are using monthly data) has a value of 0.8739 and a t-statistic of 16.28. The t-statistic on this autocorrelation is larger than the critical value (1.97) implying that we can reject the null hypothesis that the 12th autocorrelation is 0. Note also that many of the other t-statistics for autocorrelations shown in the table differ significantly from 0. Consequently, the model shown in Table 10-15 is misspecified, so we cannot rely on it to forecast sales growth.

TABLE 10-15 Monthly Real Retail Sales Growth: AR(1) Model
February 1972–December 2000

Regression Statistics			
R-squared	0.0659		
Standard error	2.3520		
Observations	347		
Durbin–Watson	2.1008		

	Coefficient	Standard Error	t-Statistic
Intercept	1.2170	0.1357	8.9666
Lag 1	−0.2577	0.0522	−4.9349

Autocorrelations of the Residual			
Lag	Autocorrelation	Standard Error	t-Statistic
1	−0.0552	0.0537	−1.0288
2	−0.1536	0.0537	−2.8619
3	0.1774	0.0537	3.3044
4	−0.1020	0.0537	−1.8996
5	−0.1320	0.0537	−2.4582
6	−0.2676	0.0537	−4.9841
7	−0.1366	0.0537	−2.5455
8	−0.0923	0.0537	−1.7186
9	0.1655	0.0537	3.0832
10	−0.1732	0.0537	−3.2273
11	−0.0623	0.0537	−1.1597
12	0.8739	0.0537	16.2793

Source: U.S. Department of Commerce.

Suppose we add the seasonal lag of sales growth (the 12th lag) to the AR(1) model to estimate the equation Sales growth$_t$ = b_0 + b_1(Sales growth$_{t-1}$) + b_2(Sales growth$_{t-12}$) + ϵ_t. Table 10-16 presents the results of estimating this equation. The estimated value of the seasonal autocorrelation (the 12th autocorrelation) has fallen to 0.0335. None of the first 12 autocorrelations has a *t*-statistic with an absolute value greater than the critical value of 1.97 at the 0.05 significance level. We can conclude that there is no significant serial correlation in the residuals from this model. Because we can reasonably believe that the model is correctly specified, we can use it to predict retail sales growth. Note that the R^2 in Table 10-16 is 0.8149, much larger than the R^2 in Table 10-15 (computed by the model without the seasonal lag).

How can we interpret the coefficients in the model? To predict growth in retail sales in this month, we need to know last month's retail sales growth and retail sales growth 12 months ago. If retail sales remained constant both last month and 12 months ago, the model in Table 10-16 predicts that retail sales will grow at an annual rate of approximately 15 percent this month. If retail sales grew at an annual rate of 5 percent last month and at an annual rate of 10 percent 12 months ago, the model in Table 10-16 predicts that retail sales will grow in the current month at an annual rate of $0.1516 - 0.0490(0.05) + 0.8857(0.10) = 0.2377$ or 23.8 percent.

TABLE 10-16   Monthly Real Retail Sales Growth: AR(1) Model with Seasonal Lag, February 1972–December 2000

Regression Statistics		
R-squared	0.8149	
Standard error	1.0487	
Observations	347	
Durbin–Watson	2.4301	

	Coefficient	Standard Error	t-Statistic
Intercept	0.1516	0.0669	2.2652
Lag 1	−0.0490	0.0239	−2.0484
Lag 12	0.8857	0.0237	37.3028

Autocorrelations of the Residual			
Lag	Autocorrelation	Standard Error	t-Statistic
1	−0.0699	0.0537	−1.3019
2	−0.0107	0.0537	−0.1985
3	0.0946	0.0537	1.7630
4	−0.0556	0.0537	−1.0355
5	−0.0319	0.0537	−0.5936
6	0.0289	0.0537	0.5386
7	−0.0933	0.0537	−1.7382
8	0.0062	0.0537	0.1150
9	−0.0111	0.0537	−0.2059
10	−0.0523	0.0537	−0.9742
11	0.0377	0.0537	0.7026
12	0.0335	0.0537	0.6231

Source: U.S. Department of Commerce.

8. AUTOREGRESSIVE MOVING-AVERAGE MODELS

So far, we have presented autoregressive and moving-average models as alternatives for modeling a time series. The time series we have considered in examples have usually been explained quite well with a simple autoregressive model (with or without seasonal lags).[36]

---

[36]For the returns on the S&P 500 (see Example 10-14), we chose a moving-average model over an autoregressive model.

Some statisticians, however, have advocated using a more general model, the autoregressive moving-average (ARMA) model. The advocates of ARMA models argue that these models may fit the data better and provide better forecasts than do plain autoregressive (AR) models. However, as we discuss later in this section, there are severe limitations to estimating and using these models. Because you may encounter ARMA models, we provide a brief overview below.

An ARMA model combines both autoregressive lags of the dependent variable and moving-average errors. The equation for such a model with p autoregressive terms and q moving-average terms, denoted ARMA(p, q), is

$$x_{t+1} = b_0 + b_1 x_t + \cdots + b_p x_{t-p} + \epsilon_t + \theta_1 \epsilon_{t-1} + \cdots + \theta_q \epsilon_{t-q} \qquad (10\text{-}16)$$

$$E(\epsilon_t) = 0, E(\epsilon_t^2) = \sigma^2, E(\epsilon_t \epsilon_s) = 0 \text{ for } t \neq s$$

where $b_1, b_2, \ldots, b_p$ are the autoregressive parameters and $\theta_1, \theta_2, \ldots, \theta_q$ are the moving-average parameters.

Estimating and using ARMA models has several limitations. First, the parameters in ARMA models can be very unstable. In particular, slight changes in the data sample or the initial guesses for the values of the ARMA parameters can result in very different final estimates of the ARMA parameters. Second, choosing the right ARMA model is more of an art than a science. The criteria for deciding on p and q for a particular time series are far from perfect. Moreover, even after a model is selected, that model may not forecast well.

To reiterate, ARMA models can be very unstable, depending on the data sample used and the particular ARMA model estimated. Therefore, you should be skeptical of claims that a particular ARMA model provides much better forecasts of a time series than any other ARMA model. In fact, in most cases, you can use an AR model to produce forecasts that are just as accurate as those from ARMA models without nearly as much complexity. Even some of the strongest advocates of ARMA models admit that these models should not be used with fewer than 80 observations, and they do not recommend using ARMA models for predicting quarterly sales or gross margins for a company using even 15 years of quarterly data.

9. AUTOREGRESSIVE CONDITIONAL HETEROSKEDASTICITY MODELS

Up to now, we have ignored any issues of heteroskedasticity in time-series models and have assumed homoskedasticity. **Heteroskedasticity** is the dependence of the error term variance on the independent variable; **homoskedasticity** is the independence of the error term variance from the independent variable. We have assumed that the error term's variance is constant and does not depend on the value of the time series itself or on the size of previous errors. At times, however, this assumption is violated and the variance of the error term is not constant. In such a situation, the standard errors of the regression coefficients in AR, MA, or ARMA models will be incorrect, and our hypothesis tests would be invalid. Consequently, we can make poor investment decisions based on those tests.

For example, suppose you are building an autoregressive model of a company's sales. If heteroskedasticity is present, then the standard errors of the regression coefficients of your model are incorrect. It is likely that due to heteroskedasticity, one or more of the lagged sales terms may appear statistically significant when in fact they are not. Therefore, if you use this model for your decision making, you may make some suboptimal decisions.

In work responsible in part for his shared Nobel Prize in Economics for 2003, Robert F. Engle in 1982 first suggested a way of testing whether the variance of the error in a particular time-series model in one period depends on the variance of the error in previous periods. He called this type of heteroskedasticity autoregressive conditional heteroskedasticity (ARCH).

As an example, consider the ARCH(1) model

$$\epsilon_t \sim N(0, a_0 + a_1 \epsilon_{t-1}^2) \tag{10-17}$$

where the distribution of ϵ_t, conditional on its value in the previous period, ϵ_{t-1}, is normal with mean 0 and variance $a_0 + a_1 \epsilon_{t-1}^2$. If $a_1 = 0$, the variance of the error in every period is just a_0. The variance is constant over time and does not depend on past errors. Now suppose that $a_1 > 0$. Then the variance of the error in one period depends on how large the squared error was in the previous period. If a large error occurs in one period, the variance of the error in the next period will be even larger.

Engle shows that we can test whether a time series is ARCH(1) by regressing the squared residuals from a previously estimated time-series model (AR, MA, or ARMA) on a constant and one lag of the squared residuals. We can estimate the linear regression equation

$$\hat{\epsilon}_t^2 = a_0 + a_1 \hat{\epsilon}_{t-1}^2 + u_t \tag{10-18}$$

where u_t is an error term. If the estimate of a_1 is statistically significantly different from zero, we conclude that the time series is ARCH(1). If a time-series model has ARCH(1) errors, then the variance of the errors in period $t + 1$ can be predicted in period t using the formula $\hat{\sigma}_{t+1}^2 = \hat{a}_0 + \hat{a}_1 \hat{\epsilon}_t^2$.

EXAMPLE 10-17   Testing for ARCH(1) in Monthly Inflation

Analyst Lisette Miller wants to test whether monthly data on CPI inflation contain autoregressive conditional heteroskedasticity. She could estimate Equation 10-18 using the residuals from the time-series model. As discussed in Example 10-8, if she modeled monthly CPI inflation from 1971 to 2000, she would conclude that an AR(1) model was the best autoregressive model to use to forecast inflation out of sample. Table 10-17 shows the results of testing whether the errors in that model are ARCH(1).

Because the t-statistic for the coefficient on the previous period's squared residuals is greater than 7.5, Miller easily rejects the null hypothesis that the variance of the error does not depend on the variance of previous errors. Consequently, the test statistics she computed in Table 10-5 are not valid, and she should not use them in deciding her investment strategy.

It is possible Miller's conclusion—that the AR(1) model for monthly inflation has ARCH in the errors—may have been due to the sample period employed (1971 to 2000). In Example 10-9, she used a shorter sample period of 1985 to 2000 and concluded that monthly CPI inflation follows an AR(1) process. (These results were shown in Table 10-8.) Table 10-17 shows that errors for a time-series model of inflation for the entire sample (1971 to 2000) have ARCH errors. Do the errors estimated with a shorter sample period (1985 to 2000) also display ARCH? For the shorter sample period, Miller estimated an AR(1) model using monthly inflation data.[37] Now she tests to see whether the errors display ARCH. Table 10-18 shows the results.

TABLE 10-17   Test for ARCH(1) in an AR(1) Model Residuals from Monthly CPI Inflation at an Annual Rate, February 1971–December 2000

Regression Statistics		
R-squared	0.1376	
Standard error	26.3293	
Observations	359	
Durbin–Watson	1.9126	
	Coefficient	Standard Error	t-Statistic
Intercept	7.2958	1.5050	4.8478
Lag 1	0.3687	0.0488	7.5483

Source: U.S. Bureau of Labor Statistics.

TABLE 10-18   Test for ARCH(1) in an AR(1) Model Monthly CPI Inflation at an Annual Rate, February 1985–December 2000

Regression Statistics		
R-squared	0.0106	
Standard error	11.2593	
Observations	191	
Durbin–Watson	1.9969	
	Coefficient	Standard Error	t-Statistic
Intercept	5.3939	0.9224	5.8479
Lag 1	0.1028	0.0724	1.4205

Source: U.S. Bureau of Labor Statistics.

In this sample, the coefficient on the previous period's squared residual is quite small and has a t-statistic of only 1.4205. Consequently, Miller fails to reject the null hypothesis that the errors in this regression have no autoregressive conditional heteroskedasticity. This is additional evidence that the AR(1) model for 1985 to 2000 is a good fit. The error variance appears to be homoskedastic, and Miller can rely on the t-statistics. This result again confirms that a single AR process for the entire 1971–2000 period is misspecified (it does not describe the data well).

---

[37] The AR(1) results are reported in Example 10-9.

Suppose a model contains ARCH(1) errors. What are the consequences of that fact? First, if ARCH exists, the standard errors for the regression parameters will not be correct. In case ARCH exists, we will need to use generalized least squares[38] or other methods that correct for heteroskedasticity to correctly estimate the standard error of the parameters in the time-series model. Second, if ARCH exists and we have it modeled, for example as ARCH(1), we can predict the variance of the errors. Suppose, for instance, that we want to predict the variance of the error in inflation using the estimated parameters from Table 10-17: $\hat{\sigma}_t^2 = 7.2958 + 0.3687\hat{\epsilon}_{t-1}^2$. If the error in one period were 0 percent, the predicted variance of the error in the next period would be $7.2958 + 0.3687(0) = 7.2958$. If the error in one period were 1 percent, the predicted variance of the error in the next period would be $7.2958 + 0.3687(1^2) = 7.6645$.

Engle and other researchers have suggested many generalizations of the ARCH(1) model, including ARCH(p) and generalized autoregressive conditional heteroskedasticity (GARCH) models. In an ARCH(p) model, the variance of the error term in the current period depends linearly on the squared errors from the previous p periods: $\sigma_t^2 = a_0 + a_1\epsilon_{t-1}^2 + \cdots + a_p\epsilon_{t-p}^2$. GARCH models are similar to ARMA models of the error variance in a time series. Just like ARMA models, GARCH models can be finicky and unstable: Their results can depend greatly on the sample period and the initial guesses of the parameters in the GARCH model. Financial analysts who use GARCH models should be well aware of how delicate these models can be, and they should examine whether GARCH estimates are robust to changes in the sample and the initial guesses about the parameters.[39]

10. REGRESSIONS WITH MORE THAN ONE TIME SERIES

Up to now, we have discussed time-series models only for one time series. Although in the chapters on correlation and regression and on multiple regression we used linear regression to analyze the relationship among different time series, in those chapters we completely ignored unit roots. A time series that contains a unit root is not covariance stationary. If any time series in a linear regression contains a unit root, ordinary least squares estimates of regression test statistics may be invalid.

To determine whether we can use linear regression to model more than one time series, let us start with a single independent variable; that is, there are two time series, one corresponding to the dependent variable and one corresponding to the independent variable. We will then extend our discussion to multiple independent variables.

We first use a unit root test, such as the Dickey–Fuller test, for each of the two time series to determine whether either of them has a unit root.[40] There are several possible scenarios related to the outcome of these tests. One possible scenario is that we find that neither of the time series has a unit root. Then we can safely use linear regression to test the relations between the two time series. Otherwise, we may have to use additional tests, as we discuss later in this section.

---

[38] See Greene (2003).

[39] For more on ARCH, GARCH, and other models of time-series variance, see Hamilton (1994).

[40] For theoretical details of unit root tests, see Greene (2003) or Hamilton (1994). Unit root tests are available in some econometric software packages, such as EViews.

EXAMPLE 10-18   Unit Roots and the Fisher Effect

In Example 9-8 in the chapter on multiple regression, we examined the Fisher effect by estimating the regression relation between expected inflation and risk-free U.S. Treasury bill (T-bill) returns. We used a sample of 137 quarterly observations from the fourth quarter of 1968 until the fourth quarter of 2002 on the expected inflation and risk-free T-bill returns. We used linear regression to analyze the relationship between the two time series. The results of this regression would be valid if both the time series are covariance stationary; that is, neither of the two time series has a unit root. So, if we compute the Dickey–Fuller *t*-test statistic of the hypothesis of a unit root separately for each time series and find that we can reject the null hypothesis that the risk-free T-bill return series has a unit root and the null hypothesis that the expected inflation time series has a unit root, then we can use linear regression to analyze the relation between the two series. In that case, the results of our analysis of the Fisher effect would be valid.

A second possible scenario is that we reject the hypothesis of a unit root for the independent variable but fail to reject the hypothesis of a unit root for the dependent variable. In this case, the error term in the regression would not be covariance stationary. Therefore, one or more of the following linear regression assumptions would be violated: (1) that the expected value of the error term is 0, (2) that the variance of the error term is constant for all observations, and (3) that the error term is uncorrelated across observations. Consequently, the estimated regression coefficients and standard errors would be inconsistent. The regression coefficients might appear significant, but those results would be spurious.[41] Thus we should not use linear regression to analyze the relation between the two time series in this scenario.

A third possible scenario is the reverse of the second scenario: We reject the hypothesis of a unit root for the dependent variable but fail to reject the hypothesis of a unit root for the independent variable. In this case also, like the second scenario, the error term in the regression would not be covariance stationary, and we cannot use linear regression to analyze the relation between the two time series.

EXAMPLE 10-19   Unit Roots and Predictability of Stock Market Returns by Price-to-Earnings Ratio

Johann de Vries is analyzing the performance of the South African stock market. He examines whether the percentage change in the Johannesburg Stock Exchange (JSE) All Share Index can be predicted by the price-to-earnings ratio (P/E) for the index. Using monthly data from January 1983 to December 2002, he runs a regression using $(P_t - P_{t-1})/P_{t-1}$ as the dependent variable and P_{t-1}/E_{t-2} as the independent variable, where P_t is the value of the JSE index at time t and E_t is the earnings on the index.

---

[41]The problem of spurious regression for nonstationary time series was first discussed by Granger and Newbold (1974).

De Vries finds that the regression coefficient is statistically significant and the value of the R-squared for the regression is quite high. What additional analysis should he perform before accepting the regression as valid?

De Vries needs to perform unit root tests for each of the two time series. If one of the two time series has a unit root, implying that it is not stationary, the results of the linear regression are not meaningful and cannot be used to conclude that stock market returns are predictable by P/E.[42]

The next possibility is that both time series have a unit root. In this case, we need to establish whether the two time series are **cointegrated** before we can rely on regression analysis.[43] Two time series are cointegrated if a long-term financial or economic relationship exists between them such that they do not diverge from each other without bound in the long run. For example, two time series are cointegrated if they share a common trend.

In the fourth scenario, both time series have a unit root but are not cointegrated. In this scenario, as in the second and third scenarios above, the error term in the linear regression will not be covariance stationary, some regression assumptions will be violated, the regression coefficients and standard errors will not be consistent, and we cannot use them for hypothesis tests. Consequently, linear regression of one variable on the other would be meaningless.

Finally, the fifth possible scenario is that both time series have a unit root, but they are cointegrated. In this case, the error term in the linear regression of one time series on the other will be covariance stationary. Accordingly, the regression coefficients and standard errors will be consistent, and we can use them for hypothesis tests. However, we should be very cautious in interpreting the results of a regression with cointegrated variables. The cointegrated regression estimates the long-term relation between the two series but may not be the best model of the short-term relation between the two series. Short-term models of cointegrated series (error correction models) are discussed in Engle and Granger (1987) and Hamilton (1994), but these are specialist topics.

Now let us look at how we can test for cointegration between two time series that each have a unit root as in the last two scenarios above.[44] Engle and Granger suggest this test: If y_t and x_t are both time series with a unit root, we should do the following.

1. Estimate the regression $y_t = b_0 + b_1 x_t + \epsilon_t$.
2. Test whether the error term from the regression in Step 1 has a unit root using a Dickey–Fuller test. Because the residuals are based on the estimated coefficients of the regression, we cannot use the standard critical values for the Dickey–Fuller test. Instead, we must use the critical values computed by Engle and Granger, which take into account the effect of uncertainty about the regression parameters on the distribution of the Dickey–Fuller test.

---

[42] Barr and Kantor (1999) contains evidence that the P/E time series is nonstationary.

[43] Engle and Granger (1987) first discussed cointegration.

[44] Consider a time series, x_t, that has a unit root. For many such financial and economic time series, the first difference of the series, $x_t - x_{t-1}$, is stationary. We say that such a series, whose first difference is stationary, has a *single* unit root. However, for some time series, even the first difference may not be stationary and further differencing may be needed to achieve stationarity. Such a time series is said to have *multiple* unit roots. In this section, we consider only the case in which each nonstationary series has a single unit root (which is quite common).

3. If the (Engle–Granger) Dickey–Fuller test fails to reject the null hypothesis that the error term has a unit root, then we conclude that the error term in the regression is not covariance stationary. Therefore, the two time series are not cointegrated. In this case any regression relation between the two series is spurious.

4. If the (Engle–Granger) Dickey–Fuller test rejects the null hypothesis that the error term has a unit root, then we conclude that the error term in the regression is covariance stationary. Therefore, the two time series are cointegrated. The parameters and standard errors from linear regression will be consistent and will let us test hypotheses about the long-term relation between the two series.

EXAMPLE 10-20   Testing for Cointegration between Intel Sales and Nominal GDP

Suppose we want to test whether the natural log of Intel's sales and the natural log of GDP are cointegrated (that is, whether there is a long-term relation between GDP and Intel sales). We want to test this hypothesis using quarterly data from the first quarter of 1985 through the fourth quarter of 1999. Here are the steps:

1. Test whether the two series each have a unit root. If we cannot reject the null hypothesis of a unit root for both series, implying that both series are nonstationary, we must then test whether the two series are cointegrated.

2. Having established that each series has a unit root, we estimate the regression ln (Intel Sales$_t$) $= b_0 + b_1$ ln GDP$_t + \epsilon_t$, then conduct the (Engle–Granger) Dickey–Fuller test of the hypothesis that there is a unit root in the error term of this regression using the residuals from the estimated regression. If we reject the null hypothesis of a unit root in the error term of the regression, we reject the null hypothesis of no cointegration. That is, the two series would be cointegrated. If the two series are cointegrated, we can use linear regression to estimate the long-term relation between the natural log of Intel Sales and the natural log of GDP.

We have so far discussed models with a single independent variable. We now extend the discussion to a model with two or more independent variables, so that there are three or more time series. The simplest possibility is that none of the time series in the model has a unit root. Then, we can safely use multiple regression to test the relation among the time series.

EXAMPLE 10-21   Unit Roots and Returns to the Fidelity Select Technology Fund

In Example 9-3 in the chapter on multiple regression, we used multiple linear regression to examine whether returns to either the S&P 500/BARRA Growth Index or the S&P

500/BARRA Value Index explain returns to the Fidelity Select Technology Fund using 60 monthly observations between January 1998 and December 2002. Of course, if any of the three time series has a unit root, then the results of our regression analysis may be invalid. Therefore, we could use a Dickey–Fuller test to determine whether any of these series has a unit root.

If we reject the hypothesis of unit roots for all three series, we can use linear regression to analyze the relation among the series. In that case the results of our analysis of the factors affecting returns to the Fidelity Select Technology Fund would be valid.

If at least one time series (the dependent variable or one of the independent variables) has a unit root while at least one time series (the dependent variable or one of the independent variables) does not, the error term in the regression cannot be covariance stationary. Consequently, we should not use multiple linear regression to analyze the relation among the time series in this scenario.

Another possibility is that each time series, including the dependent variable and each of the independent variables, has a unit root. If this is the case, we need to establish whether the time series are cointegrated. To test for cointegration, the procedure is similar to that for a model with a single independent variable. First, estimate the regression $y_t = b_0 + b_1 x_{1t} + b_2 x_{2t} + \cdots + b_k x_{kt} + \epsilon_t$. Then conduct the (Engle–Granger) Dickey–Fuller test of the hypothesis that there is a unit root in the errors of this regression using the residuals from the estimated regression.

If we cannot reject the null hypothesis of a unit root in the error term of the regression, we cannot reject the null hypothesis of no cointegration. In this scenario, the error term in the multiple regression will not be covariance stationary, so we cannot use multiple regression to analyze the relationship among the time series.

If we can reject the null hypothesis of a unit root in the error term of the regression, we can reject the null hypothesis of no cointegration. However, modeling three or more time series that are cointegrated may be difficult. For example, an analyst may want to predict a retirement services company's sales based on the country's GDP and the total population over age 65. Although the company's sales, GDP, and the population over 65 may each have a unit root and be cointegrated, modeling the cointegration of the three series may be difficult, and doing so is beyond the scope of this book. Analysts who have not mastered all these complex issues should avoid forecasting models with multiple time series that have unit roots: The regression coefficients may be inconsistent and may produce incorrect forecasts.

11. OTHER ISSUES IN TIME SERIES

Time-series analysis is an extensive topic and includes many highly complex issues. Our objective in this chapter has been to present those issues in time series that are the most important for financial analysts and can also be handled with relative ease. In this section, we briefly discuss some of the issues that we have not covered but could be useful for analysts.

In this chapter, we have shown how to use time-series models to make forecasts. We have also introduced the RMSE as a criterion for comparing forecasting models. However, we have not discussed measuring the uncertainty associated with forecasts made using time-series models. The uncertainty of these forecasts can be very large, and should be taken into account when making investment decisions. Fortunately, the same techniques apply to evaluating the uncertainty of time-series forecasts as they apply to evaluating the uncertainty about forecasts from linear regression models. To accurately evaluate forecast uncertainty, we need to consider both the uncertainty about the error term and the uncertainty about the estimated parameters in the time-series model. Evaluating this uncertainty is fairly complicated when using regressions with more than one independent variable.

In this chapter, we used the U.S. CPI inflation series to illustrate some of the practical challenges analysts face in using time-series models. We used information on U.S. Federal Reserve policy to explore the consequences of splitting the inflation series in two. In financial time-series work, we may suspect that a time series has more than one regime but not have the information to attempt to sort the data into different regimes. If you face such a problem, you may want to investigate other methods, especially switching regression models, to identify multiple regimes using only the time series itself.

If you are interested in these and other advanced time-series topics, you can learn more in Diebold (2004) and Hamilton (1994).

12. SUGGESTED STEPS IN TIME-SERIES FORECASTING

The following is a step-by-step guide to building a model to predict a time series.

1. Understand the investment problem you have, and make an initial choice of model. One alternative is a regression model that predicts the future behavior of a variable based on hypothesized causal relationships with other variables. Another is a time-series model that attempts to predict the future behavior of a variable based on the past behavior of the same variable.

2. If you have decided to use a time-series model, compile the time series and plot it to see whether it looks covariance stationary. The plot might show important deviations from covariance stationarity, including the following:
   - a linear trend,
   - an exponential trend,
   - seasonality, or
   - a significant shift in the time series during the sample period (for example, a change in mean or variance).

3. If you find no significant seasonality or shift in the time series, then perhaps either a linear trend or an exponential trend will be sufficient to model the time series. In that case, take the following steps:
   - Determine whether a linear or exponential trend seems most reasonable (usually by plotting the series).
   - Estimate the trend.
   - Compute the residuals.
   - Use the Durbin–Watson statistic to determine whether the residuals have significant serial correlation. If you find no significant serial correlation in the residuals, then the trend model is sufficient to capture the dynamics of the time series and you can use that model for forecasting.

4. If you find significant serial correlation in the residuals from the trend model, use a more complex model, such as an autoregressive model. First, however, reexamine whether the time series is covariance stationary. Following is a list of violations of stationarity, along with potential methods to adjust the time series to make it covariance stationary:

- If the time series has a linear trend, first-difference the time series.
- If the time series has an exponential trend, take the natural log of the time series and then first-difference it.
- If the time series shifts significantly during the sample period, estimate different time-series models before and after the shift.
- If the time series has significant seasonality, include seasonal lags (discussed in Step 7 below).

5. After you have successfully transformed a raw time series into a covariance-stationary time series, you can usually model the transformed series with a short autoregression.[45] To decide which autoregressive model to use, take the following steps:

- Estimate an AR(1) model.
- Test to see whether the residuals from this model have significant serial correlation.
- If you find no significant serial correlation in the residuals, you can use the AR(1) model to forecast.

6. If you find significant serial correlation in the residuals, use an AR(2) model and test for significant serial correlation of the residuals of the AR(2) model.

- If you find no significant serial correlation, use the AR(2) model.
- If you find significant serial correlation of the residuals, keep increasing the order of the AR model until the residual serial correlation is no longer significant.

7. Your next move is to check for seasonality. You can use one of two approaches:

- Graph the data and check for regular seasonal patterns.
- Examine the data to see whether the seasonal autocorrelations of the residuals from an AR model are significant (for example, the fourth autocorrelation for quarterly data) and whether the autocorrelations before and after the seasonal autocorrelations are significant. To correct for seasonality, add seasonal lags to your AR model. For example, if you are using quarterly data, you might add the fourth lag of a time series as an additional variable in an AR(1) or an AR(2) model.

8. Next, test whether the residuals have autoregressive conditional heteroskedasticity. To test for ARCH(1), for example, do the following:

- Regress the squared residual from your time-series model on a lagged value of the squared residual.
- Test whether the coefficient on the squared lagged residual differs significantly from 0.
- If the coefficient on the squared lagged residual does not differ significantly from 0, the residuals do not display ARCH and you can rely on the standard errors from your time-series estimates.

---

[45]Most financial time series can be modeled using an autoregressive process. For a few time series, a moving-average model may fit better. To see if this is the case, examine the first five or six autocorrelations of the time series. If the autocorrelations suddenly drop to 0 after the first q autocorrelations, a moving-average model (of order q) is appropriate. If the autocorrelations start large and decline gradually, an autoregressive model is appropriate.

- If the coefficient on the squared lagged residual does differ significantly from 0, use generalized least squares or other methods to correct for ARCH.

9. Finally, you may also want to perform tests of the model's out-of-sample forecasting performance to see how the model's out-of-sample performance compares to its in-sample performance.

Using these steps in sequence, you can be reasonably sure that your model is correctly specified.

CHAPTER 11

PORTFOLIO CONCEPTS

1. INTRODUCTION

No aspect of quantitative investment analysis is as widely studied or as vigorously debated as portfolio theory. Issues that portfolio managers have studied during the last 50 years include the following:

- What characteristics of a portfolio are important, and how may we quantify them?
- How do we model risk?
- If we could know the distribution of asset returns, how would we select an optimal portfolio?
- What is the optimal way to combine risky and risk-free assets in a portfolio?
- What are the limitations of using historical return data to predict a portfolio's future characteristics?
- What risk factors should we consider in addition to market risk?

In this chapter, we present key quantitative methods to support the management of portfolios. In Section 2, we focus on mean–variance analysis and related models and issues. Then in Section 3, we address some of the problems encountered using mean–variance analysis and how we can respond to them. We introduce a single-factor model, the market model, which explains the return on assets in terms of a single variable, a market index. In Section 4, we present models that explain the returns on assets in terms of multiple factors, and we illustrate some important applications of these models in current practice.

2. MEAN–VARIANCE ANALYSIS

When does portfolio diversification reduce risk? Are there some portfolios that all risk-averse investors would avoid? These are some of the questions that Harry Markowitz addressed in the research for which he shared the 1990 Nobel Prize in Economics.

Mean–variance portfolio theory, the oldest and perhaps most accepted part of modern portfolio theory, provides the theoretical foundation for examining the roles of risk and return in portfolio selection. In this section, we describe Markowitz's theory, illustrate the principles of portfolio diversification with several examples, and discuss several important issues in implementation.

Mean–variance portfolio theory is based on the idea that the value of investment opportunities can be meaningfully measured in terms of mean return and variance of return. Markowitz called this approach to portfolio formation **mean–variance analysis**. Mean–variance analysis is based on the following assumptions:

1. All investors are risk averse; they prefer less risk to more for the same level of expected return.[1]
2. Expected returns for all assets are known.
3. The variances and covariances of all asset returns are known.
4. Investors need only know the expected returns, variances, and covariances of returns to determine optimal portfolios. They can ignore skewness, kurtosis, and other attributes of a distribution.[2]
5. There are no transaction costs or taxes.

Note that the first assumption does not mean that all investors have the same tolerance for risk. Investors differ in the level of risk they are willing to accept; however, risk-averse investors prefer as little risk as possible for a given level of expected return. In practice, expected returns and variances and covariances of returns for assets are not known but rather estimated. The estimation of those quantities may be a source of mistakes in decision-making when we use mean–variance analysis.

The fourth assumption is a key one, as it says that we may rely on certain summary measures of assets' return distributions—expected returns, variances, and covariances—to determine which combinations of assets make an optimal portfolio.

2.1. The Minimum-Variance Frontier and Related Concepts

An investor's objective in using a mean–variance approach to portfolio selection is to choose an efficient portfolio. An **efficient portfolio** is one offering the highest expected return for a given level of risk as measured by variance or standard deviation of return. Thus if an investor quantifies her tolerance for risk using standard deviation, she seeks the portfolio that she expects will deliver the greatest return for the standard deviation of return consistent with her risk tolerance. We begin the exploration of portfolio selection by forming a portfolio from just two asset classes, government bonds and large-cap stocks.

Table 11-1 shows the assumptions we make about the expected returns of the two assets, along with the standard deviation of return for the two assets and the correlation between their returns.

To begin the process of finding an efficient portfolio, we must identify the portfolios that have minimum variance for each given level of expected return. Such portfolios are called **minimum-variance portfolios**. As we shall see, the set of efficient portfolios is a subset of the set of minimum variance portfolios.

We see from Table 11-1 that the standard deviation of the return to large-cap stocks (Asset 1) is 15 percent, the standard deviation of the return to government bonds (Asset 2) is 10 percent, and the correlation between the two asset returns is 0.5. Therefore, we can compute the variance of a portfolio's returns as a function of the fraction of the portfolio

---

[1] For more on risk aversion and its role in portfolio theory, see, for example, Sharpe, Alexander, and Bailey (1999) or Reilly and Brown (2003).

[2] This assumption could follow either from assuming that returns follow a normal distribution or from assuming that investors' attitudes toward risk and return can be mathematically represented in terms of mean and variance only.

TABLE 11-1   Assumed Expected Returns, Variances, and
Correlation: Two-Asset Case

	Asset 1 Large-Cap Stocks	Asset 2 Government Bonds
Expected return	15%	5%
Variance	225	100
Standard deviation	15%	10%
Correlation	0.5	

invested in large-cap stocks (w_1) and the fraction of the portfolio invested in government bonds (w_2). Because the portfolio contains only these two assets, we have the relationship $w_1 + w_2 = 1$. When the portfolio is 100 percent invested in Asset 1, w_1 is 1.0 and w_2 is 0; and when w_2 is 1.0, then w_1 is 0 and the portfolio is 100 percent invested in Asset 2. Also, when w_1 is 1.0, we know that our portfolio's expected return and variance of return are those of Asset 1. Conversely, when w_2 is 1.0, the portfolio's expected return and variance are those of Asset 2. In this case, the portfolio's maximum expected return is 15 percent if 100 percent of the portfolio is invested in large-cap stocks; its minimum expected return is 5 percent if 100 percent of the portfolio is invested in government bonds.

Before we can determine risk and return for all portfolios composed of large-cap stocks and government bonds, we must know how the expected return, variance, and standard deviation of the return for any two-asset portfolio depend on the expected returns of the two assets, their variances, and the correlation between the two assets' returns.

For any portfolio composed of two assets, the expected return to the portfolio, $E(R_p)$, is

$$E(R_p) = w_1 E(R_1) + w_2 E(R_2)$$

where

$E(R_1) =$ the expected return on Asset 1
$E(R_2) =$ the expected return on Asset 2

The portfolio variance of return is

$$\sigma_p^2 = w_1^2 \sigma_1^2 + w_2^2 \sigma_2^2 + 2w_1 w_2 \rho_{1,2} \sigma_1 \sigma_2$$

where

$\sigma_1 =$ the standard deviation of return on Asset 1
$\sigma_2 =$ the standard deviation of return on Asset 2
$\rho_{1,2} =$ the correlation between the two assets' returns

and $\text{Cov}(R_1, R_2) = \rho_{1,2} \sigma_1 \sigma_2$ is the covariance between the two returns, recalling the definition of correlation as the covariance divided by the individual standard deviations. The portfolio standard deviation of return is

$$\sigma_p = (w_1^2 \sigma_1^2 + w_2^2 \sigma_2^2 + 2w_1 w_2 \rho_{1,2} \sigma_1 \sigma_2)^{1/2}$$

In this case, the expected return to the portfolio is $E(R_p) = w_1(0.15) + w_2(0.05)$, and the portfolio variance is $\sigma_p^2 = w_1^2 0.15^2 + w_2^2 0.10^2 + 2w_1 w_2 (0.5)(0.15)(0.10)$.

Given our assumptions about the expected returns, variances, and return correlation for the two assets, we can determine both the variance and the expected return of the portfolio as a function of the proportion of assets invested in large-cap stocks and government bonds. Table 11-2 shows the portfolio expected return, variance, and standard deviation as the weights on large-cap stocks rise from 0 to 1.0.

TABLE 11-2   Relation Between Expected Return and Risk for a Portfolio of Stocks and Bonds

Expected Return	Portfolio Variance	Portfolio Standard Deviation	Large-Cap Stocks (w_1)	Government Bonds (w_2)
5%	100.00	10.00%	0	1.0
6%	96.75	9.84%	0.1	0.9
7%	97.00	9.85%	0.2	0.8
8%	100.75	10.04%	0.3	0.7
9%	108.00	10.39%	0.4	0.6
10%	118.75	10.90%	0.5	0.5
11%	133.00	11.53%	0.6	0.4
12%	150.75	12.28%	0.7	0.3
13%	172.00	13.11%	0.8	0.2
14%	196.75	14.03%	0.9	0.1
15%	225.00	15.00%	1.0	0

As Table 11-2 shows, when the weight on large-cap stocks is 0.1, the expected portfolio return is 6 percent and the portfolio variance is 96.75.[3] That portfolio has a higher expected return and lower variance than a portfolio with a weight of 0 on stocks—that is, a portfolio fully invested in government bonds. This improvement in risk–return characteristics illustrates the power of diversification: Because the returns to large-cap stocks are not perfectly correlated with the returns to government bonds (they do not have a correlation of 1), by putting some of the portfolio into large-cap stocks, we increase the expected return and reduce the variance of return. Furthermore, there is no cost to improving the risk–return characteristics of the portfolio in this way.

Figure 11-1 graphs the possible combinations of risk and return for a portfolio composed of government bonds and large-cap stocks. Figure 11-1 plots the expected portfolio return on the y-axis and the portfolio variance on the x-axis.

The two-asset case is special because all two-asset portfolios plot on the curve illustrated (there is a unique combination of two assets that provides a given level of expected return). This is the **portfolio possibilities curve**—a curve plotting the expected return and risk of the portfolios that can be formed using two assets. We can also call the curve in Figure 11-1 the **minimum-variance frontier** because it shows the minimum variance that can be achieved for a given level of expected return. The minimum-variance frontier is a more useful concept than the portfolio possibilities curve because it also applies to portfolios with more than two assets. In the general case of more than two assets, any portfolios plotting on an imaginary horizontal line at any expected return level have the same expected return, and as we move left on that line, we have less variance of return. The attainable portfolio farthest to the left on such a line is the minimum-variance portfolio for that level of expected return and one

---

[3] Note that the 96.75 is in units of percent squared. In decimals, the expected portfolio return is 0.06 and the portfolio variance is 0.009675.

Expected Return (%)

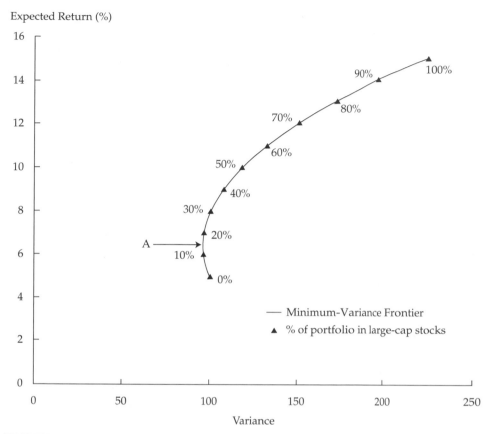

FIGURE 11-1   Minimum-Variance Frontier: Large Cap Stocks and Government Bonds

point on the minimum-variance frontier. With three or more assets, the minimum-variance frontier is a true frontier: It is the border of a region representing all combinations of expected return and risk that are possible (the border of the feasible region). The region results from the fact that with three or more assets, an unlimited number of portfolios can provide a given level of expected return.[4] In the case of three or more assets, if we move to the right from a point on the minimum-variance frontier, we reach another portfolio but one with more risk.

From Figure 11-1, note that the variance of the global minimum-variance portfolio (the one with the smallest variance) appears to be close to 96.43 (Point A) when the expected return of the portfolio is 6.43. This global minimum-variance portfolio has 14.3 percent of assets in large-cap stocks and 85.7 percent of assets in government bonds. Given these assumed returns, standard deviations, and correlation, a portfolio manager should not choose a portfolio with less than 14.3 percent of assets in large-cap stocks because any such portfolio will have both

[4]For example, if we have three assets with expected returns of 5 percent, 12 percent, and 20 percent and we want an expected return of 11 percent on the portfolio, we would use the following equation to solve for the portfolio weights (using the fact that portfolio weights must sum to 1): $11\% = (5\% \times w_1) + (12\% \times w_2) + [20\% \times (1 - w_1 - w_2)]$. This single equation with two unknowns, w_1 and w_2, has an unlimited number of possible solutions, each solution representing a portfolio.

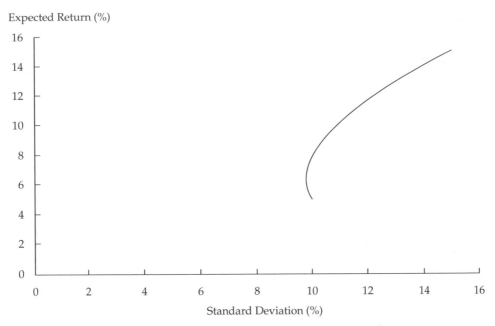

Expected Return (%)

Standard Deviation (%)

FIGURE 11-2   Minimum-Variance Frontier: Large-Cap Stocks and Government Bonds

a higher variance and a lower expected return than the global minimum-variance portfolio. All of the points on the minimum-variance frontier below Point A are inferior to the global minimum-variance portfolio, and they should be avoided.

Financial economists often say that portfolios located below the global minimum-variance portfolio (Point A in Figure 11-1) are dominated by others that have the same variances but higher expected returns. Because these dominated portfolios use risk inefficiently, they are inefficient portfolios. The portion of the minimum-variance frontier beginning with the global minimum-variance portfolio and continuing above it is called the **efficient frontier**. Portfolios lying on the efficient frontier offer the maximum expected return for their level of variance of return. Efficient portfolios use risk efficiently: Investors making portfolio choices in terms of mean return and variance of return can restrict their selections to portfolios lying on the efficient frontier. This reduction in the number of portfolios to be considered simplifies the selection process. If an investor can quantify his risk tolerance in terms of variance or standard deviation of return, the efficient portfolio for that level of variance or standard deviation will represent the optimal mean–variance choice.

Because standard deviation is easier to interpret than variance, investors often plot the expected return against standard deviation rather than variance.[5] Figure 11-2 plots the expected portfolio return for this example on the y-axis and the portfolio standard deviation of return on the x-axis.[6] The curve graphed is still called the minimum variance frontier.

Example 11-1 illustrates the process of determining a historical minimum-variance frontier.

---

[5] Expected return and standard deviation are measured in the same units, percent.

[6] For the remainder of this chapter, we will plot the expected return against standard deviation of return.

EXAMPLE 11-1   A Two-Asset Minimum-Variance Frontier Using Historical U.S. Return Data

Susan Fitzsimmons has decided to invest her retirement plan assets in a U.S. small-cap equity index fund and a U.S. long-term government bond index fund. Fitzsimmons decides to use mean–variance analysis to help determine the fraction of her funds to invest in each fund. Assuming that expected returns and variances can be estimated accurately using monthly historical returns from 1970 through 2002, she computes the average returns, variances of returns, and correlation of returns for the indexes that the index funds attempt to track. Table 11-3 shows those historical statistics.

TABLE 11-3   Average Returns and Variances of Returns (Annualized, Based on Monthly Data, January 1970–December 2002)1-3

Asset Class	Average Return	Variance
U.S. small-cap stocks	14.63%	491.8
U.S. long-term government bonds	9.55%	109.0
Correlation	0.138	

Source: Ibbotson Associates.

Given these statistics, Fitzsimmons can determine the allocation of the portfolio between the two assets using the expected return and variance. To do so, she must calculate

- the range of possible expected returns for the portfolio (minimum and maximum),
- the proportion of each of the two assets (asset weights) in the minimumvariance portfolio for each possible level of expected return, and
- the variance[7] for each possible level of expected return.

Because U.S. government bonds have a lower expected return than U.S. small-cap stocks, the minimum expected return portfolio has 100 percent weight in U.S. long-term government bonds, 0 percent weight in U.S. small-cap stocks, and an expected return of 9.55 percent. In contrast, the maximum expected return portfolio has 100 percent weight in U.S. small-cap stocks, 0 percent weight in U.S. long-term government bonds, and an expected return of 14.63 percent. Therefore, the range of possible expected portfolio returns is 9.55 percent to 14.63 percent.

Fitzsimmons now determines the asset weights of the two asset classes at different levels of expected return, starting at the minimum expected return of 9.55 percent and concluding at the maximum level of expected return of 14.63 percent. The weights at each level of expected return determine the variance for the portfolio consisting of these two asset classes. Table 11-4 shows the composition of portfolios for various levels of expected return.

---

[7]In the two-asset case, as previously stated, there is a unique combination of the two assets that provides a given level of expected return, so there is a unique variance for a given level of expected return. Thus the portfolio variance calculated for each level of expected return is trivially the minimum-variance portfolio for that level of expected return.

TABLE 11-4   Points on the Minimum-Variance Frontier for
U.S. Small-Cap Stocks and U.S. Long-Term Government Bonds

Expected Return	Variance	Standard Deviation	Small-Cap Stocks, w_1	Government Bonds, w_2
9.55%	109.0	10.4%	0.000	1.000
9.65%	106.2	10.3%	0.020	0.980
9.95%	100.2	10.0%	0.079	0.921
10.25%	98.0	9.9%	0.138	0.862
10.55%	99.5	10.0%	0.197	0.803
10.75%	102.6	10.1%	0.236	0.764
14.63%	491.8	22.2%	1.000	0.000

Table 11-4 illustrates what happens to the weights in the individual asset classes as we move from the minimum expected return to the maximum expected return. When the expected return is 9.55 percent, the weight for the long-term government bonds is 100 percent. As we increase the expected return, the weight in long-term government bonds decreases; at the same time, the weight for U.S. small stocks increases. This result makes sense because we know that the maximum expected return of 14.63 percent must have a weight of 100 percent in U.S. small stocks. The weights in Table 11-4 reflect that property. Note that the global minimum-variance portfolio (which is also the global minimum-standard-deviation portfolio) contains some of both assets. A portfolio consisting only of bonds has more risk and a lower expected return than the global minimum-variance portfolio because diversification can reduce total portfolio risk, as we discuss shortly.

Figure 11-3 illustrates the minimum-variance frontier (in the two-asset-class case, merely a portfolio possibilities curve) over the period 1970 to 2002 by graphing expected return as a function of standard deviation.

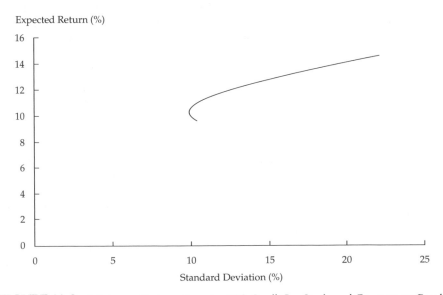

FIGURE 11-3   Minimum-Variance Frontier: U.S. Small-Cap Stocks and Government Bonds

If Fitzsimmons quantifies her risk tolerance as a standard deviation of 10 percent, for example, mean–variance analysis suggests that she choose a portfolio with an approximate weighting of 0.20 in small-cap stocks and 0.80 in long-term government bonds. One major caution that we shall discuss later in this chapter is that even small changes in inputs can have a significant effect on the minimum-variance frontier, and the future may obviously be very different from the past. The historical record is only a starting point in developing inputs for calculating the minimum-variance frontier.[8]

The trade-off between risk and return for a portfolio depends not only on the expected asset returns and variances but also on the correlation of asset returns. Returning to the case of large-cap stocks and government bonds, we assumed that the correlation was 0.5. The risk–return trade-off is quite different for other correlation values. Figure 11-4 shows the minimum-variance frontiers for portfolios containing large-cap stocks and government bonds for varying weights.[9] The weights go from 100 percent in government bonds and 0 percent in large-cap stocks to 0 percent in government bonds and 100 percent in large-cap stocks, for four different values of the correlation coefficient. The correlations illustrated in Figure 11-4 are −1, 0, 0.5, and 1.

Figure 11-4 illustrates a number of interesting characteristics about minimum-variance frontiers and diversification:[10]

- The endpoints for all of the frontiers are the same. This fact should not be surprising, because at one endpoint all of the assets are in government bonds and at the other endpoint all of the assets are in large-cap stocks. At each endpoint, the expected return and standard deviation are simply the return and standard deviation for the relevant asset (stocks or bonds).
- When the correlation is +1, the minimum-variance frontier is an upward-sloping straight line. If we start at any point on the line, for each one percentage point increase in standard deviation we achieve the same constant increment in expected return. With a correlation of +1, the return (not just the expected return) on one asset is an exact positive linear function of the return on the other asset.[11] Because fluctuations in the returns on the two assets track each other in this way, the returns on one asset cannot dampen or smooth out the fluctuations in the returns on the other asset. For a correlation of +1, diversification has no potential benefits.

---

[8]Note also that the historical data are monthly, corresponding to a monthly investment horizon. The minimum-variance frontier could be quite different if we used data with a different horizon (say quarterly).

[9]Recall from Table 11-1 that large-cap stocks have an assumed expected return and standard deviation of return of 15 percent, while government bonds have an assumed expected return and standard deviation of return of 5 percent and 10 percent, respectively.

[10]We are examining, and our observations generally pertain to, the case in which neither of the two assets is dominated. In mean–variance analysis, an asset A is dominated by an asset B if (1) the mean return on B is equal to or larger than that on A, but B has a smaller standard deviation of return than A; or (2) the mean return on B is strictly larger than that on A, but A and B have the same standard deviation of return. The slope of a straight line connecting two assets, neither of which is dominated, is positive.

[11]If the correlation is +1, $R_1 = a + bR_2$, with $b > 0$.

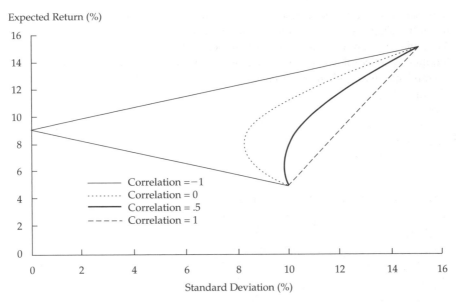

FIGURE 11-4 Minimum-Variance Frontier for Varied Correlations: Large-Cap Stocks and Government Bonds

- When we move from a correlation of +1 to a correlation of 0.5, the minimum-variance frontier bows out to the left, in the direction of smaller standard deviation. With any correlation less than +1, we can achieve any feasible level of expected return with a smaller standard deviation of return than for the +1 correlation case. As we move from a correlation of 0.5 to each smaller value of correlation, the minimum-variance frontier bows out farther to the left.
- The frontiers for correlation of 0.5, 0, and −1 have a negatively sloped part.[12] This means that if we start at the lowest point (100 percent in government bonds) and shift money into stocks until we reach the global minimum-variance portfolio, we can get more expected return with less risk. Therefore, relative to an initial position fully invested in government bonds, there are diversification benefits in each of these correlation cases. A diversification benefit is a reduction in portfolio standard deviation of return through diversification without an accompanying decrease in expected return. Because the minimum-variance frontier bows out further to the left as we lower correlation, we can also conclude that as we lower correlation, holding all other values constant, there are increasingly larger potential benefits to diversification.
- When the correlation is −1, the minimum-variance frontier has two linear segments. The two segments join at the global minimum-variance portfolio, which has a standard deviation of 0. With a correlation of −1, portfolio risk can be reduced to zero, if desired.

---

[12]For positive correlations (between 0 and 1), a negatively sloped part is present when correlation is less than the standard deviation of the less risky asset divided by the standard deviation of the riskier asset. In our case, this ratio is equal to the standard deviation of long-term government bonds to large-cap stocks, or $10/15 = 0.6667$. Because 0.5 is less than 0.6667, the minimum-variance frontier for 0.5 has a negatively sloped part. We have not allowed short sales (negative asset weights). If we allow short sales, frontiers for any positive correlation will have a negatively sloped part, which may involve the short sale of the more risky asset. For details, see Elton, Gruber, Brown, and Goetzmann (2003).

- Between the two extreme correlations of $+1$ and -1, the minimum-variance frontier has a bullet-like shape. Thus the minimum-variance frontier is sometimes called the "bullet."
- The efficient frontier is the positively sloped part of the minimum-variance frontier. Holding all other values constant, as we lower correlation, the efficient frontier improves in the sense of offering a higher expected return for a given feasible level of standard deviation of return.

In summary, when the correlation between two portfolios is less than $+1$, diversification offers potential benefits. As we lower the correlation coefficient toward -1, holding other values constant, the potential benefits to diversification increase.

2.2. Extension to the Three-Asset Case

Earlier we considered forming a portfolio composed of two assets: large-cap stocks and government bonds. For investors in our example who want to maximize expected return for a given level of risk (hold an efficient portfolio), the optimal portfolio combination of two assets contains some of each asset, unless the portfolio is placed entirely in stocks.

Now we may ask, would adding another asset to the possible investment choices improve the available trade-offs between risk and return? The answer to this question is very frequently yes. A fundamental economic principle states that one is never worse off for having additional choices. At worst, an investor can ignore the additional choices and be no worse off than initially. Often, however, a new asset permits us to move to a superior minimum-variance frontier. We can illustrate this common result by contrasting the minimum-variance frontier for two assets (here, large-cap stocks and government bonds) with the minimum-variance frontier for three assets (large-cap stocks, government bonds, and small-cap stocks).

In our initial two-asset case shown in Table 11-1, we assumed expected returns, variances, and correlations for large-cap stocks and government bonds. Now suppose we have an additional investment option, small-cap stocks. Can we achieve a better trade-off between risk and return than when we could choose between only two assets, large-cap stocks and government bonds?

Table 11-5 shows our assumptions about the expected returns of all three assets, along with the standard deviations of the asset returns and their correlations.

Now we can consider the relation between these statistics and the expected return and

TABLE 11-5   Assumed Expected Returns, Variances, and Correlations: Three-Asset Case

	Asset 1 Large-Cap Stocks	Asset 2 Government Bonds	Asset 3 Small-Cap Stocks
Expected return	15%	5%	15%
Variance	225	100	225
Standard deviation	15%	10%	15%
Correlations			
Large-cap stocks and bonds		0.5	
Large-cap stocks and small-cap stocks		0.8	
Bonds and small-cap stocks		0.5	

variance for the portfolio. For any portfolio composed of three assets with portfolio weights w_1, w_2, and w_3, the expected return on the portfolio, $E(R_p)$, is

$$E(R_p) = w_1 E(R_1) + w_2 E(R_2) + w_3 E(R_3)$$

where

$E(R_1) =$ the expected return on Asset 1 (here, large-cap stocks)
$E(R_2) =$ the expected return on Asset 2 (government bonds)
$E(R_3) =$ the expected return on Asset 3 (small-cap stocks)

The portfolio variance is

$$\sigma_p^2 = w_1^2 \sigma_1^2 + w_2^2 \sigma_2^2 + w_3^2 \sigma_3^2 + 2w_1 w_2 \rho_{1,2} \sigma_1 \sigma_2 + 2w_1 w_3 \rho_{1,3} \sigma_1 \sigma_3 + 2w_2 w_3 \rho_{2,3} \sigma_2 \sigma_3$$

where

$\sigma_1 =$ the standard deviation of the return on Asset 1
$\sigma_2 =$ the standard deviation of the return on Asset 2
$\sigma_3 =$ the standard deviation of the return on Asset 3
$\rho_{1,2} =$ the correlation between returns on Asset 1 and Asset 2
$\rho_{1,3} =$ the correlation between returns on Asset 1 and Asset 3
$\rho_{2,3} =$ the correlation between returns on Asset 2 and Asset 3

The portfolio standard deviation is

$$\sigma_p = [w_1^2 \sigma_1^2 + w_2^2 \sigma_2^2 + w_3^2 \sigma_3^2 + 2w_1 w_2 \rho_{1,2} \sigma_1 \sigma_2 + 2w_1 w_3 \rho_{1,3} \sigma_1 \sigma_3 \\ + 2w_2 w_3 \rho_{2,3} \sigma_2 \sigma_3]^{1/2}$$

Given our assumptions, the expected return on the portfolio is

$$E(R_p) = w_1(0.15) + w_2(0.05) + w_3(0.15)$$

The portfolio variance is

$$\sigma_p^2 = w_1^2 0.15^2 + w_2^2 0.10^2 + w_3^2 0.15^2 + 2w_1 w_2 (0.5)(0.15)(0.10) \\ + 2w_1 w_3 (0.8)(0.15)(0.15) + 2w_2 w_3 (0.5)(0.10)(0.15)$$

The portfolio standard deviation is

$$\sigma_p = [w_1^2 0.15^2 + w_2^2 0.10^2 + w_3^2 0.15^2 + 2w_1 w_2 (0.5)(0.15)(0.10) \\ + 2w_1 w_3 (0.8)(0.15)(0.15) + 2w_2 w_3 (0.5)(0.10)(0.15)]^{1/2}$$

In this three-asset case, however, determining the optimal combinations of assets is much more difficult than it was in the two-asset example. In the two-asset case, the percentage of assets in large-cap stocks was simply 100 percent minus the percentage of assets in government bonds. But with three assets, we need a method to determine what combination of assets will produce the lowest variance for any particular expected return. At least we know the minimum expected return (the return that would result from putting all assets in government

TABLE 11-6   Points on the Minimum-Variance Frontier for the Three-Asset Case

Expected Return	Portfolio Variance	Portfolio Standard Deviation	Large-Cap Stocks (w_1)	Government Bonds (w_2)	Small-Cap (w_3)
5%	100.00	10.00%	0	1.00	0
6%	96.53	9.82%	0.05	0.90	0.05
7%	96.10	9.80%	0.10	0.80	0.10
8%	98.72	9.94%	0.15	0.70	0.15
9%	104.40	10.22%	0.20	0.60	0.20
10%	113.13	10.64%	0.25	0.50	0.25
11%	124.90	11.18%	0.30	0.40	0.30
12%	139.73	11.82%	0.35	0.30	0.35
13%	157.60	12.55%	0.40	0.20	0.40
14%	178.53	13.36%	0.45	0.10	0.45
15%	202.50	14.23%	0.50	0	0.50

bonds, 5 percent) and the maximum expected return (the return from putting no assets in government bonds, 15 percent). For any level of expected return between the minimum and maximum levels, we must solve for the portfolio weights that will result in the lowest risk for that level of expected return. We use an **optimizer** (a specialized computer program or a spreadsheet with this capability) to provide these weights.[13]

Notice that the new asset, small-cap stocks, has a correlation of less than +1 with both large-cap stocks and bonds, suggesting that small-cap stocks may be useful in diversifying risk.

Table 11-6 shows the portfolio expected return, variance, standard deviation, and portfolio weights for the minimum-variance portfolio as the expected return rises from 5 percent to 15 percent.

As Table 11-6 shows, the proportion of the portfolio in large-cap stocks and small-cap stocks is the same in all the minimum-variance portfolios. This proportion results from the simplifying assumption in Table 11-5 that large-cap stocks and small-cap stocks have identical expected returns and standard deviations of return, as well as the same correlation with government bonds. With a different, more realistic combination of returns, variances, and correlations, the minimum-variance portfolios in this example would contain different proportions of the large-cap stocks and small-cap stocks, but we would reach a similar conclusion about the possibility of improving the available risk–return trade-offs.

How does the minimum variance for each level of expected return in the three-asset case compare with the minimum variance for each level of expected return in the two-asset case? Figure 11-5 shows the comparison.

When 100 percent of the portfolio is invested in government bonds, the minimum-variance portfolio has the same expected return (5 percent) and standard deviation (10 percent) in both cases. For every other level of expected return, however, the minimum-variance portfolio in the three-asset case has a lower standard deviation than the minimum-variance portfolio in the two-asset case for the same expected return. Note also that the efficient frontier with three assets dominates the efficient frontier with two assets (we would choose our optimal portfolio from those on the superior efficient frontier).

From this three-asset example, we can draw two conclusions about the theory of portfolio diversification. First, we generally can improve the risk–return trade-off by expanding the set

---

[13]These programs use a solution method called quadratic programming.

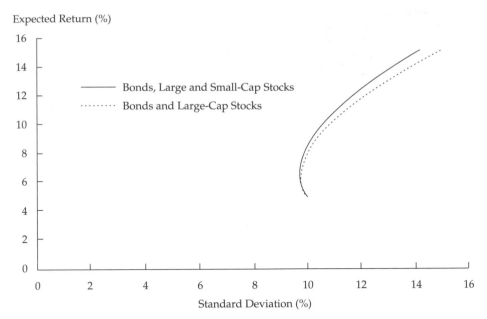

FIGURE 11-5   Comparing Minimum-Variance Frontiers: Three Assets versus Two Assets

of assets in which we can invest. Second, the composition of the minimum-variance portfolio for any particular level of expected return depends on the expected returns, the variances and correlations of those returns, and the number of assets.

2.3. Determining the Minimum-Variance Frontier for Many Assets

We have shown examples of mean–variance analysis with two and three assets. Typically, however, portfolio managers form optimal portfolios using a larger number of assets. In this section, we show how to determine the minimum-variance frontier for a portfolio composed of many assets.

For a portfolio of n assets, the expected return on the portfolio is[14]

$$E(R_p) = \sum_{j=1}^{n} w_j E(R_j) \tag{11-1}$$

The variance of return on the portfolio is[15]

$$\sigma_p^2 = \sum_{i=1}^{n} \sum_{j=1}^{n} w_i w_j \text{Cov}(R_i, R_j) \tag{11-2}$$

---

[14]The summation notation says that we set j equal to 1 through n, and then we sum the resulting terms.
[15]The double summation notation says that we set i equal to 1 and let j run from 1 through n, then we set i equal to 2 and let j run from 1 through n, and so forth until i equals n; then we sum all the terms.

Before determining the optimal portfolio weights, remember that the weights of the individual assets in the portfolio must sum to 1:

$$\sum_{j=1}^{n} w_j = 1$$

To determine the minimum-variance frontier for a set of n assets, we must first determine the minimum and maximum expected returns possible with the set of assets (these are the minimum, r_{min}, and the maximum, r_{max}, expected returns for the individual assets). Then we must determine the portfolio weights that will create the minimumvariance portfolio for values of expected return between r_{min} and r_{max}. In mathematical terms, we must solve the following problem for specified values of z, $r_{min} \leq z \leq r_{max}$:

$$\underset{\text{by choice of } w's}{\text{Minimize}} \ \sigma_p^2 = \sum_{i=1}^{n} \sum_{j=1}^{n} w_i w_j \text{Cov}(R_i, R_j) \qquad (11\text{-}3)$$

subject to $E(R_p) = \sum_{j=1}^{n} w_j E(R_j) = z$ and subject to $\sum_{j=1}^{n} w_j = 1$

This optimization problem says that we solve for the portfolio weights $(w_1, w_2, w_3, \ldots, w_n)$ that minimize the variance of return for a given level of expected return z, subject to the constraint that the weights sum to 1. The weights define a portfolio, and the portfolio is the minimum-variance portfolio for its level of expected return. Equation 11-3 shows the simplest case in which the only constraint on portfolio weights is that they sum to 1; this case allows assets to be sold short. A constraint against short sales would require adding a further constraint that $w_j \geq 0$. We trace out the minimum-variance frontier by varying the value of expected return from the minimum to the maximum level. For example, we could determine the optimal portfolio weights for a small set of z values by starting with $z = r_{min}$, then increasing z by 10 basis points (0.10 percent) and solving for the optimal portfolio weights until we reach $z = r_{max}$.[16] We use an optimizer to actually solve the optimization problem. Example 11-2 shows a minimum-variance frontier that results from using historical data for non-U.S. stocks and three U.S. asset classes.

EXAMPLE 11-2   A Minimum-Variance Frontier Using International Historical Return Data

In this example, we examine a historical minimum-variance frontier with four asset classes. The three U.S. asset classes are the S&P 500 Index, U.S. small-cap stocks, and

---

[16]There is a shortcut in the case of no constraints against short sales. According to Black's (1972) two-fund theorem, all portfolios on the minimum-variance frontier of risky assets are a linear combination of any two other minimum-variance portfolios, assuming that short sales are allowed. The implication is that we can trace out the minimum-variance frontier if we have calculated the portfolio weights of two minimum-variance portfolios. The procedure in the text, however, works even when we add the constraint against short sales, which many investors face.

U.S. long-term government bonds. To these we add non-U.S. stocks (MSCI World ex-United States). We estimate the minimum-variance frontier based on historical monthly return data from January 1970 to December 2002. Table 11-7 presents the mean returns, variances, and correlations of these four assets for the entire sample period.

TABLE 11-7 Mean Annual Returns, Standard Deviations, and Correlation Matrix for Four Asset Classes, January 1970–December 2002

	S&P 500	U.S. Small-Cap Stocks	MSCI World ex-United States	U.S. Long-Term Government Bonds
Mean Annual Returns	11.6%	14.6%	11.1%	19.6%
Standard deviation	15.83%	22.18%	17.07%	10.44%
Correlations				
S&P 500	1			
U.S. small-cap stocks	0.731	1		
MSCI World ex-U.S.	0.573	0.475	1	
U.S. long-term bonds	0.266	0.138	0.155	1

Source: Ibbotson Associates.

Table 11-7 shows that the minimum average historical return from these four asset classes was 9.6 percent a year (bonds) and the maximum average historical return was 14.6 percent (U.S. small-cap stocks). To trace out the minimum-variance frontier, we use the optimization model. The optimization program with a short sales constraint solves for the mean–variance frontier using the following equations:

$$\text{Min } \sigma_p^2(R) = w_1^2\sigma_1^2 + w_2^2\sigma_2^2 + w_3^2\sigma_3^2 + w_4^2\sigma_4^2 + 2w_1w_2\rho_{1,2}\sigma_1\sigma_2$$
$$+ 2w_1w_3\rho_{1,3}\sigma_1\sigma_3 + 2w_1w_4\rho_{1,4}\sigma_1\sigma_4 + 2w_2w_3\rho_{2,3}\sigma_2\sigma_3$$
$$+ 2w_2w_4\rho_{2,4}\sigma_2\sigma_4 + 2w_3w_4\rho_{3,4}\sigma_3\sigma_4$$

subject to $E(R_p) = w_1E(R_1) + w_2E(R_2) + w_3E(R_3) + w_4E(R_4) = z$ (repeated for specified values of z, $0.096 \leq z \leq 0.146$), $w_1 + w_2 + w_3 + w_4 = 1$, and $w_j \geq 0$.

The weights w_1, w_2, w_3, and w_4 represent the four asset classes in the order listed in Table 11-7. The optimizer chooses the weights (allocations to the four asset classes) that result in the minimum-variance portfolio for each level of average return as we move from the minimum level ($r_{\min} = 9.6$ percent) to the maximum level ($r_{\max} = 14.6$ percent). In this example, $E(R_j)$ is represented by the sample mean return on asset class j, and the variances and covariances are also sample statistics. Unless we deliberately chose to use these historical data as our forward looking estimates, we would not interpret the results of the optimization as a prediction about the future.

Figure 11-6 shows the minimum-variance frontier for these four asset classes based on the historical means, variances, and covariances from 1970 to 2002. The figure also shows the means and standard deviations of the four asset classes separately.

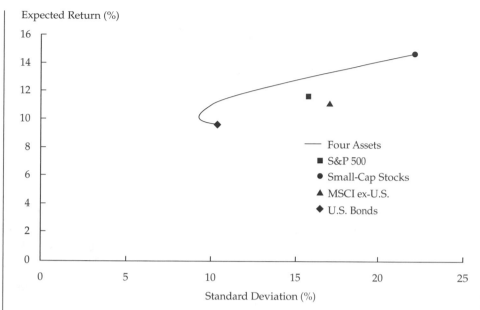

FIGURE 11-6   Minimum-Variance Frontier for Four Asset Classes, 1970–2002

Although U.S. government bonds lie on the minimum-variance frontier, they are dominated by other asset classes that offer a better mean return for the same level of risk. Note that the points representing S & P 500 and the MSCI World ex-U.S. stocks plotted off and to the right of the minimum-variance frontier. If we move directly to the left from either the S & P 500 or MSCI ex-U.S. stock portfolio, we reach a portfolio on the efficient frontier that has smaller risk without affecting the mean return. If we move directly up from either, we reach a portfolio that has greater mean return with the same level of risk. After the fact, at least, these two portfolios were not efficient for an investor who could invest in all four asset classes. Despite the fact that MSCI World ex-U.S. stocks is itself a very broad index, for example, there were benefits to further diversifying. Of the four asset classes, only U.S. small-cap stocks as the highest-mean-return portfolio plotted on the efficient frontier; in general, the highest-mean-return portfolio appears as an endpoint of the efficient frontier in an optimization with a constraint against short sales, as in this case.

In this section, we showed the process for tracing out a minimum-variance frontier. We also analyzed a frontier generated from actual data. In the next section, we address the relationship between portfolio size and diversification.

2.4. Diversification and Portfolio Size

Earlier, we illustrated the diversification benefits of adding a third asset to a two-asset portfolio. That discussion opened a question of practical interest that we explore in this section: How many different stocks must we hold in order to have a well-diversified portfolio? How does covariance or correlation interact with portfolio size in determining a portfolio's risk?

We address these questions using the example of an investor who holds an equally weighted portfolio. Suppose we purchase a portfolio of n stocks and put an equal fraction of the value of the portfolio into each of the stocks ($w_i = 1/n, i = 1, 2, \ldots, n$). The variance of return is

$$\sigma_p^2 = \sum_{i=1}^{n} \sum_{j=1}^{n} w_i w_j \text{Cov}(R_i, R_j) = \frac{1}{n^2} \sum_{i=1}^{n} \sum_{j=1}^{n} \text{Cov}(R_i, R_j) \qquad (11\text{-}4)$$

Suppose we call the average variance of return across all stocks $\overline{\sigma}^2$ and the average covariance between all pairs of two stocks $\overline{\text{Cov}}$. It is possible to show[17] that Equation 11-4 simplifies to

$$\sigma_p^2 = \frac{1}{n}\overline{\sigma}^2 + \frac{n-1}{n}\overline{\text{Cov}} \qquad (11\text{-}5)$$

As the number of stocks, n, increases, the contribution of the variance of the individual stocks becomes very small because $(1/n)\overline{\sigma}^2$ has a limit of 0 as n becomes large. Also, the contribution of the average covariance across stocks to the portfolio variance stays nonzero because $\dfrac{n-1}{n}\overline{\text{Cov}}$ has a limit of $\overline{\text{Cov}}$ as n becomes large. Therefore, as the number of assets in the portfolio becomes large, portfolio variance approximately equals average covariance. In large portfolios, average covariance—capturing how assets move together—becomes more important than average individual risk or variance.

In addition to this insight, Equation 11-5 allows us to gauge the reduction in portfolio variance from the completely undiversified position of holding only one stock. If the portfolio contained only one stock, then of course its variance would be the individual stock's variance, which is the position of maximum variance.[18] If the portfolio contained a very large number of stocks, the variance of the portfolio would be close to the average covariance of any two of the stocks, known as the position of minimum variance. How large is the difference between these two levels of variance, and how much of the maximum benefit can we obtain with a relatively small number of stocks?

The answers depend on the sizes of the average variance and the average covariance. Because correlation is easier to interpret than covariance, we will work with correlation. Suppose, for simplicity's sake, that the correlation between the returns for any two stocks is the same and that all stocks have the same standard deviation. Chan, Karceski, and Lakonishok (1999) found that for U.S. NYSE and Amex stocks over the 1968–98 period, the average correlation of small-stock returns was 0.24, the average correlation of large-stock returns was 0.33, and the average correlation of stock returns across the entire sample of stocks was 0.28. Assume that the common correlation is 0.30, which is in the approximate range for the average correlation of U.S. equities for many time periods. The covariance of two random variables is the correlation of those variables multiplied by the standard deviations of the two variables, so $\overline{\text{Cov}} = 0.30\sigma^2$ (using our assumption that all stocks have the same standard deviation of returns, denoted σ).

Look back at Equation 11-5 and replace $\overline{\text{Cov}}$ with $0.30\sigma^2$:

$$\sigma_p^2 = \frac{1}{n}\sigma^2 + \frac{n-1}{n}(0.30\sigma^2)$$

$$= \frac{\sigma^2}{n}[1 + 0.30(n-1)]$$

---

[17] See Bodie, Kane, and Marcus (2001).

[18] For realistic values of correlation, average variance is greater than average covariance.

$$= \frac{\sigma^2}{n}(0.70 + 0.30n)$$

$$= \sigma^2 \left(\frac{0.70}{n} + 0.30 \right)$$

which provides an example of the more general expression (assuming stocks have the same standard deviation of returns)

$$\sigma_p^2 = \sigma^2 \left(\frac{1 - \rho}{n} + \rho \right) \tag{11-6}$$

If the portfolio contains one stock, the portfolio variance is σ^2. As n increases, portfolio variance drops rapidly. In our example, if the portfolio contains 15 stocks, the portfolio variance is $0.347\sigma^2$, or only 34.7 percent of the variance of a portfolio with one stock. With 30 stocks, the portfolio variance is 32.3 percent of the variance of a single-stock portfolio. The smallest possible portfolio variance in this case is 30 percent of the variance of a single stock, because $\sigma_p^2 = 0.30\sigma^2$ when n is extremely large. With only 30 stocks, for example, the portfolio variance is only approximately 8 percent larger than minimum possible value $(0.323\sigma^2/0.30\sigma^2 - 1 = 0.077)$, and the variance is 67.7 percent smaller than the variance of a portfolio that contains only one stock.

For a reasonable assumed value of correlation, the previous example shows that a portfolio composed of many stocks has far less total risk than a portfolio composed of only one stock. In this example, we can diversify away 70 percent of an individual stock's risk by holding many stocks. Furthermore, we may be able to obtain a large part of the risk reduction benefits of diversification with a surprisingly small number of securities.

What if the correlation among stocks is higher than 0.30? Suppose an investor wanted to be sure that his portfolio variance was only 110 percent of the minimum possible portfolio variance of a diversified portfolio. How many stocks would the investor need? If the average correlation among stocks were 0.5, he would need only 10 stocks for the portfolio to have 110 percent of the minimum possible portfolio variance. With a higher correlation, the investor would need fewer stocks to obtain the same percentage of minimum possible portfolio variance. What if the correlation is lower than 0.30? If the correlation among stocks were 0.1, the investor would need 90 stocks in the portfolio to obtain 110 percent of the minimum possible portfolio variance.

One common belief among investors is that almost all of the benefits of diversification can be achieved with a portfolio of only 30 stocks. In fact, Fisher and Lorie (1970) showed that 95 percent of the benefits of diversification among NYSE-traded stocks from 1926 to 1965 were achieved with a portfolio of 32 stocks.

As shown above, the number of stocks needed to achieve a particular diversification gain depends on the average correlation among stock returns: The lower the average correlation, the greater the number of stocks needed. Campbell, Lettau, Malkiel, and Xu (2001) showed that although overall market volatility has not increased since 1963, individual stock returns have been more volatile recently (1986–97) and individual stock returns have been less correlated with each other. Consequently, to achieve the same percentage of the risk-reducing benefits of diversification during the more recent period, more stocks were needed in a portfolio than in the period studied by Fisher and Lorie. Campbell et al. conclude that during the 1963–85 period, "a portfolio of 20 stocks reduced annualized excess standard deviation to about five percent, but in the 1986–1997 subsample, this level of excess standard deviation required almost 50 stocks."[19]

EXAMPLE 11-3   Diversification at Berkshire Hathaway

Berkshire Hathaway's highly successful CEO, Warren Buffett, is one of the harshest critics of modern portfolio theory and diversification. Buffett has said, for example, that "[I]f you are a know-something investor, able to understand business economics, and find 5 to 10 sensibly priced companies that possess important long-term competitive advantages, conventional diversification makes no sense for you. It is apt simply to hurt your results and increase your risk."[20]

Does Buffett avoid diversification altogether? Certainly his investment record is phenomenal, but even Buffett engages in diversification to some extent. For example, consider Berkshire Hathaway's top three investment holdings at the end of 2002.[21]

American Express Company	$ 5.6 billion (32%)
The Coca-Cola Company	$ 8.8 billion (51%)
The Gillette Company	$ 2.9 billion (17%)
Total	$17.3 billion

How much diversification do these three stocks provide? How much lower is this portfolio's standard deviation than that of a portfolio consisting only of Coca-Cola stock? To answer these questions, assume that the historical mean returns, return standard deviations, and return correlations of these stocks are the best estimates of the future expected returns, return standard deviations, and return correlations. Table 11-8 shows these historical statistics, based on monthly return data from 1990 through 2002.

TABLE 11-8   Historical Returns, Variances, and Correlations: Berkshire Hathaway's Largest Equity Holdings (Monthly Data, January 1990–December 2002)

	American Express	Coca-Cola	Gillette
Mean annual return	16.0%	16.1%	17.6%
Standard deviation	29.0%	24.7%	27.3%
Correlations			
American Express and Coca-Cola	0.361		
American Express and Gillette	0.317		
Coca-Cola and Gillette	0.548		

Source: FactSet.

---

[19] Campbell et al. defined "excess standard deviation" as the standard deviation of a randomly selected portfolio of a given size minus the standard deviation of an equally weighted market index.

[20] Buffett (1993).

[21] We consider only the top three holdings in order to simplify the computations in this example. Also for simplicity, we rounded the percentage allocations in the portfolio. The weights shown here are the relative weights among these three stocks, not their actual weights in the Berkshire Hathaway portfolio.

Table 11-8 shows that for Coca-Cola's stock during this period, the mean annual return was 16.1 percent and the annualized standard deviation of the return was 24.7 percent. In contrast, a portfolio consisting of 32 percent American Express stock, 51 percent Coca-Cola stock, and 17 percent Gillette stock had an expected return of $0.32(0.16) + 0.51(0.161) + 0.17(0.176) = 0.163$, or 16.3 percent.

The portfolio's expected standard deviation, based on these weights and the statistics in Table 11-8, was

$$\sigma_p = [w_1^2\sigma_1^2 + w_2^2\sigma_2^2 + w_3^2\sigma_3^2 + 2w_1w_2\rho_{1,2}\sigma_1\sigma_2 + 2w_1w_3\rho_{1,3}\sigma_1\sigma_3$$
$$+ 2w_2w_3\rho_{2,3}\sigma_2\sigma_3]^{1/2}$$

or

$$\sigma_p = [(0.32^2)(0.290^2) + (0.51^2)(0.247^2) + (0.17^2)(0.273^2)$$
$$+ 2(0.32)(0.51)(0.361)(0.290)(0.247)$$
$$+ 2(0.32)(0.17)(0.317)(0.290)(0.273)$$
$$+ 2(0.51)(0.17)(0.548)(0.247)(0.273)]^{1/2}$$
$$= 0.210 \text{ or } 21.0 \text{ percent}$$

The standard deviation of a portfolio with these three stocks is only $21.0/24.7 = 85.0$ percent of the standard deviation of a portfolio composed exclusively of Coca-Cola stock. Therefore, Berkshire Hathaway actually achieved substantial diversification in the sense of risk reduction, even considering only its top three holdings.

2.5. Portfolio Choice with a Risk-Free Asset

So far, we have considered only portfolios of risky securities, implicitly assuming that investors cannot also invest in a risk-free asset. But investors can hold their own government's securities such as Treasury bills, which are virtually risk-free in nominal terms over appropriate time horizons. For example, the purchaser of a one-year Treasury bill knows his nominal return if he holds the bill to maturity. What is the trade-off between risk and return when we can invest in a risk-free asset?

A risk-free asset's standard deviation of return is 0 because the return is certain and there is no risk of default. Suppose, for example, that the return to the risk-free asset is 4 percent a year. If we take the Treasury bill as risk-free, then 4 percent is the actual return, known in advance; it is not an expected return.[22] Because the risk-free asset's standard deviation of return is 0, the covariance between the return of the risk-free asset and the return of any other asset must also be 0. These observations help us understand how adding a risk-free asset to a portfolio can affect the mean–variance trade-off among assets.

---

[22]We assume here that the maturity of the T-bills is the same as the investment horizon so that there is no interest rate risk.

2.5.1. The Capital Allocation Line   The **capital allocation line** (CAL) describes the combinations of expected return and standard deviation of return available to an investor from combining her optimal portfolio of risky assets with the risk-free asset. Thus the CAL describes the expected results of the investor's decision on how to optimally allocate her capital among risky and risk-free assets.

What graph in mean return–standard deviation space satisfies the definition of the CAL? The CAL must be the line from the risk-free rate of return that is tangent to the efficient frontier of risky assets; of all lines we could extend from the risk-free rate to the efficient frontier of risky assets, the tangent line has the maximum slope and best risk–return tradeoff ("tangent" means touching without intersecting). The tangency portfolio is the investor's optimal portfolio of risky assets. The investor's risk tolerance determines which point on the line he or she will choose. Example 11-4 and the ensuing discussion clarify and illustrate these points.

EXAMPLE 11-4   An Investor's Trade-Off Between Risk and Return with a Risk-Free Asset

Suppose that we want to determine the effect of including a risk-free asset in addition to large-cap stocks and government bonds in our portfolio. Table 11-9 shows the hypothetical expected returns and correlations for the three asset classes.

TABLE 11-9   Expected Returns, Variances, and Correlations: Three-Asset Case with Risk-Free Asset

	Large-Cap Stocks	Government Bonds	Risk-Free Asset
Expected return	15%	5%	4%
Variance	225	100	0
Standard deviation	15%	10%	0%
Correlations			
Large-cap stocks and government bonds	0.5		
Large-cap stocks and risk-free asset	0		
Government bonds and risk-free asset	0		

Suppose we decide to invest the entire portfolio in the risk-free asset with a return of 4 percent. In this case, the expected return to the portfolio is 4 percent and the expected standard deviation is 0. Now assume that we put the entire portfolio into large-cap stocks. The expected return is now 15 percent, and the standard deviation of the portfolio is 15 percent. What will happen if we divide the portfolio between the risk-free asset and large-cap stocks? If the proportion of assets in large-cap stocks is w_1 and the proportion of assets in the risk-free asset is $(1 - w_1)$, then the expected portfolio return is

$$E(R_p) = w_1(0.15) + (1 - w_1)(0.04)$$

and the portfolio standard deviation is

$$\sigma_p = [w_1^2(0.15)^2 + (1 - w_1)^2(0)^2]^{1/2} = w_1(0.15)$$

Note that both the expected return and the standard deviation of return are linearly related to w_1, the percentage of the portfolio in large-cap stocks. Figure 11-7 illustrates the trade-off between risk and return for the risk-free asset and large-cap stocks in this example.

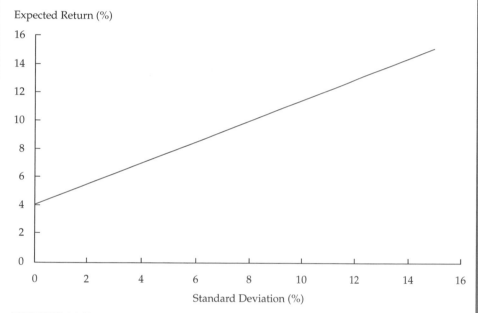

Expected Return (%)

Standard Deviation (%)

FIGURE 11-7   Portfolios of the Risk-Free Asset and Large-Cap Stocks

Now let us consider the trade-off between risk and return for a portfolio containing the risk-free asset and U.S. government bonds. Suppose we decide to put the entire portfolio in the risk-free asset. In this case, the expected return to the portfolio is 4 percent and the expected standard deviation of the portfolio is 0. Now assume that we put the entire portfolio into U.S. government bonds. The expected return is now 5 percent, and the standard deviation of the portfolio is 10 percent. What will happen if we divide the portfolio between the risk-free asset and government bonds? If the proportion of assets in government bonds is w_1 and the proportion of assets in the risk-free asset is $(1 - w_1)$, then the expected portfolio return is

$$E(R_p) = w_1(0.05) + (1 - w_1)(0.04)$$

and the portfolio standard deviation is

$$\sigma_p = [w_1^2(0.10)^2 + (1 - w_1)^2(0)^2]^{1/2} = w_1(0.10)$$

Note that both the expected return and the standard deviation of return are linearly related to w_1, the percentage of the portfolio in the government bonds. Figure 11-8 shows the trade-off between risk and return for the risk-free asset and government bonds in this example.

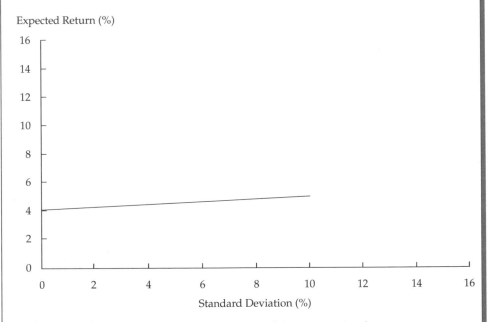

FIGURE 11-8   Portfolios of the Risk-Free Asset and Government Bonds

We have just seen the trade-off between risk and return for two different portfolios: one with the risk-free asset and large-cap stocks, the other with the risk-free asset and government bonds. How do these trade-offs between risk and return compare with the original risk–return trade-off between government bonds and large-cap stocks? Figure 11-9 illustrates the risk–return trade-off for all three portfolios.

Notice that the line describing portfolios of the risk-free asset and government bonds touches the minimum-variance frontier for bonds and stocks at the point of lowest return on the bond–stock minimum-variance frontier—that is, the point where 100 percent of the portfolio is invested in bonds. Some points on the risk-free asset–bond line have lower risk and return than points on the bond–stock frontier; however, we can

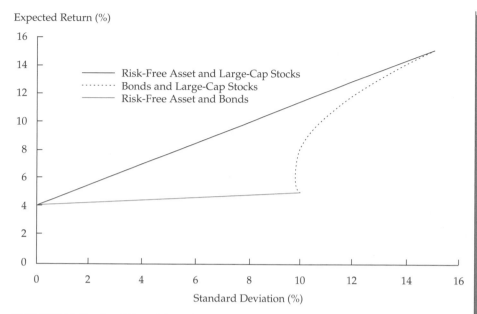

FIGURE 11-9   Portfolios of the Risk-Free Asset, Large-Cap Stocks, and Government Bonds

find no point where, for a given level of risk, the expected return is higher on the risk-free asset–bond line than on the bond–stock frontier. In this case, if we draw the line with the highest slope from the risk-free asset to the bond–stock frontier, that line is tangent to the bond–stock frontier at a point representing a portfolio 100 percent invested in stocks.[23] This CAL is labeled Risk-Free Asset and Large-Cap Stocks in Figure 11-9. For given assumptions about expected returns, variances, and covariances, that capital allocation line identifies portfolios with the maximum expected return for a given level of risk, if we can spread our money between an optimal risky portfolio and a risk-free asset. Of all lines we could extend from the risk-free rate to the minimum-variance frontier of risky assets, the CAL has maximum slope. Slope defined as rise (expected return) over run (standard deviation) measures the expected risk–return trade-off. The CAL is the line of maximum slope that touches the minimum-variance frontier; consequently, the capital allocation line offers the best risk–return trade-off achievable, given our expectations.

The previous example showed three important general principles concerning the risk–return trade-off in a portfolio containing a risk-free asset:

- If we can invest in a risk-free asset, then the CAL represents the best risk return trade-off achievable.

---

[23] In a typical case with many assets, however, the point where the line with maximum slope from the risk-free asset touches the minimum-variance frontier of risky assets does not represent a portfolio composed of only the highest expected return asset. In such typical cases, the CAL represents combinations of the risk-free asset and a broad combination of risky assets.

- The CAL has a *y*-intercept equal to the risk-free rate.
- The CAL is tangent to the efficient frontier of risky assets.[24]

EXAMPLE 11-5A   The CAL with Multiple Assets

In Example 11-4, the CAL was tangent to the efficient frontier for all risky assets. We now illustrate how the efficient frontier changes depending on the **opportunity set** (the set of assets available for investment) and whether the investor wants to borrow to leverage his investments. We can illustrate this point by reconsidering our earlier example (Example 11-2) of optimal portfolio choice among the S&P 500, U.S. small-cap stocks, non-U.S. stocks (the MSCI World ex-U.S.), and U.S. government bonds, adding a risk-free asset.

   We now assume that the risk-free rate is 5 percent. The standard deviation of the risk-free rate of return is 0, because the return is certain; the covariance between returns to the risk-free asset and returns to the other assets is also 0. We demonstrate the following principles:

- The point of maximum expected return is not the point of tangency between the CAL and the efficient frontier of risky assets.

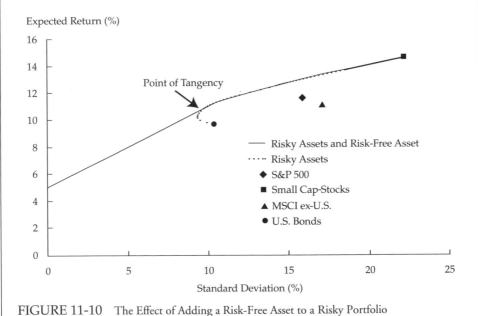

FIGURE 11-10   The Effect of Adding a Risk-Free Asset to a Risky Portfolio

---

[24]Note that that when we expand the set of assets to include the risk-free asset, an investor's CAL becomes the efficient frontier defined in relation to the expanded set of assets. The efficient frontier of risky assets is the efficient frontier considering risky assets alone. It is critical to understand that the efficient frontier is always defined in relationship to a specified set of assets.

- The point of tangency between the CAL and the efficient frontier for risky assets represents a portfolio containing risky assets and none of the risk-free asset.
- If we rule out borrowing at the risk-free rate, then the efficient frontier for all the assets (including the risk-free asset) cannot be completely linear.

Figure 11-10 shows the mean–variance frontier for all five assets (the original four plus the risk-free asset), assuming borrowing at the risk-free rate is not possible.

As the figure shows, the efficient frontier is linear from the *y*-intercept (the combination of risk and return for placing the entire portfolio in the risk-free asset) to the point of tangency. If the investor wants additional return (and risk) beyond the point of tangency without borrowing, however, the investor's efficient frontier is the portion of the efficient frontier for the four risky assets that lies to the right of the point of tangency. The investor's efficient frontier has linear and curved portions.[25]

2.5.2. The Capital Allocation Line Equation   In the previous section, we discussed the graph of the CAL and illustrated how the efficient frontier can change depending on the set of assets available for investment as well as the portfolio manager's expectations. We now provide the equation for this line.

Suppose that an investor, given expectations about means, variances, and covariances for risky assets, plots the efficient frontier of risky assets. There is a risk-free asset offering a risk-free rate of return, R_F. If w_T is the proportion of the portfolio the investor places in the tangency portfolio, then the expected return for the entire portfolio is

$$E(R_p) = (1 - w_T)R_F + w_T E(R_T)$$

and the standard deviation of the portfolio is

$$\sigma_p = [(1 - w_T)^2 \sigma_{R_F}^2 + w_T^2 \sigma_{R_T}^2 + 2(1 - w_T)w_T \sigma_{R_F} \sigma_{R_T} \rho_{R_F,R_T}]^{1/2}$$
$$= [(1 - w_T)^2(0) + w_T^2 \sigma_{R_T}^2 + 2(1 - w_T)w_T(0)(\sigma_{R_T})(0)]^{1/2}$$
$$= (w_T^2 \sigma_{R_T}^2)^{1/2}$$
$$= w_T \sigma_{R_T}$$

An investor can choose to invest any fraction of his assets in the risk-free asset or in the tangency portfolio; therefore, he can choose many combinations of risk and return. If he puts the entire portfolio in the risk-free asset, then

$$w_T = 0$$
$$E(R_p) = (1 - 0)R_F + 0E(R_T) = R_F, \text{ and}$$
$$\sigma_p = 0\sigma_{R_T}$$
$$= 0$$

---

[25] If borrowing at the risk-free rate were possible (equivalent to buying on margin at the risk-free rate), the efficient frontier would be the straight line from the risk-free rate, now continued past the point of tangency.

If he puts his entire portfolio in the tangency portfolio, then

$$w_T = 1$$

$$E(R_p) = (1 - 1)R_F + 1E(R_T) = E(R_T), \text{ and}$$

$$\sigma_p = 1\sigma_{R_T} = \sigma_{R_T}$$

In general, if he puts w_T percent of his portfolio in the tangency portfolio, his portfolio standard deviation will be $\sigma_p = w_T\sigma_{R_T}$.

To see how the portfolio weights, expected return, and risk are related, we use the relationship $w_T = \sigma_p/\sigma_{R_T}$. If we substitute this value of w_T back into the expression for expected return, $E(R_p) = (1 - w_T)R_F + w_T E(R_T)$, we get

$$E(R_p) = \left(1 - \frac{\sigma_p}{\sigma_{R_T}}\right)R_F + \frac{\sigma_p}{\sigma_{R_T}}E(R_T)$$

or

$$E(R_p) = R_F + \frac{E(R_T) - R_T}{\sigma_{R_T}}\sigma_p \qquad (11\text{-}7)$$

This equation shows the best possible trade-off between expected risk and return, given this investor's expectations. The term $[E(R_T) - R_F]/\sigma_{R_T}$ is the return that the investor demands in order to take on an extra unit of risk. Example 11-5B illustrates how to calculate the investor's price of risk and other aspects of his investment using the capital allocation line.

EXAMPLE 11-5B   CAL Calculations

Suppose that the risk-free rate, R_F, is 5 percent; the expected return to an investor's tangency portfolio, $E(R_T)$, is 15 percent; and the standard deviation of the tangency portfolio is 25 percent.

1. How much return does this investor demand in order to take on an extra unit of risk?
2. Suppose the investor wants a portfolio standard deviation of return of 10 percent. What percentage of the assets should be in the tangency portfolio, and what is the expected return?
3. Suppose the investor wants to put 40 percent of the portfolio in the risk-free asset. What is the portfolio expected return? What is the standard deviation?
4. What expected return should the investor demand for a portfolio with a standard deviation of 35 percent?
5. What combination of the tangency portfolio and the risk-free asset does the investor need to hold in order to have a portfolio with an expected return of 19 percent?

6. If the investor has \$10 million to invest, how much must she borrow at the risk-free rate to have a portfolio with an expected return of 19%?

Solution to 1:   In this case, $[E(R_T) - R_F]/\sigma_{R_T} = (0.15 - 0.05)/0.25 = 0.4$. The investor demands an additional 40 basis points of expected return of the portfolio for every 1 percentage point increase in the standard deviation of portfolio returns.

Solution to 2: Because $\sigma_p = w_T \sigma_{R_T}$, then $w_T = 0.1/0.25 = 0.4$, or 40 percent. In other words, 40 percent of the assets are in the tangency portfolio and 60 percent are in the risk-free asset. The expected return for the portfolio is $E(R_p) = R_F + \dfrac{E(R_T) - R_F}{\sigma_{R_T}}\sigma_p = 0.05 + (0.4)(0.1) = 0.09$, or 9 percent.

Solution to 3:   In this case, $w_T = 1 - 0.4 = 0.6$. Therefore, the expected portfolio return is $E(R_p) = (1 - w_T)R_F + w_T E(R_T) = (1 - 0.6)(0.05) + (0.6)(0.15) = 0.11$, or 11 percent. The portfolio standard deviation is $\sigma_p = w_T \sigma_{R_T} = (0.6)(0.25) = 0.15$ or 15 percent.

Solution to 4:   We know that the relation between risk and expected return for this portfolio is $E(R_p) = R_F + \dfrac{E(R_T) - R_F}{\sigma_{R_T}}\sigma_p = 0.05 + [(0.15 - 0.05)/0.25]\sigma_p = 0.05 + 0.4\sigma_p$. If the standard deviation for the portfolio's returns is 35 percent, then the investor can demand an expected return of $E(R_p) = 0.05 + 0.4\sigma_p = 0.05 + 0.4(0.35) = 0.19$, or 19 percent.

Solution to 5: With an expected return of 19 percent, the asset allocation must be as follows:

$$E(R_p) = (1 - w_T)R_F + w_T E(R_T) \text{ or}$$

$$0.19 = (1 - w_T)(0.05) + w_T(0.15) = 0.05 + 0.10 w_T$$

$$w_T = 1.4$$

How can the weight on the tangency portfolio be 140 percent? The interpretation of $w_T = 1.4$ is that the investment in the tangency portfolio consists of (1) the entire amount of initial wealth and (2) an amount equal to 40 percent of initial wealth that has been borrowed at the risk-free rate. We can confirm that the expected return is $(-0.4)(0.05) + (1.4)(0.15) = 0.19$ or 19 percent.

Solution to 6:   The investor must borrow \$4 million dollars at the risk-free rate to increase the holdings of the tangency-asset portfolio to \$14 million dollars. Therefore, the net value of the portfolio will be \$14million − \$4million = \$10 million.

In this section, we have assumed that investors may have different views about risky assets' mean returns, variances of returns, and correlations. Thus each investor may perceive a different efficient frontier of risky assets and have a different tangency portfolio, the optimal portfolio of risky assets which the investor may combine with risk-free borrowing or lending. In the next two sections, we examine the consequences when mean–variance investors share identical expectations.

2.5.3. The Capital Market Line   When investors share identical expectations about the mean returns, variance of returns, and correlations of risky assets, the CAL for all investors is the same and is known as the **capital market line** (CML). With identical expectations, the tangency portfolio must be the same portfolio for all investors. In equilibrium, this tangency portfolio must be a portfolio containing all risky assets in proportions reflecting their market value weights; the tangency portfolio is the market portfolio of all risky assets. The CML is a capital allocation line with the market portfolio as the tangency portfolio. The equation of the CML is

$$E(R_p) = R_F + \frac{E(R_M) - R_F}{\sigma_M}\sigma_p \qquad (11\text{-}8)$$

where

$E(R_p) =$ the expected return of portfolio p lying on the capital market line
$R_F =$ the risk-free rate
$E(R_M) =$ the expected rate of return on the market portfolio
$\sigma_M =$ the standard deviation of return on the market portfolio
$\sigma_p =$ the standard deviation of return on portfolio p

The slope of the CML, $[E(R_M) - R_F]/\sigma_M$, is called the **market price of risk** because it indicates the market risk premium for each unit of market risk. As noted, the CML describes the expected return of only efficient portfolios. The implication of the capital market line is that all mean–variance investors, whatever their risk tolerance, can satisfy their investment needs by combining the risk-free asset with a single risky portfolio, the market portfolio of all risky assets.

In the next section we present a mean–variance theory describing the expected return of any asset or portfolio, efficient or inefficient.

2.6. The Capital Asset Pricing Model

The capital asset pricing model (CAPM) has played a pivotal role in the development of quantitative investment management since its introduction in the early 1960s. In this section, we review some of its key aspects.

The CAPM makes the following assumptions:[26]

- Investors need only know the expected returns, the variances, and the covariances of returns to determine which portfolios are optimal for them. (This assumption appears throughout all of mean–variance theory.)
- Investors have identical views about risky assets' mean returns, variances of returns, and correlations.
- Investors can buy and sell assets in any quantity without affecting price, and all assets are marketable (can be traded).
- Investors can borrow and lend at the risk-free rate without limit, and they can sell short any asset in any quantity.
- Investors pay no taxes on returns and pay no transaction costs on trades.

---

[26]For a complete list of assumptions, see Elton, Gruber, Brown, and Goetzmann (2003).

The CML represents the efficient frontier when the assumptions of the CAPM hold. In a CAPM world, therefore, all investors can satisfy their investment needs by combining the risk-free asset with the identical tangency portfolio, which is the market portfolio of all risky assets (no risky asset is excluded).

The following equation describes the expected returns on all assets and portfolios, whether efficient or not:

$$E(R_i) = R_F + \beta_i[E(R_M) - R_F] \tag{11-9}$$

where

$E(R_i) =$ the expected return on asset i
$R_F =$ the risk-free rate of return
$E(R_M) =$ the expected return on the market portfolio
$\beta_i = \text{Cov}(R_i, R_M)/\text{Var}(R_M)$

Equation 11-9 itself is referred to as the **capital asset pricing model**, and its graph is called the **security market line** (SML). The CAPM is an equation describing the expected return on any asset (or portfolio) as a linear function of its **beta**, β_i, which is a measure of the asset's sensitivity to movements in the market. The CAPM says that expected return has two components: first, the risk-free rate, R_F, and second, an extra return equal to $\beta_i[E(R_M) - R_F]$. The term $[E(R_M) - R_F]$ is the expected excess return on the market. This amount is the **market risk premium**; if we are 100 percent invested in the market, the market risk premium is the extra return we expect to obtain, on average, compared with the risk-free rate of return.

The market risk premium is multiplied by the asset's beta. A beta of 1 represents average market sensitivity, and we expect an asset with that beta to earn the market risk premium exactly.[27] A beta greater than 1 indicates greater than average market risk and, according to the CAPM, earns a higher expected excess return. Conversely, a beta less than 1 indicates less than average market risk and, according to the CAPM, earns a smaller expected excess return. Expected excess returns are related only to market risk, represented by beta. Sensitivity to the market return is the only source of difference in expected excess returns across assets.[28]

Like all theory-based models, the CAPM comes from a set of assumptions. The CAPM describes a financial market equilibrium in the sense that, if the model is correct and any asset's expected return differs from its expected return as given by the CAPM, market forces will come into play to restore the relationships specified by the model. For example, a stock that offers a higher expected return than justified by its beta will be bid up in price, lowering the stock's expected return; investors would expect that a broad-based portfolio would offset any non-market risk the stock might carry.

Because it is all-inclusive, the market portfolio defined in the CAPM is unobservable. In practice, we must use some broad index to represent it. The CAPM has been used primarily

---

[27]The market portfolio itself has a beta of 1, as $\beta_M = \text{Cov}(R_M, R_M)/\text{Var}(R_M) = \text{Var}(R_M)/\text{Var}(R_M) = 1$. Because the market portfolio includes all assets, the average asset must have a beta of 1. The same argument applies if we compute the betas of assets in an index, using the index to represent the market.

[28]One intuition for this idea is that the market is the perfectly diversified portfolio. We can cancel out any other risk by holding the market portfolio, and we can costlessly hold the market portfolio (by the no-transaction-costs assumption). Even risk with respect to personal assets such as human capital (representing earning power) can be diversified away (all assets are tradable). Investors should not require extra return for risks they can costlessly hedge.

to value equities, so a common choice for the market portfolio is a broad value-weighted stock index or market proxy. The straight-line relationship between expected return and beta results from the efficiency of the market portfolio. As a result, the CAPM theory is equivalent to saying that the unobservable market portfolio is efficient, but not that any particular proxy for the market is efficient.[29] Of more interest to practitioners than the strict truth of CAPM as a theory is whether beta computed using available market proxies is useful for evaluating the expected mean returns to various investment strategies. The evidence now favors the existence of multiple sources of systematic risk affecting the mean returns to investment strategies.

2.7. Mean–Variance Portfolio Choice Rules: An Introduction

In this section, we introduce some of the principles of portfolio choice from a mean–variance perspective. One of the most basic portfolio choice decisions is the selection of an optimal asset allocation starting from a set of permissible asset classes. A second kind of decision involves modifying an existing portfolio. This type of decision is easier because we may be able to conclude that one portfolio represents a mean–variance improvement on another without necessarily establishing that the better portfolio is optimal. We begin with a brief discussion of this second decision type.

2.7.1. Decisions Related to Existing Portfolios
We examine two kinds of decisions related to existing portfolios in which mean–variance analysis may play a role.

Comparisons of Portfolios as Stand-Alone Investments The **Markowitz decision rule** provides the principle by which a mean–variance investor facing the choice of putting all her money in Asset A or all her money in Asset B can sometimes reach a decision. This investor prefers A to B if either

- the mean return on A is equal to or larger than that on B, but A has a smaller standard deviation of return than B; or
- the mean return on A is strictly larger than that on B, but A and B have the same standard deviation of return.

When A is preferred to B by the Markowitz decision rule, we say that A *mean–variance dominates* B: Asset A clearly makes more efficient use of risk than B does. For example, if an investor is presented with a choice between (1) an asset allocation A with a mean return of 9 percent and a standard deviation of return of 12 percent and (2) a second asset allocation B with a mean return of 8 percent and a standard deviation of return of 15 percent, a mean–variance investor will prefer alternative A because it is expected to provide a higher mean return with less risk. A point to note is that when asset allocation has both higher mean return and higher standard deviation, the Markowitz decision rule does not select one asset allocation as superior; rather, the preference depends on the individual investor's risk tolerance.

We can identify an expanded set of mean–variance dominance relationships if we admit borrowing and lending at the risk-free rate. Then we can use the risk-free asset to match risk among the portfolios being compared. The Sharpe ratio (the ratio of mean return in excess of the risk-free rate of return to the standard deviation of return) serves as the appropriate metric.

---

[29] See Bodie, Kane, and Marcus (2001) for more on this topic.

- If a portfolio p has a higher positive Sharpe ratio than portfolio q, then p mean–variance dominates q if borrowing and lending at the risk-free rate is possible.[30]

Suppose asset allocation A is as before but now B has a mean of 6 percent and a standard deviation of 10 percent. Allocation A has higher mean return than B (9 percent versus 6 percent) but also higher risk (12 percent versus 10 percent), so the Markowitz decision rule is inconclusive about which allocation is better. Suppose we can borrow and lend at a risk-free rate of 3 percent. The Sharpe ratio of A, $(9 - 3)/12 = 0.50$, is higher than the Sharpe ratio of B, $(6 - 3)/10 = 0.30$, so we can conclude that A mean–variance dominates B. Note that a portfolio 83.3 percent invested in A and 16.7 percent invested in the risk-free asset has the same standard deviation as B, because $0.833(12) = 10$ percent, with mean return of $0.833(9) + 0.167(3) = 8$ percent, versus 6 percent for B. In short, we combined the higher Sharpe ratio portfolio p with the risk-free asset to achieve a portfolio with the same risk as portfolio q but with higher mean return. As B was originally defined (mean return of 8 percent and standard deviation of 15 percent), B had a Sharpe ratio of 0.33 and, as expected, the decision based on Sharpe ratios is consistent with that based on the Markowitz decision rule.

Practically, the above decision-making approach is most reliable when we are considering choices among well-diversified portfolios and when the return distributions of the choices are at least approximately normal.

The Decision to Add an Investment to an Existing Portfolio   We described an approach for choosing between two asset allocations as an either/or proposition. We now discuss an approach to deciding whether to add a new asset class to an existing portfolio, or more generally to further diversify an existing portfolio.

Suppose you hold a portfolio p with expected or mean return $E(R_p)$ and standard deviation of return σ_p. Then you are offered the opportunity to add another investment to your portfolio, for example, a new asset class. Will you effect a mean–variance improvement by expanding your portfolio to include a positive position in the new investment? To answer this question, you need three inputs:

- the Sharpe ratio of the new investment,
- the Sharpe ratio of the existing portfolio, and
- the correlation between the new investment's return and portfolio p's return, $\text{Corr}(R_{new}, R_p)$.

Adding the new asset to your portfolio is optimal if the following condition is met:[31]

$$\frac{E(R_{new}) - R_F}{\sigma_{new}} > \left(\frac{E(R_p) - R_F}{\sigma_p} \right) \text{Corr}(R_{new}, R_p) \qquad (11\text{-}10)$$

This expression says that in order to gain by adding the new investment to your holdings, the Sharpe ratio of the new investment must be larger than the product of the Sharpe ratio of your existing portfolio and the correlation of the new investment's returns with the returns of

---

[30]The reverse of the proposition is also true: If a portfolio p mean–variance dominates a portfolio q, then p has a higher Sharpe ratio than q. The proof of these propositions is in Dybvig and Ross (1985b). Note that we assume a positive Sharpe ratio for the higher Sharpe ratio portfolio to rule out some counterintuitive results when negative-Sharpe-ratio portfolios are compared.

[31]See Blume (1984) and Elton, Gruber, and Rentzler (1987).

your current portfolio. If Equation 11-10 holds, we can combine the new investment with the prior holdings to achieve a superior efficient frontier of risky assets (one in which the tangency portfolio has a higher Sharpe ratio). Note that although the expression may indicate that we effect a mean–variance improvement at the margin by adding a positive amount of a new asset, it does not indicate how much of the new asset we might want to add, or more broadly, what the efficient frontier including the new asset may be—to determine it, we would need to conduct an optimization. An insight from Equation 11-10 is that, in contrast to the case in which we considered investments as stand-alone and needed to consider only Sharpe ratios (from a mean–variance perspective) in choosing among them, in the case in which we can combine two investments, we must also consider their correlation. Example 11-6 illustrates how to use Equation 11-10 in deciding whether to add an asset class.

EXAMPLE 11-6   The Decision to Add an Asset Class

Jim Regal is chief investment officer of a Canadian pension fund invested in Canadian equities, Canadian bonds, Canadian real estate, and U.S. equities. The portfolio has a Sharpe ratio of 0.25. The investment committee is considering adding one or the other (but not both) of the following asset classes:

- Eurobonds: predicted Sharpe ratio = 0.10; predicted correlation with existing portfolio = 0.42.
- Non-North American developed market equities, as represented in the MSCI EAFE (Europe, Australasia, Far East) index: predicted Sharpe ratio = 0.30; predicted correlation with existing portfolio = 0.67.

1. Explain whether the investment committee should add Eurobonds to the existing portfolio.
2. Explain whether the committee should add non-North American developed market equities to the portfolio.

Solution to 1:   (Sharpe ratio of existing portfolio) × (Correlation of Eurobonds with existing portfolio) = 0.25(0.42) = 0.105. We should add Eurobonds if their predicted Sharpe ratio exceeds 0.105. Because the investment committee predicts a Sharpe ratio of 0.10 for Eurobonds, the committee should not add them to the existing portfolio.

Solution to 2: (Sharpe ratio of existing portfolio) × (Correlation of new equity class with existing portfolio) = 0.25(0.67) = 0.1675. Because the predicted Sharpe ratio of 0.30 for non-North American equities exceeds 0.1675, the investment committee should add them to the existing portfolio.

In Example 11-6, even if the correlation between the pension fund's existing portfolio and the proposed new equity class were +1, so that adding the new asset class had no potential risk reduction benefits, Equation 11-10 would indicate that the class should be added because the condition for adding the asset class would be satisfied, as $0.30 > 0.25(1.0)$. For any portfolio, we can always effect a mean–variance improvement at the margin by adding an investment with a higher Sharpe ratio than the existing portfolio. This result is intuitive, because the higher Sharpe ratio investment would mean–variance dominate the existing portfolio in a pairwise comparison. Again, we emphasize that the assumptions of mean–variance analysis must be fulfilled for these results to be reliable.

2.7.2. Determining an Asset Allocation

Our objective in this section is to summarize the mean–variance perspective on asset allocation. In a prior section, we gave the mathematical objective and constraints for determining the minimum-variance frontier of risky assets in the simplest case in which the only constraint on portfolio weights is that they sum to 1. Determining the efficient frontier using Equation 11-3 plus a constraint $w_i \geq 0$ to reflect no short sales is a starting point for many institutional investors in determining an asset allocation.[32] Mean–variance theory then points to choosing the asset allocation represented by the perceived tangency portfolio if the investor can borrow or lend at the risk-free rate. The manager can combine the tangency portfolio with the risk-free asset to achieve an efficient portfolio at a desired level of risk. Because the tangency portfolio represents the highest-Sharpe-ratio portfolio of risky assets, it is a logical baseline for an asset allocation.

This theoretical perspective, however, views the investment in a risk-free asset as a readily available risk-adjustment variable. In practice, investors may be constrained against using margin (borrowing), may face constraints concerning minimum and maximum positive investments in a risk-free asset, or may have other reasons for not adopting the perspective of theory.[33] In such a case, the investor may establish an asset allocation among risky asset classes that differs from the tangency portfolio. Quantifying his risk tolerance in terms of standard deviation of returns, the investor could choose the portfolio on the efficient frontier of risky assets that corresponds to the chosen level of standard deviation.

The CAPM framework provides even more narrowly focused choices because it adds the assumption that investors share the same views about mean returns, variances of returns, and correlations. Then all investors would agree on the identity of the tangency portfolio, which is the market portfolio of all risky assets held in proportion to their market values. This portfolio represents the highest possible degree of diversification. The exact identity of such an all-inclusive portfolio cannot be established, of course. Practically, however, investors can own highly diversified passively managed portfolios invested in major asset classes worldwide that approximately reflect the relative market values of the included classes. This asset allocation can be adapted to account for differential expectations. For example, the Black–Litterman (1991, 1992) asset allocation model takes a well-diversified market-value-weighted asset allocation as a neutral starting point for investors. The model incorporates a procedure for deviating from market capitalization weights in directions reflecting an investor's different-from-equilibrium model (CAPM) views concerning expected returns.

Mean–variance theory in relation to portfolio construction and asset allocation has been intensively examined, and researchers have recognized a number of its limitations. We will discuss an important limitation related to the sensitivity of the optimization procedure—the

---

[32] See Grinblatt and Titman (1998) and Elton, Gruber, Brown, and Goetzmann (2003) for discussions of solution methods and mechanics. In practice, investors often place additional constraints, such as constraints on maximum percentages, to assure plausible solutions. We discuss this approach further in the section on instability of the minimum-variance frontier.

[33] For example, a risk-free asset may not be readily available if the analysis is conducted in real terms. Only short-term inflation-protected securities, if available, are potentially risk free in such a context.

instability of the efficient frontier—in a later section. We must recognize that as a single-period model, mean–variance analysis ignores the liquidity and tax considerations that arise in a multiperiod world in which investors rebalance portfolios. Relatedly, the time horizon associated with the optimization, often one year, may be shorter than an investor's actual time horizon due to difficulties in developing inputs for long horizons.[34] Mean–variance analysis takes into account the correlation of returns across asset classes over single time periods but does not address serial correlation (long and short-term dependencies) in returns for a given asset class. Monte Carlo simulation is sometimes used in asset allocation to address such multiperiod issues.[35] Despite its limitations, mean–variance analysis provides an objective and fairly adaptable procedure for narrowing the unlimited set of choices we face in selecting an asset allocation.[36]

3. PRACTICAL ISSUES IN MEAN–VARIANCE ANALYSIS

We now discuss practical issues that arise in the application of mean–variance analysis in choosing portfolios. The two areas of focus are

- estimating inputs for mean–variance optimization, and
- the instability of the minimum-variance frontier, which results from the optimization process's sensitivity to the inputs.

Relative to the first area, we must ask two principal questions concerning the prediction of expected returns, variances, and correlations. First, which methods are feasible? Second, which are most accurate? Relative to sensitivity of the optimization process, we need to ask first, what is the source of the problem, and second, what corrective measures are available to address it.

3.1. Estimating Inputs for Mean–Variance Optimization

In this section, we compare the feasibility and accuracy of several methods for computing the inputs for mean–variance optimization. These methods use one of the following:

- historical means, variances, and correlations,
- historical beta estimated using the market model, or
- adjusted betas.

---

[34] See Swenson (2000). For example, if the investor's time horizon is five years, developing an efficient frontier involves estimating the correlations of five-year returns. Many assets have a limited number of independent five-year observations for correlation that we might use to develop estimates.

[35] See the chapter on probability distributions for more information about Monte Carlo simulation.

[36] For example, Chow (1995) adapted mean–variance optimization to address managers' concerns about performance relative to a benchmark, and Chow, Jacquier, Kritzman, and Lowry (1999) adapted optimization to account for correlations that may change in times of stress.

3.1.1. Historical Estimates   This approach involves calculating means, variances, and correlations directly from historical data. The historical method requires estimating a very large number of parameters when we are optimizing for even a moderately large number of assets. As a result, it is more feasible for asset allocation than for portfolio formation involving a large number of stocks.

The number of parameters a portfolio manager needs to estimate to determine the minimum-variance frontier depends on the number of potential stocks in the portfolio. If a portfolio manager has n stocks in a portfolio and wants to use mean–variance analysis, she must estimate

- n parameters for the expected returns to the stocks,
- n parameters for the variances of the stock returns, and
- $n(n - 1)/2$ parameters for the covariances of all the stock returns with each other.

Together, the parameters total $n^2/2 + 3n/2$.

The two limitations of the historical approach involve the quantity of estimates needed and the quality of historical estimates of inputs.

The quantity of estimates needed may easily be very large, mainly because the number of covariances increases in the square of the number of securities. If the portfolio manager wanted to compute the minimum-variance frontier for a portfolio of 100 stocks, she would need to estimate $100^2/2 + 3(100)/2 = 5,150$ parameters. If she wanted to compute the minimum-variance frontier for 1,000 stocks, she would need to estimate 501,500 parameters. Not only is this task unappealing, it might be impossible.[37]

The second limitation is that historical estimates of return parameters typically have substantial estimation error. The problem is least severe for estimates of variances.[38] The problem is acute with historical estimates of mean returns because the variability of risky asset returns is high relative to the mean, and the problem cannot be ameliorated by increasing the frequency of observations. Estimation error is also serious with historical estimates of covariances. The intuition in the case of covariances is that the historical method essentially tries to capture every random feature of a historical data set, reducing the usefulness of the estimates in a predictive mode. In a study based on monthly returns for U.S. stocks over the period 1973–1997, Chan, Karceski, and Lakonishok (1999) found that the correlation between past and future sample covariances was 0.34 at the 36-month horizon but only 0.18 at the 12-month horizon.

In current industry practice, the historical sample covariance matrix is not used without adjustment in mean–variance optimization. Adjusted values of variance and covariance may be weighted averages of the raw sample values and the average variance or covariance, respectively. For example, if a stock's variance of monthly returns is 0.0210 and the average stock's variance of monthly returns is 0.0098, the procedure might adjust 0.0210 downward, in the direction of the mean. Adjusting values in the direction of the mean reduces the dispersion in the estimates that may be caused by sampling error.[39]

---

[37]The number of time-series observations must exceed the number of securities for the covariances (including variances) to be estimated.

[38]See Chan, Karceski, and Lakonishok (1999) for empirical evidence that future variances are relatively more predictable from past variances than is the case for future covariances.

[39]For more information on this approach, called shrinkage estimators, see Michaud (1998) and Ledoit and Wolf (2004).

In estimating mean returns, analysts use a variety of approaches. They may adjust historical mean returns to reflect perceived contrasts between current market conditions and past average experience. They frequently use valuation models, such as models based on expected future cash flows, or equilibrium models, such as the CAPM, to develop forward-looking mean return estimates. Their use of these approaches reflects not only the technical issue of estimation error but also the risk in assuming that future performance will mirror past average performance.

3.1.2. Market Model Estimates: Historical Beta (Unadjusted)

A simpler way to compute the variances and covariances of asset returns involves the insight that asset returns may be related to each other through their correlation with a limited set of variables or factors. The simplest such model is the market model, which describes a regression relationship between the returns on an asset and the returns on the market portfolio. For asset i, the return to the asset can be modeled as

$$R_i = \alpha_i + \beta_i R_M + \epsilon_i \qquad (11\text{-}11)$$

where

R_i = the return on asset i

R_M = the return on the market portfolio

α_i = average return on asset i unrelated to the market return

β_i = the sensitivity of the return on asset i to the return on the market portfolio

ϵ_i = an error term

Consider first how to interpret β_i. If the market return increases by one percentage point, the market model predicts that the return to asset i will increase by β_i percentage points. (Recall that β_i is the slope in the market model.)

Now consider how to interpret α_i. If the market return is 0, the market model predicts that the return to asset i will be α_i, the intercept in the market model.

The market model makes the following assumptions about the terms in Equation 11-11:

- The expected value of the error term is 0, so $E(\epsilon_i) = 0$.
- The market return (R_M) is uncorrelated with the error term, $\text{Cov}(R_M, \epsilon_i) = 0$.
- The error terms, ϵ_i, are uncorrelated among different assets. For example, the error term for asset i is uncorrelated with the error term for asset j. Consequently, $E(\epsilon_i \epsilon_j) = 0$ for all i not equal to j.[40]

Note that some of these assumptions are very similar to those we made about the single-variable linear regression model in the chapter on correlation and regression. The market model, however, does not assume that the error term is normally distributed or that the variance of the error term is identical across assets.

Given these assumptions, the market model makes the following predictions about the expected returns of assets as well as the variances and covariances of asset returns.[41]

---

[40] $\text{Cov}(\epsilon_i, \epsilon_j) = E\{[\epsilon_i - E(\epsilon_i)][\epsilon_j - E(\epsilon_j)]\} = E[(\epsilon_i - 0)(\epsilon_j - 0)] = E(\epsilon_i \epsilon_j) = 0$. The assumption of uncorrelated errors is not innocuous. If we have more than one factor that affects returns for assets, then this assumption will be incorrect and single-factor models will produce inaccurate estimates for the covariance of asset returns.

[41] See Elton, Gruber, Brown, and Goetzmann (2003) for derivations of these results.

First, the expected return for asset i depends on the expected return to the market, $E(R_M)$, the sensitivity of the return on asset i to the return on the market, β_i, and the part of returns on asset i that are independent of market returns, α_i.

$$E(R_i) = \alpha_i + \beta_i E(R_M) \qquad (11\text{-}12)$$

Second, the variance of the return to asset i depends on the variance of the return to the market, σ_M^2, the variance of the error for the return of asset i in the market model, $\sigma_{\epsilon_i}^2$, and the sensitivity, β_i.

$$\mathrm{Var}(R_i) = \beta_i^2 \sigma_M^2 + \sigma_{\epsilon_i}^2 \qquad (11\text{-}13)$$

In the context of a model in which the market portfolio is the only source of risk, the first term in Equation 11-13, $\beta_i^2 \sigma_M^2$, is sometimes referred to as the systematic risk of asset i. The error variance term in Equation 11-13, $\sigma_{\epsilon_i}^2$, is sometimes referred to as the nonsystematic risk of asset i.

Third, the covariance of the return to asset i and the return to asset j depends on the variance of the return to the market, σ_M^2, and on the sensitivities β_i and β_j.

$$\mathrm{Cov}(R_i, R_j) = \beta_i \beta_j \sigma_M^2 \qquad (11\text{-}14)$$

We can use the market model to greatly reduce the computational task of providing the inputs to a mean–variance optimization. For each of the n assets, we need to know $\alpha_i, \beta_i, \sigma_{\epsilon_i}^2$, as well as the expected return and variance for the market. Because we need to estimate only $3n + 2$ parameters with the market model, we need far fewer parameters to construct the minimum-variance frontier than we would if we estimated the historical means, variances, and covariances of asset returns. For example, if we estimated the minimum-variance frontier for 1,000 assets (say, 1,000 different stocks), the market model would use 3,002 parameters for computing the minimum-variance frontier, whereas the historical estimates approach would require 501,500 parameters, as discussed earlier.

We do not know the parameters of the market model, so we must estimate them. But what method do we use? The most convenient way is to estimate a linear regression using time-series data on the returns to the market and the returns to each asset.

We can use the market model to estimate α_i and β_i by using a separate linear regression for each asset, using historical data on asset returns and market returns.[42] The regression output produces an estimate, $\hat{\beta}_i$, of β_i; we call this estimate an unadjusted beta. Later we will introduce an adjusted beta. We can use these estimates to compute the expected returns and the variances and covariances of those returns for mean–variance optimization.

EXAMPLE 11-7   Computing Stock Correlations Using the Market Model

You are estimating the correlation of returns between Cisco Systems (Nasdaq: CSCO) and Microsoft (Nasdaq: MSFT) as of late 2003. You run a market-model regression for

---

[42] One common practice is to use 60 monthly returns to estimate this model. The default setting on Bloomberg terminals uses two years of weekly data to estimate this model.

each of the two stocks based on monthly returns, using the S&P 500 to represent the market. You obtain the following regression results:

- The estimated beta for Cisco, $\hat{\beta}_{CSCO}$, is 2.09, and the residual standard deviation, $\hat{\sigma}_{\epsilon_{CSCO}}$, is 11.52.
- The estimated beta for Microsoft, $\hat{\beta}_{MSFT}$, is 1.75, and the residual standard deviation, $\sigma_{\epsilon_{MSFT}}$, is 11.26.

Your estimate of the variance of monthly returns on the S&P 500 is $\sigma_M^2 = 29.8$, which corresponds to an annual standard deviation of returns of about 18.9 percent. Using the data given, estimate the correlation of returns between Cisco and Microsoft.

Solution: We compute $\sigma_{\epsilon_{CSCO}}^2 = 132.71$ and $\sigma_{\epsilon_{MSFT}}^2 = 126.79$. Using the definition of correlation as covariance divided by the individual standard deviations, and using Equations 11-13 and 11-14, we have

$$\frac{\text{Cov}(R_{CSCO}, R_{MSFT})}{\text{Var}(R_{CSCO})^{1/2}\text{Var}(R_{MSFT})^{1/2}}$$

$$= \frac{\hat{\beta}_{CSCO}\hat{\beta}_{MSFT}(\hat{\sigma}_M^2)}{[\hat{\beta}_{CSCO}^2(\hat{\sigma}_M^2) + \hat{\sigma}_{\epsilon_{CSCO}}^2]^{1/2}[\hat{\beta}_{MSFT}^2(\hat{\sigma}_M^2) + \hat{\sigma}_{\epsilon_{MSFT}}^2]^{1/2}}$$

$$= \frac{(2.09)(1.75)(29.8)}{[(2.09)^2(29.8) + 132.71]^{1/2}[(1.75)^2(29.8) + 126.79]^{1/2}} = 0.4552$$

Thus the market model predicts that the correlation between the two asset returns is 0.4552.

One difficulty with using the market model is determining an appropriate index to represent the market. Typically, analysts who use the market model to determine the risk of individual domestic equities use returns on a domestic equity market index. In the United States, such an index might be the S&P 500 or the Wilshire 5000 Index; in the United Kingdom, the Financial Times Stock Exchange 100 Index might be used. Using returns on an equity market index may create a reasonable market model for equities, but it may not be reasonable for modeling the risk of other asset classes.[43]

3.1.3. Market Model Estimates: Adjusted Beta

Should we use historical betas from a market model for mean–variance optimization? Before we can answer this question, we need to restate our goal: We want to predict expected returns for a set of assets and the variances and covariances of those returns so that we can estimate the minimum-variance frontier for those assets. Estimates based on historical beta depend on the crucial assumption that the historical beta for a particular asset is the best predictor of the future beta for that asset. If beta

---

[43] Using this model to estimate the risk of other asset classes may violate two assumptions of single-factor models discussed earlier: The market return, R_M, is independent of the error term, ϵ_i; and the error terms, ϵ_i, are independent across assets. If either of these assumptions is violated, the market model will not produce accurate predictions of expected returns or the variances and covariances of returns.

changes over time, then this assumption is untrue. Therefore, we may want to use some other measure instead of historical beta to estimate an asset's future beta. These other forecasts are known by the general term **adjusted beta**. Researchers have shown that adjusted beta is often a better forecast of future beta than is historical beta. As a consequence, practitioners often use adjusted beta.

Suppose, for example, we are in period t and we want to estimate the minimum-variance frontier for period $t + 1$ for a set of stocks. We need to use data available in period t to predict the expected stock returns and the variances and covariances of those returns in period $t + 1$. Note, however, that the historical estimate of beta in period t for a particular stock may not be the best estimate we can make in period t of beta in period $t + 1$ for that stock. And the minimum-variance frontier for period $t + 1$ must be based on the forecast of beta for period $t + 1$.

If beta for each stock were a random walk from one period to the next, then we could write the relation between the beta for stock i in period t and the beta for stock i in period $t + 1$ as

$$\beta_{i,t+1} = \beta_{i,t} + \epsilon_{i,t+1}$$

where $\epsilon_{i,t+1}$ is an error term. If beta followed a random walk, the best predictor of $\beta_{i,t+1}$ would be $\beta_{i,t}$ because the error term has a mean value of 0. The historical beta would be the best predictor of the future beta, and the historical beta need not be adjusted.

In reality, beta for each stock often is not a random walk from one period to the next, and therefore, historical beta is not necessarily the best predictor of the future beta. For example, if beta can be represented as a first-order autoregression, then

$$\beta_{i,t+1} = \alpha_0 + \alpha_1 \beta_{i,t} + \epsilon_{i,t+1} \qquad (11\text{-}15)$$

If we estimate Equation 11-15 using time-series data on historical betas, the best predictor of $\beta_{i,t+1}$ is $\hat{\alpha}_0 + \hat{\alpha}_1 \beta_{i,t}$. In this case, the historical beta needs to be adjusted because the best prediction of beta in the next period is $\hat{\alpha}_0 + \hat{\alpha}_1 \beta_{i,t}$, not $\beta_{i,t}$.

Adjusted betas predict future betas better than historical betas do because betas are, on average, mean reverting.[44] Therefore, we should use adjusted, rather than historical, betas. One common method that practitioners use to adjust historical beta is to assume that $\alpha_0 = 0.333$ and $\alpha_1 = 0.667$. With this adjustment,

- if the historical beta equals 1.0, then the adjusted beta will be $0.333 + 0.667(1.0) = 1.0$.
- if the historical beta equals 1.5, then adjusted beta will be $0.333 + 0.667(1.5) = 1.333$.
- if the historical beta equals 0.5, then adjusted beta will be $0.333 + 0.667(0.5) = 0.667$.

Thus the mean-reverting level of beta is 1.0. If the historical beta is above 1.0, then adjusted beta will be below historical beta; if historical beta is below 1.0, then adjusted beta will be above historical beta.[45]

---

[44]See, for example, Klemkosky and Martin (1975).

[45]Although practitioners regularly use this method for computing adjusted beta, we are unaware of any published research suggesting that $\alpha_0 = 0.333$ and $\alpha_1 = 0.667$ are the best coefficient values to use in computing adjusted beta. Some researchers suggest an additional adjustment to historical betas called fundamental betas. **Fundamental betas** predict beta based on fundamental data for a company (price–earnings ratio, earnings growth, market capitalization, volatility, and so forth). Consulting firms such as BARRA sell estimates of fundamental betas.

3.2. Instability in the Minimum-Variance Frontier

Although standard mean–variance optimization, as represented by Equation 11-3, is a convenient and objective procedure for portfolio formation, we must use care when interpreting its results in practice. In this section, we discuss cautions regarding the use of mean–variance optimization. The problems that can arise have been widely studied, and remedies for them have been developed. With this knowledge, mean–variance optimization can still be a useful tool.

The chief problem with mean–variance optimization is that small changes in input assumptions can lead to large changes in the minimum-variance (and efficient) frontier. This problem is called **instability in the minimum-variance frontier**. It arises because, in practice, uncertainty exists about the expected returns, variances, and covariances used in tracing out the minimum-variance frontier.

Suppose, for example, that we use historical data to compute estimates to be used in an optimization. These means, variances, and covariances are sample quantities that are subject to random variation. In the chapter on sampling, for instance, we discussed how the sample mean has a probability distribution, called its sampling distribution. The sample mean is only a point estimate of the underlying or population mean.[46] The optimization process attempts to maximally exploit differences among assets. When these differences are statistically (and economically) insignificant (e.g., representing random variation), the resulting minimum-variance frontiers are misleading and not practically useful. Mean–variance optimization then overfits the data: It does too much with differences that are actually not meaningful. In an optimization with no limitation on short sales, assets can appear with very large negative weights, reflecting this overfitting (a negative weight for an asset means that the asset is sold short). Portfolios with very large short positions are of little practical interest.[47] Because of sensitivity to small changes in inputs, mean–variance optimizations may suggest too-frequent portfolio rebalancing, which is costly. Responses to instability include the following:

- Adding constraints against short sales (which is sometimes an institutional investment policy constraint as well). In Equation 11-3, we can add a no-short-sales constraint specifying that all asset weights must be positive: $w_j \geq 0, j = 1, 2, 3, \ldots, n$.[48]
- Improving the statistical quality of inputs to optimization.
- Using a statistical concept of the efficient frontier, reflecting the fact that the inputs to the optimization are random variables rather than constants.[49]

We stated above that mean–variance optimizations can recommend too-frequent portfolio rebalancing. Similarly, we find that the minimum-variance frontier is generally unstable when calculated using historical data for different time periods. One possible explanation is that the different frontiers reflect shifts in the parameters of asset return distribution between sample time periods. Time instability of the minimum-variance frontier can also result from random variation in means, variances, and covariances, when the underlying parameters are actually unchanged. Small differences in sample periods used for mean–variance optimization may

---

[46] The underlying means of asset returns are particularly difficult to estimate accurately. See Luenberger (1998) for an introduction to this problem, as well as Black (1993).

[47] In practice, few investors that engage in short sales would take a large short position as a result of an analysis restricted to means, variances, and correlations. Unlimited losses are possible in a short position.

[48] In practice, other ad hoc constraints on the size of positions are sometimes used as well.

[49] For example, Michaud (1998) defines a region of efficient portfolios that are statistically equivalent at a given confidence level. A portfolio falling in the region is consistent with being efficient and does not need to be rebalanced.

greatly affect a model even if the distribution of asset returns is stationary. Example 11-8 illustrates time instability with the data used for optimization.

EXAMPLE 11-8   Time Instability of the Minimum-Variance Frontier

In Example 11-2, we calculated a minimum-variance frontier for four asset classes for the period 1970 through 2002. What variation would we find among minimum-variance frontiers for subperiods of 1970 to 2002? To find out, we take the data for decades within the entire period, calculate the sample statistics, and then trace out the minimum-variance frontier for each decade. Table 11-10 shows the sample statistics of the monthly asset returns to these four asset classes for 1970 to 1979, 1980 to 1989, 1990 to 2002, and the combined sample period.

TABLE 11-10   Average Returns, Standard Deviations, and Correlation Matrixes

	S&P 500	U.S. Small-Cap Stocks	MSCI World ex-United States	U.S. Long-Term Government Bonds
A. *Average Returns*				
Time Period				
1970–1979	7.0%	14.4%	11.8%	5.7%
1980–1989	17.6%	16.7%	21.1%	12.9%
1990–2002	10.4%	13.2%	2.7%	9.9%
Overall period	11.6%	14.6%	11.1%	9.6%
B. *Standard Deviations*				
Time Period				
1970–1979	15.93%	26.56%	16.68%	8.25%
1980–1989	16.41%	19.17%	17.32%	14.19%
1990–2002	15.27%	20.71%	16.93%	8.31%
Overall period	15.83%	22.18%	17.07%	10.44%
C. *Correlation Matrixes*				
1970–1979				
S&P 500	1			
U.S. Small-cap	0.787	1		
MSCI ex-U.S.	0.544	0.490	1	
U.S. LT Bonds	0.415	0.316	0.218	1
1980–1989				
S&P 500	1			
U.S. Small-cap	0.844	1		
MSCI ex-U.S.	0.512	0.483	1	
U.S. LT Bonds	0.310	0.171	0.229	1

(continued)

TABLE 11-10 *(continued)*

	S&P 500	U.S. Small-Cap Stocks	MSCI World ex-United States	U.S. Long-Term Government Bonds
1990–1999				
S&P 500	1			
U.S. Small-cap	0.611	1		
MSCI ex-U.S.	0.647	0.473	1	
U.S. LT Bonds	0.097	−0.047	0.017	1
Overall Period				
S&P 500	1			
U.S. Small-cap	0.731	1		
MSCI ex-U.S.	0.573	0.475	1	
U.S. LT Bonds	0.266	0.138	0.155	1

Source: Ibbotson Associates.

As we might expect, variation occurs within subperiods in the sample means, variances, and covariances for all asset classes. Initially, the correlations offer the impression of relative stability over time. For example, the correlation of the S&P 500 with the MSCI World ex-U.S. was 0.544, 0.512, and 0.647 for 1970 to 1979, 1980 to 1989, and 1990 to 2002, respectively. In contrast to ranking by mean returns, the ranking of asset classes by standard deviation was the same in each decade, with U.S. small-cap stocks the riskiest asset class and bonds the least risky. We could use statistical inference to explore interperiod differences. With these initial impressions in mind, however, let us view the decades' minimum-variance frontiers.

Figure 11-11 shows the minimum-variance frontiers computed using the historical return statistics shown in Table 11-10 for 1970 to 1979, 1980 to 1989, 1990 to 2002, and the entire sample period. As this figure shows, the minimum-variance frontiers can differ dramatically in different periods. For example, note that the minimum-variance frontiers based on data from 1970 to 1979 and 1980 to 1989 do not overlap at all.

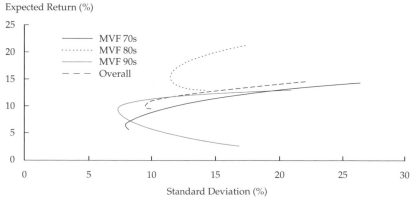

FIGURE 11-11   Historical Minimum–Variance Frontier Comparison

As mentioned, researchers have developed various methods to address portfolio managers' concerns about the issue of instability.

EXAMPLE 11-9   How Yale University's Endowment Fund Uses Mean–Variance Analysis

David Swensen, Yale University's chief investment officer (who also teaches portfolio management at Yale), wrote that "unconstrained mean–variance [optimization] usually provide[s] solutions unrecognizable as reasonable portfolios . . . . Because the process involves material simplifying assumptions, adopting the unconstrained asset allocation point estimates produced by mean–variance optimization makes little sense."[50]

Swensen's remarks highlight practitioners' concerns about the usefulness of standard mean–variance optimization. Among the most important simplifying assumptions of mean–variance analysis is that the means, variances, and covariances of assets in a portfolio are known. Because the optimization process tries to make much of small differences, and the true values of the means and other parameters are uncertain, this simplifying assumption has a large impact. As mentioned earlier, responses to instability include adding constraints on asset weights and modifying historical sample estimates of the inputs. Despite Swensen's criticism, Yale uses mean–variance analysis for allocating its portfolio; however, the Yale Investment Office adds constraints on weights and does not use raw historical inputs.

---

4. MULTIFACTOR MODELS

Earlier we discussed the market model, which was historically the first attempt to describe the process that drives asset returns. The market model assumes that all explainable variation in asset returns is related to a single factor, the return to the market. Yet asset returns may be related to factors other than market return, such as interest rate movements, inflation, or industry-specific returns. For many years, investment professionals have used multifactor models in portfolio management, risk analysis, and the evaluation of portfolio performance.

Multifactor models have gained importance for the practical business of portfolio management for two main reasons. First, multifactor models explain asset returns better than the market model does.[51] Second, multifactor models provide a more detailed analysis of risk than does a single factor model. That greater level of detail is useful in both passive and active management.

- *Passive management.* In managing a fund that seeks to track an index with many component securities, portfolio managers may need to select a sample of securities from the index.

---

[50] Swensen (2000).

[51] See, for example, Burmeister and McElroy (1988). These authors show that at the 1 percent significance level, the CAPM can be rejected in favor of an arbitrage pricing theory model with several factors. We discuss arbitrage pricing theory later in the chapter.

Analysts can use multifactor models to match an index fund's factor exposures to the factor exposures of the index tracked.

- *Active management.* Multifactor models are used in portfolio formation to model the expected returns and risks of securities and portfolio. Many quantitative investment managers rely on multifactor models in predicting alpha (excess risk-adjusted returns) or relative return (the return on one asset or asset class relative to that of another) as part of a variety of active investment strategies. In evaluating portfolios, analysts use multifactor models to understand the sources of active managers' returns and assess the risks assumed relative to the manager's **benchmark** (comparison portfolio).

In the following sections, we explain the basic principles of factor models and discuss various types of models and their application. We also present the arbitrage pricing theory developed by Ross (1976), which relates the expected return of investments to their risk with respect to a set of factors.

4.1. Factors and Types of Multifactor Models

To begin by defining terms, a **factor** is a common or underlying element with which several variables are correlated. For example, the market factor is an underlying element with which individual share returns are correlated. We search for **systematic factors**, which affect the average returns of a large number of different assets. These factors represent **priced risk**, risk for which investors require an additional return for bearing. Systematic factors should thus help explain returns.

Many varieties of multifactor models have been proposed and researched. We can categorize most of them into three main groups, according to the type of factor used:

- In **macroeconomic factor models**, the factors are surprises in macroeconomic variables that significantly explain equity returns. The factors can be understood as affecting either the expected future cash flows of companies or the interest rate used to discount these cash flows back to the present.
- In **fundamental factor models**, the factors are attributes of stocks or companies that are important in explaining cross-sectional differences in stock prices. Among the fundamental factors that have been used are the book-value-to-price ratio, market capitalization, the price–earnings ratio, and financial leverage.
- In **statistical factor models**, statistical methods are applied to a set of historical returns to determine portfolios that explain historical returns in one of two senses. In factor analysis models, the factors are the portfolios that best explain (reproduce) historical return covariances. In principal-components models, the factors are portfolios that best explain (reproduce) the historical return variances.

Some practical factor models have the characteristics of more than one of the above categories. We can call such models **mixed factor models**.

Our discussion concentrates on macroeconomic factor models and fundamental factor models. Industry use has generally favored fundamental and macroeconomic models, perhaps because such models are much more easily interpreted; nevertheless, statistical factor models have proponents and are used in practical applications.

4.2. The Structure of Macroeconomic Factor Models

The representation of returns in macroeconomic factor models assumes that the returns to each asset are correlated with only the surprises in some factors related to the aggregate economy, such as inflation or real output.[52] We can define **surprise** in general as the actual value minus predicted (or expected) value. A factor's surprise is the component of the factor's return that was unexpected, and the factor surprises constitute the model's independent variables. This idea contrasts to the representation of independent variables as returns (as opposed to the surprise in returns) in fundamental factor models, or for that matter in the market model.

Suppose that K factors explain asset returns. Then in a macroeconomic factor model, the following equation expresses the return of asset i:

$$R_i = a_i + b_{i1}F_1 + b_{i2}F_2 + \cdots + b_{iK}F_K + \epsilon_i \qquad (11\text{-}16)$$

where

> R_i = the return to asset i
>
> a_i = the expected return to asset i
>
> F_k = the surprise in the factor $k, k = 1, 2, \ldots, K$
>
> b_{ik} = the sensitivity of the return on asset i to a surprise in factor $k, k = 1, 2, \ldots, K$
>
> ϵ_i = an error term with a zero mean that represents the portion of the return to asset i not explained by the factor model

What exactly do we mean by the surprise in a macroeconomic factor? Suppose we are analyzing monthly returns for stocks. At the beginning of each month, we have a prediction of inflation for the month. The prediction may come from an econometric model or a professional economic forecaster, for example. Suppose our forecast at the beginning of the month is that inflation will be 0.4 percent during the month. At the end of the month, we find that inflation was actually 0.5 percent during the month. During any month,

Actual inflation = Predicted inflation + Surprise inflation

In this case, actual inflation was 0.5 percent and predicted inflation was 0.4 percent. Therefore, the surprise in inflation was $0.5 - 0.4 = 0.1$ percent.

What is the effect of defining the factors in terms of surprises? Suppose we believe that inflation and gross domestic product (GDP) growth are priced risk. (GDP is a money measure of the goods and services produced within a country's borders.) We do not use the predicted values of these variables because the predicted values are already reflected in stock prices and thus in their expected returns. The intercept a_i, the expected return to asset i, reflects the effect of the predicted values of the macroeconomic variables on expected stock returns. The surprise in the macroeconomic variables during the month, on the other hand, contains new information about the variable. As a result, this model structure analyzes the return to an asset into three components: the asset's expected return, its unexpected return resulting from new information about the factors, and an error term.

Consider a factor model in which the returns to each asset are correlated with two factors. For example, we might assume that the returns for a particular stock are correlated with

---

[52]See, for example, Burmeister, Roll, and Ross (1994).

surprises in interest rates and surprises in GDP growth. For stock i, the return to the stock can be modeled as

$$R_i = a_i + b_{i1}F_{INT} + b_{i2}F_{GDP} + \epsilon_i \qquad (11\text{-}17)$$

where

R_i = the return to stock i

a_i = the expected return to stock i

b_{i1} = the sensitivity of the return to stock i to interest rate surprises

F_{INT} = the surprise in interest rates

b_{i2} = the sensitivity of the return to stock i to GDP growth surprises

F_{GDP} = the surprise in GDP growth

ϵ_i = an error term with a zero mean that represents the portion of the return to asset i not explained by the factor model

Consider first how to interpret b_{i1}. The factor model predicts that a one percentage point surprise in interest rates will contribute b_{i1} percentage points to the return to stock i. The slope coefficient b_{i2} has a similar interpretation relative to the GDP growth factor. Thus slope coefficients are naturally interpreted as the factor sensitivities of the asset.[53] A **factor sensitivity** is a measure of the response of return to each unit of increase in a factor, holding all other factors constant.

Now consider how to interpret the intercept a_i. Recall that the error term has a mean or average value of 0. If the surprises in both interest rates and GDP growth are 0, the factor model predicts that the return to asset i will be a_i. Thus a_i is the expected value of the return to stock i.

Finally, consider the error term ϵ_i. The intercept a_i represents the asset's expected return. The amount $(b_{i1}F_{INT} + b_{i2}F_{GDP})$ represents the return resulting from factor surprises, and we have interpreted these as the sources of risk shared with other assets. The term ϵ_i is the part of return that is unexplained by expected return or the factor surprises. If we have adequately represented the sources of common risk (the factors), then ϵ_i must represent an asset-specific risk. For a stock, it might represent the return from an unanticipated company-specific event.

We will discuss expected returns further when we present the arbitrage pricing theory. In macroeconomic factor models, the time series of factor surprises are developed first. We use regression analysis to estimate assets' sensitivities to the factors. In our discussion, we assume that you do not estimate sensitivities and intercepts yourself; instead you use estimates from another source (for example, one of the many consulting companies that specialize in factor models).[54] When we have the parameters for the individual assets in a portfolio, we can calculate the portfolio's parameters as a weighted average of the parameters of individual assets. An individual asset's weight in that calculation is the proportion of the total market value of the portfolio that the individual asset represents.

---

[53]Factor sensitivities are sometimes called **factor betas** or **factor loadings**.

[54]If you want to estimate your own macroeconomic factor model, follow these steps. First, estimate a time series for each macroeconomic surprise (for example, you could use the residuals from a time-series model for each different macroeconomic series). Then, use time-series data to regress the returns for a particular asset on the surprises to the different macroeconomic factors.

EXAMPLE 11-10 Factor Sensitivities for a Two-Stock Portfolio

Suppose that stock returns are affected by two common factors: surprises in inflation and surprises in GDP growth. A portfolio manager is analyzing the returns on a portfolio of two stocks, Manumatic (MANM) and Nextech (NXT). The following equations describe the returns for those stocks, where the factors F_{INFL} and F_{GDP} represent the surprise in inflation and GDP growth, respectively:

$$R_{MANM} = 0.09 - 1F_{INFL} + 1F_{GDP} + \epsilon_{MANM}$$

$$R_{NXT} = 0.12 + 2F_{INFL} + 4F_{GDP} + \epsilon_{NXT}$$

In evaluating the equations for surprises in inflation and GDP, amounts stated in percent terms need to be converted to decimal form. One-third of the portfolio is invested in Manumatic stock, and two-thirds is invested in Nextech stock.

1. Formulate an expression for the return on the portfolio.
2. State the expected return on the portfolio.
3. Calculate the return on the portfolio given that the surprises in inflation and GDP growth are 1 percent and 0 percent, respectively, assuming that the error terms for MANM and NXT both equal 0.5 percent.

Solution to 1: The portfolio's return is the following weighted average of the returns to the two stocks:

$$R_P = (1/3)(0.09) + (2/3)(0.12) + [(1/3)(-1) + (2/3)(2)]F_{INFL} + [(1/3)(1)$$
$$+ (2/3)(4)]F_{GDP} + (1/3)\epsilon_{MANM} + (2/3)\epsilon_{NXT}$$
$$= 0.11 + 1F_{INFL} + 3F_{GDP} + (1/3)\epsilon_{MANM} + (2/3)\epsilon_{NXT}$$

Solution to 2: The expected return on the portfolio is 11 percent, the value of the intercept in the expression obtained in Part 1.

Solution to 3:

$$R_P = 0.11 + 1F_{INFL} + 3F_{GDP} + (1/3)\epsilon_{MANM} + (2/3)\epsilon_{NXT}$$
$$= 0.11 + 1(0.01) + 3(0) + (1/3)(0.005) + (2/3)(0.005)$$
$$= 0.125 \text{ or } 12.5 \text{ percent}$$

4.3. Arbitrage Pricing Theory and the Factor Model

In the 1970s, Stephen Ross developed the arbitrage pricing theory (APT) as an alternative to the CAPM. APT describes the expected return on an asset (or portfolio) as a linear function of the risk of the asset (or portfolio) with respect to a set of factors. Like the CAPM, the APT describes a financial market equilibrium. However, the APT makes less-strong assumptions than the CAPM. The APT relies on three assumptions:

1. A factor model describes asset returns.
2. There are many assets, so investors can form well-diversified portfolios that eliminate asset-specific risk.
3. No arbitrage opportunities exist among well-diversified portfolios.

Arbitrage is a risk-free operation that earns an expected positive net profit but requires no net investment of money.[55] An **arbitrage opportunity** is an opportunity to conduct an arbitrage—an opportunity to earn an expected positive net profit without risk and with no net investment of money.

In the first assumption, the number of factors is not specified. The second assumption allows us to form portfolios with factor risk but without asset-specific risk. The third assumption is the condition of financial market equilibrium.

Empirical evidence indicates that Assumption 2 is reasonable. When a portfolio contains many stocks, the asset-specific or nonsystematic risk of individual stocks makes almost no contribution to the variance of portfolio returns. Roll and Ross (2001) found that only 1 percent to 3 percent of a well-diversified portfolio's variance comes from the nonsystematic variance of the individual stocks in the portfolio, as Figure 11-12 shows.

According to the APT, if the above three assumptions hold, the following equation holds:[56]

$$E(R_p) = R_F + \lambda_1 \beta_{p,1} + \cdots + \lambda_K \beta_{p,K} \tag{11-18}$$

where

$$\begin{aligned}
E(R_p) &= \text{the expected return to portfolio } p \\
R_F &= \text{the risk-free rate} \\
\lambda_j &= \text{the risk premium for factor } j \\
\beta_{p,j} &= \text{the sensitivity of the portfolio to factor } j \\
K &= \text{the number of factors}
\end{aligned}$$

The APT equation, Equation 11-18, says that the expected return on any well-diversified portfolio is linearly related to the factor sensitivities of that portfolio.[57]

---

[55] As we will see, arbitrage typically involves funding the investment in assets with proceeds from the short sale of other assets, so that net, no money is invested. A short sale is the sale of a borrowed asset. Note that the word "arbitrage" is also sometimes used to describe investment operations in which significant risk is present.

[56] A risk-free asset is assumed. If no risk-free asset exists, in place of R_F we write λ_0 to represent the expected return on a risky portfolio with zero sensitivity to all the factors. The number of factors is not specified but must be much lower than the number of assets, a condition fulfilled in practice.

[57] The APT equation can also describe (at least approximately) the expected return on investments with asset-specific risk, under certain conditions.

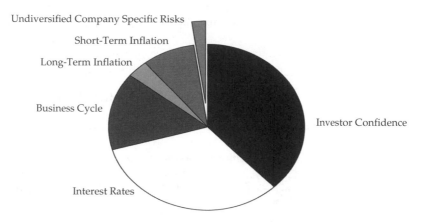

From *What Is the Arbitrage Pricing Theory.*
Retrieved May 25, 2001, from the World Wide Web: www.rollross.com/apt.html.
Reprinted with permission of Richard Roll.

FIGURE 11-12   Sources of Volatility: The Case of a Well Diversified Portfolio

The **factor risk premium** (or **factor price**) λ_j represents the expected return in excess of the risk-free rate for a portfolio with a sensitivity of 1 to factor j and a sensitivity of 0 to all other factors. Such a portfolio is called a **pure factor portfolio** for factor j.

For example, suppose we have a portfolio with a sensitivity of 1 with respect to Factor 1 and a sensitivity of 0 to all other factors. With E_1 being the expected return on this portfolio, Equation 11-18 shows that the expected return on this portfolio is $E_1 = R_F + \lambda_1 \times 1$, so $\lambda_1 = E_1 - R_F$. Suppose that $E_1 = 0.12$ and $R_F = 0.04$. Then the risk premium for Factor 1 is $\lambda_1 = 0.12 - 0.04 = 0.08$ or 8 percent. We obtain an eight percentage point increase in expected return for an increase of 1 in the sensitivity to first factor.

What is the relationship between the APT equation and the equation for a multifactor model, Equation 11-17? In discussing the multifactor model, we stated that the intercept term is the investment's expected return. The APT equation explains what an investment's expected return is in equilibrium. Thus if the APT holds, it places a restriction on the intercept term in the multifactor model in the sense that the APT model tells us what the intercept's value should be. For instance, in Example 11-10, the APT would explain the intercept of 0.09 in the model for MANM returns as the expected return on MANM given the stock's sensitivities to the inflation and GDP factors and the risk premiums of the those factors. We can in fact substitute the APT equation into the multifactor model to produce what is known as an APT model in returns form.[58]

To use the APT equation, we need to estimate its parameters. The parameters of the APT equation are the risk-free rate and the factor risk premiums (the factor sensitivities are

---

[58]An interesting issue is the relationship between the APT and the CAPM. If the market is the factor in a single-factor model, APT (Equation 11-18) is consistent with the CAPM. The CAPM can also be consistent with multiple factors in an APT model, if the risk premiums in the APT model satisfy certain restrictions; these CAPM-related restrictions have been repeatedly rejected in statistical tests. See Burmeister and McElroy (1988), for example.

specific to individual investments). Example 11-11 shows how the expected returns and factor sensitivities of a set of portfolios can determine the parameters of the APT model assuming a single factor.

EXAMPLE 11-11   Determining the Parameters in a One-Factor APT Model

Suppose we have three well-diversified portfolios that are each sensitive to the same single factor. Table 11-11 shows the expected returns and factor sensitivities of these portfolios. Assume that the expected returns reflect a one-year investment horizon.

TABLE 11-11   Sample Portfolios for a One-Factor Model

Portfolio	Expected Return	Factor Sensitivity
A	0.075	0.5
B	0.150	2.0
C	0.070	0.4

We can use these data to determine the parameters of the APT equation. According to Equation 11-18, for any well-diversified portfolio and assuming a single factor explains returns, we have $E(R_p) = R_F + \lambda_1 \beta_{p,1}$. The factor sensitivities and expected returns are known; thus there are two unknowns, the parameters R_F and λ_1. Because two points define a straight line, we need to set up only two equations. Selecting Portfolios A and B, we have

$$E(R_A) = 0.075 = R_F + 0.5\lambda_1$$

and

$$E(R_B) = 0.150 = R_F + 2\lambda_1$$

From the equation for Portfolio A, we have $R_F = 0.075 - 0.5\lambda_1$. Substituting this expression for the risk-free rate into the equation for Portfolio B gives

$$0.15 = 0.075 - 0.5\lambda_1 + 2\lambda_1$$

$$0.15 = 0.075 + 1.5\lambda_1$$

So we have $\lambda_1 = (0.15 - 0.075)/1.5 = 0.05$. Substituting this value for λ_1 back into the equation for the expected return to Portfolio A yields

$$0.075 = R_F + 0.05 \times 0.5$$

$$R_F = 0.05$$

So the risk-free rate is 0.05 or 5 percent, and the factor premium for the common factor is also 0.05 or 5 percent. The APT equation is

$$E(R_p) = 0.05 + 0.05\beta_{p,1}$$

Portfolio C has a factor sensitivity of 0.4. Accordingly, $0.05 + (0.05 \times 0.4) = 0.07$ or 7 percent if no arbitrage opportunity exists. The expected return for Portfolio C given in Table 11-11 is 7 percent. Therefore, in this example no arbitrage opportunity exists.

EXAMPLE 11-12   Checking Whether Portfolio Returns Are Consistent with No Arbitrage

In this example, we demonstrate how to tell whether a set of expected returns for well-diversified portfolios is consistent with the APT by testing whether an arbitrage opportunity exists. In Example 11-11, we had three portfolios with expected returns and factor sensitivities that were consistent with the one-factor APT model $E(R_p) = 0.05 + 0.05\beta_{p,1}$. Suppose we expand the set of portfolios to include a fourth well-diversified portfolio, Portfolio D. Table 11-12 repeats the data given in Table 11-11 for Portfolios A, B, and C, in addition to providing data on Portfolio D and a portfolio we form using A and C.

TABLE 11-12   Sample Portfolios for a One-Factor Model

Portfolio	Expected Return	Factor Sensitivity
A	0.0750	0.50
B	0.1500	2.00
C	0.0700	0.40
D	0.0800	0.45
0.5A + 0.5C	0.0725	0.45

The expected return and factor sensitivity of a portfolio is the weighted average of the expected returns and factor sensitivities of the assets in the portfolio. Suppose we construct a portfolio consisting of 50 percent Portfolio A and 50 percent Portfolio C. Table 11-12 shows that the expected return of this portfolio is $(0.50)(0.0750) + (0.50)(0.07) = 0.0725$, or 7.25 percent. The factor sensitivity of this portfolio is $(0.50)(0.50) + (0.50)(0.40) = 0.45$.

Arbitrage pricing theory assumes that well-diversified portfolios present no arbitrage opportunities. If the initial investment is 0 and we bear no risk, the final expected cash flow should be 0. In this case, the configuration of expected returns in relation to factor risk presents an arbitrage opportunity involving Portfolios A, C, and D. Portfolio D offers too high an expected rate of return given its factor sensitivity.

According to the APT model estimated in Example 11-11, an arbitrage opportunity exists unless $E(R_D) = 0.05 + 0.05\beta_{D,1} = 0.05 + (0.05 \times 0.45) = 0.0725$, so that the expected return on D is 7.25 percent. In fact, the expected return on D is 8 percent. Portfolio D is undervalued relative to its factor risk. We will buy D (hold it long) in the portfolio that exploits the arbitrage opportunity (the **arbitrage portfolio**). We purchase D using the proceeds from selling short a portfolio consisting of A and C with exactly the same 0.45 factor sensitivity as D. As we showed above, an equally weighted portfolio of A and C has a factor sensitivity of 0.45.

The arbitrage thus involves the following strategy: Invest $10,000 in Portfolio D and fund that investment by selling short an equally weighted portfolio of Portfolios A and C; then close out the investment position at the end of one year (the investment horizon for expected returns). Table 11-13 demonstrates the arbitrage profits to the arbitrage strategy. The final row of the table shows the net cash flow to the arbitrage portfolio.

TABLE 11-13   Arbitrage Opportunity within Sample Portfolios

	Initial Cash Flow	Final Cash Flow	Factor Sensitivity
Portfolio D	−$10,000.00	$10,800.00	0.45
Portfolios A and C	$10,000.00	−$10,725.00	−0.45
Sum	$0.00	$75.00	0.00

As Table 11-13 shows, if we buy $10,000 of Portfolio D and sell $10,000 of an equally weighted portfolio of Portfolios A and C, we have an initial net cash flow of $0. The expected value of our investment in Portfolio D at the end of one year is $10,000(1 + 0.08) = \$10,800$. The expected value of our short position in Portfolios A and C at the end of one year is $-\$10,000(1.0725) = -\$10,725$. So the combined expected cash flow from our investment position in one year is $75.

What about the risk? Table 11-13 shows that the factor risk has been eliminated: Purchasing D and selling short an equally weighted portfolio of A and C creates a portfolio with a factor sensitivity of $0.45 - 0.45 = 0$. The portfolios are well diversified, and we assume any asset-specific risk is negligible.

Because the arbitrage is possible, Portfolios A, C, and D cannot all be consistent with the same equilibrium. A unique set of parameters for the APT model does not describe the returns on these three portfolios. If Portfolio D actually had an expected return of 8 percent, investors would bid up its price until the expected return fell and the arbitrage opportunity vanished. Thus arbitrage restores equilibrium relationships among expected returns.

In Example 11-11, we illustrated how the parameters of a single-factor APT model can be determined from data. Example 11-13 shows how to determine the model parameters in a model with more than one factor.

EXAMPLE 11-13   Determining the Parameters in a Two-Factor Model

Suppose that two factors, surprise in inflation (Factor 1) and surprise in GDP growth (Factor 2), explain returns. According to the APT, an arbitrage opportunity exists unless

$$E(R_p) = R_F + \lambda_1 \beta_{p,1} + \lambda_2 \beta_{p,2}$$

Our goal is to estimate the three parameters of the model, R_F, λ_1, and λ_2. We also have hypothetical data on three well-diversified portfolios, J, K, and L, given in Table 11-14.

TABLE 11-14   Sample Portfolios for a Two-Factor Model

Portfolio	Expected Return	Sensitivity to Inflation Factor	Sensitivity to GDP Factor
J	0.14	1.0	1.5
K	0.12	0.5	1.0
L	0.11	1.3	1.1

If the market is in equilibrium (no arbitrage opportunities exist), the expected returns to the three portfolios should be described by the two-factor APT with the same set of parameters. Using the expected returns and the return sensitivities shown in Table 11-14 yields

$$E(R_J) = 0.14 = R_F + 1.0\lambda_1 + 1.5\lambda_2$$

$$E(R_K) = 0.12 = R_F + 0.5\lambda_1 + 1.0\lambda_2$$

$$E(R_L) = 0.11 = R_F + 1.3\lambda_1 + 1.1\lambda_2$$

We have three equations with three unknowns, so we can solve for the parameters using the method of substitution. We first want to get two equations with two unknowns. Solving the equation for $E(R_J)$ for the risk-free rate,

$$R_F = 0.14 - 1.0\lambda_1 - 1.5\lambda_2$$

Substituting this expression for the risk-free rate into the equation for $E(R_K)$, we find, after simplification, that $\lambda_1 = 0.04 - \lambda_2$. Using $\lambda_1 = 0.04 - \lambda_2$ to eliminate λ_1 in the equation for $E(R_J)$,

$$0.10 = R_F + 0.5\lambda_2$$

Using $\lambda_1 = 0.04 - \lambda_2$ to eliminate λ_1 in the equation for $E(R_L)$,

$$0.058 = R_F - 0.2\lambda_2$$

Using the two equations in R_F and λ_2 immediately above, we find that $\lambda_2 = 0.06$ (we solved for the risk-free rate in the first of these two equations and used the expression in the second equation). Because $\lambda_1 = 0.04 - \lambda_2, \lambda_1 = -0.02$. Finally, $R_F = 0.14 - 1.0 \times (-0.02) - 1.5 \times (0.06) = 0.07$. To summarize:

$R_F = 0.07$ (The risk-free rate is 7 percent.)

$\lambda_1 = -0.02$ (The inflation risk premium is -2 percent per unit of sensitivity.)

$\lambda_2 = 0.06$ (The GDP risk premium is 6 percent per unit of sensitivity.)

So, the APT equation for these three portfolios is

$$E(R_p) = 0.07 - 0.02\beta_{p,1} + 0.06\beta_{p,2}$$

This example illustrates the calculations for determining the parameters of an APT model. It also shows that the risk premium for a factor can actually be negative.

In Example 11-13, we computed a *negative* risk premium for the inflation factor. One explanation for a negative inflation risk premium is that most equities have negative sensitivities to inflation risk (their returns tend to decrease with a positive inflation surprise). An asset with a positive inflation sensitivity would be in demand as an inflation-hedging asset; the premium associated with a factor portfolio for inflation risk could be negative as a result.

4.4. The Structure of Fundamental Factor Models

We earlier gave the equation of a macroeconomic factor model as

$$R_i = a_i + b_{i1}F_1 + b_{i2}F_2 + \cdots + b_{iK}F_K + \epsilon_i$$

We can also represent the structure of fundamental factor models with this equation, but we need to interpret the terms differently.

In fundamental factor models, the factors are stated as returns rather than return surprises in relation to predicted values, so they do not generally have expected values of zero. This approach changes the interpretation of the intercept, which we no longer interpret as the expected return.[59]

We also interpret the factor sensitivities differently in most fundamental factor models. In fundamental factor models, the factor sensitivities are attributes of the security. Consider a fundamental model for equities with a dividend yield factor. An asset's sensitivity to the dividend factor is the value of the attribute itself, its dividend yield; the sensitivity is typically standardized. Specifically, an asset i's sensitivity to a given factor would be calculated as the

---

[59] If the coefficients were not standardized as described in the following paragraph, the intercept could be interpreted as the risk-free rate, because it would be the return to an asset with no factor risk (zero factor betas) and no asset-specific risk. With standardized coefficients, the intercept is not interpreted beyond being an intercept in a regression included so that the expected asset-specific risk equals 0.

value of the attribute for the asset minus the average value of the attribute across all stocks, divided by the standard deviation of the attribute across all stocks. The **standardized beta** is

$$b_{ij} = \frac{\text{Asset } i\text{'s attribute value} - \text{Average attribute value}}{\sigma(\text{Attribute values})} \tag{11-19}$$

Continuing with the dividend yield example, after standardization a stock with an average dividend yield will have a factor sensitivity of 0, a stock with a dividend yield one standard deviation above the average will have a factor sensitivity of 1, and a stock with a dividend yield one standard deviation below the average will have a factor sensitivity of -1. Suppose, for example, that an investment has a dividend yield of 3.5 percent and that the average dividend yield across all stocks being considered is 2.5 percent. Further, suppose that the standard deviation of dividend yields across all stocks is 2 percent. The investment's sensitivity to dividend yield is $(3.5\% - 2.5\%)/2\% = 0.50$, or one-half standard deviation above average. The scaling permits all factor sensitivities to be interpreted similarly, despite differences in units of measure and scale in the variables. The exception to this interpretation is factors for binary variables such as industry membership. A company either participates in an industry or it does not. The industry factor sensitivities would be $0 - 1$ dummy variables; in models that recognize that companies frequently operate in multiple industries, the value of the sensitivity would be 1 for each industry in which a company operated.[60]

A second distinction between macroeconomic multifactor models and fundamental factor models is that with the former, we develop the factor (surprise) series first and then estimate the factor sensitivities through regressions; with the latter, we generally specify the factor sensitivities (attributes) first and then estimate the factor returns through regressions.[61]

4.5. Multifactor Models in Current Practice

In the previous sections, we explained the basic concepts of multifactor models and the APT. We now describe some models in actual industry use.

4.5.1. Macroeconomic Factor Models
Chen, Roll, and Ross (1986) pioneered the development of macroeconomic factor models. Following statistically based research suggesting that more than one factor was important in explaining the average returns on U.S. stocks, Chen et al. suggested that a relatively small set of macro factors was the primary influence on the U.S. stock market. The factors in the Chen et al. study were (1) inflation, including unanticipated inflation and changes in expected inflation, (2) a factor related to the term structure of interest rates, represented by long-term government bond returns minus one-month Treasury-bill rates, (3) a factor reflecting changes in market risk and investors' risk aversion, represented by the difference between the returns on low-rated and high-rated bonds, and (4) changes in industrial production.

The usefulness of any factor for explaining asset returns is generally evaluated using historical data. Our confidence that a factor will explain future returns increases if we can

---

[60]To further explain $0 - 1$ variables, industry membership is measured on a nominal scale because we can name the industry to which a company belongs but no more. A nominal variable can be represented in a regression by a dummy variable (a variable that takes on the value of 0 or 1). For more on dummy variables, see the chapter on multiple regression.

[61]In some models that may be classed as fundamental, the factor sensitivities are regression coefficients and are not specified first.

give an economic explanation of why a factor should be important in explaining average returns. We can plausibly explain all of Chen et al.'s four factors. For example, inflation affects the cash flows of businesses as well as the level of the discount rate applied to these cash flows by investors. Changes in industrial production affect the cash flows of businesses and the opportunities faced by investors. Example 11-14 details a current macroeconomic factor model that expanded on the model of Chen et al.

EXAMPLE 11-14   Expected Return in a Macroeconomic Factor Model

Burmeister, Roll, and Ross (1994) presented a macroeconomic factor model to explain the returns on U.S. equities. The model is known as the BIRR model for short. The BIRR model includes five factors:

1. Confidence risk: the unanticipated change in the return difference between risky corporate bonds and government bonds, both with maturities of 20 years. Risky corporate bonds bear greater default risk than does government debt. Investors' attitudes toward this risk should affect the average returns on equities. To explain the factor's name, when their confidence is high, investors are willing to accept a smaller reward for bearing this risk.
2. Time horizon risk: the unanticipated change in the return difference between 20-year government bonds and 30-day Treasury bills. This factor reflects investors' willingness to invest for the long term.
3. Inflation risk: the unexpected change in the inflation rate. Nearly all stocks have negative exposure to this factor, as their returns decline with positive surprises in inflation.
4. Business cycle risk: the unexpected change in the level of real business activity. A positive surprise or unanticipated change indicates that the expected growth rate of the economy, measured in constant dollars, has increased.
5. Market timing risk: the portion of the S&P 500's total return that remains unexplained by the first four risk factors.[62] Almost all stocks have positive sensitivity to this factor.

The first four factors are quite similar to Chen et al.'s factors with respect to the economic influences they seek to capture. The fifth factor acknowledges the uncertainty surrounding the correct set of underlying variables for asset pricing; this factor captures influences on the returns to the S&P 500 not explained by the first four factors.

　　The S&P 500 is a widely used index of 500 U.S. stocks of leading companies in leading industries. Burmeister et al. used the S&P 500 to gauge the influence of their five factors on the mean excess returns (above the Treasury bill rate) to the S&P 500. Table 11-15 shows their results.

---

[62] Because of the way the factor is constructed, the S&P 500 itself has a sensitivity of 1 to market timing risk.

TABLE 11-15   Explaining the Annual Expected Excess Return for the S&P 500

Risk Factor	Factor Sensitivity	Risk Premium	Effect of Factor on Expected Return
Confidence risk	0.27	2.59%	0.70%
Time horizon risk	0.56	−0.66%	−0.37%
Inflation risk	−0.37	−4.32%	1.60%
Business cycle risk	1.71	1.49%	2.55%
Market timing risk	1.00	3.61%	3.61%
Expected excess return			8.09%

Source: Burmeister et al.

The estimated APT model is $E(R_p)$ = T-bill rate + 2.59(Confidence risk) − 0.66(Time horizon risk) − 4.32(Inflation risk) + 1.49(Business cycle risk) + 3.61 (Market timing risk). The table shows that the S&P 500 had positive exposure to every risk factor except inflation risk. The two largest contributions to excess return came from market timing risk and business cycle risk. According to the table, this model predicts that the S&P 500 will have an expected excess return of 8.09 percent above the T-bill rate. Therefore, if the 30-day Treasury bill rate were 4 percent, for example, the forecasted return for the S&P 500 would be 4 + 8.09 = 12.09 percent a year.

In Example 11-15, we illustrate how we might use the Burmeister et al. factor model to assess the factor bets placed by a portfolio manager managing a U.S. active core equity portfolio (an actively managed portfolio invested in large-cap stocks).

EXAMPLE 11-15   Exposures to Economy-Wide Risks

William Hughes is the portfolio manager of a U.S. core equity portfolio that is being evaluated relative to its benchmark, the S&P 500. Because Hughes's performance will be evaluated relative to this benchmark, it is useful to understand the active factor bets that Hughes took relative to the S&P 500. With a focus on exposures to economy-wide risk, we use the Burmeister et al. model already presented. Table 11-16 displays Hughes's data.

We see that the portfolio manager tracks the S&P 500 exactly on confidence and time horizon risk but tilts toward greater business cycle risk. The portfolio also has a small positive excess exposure to the market timing factor.

We can use the excess exposure to business cycle risk to illustrate the numerical interpretation of the excess sensitivities. Ignoring nonsystematic risk and holding the values of the other factors constant, if there is a +1 percent surprise in the business cycle factor, we expect the return on the portfolio to be 0.01 × 0.54 = 0.0054 or 0.54 percent higher than the return on the S&P 500. Conversely, we expect the return on the portfolio to be lower than the S&P 500's return by an equal amount for a −1 percent surprise in business cycle risk.

TABLE 11-16   Excess Factor Sensitivities for a Core Equity Portfolio

Risk Factor	Core Portfolio's Factor Sensitivity	S&P 500 Factor Sensitivity	Core Portfolio's Excess Factor Sensitivity
Confidence risk	0.27	0.27	0.00
Time horizon risk	0.56	0.56	0.00
Inflation risk	−0.12	−0.37	0.25
Business cycle risk	2.25	1.71	0.54
Market timing risk	1.10	1.00	0.10

Because of the excess exposure of 0.54, the portfolio manager appears to be placing a bet on economic expansion, relative to the benchmark. If the factor bet is inadvertent, Hughes is perhaps assuming an unwanted risk. If he is aware of the bet, what are the reasons for the bet?

Care must be taken in interpreting the portfolio manager's excess sensitivity of 0.25 to the inflation factor. The S&P 500 has a negative inflation factor exposure. The value of 0.25 represents a smaller negative exposure to inflation for the core portfolio—that is, less rather than more exposure to inflation risk. Note from Table 11-16 that because the risk premium for inflation risk is negative, Hughes is giving up expected return relative to the benchmark by his bet on inflation. Again, what are his reasons for the inflation factor bet?

The market timing factor has an interpretation somewhat similar to that of the CAPM beta about how a stock tends to respond to changes in the broad market, with a higher value indicating higher sensitivity to market returns, all else equal. But the market timing factor reflects only the portion of the S&P 500's returns not explained by the other four factors, and the two concepts are distinct. Whereas we would expect S&P 500 returns to be correlated with one or more of the first four factors, the market timing factor is constructed to be uncorrelated with the first four factors. Because the market timing factor and the S&P 500 returns are distinct, we would not expect market timing factor sensitivity to be proportional to CAPM beta computed relative to the S&P 500, in general.

Another major macroeconomic factor model is the Salomon Smith Barney U.S. Equity Risk Attribute Model, or Salomon RAM, for short.

EXAMPLE 11-16   Expected Return in the Salomon RAM

The Salomon RAM model explains returns to U.S. stocks in terms of nine factors: six macroeconomic factors, a residual market factor, a residual size factor, and a residual sector factor:

1. Economic growth: the monthly change in industrial production.
2. Credit quality: the monthly change in the yield of the Salomon Smith Barney High-Yield Market 10+ year index, after removing the component of the change

that is correlated with the monthly changes in the yields of 30-year Treasury bonds.

3. Long rates: the monthly change in the yield of the 30-year Treasury bond.
4. Short rates: the monthly change in the yield of the 3-month Treasury bill.
5. Inflation shock: the unexpected component of monthly change in the consumer price index (CPI).
6. Dollar: the monthly change in the trade-weighted dollar.
7. Residual market: the monthly return on the S&P 500 after removing the effects of the six factors above.
8. Small-cap premium: the monthly difference between the return on the Russell 2000 Index and the S&P 500, after removing the effect of the seven factors above.
9. Residual sector: the monthly return on a sector membership index after removing the effect of the eight factors above.

Some noteworthy points concerning this model are as follows:[63]

- In contrast to the BIRR model and the general model (Equation 11-16), all the factors except inflation are stated in terms of returns rather than surprises.
- Factors 7, 8, and 9 attempt to isolate the net or unique contribution of the factor by removing the component of the factor return that is correlated with the group of preceding factors. Factors 7, 8, and 9 are each uncorrelated among themselves and with the other factors; they are said to be **orthogonal** (uncorrelated) factors. In addition, the credit quality factor is constructed to be uncorrelated with the long-rate factor.
- Based on the explanatory power of the model, each stock receives a RAM ranking that reflects its coefficient of determination, with 1 the highest and 5 the lowest rank.
- The factor sensitivities are presented in standardized form.

In Table 11-17, the factor sensitivities are standardized with the same interpretation as Equation 11-19.

TABLE 11-17   Factor Sensitivities for Four Stocks

	Bank	Cable TV Provider	Department Store	Computer Manufacturer
Economic growth	1.48	−1.30	−0.88	0.88
Credit quality	−1.62	−0.77	−3.19	0.12
Long rates	−0.01	−1.65	1.83	0.78
Short rates	1.00	1.53	1.10	1.17
Inflation shock	−0.97	−1.99	−1.57	0.80
Dollar	0.82	1.47	0.87	−1.63
Residual market	0.06	0.30	0.13	0.26
Small-cap premium	0.13	1.44	0.92	−1.19
Residual sector	0.02	0.00	−0.03	0.00

Note: Entries are standardized factor sensitivities.

---

[63] See Sorenson, Samak, and Miller (1998) for more information on this model.

The bank and the computer manufacturer have investment-grade debt. The cable TV provider and department store are relatively heavy users of debt that is rated below investment grade. The computer manufacturer uses little debt in its capital structure. Based only on the information given, answer the following questions.

1. Contrast the factor sensitivities of the cable TV provider stock to those of the average stock.
2. State which stocks are expected to do well in an economy showing strong economic growth coupled with an improving credit environment, all else equal.
3. Explain a possible business reason or a reason related to company fundamentals to explain negative sensitivity of the cable TV provider's stock to the credit quality factor.

Solution to 1:   The factor sensitivities to short rates, the trade-weighted dollar, the residual market factor, and the small-cap premium factor are above average, as indicated by positive factor sensitivities. The sensitivity to the residual sector factor is average, as indicated by zero factor sensitivity. By contrast, the cable TV provider's stock has below-average sensitivity to the economic growth, credit quality, long-rate, and inflation factors, as indicated by negative factor sensitivities.

Solution to 2:   Both the bank and the computer manufacturer have positive sensitivity to the economic growth factor, which is the monthly change in industrial production. As the factor and factor sensitivity are defined, the positive sensitivity implies above-average returns for these two stocks in an environment of strong economic growth, all else equal. The bank has a negative coefficient on the credit quality factor, whereas the computer manufacturer has a positive sensitivity. An improving credit environment means that the yields of high-yield bonds are declining. Thus we would observe a negative value for the credit quality factor in that environment. Of the two stocks, we expect that only the bank stock with a negative sensitivity should give above-average returns in an improving credit environment. Thus the bank stock is expected to do well in the stated scenario.

Solution to 3:   The credit quality factor essentially measures the change in the premium for bearing default risk. A negative coefficient on the credit quality factor means that the stock should do well when the premium for bearing default risk declines (an improving credit environment). One explanation for the negative sensitivity of the cable TV provider's stock to the credit quality factor is that the company is a heavy borrower with less than investment-grade debt. The cost of such debt reflects a significant default premium. The cable TV provider's borrowing costs should decline in an improving credit environment; that decline should positively affect its stock price.

4.5.2. Fundamental Factor Models   Financial analysts frequently use fundamental factor models for a variety of purposes, including portfolio performance attribution and risk analysis.[64] Fundamental factor models focus on explaining the returns to individual stocks

---

[64]**Portfolio performance attribution** analyzes the performance of portfolios in terms of the contributions from various sources of risk.

using observable fundamental factors that describe either attributes of the securities them-selves or attributes of the securities' issuers. Industry membership, price–earnings ratio, book value-to-price ratio, size, and financial leverage are examples of fundamental factors.

Example 11-17 reports a study that examined macroeconomic, fundamental, and statistical factor models.

EXAMPLE 11-17   Alternative Factor Models

Connor (1995) contrasted a macroeconomic factor model with a fundamental factor model to compare how well the models explain stock returns.[65]

Connor reported the results of applying a macroeconomic factor model to the returns for 779 large-cap U.S. stocks based on monthly data from January 1985 through December 1993. Using five macroeconomic factors, Connor was able to explain approximately 11 percent of the variance of return on these stocks.[66] Table 11-18 shows his results.

TABLE 11-18   The Explanatory Power of the Macroeconomic Factors

Factor	Explanatory Power from Using Each Factor Alone	Increase in Explanatory Power from Adding Each Factor to All the Others
Inflation	1.3%	0.0%
Term structure	1.1%	7.7%
Industrial production	0.5%	0.3%
Default premium	2.4%	8.1%
Unemployment	−0.3%	0.1%
All factors		10.9%

Source: Connor (1995).

Connor also reported a fundamental factor analysis of the same companies for which he conducted a macroeconomic factor analysis. The factor model employed was the BARRA US-E2 model (the current version is E3). Table 11-19 shows these results. In the table, "variability in markets" represents the stock's volatility, "success" is a price momentum variable, "trade activity" distinguishes stocks by how often their shares trade, and "growth" distinguishes stocks by past and anticipated earnings growth.[67]

---

[65] We do not discuss results for statistical factor models also reported in Connor (1995).

[66] The explanatory power of a given model was computed as 1 − [(Average asset-specific variance of return across stocks)/(Average total variance of return across stocks)]. The variance estimates were corrected for degrees of freedom, so the marginal contribution of a factor to explanatory power can be 0 or negative. Explanatory power captures the proportion of the total variance of return that a given model explains for the average stock.

[67] The explanations of the variables are from Grinold and Kahn (1994); Connor did not supply definitions.

TABLE 11-19   The Explanatory Power of the Fundamental Factors

Factor	Explanatory Power from Using Each Factor Alone	Increase in Explanatory Power from Adding Each Factor to All the Others
Industries	16.3%	18.0%
Variability in markets	4.3%	0.9%
Success	2.8%	0.8%
Size	1.4%	0.6%
Trade activity	1.4%	0.5%
Growth	3.0%	0.4%
Earnings to price	2.2%	0.6%
Book to price	1.5%	0.6%
Earnings variability	2.5%	0.4%
Financial leverage	0.9%	0.5%
Foreign investment	0.7%	0.4%
Labor intensity	2.2%	0.5%
Dividend yield	2.9%	0.4%
All factors		42.6%

Source: Connor (1995).

As Table 11-19 shows, the most important fundamental factor is "industries," represented by 55 industry dummy variables. The fundamental factor model explained approximately 43 percent of the variation in stock returns, compared with approximately 11 percent for the macroeconomic factor model. Connor's article does not provide tests of the statistical significance of the various factors in either model; however, Connor did find strong evidence for the usefulness of fundamental factor models, and this evidence is mirrored by the wide use of those models in the investment community. Fundamental factor models are frequently used in portfolio performance attribution, for example. We shall illustrate this use later in the chapter. Typically, fundamental factor models employ many more factors than macroeconomic factor models, giving a more detailed picture of the sources of a portfolio manager's results.

We cannot conclude from this study that fundamental factor models are inherently superior to macroeconomic factors, however. Each of the major types of models has its uses. The factors in various macroeconomic factor models are individually backed by statistical evidence that they represent systematic risk (i.e., risk that cannot be diversified away). In contrast, a portfolio manager can easily construct a portfolio that excludes a particular industry, so exposure to a particular industry is not systematic risk. The two types of factors, macroeconomic and fundamental, have different implications for measuring and managing risk, in general. The macroeconomic factor set is parsimonious (five variables). The fundamental factor set is large (67 variables including the 55 industry dummy variables), and at the expense of greater complexity, it can give a more detailed picture of risk in terms that are easily related to company and security characteristics. Connor found that the macroeconomic factor model had no marginal explanatory power when added to the fundamental factor model, implying that the fundamental risk attributes capture all the risk characteristics represented by the macroeconomic factor betas. Because the fundamental factors supply such a detailed description of the characteristics of a stock and its issuer, however, this finding is not necessarily surprising.

We encounter a range of distinct representations of risk in the fundamental models that are currently used in practical applications. Diversity exists in both the identity and exact definition of factors as well as in the underlying functional form and estimation procedures. Despite the diversity, we can place the factors of most fundamental factor models for equities into three broad groups:

- **Company fundamental factors**. These are factors related to the company's internal performance. Examples are factors relating to earnings growth, earnings variability, earnings momentum, and financial leverage.
- **Company share-related factors**. These factors include valuation measures and other factors related to share price or the trading characteristics of the shares. In contrast to the previous category, these factors directly incorporate investors' expectations concerning the company. Examples include price multiples such as earnings yield, dividend yield, and book-to-market. Market capitalization falls under this heading. Various models incorporate variables relating to share price momentum, share price volatility, and trading activity that fall in this category.
- **Macroeconomic factors**. Sector or industry membership factors come under this heading. Various models include factors such as CAPM beta, other similar measures of systematic risk, and yield curve level sensitivity, all of which can be placed in this category.

4.6. Applications

The following sections present some of the major applications of multifactor models in investment practice.

We begin by discussing portfolio performance attribution and risk analysis. We could frame the discussion in terms of raw returns or in terms of returns relative to a portfolio's benchmark. Because they provide a reference standard for risk and return, benchmarks play an important role in many institutional investors' plans for quantitatively risk-controlled returns. We shall thus focus on analyzing returns relative to a benchmark.

Multifactor models can also help portfolio managers form portfolios with specific desired risk characteristics. After discussing performance attribution and risk analysis, we explain the use of multifactor models in creating a portfolio with risk exposures that are similar to those of another portfolio.

4.6.1. Analyzing Sources of Returns   Multifactor models can help us understand in detail the sources of a manager's returns relative to a benchmark. For simplicity, in this section we analyze the sources of the returns of a portfolio fully invested in the equities of a single national equity market.[68]

Analysts frequently favor fundamental multifactor models in decomposing (separating into basic elements) the sources of returns. In contrast to statistical factor models, fundamental factor models allow the sources of portfolio performance to be described by name. Also, in contrast to macroeconomic factor models, fundamental models suggest investment style choices and security characteristics more directly, and often in greater detail.

We first need to understand the objectives of active managers. As mentioned, managers are commonly evaluated relative to a specified benchmark. Active portfolio managers hold

---

[68]The assumption allows us to ignore the roles of country selection, asset allocation, market timing, and currency hedging, greatly simplifying the analysis. Even in a more general context, however, we can perform similar analyses using multifactor models.

securities in different-from-benchmark weights in an attempt to add value to their portfolios relative to a passive investment approach. Securities held in different-from-benchmark weights reflect portfolio manager expectations that differ from consensus expectations. For an equity manager, those expectations may relate to common factors driving equity returns or to considerations unique to a company. Thus when we evaluate an active manager, we want to ask questions such as "Did the manager have insights that were valuable in the sense of adding value above a passive strategy?" Analyzing the sources of returns using multifactor models can help answer these questions.

The return on a portfolio, R_p, can be viewed as the sum of the benchmark's return, R_B, and the **active return** (portfolio return minus benchmark return):

$$\text{Active return} = R_p \mid R_B \tag{11-20}$$

With a factor model in hand, we can analyze a portfolio manager's active return as the sum of two components. The first component is the product of portfolio manager's factor tilts (active factor sensitivities) and the factor returns; we may call that component the return from factor tilts. The second component is the part of active return reflecting the manager's skill in individual asset selection; we may call that component asset selection. Equation 11-21 shows the decomposition of active return into those two components:

$$\text{Active return} = \sum_{j=1}^{K} [(\text{Portfolio sensitivity})_j - (\text{Benchmark sensitivity})_j] \\ \times (\text{Factor return})_j + \text{Asset selection} \tag{11-21}$$

In Equation 11-21, we measure the portfolio's and benchmark's sensitivities to each factor in our risk model at the beginning of an evaluation period.

Example 11-18 illustrates the use of a relatively parsimonious fundamental factor model in decomposing and interpreting returns.

EXAMPLE 11-18   Active Return Decomposition of an Equity Portfolio Manager

As an equity analyst at a pension fund sponsor, Ronald Service uses the following multifactor model to evaluate U.S. equity portfolios:

$$R_p - R_F = a_p + b_{p1}\text{RMRF} + b_{p2}\text{SMB} + b_{p3}\text{HML} + b_{p4}\text{WML} + \epsilon_p \tag{11-22}$$

where

R_p and R_F = the return on the portfolio and the risk-free rate of return, respectively

RMRF = the return on a value-weighted equity index in excess of the one-month T-bill rate

SMB = small minus big, a size (market capitalization) factor. SMB is the average return on three small-cap portfolios minus the average return on three large-cap portfolios.

HML = high minus low, the average return on two high book-to-market portfolios minus the average return on two low book-to-market portfolios

WML = winners minus losers, a momentum factor. WML is the return on a portfolio of the past year's winners minus the return on a portfolio of the past year's losers.[69]

In Equation 11-22, the sensitivities are interpreted as regression coefficients and are not standardized.

Service's current task is evaluating the performance of the most recently hired U.S. equity manager. That manager's benchmark is the Russell 1000, an index representing the performance of U.S. large-cap stocks. The manager describes herself as a "stock picker" and points to her performance in beating the benchmark as evidence that she is successful. Table 11-20 presents an analysis based on Equation 11-21 of the sources of that manager's active return during the year. In Table 11-20, "A. Return from Factor Tilts," equal to 2.1241 percent, sums the four numbers above it in the column; the return from factor tilts is the first component of the Equation 11-21. Table 11-20 lists asset selection as equal to −0.05 percent. Active return is found as 2.1241% + (−0.05%) = 2.0741%.

TABLE 11-20   Active Return Decomposition

	Factor Sensitivity				Contribution to Active Return	
Factor	Portfolio (1)	Benchmark (2)	Difference (3) = (1) − (2)	Factor Return (4)	Absolute (3) × (4)	Proportion of Total Active
RMRF	0.85	0.90	−0.05	5.52%	−0.2760	−13.3%
SMB	0.05	0.10	−0.05	−3.35%	0.1675	8.1%
HML	1.40	1.00	0.40	5.10%	2.0400	98.4%
WML	0.08	0.06	0.02	9.63%	0.1926	9.3%
			A. Return from Factor Tilts =		2.1241	102.4%
			B. Asset Selection =		−0.0500	−2.4%
			C. Active Return (A + B) =		2.0741	100.0%

From his previous work, Service knows that the returns to growth-style portfolios often have a positive sensitivity to the momentum factor (WML) in Equation 11-22. By contrast, the returns to certain value-style portfolios, such as those following a contrarian strategy, often have low or negative sensitivity to the momentum factor.

Using the information given, address the following:

1. Determine the manager's investment style mandate.
2. Evaluate the sources of the manager's active return for the year.
3. What concerns might Service discuss with the manager as a result of the return decomposition?

---

[69] WML is an equally weighted average of the stocks with the highest 30 percent 11-month returns lagged 1 month minus the equally weighted average of the stocks with the lowest 30 percent 11-month returns lagged 1 month. The model is based on Carhart (1997); WML is Carhart's PR1YR factor.

Solution to 1: The benchmark's sensitivities reflect the baseline risk characteristics of a manager's investment opportunity set. We can infer the manager's anticipated style by examining the characteristics of the benchmark selected for her. We then confirm these inferences by examining the portfolio's actual factor exposures:

- Stocks with high book-to-market are generally viewed as value stocks. Because the pension sponsor selected a benchmark with a high sensitivity (1.0) to HML (the high book-to-market minus low book-to-market factor), we can infer that the manager has a value orientation. The actual sensitivity of 1.4 to HML indicates that the manager had even more exposure to high book-to-market stocks than the benchmark.
- The benchmark's and portfolio's approximate neutrality to the momentum factor is consistent with a value orientation.
- The benchmark's and portfolio's low exposure to SMB suggests essentially no net exposure to small-cap stocks.

The above considerations as a group suggest that the manager has a large-cap value orientation.

Solution to 2: The dominant source of the manager's positive active return was her positive active exposure to the HML factor. The bet contributed $(1.40 - 1.00)(5.10\%) = 2.04\%$ or approximately 98 percent of the realized active return of about 2.07 percent. During the evaluation period, the manager sharpened her value orientation, and that bet paid off. The manager's active exposure to the overall market (RMRF) was unprofitable, but her active exposures to small stocks (SMB) and to momentum (WML) were profitable; however, the magnitudes of the manager's active exposures to RMRF, SMB, and WML were relatively small, so the effects of those bets on active return was minor compared with her large and successful bet on HML.

Solution to 3: Although the manager is a self-described "stock picker," her active return from asset selection in this period was actually negative. Her positive active return resulted from the concurrence of a large active bet on HML and a high return to that factor during the period. If the market had favored growth rather than value without the manager doing better in individual asset selection, the manager's performance would have been unsatisfactory. Can the manager supply evidence that she can predict changes in returns to the HML factor? Is she overconfident about her stock selection ability? Service may want to discuss these concerns with the manager. The return decomposition has helped Service distinguish between the return from positioning along the value–growth spectrum and return from insights into individual stocks within the investment approach the manager has chosen.

4.6.2. Analyzing Sources of Risk

Continuing with our focus on active returns, in this section we explore analysis of active risk. **Active risk** is the standard deviation of active returns. Many terms in use refer to exactly the same concept, so we need to take a short detour to mention them. A traditional synonym is **tracking error** (TE), but the term may be confusing unless *error* is associated by the reader with *standard deviation*; tracking-error volatility (TEV) has been used (where *error* is understood as a *difference*); and **tracking risk** is now in common use (but the natural abbreviation TR could be misunderstood to refer to total return). We will use the abbreviation TE for the concept of tracking risk, and we will refer to it usually as tracking risk:

$$\text{TE} = s(R_p - R_B) \tag{11-23}$$

In Equation 11-23, $s(R_p - R_B)$ indicates that we take the sample standard deviation (indicated by s) of the time series of differences between the portfolio return, R_p, and the benchmark return, R_B. We should be careful that active return and tracking risk are stated on the same time basis.[70]

As a broad indication of ranges for tracking risk, in U.S. equity markets a well executed passive investment strategy can often achieve tracking risk on the order of 1 percent or less per annum. A semi-active or enhanced index investment strategy, which makes tightly controlled use of managers' expectations, often has a tracking risk goal of 2 percent per annum. A diversified active U.S. large-cap equity strategy that might be benchmarked on the S&P 500 would commonly have tracking risk in the range of 2 percent to 6 percent per annum. An aggressive active equity manager might have tracking risk in the range of 6 percent to 9 percent or more.

Somewhat analogous to use of the traditional Sharpe measure in evaluating absolute returns, the ratio of mean active return to active risk, the **information ratio** (IR), is a tool for evaluating mean active returns per unit of active risk. The historical or *ex post* IR has the form

$$\text{IR} = \frac{\overline{R}_p - \overline{R}_B}{s(R_p - R_B)} \tag{11-24}$$

In the numerator of Equation 11-24, $\overline{R}_p$ and $\overline{R}_B$ stand for the sample mean return on the portfolio and the sample mean return on the benchmark, respectively. To illustrate the calculation, if a portfolio achieved a mean return of 9 percent during the same period that its benchmark earned a mean return of 7.5 percent, and the portfolio's tracking risk was 6 percent, we would calculate an information ratio of $(9\% - 7.5\%)/6\% = 0.25$. Setting guidelines for acceptable active risk or tracking risk is one of the ways that some institutional investors attempt to assure that the overall risk and style characteristics of their investments are in line with those desired.

EXAMPLE 11-19   Communicating with Investment Managers

The framework of active return and active risk is appealing to investors who want to closely control the risk of investments. The benchmark serves as a known and continuously observable reference standard in relation to which quantitative risk and

---

[70]To annualize a daily TE based on daily returns, we multiply daily TE by $(250)^{1/2}$ based on 250 trading days in a year; to annualize a monthly TE based on monthly returns, we multiply monthly TE by $(12)^{1/2}$.

return objectives may be stated and communicated. For example, a U.S. public employee retirement system issued a solicitation (or request for proposal) to prospective investment managers for a "risk-controlled U.S. large-cap equity fund" that included the following requirements:

- Shares must be components of the S&P 500.
- The portfolio should have a minimum of 200 issues. At time of purchase, the maximum amount that may be invested in any one issuer is 5 percent of the portfolio at market value or 150 percent of the issuers' weight within the S&P 500 Index, whichever is greater.
- The portfolio must have a minimum 0.30 percent information ratio either since inception or over the last seven years.
- The portfolio must also have tracking risk of less than 4.0 percent with respect to the S&P 500 either since inception or over the last seven years.

Analysts use multifactor models to understand in detail a portfolio manager's risk exposures. In decomposing active risk, the analyst's objective is to measure the portfolio's active exposure along each dimension of risk—in other words, to understand the sources of tracking risk.[71] Among the questions analysts will want to answer are the following:

- What active exposures contributed most to the manager's tracking risk?
- Was the portfolio manager aware of the nature of his active exposures, and if so, can he articulate a rationale for assuming them?
- Are the portfolio's active risk exposures consistent with the manager's stated investment philosophy?
- Which active bets earned adequate returns for the level of active risk taken?

In addressing these questions, analysts often choose fundamental factor models because they can be used to relate active risk exposures to a manager's portfolio decisions in a fairly direct and intuitive way. In this section, we explain how to decompose or explain a portfolio's active risk using a multifactor model.

We previously addressed the decomposition of active return; now we address the decomposition of active risk. In analyzing risk, it is convenient to use variances rather than standard deviations because the variances of uncorrelated variables are additive. We refer to the variance of active risk as **active risk squared**:

$$\text{Active risk squared} = s^2(R_p - R_B) \qquad (11\text{-}25)$$

We can separate a portfolio's active risk squared into two components:

---

[71] The portfolio's active risks are weighted averages of the component securities' active risk. Therefore, we may also perform the analysis at the level of individual holdings. A portfolio manager may find this approach useful in making adjustments to his active risk profile.

- **Active factor risk** is the contribution to active risk squared resulting from the portfolio's different-than-benchmark exposures relative to factors specified in the risk model.[72]
- **Active specific risk** or **asset selection risk** is the contribution to active risk squared resulting from the portfolio's active weights on individual assets as those weights interact with assets' residual risk.[73]

When applied to an investment in a single asset class, active risk squared has two components. The decomposition of active risk squared into two components is

$$\text{Active risk squared} = \text{Active factor risk} + \text{Active specific risk} \qquad (11\text{-}26)$$

Active factor risk represents the part of active risk squared explained by the portfolio active factor exposures. Active factor risk can be found indirectly as the difference between active risk squared and active specific risk, which has the expression[74]

$$\text{Active specific risk} = \sum_{i=1}^{n} w_i^a \sigma_{\epsilon_i}^2$$

where w_i^a is the ith asset's active weight in the portfolio (that is, the difference between the asset's weight in the portfolio and its weight in the benchmark) and $\sigma_{\epsilon_i}^2$ is the residual risk of the ith asset (the variance of the ith asset's returns left unexplained by the factors).[75] Active specific risk identifies the active nonfactor or residual risk assumed by the manager. We should look for a positive average return from asset selection as compensation for bearing active specific risk.

EXAMPLE 11-20   A Comparison of Active Risk

Richard Gray is comparing the risk of four U.S. equity managers who share the same benchmark. He uses a fundamental factor model, the BARRA US-E3 model, which incorporates 13 risk indexes and a set of 52 industrial categories. The risk indexes measure various fundamental aspects of companies and their shares such as size, leverage, and dividend yield. In the model, companies have nonzero exposures to all industries in which the company operates. Table 11-21 presents Gray's analysis of the active risk squared of the four managers, based on Equation 11-26.[76] In Table 11-21, the column

---

[72]Throughout this discussion, "active" means "different than benchmark."

[73]As we use the terms, "active specific risk" and "active factor risk" refer to variances rather than standard deviations.

[74]The direct procedure for calculating active factor risk is as follows. A portfolio's active factor exposure to a given factor j, b_j^a, is found by weighting each asset's sensitivity to factor j by its active weight and summing the terms $b_j^a = \sum_{i=1}^{n} w_i^a b_{ji}$. Then active factor risk equals $\sum_{i=1}^{K} \sum_{j=1}^{K} b_i^a b_j^a \text{Cov}(F_i, F_j)$.

[75]The residual returns of the assets are assumed to be uncorrelated with each other and with the factor returns.

[76]There is a covariance term in active factor risk, reflecting the correlation of industry membership and the risk indexes, which we assume is negligible in this example.

labeled "Industry" gives the portfolio's active factor risk associated with the industry exposures of its holdings; the column "Risk Indexes" gives the portfolio's active factor risk associated with the exposures of its holdings to the 13 risk indexes.

TABLE 11-21   Active Risk Squared Decomposition

| | Active Factor | | | | |
| | Industry | Risk Indexes | Total Factor | Active Specific | Active Risk Squared |
Portfolio					
A	12.25	17.15	29.40	19.60	49
B	1.25	13.75	15.00	10.00	25
C	1.25	17.50	18.75	6.25	25
D	0.03	0.47	0.50	0.50	1

Note: Entries are percent squared.

Using the information in Table 11-21, address the following:

1. Contrast the active risk decomposition of Portfolios A and B.
2. Contrast the active risk decomposition of Portfolios B and C.
3. Characterize the investment approach of Portfolio D.

Solution to 1:   Table 11-22 restates the information in Table 11-21 to show the proportional contributions of the various sources of active risk. In the last column of Table 11-22, we now give the square root of active risk squared—that is, active risk or tracking risk. To explain the middle set of columns in Table 11-22, Portfolio A's value of 25 percent under the Industry column is found as $12.25/49 = 0.25$. So Portfolio A's active risk related to industry exposures is 25 percent of active risk squared.

TABLE 11-22   Active Risk Decomposition (re-stated)

| | Active Factor (% of total active) | | | Active Specific (% of total active) | Active Risk |
Portfolio	Industry	Risk Indexes	Total Factor		
A	25%	35%	60%	40%	7%
B	5%	55%	60%	40%	5%
C	5%	70%	75%	25%	5%
D	3%	47%	50%	50%	1%

Portfolio A has assumed a higher level of active risk than B (tracking risk of 7 percent versus 5 percent). Portfolios A and B assumed the same proportions of active factor and active specific risk, but a sharp contrast exists between the two in terms of type of active factor risk exposure. Portfolio A assumed substantial active industry risk, whereas Portfolio B was approximately industry neutral relative to the benchmark. By contrast, Portfolio B had higher active bets on the risk indexes representing company and share characteristics.

Solution to 2:   Portfolios B and C were similar in their absolute amounts of active risk. Furthermore, both Portfolios B and C were both approximately industry neutral relative to the benchmark. Portfolio C assumed more active factor risk related to the risk indexes, but B assumed more active specific risk. We can also infer from the second point that B is somewhat less diversified than C.

Solution to 3:   Portfolio D appears to be a passively managed portfolio, judging by its negligible level of active risk. Referring to Table 11-21, Portfolio D's active factor risk of 0.50, equal to 0.707 percent expressed as a standard deviation, indicates that the portfolio very closely matches the benchmark along the dimensions of risk that the model identifies as driving average returns.

Example 11-20 presented a set of hypothetical portfolios with differing degrees of tracking risk in which active factor risk tended to be larger than active specific risk. Given a well-constructed multifactor model and a well-diversified portfolio, this relationship is fairly commonplace. For well-diversified portfolios, managing active factor risk is typically the chief task in managing tracking risk.

Example 11-20 presented an analysis of active risk at an aggregated level; a portfolio's active factor risks with respect to the multifactor model's 13 risk indexes was aggregated into a single number. In appraising performance, an analyst may be interested in a much more detailed analysis of a portfolio's active risk. How can an analyst appraise the individual contributions of a manager's active factor exposures to active risk squared?

Whatever the set of factors, the procedure for evaluating the contribution of an active factor exposure to active risk squared is the same. This quantity has been called a factor's marginal contribution to active risk squared (FMCAR). With K factors, the marginal contribution to active risk squared for a factor j, $FMCAR_j$ is

$$\text{FMCAR}_j = \frac{b_j^a \sum_{i=1}^{K} b_i^a \text{Cov}(F_j, F_i)}{\text{Active risk squared}} \tag{11-27}$$

where b_j^a is the portfolio's active exposure to factor j. The numerator is the active factor risk for factor j.[77] The numerator is similar to expressions involving beta that we encountered earlier in discussing the market model, but with multiple factors, factor covariances as well as variances are relevant. To illustrate Equation 11-27 in a simple setting, suppose we have a two-factor model:

---

[77] If we summed the numerator over $j = 1$ to K, we would have the expression for active factor risk given in Footnote 74.

- The manager's active exposure to the first factor is 0.50; that is, $b_1^a = 0.50$. The other active factor exposure is $b_2^a = 0.15$.
- The variance–covariance matrix of the factors is described by $\mathrm{Cov}(F_1, F_1) = \sigma^2(F_1) = 225, \mathrm{Cov}(F_1, F_2) = 12$, and $\mathrm{Cov}(F_2, F_2) = \sigma^2(F_2) = 144$.
- Active specific risk is 53.71.

We first compute active factor risk for each factor; that calculation is the numerator in Equation 11-27. Then we find active risk squared by summing the active factor risks and active specific risk, and form the ratio indicated in Equation 11-27. For the first factor, we calculate the numerator of FMCAR_1 as

$$b_1^a \sum_{i=1}^{2} b_i^a \mathrm{Cov}(F_1, F_i) = 0.50[0.50(225) + 0.15(12)] = 57.15$$

For the second factor, we have

$$b_2^a \sum_{i=1}^{2} b_i^a \mathrm{Cov}(F_2, F_i) = 0.15[0.50(12) + 0.15(144)] = 4.14$$

Active factor risk is $57.15 + 4.14 = 61.29$. Adding active specific risk, we find that active risk squared is $61.29 + 53.71 = 115$. Thus we have $\mathrm{FMCAR}_1 = 57.15/115 = 0.497$ or 49.7 percent, and $\mathrm{FMCAR}_2 = 4.14/115 = 0.036$ or 3.6 percent. Active factor risk as a fraction of total risk is $\mathrm{FMCAR}_1 + \mathrm{FMCAR}_2 = 49.7\% + 3.6\% = 53.3\%$. Active specific risk contributes $100\% - 53.3\% = 46.7\%$ to active risk squared. Example 11-21 illustrates the application of these concepts.

EXAMPLE 11-21   An Analysis of Individual Active Factor Risk

William Whetzell is responsible for a monthly internal performance attribution and risk analysis of a domestic core equity fund managed internally by his organization, a Canadian endowment. In his monthly analyses, Whetzell uses a risk model incorporating the following factors:

- Log of market cap
- E/P, the earnings yield
- B/P, the book-to-price ratio
- Earnings growth
- Average dividend yield
- D/A, the long-term debt-to-asset ratio
- Volatility of return on equity (ROE)
- Volatility of EPS

The factor sensitivities in the model have the standard interpretation of factor sensitivities in fundamental factor models.

Having determined that he earned an active return of 0.75 percent during the last fiscal year, Whetzell turns to the task of analyzing the portfolio's risk. At the start of that fiscal year, the investment committee made the following decisions:

- to tactically tilt the portfolio in the direction of small-cap stocks;
- to implement an "earnings growth at a reasonable price" (GARP) bias in security selection;
- to keep any active factor risk, expressed as a standard deviation, under 5 percent per annum;
- to keep active specific risk at no more than 50 percent of active risk squared; and
- to achieve an information ratio of 0.15 or greater.

Before Whetzell presented his report, one investment committee member reviewing his material commented that the investment committee should adopt a passive investment strategy for domestic equities if the equity fund continues to perform as it did during the last fiscal year.

Table 11-23 presents information on the equity fund. The factor returns were constructed to be approximately mutually uncorrelated.

TABLE 11-23   Risk Analysis Data

	Sensitivity		
Factor	Portfolio	Benchmark	Factor Variance
Log of market cap	0.05	0.25	225
E/P	−0.05	0.05	144
B/P	−0.25	−0.02	100
Earnings growth	0.25	0.10	196
Dividend yield	0.01	0.00	169
D/A	0.03	0.03	81
Vol of ROE	−0.25	0.02	121
Vol of EPS	−0.10	0.03	64
		Active specific risk =	29.9406
		Active specific return =	−0.5%
		Active return =	0.75%

Based on the information in Table 11-23, address the following:

1. For each factor, calculate (A) the active factor risk and (B) the marginal contribution to active risk squared.
2. Discuss whether the data are consistent with the objectives of the investment committee having been met.
3. Appraise the endowment's risk-adjusted performance for the year.

4. Explain two pieces of evidence supporting the committee member's statement concerning a passive investment strategy.

Solution to 1:

(A) Active factor risk for a factor = (Active sensitivity to the factor)^2(Factor variance) in Equation 11-27 with zero factor correlations.

$$\text{Log of market cap} = (0.05 - 0.25)^2(225) = 9.0$$

$$\text{E/P} = (-0.05 - 0.05)^2(144) = 1.44$$

$$\text{B/P} = [-0.25 - (-0.02)]^2(100) = 5.29$$

$$\text{Earnings growth} = (0.25 - 0.10)^2(196) = 4.41$$

$$\text{Dividend yield} = (0.01 - 0.00)^2(169) = 0.0169$$

$$\text{D/A} = (0.03 - 0.03)^2(81) = 0.0$$

$$\text{Volatility of ROE} = (-0.25 - 0.02)^2(121) = 8.8209$$

$$\text{Volatility of EPS} = (-0.10 - 0.03)^2(64) = 1.0816$$

(B) The sum of the individual active factor risks equals 30.0594. We add active specific risk to this sum to obtain active risk squared of $30.0594 + 29.9406 = 60$. Thus FMCAR for the factors is as follows:

$$\text{Log of market cap} = 9/60 = 0.15$$

$$\text{E/P} = 1.44/60 = 0.024$$

$$\text{B/P} = 5.29/60 = 0.0882$$

$$\text{Earnings growth} = 4.41/60 = 0.0735$$

$$\text{Dividend yield} = 0.0169/60 = 0.0003$$

$$\text{D/A} = 0.0/60 = 0.0$$

$$\text{Volatility of ROE} = 8.8209/60 = 0.1470$$

$$\text{Volatility of EPS} = 1.0816/60 = 0.0180$$

Solution to 2: We consider each investment committee objective in turn. The first objective was *to tactically tilt the portfolio in the direction of small-cap stocks*. A zero sensitivity to the log market cap factor would indicate average exposure to size. An exposure of 1 would indicate a positive exposure to returns to increasing size that is one standard deviation above the mean, given the standard interpretation of factor sensitivities in fundamental factor models. Although the equity fund's exposure to size is positive, the *active* exposure is negative. This result is consistent with tilting toward small-cap stocks.

The second objective was *to implement an "earnings growth at a reasonable price" bias in security selection.* The equity fund has a positive active exposure to earnings growth consistent with seeking companies with high earnings growth rates. It is questionable, however, whether the "reasonable price" part of the approach is being satisfied. The fund's absolute E/P and B/P sensitivities are negative, indicating below average earning yield and B/P (higher than average P/E and P/B). The active exposures to these factors are also negative. If above-average earnings growth is priced in the marketplace, the fund may need to bear negative active exposures, so we cannot reach a final conclusion. We can say, however, that none of the data positively supports a conclusion that the GARP strategy was implemented.

The third objective was *to keep any active factor risk, expressed as a standard deviation, under 5 percent per annum.* The largest active factor risk was on the log of market cap factor. Expressed as a standard deviation, that risk was $(9)^{1/2} = 3$ percent per annum, so this objective was met.

The fourth objective was *to keep active specific risk at no more than 50 percent of active risk squared.* Active specific risk as a fraction of active risk squared was $29.9406/60 = 0.4990$ or 49.9 percent, so this objective was met.

The fifth objective was *to achieve an information ratio of 0.15 or greater.* The information ratio is active return divided by active risk (tracking risk). Active return was given as 0.75 percent. Active risk is the square root of active risk squared: $(60)^{1/2} = 7.7460\%$. Thus IR $= 0.75\%/7.7460\% = 0.0968$ or approximately 0.10, which is short of the stated objective of 0.15.

Solution to 3: The endowment's realized information ratio of 0.10 means its risk-adjusted performance for the year was inadequate.

Solution to 4: The active specific return for the year was negative, although the fund incurred substantial active specific risk. Therefore, specific risk had a negative reward. Furthermore, the realized information ratio fell short of the investment committee's objective. With the qualification that this analysis is based on only one year, these facts would argue for the cost-efficient alternative of indexing.

In our discussion of performance attribution and risk analysis, we have given examples related to common stock. Multifactor models have also been used in similar roles for portfolios of bonds and other asset classes.

We have illustrated the use of multifactor models in analyzing a portfolio's active returns and active risk. At least equally important is the use of multifactor models in portfolio construction. At that stage of the portfolio management process, multifactor models permit the portfolio manager to make focused bets or to control portfolio risk relative to her benchmark's risk. In the remaining sections, we discuss these uses of multifactor models.

4.6.3. Factor Portfolios   A portfolio manager can use multifactor models to establish a specific desired risk profile for his portfolio. For example, he may want to create and use a factor portfolio. A factor portfolio for a particular factor has a sensitivity of 1 for that factor and a sensitivity of 0 for all other factors. It is thus a portfolio with exposure to only one risk factor and exactly represents the risk of that factor. As a pure bet on a source of risk, factor portfolios are of interest to a portfolio manager who wants to hedge that risk (offset it) or speculate on it. Example 11-22 illustrates the use of factor portfolios.

EXAMPLE 11-22   Factor Portfolios

Analyst Wanda Smithfield has constructed six portfolios for possible use by portfolio managers in her firm. The portfolios are labeled A, B, C, D, E, and F in Table 11-24.

TABLE 11-24   Factor Portfolios

Risk Factor	Portfolios					
	A	B	C	D	E	F
Confidence risk	0.50	0.00	1.00	0.00	0.00	0.80
Time horizon risk	1.92	0.00	1.00	1.00	1.00	1.00
Inflation risk	0.00	0.00	1.00	0.00	0.00	−1.05
Business cycle risk	1.00	1.00	0.00	0.00	1.00	0.30
Market timing risk	0.90	0.00	1.00	0.00	0.00	0.75

Note: Entries are factor sensitivities.

1. A portfolio manager wants to place a bet that real business activity will increase.

   A. Determine and justify the portfolio among the six given that would be most useful to the manager.
   B. What type of position would the manager take in the portfolio chosen in Part A?

2. A portfolio manager wants to hedge an existing positive exposure to time horizon risk.

   A. Determine and justify the portfolio among the six given that would be most useful to the manager.
   B. What type of position would the manager take in the portfolio chosen in Part A?

Solution to 1A: Portfolio B is the most appropriate choice. Portfolio B is the factor portfolio for business cycle risk because it has a sensitivity of 1 to business cycle risk and a sensitivity of 0 to all other risk factors. Portfolio B is thus efficient for placing a pure bet on an increase in real business activity.

Solution to 1B: The manager would take a long position in Portfolio B to place a bet on an increase in real business activity.

Solution to 2A: Portfolio D is the appropriate choice. Portfolio D is the factor portfolio for time horizon risk because it has a sensitivity of 1 to time horizon risk and a sensitivity of 0 to all other risk factors. Portfolio D is thus efficient for hedging an existing positive exposure to time horizon risk.

Solution to 2B: The manager would take a short position in Portfolio D to hedge the positive exposure to time horizon risk.

The next section illustrates the procedure for constructing a portfolio with a desired configuration of factor sensitivities.

4.6.4. Creating a Tracking Portfolio

In the previous section, we discussed the use of multifactor models to speculate on or hedge a specific factor risk. Perhaps even more commonly, portfolio managers use multifactor models to control the risk of portfolios relative to their benchmarks. For example, in a risk-controlled active or enhanced index strategy, the portfolio manager may attempt to earn a small incremental return relative to her benchmark while controlling risk by matching the factor sensitivities of her portfolio to her benchmark. That portfolio would be an example of a tracking portfolio. A **tracking portfolio** is a portfolio having factor sensitivities that are matched to those of a benchmark or other portfolio.

The technique of constructing a portfolio with a target set of factor sensitivities involves the solution of a system of equations using algebra.

- Count the number of constraints. Each target value of beta represents a constraint on the portfolio, and another constraint is that the weights of the investments in the portfolio must sum to one. *As many investments are needed as there are constraints.*
- Set up an equation for the weights of the portfolio's investments reflecting each constraint on the portfolio. We have an equation stating that the portfolio weights sum to 1. We have an equation for each target factor sensitivity; on the left-hand side of the equal sign, we have a weighted average of the factor sensitivities of the investments to the factor, and on the right-hand side of the equal sign we have the target factor sensitivity.
- Solve the system of equations for the weights of the investments in the portfolio.

In Example 11-23, we illustrate how a tracking portfolio can be created.

EXAMPLE 11-23   Creating a Tracking Portfolio

Suppose that a pension plan sponsor wants to be fully invested in U.S. common stocks. The plan sponsor has specified an equity benchmark for a portfolio manager, who has decided to create a tracking portfolio for the benchmark. For the sake of using familiar data, let us continue with the three portfolios J, K, and L, as well as the same two-factor model from Example 11-13.

The portfolio manager determines that the benchmark has a sensitivity of 1.3 to the surprise in inflation and a sensitivity of 1.975 to the surprise in GDP. There are three constraints. One constraint is that portfolio weights sum to 1, a second is that the weighted sum of sensitivities to the inflation factor equals 1.3 (to match the benchmark), and a third is that the weighted sum of sensitivities to the GDP factor equals 1.975 (to match the benchmark). Thus we need three investments to form the portfolio, which we take to be Portfolios J, K, and L. We repeat Table 11-14 below.

TABLE 11-14   (repeated) Sample Portfolios for a
Two-Factor Model

Portfolio	Expected Return	Sensitivity to Inflation Factor	Sensitivity to GDP Factor
J	0.14	1.0	1.5
K	0.12	0.5	1.0
L	0.11	1.3	1.1

As mentioned, we need three equations to determine the portfolio weights w_J, w_K, and w_L in the tracking portfolio.

- *Equation 1.* This equation states that portfolio weights must sum to 1.

$$w_J + w_K + w_L = 1$$

- *Equation 2.* The second equation states that the weighted average of the sensitivities of J, K, and L to the surprise in inflation must equal the benchmark's sensitivity to the surprise in inflation, 1.3. This requirement ensures that the tracking portfolio has the same inflation risk as the benchmark.

$$1.0w_J + 0.5w_K + 1.3w_L = 1.3$$

- *Equation 3.* The third equation states that the weighted average of the sensitivities of J, K, and L to the surprise in GDP must equal the benchmark's sensitivity to the surprise in GDP, 1.975. This requirement ensures that the tracking portfolio has the same GDP risk as the benchmark.

$$1.5w_J + 1.0w_K + 1.1w_L = 1.975$$

We can solve for the weights as follows. From Equation 1, $w_L = (1 - w_J - w_K)$. We substitute this result in the other two equations to find

$$1.0w_J + 0.5w_K + 1.3(1 - w_J - w_K) = 1.3, \text{ simplifying to } w_K = -0.375w_J$$

and

$$1.5w_J + 1.0w_K + 1.1(1 - w_J - w_K) = 1.975,$$

$$\text{simplifying to } 0.4w_J - 0.1w_K = 0.875$$

We next substitute $w_K = -0.375w_J$ into $0.4w_J - 0.1w_K = 0.875$, obtaining $0.4w_J - 0.1(-0.375w_J) = 0.875$ or $0.4w_J + 0.0375w_J = 0.875$, so $w_J = 2$.

Using $w_K = -0.375w_J$ obtained earlier, $w_K = -0.375 \times 2 = -0.75$. Finally, from $w_L = (1 - w_J - w_K) = [1 - 2 - (-0.75)] = -0.25$. To summarize,

$$w_J = 2$$

$$w_K = -0.75$$

$$w_L = -0.25$$

The tracking portfolio has an expected return of $0.14w_J + 0.12w_K + 0.11w_L = 0.14(2) + (0.12)(-0.75) + 0.11(-0.25) = 0.28 - 0.09 - 0.0275 = 0.1625$. In Example 11-13 using the same inputs, we calculated the APT model as $E(R_p) = 0.07 - 0.02\beta_{p,1} + 0.06\beta_{p,2}$. For the tracking portfolio, $\beta_{p,1} = 1.3$ and $\beta_{p,2} = 1.975$. As $E(R_p) = 0.07 - 0.02(1.3) + 0.06(1.975) = 0.1625$, we have confirmed the expected return calculation.

4.7. Concluding Remarks

In earlier sections, we showed how models with multiple factors can help portfolio managers solve practical tasks in measuring and controlling risk. We now draw contrasts between the CAPM and the APT, providing additional insight into why some risks may be priced and how, as a result, the portfolio implications of a multifactor world differ from those of the world described by the CAPM. An investor may be able to make better portfolio decisions with a multifactor model than with a single-factor model.

The CAPM provides investors with useful and influential concepts for thinking about investments. Considerable evidence has accumulated, however, that shows that the CAPM provides an incomplete description of risk.[78] What is the portfolio advice of CAPM, and how can we improve on it when more than one source of systematic risk drives asset returns? An investor who believes that the CAPM explains asset returns would hold a portfolio consisting only of the risk-free asset and the market portfolio of risky assets. If the investor had a high tolerance for risk, she would put a greater proportion in the market portfolio. But to the extent the investor held risky assets, she would hold them in amounts proportional to their market-value weights, without consideration for any other dimension of risk. In reality, of course, not everyone holds the same portfolio of risky assets. Practically speaking, this CAPM-oriented investor might hold a money market fund and a portfolio indexed on a broad market index.[79]

With more than one source of systematic risk, the average investor might still want to hold a broadly based portfolio and the risk-free asset. Other investors, however, may find it appropriate to tilt away from an index fund after considering dimensions of risk ignored by the CAPM. To make this argument, let us explore why, for example, the business cycle is a source

---

[78] See Bodie, Kane, and Marcus (2001) for an introduction to the empirical evidence.

[79] Passive management is a distinct issue from holding a single portfolio. There are efficient-markets arguments for holding indexed investments that are separate from the CAPM. An index fund is reasonable for this investor, however.

of systematic risk, as in the Burmeister et al. model discussed earlier. There is an economic intuition for why this risk is systematic:[80] Most investors hold jobs and are thus sensitive to recessions. Suppose, for example, that a working investor faces the risk of a recession. If this investor compared two stocks with the same CAPM beta, given his concern about recession risk, he would accept a lower return from the counter cyclical stock and require a risk premium on the procyclical one. In contrast, an investor with independent wealth and no job-loss concerns would be willing to accept the recession risk.

If the average investor holding a job bids up the price of the counter cyclical stocks, then recession risk will be priced. In addition, procyclical stocks would have lower prices than if the recession factor were not priced. Investors can thus, as Cochrane (1999a) notes, "earn a substantial premium for holding dimensions of risk unrelated to market movements."

This view of risk has portfolio implications. The average investor is exposed to and negatively affected by cyclical risk, which is a priced factor. (Risks that do not affect the average investor should not be priced.) Investors who hold jobs (and thus receive labor income) want lower cyclical risk and create a cyclical risk premium, whereas investors without labor income will accept more cyclical risk to capture a premium for a risk that they do not care about. As a result, an investor who faces lower-than-average recession risk optimally tilts towards greater-than-average exposure to the business cycle factor, all else equal.

In summary, investors should know which priced risks they face and analyze the extent of their exposure. Compared with single-factor models, multifactor models offer a rich context for investors to search for ways to improve portfolio selection.

---

[80]This discussion follows Cochrane (1999a) and (1999b).

APPENDICES

Appendix A   Cumulative Probabilities for a Standard Normal Distribution
$P(Z \leq x) = N(x)$ for $x \geq 0$ or $P(Z \leq z) = N(z)$ for $z \geq 0$

Appendix B   Table of the Student's t-Distribution (One-Tailed Probabilities)

Appendix C   Values of χ^2 (Degrees of Freedom, Level of Significance)

Appendix D   Table of the F-Distribution

Appendix E   Critical Values for the Durbin-Watson Statistic ($\alpha = .05$)

Appendix A   Cumulative Probabilities for a Standard Normal Distribution
$P(Z \leq x) = N(x)$ for $x \geq 0$ or $P(Z \leq z) = N(z)$ for $z \geq 0$

x or z	0	0.01	0.02	0.03	0.04	0.05	0.06	0.07	0.08	0.09
0.00	0.5000	0.5040	0.5080	0.5120	0.5160	0.5199	0.5239	0.5279	0.5319	0.5359
0.10	0.5398	0.5438	0.5478	0.5517	0.5557	0.5596	0.5636	0.5675	0.5714	0.5753
0.20	0.5793	0.5832	0.5871	0.5910	0.5948	0.5987	0.6026	0.6064	0.6103	0.6141
0.30	0.6179	0.6217	0.6255	0.6293	0.6331	0.6368	0.6406	0.6443	0.6480	0.6517
0.40	0.6554	0.6591	0.6628	0.6664	0.6700	0.6736	0.6772	0.6808	0.6844	0.6879
0.50	0.6915	0.6950	0.6985	0.7019	0.7054	0.7088	0.7123	0.7157	0.7190	0.7224
0.60	0.7257	0.7291	0.7324	0.7357	0.7389	0.7422	0.7454	0.7486	0.7517	0.7549
0.70	0.7580	0.7611	0.7642	0.7673	0.7704	0.7734	0.7764	0.7794	0.7823	0.7852
0.80	0.7881	0.7910	0.7939	0.7967	0.7995	0.8023	0.8051	0.8078	0.8106	0.8133
0.90	0.8159	0.8186	0.8212	0.8238	0.8264	0.8289	0.8315	0.8340	0.8365	0.8389
1.00	0.8413	0.8438	0.8461	0.8485	0.8508	0.8531	0.8554	0.8577	0.8599	0.8621
1.10	0.8643	0.8665	0.8686	0.8708	0.8729	0.8749	0.8770	0.8790	0.8810	0.8830
1.20	0.8849	0.8869	0.8888	0.8907	0.8925	0.8944	0.8962	0.8980	0.8997	0.9015
1.30	0.9032	0.9049	0.9066	0.9082	0.9099	0.9115	0.9131	0.9147	0.9162	0.9177
1.40	0.9192	0.9207	0.9222	0.9236	0.9251	0.9265	0.9279	0.9292	0.9306	0.9319
1.50	0.9332	0.9345	0.9357	0.9370	0.9382	0.9394	0.9406	0.9418	0.9429	0.9441
1.60	0.9452	0.9463	0.9474	0.9484	0.9495	0.9505	0.9515	0.9525	0.9535	0.9545
1.70	0.9554	0.9564	0.9573	0.9582	0.9591	0.9599	0.9608	0.9616	0.9625	0.9633
1.80	0.9641	0.9649	0.9656	0.9664	0.9671	0.9678	0.9686	0.9693	0.9699	0.9706
1.90	0.9713	0.9719	0.9726	0.9732	0.9738	0.9744	0.9750	0.9756	0.9761	0.9767
2.00	0.9772	0.9778	0.9783	0.9788	0.9793	0.9798	0.9803	0.9808	0.9812	0.9817
2.10	0.9821	0.9826	0.9830	0.9834	0.9838	0.9842	0.9846	0.9850	0.9854	0.9857
2.20	0.9861	0.9864	0.9868	0.9871	0.9875	0.9878	0.9881	0.9884	0.9887	0.9890
2.30	0.9893	0.9896	0.9898	0.9901	0.9904	0.9906	0.9909	0.9911	0.9913	0.9916
2.40	0.9918	0.9920	0.9922	0.9925	0.9927	0.9929	0.9931	0.9932	0.9934	0.9936
2.50	0.9938	0.9940	0.9941	0.9943	0.9945	0.9946	0.9948	0.9949	0.9951	0.9952
2.60	0.9953	0.9955	0.9956	0.9957	0.9959	0.9960	0.9961	0.9962	0.9963	0.9964
2.70	0.9965	0.9966	0.9967	0.9968	0.9969	0.9970	0.9971	0.9972	0.9973	0.9974
2.80	0.9974	0.9975	0.9976	0.9977	0.9977	0.9978	0.9979	0.9979	0.9980	0.9981
2.90	0.9981	0.9982	0.9982	0.9983	0.9984	0.9984	0.9985	0.9985	0.9986	0.9986
3.00	0.9987	0.9987	0.9987	0.9988	0.9988	0.9989	0.9989	0.9989	0.9990	0.9990
3.10	0.9990	0.9991	0.9991	0.9991	0.9992	0.9992	0.9992	0.9992	0.9993	0.9993
3.20	0.9993	0.9993	0.9994	0.9994	0.9994	0.9994	0.9994	0.9995	0.9995	0.9995
3.30	0.9995	0.9995	0.9995	0.9996	0.9996	0.9996	0.9996	0.9996	0.9996	0.9997
3.40	0.9997	0.9997	0.9997	0.9997	0.9997	0.9997	0.9997	0.9997	0.9997	0.9998
3.50	0.9998	0.9998	0.9998	0.9998	0.9998	0.9998	0.9998	0.9998	0.9998	0.9998
3.60	0.9998	0.9998	0.9999	0.9999	0.9999	0.9999	0.9999	0.9999	0.9999	0.9999
3.70	0.9999	0.9999	0.9999	0.9999	0.9999	0.9999	0.9999	0.9999	0.9999	0.9999
3.80	0.9999	0.9999	0.9999	0.9999	0.9999	0.9999	0.9999	0.9999	0.9999	0.9999
3.90	1.0000	1.0000	1.0000	1.0000	1.0000	1.0000	1.0000	1.0000	1.0000	1.0000
4.00	1.0000	1.0000	1.0000	1.0000	1.0000	1.0000	1.0000	1.0000	1.0000	1.0000

For example, to find the z-value leaving 2.5 percent of the area/probability in the upper tail, find the element 0.9750 in the body of the table. Read 1.90 at the left end of the element's row and 0.06 at the top of the element's column, to give $1.90 + 0.06 = 1.96$. *Table generated with Excel.*

Appendix A   Cumulative Probabilities for a Standard Normal Distribution
$P(Z \leq x) = N(x)$ for $x \leq 0$ or $P(Z \leq z) = N(z)$ for $z \leq 0$

x or z	0	0.01	0.02	0.03	0.04	0.05	0.06	0.07	0.08	0.09
0.00	0.5000	0.4960	0.4920	0.4880	0.4840	0.4801	0.4761	0.4721	0.4681	0.4641
−0.10	0.4602	0.4562	0.4522	0.4483	0.4443	0.4404	0.4364	0.4325	0.4286	0.4247
−0.20	0.4207	0.4168	0.4129	0.4090	0.4052	0.4013	0.3974	0.3936	0.3897	0.3859
−0.30	0.3821	0.3783	0.3745	0.3707	0.3669	0.3632	0.3594	0.3557	0.3520	0.3483
−0.40	0.3446	0.3409	0.3372	0.3336	0.3300	0.3264	0.3228	0.3192	0.3156	0.3121
−0.50	0.3085	0.3050	0.3015	0.2981	0.2946	0.2912	0.2877	0.2843	0.2810	0.2776
−0.60	0.2743	0.2709	0.2676	0.2643	0.2611	0.2578	0.2546	0.2514	0.2483	0.2451
−0.70	0.2420	0.2389	0.2358	0.2327	0.2296	0.2266	0.2236	0.2206	0.2177	0.2148
−0.80	0.2119	0.2090	0.2061	0.2033	0.2005	0.1977	0.1949	0.1922	0.1894	0.1867
−0.90	0.1841	0.1814	0.1788	0.1762	0.1736	0.1711	0.1685	0.1660	0.1635	0.1611
−1.00	0.1587	0.1562	0.1539	0.1515	0.1492	0.1469	0.1446	0.1423	0.1401	0.1379
−1.10	0.1357	0.1335	0.1314	0.1292	0.1271	0.1251	0.1230	0.1210	0.1190	0.1170
−1.20	0.1151	0.1131	0.1112	0.1093	0.1075	0.1056	0.1038	0.1020	0.1003	0.0985
−1.30	0.0968	0.0951	0.0934	0.0918	0.0901	0.0885	0.0869	0.0853	0.0838	0.0823
−1.40	0.0808	0.0793	0.0778	0.0764	0.0749	0.0735	0.0721	0.0708	0.0694	0.0681
−1.50	0.0668	0.0655	0.0643	0.0630	0.0618	0.0606	0.0594	0.0582	0.0571	0.0559
−1.60	0.0548	0.0537	0.0526	0.0516	0.0505	0.0495	0.0485	0.0475	0.0465	0.0455
−1.70	0.0446	0.0436	0.0427	0.0418	0.0409	0.0401	0.0392	0.0384	0.0375	0.0367
−1.80	0.0359	0.0351	0.0344	0.0336	0.0329	0.0322	0.0314	0.0307	0.0301	0.0294
−1.90	0.0287	0.0281	0.0274	0.0268	0.0262	0.0256	0.0250	0.0244	0.0239	0.0233
−2.00	0.0228	0.0222	0.0217	0.0212	0.0207	0.0202	0.0197	0.0192	0.0188	0.0183
−2.10	0.0179	0.0174	0.0170	0.0166	0.0162	0.0158	0.0154	0.0150	0.0146	0.0143
−2.20	0.0139	0.0136	0.0132	0.0129	0.0125	0.0122	0.0119	0.0116	0.0113	0.0110
−2.30	0.0107	0.0104	0.0102	0.0099	0.0096	0.0094	0.0091	0.0089	0.0087	0.0084
−2.40	0.0082	0.0080	0.0078	0.0075	0.0073	0.0071	0.0069	0.0068	0.0066	0.0064
−2.50	0.0062	0.0060	0.0059	0.0057	0.0055	0.0054	0.0052	0.0051	0.0049	0.0048
−2.60	0.0047	0.0045	0.0044	0.0043	0.0041	0.0040	0.0039	0.0038	0.0037	0.0036
−2.70	0.0035	0.0034	0.0033	0.0032	0.0031	0.0030	0.0029	0.0028	0.0027	0.0026
−2.80	0.0026	0.0025	0.0024	0.0023	0.0023	0.0022	0.0021	0.0021	0.0020	0.0019
−2.90	0.0019	0.0018	0.0018	0.0017	0.0016	0.0016	0.0015	0.0015	0.0014	0.0014
−3.00	0.0013	0.0013	0.0013	0.0012	0.0012	0.0011	0.0011	0.0011	0.0010	0.0010
−3.10	0.0010	0.0009	0.0009	0.0009	0.0008	0.0008	0.0008	0.0008	0.0007	0.0007
−3.20	0.0007	0.0007	0.0006	0.0006	0.0006	0.0006	0.0006	0.0005	0.0005	0.0005
−3.30	0.0005	0.0005	0.0005	0.0004	0.0004	0.0004	0.0004	0.0004	0.0004	0.0003
−3.40	0.0003	0.0003	0.0003	0.0003	0.0003	0.0003	0.0003	0.0003	0.0003	0.0002
−3.50	0.0002	0.0002	0.0002	0.0002	0.0002	0.0002	0.0002	0.0002	0.0002	0.0002
−3.60	0.0002	0.0002	0.0001	0.0001	0.0001	0.0001	0.0001	0.0001	0.0001	0.0001
−3.70	0.0001	0.0001	0.0001	0.0001	0.0001	0.0001	0.0001	0.0001	0.0001	0.0001
−3.80	0.0001	0.0001	0.0001	0.0001	0.0001	0.0001	0.0001	0.0001	0.0001	0.0001
−3.90	0.0000	0.0000	0.0000	0.0000	0.0000	0.0000	0.0000	0.0000	0.0000	0.0000
−4.00	0.0000	0.0000	0.0000	0.0000	0.0000	0.0000	0.0000	0.0000	0.0000	0.0000

For example, to find the z-value leaving 2.5 percent of the area/probability in the lower tail, find the element 0.0250 in the body of the table. Read −1.90 at the left end of the element's row and 0.06 at the top of the element's column, to give $-1.90 - 0.06 = -1.96$. *Table generated with Excel.*

Appendix B Table of the Student's t-Distribution (One-Tailed Probabilities)

df	$p=0.10$	$p=0.05$	$p=0.025$	$p=0.01$	$p=0.005$	df	$p=0.10$	$p=0.05$	$p=0.025$	$p=0.01$	$p=0.005$
1	3.078	6.314	12.706	31.821	63.657	31	1.309	1.696	2.040	2.453	2.744
2	1.886	2.920	4.303	6.965	9.925	32	1.309	1.694	2.037	2.449	2.738
3	1.638	2.353	3.182	4.541	5.841	33	1.308	1.692	2.035	2.445	2.733
4	1.533	2.132	2.776	3.747	4.604	34	1.307	1.691	2.032	2.441	2.728
5	1.476	2.015	2.571	3.365	4.032	35	1.306	1.690	2.030	2.438	2.724
6	1.440	1.943	2.447	3.143	3.707	36	1.306	1.688	2.028	2.434	2.719
7	1.415	1.895	2.365	2.998	3.499	37	1.305	1.687	2.026	2.431	2.715
8	1.397	1.860	2.306	2.896	3.355	38	1.304	1.686	2.024	2.429	2.712
9	1.383	1.833	2.262	2.821	3.250	39	1.304	1.685	2.023	2.426	2.708
10	1.372	1.812	2.228	2.764	3.169	40	1.303	1.684	2.021	2.423	2.704
11	1.363	1.796	2.201	2.718	3.106	41	1.303	1.683	2.020	2.421	2.701
12	1.356	1.782	2.179	2.681	3.055	42	1.302	1.682	2.018	2.418	2.698
13	1.350	1.771	2.160	2.650	3.012	43	1.302	1.681	2.017	2.416	2.695
14	1.345	1.761	2.145	2.624	2.977	44	1.301	1.680	2.015	2.414	2.692
15	1.341	1.753	2.131	2.602	2.947	45	1.301	1.679	2.014	2.412	2.690
16	1.337	1.746	2.120	2.583	2.921	46	1.300	1.679	2.013	2.410	2.687
17	1.333	1.740	2.110	2.567	2.898	47	1.300	1.678	2.012	2.408	2.685
18	1.330	1.734	2.101	2.552	2.878	48	1.299	1.677	2.011	2.407	2.682
19	1.328	1.729	2.093	2.539	2.861	49	1.299	1.677	2.010	2.405	2.680
20	1.325	1.725	2.086	2.528	2.845	50	1.299	1.676	2.009	2.403	2.678
21	1.323	1.721	2.080	2.518	2.831	60	1.296	1.671	2.000	2.390	2.660
22	1.321	1.717	2.074	2.508	2.819	70	1.294	1.667	1.994	2.381	2.648
23	1.319	1.714	2.069	2.500	2.807	80	1.292	1.664	1.990	2.374	2.639
24	1.318	1.711	2.064	2.492	2.797	90	1.291	1.662	1.987	2.368	2.632
25	1.316	1.708	2.060	2.485	2.787	100	1.290	1.660	1.984	2.364	2.626
26	1.315	1.706	2.056	2.479	2.779	110	1.289	1.659	1.982	2.361	2.621
27	1.314	1.703	2.052	2.473	2.771	120	1.289	1.658	1.980	2.358	2.617
28	1.313	1.701	2.048	2.467	2.763	200	1.286	1.653	1.972	2.345	2.601
29	1.311	1.699	2.045	2.462	2.756	∞	1.282	1.645	1.960	2.326	2.576
30	1.310	1.697	2.042	2.457	2.750						

To find a critical t-value, enter the table with df and a specified value for α, the significance level. For example, with 5 df, α = 0.05 and a one-tailed test, the desired probability in the tail would be $p = 0.05$ and the critical t-value would be $t(5, 0.05) = 2.015$. With α = 0.05 and a two-tailed test, the desired probability in each tail would be $p = 0.025 = α/2$, giving $t(0.025) = 2.571$. *Table generated using Excel.*

Appendix C   Values of χ^2 (Degrees of Freedom, Level of Significance)

Degrees of Freedom	Probability in Right Tail								
	0.99	**0.975**	**0.95**	**0.9**	**0.1**	**0.05**	**0.025**	**0.01**	**0.005**
1	0.000157	0.000982	0.003932	0.0158	2.706	3.841	5.024	6.635	7.879
2	0.020100	0.050636	0.102586	0.2107	4.605	5.991	7.378	9.210	10.597
3	0.1148	0.2158	0.3518	0.5844	6.251	7.815	9.348	11.345	12.838
4	0.297	0.484	0.711	1.064	7.779	9.488	11.143	13.277	14.860
5	0.554	0.831	1.145	1.610	9.236	11.070	12.832	15.086	16.750
6	0.872	1.237	1.635	2.204	10.645	12.592	14.449	16.812	18.548
7	1.239	1.690	2.167	2.833	12.017	14.067	16.013	18.475	20.278
8	1.647	2.180	2.733	3.490	13.362	15.507	17.535	20.090	21.955
9	2.088	2.700	3.325	4.168	14.684	16.919	19.023	21.666	23.589
10	2.558	3.247	3.940	4.865	15.987	18.307	20.483	23.209	25.188
11	3.053	3.816	4.575	5.578	17.275	19.675	21.920	24.725	26.757
12	3.571	4.404	5.226	6.304	18.549	21.026	23.337	26.217	28.300
13	4.107	5.009	5.892	7.041	19.812	22.362	24.736	27.688	29.819
14	4.660	5.629	6.571	7.790	21.064	23.685	26.119	29.141	31.319
15	5.229	6.262	7.261	8.547	22.307	24.996	27.488	30.578	32.801
16	5.812	6.908	7.962	9.312	23.542	26.296	28.845	32.000	34.267
17	6.408	7.564	8.672	10.085	24.769	27.587	30.191	33.409	35.718
18	7.015	8.231	9.390	10.865	25.989	28.869	31.526	34.805	37.156
19	7.633	8.907	10.117	11.651	27.204	30.144	32.852	36.191	38.582
20	8.260	9.591	10.851	12.443	28.412	31.410	34.170	37.566	39.997
21	8.897	10.283	11.591	13.240	29.615	32.671	35.479	38.932	41.401
22	9.542	10.982	12.338	14.041	30.813	33.924	36.781	40.289	42.796
23	10.196	11.689	13.091	14.848	32.007	35.172	38.076	41.638	44.181
24	10.856	12.401	13.848	15.659	33.196	36.415	39.364	42.980	45.558
25	11.524	13.120	14.611	16.473	34.382	37.652	40.646	44.314	46.928
26	12.198	13.844	15.379	17.292	35.563	38.885	41.923	45.642	48.290
27	12.878	14.573	16.151	18.114	36.741	40.113	43.195	46.963	49.645
28	13.565	15.308	16.928	18.939	37.916	41.337	44.461	48.278	50.994
29	14.256	16.047	17.708	19.768	39.087	42.557	45.722	49.588	52.335
30	14.953	16.791	18.493	20.599	40.256	43.773	46.979	50.892	53.672
50	29.707	32.357	34.764	37.689	63.167	67.505	71.420	76.154	79.490
60	37.485	40.482	43.188	46.459	74.397	79.082	83.298	88.379	91.952
80	53.540	57.153	60.391	64.278	96.578	101.879	106.629	112.329	116.321
100	70.065	74.222	77.929	82.358	118.498	124.342	129.561	135.807	140.170

To have a probability of 0.05 in the right tail when df $= 5$, the tabled value is $\chi^2(5, 0.05) = 11.070$.

Appendix D Table of the F-Distribution
Panel A. Critical values for right-hand tail area equal to **0.05**

Numerator: df$_1$ and Denominator: df$_2$

df1:	1	2	3	4	5	6	7	8	9	10	11	12	15	20	21	22	23	24	25	30	40	60	120	∞
df2: 1	161	200	216	225	230	234	237	239	241	242	243	244	246	248	248	249	249	249	249	250	251	252	253	254
2	18.5	19.0	19.2	19.2	19.3	19.3	19.4	19.4	19.4	19.4	19.4	19.4	19.4	19.4	19.4	19.5	19.5	19.5	19.5	19.5	19.5	19.5	19.5	19.5
3	10.1	9.55	9.28	9.12	9.01	8.94	8.89	8.85	8.81	8.79	8.76	8.74	8.70	8.66	8.65	8.65	8.64	8.64	8.63	8.62	8.59	8.57	8.55	8.53
4	7.71	6.94	6.59	6.39	6.26	6.16	6.09	6.04	6.00	5.96	5.94	5.91	5.86	5.80	5.79	5.79	5.78	5.77	5.77	5.75	5.72	5.69	5.66	5.63
5	6.61	5.79	5.41	5.19	5.05	4.95	4.88	4.82	4.77	4.74	4.70	4.68	4.62	4.56	4.55	4.54	4.53	4.53	4.52	4.50	4.46	4.43	4.40	4.37
6	5.99	5.14	4.76	4.53	4.39	4.28	4.21	4.15	4.10	4.06	4.03	4.00	3.94	3.87	3.86	3.86	3.85	3.84	3.83	3.81	3.77	3.74	3.70	3.67
7	5.59	4.74	4.35	4.12	3.97	3.87	3.79	3.73	3.68	3.64	3.60	3.57	3.51	3.44	3.43	3.43	3.42	3.41	3.40	3.38	3.34	3.30	3.27	3.23
8	5.32	4.46	4.07	3.84	3.69	3.58	3.50	3.44	3.39	3.35	3.31	3.28	3.22	3.15	3.14	3.13	3.12	3.12	3.11	3.08	3.04	3.01	2.97	2.93
9	5.12	4.26	3.86	3.63	3.48	3.37	3.29	3.23	3.18	3.14	3.10	3.07	3.01	2.94	2.93	2.92	2.91	2.90	2.89	2.86	2.83	2.79	2.75	2.71
10	4.96	4.10	3.71	3.48	3.33	3.22	3.14	3.07	3.02	2.98	2.94	2.91	2.85	2.77	2.76	2.75	2.75	2.74	2.73	2.70	2.66	2.62	2.58	2.54
11	4.84	3.98	3.59	3.36	3.20	3.09	3.01	2.95	2.90	2.85	2.82	2.79	2.72	2.65	2.64	2.63	2.62	2.61	2.60	2.57	2.53	2.49	2.45	2.40
12	4.75	3.89	3.49	3.26	3.11	3.00	2.91	2.85	2.80	2.75	2.72	2.69	2.62	2.54	2.53	2.52	2.51	2.51	2.50	2.47	2.43	2.38	2.34	2.30
13	4.67	3.81	3.41	3.18	3.03	2.92	2.83	2.77	2.71	2.67	2.63	2.60	2.53	2.46	2.45	2.44	2.43	2.42	2.41	2.38	2.34	2.30	2.25	2.21
14	4.60	3.74	3.34	3.11	2.96	2.85	2.76	2.70	2.65	2.60	2.57	2.53	2.46	2.39	2.38	2.37	2.36	2.35	2.34	2.31	2.27	2.22	2.18	2.13
15	4.54	3.68	3.29	3.06	2.90	2.79	2.71	2.64	2.59	2.54	2.51	2.48	2.40	2.33	2.32	2.31	2.30	2.29	2.28	2.25	2.20	2.16	2.11	2.07
16	4.49	3.63	3.24	3.01	2.85	2.74	2.66	2.59	2.54	2.49	2.46	2.42	2.35	2.28	2.26	2.25	2.24	2.24	2.23	2.19	2.15	2.11	2.06	2.01
17	4.45	3.59	3.20	2.96	2.81	2.70	2.61	2.55	2.49	2.45	2.41	2.38	2.31	2.23	2.22	2.21	2.20	2.19	2.18	2.15	2.10	2.06	2.01	1.96
18	4.41	3.55	3.16	2.93	2.77	2.66	2.58	2.51	2.46	2.41	2.37	2.34	2.27	2.19	2.18	2.17	2.16	2.15	2.14	2.11	2.06	2.02	1.97	1.92
19	4.38	3.52	3.13	2.90	2.74	2.63	2.54	2.48	2.42	2.38	2.34	2.31	2.23	2.16	2.14	2.13	2.12	2.11	2.11	2.07	2.03	1.98	1.93	1.88
20	4.35	3.49	3.10	2.87	2.71	2.60	2.51	2.45	2.39	2.35	2.31	2.28	2.20	2.12	2.11	2.10	2.09	2.08	2.07	2.04	1.99	1.95	1.90	1.84
21	4.32	3.47	3.07	2.84	2.68	2.57	2.49	2.42	2.37	2.32	2.28	2.25	2.18	2.10	2.08	2.07	2.06	2.05	2.05	2.01	1.96	1.92	1.87	1.81
22	4.30	3.44	3.05	2.82	2.66	2.55	2.46	2.40	2.34	2.30	2.26	2.23	2.15	2.07	2.06	2.05	2.04	2.03	2.02	1.98	1.94	1.89	1.84	1.78
23	4.28	3.42	3.03	2.80	2.64	2.53	2.44	2.37	2.32	2.27	2.24	2.20	2.13	2.05	2.04	2.02	2.01	2.01	2.00	1.96	1.91	1.86	1.81	1.76
24	4.26	3.40	3.01	2.78	2.62	2.51	2.42	2.36	2.30	2.25	2.22	2.18	2.11	2.03	2.01	2.00	1.99	1.98	1.97	1.94	1.89	1.84	1.79	1.73
25	4.24	3.39	2.99	2.76	2.60	2.49	2.40	2.34	2.28	2.24	2.20	2.16	2.09	2.01	2.00	1.98	1.97	1.96	1.96	1.92	1.87	1.82	1.77	1.71
30	4.17	3.32	2.92	2.69	2.53	2.42	2.33	2.27	2.21	2.16	2.13	2.09	2.01	1.93	1.92	1.91	1.90	1.89	1.88	1.84	1.79	1.74	1.68	1.62
40	4.08	3.23	2.84	2.61	2.45	2.34	2.25	2.18	2.12	2.08	2.04	2.00	1.92	1.84	1.83	1.81	1.80	1.79	1.78	1.74	1.69	1.64	1.58	1.51
60	4.00	3.15	2.76	2.53	2.37	2.25	2.17	2.10	2.04	1.99	1.95	1.92	1.84	1.75	1.73	1.72	1.71	1.70	1.69	1.65	1.59	1.53	1.47	1.39
120	3.92	3.07	2.68	2.45	2.29	2.18	2.09	2.02	1.96	1.91	1.87	1.83	1.75	1.66	1.64	1.63	1.62	1.61	1.60	1.55	1.50	1.43	1.35	1.25
Infinity	3.84	3.00	2.60	2.37	2.21	2.10	2.01	1.94	1.88	1.83	1.79	1.75	1.67	1.57	1.56	1.54	1.53	1.52	1.51	1.46	1.39	1.32	1.22	1.00

With 1 degree of freedom (df) in the numerator and 3 df in the denominator, the critical F-value is 10.1 for a right-hand tail area equal to 0.05.

Appendix D   Table of the *F*-Distribution
Panel B. Critical values for right-hand tail area equal to **0.025**

Numerator: df$_1$ and Denominator: df$_2$

df2:	1	2	3	4	5	6	7	8	9	10	11	12	15	20	21	22	23	24	25	30	40	60	120	∞
df2: 1	648	799	864	900	922	937	948	957	963	969	973	977	985	993	994	995	996	997	998	1001	1006	1010	1014	1018
2	38.51	39.00	39.17	39.25	39.30	39.33	39.36	39.37	39.39	39.40	39.41	39.41	39.43	39.45	39.45	39.45	39.45	39.46	39.46	39.46	39.47	39.48	39.49	39.50
3	17.44	16.04	15.44	15.10	14.88	14.73	14.62	14.54	14.47	14.42	14.37	14.34	14.25	14.17	14.16	14.14	14.13	14.12	14.12	14.08	14.04	13.99	13.95	13.90
4	12.22	10.65	9.98	9.60	9.36	9.20	9.07	8.98	8.90	8.84	8.79	8.75	8.66	8.56	8.55	8.53	8.52	8.51	8.50	8.46	8.41	8.36	8.31	8.26
5	10.01	8.43	7.76	7.39	7.15	6.98	6.85	6.76	6.68	6.62	6.57	6.52	6.43	6.33	6.31	6.30	6.29	6.28	6.27	6.23	6.18	6.12	6.07	6.02
6	8.81	7.26	6.60	6.23	5.99	5.82	5.70	5.60	5.52	5.46	5.41	5.37	5.27	5.17	5.15	5.14	5.13	5.12	5.11	5.07	5.01	4.96	4.90	4.85
7	8.07	6.54	5.89	5.52	5.29	5.12	4.99	4.90	4.82	4.76	4.71	4.67	4.57	4.47	4.45	4.44	4.43	4.41	4.40	4.36	4.31	4.25	4.20	4.14
8	7.57	6.06	5.42	5.05	4.82	4.65	4.53	4.43	4.36	4.30	4.24	4.20	4.10	4.00	3.98	3.97	3.96	3.95	3.94	3.89	3.84	3.78	3.73	3.67
9	7.21	5.71	5.08	4.72	4.48	4.32	4.20	4.10	4.03	3.96	3.91	3.87	3.77	3.67	3.65	3.64	3.63	3.61	3.60	3.56	3.51	3.45	3.39	3.33
10	6.94	5.46	4.83	4.47	4.24	4.07	3.95	3.85	3.78	3.72	3.66	3.62	3.52	3.42	3.40	3.39	3.38	3.37	3.35	3.31	3.26	3.20	3.14	3.08
11	6.72	5.26	4.63	4.28	4.04	3.88	3.76	3.66	3.59	3.53	3.47	3.43	3.33	3.23	3.21	3.20	3.18	3.17	3.16	3.12	3.06	3.00	2.94	2.88
12	6.55	5.10	4.47	4.12	3.89	3.73	3.61	3.51	3.44	3.37	3.32	3.28	3.18	3.07	3.06	3.04	3.03	3.02	3.01	2.96	2.91	2.85	2.79	2.72
13	6.41	4.97	4.35	4.00	3.77	3.60	3.48	3.39	3.31	3.25	3.20	3.15	3.05	2.95	2.93	2.92	2.91	2.89	2.88	2.84	2.78	2.72	2.66	2.60
14	6.30	4.86	4.24	3.89	3.66	3.50	3.38	3.29	3.21	3.15	3.09	3.05	2.95	2.84	2.83	2.81	2.80	2.79	2.78	2.73	2.67	2.61	2.55	2.49
15	6.20	4.77	4.15	3.80	3.58	3.41	3.29	3.20	3.12	3.06	3.01	2.96	2.86	2.76	2.74	2.73	2.71	2.70	2.69	2.64	2.59	2.52	2.46	2.40
16	6.12	4.69	4.08	3.73	3.50	3.34	3.22	3.12	3.05	2.99	2.93	2.89	2.79	2.68	2.67	2.65	2.64	2.63	2.61	2.57	2.51	2.45	2.38	2.32
17	6.04	4.62	4.01	3.66	3.44	3.28	3.16	3.06	2.98	2.92	2.87	2.82	2.72	2.62	2.60	2.59	2.57	2.56	2.55	2.50	2.44	2.38	2.32	2.25
18	5.98	4.56	3.95	3.61	3.38	3.22	3.10	3.01	2.93	2.87	2.81	2.77	2.67	2.56	2.54	2.53	2.52	2.50	2.49	2.44	2.38	2.32	2.26	2.19
19	5.92	4.51	3.90	3.56	3.33	3.17	3.05	2.96	2.88	2.82	2.76	2.72	2.62	2.51	2.49	2.48	2.46	2.45	2.44	2.39	2.33	2.27	2.20	2.13
20	5.87	4.46	3.86	3.51	3.29	3.13	3.01	2.91	2.84	2.77	2.72	2.68	2.57	2.46	2.45	2.43	2.42	2.41	2.40	2.35	2.29	2.22	2.16	2.09
21	5.83	4.42	3.82	3.48	3.25	3.09	2.97	2.87	2.80	2.73	2.68	2.64	2.53	2.42	2.41	2.39	2.38	2.37	2.36	2.31	2.25	2.18	2.11	2.04
22	5.79	4.38	3.78	3.44	3.22	3.05	2.93	2.84	2.76	2.70	2.65	2.60	2.50	2.39	2.37	2.36	2.34	2.33	2.32	2.27	2.21	2.14	2.08	2.00
23	5.75	4.35	3.75	3.41	3.18	3.02	2.90	2.81	2.73	2.67	2.62	2.57	2.47	2.36	2.34	2.33	2.31	2.30	2.29	2.24	2.18	2.11	2.04	1.97
24	5.72	4.32	3.72	3.38	3.15	2.99	2.87	2.78	2.70	2.64	2.59	2.54	2.44	2.33	2.31	2.30	2.28	2.27	2.26	2.21	2.15	2.08	2.01	1.94
25	5.69	4.29	3.69	3.35	3.13	2.97	2.85	2.75	2.68	2.61	2.56	2.51	2.41	2.30	2.28	2.27	2.26	2.24	2.23	2.18	2.12	2.05	1.98	1.91
30	5.57	4.18	3.59	3.25	3.03	2.87	2.75	2.65	2.57	2.51	2.46	2.41	2.31	2.20	2.18	2.16	2.15	2.14	2.12	2.07	2.01	1.94	1.87	1.79
40	5.42	4.05	3.46	3.13	2.90	2.74	2.62	2.53	2.45	2.39	2.33	2.29	2.18	2.07	2.05	2.03	2.02	2.01	1.99	1.94	1.88	1.80	1.72	1.64
60	5.29	3.93	3.34	3.01	2.79	2.63	2.51	2.41	2.33	2.27	2.22	2.17	2.06	1.94	1.93	1.91	1.90	1.88	1.87	1.82	1.74	1.67	1.58	1.48
120	5.15	3.80	3.23	2.89	2.67	2.52	2.39	2.30	2.22	2.16	2.10	2.05	1.94	1.82	1.81	1.79	1.77	1.76	1.75	1.69	1.61	1.53	1.43	1.31
Infinity	5.02	3.69	3.12	2.79	2.57	2.41	2.29	2.19	2.11	2.05	1.99	1.94	1.83	1.71	1.69	1.67	1.66	1.64	1.63	1.57	1.48	1.39	1.31	1.00

Appendix D   Table of the *F*-Distribution
Panel C. Critical values for right-hand tail area equal to **0.01**

Numerator: df_1 and Denominator: df_2

df2: \ df1:	1	2	3	4	5	6	7	8	9	10	11	12	15	20	21	22	23	24	25	30	40	60	120	∞
1	4052	5000	5403	5625	5764	5859	5928	5982	6023	6056	6083	6106	6157	6209	6216	6223	6229	6235	6240	6261	6287	6313	6339	6366
2	98.5	99.0	99.2	99.2	99.3	99.3	99.4	99.4	99.4	99.4	99.4	99.4	99.4	99.4	99.5	99.5	99.5	99.5	99.5	99.5	99.5	99.5	99.5	99.5
3	34.1	30.8	29.5	28.7	28.2	27.9	27.7	27.5	27.3	27.2	27.1	27.1	26.9	26.7	26.7	26.6	26.6	26.6	26.6	26.5	26.4	26.3	26.2	26.1
4	21.2	18.0	16.7	16.0	15.5	15.2	15.0	14.8	14.7	14.5	14.5	14.4	14.2	14.0	14.0	14.0	13.9	13.9	13.9	13.8	13.7	13.7	13.6	13.5
5	16.3	13.3	12.1	11.4	11.0	10.7	10.5	10.3	10.2	10.1	10.0	9.89	9.72	9.55	9.53	9.51	9.49	9.47	9.45	9.38	9.29	9.20	9.11	9.02
6	13.7	10.9	9.78	9.15	8.75	8.47	8.26	8.10	7.98	7.87	7.79	7.72	7.56	7.40	7.37	7.35	7.33	7.31	7.30	7.23	7.14	7.06	6.97	6.88
7	12.2	9.55	8.45	7.85	7.46	7.19	6.99	6.84	6.72	6.62	6.54	6.47	6.31	6.16	6.13	6.11	6.09	6.07	6.06	5.99	5.91	5.82	5.74	5.65
8	11.3	8.65	7.59	7.01	6.63	6.37	6.18	6.03	5.91	5.81	5.73	5.67	5.52	5.36	5.34	5.32	5.30	5.28	5.26	5.20	5.12	5.03	4.95	4.86
9	10.6	8.02	6.99	6.42	6.06	5.80	5.61	5.47	5.35	5.26	5.18	5.11	4.96	4.81	4.79	4.77	4.75	4.73	4.71	4.65	4.57	4.48	4.40	4.31
10	10.0	7.56	6.55	5.99	5.64	5.39	5.20	5.06	4.94	4.85	4.77	4.71	4.56	4.41	4.38	4.36	4.34	4.33	4.31	4.25	4.17	4.08	4.00	3.91
11	9.65	7.21	6.22	5.67	5.32	5.07	4.89	4.74	4.63	4.54	4.46	4.40	4.25	4.10	4.08	4.06	4.04	4.02	4.01	3.94	3.86	3.78	3.69	3.60
12	9.33	6.93	5.95	5.41	5.06	4.82	4.64	4.50	4.39	4.30	4.22	4.16	4.01	3.86	3.84	3.82	3.80	3.78	3.76	3.70	3.62	3.54	3.45	3.36
13	9.07	6.70	5.74	5.21	4.86	4.62	4.44	4.30	4.19	4.10	4.02	3.96	3.82	3.66	3.64	3.62	3.60	3.59	3.57	3.51	3.43	3.34	3.25	3.17
14	8.86	6.51	5.56	5.04	4.70	4.46	4.28	4.14	4.03	3.94	3.86	3.80	3.66	3.51	3.48	3.46	3.44	3.43	3.41	3.35	3.27	3.18	3.09	3.00
15	8.68	6.36	5.42	4.89	4.56	4.32	4.14	4.00	3.89	3.80	3.73	3.67	3.52	3.37	3.35	3.33	3.31	3.29	3.28	3.21	3.13	3.05	2.96	2.87
16	8.53	6.23	5.29	4.77	4.44	4.20	4.03	3.89	3.78	3.69	3.62	3.55	3.41	3.26	3.24	3.22	3.20	3.18	3.16	3.10	3.02	2.93	2.84	2.75
17	8.40	6.11	5.19	4.67	4.34	4.10	3.93	3.79	3.68	3.59	3.52	3.46	3.31	3.16	3.14	3.12	3.10	3.08	3.07	3.00	2.92	2.83	2.75	2.65
18	8.29	6.01	5.09	4.58	4.25	4.01	3.84	3.71	3.60	3.51	3.43	3.37	3.23	3.08	3.05	3.03	3.02	3.00	2.98	2.92	2.84	2.75	2.66	2.57
19	8.19	5.93	5.01	4.50	4.17	3.94	3.77	3.63	3.52	3.43	3.36	3.30	3.15	3.00	2.98	2.96	2.94	2.92	2.91	2.84	2.76	2.67	2.58	2.49
20	8.10	5.85	4.94	4.43	4.10	3.87	3.70	3.56	3.46	3.37	3.29	3.23	3.09	2.94	2.92	2.90	2.88	2.86	2.84	2.78	2.69	2.61	2.52	2.42
21	8.02	5.78	4.87	4.37	4.04	3.81	3.64	3.51	3.40	3.31	3.24	3.17	3.03	2.88	2.86	2.84	2.82	2.80	2.79	2.72	2.64	2.55	2.46	2.36
22	7.95	5.72	4.82	4.31	3.99	3.76	3.59	3.45	3.35	3.26	3.18	3.12	2.98	2.83	2.81	2.78	2.77	2.75	2.73	2.67	2.58	2.50	2.40	2.31
23	7.88	5.66	4.76	4.26	3.94	3.71	3.54	3.41	3.30	3.21	3.14	3.07	2.93	2.78	2.76	2.74	2.72	2.70	2.69	2.62	2.54	2.45	2.35	2.26
24	7.82	5.61	4.72	4.22	3.90	3.67	3.50	3.36	3.26	3.17	3.09	3.03	2.89	2.74	2.72	2.70	2.68	2.66	2.64	2.58	2.49	2.40	2.31	2.21
25	7.77	5.57	4.68	4.18	3.86	3.63	3.46	3.32	3.22	3.13	3.06	2.99	2.85	2.70	2.68	2.66	2.64	2.62	2.60	2.53	2.45	2.36	2.27	2.17
30	7.56	5.39	4.51	4.02	3.70	3.47	3.30	3.17	3.07	2.98	2.91	2.84	2.70	2.55	2.53	2.51	2.49	2.47	2.45	2.39	2.30	2.21	2.11	2.01
40	7.31	5.18	4.31	3.83	3.51	3.29	3.12	2.99	2.89	2.80	2.73	2.66	2.52	2.37	2.35	2.33	2.31	2.29	2.27	2.20	2.11	2.02	1.92	1.80
60	7.08	4.98	4.13	3.65	3.34	3.12	2.95	2.82	2.72	2.63	2.56	2.50	2.35	2.20	2.17	2.15	2.13	2.12	2.10	2.03	1.94	1.84	1.73	1.60
120	6.85	4.79	3.95	3.48	3.17	2.96	2.79	2.66	2.56	2.47	2.40	2.34	2.19	2.03	2.01	1.99	1.97	1.95	1.93	1.86	1.76	1.66	1.53	1.38
Infinity	6.63	4.61	3.78	3.32	3.02	2.80	2.64	2.51	2.41	2.32	2.25	2.18	2.04	1.88	1.85	1.83	1.81	1.79	1.77	1.70	1.59	1.47	1.32	1.00

Appendix D Table of the F-Distribution

Panel D. Critical values for right-hand tail area equal to **0.005**

Numerator: df$_1$ and Denominator: df$_2$

df2: \ df1:	1	2	3	4	5	6	7	8	9	10	11	12	15	20	21	22	23	24	25	30	40	60	120	∞
1	16211	20000	21615	22500	23056	23437	23715	23925	24091	24222	24334	24426	24630	24836	24863	24892	24915	24940	24959	25044	25146	25253	25359	25464
2	198.5	199.0	199.2	199.2	199.3	199.3	199.4	199.4	199.4	199.4	199.4	199.4	199.4	199.4	199.4	199.4	199.4	199.4	199.4	199.5	199.5	199.5	199.5	199.5
3	55.55	49.80	47.47	46.20	45.39	44.84	44.43	44.13	43.88	43.68	43.52	43.39	43.08	42.78	42.73	42.69	42.66	42.62	42.59	42.47	42.31	42.15	41.99	41.83
4	31.33	26.28	24.26	23.15	22.46	21.98	21.62	21.35	21.14	20.97	20.82	20.70	20.44	20.17	20.13	20.09	20.06	20.03	20.00	19.89	19.75	19.61	19.47	19.32
5	22.78	18.31	16.53	15.56	14.94	14.51	14.20	13.96	13.77	13.62	13.49	13.38	13.15	12.90	12.87	12.84	12.81	12.78	12.76	12.66	12.53	12.40	12.27	12.14
6	18.63	14.54	12.92	12.03	11.46	11.07	10.79	10.57	10.39	10.25	10.13	10.03	9.81	9.59	9.56	9.53	9.50	9.47	9.45	9.36	9.24	9.12	9.00	8.88
7	16.24	12.40	10.88	10.05	9.52	9.16	8.89	8.68	8.51	8.38	8.27	8.18	7.97	7.75	7.72	7.69	7.67	7.64	7.62	7.53	7.42	7.31	7.19	7.08
8	14.69	11.04	9.60	8.81	8.30	7.95	7.69	7.50	7.34	7.21	7.10	7.01	6.81	6.61	6.58	6.55	6.53	6.50	6.48	6.40	6.29	6.18	6.06	5.95
9	13.61	10.11	8.72	7.96	7.47	7.13	6.88	6.69	6.54	6.42	6.31	6.23	6.03	5.83	5.80	5.78	5.75	5.73	5.71	5.62	5.52	5.41	5.30	5.19
10	12.83	9.43	8.08	7.34	6.87	6.54	6.30	6.12	5.97	5.85	5.75	5.66	5.47	5.27	5.25	5.22	5.20	5.17	5.15	5.07	4.97	4.86	4.75	4.64
11	12.23	8.91	7.60	6.88	6.42	6.10	5.86	5.68	5.54	5.42	5.32	5.24	5.05	4.86	4.83	4.80	4.78	4.76	4.74	4.65	4.55	4.45	4.34	4.23
12	11.75	8.51	7.23	6.52	6.07	5.76	5.52	5.35	5.20	5.09	4.99	4.91	4.72	4.53	4.50	4.48	4.45	4.43	4.41	4.33	4.23	4.12	4.01	3.90
13	11.37	8.19	6.93	6.23	5.79	5.48	5.25	5.08	4.94	4.82	4.72	4.64	4.46	4.27	4.24	4.22	4.19	4.17	4.15	4.07	3.97	3.87	3.76	3.65
14	11.06	7.92	6.68	6.00	5.56	5.26	5.03	4.86	4.72	4.60	4.51	4.43	4.25	4.06	4.03	4.01	3.98	3.96	3.94	3.86	3.76	3.66	3.55	3.44
15	10.80	7.70	6.48	5.80	5.37	5.07	4.85	4.67	4.54	4.42	4.33	4.25	4.07	3.88	3.86	3.83	3.81	3.79	3.77	3.69	3.59	3.48	3.37	3.26
16	10.58	7.51	6.30	5.64	5.21	4.91	4.69	4.52	4.38	4.27	4.18	4.10	3.92	3.73	3.71	3.68	3.66	3.64	3.62	3.54	3.44	3.33	3.22	3.11
17	10.38	7.35	6.16	5.50	5.07	4.78	4.56	4.39	4.25	4.14	4.05	3.97	3.79	3.61	3.58	3.56	3.53	3.51	3.49	3.41	3.31	3.21	3.10	2.98
18	10.22	7.21	6.03	5.37	4.96	4.66	4.44	4.28	4.14	4.03	3.94	3.86	3.68	3.50	3.47	3.45	3.42	3.40	3.38	3.30	3.20	3.10	2.99	2.87
19	10.07	7.09	5.92	5.27	4.85	4.56	4.34	4.18	4.04	3.93	3.84	3.76	3.59	3.40	3.37	3.35	3.33	3.31	3.29	3.21	3.11	3.00	2.89	2.78
20	9.94	6.99	5.82	5.17	4.76	4.47	4.26	4.09	3.96	3.85	3.76	3.68	3.50	3.32	3.29	3.27	3.24	3.22	3.20	3.12	3.02	2.92	2.81	2.69
21	9.83	6.89	5.73	5.09	4.68	4.39	4.18	4.01	3.88	3.77	3.68	3.60	3.43	3.24	3.22	3.19	3.17	3.15	3.13	3.05	2.95	2.84	2.73	2.61
22	9.73	6.81	5.65	5.02	4.61	4.32	4.11	3.94	3.81	3.70	3.61	3.54	3.36	3.18	3.15	3.12	3.10	3.08	3.06	2.98	2.88	2.77	2.66	2.55
23	9.63	6.73	5.58	4.95	4.54	4.26	4.05	3.88	3.75	3.64	3.55	3.47	3.30	3.12	3.09	3.06	3.04	3.02	3.00	2.92	2.82	2.71	2.60	2.48
24	9.55	6.66	5.52	4.89	4.49	4.20	3.99	3.83	3.69	3.59	3.50	3.42	3.25	3.06	3.04	3.01	2.99	2.97	2.95	2.87	2.77	2.66	2.55	2.43
25	9.48	6.60	5.46	4.84	4.43	4.15	3.94	3.78	3.64	3.54	3.45	3.37	3.20	3.01	2.99	2.96	2.94	2.92	2.90	2.82	2.72	2.61	2.50	2.38
30	9.18	6.35	5.24	4.62	4.23	3.95	3.74	3.58	3.45	3.34	3.25	3.18	3.01	2.82	2.80	2.77	2.75	2.73	2.71	2.63	2.52	2.42	2.30	2.18
40	8.83	6.07	4.98	4.37	3.99	3.71	3.51	3.35	3.22	3.12	3.03	2.95	2.78	2.60	2.57	2.55	2.52	2.50	2.48	2.40	2.30	2.18	2.06	1.93
60	8.49	5.79	4.73	4.14	3.76	3.49	3.29	3.13	3.01	2.90	2.82	2.74	2.57	2.39	2.36	2.33	2.31	2.29	2.27	2.19	2.08	1.96	1.83	1.69
120	8.18	5.54	4.50	3.92	3.55	3.28	3.09	2.93	2.81	2.71	2.62	2.54	2.37	2.19	2.16	2.13	2.11	2.09	2.07	1.98	1.87	1.75	1.61	1.43
Infinity	7.88	5.30	4.28	3.72	3.35	3.09	2.90	2.74	2.62	2.52	2.43	2.36	2.19	2.00	1.97	1.95	1.92	1.90	1.88	1.79	1.67	1.53	1.36	1.00

Appendix E   Critical Values for the Durbin-Watson Statistic ($\alpha = .05$)

n	$K = 1$ d_l	d_u	$K = 2$ d_l	d_u	$K = 3$ d_l	d_u	$K = 4$ d_l	d_u	$K = 5$ d_l	d_u
15	1.08	1.36	0.95	1.54	0.82	1.75	0.69	1.97	0.56	2.21
16	1.10	1.37	0.98	1.54	0.86	1.73	0.74	1.93	0.62	2.15
17	1.13	1.38	1.02	1.54	0.90	1.71	0.78	1.90	0.67	2.10
18	1.16	1.39	1.05	1.53	0.93	1.69	0.82	1.87	0.71	2.06
19	1.18	1.40	1.08	1.53	0.97	1.68	0.86	1.85	0.75	2.02
20	1.20	1.41	1.10	1.54	1.00	1.68	0.90	1.83	0.79	1.99
21	1.22	1.42	1.13	1.54	1.03	1.67	0.93	1.81	0.83	1.96
22	1.24	1.43	1.15	1.54	1.05	1.66	0.96	1.80	0.86	1.94
23	1.26	1.44	1.17	1.54	1.08	1.66	0.99	1.79	0.90	1.92
24	1.27	1.45	1.19	1.55	1.10	1.66	1.01	1.78	0.93	1.90
25	1.29	1.45	1.21	1.55	1.12	1.66	1.04	1.77	0.95	1.89
26	1.30	1.46	1.22	1.55	1.14	1.65	1.06	1.76	0.98	1.88
27	1.32	1.47	1.24	1.56	1.16	1.65	1.08	1.76	1.01	1.86
28	1.33	1.48	1.26	1.56	1.18	1.65	1.10	1.75	1.03	1.85
29	1.34	1.48	1.27	1.56	1.20	1.65	1.12	1.74	1.05	1.84
30	1.35	1.49	1.28	1.57	1.21	1.65	1.14	1.74	1.07	1.83
31	1.36	1.50	1.30	1.57	1.23	1.65	1.16	1.74	1.09	1.83
32	1.37	1.50	1.31	1.57	1.24	1.65	1.18	1.73	1.11	1.82
33	1.38	1.51	1.32	1.58	1.26	1.65	1.19	1.73	1.13	1.81
34	1.39	1.51	1.33	1.58	1.27	1.65	1.21	1.73	1.15	1.81
35	1.40	1.52	1.34	1.58	1.28	1.65	1.22	1.73	1.16	1.80
36	1.41	1.52	1.35	1.59	1.29	1.65	1.24	1.73	1.18	1.80
37	1.42	1.53	1.36	1.59	1.31	1.66	1.25	1.72	1.19	1.80
38	1.43	1.54	1.37	1.59	1.32	1.66	1.26	1.72	1.21	1.79
39	1.43	1.54	1.38	1.60	1.33	1.66	1.27	1.72	1.22	1.79
40	1.44	1.54	1.39	1.60	1.34	1.66	1.29	1.72	1.23	1.79
45	1.48	1.57	1.43	1.62	1.38	1.67	1.34	1.72	1.29	1.78
50	1.50	1.59	1.46	1.63	1.42	1.67	1.38	1.72	1.34	1.77
55	1.53	1.60	1.49	1.64	1.45	1.68	1.41	1.72	1.38	1.77
60	1.55	1.62	1.51	1.65	1.48	1.69	1.44	1.73	1.41	1.77
65	1.57	1.63	1.54	1.66	1.50	1.70	1.47	1.73	1.44	1.77
70	1.58	1.64	1.55	1.67	1.52	1.70	1.49	1.74	1.46	1.77
75	1.60	1.65	1.57	1.68	1.54	1.71	1.51	1.74	1.49	1.77
80	1.61	1.66	1.59	1.69	1.56	1.72	1.53	1.74	1.51	1.77
85	1.62	1.67	1.60	1.70	1.57	1.72	1.55	1.75	1.52	1.77
90	1.63	1.68	1.61	1.70	1.59	1.73	1.57	1.75	1.54	1.78
95	1.64	1.69	1.62	1.71	1.60	1.73	1.58	1.75	1.56	1.78
100	1.65	1.69	1.63	1.72	1.61	1.74	1.59	1.76	1.57	1.78

Source: From J. Durbin and G. S. Watson, "Testing for Serial Correlation in Least Squares Regression, II." *Biometrika* 38 (1951): 159– 178. Reproduced by permission of the *Biometrika* trustees.

Note: $K =$ the number of slope parameters in the model.

REFERENCES

Ackerman, Carl, Richard McEnally, and David Ravenscraft. 1999. "The Performance of Hedge Funds: Risk, Return, and Incentives." *Journal of Finance.* Vol. 54, No. 3: 833–874.

Altman, Edward I. 1968. "Financial Ratios, Discriminant Analysis and the Prediction of Corporate Bankruptcy." *Journal of Finance.* Vol. 23: 589–699.

Altman, Edward I., and Vellore M. Kishore. 1996. "Almost Everything You Wanted to Know about Recoveries on Defaulted Bonds." *Financial Analysts Journal.* Vol. 52, No. 6: 57–63.

Altman, Edward I., R. Haldeman, and P. Narayanan. 1977. "Zeta Analysis: A New Model to Identify Bankruptcy Risk of Corporations." *Journal of Banking and Finance.* Vol. 1: 29–54.

Ambachtsheer, Keith, Ronald Capelle, and Tom Scheibelhut. 1998. "Improving Pension Fund Performance." *Financial Analysts Journal.* Vol. 54, No. 6: 15–21.

American Association of Individual Investors. 2003. *The Individual Investor's Guide to the Top Mutual Funds,* 22nd edition. Chicago: AAII.

Amihud, Yakov, and Kefei Li. 2002. "The Declining Information Content of Dividend Announcements and the Effect of Institutional Holdings." New York University Stern School of Business Working Paper No. SC-AM-02-11.

Amin, Gaurav S., and Harry M. Kat. 2003. "Stocks, Bonds, and Hedge Funds." *Journal of Portfolio Management.* Vol. 29, No. 4: 113–120.

Baks, Klaas P., Andres Metrick, and Jessica Wachter. 2001. "Should Investors Avoid All Actively Managed Mutual Funds?" *Journal of Finance.* Vol. 56: 45–85.

Barr, G.D.I., and Kantor, B.S. 1999. "Price-Earnings Ratios on the Johannesburg Stock Exchange—Are They a Guide to Value?" *SA Journal of Accounting Research.* Vol. 13, No. 1: 1–23.

Bauman, W. Scott, C. Mitchell Conover, and Robert E. Miller. 1998. "Growth versus Value and Large-Cap versus Small-Cap Stocks in International Markets." *Financial Analysts Journal.* Vol. 54, No. 2: 75–89.

Black, Fischer. 1972. "Capital Market Equilibrium with Restricted Borrowing." *Journal of Business.* Vol. 45, No. 3: 444–455.

——. 1993. "Estimating Expected Return." *Financial Analysts Journal.* Vol. 49, No. 5: 36–38.

Black, Fischer, and Robert Litterman. 1991. "Asset Allocation: Combining Investor Views with Market Equilibrium." *Journal of Fixed Income.* Vol. 1, No. 2: 7–18.

——. 1992. "Global Portfolio Optimization." *Financial Analysts Journal.* Vol. 48, No. 5: 28–43.

Block, Stanley B. 1999. "A Study of Financial Analysts: Practice and Theory." *Financial Analysts Journal.* Vol. 55, No. 4: 86–95.

Blume, Marshall. 1984. "The Use of 'Alphas' to Improve Performance." *Journal of Portfolio Management.* Vol. 11: 86–92.

Bodie, Zvi, Alex Kane, and Alan J. Marcus. 2001. *Investments,* 5th edition. Boston: Irwin/McGraw-Hill.

Bowerman, Bruce L., and Richard T. O'Connell. 1997. *Applied Statistics: Improving Business Practices.* Chicago: Irwin.

Brealey, Richard A., and Stewart C. Myers. 2003. *Principles of Corporate Finance.* 7th ed. New York: McGraw-Hill.

Breusch, T., and A. Pagan. 1979. "A Simple Test for Heteroscedasticity and Random Coefficient Variation." *Econometrica.* Vol. 47: 1287–1294.

Brown, Stephen, William Goetzmann, and Stephen Ross. 1995. "Survival." *Journal of Finance*. Vol. 50: 853–873.

Buetow, Gerald W., Jr., Robert R. Johnson, and David E. Runkle. 2000. "The Inconsistency of Return-Based Style Analysis." *Journal of Portfolio Management*. Vol. 26, No. 3: 61–77.

Buffett, Warren. 1993. *Berkshire Hathaway Chairman's Letter*. Retrieved May 25, 2001, from the World Wide Web: www.berkshirehathaway.com/letters/1983.html.

Burmeister, Edwin, and Marjorie B. McElroy. 1988. "Joint Estimation of Factor Sensitivities and Risk Premia for the Arbitrage Pricing Theory." *Journal of Finance*. Vol. 43, No. 3: 721–733.

Burmeister, Edwin, Richard Roll, and Stephen A. Ross. 1994. "A Practitioner's Guide to Arbitrage Pricing Theory." In *A Practitioner's Guide to Factor Models*. Charlottesville, VA: Research Foundation of the Institute of Chartered Financial Analysts.

Campbell, John Y., Andrew W. Lo, and A. Craig MacKinlay. 1997. *The Econometrics of Financial Markets*. Princeton, NJ: Princeton University Press.

Campbell, John Y., Martin Lettau, Burton G. Malkiel, and Yexiao Xu. 2001. "Have Individual Stocks Become More Volatile? An Empirical Exploration of Idiosyncratic Risk." *Journal of Finance*. Vol. 56, No. 1: 1–43.

Campbell, Stephen K. 1974. *Flaws and Fallacies in Statistical Thinking*. Englewood Cliffs, NJ: Prentice-Hall.

Carhart, Mark M. 1997. "On Persistence in Mutual Fund Performance." *Journal of Finance*. Vol. 52, No. 1: 57–82.

Chan, Louis K.C., Jason Karceski, and Josef Lakonishok. 1999. "On Portfolio Optimization: Forecasting Covariances and Choosing the Risk Model." *Review of Financial Studies*. Vol. 12, No. 5: 937–974.

Chance, Don M. 2003. *Analysis of Derivatives for the CFA® Program*. Charlottesville, VA: AIMR.

Chen, Nai-fu, Richard Roll, and Stephen Ross. 1986. "Economic Forces and the Stock Market." *Journal of Business*. Vol. 59, No. 3: 383–403.

Chow, George. 1995. "Portfolio Selection Based on Return, Risk, and Relative Performance." *Financial Analysts Journal*. Vol. 51, No. 2: 54–60.

Chow, George, Eric Jacquier, Mark Kritzman, and Kenneth Lowry. 1999. "Optimal Portfolios in Good Times and Bad." *Financial Analysts Journal*. Vol. 55, No. 3: 65–73.

Chua, Jess H., Richard S. Woodward, and Eric C. To. 1987. "Potential Gains from Stock Market Timing in Canada." *Financial Analysts Journal*. Vol. 43, No. 5: 50–56.

Clarke, Roger G., and Mark P. Kritzman. 1996. *Currency Management: Concepts and Practices*. Charlottesville, VA: Research Foundation of AIMR.

Cochrane, John H. 1999a. "New Facts in Finance." *Economic Perspectives*. Federal Reserve Bank of Chicago. Vol. 23, No. 3: 36–58. (Revision of NBER Working Paper 7169.)

———. 1999b. "Portfolio Advice for a Multifactor World." *Economic Perspectives*. Federal Reserve Bank of Chicago. Vol. 23, No. 3: 59–78. (Revision of NBER Working Paper 7170.)

Connor, Gregory. 1995. "The Three Types of Factor Models: A Comparison of Their Explanatory Power." *Financial Analysts Journal*. Vol. 51, No. 3: 42–46.

Cox, Jonathan, Stephen Ross, and Mark Rubinstein. 1979. "Options Pricing: A Simplified Approach." *Journal of Financial Economics*. Vol. 7: 229–263.

Daniel, Wayne W., and James C. Terrell. 1986. *Business Statistics, Basic Concepts and Methodology*, 4th edition. Boston: Houghton Mifflin.

———. 1995. *Business Statistics for Management & Economics*, 7th edition. Boston: Houghton-Mifflin.

Davidson, Russell, and James G. MacKinnon. 1993. *Estimation and Inference in Econometrics*. New York: Oxford University Press.

Dickey, David A., and Wayne A. Fuller. 1979. "Distribution of the Estimators for Autoregressive Time Series with a Unit Root." *Journal of the American Statistical Association*. Vol. 74: 427–431.

Diebold, Francis X. 2004. *Elements of Forecasting*, 3rd edition. Cincinnati, OH: South-Western.

Dimson, Elroy, Paul Marsh, and Mike Staunton. 2002. *Triumph of the Optimists: 101 Years of Global Investment Returns*. Princeton, NJ: Princeton University Press.

Durbin, J., and G.S. Watson. 1951. "Testing for Serial Correlation in Least Squares Regression, II." *Biometrika*. Vol. 38: 159–178.

Dybvig, Philip H., and Stephen A. Ross. 1985a. "Differential Information and Performance Measurement Using a Security Market Line." *Journal of Finance*. Vol. 40, No. 2: 383–399.

———. 1985b. "The Analytics of Performance Measurement Using a Security Market Line." *Journal of Finance*. Vol. 40, No. 2: 401–416.

Edwards, Franklin R. 1988. "Does Futures Trading Increase Stock Market Volatility?" *Financial Analysts Journal*. Vol. 44, No. 1: 63–69.

Elton, Edwin J., Martin J. Gruber, and Joel Rentzler. 1987. "Professionally Managed Publicly Traded Commodity Funds." *Journal of Business*. Vol. 60, No. 2: 175–199.

———. 1990. "The Performance of Publicly Offered Commodity Funds." *Financial Analysts Journal*. Vol. 46, No. 4: 23–30.

Elton, Edwin J., Martin J. Gruber, Stephen J. Brown, and William N. Goetzmann. 2003. *Modern Portfolio Theory and Investment Analysis*, 6th edition. New York: Wiley.

Engle, Robert F. 1982. "Autoregressive Conditional Heteroscedasticity with Estimates of the Variance of United Kingdom Inflation." *Econometrica*. Vol. 50, No. 4: 987–1007.

Engle, Robert F., and Clive W.J. Granger. 1987. "Co-Integration and Error Correction: Representation, Estimation, and Testing." *Econometrica*. Vol. 55, No. 2: 251–276.

Estrada, Javier. 2003. "Mean-Semivariance Behavior: A Note." *Finance Letters*. Vol. 1, Issue 1: 9–14.

Fabozzi, Frank J. 2004a. *Fixed Income Analysis for the Chartered Financial Analyst® Program*, 2nd edition. New Hope, PA: Frank J. Fabozzi Associates.

———. 2004b. *Fixed Income Readings for the Chartered Financial Analyst® Program*, 2nd edition. New Hope, PA: Frank J. Fabozzi Associates.

Fama, Eugene. 1976. *Foundations of Finance*. New York: Basic Books.

Fama, Eugene F., and Kenneth R. French. 1992. "The Cross-Section of Expected Stock Returns." *Journal of Finance*. Vol. 47, No. 2: 427–466.

———. 1993. "Common Risk Factors in the Returns on Stocks and Bonds." *Journal of Financial Economics*. Vol. 33, No. 1: 3–56.

———. 1996. "Multifactor Explanations of Asset Pricing Anomalies." *Journal of Finance*, Vol. 51, No. 1: 55–84.

Feller, William. 1957. *An Introduction to Probability Theory and Its Applications, Vol. I*, 2nd edition. New York: Wiley.

Ferguson, Robert. 1993. "Some Formulas for Evaluating Two Popular Option Strategies." *Financial Analysts Journal*. Vol. 49, No. 5: 71–76.

Fisher, Lawrence, and James H. Lorie. 1970. "Some Studies of Variability of Returns on Investments in Common Stocks." *Journal of Business*. Vol. 43, No. 2: 99–134.

Forbes. 16 September 2003. "The Honor Roll." New York: Forbes Management Co., Inc.

Freeley, Austin J., and David L. Steinberg. 1999. *Argumentation and Debate: Critical Thinking for Reasoned Decision Making*. Wadsworth Publishing.

French, Kenneth R., and James M. Poterba. 1991. "Investor Diversification and International Equity Markets." *American Economic Review*. Vol. 81, No. 2: 222–226.

Freund, John E., and Frank J. Williams. 1977. *Elementary Business Statistics*, 3rd edition. Englewood Cliffs, NJ: Prentice-Hall.

Fridson, Martin S., and M. Christopher Garman. 1998. "Determinants of Spreads on New High-Yield Bonds." *Financial Analysts Journal*. Vol. 54, No. 2: 28–39.

Fung, William, and David A. Hsieh. 2002. "Hedge-Fund Benchmarks: Information Content and Biases." *Financial Analysts Journal*. Vol. 58, No. 1: 22–34.

Garbade, Kenneth. 1982. *Securities Markets*. New York: McGraw-Hill.

Goetzmann, William N., and Philippe Jorion. 1999. "Re-Emerging Markets." *Journal of Financial and Quantitative Analysis*. Vol. 34, No. 1: 1–32.

Goldberger, Arthur S. 1998. *Introductory Econometrics*. Cambridge, MA: Harvard University Press.

Granger, Clive W.J., and Paul Newbold. 1974. "Spurious Regressions in Econometrics." *Journal of Econometrics.* Vol. 2: 111–120.

Greene, William H. 2003. *Econometric Analysis,* 5th edition. Upper Saddle River, NJ: Prentice-Hall.

Grinblatt, Mark, and Sheridan Titman. 1998. *Financial Markets and Corporate Strategy.* New York: Irwin/McGraw-Hill.

Grinold, Richard, and Ronald N. Kahn. 1994. "Multi-Factor Models for Portfolio Risk." In *A Practitioner's Guide to Factor Models.* Charlottesville, VA: Research Foundation of the Institute of Chartered Financial Analysts.

Gujarati, Damodar N. 2003. *Basic Econometrics,* 4th edition. New York: McGraw-Hill.

Hamilton, James D. 1994. *Time Series Analysis.* Princeton, NJ: Princeton University Press.

Hansen, Lars Peter. 1982. "Large Sample Properties of Generalized Method of Moments Estimators." *Econometrica.* Vol. 50, No. 4: 1029–1054.

Heaney, Richard, Chitoshi Koga, Barry Oliver, and Alfred Tran. 1999. "The Size Effect and Derivative Usage in Japan." Working paper: The Australian National University.

Henriksson, Roy D., and Robert C. Merton. 1981. "On Market Timing and Investment Performance, II. Statistical Procedures for Evaluating Forecasting Skills." *Journal of Business.* Vol. 54, No. 4: 513–533.

Hettmansperger, T.P., and J.W. McKean. 1998. *Robust Nonparametric Statistical Methods.* London: Oxford University Press.

Hillier, Frederick S., and Gerald J. Lieberman. 2000. *Introduction to Operations Research,* 7th edition. New York: McGraw-Hill.

Hull, John. 2003. *Options, Futures, and Other Derivatives,* 5th edition. Upper Saddle River, NJ: Prentice-Hall.

Kahn, Ronald N., and Andrew Rudd. 1995. "Does Historical Performance Predict Future Performance?" *Financial Analysts Journal.* Vol. 51, No. 6: 43–52.

Keane, Michael P., and David E. Runkle. 1990. "Testing the Rationality of Price Forecasts: New Evidence from Panel Data." *American Economic Review.* Vol. 80, No. 4: 714–735.

———. 1998. "Are Financial Analysts' Forecasts of Corporate Profits Rational?" *Journal of Political Economy.* Vol. 106, No. 4: 768–805.

Kemeny, John G., Arthur Schleifer, Jr., J. Laurie Snell, and Gerald L. Thompson. 1972. *Finite Mathematics with Business Applications,* 2nd edition. Englewood Cliffs, NJ: Prentice-Hall.

Klemkosky, Robert C., and John D. Martin. 1975. "The Adjustment of Beta Forecasts." *Journal of Finance.* Vol. 30, No. 4: 1123–1128.

Kmenta, Jan. 1986. *Elements of Econometrics,* 2nd edition. New York: Macmillan.

Kolb, Robert W., Gerald D. Gay, and William C. Hunter. 1985. "Liquidity Requirements for Financial Futures Investments." *Financial Analysts Journal.* Vol. 41, No. 3: 60–68.

Kon, Stanley J. 1984. "Models of Stock Returns—A Comparison." *Journal of Finance.* Vol. 39: 147–165.

Kool, Clemens J.M. 2000. "International Bond Markets and the Introduction of the Euro." *Review* of the Federal Reserve Bank of St. Louis. Vol. 82, No. 5: 41–56.

Kothari, S.P., Jay Shanken, and Richard G. Sloan. 1995. "Another Look at the Cross-Section of Expected Stock Returns." *Journal of Finance.* Vol. 50, No. 1: 185–224.

Ledoit, Olivier, and Michael Wolf. 2004. "Honey, I Shrunk the Sample Covariance Matrix." *Journal of Portfolio Management.* Vol. 31, No. 1.

Leibowitz, Martin L., and Roy D. Henriksson. 1989. "Portfolio Optimization with Shortfall Constraints: A Confidence-Limit Approach to Managing Downside Risk." *Financial Analysts Journal.* Vol. 45, No. 2: 34–41.

Leinweber, David. 1997. *Stupid Data Mining Tricks: Over-Fitting the S&P 500.* Monograph. Pasadena, CA: First Quadrant.

Liang, Bing. 1999. "On the Performance of Hedge Funds." *Financial Analysts Journal.* Vol. 55, No. 4: 72–85.

Linsmeier, Thomas J., and Neil D. Pearson. 2000. "Value at Risk." *Financial Analysts Journal.* Vol. 56, No. 2: 47–67.

Lo, Andrew W. 1999. "The Three P's of Total Risk Management." *Financial Analysts Journal.* Vol. 55, No. 1: 13–26.

Lo, Andrew W., and A. Craig MacKinlay. 1990. "Data Snooping Biases in Tests of Financial Asset Pricing Models." *Review of Financial Studies.* Vol. 3: 175–208.

Luenberger, David G. 1998. *Investment Science.* New York: Oxford University Press.

MacKinlay, A. Craig, and Matthew P. Richardson. 1991. "Using Generalized Methods of Moments to Test Mean–Variance Efficiency." *Journal of Finance.* Vol. 46, No. 2: 511–527.

Mankiw, N. Gregory. 2000. *Macroeconomics,* 4th edition. New York: Worth Publishers.

Mauboussin, Michael J., and Shelby Heard. 1996. *Packaged Food Industry Rate of Return Analysis.* New York: Credit Suisse First Boston.

——. 1975. "Selecting Economic Hypotheses by Goodness of Fit." *Economic Journal.* Vol. 85, Issue 340: 877–883.

Mayer, Thomas. 1980. "Economics as a Hard Science: Realistic Goal or Wishful Thinking?" *Economic Inquiry.* Vol. 18, No. 2: 165–178.

McQueen, Grant, and Steven Thorley. 1999. "Mining Fools Gold." *Financial Analysts Journal.* Vol. 55, No. 2: 61–72.

McQueen, Grant, Kay Shields, and Steven R. Thorley. 1997. "Does the 'Dow-10 Investment Strategy' Beat the Dow Statistically and Economically?" *Financial Analysts Journal.* Vol. 53, No. 4: 66–72.

Michaud, Richard O. 1998. *Efficient Asset Management.* Boston: Harvard Business School Press.

Moore, David S., and George P. McCabe. 1998. *Introduction to the Practice of Statistics,* 3rd edition. New York: W.H. Freeman.

Nayar, Nandkumar, and Michael S. Rozeff. 1994. "Ratings, Commercial Paper, and Equity Returns." *Journal of Finance.* Vol. 49, No. 4: 1431–1449.

Nelson, David C., Robert B. Moskow, Tiffany Lee, and Gregg Valentine. 2003. *Food Investor's Handbook.* New York: Credit Suisse First Boston.

Oppenheimer, Henry R., and Sanjiv Sabherwal. 2003. "The Competitive Effects of U.S. Decimalization: Evidence from the U.S.-Listed Canadian Stocks." *Journal of Banking and Finance.* Vol. 27, No. 9.

Pindyck, Robert S., and Daniel L. Rubinfeld. 1998. *Econometric Models and Economic Forecasts,* 4th edition. Boston: Irwin/McGraw-Hill.

Ramsey, Frank P. 1931. "Truth and Probability." In *The Foundations of Mathematics and Other Logical Essays,* edited by R.B. Braithwaite. London: Routledge and Keegan Paul.

Reilly, Frank K., and Keith C. Brown. 2003. *Investment Analysis and Portfolio Management,* 7th edition. Mason, OH: South-Western.

Roll, Richard, and Stephen A. Ross. 2001. *What Is the Arbitrage Pricing Theory?* Retrieved May 25, 2001, from the World Wide Web: www.rollross.com/apt.html.

Ross, Sheldon M. 1997. *A First Course in Probability,* 5th edition. Englewood, NJ: Prentice-Hall.

Ross, Stephen A. 1976. "The Arbitrage Theory of Capital Asset Pricing." *Journal of Economic Theory.* December: 341–360.

Roy, A.D. 1952. "Safety-First and the Holding of Assets." *Econometrica.* Vol. 20: 431–439.

Sharpe, William F. 1988. "Determining a Fund's Effective Asset Mix." *Investment Management Review.* November/December: 59–69.

——. 1992. "Asset Allocation: Management Style and Performance Measurement." *Journal of Portfolio Management.* Vol. 18, No. 2: 7–19.

——. 1994. "The Sharpe Ratio." *Journal of Portfolio Management.* Vol. 21, No. 1: 49–59.

Sharpe, William F., Gordon J. Alexander, and Jeffery V. Bailey. 1999. *Investments,* 6th edition. Upper Saddle River, NJ: Prentice-Hall.

Shumway, Tyler, and Vincent A. Warther. 1999. "The Delisting Bias in CRSP's Nasdaq Data and Its Implications for the Size Effect." *Journal of Finance.* Vol. 54, No. 6: 2361–2379.

Siegel, Jeremy J. 1998. *Stocks for the Long Run,* 2nd edition. New York: McGraw-Hill.

Siegel, Sidney. 1956. *Nonparametric Statistics for the Behavioral Sciences.* New York: McGraw-Hill.

Sorenson, Eric H., Vele Samak, and Keith Miller. 1998. "U.S. Equity Risk Attribute Model (RAM): A New Look at a Classic Model." *Quantitative Research.* Salomon Smith Barney.

Standard Life Investment, Inc. 2003. "Pooled Investment Funds Performance Review: First Quarter 2003."

Stewart, G. Bennett. 1991. *The Quest for Value.* New York: HarperBusiness.

Stoll, Hans R. 1978. "The Pricing of Security Dealer Services: An Empirical Study of Nasdaq Stocks." *Journal of Finance.* Vol. 33, No. 4: 1153–1172.

Stowe, John D., Thomas R. Robinson, Jerald E. Pinto, and Dennis W. McLeavey. 2002. *Analysis of Equity Investments: Valuation.* Charlottesville, VA: AIMR.

Stuart, Alan, and J. Keith Ord. 1994. *Kendall's Advanced Theory of Statistics, Vol. 1: Distribution Theory,* 6th edition. London: Arnold.

Swensen, David F. 2000. *Pioneering Portfolio Management: An Unconventional Approach to Institutional Investment.* New York: Free Press.

Treynor, Jack L., and Kay Mazuy. 1966. "Can Mutual Funds Outguess the Market?" *Harvard Business Review.* Vol. 44: 131–136.

White, Gerald I., Ashwinpaul C. Sondhi, and Dov Fried. 2003. *The Analysis and Use of Financial Statements,* 3rd edition. New York: Wiley.

White, Halbert. 1980. "A Heteroskedasticity-Consistent Covariance Matrix Estimator and a Direct Test for Heteroskedasticity." *Econometrica.* Vol. 48, No. 4: 817–838.

GLOSSARY

A priori probability   A probability based on logical analysis rather than on observation or personal judgment.

Absolute dispersion   The amount of variability present without comparison to any reference point or benchmark.

Absolute frequency   The number of observations in a given interval (for grouped data).

Accrued interest   Interest earned but not yet paid.

Active factor risk   The contribution to active risk squared resulting from the portfolio's different-than-benchmark exposures relative to factors specified in the risk model.

Active return   The return on a portfolio minus the return on the portfolio's benchmark.

Active risk   The standard deviation of active returns.

Active risk squared   The variance of active returns; active risk raised to the second power.

Active specific risk or asset selection risk   The contribution to active risk squared resulting from the portfolio's active weights on individual assets as those weights interact with assets' residual risk.

Addition rule for probabilities   A principle stating that the probability that A or B occurs (both occur) equals the probability that A occurs, plus the probability that B occurs, minus the probability that both A and B occur.

Adjusted beta   Historical beta adjusted to reflect the tendency of beta to be mean reverting.

Adjusted R^2   A measure of goodness-of-fit of a regression that is adjusted for degrees of freedom and hence does not automatically increase when another independent variable is added to a regression.

Alternative hypothesis   The hypothesis accepted when the null hypothesis is rejected.

Analysis of variance (ANOVA)   The analysis of the total variability of a dataset (such as observations on the dependent variable in a regression) into components representing different sources of variation; with reference to regression, ANOVA provides the inputs for an F-test of the significance of the regression as a whole.

Annual percentage rate   The cost of borrowing expressed as a yearly rate.

Annuity   A finite set of level sequential cash flows.

Annuity due   An annuity having a first cash flow that is paid immediately.

Arbitrage   A risk-free operation that earns an expected positive net profit but requires no net investment of money.

Arbitrage opportunity   An opportunity to conduct an arbitrage; an opportunity to earn an expected positive net profit without risk and with no net investment of money.

Arbitrage portfolio   The portfolio that exploits an arbitrage opportunity.

Arithmetic mean   The sum of the observations divided by the number of observations.

Asian call option   A European-style option with a value at maturity equal to the difference between the stock price at maturity and the average stock price during the life of the option, or $0, whichever is greater.

Autocorrelation   The correlation of a time series with its own past values.

Autoregressive (AR) model   A time series regressed on its own past values, in which the independent variable is a lagged value of the dependent variable.

Bank discount basis   A quoting convention that annualizes, on a 360-day year, the discount as a percentage of face value.

Bayes' formula A method for updating probabilities based on new information.

Benchmark A comparison portfolio; a point of reference or comparison.

Bernoulli random variable A random variable having the outcomes 0 and 1.

Bernoulli trial An experiment that can produce one of two outcomes.

Beta A measure of an asset's sensitivity to movements in the market.

Binomial random variable The number of successes in n Bernoulli trials for which the probability of success is constant for all trials and the trials are independent.

Binomial tree The graphical representation of a model of asset price dynamics in which, at each period, the asset moves up with probability p or down with probability $(1 - p)$.

Block Orders to buy or sell that are too large for the liquidity ordinarily available in dealer networks or stock exchanges.

Bond-equivalent basis A basis for stating an annual yield that annualizes a semiannual yield by doubling it.

Bond-equivalent yield The yield to maturity on a basis that ignores compounding.

Breusch–Pagan test A test for conditional heteroskedasticity in the error term of a regression.

Capital allocation line (CAL) A graph line that describes the combinations of expected return and standard deviation of return available to an investor from combining the optimal portfolio of risky assets with the risk-free asset.

Capital asset pricing model (CAPM) An equation describing the expected return on any asset (or portfolio) as a linear function of its beta.

Capital budgeting The allocation of funds to relatively long-range projects or investments.

Capital market line (CML) A form of the capital allocation line in which investors share identical expectations about the mean returns, variance of returns, and correlations of risky assets.

Capital structure A company's specific mixture of long-term financing.

Cash flow additivity principle The principle that dollar amounts indexed at the same point in time are additive.

Central limit theorem A result in statistics that states that the sample mean computed from large samples of size n from a population with finite variance will follow an approximate normal distribution with a mean equal to the population mean and a variance equal to the population variance divided by n.

Chain rule of forecasting A forecasting process in which the next period's value as predicted by the forecasting equation is substituted into the right-hand side of the equation to give a predicted value two periods ahead.

Coefficient of variation (CV) The ratio of a set of observations' standard deviation to the observations' mean value.

Cointegrated Describes two time series that have a long-term financial or economic relationship such that they do not diverge from each other without bound in the long run.

Combination A listing in which the order of the listed items does not matter.

Commercial paper Unsecured short-term corporate debt that is characterized by a single payment at maturity.

Common size statements Financial statements in which all elements (accounts) are stated as a percentage of a key figure such as revenue for an income statement or total assets for a balance sheet.

Company fundamental factors Factors related to the company's internal performance, such as factors relating to earnings growth, earnings variability, earnings momentum, and financial leverage.

Company share-related factors Valuation measures and other factors related to share price or the trading characteristics of the shares, such as earnings yield, dividend yield, and book-to-market value.

Complement With reference to an event S, the event that S does not occur.

Compounding The process of accumulating interest on interest.

Conditional expected value The expected value of a stated event given that another event has occurred.

Conditional heteroskedasticity Heteroskedasticity in the error variance that is correlated with the values of the independent variable(s) in the regression.

Conditional probability   The probability of an event given (conditioned on) another event.

Conditional variances   The variance of one variable, given the outcome of another.

Confidence interval   A range that has a given probability that it will contain the population parameter it is intended to estimate.

Consistency   A desirable property of estimators; a consistent estimator is one for which the probability of estimates close to the value of the population parameter increases as sample size increases.

Consistent   With reference to estimators, describes an estimator for which the probability of estimates close to the value of the population parameter increases as sample size increases.

Continuous random variable   A random variable for which the range of possible outcomes is the real line (all real numbers between $-\infty$ and $+\infty$) or some subset of the real line.

Continuously compounded return   The natural logarithm of 1 plus the holding period return, or equivalently, the natural logarithm of the ending price over the beginning price.

Correlation   A number between -1 and $+1$ that measures the co-movement (linear association) between two random variables.

Correlation analysis   The analysis of the strength of the linear relationship between two data series.

Cost averaging   The periodic investment of a fixed amount of money.

Covariance   A measure of the co-movement (linear association) between two random variables.

Covariance matrix   A matrix or square array whose entries are covariances; also known as a variance–covariance matrix.

Covariance stationary   Describes a time series when its expected value and variance are constant and finite in all periods and when its covariance with itself for a fixed number of periods in the past or future is constant and finite in all periods.

Cross-sectional data   Observations over individual units at a point in time, as opposed to time-series data.

Cumulative distribution function   A function giving the probability that a random variable is less than or equal to a specified value.

Cumulative relative frequency   For data grouped into intervals, the fraction of total observations that are less than the value of the upper limit of a stated interval.

Data mining   The practice of determining a model by extensive searching through a dataset for statistically significant patterns.

Deciles   Quantiles that divide a distribution into 10 equal parts.

Decision rule   With respect to hypothesis testing, the rule according to which the null hypothesis will be rejected or not rejected; involves the comparison of the test statistic to rejection point(s).

Default risk premium   An extra return that compensates investors for the possibility that the borrower will fail to make a promised payment at the contracted time and in the contracted amount.

Degree of confidence   The probability that a confidence interval includes the unknown population parameter.

Degrees of freedom (df)   The number of independent observations used.

Dependent   With reference to events, the property that the probability of one event occurring depends on (is related to) the occurrence of another event.

Dependent variable   The variable whose variation about its mean is to be explained by the regression; the left-hand-side variable in a regression equation.

Descriptive statistics   The study of how data can be summarized effectively.

Diffuse prior   The assumption of equal prior probabilities.

Discount   To reduce the value of a future payment in allowance for how far away it is in time; to calculate the present value of some future amount. Also, the amount by which an instrument is priced below its face value.

Discrete random variable   A random variable that can take on at most a countable number of possible values.

Discriminant analysis   A multivariate classification technique used to discriminate between groups, such as companies that either will or will not become bankrupt during some time frame.

Dispersion   The variability around the central tendency.

Down transition probability　The probability that an asset's value moves down in a model of asset price dynamics.

Dummy variable　A type of qualitative variable that takes on a value of 1 if a particular condition is true and 0 if that condition is false.

Dutch Book Theorem　A result in probability theory stating that inconsistent probabilities create profit opportunities.

Effective annual rate　The amount by which a unit of currency will grow in a year with interest on interest included.

Effective annual yield (EAY)　An annualized return that accounts for the effect of interest on interest; EAY is computed by compounding 1 plus the holding period yield forward to one year, then subtracting 1.

Efficiency　A desirable property of estimators; an efficient estimator is the unbiased estimator with the smallest variance among unbiased estimators of the same parameter.

Efficient frontier　The portion of the minimum-variance frontier beginning with the global minimum-variance portfolio and continuing above it; the graph of the set of portfolios offering the maximum expected return for their level of variance of return.

Efficient portfolio　A portfolio offering the highest expected return for a given level of risk as measured by variance or standard deviation of return.

Empirical probability　The probability of an event estimated as a relative frequency of occurrence.

Error autocorrelation　The autocorrelation of the error term.

Error term　The portion of the dependent variable that is not explained by the independent variable(s) in the regression.

Estimate　The particular value calculated from sample observations using an estimator.

Estimated (or fitted) parameters　With reference to regression analysis, the estimated values of the population intercept and population slope coefficient(s) in a regression.

Estimation　With reference to statistical inference, the subdivision dealing with estimating the value of a population parameter.

Estimator　An estimation formula; the formula used to compute the sample mean and other sample statistics are examples of estimators.

European-style option or European option　An option exercisable only at maturity.

Event　Any outcome or specified set of outcomes of a random variable.

Excess kurtosis　Degree of peakedness (fatness of tails) in excess of the peakedness of the normal distribution.

Exhaustive　Covering or containing all possible outcomes.

Expected value　The probability-weighted average of the possible outcomes of a random variable.

Face value　The promised payment at maturity separate from any coupon payment.

Factor　A common or underlying element with which several variables are correlated.

Factor risk premium (or factor price)　The expected return in excess of the risk-free rate for a portfolio with a sensitivity of 1 to one factor and a sensitivity of 0 to all other factors.

Factor sensitivity (also factor betas or factor loadings)　A measure of the response of return to each unit of increase in a factor, holding all other factors constant.

Financial risk　Risk relating to asset prices and other financial variables.

First-differencing　A transformation that subtracts the value of the time series in period $t - 1$ from its value in period t.

First-order serial correlation　Correlation between adjacent observations in a time series.

Frequency distribution　A tabular display of data summarized into a relatively small number of intervals.

Frequency polygon　A graph of a frequency distribution obtained by drawing straight lines joining successive points representing the class frequencies.

Full price　The price of a security with accrued interest.

Fundamental beta　A beta that is based at least in part on fundamental data for a company.

Fundamental factor models　A multifactor model in which the factors are attributes of stocks or companies that are important in explaining cross-sectional differences in stock prices.

Future value (FV)   The amount to which a payment or series of payments will grow by a stated future date.

Generalized least squares   A regression estimation technique that addresses heteroskedasticity of the error term.

Geometric mean   A measure of central tendency computed by taking the nth root of the product of n non-negative values.

Harmonic mean   A type of weighted mean computed by averaging the reciprocals of the observations, then taking the reciprocal of that average.

Heteroskedastic   With reference to the error term of a regression, having a variance that differs across observations.

Heteroskedasticity   The property of having a nonconstant variance; refers to an error term with the property that its variance differs across observations.

Heteroskedasticity-consistent standard errors   Standard errors of the estimated parameters of a regression that correct for the presence of heteroskedasticity in the regression's error term.

Histogram   A bar chart of data that have been grouped into a frequency distribution.

Historical simulation (or back simulation)   Simulation involving sampling from a historical data series.

Holding period return   The return that an investor earns during a specified holding period; a synonym for total return.

Holding period yield (HPY)   The return that an investor earns during a specified holding period; holding period return with reference to a fixed-income instrument.

Homoskedasticity   The property of having a constant variance; refers to an error term that is constant across observations.

Hurdle rate   The rate of return that must be met for a project to be accepted.

Hypothesis   With reference to statistical inference, a statement about one or more populations.

Hypothesis testing   With reference to statistical inference, the subdivision dealing with the testing of hypotheses about one or more populations.

Incremental cash flows   The changes or increments to cash flows resulting from a decision or action.

Independent   With reference to events, the property that the occurrence of one event does not affect the probability of another event occurring.

Independent and identically distributed (IID)   With respect to random variables, the property of random variables that are independent of each other but follow the identical probability distribution.

Independent variable   A variable used to explain the dependent variable in a regression; a right-hand-side variable in a regression equation.

Indexing   An investment strategy in which an investor constructs a portfolio to mirror the performance of a specified index.

Inflation premium   An extra return that compensates investors for expected inflation.

Information ratio (IR)   Mean active return divided by active risk.

In-sample forecast errors   The residuals from a fitted time-series model within the sample period used to fit the model.

Instability in the minimum-variance frontier   The characteristic of minimum-variance frontiers that they are sensitive to small changes in inputs.

Interest rate   A rate of return that reflects the relationship between differently dated cash flows; a discount rate.

Intergenerational data mining   A form of data mining that applies information developed by previous researchers using a dataset to guide current research using the same or a related dataset.

Internal rate of return (IRR)   The discount rate that makes net present value equal 0; the discount rate that makes the present value of an investment's costs (outflows) equal to the present value of the investment's benefits (inflows).

Interquartile range   The difference between the third and first quartiles of a dataset.

Interval   With reference to grouped data, a set of values within which an observation falls.

Interval scale   A measurement scale that not only ranks data but also gives assurance that the differences between scale values are equal.

IRR rule   An investment decision rule that accepts projects or investments for which the IRR is greater than the opportunity cost of capital.

Joint probability   The probability of the joint occurrence of stated events.

Joint probability function   A function giving the probability of joint occurrences of values of stated random variables.

kth Order autocorrelation   The correlation between observations in a time series separated by k periods.

Kurtosis   The statistical measure that indicates the peakedness of a distribution.

Leptokurtic   Describes a distribution that is more peaked than a normal distribution.

Level of significance   The probability of a Type I error in testing a hypothesis.

Likelihood   The probability of an observation, given a particular set of conditions.

Linear association   A straight-line relationship, as opposed to a relationship that cannot be graphed as a straight line.

Linear interpolation   The estimation of an unknown value on the basis of two known values that bracket it, using a straight line between the two known values.

Linear regression   Regression that models the straight-line relationship between the dependent and independent variable(s).

Linear trend   A trend in which the dependent variable changes at a constant rate with time.

Liquidity premium   An extra return that compensates investors for the risk of loss relative to an investment's fair value if the investment needs to be converted to cash quickly.

Logit model   A qualitative-dependent-variable multiple regression model based on the logistic probability distribution.

Log-linear model   With reference to time-series models, a model in which the growth rate of the time series as a function of time is constant.

Log-log regression model   A regression that expresses the dependent and independent variables as natural logarithms.

Longitudinal data   Observations on characteristic(s) of the same observational unit through time.

Look-ahead bias   A bias caused by using information that was unavailable on the test date.

Macroeconomic factor   A factor related to the economy, such as the inflation rate, industrial production, or economic sector membership.

Macroeconomic factor model   A multifactor model in which the factors are surprises in macroeconomic variables that significantly explain equity returns.

Market price of risk   The slope of the capital market line, indicating the market risk premium for each unit of market risk.

Market risk premium   The expected excess return on the market over the risk-free rate.

Markowitz decision rule   A decision rule for choosing between two investments based on their means and variances.

Maturity premium   An extra return that compensates investors for the increased sensitivity of the market value of debt to a change in market interest rates as maturity is extended.

Mean   The sum of all values in a distribution or dataset, divided by the number of values summed; a synonym of arithmetic mean.

Mean absolute deviation   With reference to a sample, the mean of the absolute values of deviations from the sample mean.

Mean excess return   The average rate of return in excess of the risk-free rate.

Mean reversion   The tendency of a time series to fall when its level is above its mean and rise when its level is below its mean; a mean-reverting time series tends to return to its long-term mean.

Mean–variance analysis   An approach to portfolio analysis using expected means, variances, and covariances of asset returns.

Measure of central tendency   A quantitative measure that specifies where data are centered.

Measure of location   A quantitative measure that describes the location or distribution of data; includes not only measures of central tendency but also other measures such as percentiles.

Measurement scales   A scheme of measuring differences. The four types of measurement scales are nominal, ordinal, interval, and ratio.

Median   The value of the middle item of a set of items that has been sorted into ascending or descending order; the 50th percentile.

Mesokurtic   Describes a distribution with kurtosis identical to that of the normal distribution.

Minimum-variance frontier   The graph of the set of portfolios that have minimum variance for their level of expected return.

Minimum-variance portfolio   The portfolio with the minimum variance for each given level of expected return.

Mixed factor models   Factor models that combine features of more than one type of factor model.

Modal interval   With reference to grouped data, the most frequently occurring interval.

Mode   The most frequently occurring value in a set of observations.

Model specification   With reference to regression, the set of variables included in the regression and the regression equation's functional form.

Money market   The market for short-term debt instruments (one-year maturity or less).

Money market yield (or CD equivalent yield)   A yield on a basis comparable to the quoted yield on an interest-bearing money market instrument that pays interest on a 360-day basis; the annualized holding period yield, assuming a 360-day year.

Money-weighted rate of return   The internal rate of return on a portfolio, taking account of all cash flows.

Monte Carlo simulation   A methodology involving the use of a computer to find approximate solutions to complex problems.

Multicollinearity   A regression assumption violation that occurs when two or more independent variables (or combinations of independent variables) are highly but not perfectly correlated with each other.

Multiple linear regression   Linear regression involving two or more independent variables.

Multiple linear regression model   A linear regression model with two or more independent variables.

Multiple R   The correlation between the actual and forecasted values of the dependent variable in a regression.

Multiplication rule for probabilities   The rule that the joint probability of events A and B equals the probability of A given B times the probability of B.

Multivariate distribution   A probability distribution that specifies the probabilities for a group of related random variables.

Multivariate normal distribution   A probability distribution for a group of random variables that is completely defined by the means and variances of the variables plus all the correlations between pairs of the variables.

Mutually exclusive events   Events such that only one can occur at a time.

n Factorial   For a positive integer n, the product of the first n positive integers; 0 factorial equals 1 by definition. n factorial is written as $n!$.

Negative serial correlation   Serial correlation in which a positive error for one observation increases the chance of a negative error for another observation, and vice versa.

Net present value (NPV)   The present value of an investment's cash inflows (benefits) minus the present value of its cash outflows (costs).

Node   Each value on a binomial tree from which successive moves or outcomes branch.

Nominal risk-free interest rate   The sum of the real risk-free interest rate and the inflation premium.

Nominal scale   A measurement scale that categorizes data but does not rank them.

Nonlinear relation   An association or relationship between variables that cannot be graphed as a straight line.

Nonparametric test   A test that is not concerned with a parameter, or that makes minimal assumptions about the population from which a sample comes.

Nonstationarity   With reference to a random variable, the property of having characteristics such as mean and variance that are not constant through time.

Normal distribution   A continuous, symmetric probability distribution that is completely described by its mean and its variance.

***n*-Period moving average**   The average of the current and immediately prior $n - 1$ values of a time series.

NPV rule   An investment decision rule that states that an investment should be undertaken if its NPV is positive but not undertaken if its NPV is negative.

Null hypothesis   The hypothesis to be tested.

Objective probabilities   Probabilities that generally do not vary from person to person; includes a priori and objective probabilities.

One-sided hypothesis test (or one-tailed hypothesis test)   A test in which the null hypothesis is rejected only if the evidence indicates that the population parameter is greater than (smaller than) θ_0. The alternative hypothesis also has one side.

Opportunity cost   The value that investors forgo by choosing a particular course of action; the value of something in its best alternative use.

Opportunity set   The set of assets available for investment.

Optimizer   A specialized computer program or a spreadsheet that solves for the portfolio weights that will result in the lowest risk for a specified level of expected return.

Ordinal scale   A measurement scale that sorts data into categories that are ordered (ranked) with respect to some characteristic.

Ordinary annuity   An annuity with a first cash flow that is paid one period from the present.

Ordinary least squares (OLS)   An estimation method based on the criterion of minimizing the sum of the squared residuals of a regression.

Orthogonal   Uncorrelated; at a right angle.

Outcome   A possible value of a random variable.

Outliers   Small numbers of observations at either extreme (small or large) of a sample.

Out-of-sample forecast errors   The differences between actual and predicted value of time series outside the sample period used to fit the model.

Out-of-sample test   A test of a strategy or model using a sample outside the time period on which the strategy or model was developed.

Paired comparisons test   A statistical test for differences based on paired observations drawn from samples that are dependent on each other.

Paired observations   Observations that are dependent on each other.

Pairs arbitrage trade   A trade in two closely related stocks involving the short sale of one and the purchase of the other.

Panel data   Observations through time on a single characteristic of multiple observational units.

Parameter   A descriptive measure computed from or used to describe a population of data, conventionally represented by Greek letters.

Parameter instability   The problem or issue of population regression parameters that have changed over time.

Parametric test   Any test (or procedure) concerned with parameters or whose validity depends on assumptions concerning the population generating the sample.

Partial regression coefficients or partial slope coefficients   The slope coefficients in a multiple regression.

Percentiles   Quantiles that divide a distribution into 100 equal parts.

Perfect collinearity   The existence of an exact linear relation between two or more independent variables or combinations of independent variables.

Performance appraisal   The evaluation of risk adjusted performance; the evaluation of investment skill.

Performance measurement   The calculation of returns in a logical and consistent manner.

Periodic rate   The quoted interest rate per period; the stated annual interest rate divided by the number of compounding periods per year.

Permutation   An ordered listing.

Perpetuity   A perpetual annuity, or a set of never ending level sequential cash flows, with the first cash flow occurring one period from now.

Platykurtic Describes a distribution that is less peaked than the normal distribution.

Point estimate A single numerical estimate of an unknown quantity, such as a population parameter.

Pooled estimate An estimate of a parameter that involves combining (pooling) observations from two or more samples.

Population All members of a specified group.

Population mean The arithmetic mean value of a population; the arithmetic mean of all the observations or values in the population.

Population standard deviation A measure of dispersion relating to a population in the same unit of measurement as the observations, calculated as the positive square root of the population variance.

Population variance A measure of dispersion relating to a population, calculated as the mean of the squared deviations around the population mean.

Portfolio performance attribution The analysis of portfolio performance in terms of the contributions from various sources of risk.

Portfolio possibilities curve A graphical representation of the expected return and risk of all portfolios that can be formed using two assets.

Positive serial correlation Serial correlation in which a positive error for one observation increases the chance of a positive error for another observation, and a negative error for one observation increases the chance of a negative error for another observation.

Posterior probability An updated probability that reflects or comes after new information.

Power of a test The probability of correctly rejecting the null—that is, rejecting the null hypothesis when it is false.

Present value (PV) The current (discounted) value of a future cash flow or flows.

Price relative A ratio of an ending price over a beginning price; it is equal to 1 plus the holding period return on the asset.

Priced risk Risk that investors require an additional return for bearing.

Principal The amount of funds originally invested in a project or instrument; the face value to be paid at maturity.

Prior probabilities Probabilities reflecting beliefs prior to the arrival of new information.

Probability A number between 0 and 1 describing the chance that a stated event will occur.

Probability density function A function with non-negative values such that probability can be described by areas under the curve graphing the function.

Probability distribution A distribution that specifies the probabilities of a random variable's possible outcomes.

Probability function A function that specifies the probability that the random variable takes on a specific value.

Probit model A qualitative-dependent-variable multiple regression model based on the normal distribution.

Pseudo-random numbers Numbers produced by random number generators.

Pure discount instruments Instruments that pay interest as the difference between the amount borrowed and the amount paid back.

Pure factor portfolio A portfolio with sensitivity of 1 to the factor in question and a sensitivity of 0 to all other factors.

p-**Value** The smallest level of significance at which the null hypothesis can be rejected; also called the marginal significance level.

Qualitative dependent variables Dummy variables used as dependent variables rather than as independent variables.

Quantile (or fractile) A value at or below which a stated fraction of the data lies.

Quartiles Quantiles that divide a distribution into four equal parts.

Quintiles Quantiles that divide a distribution into five equal parts.

Random number An observation drawn from a uniform distribution.

Random number generator An algorithm that produces uniformly distributed random numbers between 0 and 1.

Random variable   A quantity whose future outcomes are uncertain.

Random walk   A time series in which the value of the series in one period is the value of the series in the previous period plus an unpredictable random error.

Range   The difference between the maximum and minimum values in a dataset.

Ratio scales   A measurement scale that has all the characteristics of interval measurement scales as well as a true zero point as the origin.

Real risk-free interest rate   The single-period interest rate for a completely risk-free security if no inflation were expected.

Regime   With reference to a time series, the underlying model generating the times series.

Regression coefficients   The intercept and slope coefficient(s) of a regression.

Rejection point (or critical value)   A value against which a computed test statistic is compared to decide whether to reject or not reject the null hypothesis.

Relative dispersion   The amount of dispersion relative to a reference value or benchmark.

Relative frequency   With reference to an interval of grouped data, the number of observations in the interval divided by the total number of observations in the sample.

Residual autocorrelations   The sample autocorrelations of the residuals.

Risk premium   The expected return on an investment minus the risk-free rate.

Robust   The quality of being relatively unaffected by a violation of assumptions.

Robust standard errors   Standard errors of the estimated parameters of a regression that correct for the presence of heteroskedasticity in the regression's error term.

Root mean squared error (RMSE)   The square root of the average squared forecast error; used to compare the out-of-sample forecasting performance of forecasting models.

Roy's safety first criterion   A criterion asserting that the optimal portfolio is the one that minimizes the probability that portfolio return falls below a threshold level.

Rule of 72   The principle that the approximate number of years necessary for an investment to double is 72 divided by the stated interest rate.

Safety-first rules   Rules for portfolio selection that focus on the risk that portfolio value will fall below some minimum acceptable level over some time horizon.

Sample   A subset of a population.

Sample excess kurtosis   A sample measure of the degree of a distribution's peakedness in excess of the normal distribution's peakedness.

Sample kurtosis   A sample measure of the degree of a distribution's peakedness.

Sample mean   The sum of the sample observations, divided by the sample size.

Sample selection bias   Bias introduced by systematically excluding some members of the population according to a particular attribute—for example, the bias introduced when data availability leads to certain observations being excluded from the analysis.

Sample skewness   A sample measure of degree of asymmetry of a distribution.

Sample standard deviation   The positive square root of the sample variance.

Sample statistic or statistic   A quantity computed from or used to describe a sample.

Sample variance   A sample measure of the degree of dispersion of a distribution, calculated by dividing the sum of the squared deviations from the sample mean by the sample size (n) minus 1.

Sampling   The process of obtaining a sample.

Sampling distribution   The distribution of all distinct possible values that a statistic can assume when computed from samples of the same size randomly drawn from the same population.

Sampling error   The difference between the observed value of a statistic and the quantity it is intended to estimate.

Sampling plan   The set of rules used to select a sample.

Scatter plot   A two-dimensional plot of pairs of observations on two data series.

Security market line (SML)   The graph of the capital asset pricing model.

Semideviation   The positive square root of semivariance (sometimes called semistandard deviation).

Semilogarithmic   Describes a scale constructed so that equal intervals on the vertical scale represent equal rates of change, and equal intervals on the horizontal scale represent equal amounts of change.

Semivariance The average squared deviation below the mean.

Serially correlated With reference to regression errors, errors that are correlated across observations.

Sharpe ratio The average return in excess of the risk-free rate divided by the standard deviation of return; a measure of the average excess return earned per unit of standard deviation of return.

Shortfall risk The risk that portfolio value will fall below some minimum acceptable level over some time horizon.

Simple interest The interest earned each period on the original investment; interest calculated on the principal only.

Simple random sample A subset of a larger population created in such a way that each element of the population has an equal probability of being selected to the subset.

Simple random sampling The procedure of drawing a sample to satisfy the definition of a simple random sample.

Simulation trial A complete pass through the steps of a simulation.

Skewed Not symmetrical.

Skewness A quantitative measure of skew (lack of symmetry); a synonym of skew.

Spearman rank correlation coefficient A measure of correlation applied to ranked data.

Spurious correlation A correlation that misleadingly points towards associations between variables.

Standard deviation The positive square root of the variance; a measure of dispersion in the same units as the original data.

Standard normal distribution (or unit normal distribution) The normal density with mean (μ) equal to 0 and standard deviation (σ) equal to 1.

Standardized beta With reference to fundamental factor models, the value of the attribute for an asset minus the average value of the attribute across all stocks, divided by the standard deviation of the attribute across all stocks.

Standardizing A transformation that involves subtracting the mean and dividing the result by the standard deviation.

Stated annual interest rate or quoted interest rate A quoted interest rate that does not account for compounding within the year.

Statistic A quantity computed from or used to describe a sample of data.

Statistical factor models A multifactor model in which statistical methods are applied to a set of historical returns to determine portfolios that best explain either historical return covariances or variances.

Statistical inference Making forecasts, estimates, or judgments about a larger group from a smaller group actually observed; using a sample statistic to infer the value of an unknown population parameter.

Statistically significant A result indicating that the null hypothesis can be rejected; with reference to an estimated regression coefficient, frequently understood to mean a result indicating that the corresponding population regression coefficient is different from 0.

Statistics The science of describing, analyzing, and drawing conclusions from data; also, a collection of numerical data.

Stratified random sampling A procedure by which a population is divided into subpopulations (strata) based on one or more classification criteria. Simple random samples are then drawn from each stratum in sizes proportional to the relative size of each stratum in the population. These samples are then pooled.

Stress testing/scenario analysis A set of techniques for estimating losses in extremely unfavorable combinations of events or scenarios.

Subjective probability A probability drawing on personal or subjective judgment.

Surprise The actual value of a variable minus its predicted (or expected) value.

Survivorship bias The bias resulting from a test design that fails to account for companies that have gone bankrupt, merged, or are otherwise no longer reported in a database.

Systematic factors Factors that affect the average returns of a large number of different assets.

Systematic sampling   A procedure of selecting every kth member until reaching a sample of the desired size. The sample that results from this procedure should be approximately random.

Target semideviation   The positive square root of target semivariance.

Target semivariance   The average squared deviation below a target value.

***t*-Distribution**   A symmetrical distribution defined by a single parameter, degrees of freedom, that is largely used to make inferences concerning the mean of a normal distribution whose variance is unknown.

Test statistic   A quantity, calculated based on a sample, whose value is the basis for deciding whether or not to reject the null hypothesis.

Time series   A set of observations on a variable's outcomes in different time periods.

Time value of money   The principles governing equivalence relationships between cash flows with different dates.

Time-period bias   The possibility that when we use a time-series sample, our statistical conclusion may be sensitive to the starting and ending dates of the sample.

Time-series data   Observations of a variable over time.

Time-weighted rate of return   The compound rate of growth of one unit of currency invested in a portfolio during a stated measurement period; a measure of investment performance that is not sensitive to the timing and amount of withdrawals or additions to the portfolio.

Total probability rule   A rule explaining the unconditional probability of an event in terms of probabilities of the event conditional on mutually exclusive and exhaustive scenarios.

Total probability rule for expected value   A rule explaining the expected value of a random variable in terms of expected values of the random variable conditional on mutually exclusive and exhaustive scenarios.

Tracking error   A synonym for tracking risk and active risk; also, the total return on a portfolio (gross of fees) minus the total return on a benchmark.

Tracking portfolio   A portfolio having factor sensitivities that are matched to those of a benchmark or other portfolio.

Tracking risk   The standard deviation of the differences between a portfolio's returns and its benchmark's returns; a synonym of active risk.

Tree diagram   A diagram with branches emanating from nodes representing either mutually exclusive chance events or mutually exclusive decisions.

Trend   A long-term pattern of movement in a particular direction.

Trimmed mean   A mean computed after excluding a stated small percentage of the lowest and highest observations.

***t*-Test**   A hypothesis test using a statistic (t-statistic) that follows a t-distribution.

Two-sided hypothesis test (or two-tailed hypothesis test)   A test in which the null hypothesis is rejected in favor of the alternative hypothesis if the evidence indicates that the population parameter is either smaller or larger than a hypothesized value.

Type I error   The error of rejecting a true null hypothesis.

Type II error   The error of not rejecting a false null hypothesis.

Unbiasedness   Lack of bias. A desirable property of estimators, an unbiased estimator is one whose expected value (the mean of its sampling distribution) equals the parameter it is intended to estimate.

Unconditional heteroskedasticity   Heteroskedasticity of the error term that is not correlated with the values of the independent variable(s) in the regression.

Unconditional probability (or marginal probability)   The probability of an event *not* conditioned on another event.

Unit root   A time series that is not covariance stationary is said to have a unit root.

Univariate distribution   A distribution that specifies the probabilities for a single random variable.

Up transition probability   The probability that an asset's value moves up.

Value at Risk (VAR)   A money measure of the minimum value of losses expected during a specified time period at a given level of probability.

Variance The expected value (the probability-weighted average) of squared deviations from a random variable's expected value.

Volatility As used in option pricing, the standard deviation of the continuously compounded returns on the underlying asset.

Weighted mean An average in which each observation is weighted by an index of its relative importance.

Weighted-average cost of capital A weighted average of the after-tax required rates of return on a company's common stock, preferred stock, and long-term debt, where the weights are the fraction of each source of financing in the company's target capital structure.

White-corrected standard errors A synonym for robust standard errors.

Winsorized mean A mean computed after assigning a stated percent of the lowest values equal to one specified low value, and a stated percent of the highest values equal to one specified high value.

Working capital management The management of a company's short-term assets (such as inventory) and short-term liabilities (such as money owed to suppliers).

ABOUT THE
CFA PROGRAM

The Chartered Financial Analyst® designation (CFA®) is a globally recognized standard of excellence for measuring the competence and integrity of investment professionals. To earn the CFA charter, candidates must successfully pass through the CFA Program, a global graduate-level self-study program that combines a broad curriculum with professional conduct requirements as preparation for a wide range of investment specialties.

Anchored by a practice-based curriculum, the CFA Program is focused on the knowledge identified by professionals as essential to the investment decision-making process. This body of knowledge maintains current relevance through a regular, extensive survey of practicing CFA charterholders across the globe. The curriculum covers 10 general topic areas ranging from equity and fixed-income analysis to portfolio management to corporate finance, all with a heavy emphasis on the application of ethics in professional practice. Known for its rigor and breadth, the CFA Program curriculum highlights principles common to every market so that professionals who earn the CFA designation have a thoroughly global investment perspective and a profound understanding of the global marketplace.

www.cfainstitute.org

ABOUT THE AUTHORS

Richard A. DeFusco, CFA, is an associate professor of finance at the University of Nebraska-Lincoln (UNL). He earned his CFA charter in 1999. A member of the Omaha-Lincoln Society of Financial Analysts he also serves on committees for CFA Institute. Dr. DeFusco's primary teaching interest is investments, and he coordinates the Cornhusker Fund, UNL's student-managed investment fund. He has published a number of journal articles, primarily in the field of finance. Dr. DeFusco earned his bachelor's degree in management science from the University of Rhode Island and his doctoral degree in finance from the University of Tennessee-Knoxville.

Dennis W. McLeavey, CFA, is Head of Professional Development Products at CFA Institute. He earned his CFA charter in 1990. Prior to joining CFA Institute in 2000, he served on various organization committees. Most recently, he co-authored the fifth edition of *International Investments* with Bruno Solnik. He is also a co-author of the CFA Institute textbooks *Quantitative Investment Analysis* and *Equity Asset Valuation,* as well as two college textbooks, *Production Planning and Inventory Control* and *Operations Research for Management Decisions.* During his 25-year academic career, he has taught at the University of Western Ontario, the University of Connecticut, the University of Rhode Island (where he founded a student-managed fund), and Babson College. He serves as a New York Stock Exchange Arbitrator. After receiving his bachelor's degree in economics at the University of Western Ontario, he completed a doctorate in production management and industrial engineering at Indiana University.

Jerald E. Pinto, CFA, is Director in the CFA and CIPM Programs Division at CFA Institute. His immediate prior affiliation was as principal of TRM Services in New York City. In that role, he consulted to corporations, foundations, and partnerships in investment planning, portfolio analysis, and quantitative analysis. Dr. Pinto previously taught finance at the New York University Stern School of Business after working in the banking and investment industries in New York City. He is a co-author of the textbook *Equity Asset Valuation.* He holds an MBA from Baruch College and a Ph.D. in finance from the Stern School.

David E. Runkle, CFA, is Principal and Research Manager at Piper Jaffray. He has been an adjunct professor of finance in the Carlson School of Management at the University of Minnesota since 1989, where he teaches equity security analysis. Before joining Piper Jaffray, Dr. Runkle was a research officer at the Federal Reserve Bank of Minneapolis. He has published more than 20 academic articles and has won a number of awards, including the Wriston Prize for Outstanding Teaching (Brown University), an Elija Watt Sells Award for outstanding performance on the Certified Public Accountant examination, and a four-star rating as an outstanding professor in the Business Week Guide to the Best Business Schools. Dr. Runkle is a member of the Minnesota Society of Certified Public Accountants and a member of the CFA Institute Financial Accounting Policy Committee. He received a B.A. in economics, summa cum laude, from Carleton College and a Ph.D. in economics from M.I.T.

Index

A

Abnormal returns, 259–261
Absolute dispersion, 100
Absolute frequency, 66, 71, 73, 75–76
Absolute returns, 497
Absolute value, 336, 343, 374, 386n, 393
Account receivables, hypothesis testing case illustration, 256–257
Accrued interest, 57
Active factor risk, 499, 501–505
Active investors, 209
Active management, 474–475, 493–494
Active return, 494, 497
Active risk
    comparison of, 499–501
    decomposition, 494–496, 500
    defined, 497
    source analysis, 496
    squared, 498–502
Active specific risk, 499, 503, 505
Adjusted R^2, 340–341
Algebraic applications, 251, 337
Alpha, 314, 319n, 320–321
Alternative factor models, 491–492
Alternative hypothesis, 245, 271–273, 297–298, 320, 328, 349, 374
American Express, 191n, 448–449
American options, 185
American Stock Exchange (AMEX), 446
Amortized loans, 35
Analysis of variance (ANOVA), 253n, 318–321, 328, 338–339, 342, 357, 361–362, 365, 367
Analyst(s)
    coverage, 373–374
    data mining tips for, 238

functions of, 98, 128, 138, 219–221, 243, 312, 321, 324, 328, 341, 356, 362, 366, 370, 372, 378, 424, 490, 493
Annualized returns, 57, 117, 204
Annualized yield, 55
Annual percentage rate (APR), 12n
Annual percentage yield (APY), 12
Annual rate of return, 66
Annual returns, 50, 53, 100, 102, 121, 192, 444, 448
Annuity/annuities, *see specific types of annuities*
    defined, 13
    funding future inflow, 32–35
    future value of, 14
    present value of, 44
    size of payments, 30–35
Antilogarithm, 330
A priori probability, 131, 135, 141
Arbitrage opportunities, 478, 481–483
Arbitrage portfolio, 482
Arbitrage pricing theory (APT), multifactor models, 478–484, 509
Arithmetic mean
    applications of, 127–128
    center of gravity analogy, 80
    defined, 77
    equity market returns, 109
    harmonic mean compared with, 94
    normal distribution and, 192
    population mean, 77
    properties of, 71n, 80–81
    sample mean, 77–80
    asset classes, 114
Asian call option, 207
Asset allocation, 318, 460, 463–464
Asset classes, 114, 153, 239, 444–445, 462

Asset pricing model, multiple regression analysis case illustration, 347
Asset selection risk, 499
Asymptotic theory, 305
Audits, 373
Auto loans, 30, 35
Autocorrelations, time-series analysis, 387–390, 393–394, 398, 402, 407, 410, 412–414, 426
Autoregressive conditional heteroskedasticity (ARCH), 417–420, 426–427
Autoregressive moving-average models (ARMA), time-series analysis, 416–417
Autoregressive (AR) time-series analysis
    characteristics of, 376–377, 386–399, 426
    covariance-stationary series models, 386–387, 397, 400–401, 404–405
    forecasting models, 391–397
    mean reversion, 391, 403
    models, 386–399
    regression coefficients, instability of, 397–399
    serially correlated errors, detection of, 387–390
Average, defined, 71n, 72
Average returns, 219, 239, 471, 486

B
Back simulation, 212
Bank discount
    basis, 55
    rate, 55
    yield, 55–59
BankCorp, 139, 142–147, 149–150, 159–160
Bankers' acceptances, 55
BARRA US-E2, 491–492
BARRA US-E3, 499
Basis points
    implications of, 337
    spread, 151
Bayes' formula, 150, 161–166
Bear markets, 116, 210–213
Bell curve, *see* Normal distribution
Below-investment-grade borrower, 188–189
Benchmark, 474
Benedict, Ray, 381, 389–390
Berkshire Hathaway, 448–449

Bernoulli random variable, 175–176, 183–184
Bernoulli trial, 175, 177, 184
Beta, 111, 259, 310, 313–314, 320–321, 459–460, 476n, 479, 485, 488, 493, 510
Bias
    data-mining, 236–238
    look-ahead, 240
    sample selection, 251
    time-bias, 240–241
    time-period, 252
    variable, 360–361
Bid-ask spread, 326–327, 331, 362–363
Binomial distribution illustrations
    block brokers, trading desk evaluation of, 179–181
    tracking error, 181–182
Binomial formula, 167–168
Binomial random variables, 177–179, 183–185
Binomial trees, 184–185
Bins, 66n
BIRR model, 486, 489
Black-Scholes-Merton option pricing, 171, 200–201, 204, 212
Block brokers, 176–177, 179–181
Bond-equivalent basis, 59
Bond-equivalent yield, 59
Bond indexes, 217–218
Bond market, 56n
Bond portfolio
    expected number of defaults, 183–184
    probability case illustration, 150–152
Bonds, *see specific types of bonds*
    default on, *see* Defaulted bonds
    high-yield, 343–345, 490
    long-term, 444
    maturity, 64
    price distribution, 172–173
    ratings, 343–344
    returns, correlation with T-bill returns, 299
    seniority of, 343–344
Book-to-market ratio, 493, 496
Book-to-price (B/P) ratio, 474, 502–504
Book value per share, 98
Breusch-Pagan test, 350

British pound, 291–293
Bull markets, 209–213
Business cycle(s)
    implications of, 83, 188
    risk, 486–488, 506
Buy-and-hold strategy, 210, 212, 268

C
CAC-40, 88
Callability, 343–344
Call options, 207
Canadian investments
    bonds, 86, 89–90, 462
    equities, 252, 462
    real estate, 462
    stock, 82, 89–90, 209
    Treasury bills, 58n
Canadian dollar, 291–292
Capital allocation line (CAL)
    calculations, 456–457
    characteristics of, 450
    equation, 455–457
    with multiple assets, 454–455
    risk-return tradeoff, 453–454
    Capital asset pricing model (CAPM)
    characteristics of, 319–320
    heteroskedasticity case illustration, 347, 351
    mean-variance analysis, 463
    multifactor models, 478–479, 488, 493,
        509–510
Capital budgeting, 39
Capital market line (CML), 458
Capital structure, 39–40
Cash dividends per share, 64
Cash flow(s)
    additivity principle, 32, 36–37
    arbitrage pricing theory (APT), 482
    equal, 13–15
    immediate, 21
    incremental, 40n
    from operations (CFO), correlation analysis,
        295–296
    present value of, 58
    scaling and relation from operations and free
        cash flow, 366–367
    series of, 13–15, 19–27
    single, 3–6, 8–3, 15–18
    unequal, 15, 26–27

Cash inflow, 48–49, 53
Cash outflow, 42, 48–49, 53
Center for Research in Security Prices (CRSP),
    University of Chicago, 239
Central limit theorem, 189, 222–225, 230,
    254, 305
Certificate of deposit (CD)
    characteristics of, 5, 8–9, 55
    equivalent yield, 57–58
Chain rule of forecasting, 391–394
Chebyshev's inequality, 111–112, 189
Chi-square distribution, 269–271
Chi-square tests, 253n
Cobb-Douglas production formula, 363n
Coca-Cola, 448–449
Coefficient of determination, 309–310, 329n
Coefficient of variance (CV), 113–115
Cointegration, time-series analysis, 422–424
Combination, defined, 167
Commercial banks, 200, 345
Commercial paper (CP) 55, 259–261
Commodity price risk, 276
Common size statements, 365–367
Common stock, 132–134, 193–194,
    196–199
Company fundamental factors, 493
Company share-related factors, 493
Company value, 315–316
Complement, 142
Compounded annual rate, 349n
Compound growth rte, 28–30
Compounding
    continuous, 10–13, 202–206, 380
    daily, 11
    defined, 4
    frequency of, 8–11, 17–18
    monthly, 10–11, 18, 31
    quarterly, 9, 11
    semiannual, 11–12
Compound interest, 56
Compound returns, 90
Conditional expected values, 146
Conditional probability, 133–136, 141–143,
    162, 165
Conditional variances, 148–149
Confidence intervals
    construction of, 227–228
    defined, 227

Confidence intervals (*continued*)
  hypothesis testing, 250–251, 256, 311
  normal distribution and, 193–194
  for population mean, 227, 229–233
  regression analysis, 308, 312–313,
     317–318, 322–323
  reliability factors for, 227–229
Confidence risk, 486–488, 506
Consistency, 226–227, 345, 351n
Consol bond, 24
Constant-proportions strategy, 87
Consumer price index (CPI), 289–290,
     305–306, 317–318, 378–380, 385,
     392–394, 398–399, 418–419, 425,
     489
Continuous compounding, 10–13, 202–206,
     380
Continuous random variables
  continuous uniform distribution, 186–189
  lognormal distribution, 188, 200–206
  normal distribution, 188–201
Continuous time finance models, 202
Continuous uniform distribution, 186–189
Continuous uniform random variable,
     223–224
Corporate bonds, 259, 295
Correlated errors, time-series analysis, 385
Correlation, *see* Correlation analysis;
     Correlation coefficient; Serial correlation
  defined, 157
  matrix, 157, 159, 291, 444, 471–472
  mean-variance analysis, 462
  minimum-variance portfolios, 431, 433,
     437–438, 440–441, 447–448
  properties of, 157–158, 253n
  risk-return tradeoff, 450
Correlation analysis
  characteristics of, 282–283
  defined, 282
  correlation coefficient, 283–287, 297–300
  limitations on, 287–289
  scatter plots, 281–283
  uses of, 289–297
Correlation coefficient
  calculation and interpretation of, 283–287
  characteristics of, 294
  hypothesis testing, 276–279
  significance tests, 297–300

Cost averaging, 93
Cost of capital, 47
Cost of goods sold, 356n, 389–390
Counter cyclical stocks, 510
Counting
  combination formula, 167–168
  multinomial formula, 167
  multiple rule of, 166–167, 218
  permutation formula, 168–169
  principles of, 166
Coupon bonds, 57
Covariance
  active factor risk, 499, 501
  characteristics of, 154–159, 283–286
  computation of, 160
  defined, 154
  matrix, 156, 158
  mean-variance analysis, 473
  minimum-variance portfolios, 444,
     446–447, 454
  two-asset portfolios, 431
Covariance-stationary time series, 386–387,
     397, 400–401, 404–405, 421–422,
     424–426
Credit
  quality factor, 488–490
  ratings, 64, 84–85, 183–184
  risk, 276
Creditworthiness, 343
Critical values, 249–251, 311, 318–319, 336,
     339, 350, 354, 356, 374, 390, 405, 422
Cross-sectional data, 78, 219–221, 301, 324
Cross-sectional mean, 78–80
Cross-sectional regression, 382
Crossover discount rate, 47
Crude oil, 408
Cubed deviation, 120–121
Cumulative absolute frequency, 73, 75–76
Cumulative distribution function (cdf),
     173–174, 179
Cumulative relative frequency, 69, 71, 75
Current P/E, 77
Cyclical risk, 510

D
Data collection, 251
Data-mining bias, 236–238
Dealer market, 363

Debt
   high-yield, 345
   investment-grade, 490
   probability case illustration, 150–152
   rating, 372
   returns, correlation analysis, 294–295
Debt-to-asset (D/A) ratio, 502–504
Debt-to-equity ratio, 372
Deciles, 94, 98
Decision rule, 249
Default
   premium, 295
   rate, 184
   risk, *see* Default risk
Defaulted bonds, hypothesis testing case
      illustration, 264–265
Default risk
   multifactor models, 486
   premium, 2–3, 150–152
Defined benefit pension plans, 206
Degree of confidence, 227
Degrees of freedom (df), 230–232, 254, 258,
      262–263, 271–273, 297, 307, 311,
      319, 329, 336, 338, 340, 343, 350,
      357–358, 389, 393, 412
Delisted companies, 239
Demographics, 373
Dependent events, 138–142
Dependent variables
   discrete, 373
   qualitative, 372–374
   regression analysis, 300–304, 306–310,
      319, 322, 325, 331–332, 336–337,
      339, 341–342, 363–364, 367–369,
      372–374
   time-series analysis, 377, 386–387, 393,
      420–421
Depreciation, 375
Derivatives, 275–276
Descriptive statistics, 62
de Vries, Johann, 421–422
Dickey-Fuller test, 403–405, 420, 421–424
Diffuse priors, 166
Disclosure, Inc., 373
Discount, defined, 2
Discounted cash flow analysis, 54–55
Discounting, 128
Discount rate, 2, 16–17, 24, 26, 47, 58–59

Discount yield, 55
Discrete dependent variable, 373
Discrete uniform probability function, 175
Discriminant analysis, 372–373
Dispersion measures
   absolute dispersion, 100
   Chebyshev's inequality, 111–112
   coefficient of variance (CV), 113–115
   defined, 100
   mean absolute deviation (MAD), 101–103,
      108–109
   normal distribution, 191
   population standard deviation,
      104–106
   population variance, 103–104
   range, 100–103
   sample standard deviation, 106–109
   sample variance, 104, 106–109
   semideviation, 110–111
   semivariance, 110–111
   Sharpe ratio, 115–118
Distribution-free tests, 275n
Diversification, 157, 293–294, 438, 441,
      445–449, 459n
Dividend(s)
   active factor risk, 502–504
   implications of, 23, 95–97
   per share, 98
   reinvestment, 48–49, 54
   yield, 95–99, 499
DJ EuroSTOXX 50, 95–96
Dogs of the Dow Strategy, 237n
Dollar-weighted return, 48n
Dow Chemical, 191n
Dow Jones Industrial Average (DJIA),
      237n
Down transition probability, 184
Dow-10 investment strategy,
      268–269
Dreyfus Appreciation Fund, 320–321
DriveMed, Inc., Bayes' formula illustration,
      162–166
Dummy variables, 341–345, 373, 485
Durbin-Watson (DW) statistic, time-series
      analysis, 350, 353–355, 369, 371, 379,
      384–385, 387, 390, 393–394, 398,
      402, 425
Dutch Book Theorem, 133

E

Earnings
  active factor risk, 502–505
  per share (EPS), 82–83, 98, 139, 142–150,
    161–166
EBITDA/interest, 188–189
Econometrics, 351n
Economic decisions, 252
Economic forecasts, evaluation of
  correlation analysis, 289–290
  linear regression, 305–306
Economic reasoning, 360
Economic theory, 219, 362
Economy-wide risk, 487–488
Effective annual rate (EAR), 12–13
Effective annual yield (EAY), 57–59
Efficiency, 226
Efficient frontier, 434, 439, 441, 454–455,
    462, 464
Efficient portfolio, 430
Empirical probability, 131, 135, 141
Engle, Robert F., 418, 422–423
Engle-Granger test, 423
Enterprise value (EV), 315–316
Enterprise value/Invested Capital (EV/IC)
    ratio, 322–324
Equal-weighted returns, 347
Equity/equities
  management style, 291
  markets, 71–72, 82
  mutual funds, 104–106, 232–233,
    255–256, 270–271
  portfolio, 191, 193, 487, 494–496
  returns, correlation analysis,
    294–295
Equivalence relationships, 1–2, 13–15,
    19–20, 35–36
Error autocorrelations, 388–389
Error term, 301
Estimation, 244
Estimators, defined, 225
Eurobonds, 462
European-style options, 207
Even-numbered samples, 81, 97
Event, defined, 130. *See specific types of events*
Excess kurtosis, 123–125, 190
Excess return(s)
  regression analysis, 313–314, 320–321, 347

  risk-adjusted, 320
  to variability measure, 115n
Exchange rate(s)
  characteristics of, 219
  Japanese yen/U.S. dollar,
    401–403
  return, 291–293
  Swiss franc/U.S. dollar, 375–376
  time-series analysis, 397
Exchanges, removal from, 239. *See also specific
    exchanges*
Ex-dividend date, 185
Exhaustive events, 130, 142–143
Expected returns
  lognormal distribution, 206
  mean-variance analysis, 463
  minimum-variance portfolios, 432–433,
    437–440, 443, 448, 456–459
  multifactor models, 476–477, 479–481,
    483, 486–490, 508
  risk-free assets, 449–450
  risk-return tradeoffs, 450–453
  two-asset portfolios, 431–432, 435, 437
Expected value
  conditional, 146
  covariance, 155–157
  implications of, 88–89, 143–145,
    147–152,
  multiplication rule for, 161
  properties of, 152–153
  total probability rule for, 146–149
Explanatory variable, time-series analysis, 377,
    393
Exponential growth, 380, 384, 406
Exponential trends, time-series analysis,
    425–426
Extreme returns, 191
Extreme value, 69, 80, 83

F

Face value, 55–56
Factor, generally
  betas, 476n
  loadings, 476n
  multifactor models, 474
  portfolios, 505–507
  price, 479
  risk premium, 479

sensitivities, multifactor models, 476–477,
        480–481, 484–485, 488–490,
        494–495, 503–504, 508
Factorial, 166–167
Factor's marginal contribution to active risk
        squared (FMCARS), 501–502
Failing stocks, 239
FashionDesigns, hypothesis testing case
        illustration, 256–258
Fat tails, 191
F-distribution, 271–272, 340
Federal Reserve, 288, 290n
Fidelity Select Technology Fund (FSPTXP),
        case illustrations
    multiple regression analysis, 334–336,
        357–358
    time-series analysis, 423–424
Financial ratios, 373
Financial risk, 200n
Financial statement analysis, 365–366,
        373
Financial theory, 116, 219, 370, 397
Financial Times Stock Exchange (FTSE) All
        Share Index, 240
Finite population correction factor (fpc), 222,
        255n
First-differencing/first-difference, time-series
        analysis, 400–401, 403–404, 412,
        422n, 426
First-order
    autoregression (AR), 386
    serial correlation, 352
    time-series model, 397
Fisher effect, 349–350, 354, 369–371,
        421
Fitzsimmons, Susan, 435, 437
Fixed income
    market, 56
    portfolios, 217–218
    strategies, 200
Floating exchange rates, 219
"Foolish Four" investment strategy, 237
Forbes Honor Roll, 104–106
Forecast(s), *see* Forecasting
    unbiased, 316–317
    error, linear regression, 323
Forecasting
    chain rule of, 391–394

linear regression analysis, 305
    moving-average time-series analysis,
        409–411
    in time-series analysis, 385, 391–394,
        409–412, 424–427
Foreign currencies, 291–293. *See also specific*
        foreign currencies
Foreign exchange risk, 276
Free cash flow (FCF),
        366–367
Free cash flow to the firm (FCFF), correlation
        analysis, 295–296, 300
French BTFs, 58n
Frequency distributions
    absolute frequency, 66, 71
    central limit theorem and, 224
    construction of, 66–69, 71–72
    cumulative, 72, 74–76
    defined, 65
    holding period return, 65–66
    relative frequency, 69–72
    S&P 500, 65, 67–70, 72–76
Frequency polygon, 74–76
F-statistics, 272, 318–319, 321, 339–340,
        357–358, 366
F-tables, 272–274
F-tests, 246, 271–272, 319, 321, 328–330,
        339–340, 343, 346, 358
Full price, 57n
Fundamental factor models, 474, 484–485,
        490–493
Fund inflows, 234–235
Fund outflows, 234–235
Future cash flows, discounting, 128
Future value (FV)
    of annuity, 14, 31
    defined, 3
    equivalence, 35–36
    future lump sum, 7
    growth rate calculation, 28
    of lump sum with interim cash reinvested at
        same rate, 5–6
    of lump sum with no interim cash, 6
    series of cash flows, 13–15,
        26–27
    single cash flow, 3–6,
        8–13
    solving for, 27–30

G

Generalized autoregressive conditional heteroskedasticity (GARCH) models, 420
Generalized least squares, 351, 420
Generally accepted accounting principles (GAAP), 296
General Motors, 313–314
Geometric mean
  applications of, 127–128
  defined, 89
  equity market returns, 109
  formula for, 90–93
  harmonic mean compared with, 94
  implications of, 50, 89–90
German Treasury discount paper, 58n
Gillette, 448–449
Goodness of fit, 340–341
Government bonds, 24, 55, 295, 430–441, 444–445, 450–452, 454, 471–472
Graphic data presentations
  frequency polygon, 74–76
  histograms, 73–74
Gray, Richard, 499–500
Gross domestic product (GDP), 341, 349n, 423–424, 475–476, 479, 508
Gross margin, 389–390, 392
Gross national product (GNP), 349n
Gross profit, 356n
Growth at a reasonable rate (GARP), 503, 505
Growth funds, 277n
Growth-led markets, 324
Growth rate
  computation of, 89
  implications of, 128, 282
  solving for, 27–30
Growth stocks, 98–99, 358

H

Hansen-White standard errors, 355n
Harmonic mean, 93–94
Hedge funds, 64, 116, 239
Hedging strategies, 291, 459n, 484
Heteroskedasticity
  autoregressive conditional (ARCH), time-series analysis, 417–420
  conditional, 347–351, 356
  consequences of, 345–347

correcting for, 350–351
  defined, 345
  implications of, 345, 359–360
  multiple regression analysis case illustration, 347
  testing for, 348–350
  unconditional, 347–348
Heteroskedasticity-consistent standard errors, 351n
Histograms, 73–74, 234
Historical returns, 434–437, 443–445, 448, 474
Historical simulation, 212
Holding period return (HPR), 47–50, 56, 65–66, 191
Holding period yield (HPY), 56–59
Homoskedasticity, 345n, 346–347, 417–420
Hughes, William, 487
Hurdle rate, 43
Hypothesis testing
  characteristics of, 171, 225, 243–244
  cointegration and, 422
  investment decision, 252
  mean, 253–269
  nonparametric inference, 275–279
  one-sided/one-tailed test, 245, 249, 251, 257
  regression analysis and, 310–318, 327, 329
  steps in, 244–253
  test statistic, 246–249
  two-sided tests, 245, 251, 272
  variance, 269–274

I

I/B/E/S, 373
Immediate cash flow, present value of, 21
In-sample forecast errors, 394–395
Income statements, 365–366
Incremental cash flows, 40n
Independence, defined, 160
Independent events, 138–142
Independently and identically distributed (IID) random variables, 203
Independent variable
  random, 189
  regression analysis, 300–304, 306, 308–309, 319, 322, 325, 331–333, 336–337, 339–340, 356–357, 360–361, 363–364, 366–371, 374

time-series analysis, 376–377, 386, 420, 423–424
Index funds, 509
Indexing, 217–218
Inference
    nonparametric, 275–279
    statistical, 243–244, 359, 386
    valid, 359
Inflation/inflation rate
    annualized, 379
    arbitrage pricing theory (APT), 483–484
    autoregressive conditional heteroskedasticity (ARCH), 418
    expected, 349–350, 370
    forecasts, 316–317
    implications of, 281–282, 286, 288, 290, 297–298
    multifactor models, 483–485
    prediction of, 351, 378
    premium, 2
    regression analysis, 302–303, 308–310, 348–350, 355, 369
    risk, 486–488, 506
    time-series analysis, 385, 387, 395–399
Inflation-adjusted returns, 71–72, 109
Information ratio (IR), 497, 505
Initial investment, 5, 36, 45
Instability, time-series analysis case illustration, 398–399
Insurance, Guaranteed Investment Contract (GIC), 16, 18
Intel case illustrations
    autoregressive time-series model, 389–390
    cointegration between sales and nominal GDP, 423
    forecasting, 392
    linear trend regression, 381–383
    log-linear regression, 383–384, 404–405
    moving-average time-series analysis, 408
Intercept
    hypothesis testing, 311
    multifactor models, 475, 479
    regression analysis, 305, 315, 317, 328–329, 333, 335, 342, 357–358, 361–362, 365–366, 369, 371, 374
    time-series analysis, 377–378, 389, 401–402, 407

Interest-bearing instruments, 57
Interest rate(s)
    bond market, 345
    correlation analysis, 288
    declining, 147
    implications of, 1–3
    multifactor models, 476
    periodic, 18
    quoted, 8
    regression analysis and, 348–350
    real, 349
    risk, 276, 343
    risk-free, 2
    solving for, 27–30
    stated annual, 8–9, 11–13
    Treasury bonds, 218
Intergenerational data mining, 237
Interim cash flow, 53
Internal rate of return (IRR)
    for bonds, 59
    defined, 42
    implications of, 39–40
    rule, 42–47
International indexes, 238–239
International stocks, 98–100
Interquartile range (IQR), 101n
Intervals
    confidence, *see* Confidence intervals
    in frequency distribution, 66–67, 69, 73–74
    modal, 84
    prediction, 371–374
    scales, 63–64
    standard deviation, 111, 112
Inventory, 221
Inverse probability, 161
Inverse relationship, 239
Inverse transformation, 209–210
Invested capital (IC), 315–316
Investment banks, 201, 345
Investment decisions, influential factors, 167, 252, 290, 399, 417, 425
Investment horizon, 437, 480
Investment managers, communication with, 497–498
Investment research, 98, 240–241
Investment style, 495
Investment theory, 411n

J

Japanese yen
  characteristics of, 44–45, 291–293, 298
  /U.S. dollar exchange rate, 401–403
Jarque-Bera (JB) statistical test of normality,
    127n
Jensen's inequality, 92n
Johannesburg Stock Exchange (JSE) All Share
    Index, 421
Joint probability function, 134–135, 159

K

Kageyama Ltd., 44
Kahn, Robert L., 243
Kolmogrov-Smirnov test, 276
kth order autocorrelation, 388
Kurtosis
  calculation of, 125–127
  characteristics of, 123–124, 190
  sample formula, 124–125

L

Labeling problems, 167
Lagged dependent variable, Fisher effect with,
    369–370
Large-cap
  equity funds, 498
  stock, 293–294, 430–434, 437, 439, 441,
    450, 452–453, 495
Lehman Brothers Government Index,
    218
Lender, breach of covenant, 188
Leptokurtic distribution, 123–125
Leverage, 474, 499
Likelihoods, 162
Limited Brands, Inc., 28–30
Linear association, 283–287, 329
Linear interpolation, 95
Linear regression
  analysis of variance (ANOVA), 318–321
  assumptions of, 303–306
  characteristics of, 300–303
  coefficient of determination, 309–310
  cointegration, 422
  defined, 300
  estimation parameters, 301
  fixed parameters, 301
  hypothesis testing, 310–318
  limitations on, 324
  multiple, *see* Multiple linear regression
  multiple time series, 420
  prediction intervals, 321–324
  problems in, 359
  standard error of estimate (SEE), 306–308,
    320, 322–323, 329
Linear relationship, 300, 332n
Linear trends, in time-series analysis, 377–380,
    425
Liquidity premium, 2–3
Log-linear trend models, 380–384,
Log-log regression model, 327
Logarithmic scales, 127
Logit regression models, 372
Long-term debt market, 59
Longitudinal data, 220
Look-ahead bias, 240–241
Lump sum
  distant future, 16–17
  future value of, 9–11

M

Macroeconomic factor/multifactor models,
    474, 475–477, 485–493
Macroeconomic time series, 387
Management styles, 474–475
Mann-Whitney Utest, 276
Manumatic, 477, 479
Margin, 455n
Marginal probabilities, 133
Marketable security price risk, 276
Market capitalization, *see* Large-cap; Small-cap
  characteristics of, 99–100, 296, 327–330,
    361–364, 370, 474, 493–494,
    502–504
  indexes, 88
Market efficiency, 204, 411n
Market makers, 328, 330, 339, 361–365
Market model regression, 159
Market price of risk, 458
Market risk
  implications of, 259, 313, 320
  premium, 459
Market timing
  characteristics of, 207, 209–213
  risk, 486–488, 506
Market-to-book ratio, 370

Market value, 98–99, 374
Markowitz, Henry, 429
Markowitz decision rule, 460–461
Matrix algebra, 337
Maturity
    bonds, 64
    money market yields, 56
    premium, 2–3
    T-bills, 55
Maximum likelihood, 372
Mean, *see specific types of means*
    excess return, 115
    lognormal distribution, 200–201, 206
    normal distribution and, 190, 194, 197
    return, 115, 120
    return spread, 400
    reversion, time-series analysis, 391, 400
    sample, 221–225
    time-series analysis, 387
    value, simulation trials, 207
    variance, *see* Mean-variance analysis;
        Mean-variance portfolio theory
Mean absolute deviation (MAD), 101–103,
    108–109
Mean regression sum of squares (MSR), 339
Mean squared error (MSE), 339, 352
Mean sum of squares (MSS), 320, 357–358
Mean-variance analysis
    capital asset pricing model (CAPM),
        458–460
    defined, 430
    diversification, 445–449
    implications of, 152n, 197
    instability for minimum-variance frontier,
        470–473
    Markowitz decision rule, 460–461
    minimum-variance frontier, 430–439,
        442–445, 470–473
    optimization, estimating inputs for,
        464–470
    portfolio choice rules, 460–464
    risk-free assets, 449–458
    size of portfolio, 445–449
    three-asset case, extension to, 439–442
Mean-variance portfolio theory
    basics of, 429–430
    development of, 429
    risk aversion, 429–430

Measurement error, Fisher effect with,
    370–371
Measurement scale(s)
    defined, 63
    identification of, 64
    types of, 63–64
Measures of central tendency
    arithmetic mean, 77–83
    defined, 76–77
    mean, types of, 85–94
    median, 81–83
    mode, 83–85
Median
    defined, 81
    determination of, 81–82
    normal distribution and, 190
    price-to-earnings ratio case illustration,
        82–83
Medtronic, Inc., 412–414
Mesokurtic distribution, 123
Michelin, 204–205
Microcap firms, 296n
Microsoft Excel, applications of, 48, 123n,
    253, 390
Miller, Lisette, 378–379, 392–393, 398–399,
    418–419
Minimum-variance frontier/portfolio
    bond-stock, 452
    as bullet, 39
    characteristics of, 432–433, 463n
    defined, 430, 432
    determination for many assets,
        442–445
    efficient frontier, 434
    global, 434, 436
    historical returns, 434–437, 443–445
    three-asset, 439–442
    two-asset, 435–437
Mixed factor models, 474
Modal interval, 84
Mode
    calculation of, 84–85
    defined, 84
    normal distribution and, 190
Model specification, multiple regression
        analysis
    case illustrations, 361–367, 369–371
    defined, 359

Model specification, multiple regression
    analysis (*continued*)
  misspecified functional form, 360–361,
    365–367
  principles of, 359–360
  time-series misspecification, 368–371
Modern portfolio theory (MPT), 152, 197
Momentum, 493
Monetary policy, 219
Money, time value of, *see* Time value of money
Money market funds, 509
Money market yields
  bank discount yield, 55–57
  characteristics of, 54–59
Money supply, 281–282, 286, 297–298,
    302–303, 308–310
Money-weighted returns, 47–50, 52–54
Monte Carlo simulation
  applications, 171, 175, 186, 206–207, 213
  central limit theorem, 223
  defined, 206
  market timing case illustration, 209–213
  mean-variance analysis, 464
  risk factors, 258n
Monthly rate of return, 65–66
Moody's Investors Service
  bond ratings, 84, 183, 343
  Bond Survey, 259
Morningstar, 98
Mortgage-backed securities, 207
Mortgage loans, 30–31, 35
Moving-average time series models
  autoregressive (ARMA), 416–417
  forecasting, 409–412
  smoothing past values, 407–409
MSCI
  EAFE Index, 78–79, 87n 152–153,
    181–182, 462
  World ex. U.S., 444–445, 454,
    471–472
Multicollinearity
  consequences of, 356
  correcting for, 358–359
  defined, 356
  detection of, 356–357
  implications of, 356, 359
  multiple regression analysis case illustration,
    357–358

Multifactor models
  applications, 493–509
  arbitrage pricing theory (APT), 478–482,
    509
  characteristics of, 473–474, 510
  current practices, 485–493
  factors and types of, 474
  fundamental factor models, 484–485,
    490–493
  macroeconomic factor models, 475–478,
    485–490
  two-factor models, parameter determination,
    483–484
Multiperiod forecasts, 391–394
Multiperiod horizon, 92
Multiple linear regression
  characteristics of, 325–326
  defined, 325
  using dummy variables, 341–345
  model, assumptions of, 326, 331–336
  model specification, *see* Model specification,
    multiple regression analysis
  qualitative dependent variables, 372–374
  violation of assumptions, 345–359, 421
Multiple R-squared, 309, 314–315, 317, 320,
    322, 328–329, 335, 350, 361–362,
    365–367, 369, 371, 394
Multivariate distribution, 190
Mutual funds
  characteristics of, 84, 135–136, 141
  counting principles, 167
  equity, *see* Equity mutual funds
  expected return, 158–159
  Forbes Honor Roll, 104–106
  hypothesis testing, 277
  mean absolute deviation, 102–103
  mean returns, 90–91
  range, 102–103
  rankings, 98
  regression analysis, 319, 360
Mutually exclusive events, 130, 142–143

N
Nasdaq, 172, 239, 330, 339, 361–362
Natural logarithms, 89, 203, 330–331,
    360–364, 373, 380, 384, 423, 426
Negative coefficients, 300
Negative correlation, 158

Negative deviations, 101, 123
Negative returns, 89
Negative serial correlation, 352n
Negative Sharpe ratio, 116
Negative skew, 111n, 118, 120
Net income (NI), 295–296, 300, 362
Net present value (NPV)
  computation of, 40
  defined, 40
  implications of, 39
  rule, 40–42, 44–45
NewBank, 159–160
Newey-West computation, 355n
New York Stock Exchange (NYSE), 172, 219,
  446
Nextech, 4787
Node, 184
Nominal gross domestic product (GDP),
  423
Nominal interest rates, 349
Nominal returns, 109
Nominal risk-free interest rate, 2
Nominal scales, 63–64
Nonlinearity, bid-ask spread,
  362–363
Nonlinear regression, 304
Nonlinear relation, 287–289
Nonparamatric test, 275
Nonstationarity, 372, 403–407
Normal distribution
  applications, 197–200
  characteristics of, 119, 123, 125, 179,
    189–193
  common stock portfolio case illustration,
    193–194, 196–197
  confidence intervals and, 194, 228
  hypothesis testing, 250–251, 254,
    266–267, 272, 276n
  multivariate, 190–191
  parameters, 190–191
  regression analysis, 304n, 347
  role of, 189
  safety-first optimal portfolio,
    198–200
  standard, 191, 194–195, 200
  types of, 190
  unit, 191
n-period moving average, 407–409

Null hypothesis, 245, 250, 252–253,
  255–265, 268–270, 273, 297–299,
  311, 313, 317–318, 320, 327–329,
  333–336, 339, 350, 354–356, 374,
  404, 412n, 421, 423–424

O
Objective probability, 131
Observations
  arithmetic means, 80–81
  correlation analysis, 282, 288
  geometric means, 92
  hypothesis testing, 272, 311
  paired, 265–266
  regression analysis, 305–306, 314, 317,
    320, 322–323, 329, 332, 335, 350,
    352, 360, 365–367, 369, 371, 373
  time-series analysis, 377, 379, 384–385,
    390, 393–394, 398, 402, 407,
    413–417, 419, 421
Odd-numbered samples, 81
Off-diagonal covariance, 155
One-factor APT model, 480–481
One-tailed test, 245, 249, 251,
  257, 329
Operating costs, 149–150
Opportunity cost, 2, 47
Opportunity set, 454
Optimal portfolio, 291, 443
Optimization, 462, 473
Optimizer, 441, 444
Option pricing models
  binomial, 168, 175
  Black-Scholes-Merton, 171, 200–201, 204,
    213
  lognormal distribution, 204
  volatility used in, 204–205
Option returns, 191
Ordinal scales, 63–64
Ordinary annuity
  equal cash flows, 13–15, 19–20
  present value of, 19–23, 25–26
Ordinary least squares (OLS), 331n, 352,
  354–355, 357, 359, 377, 390
Orthogonal factors, 489
Out-of-sample
  forecast, time-series analysis, 395–397, 427
  test, 236

Outcomes, 129–130
Outliers, 80, 254, 282

P

Paired comparisons tests, 265–266
Pairs arbitrage trade, 133
Pairwise correlations, 191, 356–357
Panel data, 220
Parameter
   implications of, 215
   instability, 324
   in population(s), 62
Parametric tests, 275–276, 279
Parsimonious regression models, 360
Partial regression coefficients, 331
Partial slope coefficients, 331
Par value, 55
Passive investment, 497, 504
Passive management, 333–334, 337,
   473–474
Pension funds, 7, 18, 333–334, 337
Pension plans, 51–52, 507–509
Percentiles, 81n, 94–98
Perfect collinearity, 332n
Performance
   appraisal, 47
   evaluation, 47n, 98
   measurement, 47
Perpetual annuity, *see* Perpetuity
Perpetuity
   defined, 13
   present value of, 23–24
   projected, 25–26
Platykurtic distribution, 123
Point estimators, 225–227
Pooled estimate, 261
Population
   covariance, 284
   defined, 62
   mean, *see* Population mean
   mode, 84n
   regression coefficients, 338–340
   sample, 62–63
   standard deviation, 104–106, 192, 254
   variance, *see* Population variance
Population mean
   confidence intervals, 227–233
   defined, 77

hypothesis tests and, 250–251, 254–265
implications of, 221
interval estimates, 225–235
parameters, 225
point estimates, 225–235
sample size, 226, 233–235
Population variance (σ^2)
   hypothesis testing, 262–263, 270, 273
   implications of, 103–104, 145, 201–202,
      204, 223, 228
Portfolio
   choice rules, 460–464
   concepts, *see* Portfolio concepts
   management/management styles, 290–291,
      492, 494–496
   performance attribution, 490n
   possibilities curve, 432
   rebalanced, 87
   returns, *see* Portfolio expected returns;
      Portfolio return measurement
   risk, 445, 447
Portfolio concepts
   mean-variance analysis, 429–473
   multifactor models, 473–510
Portfolio expected return
   calculation of, 153–154
   implications of, 152
   variance of return and, 158–159
Portfolio return measurement
   money-weighted rate of return, 47–50,
      52–54
   strategies for, 87–88
   time-weighted rate of return, 49–54
Positive coefficients, 300
Positive correlations, 158, 294, 438
Positive deviations, 101, 123
Positive serial correlations, 352, 354,
   385
Positive Sharpe ratio, 116
Positive skew, 111n, 118, 120–121
Precious metals, 267
Preferred stock, 24
Present value (PV)
   defined, 3
   equivalence, 35–36
   interest rate and, 58
   IRR rule and, 48
   money-weighted rate of return, 52–53

projected, 16–17, 22–23
solving for, 27–30
Price multiples, 493
Price relative, 202
Price-to-book value (P/BV) ratio, 98–99, 239–240
Price-to-cash flow (P/CF) ratio, 98–99
Price-to-earnings (P/E) ratio, 77, 81–83, 98–99, 104, 301, 421–422, 474
Priced risk, 474, 476
Principal, defined, 4
Principal-components models, 474
Prior probabilities/priors, 162, 166
Probability
  addition rule for, 136–137
  a priori, 131, 135, 141
  Bayes' formula, 161–166
  conditional, 133–136, 141–143, 162, 165
  counting, 166–169
  defined, 130
  dependent events, 138–142
  distribution, *see* Probability distribution
  empirical, 131, 135, 141
  EPS case illustration, 139
  events, types of, 130–131, 138–139
  expected value, 143–145, 147–152
  function, 173–175
  inconsistent, 132–133
  independent events, 138–142
  joint, 134–135
  limit order executing, 137–138
  marginal, 133
  multiplication rule for, 134–135
  objective, 131
  odds, 131–134
  outcomes, 129–130, 137
  random variables, 129–130, 143–145, 152–153, 159, 166
  standard deviation and, 145–147
  stock screening case illustration, 140
  subjective, 131
  total probability rule, 142–144, 146–152, 161
  unconditional, 133–134, 136, 141–142, 147, 163, 165
  variance, 145, 148
Probability density function (pdf), 173, 187

Probability distribution
  bond price case illustration, 172–173
  continuous random variables, 172, 185–206
  defined, 171
  discrete random variables, 171–185
  implications of, 130
  Monte Carlo simulation, 171, 175, 186, 207–213
Probability-weighted average, 152
Probit regression model, 372–374
Procyclical stocks, 510
Pseudo-random numbers, 209n
Pure discount instruments, 55
Pure factor premium, 479
p-value, 252–253, 312, 330, 343

Q
Quadratic programming, 441n
Qualitative dependent variables, 372
Quarterly returns, 267
Quartiles, 94
Quintiles
  calculation of, 95–98
  defined, 94–95
  determination of, 94–95
  implications of, 95
  investment applications, 98–100
Quoted interest rate, 8, 18

R
RAD Corporation, R&D program, 41–44
Random number, 209
Random sampling, 218
Random variables
  Bernoulli, 175–176, 183–184
  binomial, 177–179, 183–185
  characteristics of, 129–130, 143–145
  continuous, 172, 185–206
  correlation and, 284
  counting principles, 166
  covariance and 152–153, 159
  defined, 171
  discrete, 171–185
  independence for, 160
  independently and identically distributed (IID), 203

Random variables (*continued*)
  lognormal, 204
  normal, 190–191, 195
  standardizing, 194–195
Random walks, 372, 399–404
Ranges, 66n, 100–103
Rate of return, 2, 24, 39–47, 93
Ratio scales, 63–64
RBC Capital Markets Canadian Bond Market
      Index, 86
Real equity returns, 71–72
Real interest rate, 349
Real risk-free interest rate, 2
Rebalanced portfolios, 87
Regimes, defined, 398
Regression analysis, characteristics of, 171,
      189, 253n. *See also* Linear regression
      analysis; Multiple regression analysis
Regression coefficients, 301, 326, 336, 359,
      361, 397–399
Regression sum of squares (RSS), 319, 321,
      340
Reinvested interest, 4
Reinvestment/reinvestment rate, 42, 46–49,
      54
Rejection point, 249–251, 257–259, 270,
      272
Relative dispersion, 113
Relative frequency
  cumulative, 69, 71, 75
  defined, 69
  implications of, 71, 75
Relative value, hypothesis testing,
      272–273
Reliability factors, 227–229, 233, 235
Residual autocorrelations, 388–389
Residual errors, time-series analysis, 377
Residuals
  linear trend regression analysis, 382–383
  time-series analysis, 394, 426–427
Residual standard error (RSE), 328–329, 335,
      349, 357, 361–362, 365–367, 369
Retail sales, case illustrations, 375–376,
      408–409, 411–416
Retirement savings plan, 30, 32–35
Return correlation, krona-yen, 298
Return distributions
  kurtosis in, 123–127

symmetry and skewness in, 118–123
  Return on equity (ROE), 372, 502–504
Return on invested capital (ROIC), 315–316,
      322–324
Return-risk measure, 115
Returns, source analysis, 493–496
Reward-to-variability ratio, 115n
Risk
  aversion, 63, 429–430
  exposure, 276, 498
  management, influential factors, 54,
        110–111, 116, 200, 244
  premium, *see* Risk premium
  source analysis, 496–505
  tolerance, 430, 463
Risk-adjusted excess returns, 347
Risk-adjusted net value added (RANVA),
      333–334, 337
Risk-adjusted returns, 319
Risk-free assets
  capital allocation line (CAL), 450–455
  capital allocation line equation, 455–457
  capital market line (CML), 458
  characteristics of, 509
  mean-variance analysis, 463
Risk-free rate
  arbitrage pricing theory (APT), 478–481
  implications of, 115–116, 119, 219, 320
  mean-variance frontier, 453–455
  mean-variance portfolio, 460–461
  multifactor models, 484–485
  nominal, 2
  real, 2
Risk premium
  arbitrage pricing theory (APT), 483–484
  defined, 478
  test, 246, 251–253
Risk-free returns, 421
Risk-return tradeoff, 449–454
Robustness, 254
Robust standard errors, 351, 355n
Root mean squared error (RMSE), time-series
      analysis, 395, 397, 424
Ross, Stephen, 478
R-squared (R^2)
  adjusted, 340–341
  characteristics of, 314–317, 320, 322, 329,
        350, 357–358, 367

multiple, *see* Multiple R-squared
time-series analysis, 379–380, 383–384,
    390, 393–394, 398, 402–403, 407,
    413–416, 419
Rule of 72, 30n
Runs tests, 276
Russell 1000 Index, 140
Russell 2000 Index
  characteristics of, 342
  Growth Index, 291
  Value Index, 291

S
Safety-first ratio (SFRatio), 198–199
Safety-first rules, 197–199
Salomon RAM model, 488–489
Sample
  covariance, 284, 286
  defined, 62
  excess kurtosis, 124–127
  mean, *see* Sample mean
  relative skewness, 121
  selection bias, 238–239, 251
  size, 233–235, 297, 389–390
  skewness, 121, 127n
  standard deviation, 106–109, 264, 268,
      270, 284
  statistic, defined, 63
  variance (s^2), 104, 106–109, 223
Sample mean
  cross-sectional mean, 78–80
  defined, 77
  distribution of, 221–225
  efficiency, 226
  formula, 78
  standard error of, 221–223
Sampling
  data-mining bias, 236–238
  defined, 215
  distribution, 217, 226, 470
  error, 217
  look-ahead bias, 240
  plan, 216
  population mean, point and interval
      estimates, 225–235
  random, 218
  sample mean, 221–225
  sample selection bias, 238–239

  simple random, 216–217
  stratified, 217–219
  systematic, 216
  time-period bias, 240–241
  time-series and cross-sectional data,
      219–221
Savage, Sam, 207
Scatter plots, 281–283, 288, 290,
    363
Scotia Capital Markets Mortgage Index,
    87n
Seasonality, time-series analysis, 375, 408,
    412–416, 425
Second-order time-series model, 397
Security dealers, 200
Security market line (SML), 459
Selected American Shares (SLASX), 90–92,
    102–103, 107–110, 117–118
Self-selection bias, 239
Semi-active investment, 497
Semideviation, 110–111
Semilogarithmic scales, 127
Semistandard deviation, 110
Semivariance, 110–111
Sendar Equity Fund, 255–256
Serial correlation
  consequences of, 352
  correcting for, 355–356
  defined, 352
  implications of, 351–352, 359–360
  measurement errors, 371n
  testing for, 353–355
  time-series analysis, 385, 425–426
Series of cash flows
  additivity, 36–37
  future value of, 13–15, 26
  present value of, 19–27
  unequal, 26–27
Service, Ronald, 494–496
Shareholder wealth, 47
Sharpe, William F., 115
Sharpe measure, 115n
Sharpe ratio, 54, 111, 115–118, 198,
    219–220, 232–233, 277n,
    460–463
Shortfall risk, 197, 199
Short sales, 133n, 443, 470, 478
Sign test, 276

Simple interest, 4, 56

Simple random sampling, 216–217

Simulation trial, 207. *See also* Monte Carlo simulation

Single cash flow
  future value of, 3–6, 8–13
  present value of, 15–18

Single-factor models
  arbitrage portfolio theory (APT), 480
  portfolio selection and, 510

Single population mean, 254–258

Single-stock portfolio, 447

Size of portfolio, 445–449

Skewed distribution, defined, 118

Skewness
  calculation for mutual fund, 121–123
  characteristics of, 120–121, 126–127, 190–191
  defined, 120
  hypothesis testing, 254
  sample formula, 121

Slope/slope coefficient, 75–76, 115, 302, 311, 317, 319, 330, 338–340, 357, 363, 366, 379, 403, 450, 453, 476

Small-cap portfolios, 494

Small-cap stocks
  characteristics of, 291, 503–504
  minimum-variance analysis, 471–472
  minimum-variance portfolios, 436–437, 439, 441, 444
  multiple regression analysis case illustration, 341–343

Smoothing, 407–409

Software packages
  econometric, 420n
  regression analysis, 330
  statistical, 315n, 340, 351–352, 355, 389

South African stock market, 421–422

Spearman rank correlation coefficient, 276–279

Specialists, 422

Spreads
  bid-ask, 326, 361–363
  regression analysis, 315, 343–345

Spreadsheet applications, 48, 123n, 208

Spurious correlation, 289, 367, 387

Squared deviation, 120

Squared error, time-series analysis, 396

Stand-alone investments, 460–461

Standard & Poor's
  CreditWeek, 259
  as information resource, 183
  Mutual Fund Reports, 277n

S&P/BARRA Growth Index, 335–336, 357–358, 423–424

S&P/BARRA Value Index, 335–336, 357–358, 424

Standard & Poor's 500 Index (S&P 500)
  characteristics of, 84, 88–89, 112, 114, 121, 125, 152, 193, 288, 293–294, 304, 313, 407, 444, 486–488, 497–498
  frequency distributions, 65, 67–70, 72–76
  minimum-variance analysis, 471
  time-series analysis model, 410–411

S&P/TSX Composite Index, 86, 87n

Standard deviation
  confidence intervals, 231
  correlation and, 284–285
  defined, 103
  equity market returns, 109
  geometric and arithmetic means, 92n
  hypothesis testing, 274
  lognormal distribution, 201
  mean absolute, 101–103
  mean-variance analysis, 463
  minimum-variance analysis, 471
  minimum-variance portfolios, 433, 438–440, 444, 447–449, 455–457
  multifactor models, 496–497, 503
  normal distribution and, 191–194
  population, 104–106, 192, 254
  regression analysis, 307
  risk-free assets, 449–450
  risk-return tradeoff, 450–452
  sample, 106–109
  simulation trials, 207
  two-asset portfolios, 432, 436

Standard error
  heteroskedasticty, 346–347, 351
  hypothesis testing, 252, 260, 266, 311n
  of the regression, 307
  regression analysis, 312, 315, 317, 328–329, 351, 422

time-series analysis, 379, 384, 390, 393–395, 398, 402, 407, 413–416, 419, 426
Standard error of estimate (SEE)
    characteristics of, 306–307, 319, 320–323, 329
    computation of, 308
Standardized beta, 485
Standard Life Investments, 87n
Stated annual interest rate, 8–9, 11–13
Stationarity
    multiple regression analysis, 372
    time-series analysis, 422
Statistic(s), *see specific statistics*
    defined, 62, 215
    descriptive, 62
    dispersion measures, 100–118
    graphic presentation of data, 72–76
    means, 127–128
    measurement scales, 63–64
    measures of central tendency, 76–94
    nature of, 62
    populations, 62
    quantiles, 94–100
    return distributions, 118–127
    samples, 62–63
    sampling distribution of, 217
    summarizing data using frequency distributions, 65–72
    tests, 359
Statistical decision, 252
Statistical factor models, 474, 493
Statistical inference, 62, 189, 243–244, 386
Stock indexes, 293–294
Stock investments, *see specific types of stocks*
    limit orders, 137–138
    regression analysis, 324
    screening process, 140
Stock market
    crash of 1987, 273
    triple witching days, 274
Stock price movement, 176, 185
Stock return series, correlations among, 293–294
Stratified sampling, 217–219
Stubeck Corporation, 51–52
Subjective probability, 131

Summarizing data, 67, 71, 79
Sum of squared errors (SSE), 319, 343
Sum of squares (SS), 319–320, 328, 338, 357–358
Supply and demand, 2
Surprise
    defined, 475
    multifactor models, 476
Survey of Professional Forecasters (SPF), 289, 318, 349
Survivorship bias, 238–239, 241
Swedish kronor, 291–293, 298
Swensen, David, 473
Swiss franc, exchange rate, 375–376
Symmetrical relationships, 168
Symmetric distributions, 120, 179, 190
Systematic factors, 474
Systematic risk, 310, 321n, 509
Systematic sampling, 216

T
Tails, in distributions, 69, 125, 179, 191, 228
Tangency portfolio, 450, 455–457, 463
Target semideviation, 110
Target semivariance, 110
t-distributions, 230–231, 254, 269, 275n, 311–312
Technology stocks, 334
Terminal value, 50, 54
Test statistics
    alternative, 258
    characteristics of, 246–249, 296
    chi-square tests, 253n, 269–271
    data collection, 251–252
    defined, 246
    F-statistics, 272, 318–319, 321, 339–340, 357–358, 366
    F-tests, 246, 253n, 254, 257, 261, 265–266, 275, 276n, 328n, 336, 346, 350, 356
    mean, 262–269
    p-value, 252–253, 312, 330, 343
    regression analysis, 305n, 343, 347, 350
    rejection point, 249–251, 258
    risk premium test, 251–253
    statistical decisions, 252

Test statistics (*continued*)
  t-statistics, 232–234, 254–255, 264, 270,
      312, 314, 321, 328–329, 343, 347, 352,
      357, 367, 374, 389, 392–393, 398, 401,
      404–405, 413–416, 418–419, 421
  t-test, 253n, 254, 257, 261, 265–266, 275,
      276n, 328n, 336, 346, 350, 356
  z-tests, 251, 253n, 257–259, 275,
      328n
Theta, 410
Time horizon
  implications of, 92
  risk, 486–488, 506
Time-period bias, 240–241, 252
Time-series analysis
  autoregressive (AR) models, 376–377,
      386–399
  autoregressive conditional heteroskedasticity
      models, 417–420
  autoregressive moving-average models,
      416–417
  challenges of, 375–377
  characteristics of, 171, 375, 424–425
  complexity of, 424–425
  defined, 375
  forecasting, 385, 425–427
  moving average models, 407–411,
      416–417
  random walks, 399–404
  regressions with multiple time series,
      420–424
  seasonality in, 375, 412–416, 425
  trend models, 377–385, 425
  unit root test, 403–407, 420–424
Time-series data, 78, 219–221, 301,
      324
Time-series mean, 87
Time-series misspecification,
      368–371
Time-series regression, 324
Time-series sample, 252
Time value of money (TVM)
  annuities, 30–35
  defined, 1
  future value, 5–15, 35–36
  growth rates, 27–30
  interest rates, 1–3, 27–30
  number of periods, 30

present value, 19–27, 35–36
series of cash flows, 13–15, 19–27
single cash flow, future value of, 3–6,
    8–13
Time-weighted returns, 49–54
Total probability rule, 161
Total returns, 87, 102, 107–108, 288.
    See also Holding period return
    (HPR)
Total sum of squares (TSS), 319
Tracking error (TE), 181–182,
    496–497
Tracking-error volatility (TEV),
    496–497
Tracking portfolio, 507–509
Tracking risk, 182, 497, 501
Trading desk, 176–177, 179–181
Trading volume, 373
Transaction costs, 212
Treasury bills, *see* U.S. Treasury bills
    (T-bills)
Treasury bonds, *see* U.S. Treasury bonds
Treasury debt, 3
Tree diagrams, 128, 147
Trend models, time-series analysis
  correlated errors, testing for, 385
  linear, 377–380, 385
  log-linear, 380–385
Trimmed mean, 81n
Triple witching days, 274
T. Rowe Price Equity Income (PRFDX),
    90–92, 102–103, 107–109, 117–118,
    121–123, 125–127
t-statistics, 232–234, 254–255, 264, 270,
    312, 314, 321, 328–329, 343, 347, 352,
    357, 367, 374, 389, 392–393, 398, 401,
    404–405, 413–416, 418–419, 421
t-tests, 253n, 254, 257, 261, 265–266, 275,
    276n, 328n, 336, 346, 350, 356
t-values, 297, 311, 330
Two-factor models
  active risk, 501–502
  arbitrage pricing theory (APT),
      483–484
Two-fund theorem, 443n
Two-stock portfolio, 477
Type I error, 312, 352
Type II error, 312

U

Unbiasedness, 226

Uncertainty, 128, 308, 324, 337, 355, 380, 391, 422, 424–425

Unconditional probability, 133–134, 136, 141–142, 147, 163, 165

Underwriters, bond market, 343–345

Uniform distribution, 209

Unimodal distribution, 120

U.S. dollar (USD)
   characteristics of, 291–293
   exchange rate, 401–403
   foreign exchange rate, 375–376
   multifactor models, 489

U.S. equities, 462

U.S. small-cap equity index fund, 436

U.S. Small-Stock index, 293–294

U.S. Treasury bills (T-bills), 2–3, 55–58, 114, 116–117, 151, 210–211, 259, 294–295, 299, 349, 351–352, 369–371, 421, 449, 486–487, 489

U.S. Treasury bonds, 218, 343, 489

Unit root, time-series analysis
   characteristics of, 403–407, 420
   cointegration, 422
   Fisher effect and, 421
   multiple, 422–423
   stock market returns, predictability of, 421–422

Univariate distribution, 190

Unsecured debt ratings, 84–85

Up transition probability, 184

V

Validity, hypothesis testing, 275

Valuation, multifactor models, 493

Value at Risk (VaR), 200, 207

Value creation, 45

Value stocks, 98–99, 291, 358, 496

Variable bias, omitted, 360–361

Variance(s)
   arbitrage pricing theory (APT), 478
   autoregressive conditional heteroskedasticity (ARCH), 418–420
   coefficient of, 113–115
   confidence intervals and, 228

equality/inequality of, 271–274

linear regression, 304, 323

lognormal distribution, 206

minimum-variance portfolios, 439, 442, 446–447

normal distribution and, 194

population, 103–104

random walks and, 400

risk-return tradeoff, 450

sample, 104, 106–109

three-asset case, 450

time-series analysis, 387, 420–421, 425

two-asset portfolios, 431–432

Volatility
   active factor risk, 502–504
   Crash of 1987, 273
   derivatives expiration days, 274
   impact of, 185, 204–205, 219, 493, 496–497
   multifactor models, 479

W

Warning signs, in data mining, 238

Weakly stationary, *see* Covariance stationary time series

Wealth creation, 47

Weighted average, 143, 152–153, 161, 191–192, 234

Weighted-average cost of capital (WACC), 40, 315–316, 322–324

Weighted mean
   defined, 86
   expected value, 88–89
   implications of, 85–87, 143
   portfolio return as, 87–88

"What if" analysis, 212

White-corrected standard errors, 351n

Wilcoxon signed-rank test, 276

Wilshire 5000, 293–294

Winsorized mean, 81n

Withdrawals, money-weighted rate of return, 53–54

Working capital management, 40

X

x-axis, 74, 290, 434

Y

Yale University's Endowment Fund, 473
y-axis, 74, 281, 290
Yield, bank discount, *see* Bank discount
    yield
Yields to maturity (YTM), 59

Z

Zero-coupon bonds, 150–152, 343–344
Zero uncertainty, 128

Zero variance, 128
Zeta analysis, 373
Z-score, 373
z-statistic, 229–230, 270n
z-tests, 251, 253n, 257–259, 275,
    328n

0-470-06918-X • Paper
US$39.95/ CAN$51.99/UK£24.99

Master Quantitative Investment Analysis with the companion Workbook

BICENTENNIAL
1807
WILEY
2007
BICENTENNIAL

wiley.com

Available at wiley.com, cfainstitute.org, and wherever books are sold.

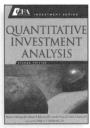
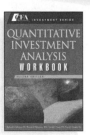

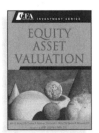